IROny IN LANGUAGE AND THOUGHT

A Cognitive Science Reader

Cover design by Katherine Houghtaling Lacey.

Cover artwork by Morgan Gibbs Colston. Father Figure, 2002; paraffin crayon on paper, 46 × 30 cm, private collection.

Lawrence Erlbaum Associates
Taylor & Francis Group
270 Madison Avenue
New York, NY 10016

Lawrence Erlbaum Associates
Taylor & Francis Group
2 Park Square
Milton Park, Abingdon
Oxon OX14 4RN

© 2007 by Taylor & Francis Group, LLC
Lawrence Erlbaum Associates is an imprint of Taylor & Francis Group, an Informa business

Printed in the United States of America on acid-free paper
10 9 8 7 6 5 4 3 2 1

International Standard Book Number-13: 978-0-8058-6062-7 (Softcover) 978-0-8058-6061-0 (Hardcover)

No part of this book may be reprinted, reproduced, transmitted, or utilized in any form by any electronic, mechanical, or other means, now known or hereafter invented, including photocopying, microfilming, and recording, or in any information storage or retrieval system, without written permission from the publishers.

Trademark Notice: Product or corporate names may be trademarks or registered trademarks, and are used only for identification and explanation without intent to infringe.

Library of Congress Cataloging-in-Publication Data

Irony in language and thought : a cognitive science reader / edited by Herbert L.
Colston and Raymond W. Gibbs, Jr.
    p. cm.
Includes bibliographical references and index.
ISBN 978-0-8058-6062-7 (pbk. : alk. paper) -- ISBN 978-0-8058-6061-0 (alk. paper)
-- ISBN 978-1-4106-1668-5 (e-book)
1. Irony. I. Colston, Herbert L. II. Gibbs, Raymond W. III. Title.

P301.5.I73I76 2007
809'.918--dc22   2006037734

Visit the Taylor & Francis Web site at
http://www.taylorandfrancis.com

and the LEA Web site at
http://www.erlbaum.com

IRONY IN LANGUAGE AND THOUGHT

A Cognitive Science Reader

Edited by

Raymond W. Gibbs, Jr.
University of California, Santa Cruz

and

Herbert L. Colston
University of Wisconsin, Parkside

Lawrence Erlbaum Associates
Taylor & Francis Group

New York   London

Contents

PART V: DEVELOPMENT OF IRONY UNDERSTANDING

PART VI: SITUATIONAL IRONY: A CONCEPT OF EVENTS GONE AWRY

PART VII: CONCLUSION

Preface

Irony is a device of both mind and language for acknowledging the gap between what is expected and what is observed. As one of the great tropes, or figures of speech, irony has been discussed and debated for thousands of years by all those interested in rhetoric. In recent decades it has been studied as a special mode of thought, perhaps used by all individuals, and thus one of many conceptual devices in the poetics of mind. Although classical studies focused on different forms of irony (e.g., tragic, Socratic, irony of fate), late 20th-century scholars, especially philosophers and linguists, have explored the ways that ironic speech conveys pragmatic meaning. One major theory is that irony is understood as a secondary meaning after the primary semantic meaning has been analyzed and rejected in the present context. Starting in the mid 1980s, experimental psycholinguists and linguists began exploring the implications of this traditional pragmatic view for psychological theories of how people understand figurative language, with irony being a special case where a speaker contextually implies, at least seemingly, the opposite of what was literally said. Over the past 25 years, dozens of experiments and many discourse studies have emerged that generally suggest a far more complicated view of irony, how it is understood, the way it is acquired, its social functions, and the ways that ironic language reflects individuals' ironic conceptualizations of their own experiences and the world around them. Unlike previous explorations of irony, in both language and thought, this recent work has a strong empirical foundation where scholars aim to compare and contrast different forms of irony use against other figurative and non-figurative modes of thinking and speaking.

The purpose of "Irony in language and thought: A cognitive science reader" is to offer students of irony an overview of the major works within cognitive science on the nature, function, and understanding of irony. This volume fills a significant gap in the literature on figurative language and thought. Although there are dozens of books on metaphor alone, very few books have been devoted exclusively to irony in its different forms, despite the increasing popularity of studies of irony and individual theories of irony use and understanding. We have collected those articles that are among the most widely cited in the interdisciplinary study of irony within disciplines encompassing the cognitive sciences, and have included several others that are likely to have impact on the conduct of research in the near future. These articles are roughly divided into five different sections: theories of irony, context in irony comprehension, the social functions of irony, development of irony understanding, and situational irony. We offer a more extensive overview of these works and situate them within the historical context of irony research in an introductory chapter. Our thoughts on the future of irony studies are provided in a concluding section. "Irony in language and thought: A cognitive science reader" surely best represents the important past on irony research. Yet we offer this collection in the hope that a comprehensive look at the complexity of irony in thought and language will generate new theories and empirical research, and give irony its proper recognition within cognitive science as a fundamental property of mind.

We thank the authors of these papers for their fine work and their agreement to republish the articles. We also thank Cathleen Petree of Lawrence Erlbaum Associates for all her assistance in making this project a reality.

PART I

INTRODUCTION

CHAPTER 1

A Brief History of Irony

Herbert L. Colston
University of Wisconsin–Parkside

Raymond W. Gibbs, Jr.
University of California, Santa Cruz

The scholarly investigation of irony has a very old history and a very broad base. Thinking and commentary about irony in all its forms goes back to some of the earliest recorded philosophical works. The historical and contemporary studies of irony can also be found in fields as diverse as anthropology, literature studies, linguistics, cognitive-, social-, language-, and even clinical-psychology, philosophy, cultural studies and more. And the topics related to irony are as widely arrayed as art, literature, dance, music, media, language, speech, image, thought, cartoons, journalism, theater, politics, situations and many others.

To offer a usable compilation of this incredible history and diversity of irony is an impossible task. We thus chose to limit our scope to the modern study of irony as predominantly related to thought and language. But even such a narrowing of the topic does not make full coverage possible. A great number of scholars, scientists and researchers of many types have published important works in the modern study of irony. We simply could not have included even a small fraction of this work and still obtain a volume not requiring a wheelbarrow. So we instead had to be incredibly selective in our choice of papers.

This volume contains what we have taken to be some of the most influential and important contributions to the modern cognitive scientific study of irony. These works come from a variety of fields and have been published in a wide diversity of international journals in a number of different disciplines. Despite this variety of venues, however, the works have all honed in on what we see as the most central topics to have been addressed. These topics correspond to the main sections of this reader: Theories of Irony—addressing primarily comprehension of its verbal form, Context in Irony Comprehension, Social Functions of Irony, the Development of Irony Understanding, and Situational Irony. We hope putting all these works under one volume will help catalyze future work on irony.

What follows is a very brief attempt at an overview of these central topics in the modern scholarly pursuit of irony. By no means should this be considered an all-inclusive review. Rather, we seek to lend some perspective to the studies we've included, to enable the reader to see how these works have furthered the field.

THEORIES OF IRONY

One might initially ask why a theory of irony is needed. Whether we are discussing verbal irony—where a speaker says something that seems to be the opposite of what they mean, or situational irony—where some situation in the world is just contradictory, why is a theory required when both of these kinds of irony seem to be relatively straightforward concepts? The answer is that for both verbal and situational irony, one simply cannot explain the phenomena with "straightforward" solutions like take-the-opposite-meaning, or irony-is-simple-contradiction. Most, and arguably all, instances of what is comprehended from an utterance of verbal irony simply does not correspond to the opposite of that utterance, because it is rarely clear, 1) what the opposite of an utterance's literal meaning is, and 2) what in fact even that literal meaning itself is (Brown, 1980; Gibbs & O'Brien, 1991). Additionally, there are a wide variety of instances subsumed under or near the umbrella of situational irony that don't necessarily fit the definition of a contradiction (e.g., coincidences, deviations from predictions, counterfactuals, frame shifts, juxtapositions of bi-coherences, hypocrisy, etc.). Moreover, the mere fact that a host of theories have been presented in an attempt to grapple with verbal and situational irony is itself indicative of the relative intractable nature of these phenomena. It is thus clear that we just cannot get away with seemingly simple solutions that, although possibly resembling what occurs in some prototypical instances of verbal or situational irony, by no means precisely explain those instances nor go anywhere near encompassing all the phenomena considered part of, or related to, the phenomena of irony.

In an attempt to theoretically corral this phenomenon of irony, several theories have been proposed from linguistic, philosophical and psychological backgrounds. Interestingly and arguably, none of these theories has predominated the interdisciplinary group of scholars studying irony, nor has any one been seriously struck down. Rather, they each offer a different perspective on the phenomenon, or use a different theoretical framework in their explication. In reality then, they are all likely explaining a portion of the phenomenon, or one of a variety of mechanisms underlying the comprehension of the phenomenon, without necessarily being incompatible with one another (Colston, 2000). Whether this means that a broader theoretical attempt is required, perhaps one based on an abstract notion such as constraint satisfaction (see Katz, 2005), or whether irony is simply a family of related phenomena that each require their own theoretical approach, remains to be seen. For now, let us just briefly discuss the key theoretical approaches in the current status of the field.

The idea that verbal irony is broader than a simple solution to a linguistic problem is key to several of the theories proposed in the included papers. For instance,

Wilson and Sperber (1992) argued that a speaker who uses verbal irony is employing a long-standing philosophical distinction between use and mention. This distinction allows for the difference between using a remark to express one's true position or feeling, versus the mention of, or reference to, a particular position or feeling that one isn't currently expressing. This use/mention distinction opens up the possibility for then making reference to some state of affairs that was predicted, expected or desired, either because of some explicit prediction or based upon a mutually shared domain of knowledge. For instance, if a basketball player uses the ironic utterance, "Nice shot" to condemn a fellow player who misses a game-winning basket, she could be mentioning an explicit prediction by say a bystander, who perhaps said, "This is going to be a nice shot," while the basketball shooter was preparing to throw the ball. Or she could be mentioning the general expectation or desire for good play. This mention or echo of predicted or known events in the midst of unexpected or undesired reality is a key contribution in our thinking about verbal irony.

In a different approach, Clark and Gerrig (1984) proposed that verbal irony is really an instance of role playing that must be recognized as such for correct comprehension. According to Clark and Gerrig, a speaker using verbal irony is "pretending to be an injudicious person speaking to an uninitiated audience; the speaker intends the addressees of the irony to discover the pretense and thereby see his or her attitude toward the speaker, the audience, and the comment" (1984). A speaker of verbal irony is thus acting out what a person other than himself or herself might feel, think, believe and say about some situation, and moreover, is portraying, at least typically, that character in an unbecoming light to essentially distance himself or herself from the position advocated by that character, and likely even to belittle that viewpoint.

One particular advantage of the pretense account is the readiness with which it handles derivation of an ironic speaker's negative (again, typically) attitude (although see Gibbs, 2000, for a treatment of jocular forms of irony, as well as Colston, 2000; Hancock, Dunham, & Purdy, 2000; Schwoebel, Dews, Winner, & Srinivas, 2000; Harris & Pexman, 2003; Anolli, Ciceri, & Infantino, 2000; Dews, Kaplan, & Winner, 1995; Kreuz & Link, 2002, for treatments of ironic praise). By basing the decryption of an ironic utterance on the recognition of the different roles in a speech-actor's portrayal, the personality characteristics given to the portrayed character are brought very much to the forefront of explanation. So a speaker/actor who portrays a character as being an idiot, for instance, with the common acting techniques of voice tone, facial expression, nonverbal cues, etc., is very clearly revealing their negative attitude toward that character and, accordingly, the position the character is advocating. The speaker/actor could just as easily have portrayed the character in a more appealing light and is thus making his or her attitude clear given that he or she has selected it from a number of possibilities.

An approach that in some ways weds the different notions of pretense and echo, but that makes some unique claims of its own is the Allusional Pretense Theory of Discourse Irony (Kumon-Nakamura, Glucksberg, & Brown, 1995). This account returned to a speech-act analysis of verbal irony comprehension based upon felicity conditions for well formed speech acts. Allusional Pretense claims that utterances of verbal irony must 1) violate the sincerity felicity condition, and 2) occur in the instance of a violation of expectations. Most accounts of verbal irony share the second condition. The first condition, however, enabled explanation of instances where a speaker does not strictly echo, because she neither re-mentions previous predictions or statements nor reminds addressees/hearers of common beliefs or desires. Utterances such as true assertions (e.g., "You sure know a lot," said to a know-it-all), questions (e.g., "How old did you say you were," spoken to someone acting childish), offerings (e.g., "How about another small slice of pizza?" said to a glutton), and over-polite requests (e.g., "Would you mind very much if I asked you to consider cleaning up your room some time this year?" said to a slob) were brought under the explanatory fold by this account.

The two claims of the Allusional Pretense account, and indeed in one form or another the dominant claims found in most of the theories of verbal irony comprehension—1) that verbal irony requires a violation of expectations, and 2) that it requires violation of felicity conditions for well-formed speech acts, was addressed by Colston (2000). This work sought to evaluate these claims with explicit empirical tests. Evidence was found to support the first claim concerning violation of expectations. Indeed, even in instances where no such violation was indicated, comprehenders of verbal irony were shown to have *inferred* such a violation on the part of the speaker. It thus appears that this condition is required for verbal irony comprehension. The second claim concerning felicity conditions for well-formed speech acts, however, was argued to be too narrow. A set of utterances of verbal irony was shown to adhere to these felicity conditions and yet still be interpreted ironically. A broader second condition was recommended that was based upon a violation of Gricean Maxims. A third condition that involved portraying a contrast of current events with expected ones was also proposed.

The Attardo (2001) article is the most recent contribution to the theoretical discussion of irony discussed here. This paper first presents a very thorough review of some of the definitional issues surrounding verbal irony, and then reviews the views of irony both as a figure of speech and as an insincere speech act. The family of "mention" theories of irony comprehension are then criticized for being unable to encompass a wide enough array of irony examples to serve as an encompassing theory of comprehension. Pretense is included in this discussion, but in our opinion is fairly treated as a much broader phenomenon, allowing explanation of dramatic and situational irony. Attardo then moves on to a criticism of psycholinguistic accounts of irony understanding, including Gibbs's (Gibbs, 1986, 1994; Gibbs & O'Brien, 1991) direct access comprehension mechanism and the Relevance theoretic approach, that call for a one-stage model of irony comprehension. The paper then concludes with an exposition of an irony comprehension account based upon relevant inappropriateness.

Most prevalent in Attardo's (2001) criticism of direct access is the argument that a one-stage processing approach "is logically incapable of accounting for novel input, since it will fail to differentiate between a semantically ill-formed sentence and a novel instance of metaphor, irony or other indirect figure of speech, etc." Certainly from a linguistic perspective such an argument seems apt. However, it fails to consider the rich body of knowledge from psycholinguistic studies of all forms of language processing and indeed much of what is known about other realms of cognitive processes, that show varieties of dependencies upon contextual sources and linguistic input, and the intricate parallel blends of processing that can occur during different kinds of cognition. Indeed, recent psycholinguistic studies have shown that the mere knowledge of the occupation of a speaker can alter the very lowest levels of online processing of figurative language (see Katz, 2005, for a review), and indeed a variety of heretofore "psychological" or "contextual" influences (e.g., mood, emotional state, physiological status, and a vast array of others) have been shown to have tremendous impact on many allegedly impenetrable cognitive, perceptual and even sensory processes. There is thus a great body of evidence against the view that processing, linguistic and otherwise, involves multiple, sequential, distinct, impenetrable stages. Rather, processing can be influenced by parallel, multiple, and interacting sources of information (see Colston, 2005, for this argument in greater detail). Thus, although there are possible instances of an ironic computation that could require a garden-path type of two-stage meaning recomputation, most instances are more likely one-stage operations where contextual information is readily-enough deterministic and available at the earliest onset of processing to enable parallel processing of context and linguistic input to produce the ironic comprehension product directly.

One of the most important contributions of the Attardo (2001) paper is the detailed explication of the emerging, generally agreed-upon, necessary condition for an instance of ironic comprehension, involving some violation of the relevance, appropriateness, or manner in which an utterance is made. Consistent with the other enclosed paper that called for a violation of the Gricean Maxim of manner as one of three needed components of irony comprehension (Colston, 2000; the other two being a violation of expectations and a contrast of expectations and reality), Attardo specifically explicated this claim and offered a detailed discussion of differences between violations of relevance and appropriateness.

CONTEXT IN IRONY COMPREHENSION

Beyond consideration of the comprehension of an utterance of verbal irony per se, other work has focused more exclusively on the role that context plays in the comprehension of verbal irony. The first paper we've selected on this topic is Gibbs's (1986) article on the comprehension and memory for sarcastic irony. This paper was among the first wave of research studies that initially challenged the standard pragmatic view that ironic and indeed all forms of figurative language first undergo an encapsulated literal meaning derivation phase that then must be subsequently overwritten by a secondary figurative meaning derivation phase once contextual information has shown the literal meaning to be incorrect. The Gibbs paper made such a challenge for verbal irony.

In six experiments the study revealed that there is no need to first derive the literal meaning from ironic utterances because contextual information comes into play early in the comprehension process (irony processing took no longer than processing of the same language used literally). Ironic language was also processed faster if it explicitly echoed previously mentioned beliefs or norms, also indicating the importance of context in irony comprehension. Memory for sarcastic utterances was also better than memory for the same utterances used literally, and explicit echo of previous information also increased memory for sarcastic utterances. The latter two memory results demonstrate the key role of context in irony cognition because, other than the greater involvement of contextual information in ironic remarks, especially ironic remarks that involve explicit echo, the utterances themselves were kept identical.

In challenging the then well-accepted standard pragmatic view of figurative language comprehension, the results of the Gibbs (1986) paper were sure to attract the attention of divergent accounts. The next paper we included is representative of works that have addressed the different claims and evidence of Gibbs's direct access account and more traditional accounts of verbal irony processing. Giora and Fein (1999) offered an account that proposed the concept of salient meaning to encompass the divergent to-date findings. Salient meanings are argued to be those that are always activated and always activated first. But they are not necessarily the same things as "literal" meanings. Instead, salient meanings are affected by conventionality, frequency, familiarity and prototypicality.

In two experiments, Giora and Fein (1999) found evidence to support the role of salient meaning in irony processing. In general, if the literal meanings of ironic utterances were coded in the lexicon (if the ironies were unfamiliar, for instance) then ironic processing took longer relative to ironies whose literal meanings were not lexically coded (familiar ironies). Giora and Fein thus concluded that direct access "may be a function of meaning salience, rather than of context effects."

The next study (Pexman, Ferretti, & Katz, 2000) took the evaluation of context, salience and processing to a new level by using a moving window paradigm than can more precisely reveal online processing of verbal irony. This study, which followed an early work on memory for sarcastic utterances that employed the same experimental materials and thus enabled correlational analysis between the two studies (Katz & Pexman, 1997), revealed a complex interaction of factors in irony processing. Contextual factors such as the occupation of the speaker, discourse factors like the nature of the discourse preceding the ironic utterance, the familiarity of the statement being made and the nature of the counterfactuality presented in the discourse, all play a role in very early processing of ironic utterances. The authors concluded that graded salience *and* contextual factors are operating in verbal irony comprehension.

The relationship between processing and memory of ironic utterances, first explored by the Gibbs (1986) paper, was also corroborated in the Pexman, Ferretti, and Katz (2000) study. Recall that Gibbs found greater memory as well as faster reading times for echoic sarcastic utterances, relative to nonechoic, suggesting that something about the enhanced processing seems to lead to greater memory. The Pexman, Ferretti, and Katz paper found that both the degree of sarcasm and the likelihood of subsequent memory are predicted by specific amounts of times spent pausing at the word stream that immediately follows the sarcastic utterances.

The next paper comes from a very different perspective in using neuropsychological work to address the role of context in irony processing. The McDonald (2000) paper discusses two kinds of brain damage and how they differentially affect people's abilities with respect to verbal irony. People with damage to their brain's right hemisphere (RH) and people who've suffered traumatic brain injury (TBI) both show deficits of various kinds in their cognitive abilities, which in turn can affect their ability to understand verbal irony.

RH patients in very general terms have difficulty incorporating prosodic cues in the processing of irony, they have a diminished ability to infer the emotional states of ironic speakers, and they may have difficulty in understanding what is on the minds of other people. TBI patients generally show a greater loss of "communication" skill, relative to full language aphasias, and as a consequence can show an increased literal-mindedness in language comprehension. Their comprehension difficulties seem less directly related to emotional assessment problems, but rather seem influenced by more general inferential reasoning deficiencies. Most interesting for issues related to context, TBI patients also seem most impaired when the contradiction inherent in an ironic utterance is restricted to other utterances. When the contradictions are against other situational contextual cues, then performance improves. As an end result, TBI patients seem least affected at detection of irony, and most impaired at gleaning the illocutionary force of ironic utterances.

What these findings show is that much of the "normal" comprehension of verbal irony lies in mechanisms outside of pure "language" processing. Abilities such as prosodic evaluation, emotional assessment, flexible incorporation of related conceptual information, inference generation and theory of mind, are all deficient to one degree or another in RH and TBI patients, without there being significant parallel deficiencies in pure language abilities (e.g., aphasias are rare in these patients). That these patients then show straightforward difficulties in aspects of verbal irony comprehension thus singles out the importance of such processes for irony cognition.

Schwoebel, Dews, Winner, and Srinivas (2000) is the next paper we included from the literature on context in irony processing. This study revisited the different claims and evidence of direct access, the standard pragmatic model, and graded salience. The study attempted to establish the exact point at which the processing of an ironic utterance would slow down because of activation of the literal meaning of the utterance. Such a lag is universally claimed to happen by the standard pragmatic model, and is also claimed to happen by graded salience if the ironic meaning of the utterance is not overly conventional. None of the items used in this study were conventional ironies in this way. The study also attempted to test whether such a literal meaning activation would linger in the processing stream and slow down subsequent processing (the spillover effect).

The study broke the key ironic utterances into three phrases, the first containing words/phrases up to the key word that made the utterance ironic. The second being the ironic words/phrases. The third was the remaining words/phrases in the utterance (e.g., said about an unintelligent person, "That guy / is brilliant / at answering questions"). Matched literal versions were also used (e.g., the same utterance as above said about an intelligent person). Participants then read through these broken sections of the utterances and reading times were recorded for each segment. The main finding was that the second phrases showed a difference between ironic and literal contexts, with ironic phrases (e.g., "is brilliant," about an unintelligent person) taking longer to read than literal phrases (e.g., "is brilliant," about an intelligent person). No differences were found in the first and third phrases. This study thus seems to show that the ironic readings are taking longer, possibly because of literal meaning activation.

There are some anomalies in this study, however, as well as some more global problems with the use of such reading time methodologies, particularly ones that so drastically dissect utterances for reading, that bear mentioning. First, the effect described above held only for ironic criticism. When ironic praise was evaluated, no significant difference was obtained. There are some well established differences between ironic praise and ironic criticism that may be at play in this discrepancy, not least that ironic criticism is more prevalent than ironic praise. This could increase the variability on reading times for ironic praise and thus weaken the statistical analysis (although not significant, there was nonetheless a non-equivalence in that ironic readings took longer). But this doesn't clearly tie in to the different claims of direct access versus graded salience/standard pragmatic model. Secondly, on the ironic praise items, a nearly significant difference was found on the initial phrases, with literal contexts actually taking longer than ironic. Most curiously, these phrases were also identical. There is thus a possibility that some other unforeseen factors are playing a role in these processing times.

As to the methodology, the harsh dissections required by this approach to measuring onsets of latencies, may produce the very effect they are seeking to evaluate. When readers are forced to read ironic phrases in isolation, and then overtly respond before moving on, the flow of contextual information for the processing of the overall utterance is drastically interrupted, where the more bottom-up lexical information is less affected. Granted, many of the previous findings on the processing of verbal irony have made use of reading time methodologies of one sort or another, most of which imbed overt responses into normal reading of text. All of these might thus be suspect to a degree. But the one used in the Schwoebel et al. (2000) study might be more vulnerable to such criticisms due to its more minute dissection of phrases requiring responses. Nonetheless, this study is a useful contribution in that it shows that despite the frequently found overall reading time equivalence of verbal irony and literal language, there may be idiosyncratic bottom-up processing differences going on that are shrouded by more global measures.

At this point, our synopsis is that more evidence is required from more natural measures such as eye-tracking, as well as very precise evaluations of the degree to which many factors may inadvertently vary between ironic utterances and their literal controls (e.g., their degree of relevance with preceding context, the prevalence of the different forms in discourses, the aptness of the utterances, the kinds of expectation sets participants might build up in responding to items counterbalanced in ways needed for experimentation [e.g., 50% literal and 50% sarcastic utterances], and many others) before the picture on verbal irony processing is entirely clear.

The final paper we consider in this section on the role of context in irony comprehension is the recent paper by Curco (2000) that evaluated the role of negation, echo, and calculations of metarepresentations in people's comprehension of verbal irony. This paper begins with a very detailed and critical analysis of the negation view advocated by Giora and colleagues (Giora 1995; Giora & Fein, 1999). Curco argued that the negation view's criticism of the relevance theoretic approach (Sperber & Wilson, 1981, 1986; Wilson & Sperber, 1992) is invalid because it draws two incorrect conclusions from that framework, 1) that attributed thoughts must come from a person other than the speaker of a verbal irony, and 2) that instances of attitudinal dissociation from a comment must necessarily be ironic. Curco then went on to argue that as far as processing issues are concerned, the negation and relevance theoretic views are more similar than Giora and colleagues claim.

The arguably most important contributions of this paper are that it 1) very concisely and convincingly eloquates the point that complexity of processing of verbal irony may not be orthogonal to the time durations required to read written utterances of verbal irony, 2) even if such processing issues could be readily gotten at, a great deal of rich "manipulation" is at work in a speaker's use of ironic contradictions (both of these points arguably among the reasons for the growth in recent work on the social functions of irony), and 3) the importance of paying attention to the notion of metarepresentations and how these may separate verbal irony from other kinds of figurative language (see also Winner & Gardner, 1993, and Colston & Gibbs, 2002, for additional treatments of this idea).

THE SOCIAL FUNCTIONS OF IRONY

The third primary topic in the contemporary cognitive science of verbal irony is what verbal irony can pragmatically and socially accomplish for speakers. This area is a relative newcomer in that most previous work on verbal irony had addressed comprehension and context. But this work holds much promise for it enables consideration of the extent to which basic cognitive, linguistic and social processes play in the social functions of verbal irony, as well as perhaps in its comprehension.

The earliest of our included papers in this section, Dews, Kaplan, and Winner (1995), opened the question as to why speakers would wish to speak ironically in a discourse (see an earlier paper, Roberts & Kreuz, 1994, that poses this question for a variety of figurative language forms). Given that irony can invite misinterpretation, why would speakers use it? This paper sought to evaluate an earlier proposed Tinge Hypothesis that verbal irony would regularly be used to diminish the criticism or condemnation brought about or intended by a speaker. This attenuated negativity is achieved by the obligatory processing of the literal positive meaning in a sarcastic utterance (Schwoebel, Dews, Winner, & Srinivas, 2000). Typically, sarcastic utterances are literally positive words used to express intended negative meanings. Listeners or readers who comprehend verbal irony are thus unable to ignore the literal (positive) meaning of a typical sarcastic (negative) utterance, which results in a diminishment of the overall degree of negativity expressed. This and another study (Dews & Winner, 1995) found evidence to support this hypothesis in that verbal irony was interpreted less negatively than direct literal commentary and thus the studies by Dews and colleagues provide supportive evidence for this account.

Another mechanism for meaning attenuation was introduced in the next included paper, Colston (1997). This work demonstrated that contrast effects can also arise in verbal irony comprehension whereby the degree of negativity expressed by a remark is actually enhanced relative to literal commentary. The mechanism for the enhancement is an influence on how negative the referent situation is seen as being. If a moderately negative situation is judged when commented upon by a literally positive remark (intended sarcastically), the perception of the situation is shifted toward the negative relative to when a literally negative remark is made. This shift is due to the ubiquitous contrast effect phenomenon whereby some perception or judgment is shifted due to a biasing contest (e.g., the temperature of a liquid feels colder after first feeling a hot liquid, relative to assessing the temperature in isolation). A speaker thus causing the negative shift is viewed as being more negative in her commentary (see also Colston, 2002; Colston & O'Brien 2000a, 2000b, for further work on contrast and assimilation effects in the social functions of verbal irony).

This Contrast mechanism is not necessarily incompatible with the Tinge Hypothesis and obligatory processing claims (Colston, 1997). Rather it might be the case that various factors influence when contrast is at play versus indirect negation or tinge. More recent work has begun to address factors that might operate to tip an instance of verbal irony comprehension toward negativity enhancement versus reduction. Among these mechanisms are the degree to which a person is influenced by a negative situation (Colston, 2002), and whether one considers the listener's impression versus speaker's intent (Pexman & Olineck, 2002). But at minimum this series of studies indicates different ways in which meanings can influence one another and produce varying levels of a pragmatic function.

The Gibbs (2000) paper takes the study of the social functions of irony in a new and important direction. This paper addresses a major concern with the authenticity of language forms used in experimental studies by focusing on actual instances of language used by real speakers in real contexts (see Colston, 2005). It thus provides a much needed impetus for researchers to work with real language in their research. This study also lays the groundwork for establishing patterns and prevalences in figurative language use in the real world. It documented quantitative differences in the frequency of different kinds of verbal irony as well as the social consequences of such use. It also moved the study of social functions of irony to discourse levels beyond that of the utterance. A key contribution of this paper is it's documentation of ironic chains where speakers in a conversation will create a pattern of ironic utterances that unfolds over many turns as well as the aforementioned jocularity irony.

The Anolli, Ciceri, and Infantino paper (2002) is representative of a different approach to the study of irony, one based upon an investigation of the acoustic and prosodic patterns to the speech form. This particular paper is important for its joint attention to acoustic/prosodic patterns and their relationship vis-à-vis semantic and pragmatic phenomena concerning irony. For instance, that verbal irony can be either critical or praiseful (Colston, 1997; Dews, Kaplan, & Winner, 1995; Dews & Winner, 1995), is a well-established finding from the comprehension and use literatures, that would also very likely show a distinctive vocal pattern. Moreover, such a pattern might enable determination of underlying cognitive or other motivations for the different vocal soundprints.

This paper analyzed the acoustic/prosodic patterns of normal speech, sarcastic irony (literally positive words spoken about negative situations/persons), and kind irony (literally negative words spoken about positive situations/persons). Male undergraduates, without acting experience, read carefully designed utterances of the described types, that controlled for the number of consonants and vowels. Three acoustic/prosodic dimensions were evaluated in the recorded spoken utterances; time, pitch and energy, with five variables measured from each dimension. The results revealed distinctive patterns for both the normal versus ironic speech categories, as well as between the two kinds of ironic utterances. The findings were modeled with a circumplex with ironic type as one dimension (labeled "context," with "cooperation" and "conflict" as poles), and "empathy" as the other ("involvement" and "estrangement" as poles). Essentially, four categories emerged. Suprasegmental traits for sarcastic irony were characteristically high and changeable pitch, strong energy and slow articulation, or, low and steady pitch, with slow articulation. The former was typical of emphatic banter where the latter was associated with blame and cold anger. For cooperative irony, suprasegmental traits were also high and changeable pitch, strong energy and slow articulation, characteristic of most instances of kind irony and also labeled emphatic banter. Or, the pattern revealed strong energy, slow articulation rate and low, monotone pitch, characteristic of a subordinate, "tender" voice.

These findings are consistent with both the previous work that has established the variable enhanced versus tinged criticism and praise of different kinds of verbal irony, as well as more recent studies that have begun to investigate factors that influence the degree of meaning enhancement/tinge (Colston, 2002; Pexman & Olineck, 2002). The additional contribution of the current paper is a testable circumplex model that encompasses multiple dimensions of context and intention. Given the influencing factors that have been proposed for enhancement and tinge strength (degree to which a listener is influenced by negative outcomes and focus of attention on listener's impression versus speaker intent), such a circumplex model may be a viable means by which to conceptualize this aspect of irony use. That such a model was gotten at by an acoustic/prosodic approach also reveals the need for multiple levels of analysis of irony and their interrelationships.

Similar to the unique and important direction taken by the Gibbs (2000) paper described above, the Kottoff (2003) article provides a refreshing and insightful perspective on the social functions of, and to a degree the comprehension of, verbal irony. This work evaluates two authentic datasets representing distinct kinds of conversational contexts (informal—dinner conversations among friends, and formal—television debates) from an interaction analysis approach. As such, the focus is placed upon the unfolding responses to verbal irony during the conversations, and what they reveal about processing and social interaction. The findings reveal that interactants are more likely to attend to the "literally said (the dictum)" in informal contexts, as a means of catalyzing humorous interaction. In informal contexts, however, interactions respond more to the figurative meaning of ironic commentary, "the implicatum," to satisfy the needs of public competition.

Such an approach to verbal irony can reveal much about how the form is used by interlocutors for a variety of cooperative and competitive social pragmatic functions, and can help inform the continuing struggle to understand the processing of verbal irony. As cognitive psychologists/psycholinguists who have been attempting to influence mainstream cognitive science experimentalists to pay attention to broad approaches such as interaction analysis (not to mention paying attention to theories outside of mainstream psychology of language), the criticism of laboratory methodology in the Kottoff paper and the call for broader approaches is well taken. We would hasten to add, though, that such broader perspectives, although clearly needed, do not serve as a panacea for the shortcomings of other methodological tools. Indeed, one can level the same flavor of criticism at interaction analysis that was directed at controlled laboratory studies—having too narrow a focus. Even interaction analysis omits crucial, rich, interactive phenomena (e.g., where a person was looking when speaking/hearing, facial expressions, nonverbal phenomena, and many others). Moreover, such broader perspectives fail to enable precise determination of causal mechanisms in verbal irony and other kinds of language online processing. Our view is that a variety of methodologies must be employed to understand different aspects of irony detection, comprehension, interpretation, chaining, use, and others (Colston & Katz, 2005).

DEVELOPMENT OF IRONY UNDERSTANDING

The development of verbal irony comprehension has also been a major topic of interest by irony scholars. The 1988 book, *The Point of Words,* by Ellen Winner, provides a review of the literature on verbal irony development up to that point, the essential findings being that children fully and correctly comprehend metaphors prior to instances of verbal irony, in part because the initial stage of comprehension, detection of a difference between sentence and speaker meaning, is more difficult for irony comprehension. Children are thus mostly unable to correctly, fully, and regularly comprehend irony prior to age 6 years. We've included some key papers that have been published since then on irony development.

The first of these papers itself serves as a very nice review of the research conducted to date on the development of cognition with respect to verbal irony. Creusere (2000) first provided this review and dissects developmental irony research into five areas: understanding, contextual influences, theory of mind influences, intonation, and social and communicative functions. The paper then makes a call for the importance of including developmental evaluations of theoretical claims concerning adult irony cognition, both as a means of providing stronger tests of the validity of such claims, as well as to uncover potential illusory beliefs about adult irony cognition (e.g., that adults always comprehend verbal irony correctly). In this spirit, the paper then evaluates whether the two tenets of the allusional pretense theory of discourse irony (Kumon-Nakamura, Glucksberg, & Brown, 1995) are at work in children's comprehension of verbal irony, allusion to violated expectations, and pragmatic insincerity. Fortunately for the allusional pretense theory, both claims were found to hold in children's comprehension of verbal irony, in participants as young as 8 years of age.

A paper by Hancock, Dunham, and Purdy (2000) continued in this vein of testing adult phenomenon on children. This paper evaluated 5- and 6-year-olds' ability to detect the nonliteral nature and intended meaning of ironic criticism and ironic praise. Most previous work had only addressed ironic criticism, and typically found that detection of nonliteralness precedes the ability to correctly infer an ironic speaker's intentions (see Dews & Winner, 1997, for a review). The current study brought ironic praise into the fold and found that the same essential pattern holds, but that it is easier to reject the literal meaning of ironic criticism than ironic praise. Additionally, the study revealed a differential enhancement of correct ironic detection with an echoic variable being introduced—in that children are aided in detecting ironic praise that explicitly echoes an earlier expectation for negativity (e.g., a speaker says, "you sure are a *bad* basketball player" after a player had said he was a bad player, but then played well), but children are not so aided with ironic criticism. Thus, the study confirmed in a developmental paradigm, the general asymmetry of verbal irony found in adults in that ironic criticism is more readily handled than ironic praise.

This study provides an important additional contribution in that it first raises but then diminishes the specter of such an asymmetry arising merely as a byproduct of children's exposure to a greater frequency of ironic criticism than ironic praise—such differential content has been observed in children's television programming (Dews, Winner, Nicolaides, & Hunt, as cited in Dews & Winner, 1997). The study instead argues that ironic asymmetry is likely due to the differential degree to which ironic criticism and praise allude to preceding events, commonly held expectations, social norms, etc., which tend toward the positive (Kreuz & Glucksberg, 1989; Kumon-Nakamura, Glucksberg, & Brown, 1995; Colston, 2000).

We concur with this position. Were it even true that ironic asymmetry arises entirely or even mostly from pure social learning, the question as to how such a systematic asymmetry got entrenched in the first place is still left begging. The ready alignment of ironic criticism with a widespread, positive, sociocognitive orientation, that is arguably universal except in cases of individuals being under extreme duress, mental illness, etc., and the concomitant lack of such correspondence by ironic praise, seems too compelling for mere coincidence.

The Harris and Pexman (2003) paper further contributed to this growing body of work on the development of ironic comprehension capacities in children, by investigating the development of the social functioning of verbal irony. This paper, in two experiments, made a parallel evaluation of the degree to which children at two stages of development (5–6-year-olds and 7–8-year-olds) can comprehend the meaning of, evaluate the speaker intent behind, and make use of the humorousness inherent in, ironic criticisms and ironic complaints. This study replicated and extended the Hancock, Dunham, and Purdy (2000) paper by revealing the asymmetry of evaluative sophistication of ironic criticism versus praise, as well as demonstrating the operation of the tinge mechanism (Dews, Kaplan, & Winner, 1995) in children's interpretation of both forms of irony. The paper additionally revealed that the humor function of verbal irony, one of the potential contributors to the muting process of verbal irony, is not fully functioning in children at the ages studied.

These studies taken together reveal, at the same time, some of the same patterns observed in adult hearers of verbal irony (asymmetry of ironic criticism/praise, the tinge mechanism, allusion to violated expectations, pragmatic insincerity, etc.), but also a progressive approach toward adult behavior vis-à-vis verbal irony, across developmental stages (accuracy of detection of ironic criticism and praise [especially the latter], detection of the humor function of verbal irony, universal sophistication with different ironic propositional forms, etc.). So clearly, adult-like abilities in comprehending and gleaning the social functions of verbal irony are emerging in relatively young children, but they also undergo a honing process as children develop.

SITUATIONAL IRONY

The last major topic we have included is that of situational irony. Situational irony is a lesser studied cousin of verbal irony, so our selections for this section are accordingly fewer. But a number of important contributions have been made to the rather fledgling field, that have begun to shape our thinking about irony in situations.

The earliest one of these papers that we've included is the Lucariello (1994) paper that was published in the *Journal of Experimental Psychology: General,* a journal specifically designed to appeal to a wide range of scholars and researchers in experimental psychology. This manuscript provided one of the first empirical demonstrations of some of the claims about the concept of situational irony that had been discussed by more historical sources. Most importantly, this study established that the general concept of situational irony is both a structured concept, and is shared and indeed prevalent among people.

The Lucariello (1994) paper first provided a discussion of the characteristics of situational irony, including how it involves unexpectedness, and given this deviation from expected normality, a "mocking" quality in that what occasionally occurs is often in direct contradiction to what is commonly expected by people. That irony also involves "human fragility" in that our expectations/desires are so readily and contradictorily violated, as well as how irony is accordingly common fodder for stories, is also discussed. The difference between situational irony and verbal irony is also briefly treated, followed by the possible internal structure of the concept of situational irony.

In the first "study" of the paper, a wide variety of instances of situational irony, taken from everyday examples, news reports, literary, and other sources is first reviewed and a detailed taxonomy of situational irony types and subtypes is provided. The second and third "studies" then address the primary empirical questions addressed by the study—is there a concept of situational irony, how similar is such a general concept to the taxonomy derived in the first study, and if such a concept exists, what is its internal structure?

Study 2 used a production task where people were asked to produce instances of situational irony that they had encountered directly or indirectly in the past. A great deal if similarity to the taxonomy produced in Study 1 was found, in that each of the subkinds of situational irony identified in Study 1 was produced by people in Study 2.

Study 3 then presented a new group of people with ironic vignettes (half of which were taken from the ironic situations produced in Study 2), along with other events that turned out unexpectedly (but not ironically), and events that turned out as expected. Subjects rated these three event types for their "goodness-as-examples" of ironic situations. The results revealed a concept structure similar to that demonstrated in the previous studies in that the most frequently produced ironic subtypes were rated as the best examples of irony, and the least frequently produced ironic subtypes in Study 2 were rated as least ironic (yet still more ironic than the nonironic unexpected foil items). Characteristics of the prototypically ironic items involved opposition and outcome (the experience of win or loss).

The greatest contribution of the Lucariello (1994) paper is thus its empirical verification of situational irony as a conceptual event type. Akin to scripts, which involve the dimension of expectedness, situational irony is also a schematized shared conceptual structure, but it instead involves unexpectedness and opposition. Situational irony thus captures the quintessential aspects of such events, their unexpectedness, but it also espouses the form that that unexpectedness takes—they're unexpected in a "culturally recognized way, making [ironic events] purportedly events for which a general knowledge structure is formed." Lucariello also briefly discussed why situational irony is humorous, and the processing of situationally ironic events.

The other two papers we selected make attempts to formally define what makes a situation and/or utterance ironic. The first of these, Utsumi (2000), offered an Implicit Display theory of verbal irony that specializes in determining the difference between irony and nonirony. The theory has three components. The first is that all instances of verbal irony involve what is termed an "ironic environment," in which there is an incongruity between a person's expectations and reality prior to an ironic remark being made, about which the speaker has a negative feeling. The second component is that such an ironic environment is implicitly displayed by a speaker by an allusion to the violated expectation, typically via pragmatic insincerity, that can reveal the speaker's negative attitude toward the discrepancy. The third component is that such ironic displays are graded in that there are very strong, obvious instances of ironic implicity display, and other less well-fitting instances. As such, verbal irony can be quantitatively analyzed as better and worse category members, to the end of predicting how ironic an utterance will be perceived as being.

This theory is offered as an extension and improvement upon the other families of theories of verbal irony, which are criticized as either being two broad or narrow to encompass all instances of verbal irony or to distinguish irony from nonirony. To offer just one example of each problem, the Pretense account is argued to be too powerful in that it would include all instances of indirect speech acts. The mention family of theories is also criticized as allowing in nonironic instances such as the example quoted from Giora (1995):

    a. Dina: I missed the last news broadcast. What did the Prime Minister say about the Palestinians?

    b. Mira (with ridiculing aversion): That we should deport them.

This example is considered problematic because it meets the purported conditions of mention with derisive attitude, yet fails to be ironic.

The criticisms of the scope of accounts of verbal irony are not necessarily new. They've been part of the reason for the progression of accounts of verbal irony and have also been discussed in various reviews of the irony literature. But the implicit display theory seems to be unique in its contribution of the notion of a prototype category structure for verbal irony. Although this too has received treatments elsewhere in somewhat different forms (see Colston, 2000; Gibbs, 1994), the specificity of the predictions enabled by Implicit Display are quite compelling.

The final paper included in this section is Shelley's (2001) paper on the bicoherence theory of situational irony. The paper bases this theory of situational irony on bicoherence conceptual relations, between either classes or elements. After first noting how most irony research has focused on topics other than situational irony, and briefly reviewing and critiquing the few treatments of situational irony, a review of the components of the bicoherence theory is offered. The nature of bicoherence, coherence, and incoherence is explained, followed by the basis of the theory on conceptual relations, salience of bicoherence relations, and emotions.

Next a corpus of situational irony cases selected from popular reporting media is thoroughly reviewed to demonstrate how the bicoherence theory provides a taxonomy to classify the cases. A discussion is then provided on how the theory is consistent with a dominant construct from social psychology—causal attribution, followed by sections on how the theory handles change in emotional reaction to situational irony over time, changes in the conceptual structure of irony, and irony in visual and musical modalities.

The most important contribution of the Shelley paper is arguably the more formalized structure lent to the general notion of contradiction, that many different accounts have struggled to define. The notion of bicoherence relations seems to bring us much closer to encapsulating this quintessential aspect of irony.

CONCLUSION

This brief review has attempted to highlight the unique contributions of the enclosed articles. This body of work, and the other papers we were unable to include, have made significant progress in our understanding of the comprehension, use, development, and make-up of irony in its various forms. This is a continuing endeavor, with many as-yet unanswered and even unaddressed questions and topics. We thus hope this collection will help inspire present and future scholars to continue this attempt at understanding this unique human phenomenon.

REFERENCES

Anolli, L., Ciceri, R., & Infantino, M. (2002). From "blame by praise" to "praise by blame": Analysis of vocal patterns in ironic communication. *International Journal of Psychology, 37,* 266–276.

Attardo, S. (2001). Irony as relevant inappropriateness. *Journal of Pragmatics, 32,* 793–826.

Brown, R. L. (1980). The pragmatics of verbal irony. In R. W. Shuy & A. Shnukal (Eds.), *Language use and the uses of language* (pp. 111–127). Washington, DC: Georgetown University Press.

Clark, H., & Gerrig, R. (1984). On the pretense theory of irony. *Journal of Experimental Psychology: General, 113,* 121–126.

Colston, H. (1997). Salting a wound or sugaring a pill: The pragmatic functions of ironic criticism. *Discourse Processes, 23,* 24–53.

Colston, H. (2000). On necessary conditions for verbal irony comprehension. *Pragmatics and Cognition, 8,* 277–324.

Colston, H. L. (2002). Contrast and assimilation in verbal irony. *Journal of Pragmatics, 34,* 111–142.

Colston, H. L. (2005). On sociocultural and nonliteral: A synopsis and a prophesy. In H. Colston & A. Katz (Eds.), *Figurative language comprehension: Social and cultural influences* (pp. 1–18). Mahwah, NJ: Lawrence Erlbaum Associates.

Colston, H. L., & Gibbs, R. W. (2002). Are irony and metaphor understood differently? *Metaphor and Symbol, 17,* 57–80.

Colston, H. L., & Katz, A. (2005). *Figurative language comprehension: Social and cultural influences.* Mahwah, NJ: Lawrence Erlbaum Associates.

Colston, H. L., & O'Brien, J. (2000a). Contrast and pragmatics in figurative language: Anything understatement can do, irony can do better. *Journal of Pragmatics, 32,* 1557–1583.

Colston, H. L., & O'Brien, J. (2000b). Contrast of kind vs. contrast of magnitude: The pragmatic accomplishments of irony and hyperbole. *Discourse Processes, 30,* 179–199.

Creusere, M. (2000). A developmental test of theoretical perspectives on the understanding of verbal irony: Children's recognition of allusion and pragmatic insincerity. *Metaphor and Symbol, 15,* 29–45.

Curco, C. (2000). Irony: Negation, echo, and metarepresentation. *Lingua, 110*, 257–280.

Dews, S., Kaplan, J., & Winner, E. (1995). Why not say it directly? The social functions of irony. *Discourse Processes, 19*, 347–367.

Dews, S., & Winner, E. (1995). Muting the meaning: A social function of irony. *Metaphor and Symbolic Activity, 10*, 3–19.

Dews, S., & Winner, E. (1997). Attributing meaning to deliberately false utterances: The case of irony. In C. Mandell & A. McCabe (Eds.), *The problem of meaning: Behavioral and cognitive perspectives* (pp. 377–414). Amsterdam: North-Holland/Elsevier Science.

Gibbs, R. (1986). On the psycholinguistics of sarcasm. *Journal of Experimental Psychology: General, 105*, 3–15.

Gibbs, R. (2000). Irony in talk among friends. *Metaphor and Symbol, 15*, 5–27.

Gibbs, R. W. (1994). *The poetics of mind.* Cambridge, England: Cambridge University Press.

Gibbs, R. W., & O'Brien, J. E. (1991). Psychological aspects of irony understanding. *Journal of Pragmatics, 16*, 523–530.

Giora, R. (1995). On irony and negation. *Discourse Processes, 19*, 239–264.

Giora, R., & Fein, O. (1999). Irony: context and salience. *Metaphor and Symbol, 14*, 241–257.

Hancock, J., Dunham, P., & Purdy, K. (2000). Children's comprehension of critical and Complimentary forms of verbal irony. *Journal of Cognition and Development, 12*, 227–240.

Harris, M., & Pexman, P. (2003). Children's perceptions of the social functions of irony. *Discourse Processes, 36*, 147–165.

Katz, A., & Pexman, P. (1997). Interpreting figurative statements: Speaker occupation can change metaphor to irony. *Metaphor and Symbol, 12*, 19–41.

Katz, A. N. (2005). Discourse and social–cultural factors in understanding nonliteral language. In H. Colston & A. Katz (Eds.), *Figurative language comprehension: Social and cultural influences* (pp. 183–208). Mahwah, NJ: Lawrence Erlbaum Associates.

Kotthoff, H. (2003). Responding to irony in different contexts: On cognition in communication. *Journal of Pragmatics, 35*, 1387–1411.

Kreuz, R. J., & Glucksberg, S. (1989). How to be sarcastic: The echoic reminder theory of verbal irony. *Journal of Experimental Psychology: General, 118*, 374–386.

Kreuz, R. J., & Link, K. E. (2002). Asymmetries in the use of verbal irony. *Journal of Language and Social Psychology, 21*, 127–143.

Kumon-Nakamura, S., Glucksberg, S., & Brown, M. (1995). How about another piece of pie: The allusional pretense theory of discourse irony. *Journal of Experimental Psychology: General, 124*, 3–12.

Lucariello, J. (1994). Situational irony: A concept of events gone awry. *Journal of Experimental Psychology: General, 123*, 129–145.

McDonald, S. (2000). Neuropsychological studies of sarcasm. *Metaphor and Symbol, 15*, 85–98.

Pexman, P., Ferretti, T., & Katz, A. (2000). Discourse factors that influence on-line reading of metaphor and irony. *Discourse Processes, 29*, 201–222.

Pexman, P. M., & Olineck, K. M. (2002). Understanding irony: How do stereotypes cue speaker intent? *Journal of Language and Social Psychology, 21*, 245–274.

Roberts, R. M., & Kreuz, R. J. (1994). Why do people use figurative language? *Psychological Science, 5*, 159–163.

Schwoebel, J., Dews, S., Winner, E., & Srinivas, K. (2000). Obligatory processing of literal meaning of ironic utterances: Further evidence. *Metaphor and Symbol, 15*, 47–61.

Shelley, C. (2001). The bicoherence theory of situational irony. *Cognitive Science, 25*, 775–818.

Sperber, D., & Wilson, D. (1981). Irony and the use-mention distinction. In P. Cole (Ed.), *Radical pragmatics* (pp. 295–318). New York: Academic.

Sperber, D., & Wilson, D. (1986). *Relevance: Communication and cognition.* Cambridge, MA: Harvard University Press.

Utsumi, A. (2000). Verbal irony as implicit display of ironic environment: Distinguishing ironic utterances from nonirony. *Journal of Pragmatics, 32,* 1777–1806.

Winner, E. (1988). *The point of words: Children's understanding of metaphor and irony.* Cambridge, MA: Harvard University Press.

Winner, E., & Gardner, H. (1993). Metaphor and irony: Two levels of understanding. In A. Ortony (Ed.), *Metaphor and thought* (2nd ed., pp. 425–443). Cambridge, England: Cambridge University Press.

Wilson, D., & Sperber, D. (1992). On verbal irony. *Lingua, 87,* 53–76.

PART II

THEORIES OF IRONY

CHAPTER 2

On the Pretense Theory of Irony

Herbert H. Clark
Richard J. Gerrig
Stanford University

We propose a pretense theory of irony based on suggestions by Grice and Fowler. In being ironic, the theory goes, a speaker is pretending to be an injudicious person speaking to an uninitiated audience; the speaker intends the addressees of the irony to discover the pretense and thereby see his or her attitude toward the speaker, the audience, and the utterance. The pretense theory, we argue, is superior to the mention theory of irony proposed by Sperber and Wilson.

What is irony? Traditional theories, according to Jorgensen, Miller, and Sperber (1984), assume "that an ironist uses a figurative meaning opposite to the literal meaning of the utterance" (p. 112). A person saying "What lovely weather" on a rainy day is using the figurative meaning, "What terrible weather." As an alternative, Sperber and Wilson (1981) offered a mention theory of irony in which a speaker is being ironic when he or she is mentioning, or echoing an earlier utterance, such as a weather forecaster's saying "The weather will be lovely today," in order to express an attitude such as contempt or ridicule toward it. Of the traditional theories, the main one with which Sperber and Wilson contrast their theory is that of Grice (1975, 1978). Sperber and Wilson marshaled a range of arguments, and Jorgensen et al. added experimental evidence, in support of the mention theory and against Grice's and the other traditional theories.

Grice's theory of irony, however, isn't what it is made out to be. It does not assume that the ironist is, technically, "*using* one proposition in order to get across its contradictory" (Jorgensen et al., 1984, p. 114; italics added), which is the main criticism leveled against it. It assumes, rather, that the ironist is *pretending* to use that proposition. In appealing to pretense, Grice appeared to be reflecting other traditional accounts of irony, the oldest perhaps going back to the Greeks. In this article, we expand Grice's few remarks on irony into a *pretense theory of irony,* argue for its

This chapter was previously published as "On the pretense theory of irony" (H. Clark & R. Gerrig) in the *Journal of Experimental Psychology: General, 113,* 121–126. Copyright © [1984] by the American Psychological Association. Reprinted with permission.

superiority to the mention theory, and describe its advantages for a psychological account of the functions and processes of irony.

A PRETENSE THEORY OF IRONY

The word *irony* comes from Greek *eironeia,* meaning "dissembling, ignorance purposely affected" (*Oxford English Dictionary*). From the beginning, it appears, irony was thought to have something to do with pretense. Grice (1978) began, like Sperber and Wilson, by assuming that "irony is intimately connected with the expression of a feeling, attitude, or evaluation. I cannot say something ironically unless what I say is intended to reflect a hostile or derogatory judgment or a feeling such as indignation or contempt" (p. 124). But Grice (1978) went on, in a crucial remark, to echo the Hellenic account: "To be ironical is, among other things, to pretend (as the etymology suggests), and while one wants the pretense to be recognized as such, to announce it as a pretense would spoil the effect" (p. 125). For Grice, then, irony is a kind of pretense.

What is the ironist pretending to do? Although Grice was silent about this, Fowler (1965), in his authoritative A *Dictionary of Modern English Usage,* hinted at an intuitively satisfying answer:

> Irony is a form of utterance that postulates a double audience, consisting of one party that hearing shall hear and shall not understand, and another party that, when more is meant than meets the ear, is aware both of that more and of the outsider's incomprehension. [It] may be defined as the use of words intended to convey one meaning to the uninitiated part of the audience and another to the initiated, the delight of it lying in the secret intimacy set up between the latter and the speaker. (pp. 305–306)

Putting Grice's pretense with Fowler's two audiences makes good sense of the irony in this example from Jorgensen et al. (1984):

> *She:* Trust the Weather Bureau! See what lovely weather it is: rain, rain, rain.
>   (p. 114)

With "See what lovely weather it is," the speaker is pretending to be an unseeing person, perhaps a weather forecaster, exclaiming to an unknowing audience how beautiful is the weather. She intends the addressee to see through the pretense—in such rain she obviously could not be making the exclamation on her own behalf—and to see that she is thereby ridiculing the sort of person who would make such an exclamation (e.g., the weather forecaster), the sort of person who would accept it, and the exclamation itself. The addressee can take "delight" in "the secret intimacy" shared with the speaker in recognizing that ignorance.

The pretense theory may be expressed as follows. Suppose S is speaking to A, the primary addressee, and to A, who may be present or absent, real or imaginary. In speaking ironically, S is pretending to be S speaking to A. What S is saying is, in one way or another, patently uniformed or injudicious, worthy of a "hostile or derogatory judgment or a feeling such as indignation or contempt" (Grice, 1978, p. 124). A in ignorance, is intended to miss this pretense, to take S as speaking sincerely. But A, as part of the "inner circle" (to use Fowler's phrase), is intended to see everything—the pretense, S's injudiciousness, A's ignorance, and hence S's attitude toward S, A, and what S said. S and A may be recognizable individuals (like the TV weather forecaster) or people of recognizable types (like opportunistic politicians).

The pretense theory provides transparent explanations for several important features of irony mentioned by Sperber and Wilson (1981).

1. *Asymmetry of affect.* An ironist is more likely to say "What a clever idea" of a bad idea than "What a stupid idea" of a good one. Why? As Jorgensen et al. (1984) pointed out, people tend to see the world according to norms of success and excellence, as Pollyannas who view the world through rose-colored glasses (Boucher & Osgood, 1969). People in ignorance should cling especially tightly to these norms. In the pretense theory, this is just the sort of person ironists pretend to be. If so, they should be more likely to make positive pretenses, "What a clever idea!" than negative ones, "What a stupid idea!"

2. *Victims of irony.* Irony generally has victims. According to the pretense theory, they should be of two kinds. The first is S, the unseeing or injudicious person the ironist is pretending to be. The second is A, the uncomprehending audience not in the inner circle. Some ironies seem to make victims of S for their misjudgments, and others, of A for their uncritical acceptance of S. The mention theory cannot distinguish these two types of victims.

3. *Ironic tone of voice.* In pretense or make-believe, people generally leave their own voices behind for new ones. An actor playing Othello assumes a voice appropriate to Othello. An ironist pretending to be S might assume a voice appropriate to S. To convey an attitude about S, however, the ironist will generally exaggerate, or caricature, S's voice, as when an ironist affects a heavily conspiratorial tone of voice in telling a well-known piece of gossip. Grice (1978) put it as follows:

If speaking ironically has to be, or at least to appear to be, the expression of a certain sort of feeling or attitude, then a tone suitable to such a feeling or attitude seems to be mandatory, at any rate for the least sophisticated examples. (p. 125)

With pretense, there is a natural account of the ironic tone of voice.

THE MENTION THEORY OF IRONY

The mention theory of irony hinges on a distinction between the *use* and *mention* of an expression, as in the following example from Jorgensen et al. (1984):

There is a cat in this room. (1)

There is a *cat* on this page. (p. 113) (2)

As Jorgensen et al. explained, *cat* in (1) is used to refer to some animal; the word *cat* in (2) is mentioned as a printed object with three letters. The idea behind the mention theory is that with irony a sentence is not used but mentioned. When the speaker in the previous example utters "See what lovely weather it is" with irony, she is mentioning some weather forecaster's words or sentiments in order to express contempt toward them. Not all ironies echo actual utterances, so the mention theory assumes that what is echoed may also be "popular wisdom or received opinions" (Jorgensen et al., 1984, p. 114). A good many ironies are explained as implicit echoes.

Sperber and Wilson (1981), in arguing against Grice, interpreted him as assuming that the speaker would be *using* the words *see what lovely weather it is* in order to implicate its opposite—that the weather was foul. That would give the wrong analysis, as they pointed out, because the speaker doesn't really mean for the hearer to believe she thinks the weather is lovely. The problem disappears, however, if she is assumed to be mentioning the words instead, as the mention theory proposes. But the problem also disappears if the speaker is assumed to be *pretending* to be a weather forecaster using those words.[1] As Ryle (1950) said about pretense

> Actors in speaking their parts before the audience are not, strictly, using their words. They are not being defiant, remorseful, loving, or desperate, but only pretending to be so. Their utterances cannot be classified as either "use" or "mention." (p. 339)

So Grice (1978) did not assume that with irony the speakers are *using* their words. As he said, "To be ironical is, among other things, to pretend" (p. 125).

How *should* irony be viewed—as echoic mention or as pretense? Is the speaker mentioning a weather forecaster's words or pretending to be a weather forecaster using those words?

Note first that all cases of ironic mention can be reinterpreted as cases of ironic pretense, often with more plausible results. Consider the echoic version of "The Hotel" by Jorgensen et al. (1984):

> "Shall we walk back to the hotel or take a taxi?" Sally asked.
> "Let's walk. It's not far. Just follow me," answered Carol. Sally felt she could have found the way herself. At one point she thought Carol had taken a wrong turn; she muttered, "We are getting lost!" and Carol heard her. But Carol seemed so self-confident that Sally followed her. They quickly reached the Campo San Stefano, and there stood the hotel.
> "We are definitely lost!" Carol said. (p. 120)

In being ironic, Carol is claimed to be mentioning Sally's words or the proposition she expressed. But is she? Sally talked about how they were *getting* lost, and Carol's words were about being definitely lost—the *result* of getting lost. It seems more perspicuous to say that Carol was entering the make-believe world of Sally's former worries and staging the next step in it by exclaiming they were definitely lost. In making that pretense, she was making light of Sally's earlier worries. All ironic mentions, we suggest, can be translated into ironic pretense along these lines.

Many ironies that are readily interpretable as pretense, however, cannot be viewed as echoic mention, for example, Jonathan Swift's (1729/1971) essay, "A Modest Proposal." The proposal was to serve up children—Irish children—as food to the rich. Methodically, and with perfect seriousness, Swift outlined the benefits of this plan, among them that these children would provide a new source of income for the poor and add a new dish to tavern menus. This essay is often pointed to as a model piece of irony. To explain the irony, the mention theory would have to say that the *entire* essay was an echoic mention. But of what? It is implausible that anyone had ever uttered the entire essay or expressed its entire contents or that dining on Irish children was ever a part of "popular wisdom or received opinions" (Jorgensen et al., 1984, p. 114). Surely Swift's irony works just because the idea is so absurd that no one could ever have entertained it seriously.

Treated as pretense, however, Swift's irony makes good sense. Swift was pretending to speak as a member of the English ruling class to an English audience. He expected his readers to recognize the pretense and to see how by affecting the pretense he was denouncing English attitudes toward the Irish. In Swift's (1729/1971) "A Modest Proposal," Grice's pretense and Fowler's double audience are particularly apparent.

The mention theory is forced to say that many ironies are merely *implicit* echoes—echoic mentions of popular wisdom or received opinion—but it does not describe any criteria for deciding what is a possible implicit echo and what is not. If Swift's proposal is considered an implicit echo, then surely almost anything goes. The predictions of the pretense theory, in contrast, are as precise for nonechoes as for explicit echoes. Ironists can pretend to use the words of any person or type of person they wish, just as long as they can get the intended audience to recognize the pretense, and, thereby, their attitude toward the speaker, audience, and sentiment of that pretense.

The rhetorical device of irony, as Fowler (1965) pointed out, is just one of several types of irony. There is also dramatic irony. In the Greek drama of Oedipus, for example, an utterance by Oedipus would seem insignificant to one of his companions but of great import to the audience, who realized its meaning for Oedipus's impending doom. And there is irony of fate, as in the statement, "Ironically, George bought a brand new Studebaker the day before the automobile company announced it was going out of business." What ties the three types of irony together, Fowler argued, is the presence of two audiences—one in on the secret and the other not. The mention theory of irony doesn't allow for the resemblance among the three types of irony. The pretense theory does.

ON THE PSYCHOLOGY OF IRONY

Psychological models of language use—saying and understanding, broadly conceived—tend to be of two sorts. Some specify the functions an aspect of language plays in saying and understanding, and others specify the mental processes by which those functions are realized. The two models of irony we have been discussing are both functional ones, and so each needs to be rounded out with models for the processes by which irony is designed and recognized. Our interest is in the recognition of irony.

A listener's understanding of an ironic utterance depends crucially on the common ground he or she believes is shared by the ironist and the audience—their mutual beliefs, mutual knowledge, and mutual suppositions (see Clark & Carlson, 1981; Clark & Marshall, 1981). The pretense theory makes clear how common ground will be needed. The mention theory does not.

Speakers are not just ironic: They are ironic only to certain listeners. Suppose it is common ground to Harry, Tom, and Anne that none of them can abide the poetry of Ezra Pound. Now suppose that Harry and Tom have just been to a lecture on Pound that they agreed was unexpectedly fascinating. As they meet Anne coming out of the lecture, Harry says either of the following:

Harry to Tom: Tedious lecture, wasn't it? (3)

Harry to Anne: Tedious lecture, wasn't it? (4)

With (3), Harry is being ironic to Tom, but not to Anne. Without knowing that they enjoyed the lecture, Anne cannot be a party to Harry's irony, because as far as she can tell, he is completely serious. Uttering (4) can only lead to confusion. Harry recognizes that Anne will take him seriously, based on their common ground, and so to utter (4) would be to deceive her. She has no way of recognizing his pretense.

As this example illustrates, the perception of irony often hangs on subtle judgments of what is common ground to whom (compare Clark & Carlson, 1982), so a listener or reader not supplied with the right information may not make these judgments accurately. Just such a thing may have happened in Jorgensen et al.'s (1984) echoic version of "The Lecture:"

> The instructor asked the whole class to attend a special evening lecture by a visiting professor.
> "How tedious!" Anne complained to Harry and Tom.
> Harry and Tom attended together and were both impressed by the high quality of the lecture, which was both educational and amusing. As they were leaving the lecture hall, they bumped into Anne.
> "Tedious, wasn't it?" Harry said. (p. 119)

The story fails to give one crucial piece of information: Did all three share knowledge that Anne, too, unexpectedly enjoyed the lecture? If they did, Harry's utterance would have been ironic to Anne; if they didn't, it would not have been, as just illustrated. According to the pretense theory, it should make little difference in this instance whether or not Anne had complained earlier, and it didn't. About half the students in Jorgensen et al.'s (1984) study saw irony in Harry's question, and half did not, whether or not Anne's complaint was mentioned earlier. According to the mention theory, Anne's prior complaint should make an ironic echo especially salient, but, as Jorgensen et al. noted, it did not. What appears to be critical is the pattern of shared knowledge and beliefs and not the presence of an utterance to be echoed per se.

In the pretense theory, ironists do not tell their listeners they are making a pretense but let them discover it for themselves. As Grice (1978) put it, "while one wants the pretense to be recognized as such, to announce it was a pretense would spoil the effect" (p. 125). But what do they need to be able to discover it? Again the crucial notion is common ground.

Listeners must see how the speaker's utterance is relevant to the common ground already established between speaker and addressees. If they cannot, they may not be able to discover the pretense. Consider Jorgensen et al.'s (1984) story, "The Party," both with their ending and with our alternative ending:

> The party was at the Clarks', but Joe didn't know where Mr. Clark lived.
> "It's on Lee Street," Irma told him. ("It's the house with the big maple tree on the front lawn.") You can't miss it."
> But Joe did miss it. He never would have found it if Ken hadn't seen him wandering down the street and led him to the Clarks' apartment. They lived over a store, and their apartment door was right on the sidewalk.
> Irma was already there when they arrived. "You're late," she called to Joe.

> "The Clarks have a beautiful lawn," he replied. (p. 117) (5)

> *Proposed alternative:*
> "You give wonderful directions," he replied. (6)

When the material in parentheses is absent, Joe and Irma share no knowledge against which they can make sense of (5). But when it is present, they do share the knowledge, and Irma can therefore discover Joe's pretense. That is just what Jorgensen et al. (1984) found. For ending (6), however, Joe and Irma's shared knowledge should be sufficient for her to discover the pretense with or without the material in parentheses. Ending (6), we venture, would be judged ironic even without any previous utterance to echo. If so, the reason that (5) isn't ironic without the previous material to echo is not that there is no previous material to echo. It is because (5) cannot be related to anything in Joe and Irma's shared knowledge. It violates one of Grice's most important maxims to speakers: Be relevant.

CONCLUSION

The mention theory appears at first to solve the most obvious problem about ironic utterances—that speakers are not really saying what they appear to be saying. What they are doing, the theory asserts, is mentioning, or echoing, prior utterances or sentiments. The solution is to treat irony as echoic mention.

Mentioning prior utterances, however, is not powerful enough to do the job: It does not do justice to what the ironist is trying to do. When Swift (1729/1971) begins describing his modest proposal, he wants his readers to think he is serious, and indeed, he is taken seriously—for a few pages. But as readers begin to see the point of his proposal, they realize that he is only pretending to make the proposal and that less astute readers, not privy to their shared understanding, will continue to take it seriously. They can take delight in being in on the pretense, in being a member of the inner circle. It is this way that Swift belittles the speaker, audience, and attitudes of his make-believe world. In some of the most effective examples of irony, the audience is intended to be taken in at first and to catch on only as the pretense is developed. So although irony, as the mention theory assumes, often involves other people's sentiments and a belittling attitude toward them, its spirit really comes from certain added ingredients: the inner and outer circles, the several types of victims, and the game of deception and discovery with the intended audience. All these come only with the more powerful notion of pretense.

ACKNOWLEDGMENTS

Preparation of this article was supported in part by National Institute of Mental Health Grant MH-20021 and by a National Science Foundation Graduate Fellowship.

We thank Eve V. Clark, Ellen P. Francik, Heather Stark, Kendall L. Walton, and Deanna L. Wilkes-Gibbs for their counsel on the article and Geoffrey Nunberg for leading us to Henry Fowler.

Requests for reprints should be sent to Herbert H. Clark, Department of Psychology, Jordon Hall, Stanford University, Stanford, CA 94305.

ENDNOTE

1. For a characterization of pretense, or of engaging in make-believe, see Walton (1973).

REFERENCES

Boucher, J., & Osgood, C. E. (1969). The Pollyanna hypothesis. *Journal of Verbal Learning and Verbal Behavior, 8,* 1–8.

Clark, H. H., & Carlson, T. B. (1981). Context for comprehension. In J. Long & A. Baddeley (Eds.), *Attention and performance, IX* (pp. 313–330). Hillsdale, NJ: Lawrence Erlbaum Associates.

Clark, H. H., & Carlson, T. B. (1982). Hearers and speech acts. *Language, 58,* 332–373.

Clark, H. H., & Marshall, C. R. (1981). Definite reference and mutual knowledge. In A. K. Joshi, B. Webber, & I. Sag (Eds.), *Linguistic structure and discourse setting* (pp. 10–63). Cambridge, MA: Cambridge University Press.

Fowler, H. W. (1965). *A dictionary of modern English usage* (2nd ed.). Oxford, England: Oxford University Press.

Grice, H. P. (1975). Logic and conversation. In P. Cole & J. L. Morgan (Eds.), *Syntax and semantics: Vol. 3. Speech acts* (pp. 41–58). New York: Academic.

Grice, H. P. (1978). Further notes on logic and conversation. In P. Cole (Ed.), *Syntax and semantics: Vol. 9. Pragmatics* (pp. 113–128). New York: Academic.

Jorgensen, J., Miller, G. A., & Sperber, D. (1984). Test of the mention theory of irony. *Journal of Experimental Psychology: General, 113,* 112–120.

Ryle, G. (1950). "If," "so," and "because." In M. Black (Ed.), *Philosophical analysis* (pp. 323–340). Ithaca, NY: Cornell University Press.

Swift, J. S. (1971). A modest proposal for preventing the children of the poor people from being a burthen to their parents or country, and for making them beneficial to the public. In T. Scott (Ed.), *The prose works of Jonathan Swift* (Vol. 7, pp. 205–216). New York: AMS Press. (Original work published 1729)

Sperber, D., & Wilson, D. (1981). Irony and the use–mention distinction. In P. Cole (Ed.), *Radical pragmatics* (pp. 295–318). New York: Academic.

Walton, K. L. (1973). Pictures and make-believe. *Philosophical Review, 82,* 283–319.

CHAPTER 3

On Verbal Irony

Deirdre Wilson
University College London

Dan Sperber
Ecole Polytechnique, Paris

Some years ago, a referendum was held on whether Britain should enter the Common Market. There was a long campaign beforehand: television programs were devoted to it, news magazines brought out special issues. At the height of the campaign, an issue of the satirical magazine *Private Eye* appeared. On the cover was a photograph of spectators at a village cricket match, sprawled in deckchairs, heads lolling, fast asleep and snoring; underneath was the following caption: "The Common Market—The Great Debate."

This is a typical example of verbal irony. As such, it is of interest not only to linguists analyzing spontaneous discourse, and to critics analyzing literary texts, but also to students of humor. It is curious, though, how little attention has been paid, by linguists, philosophers, and literary theorists, to the nature of verbal irony. Theories of metaphor abound. By contrast, while there are many illuminating discussions of particular literary examples, the nature of verbal irony is generally taken for granted. Where theoretical definitions are attempted, irony is still essentially seen as a figure of speech which communicates the opposite of what was literally said. In an earlier paper, "Irony and the Use–Mention Distinction" (Sperber & Wilson, 1981), we drew attention to some problems with this definition, and sketched an alternative account. We would now like to return to some of the issues raised in that paper, and propose some developments and modifications.

This chapter was previously published as "On verbal irony" (D. Wilson & D. Sperber) in *Lingua, 87,* 53–76. Copyright © [1992] by Elsevier. Reprinted with permission.

TRADITIONAL ACCOUNTS OF VERBAL IRONY

In classical rhetoric, verbal irony is a trope, and as such involves the substitution of a figurative for a literal meaning. Irony is defined as the trope in which the figurative meaning is the opposite of the literal meaning:

> Irony is the figure used to convey the opposite of what is said: in irony, the words are not taken in their basic literal sense.
> (Du Marsais, *Des Tropes,* chapter XIV)

Or, as Dr Johnson put it, irony is "a mode of speech in which the meaning is contrary to the words."

Modern pragmatic definitions of verbal irony remain firmly in the classical tradition. According to Grice (1975, p. 53), the ironist deliberately flouts the maxim of truthfulness, implicating the opposite of what was literally said. The only significant difference between this and the classical rhetorical account is that what was classically analyzed as a figurative meaning is re-analyzed as a figurative implication or implicature.

Yet the traditional definition of irony has many weaknesses. In the first place, there are obvious counterexamples to the claim that an ironical utterance invariably communicates the opposite of what is literally said. Here are some illustrations:

Ironical Understatements

We come upon a customer complaining in a shop, blind with rage and making a public exhibition of himself. I turn to you and say the following:

(1)   You can tell he's upset.

This is a typical example of ironical understatement. Understatements are traditionally analyzed as saying, not the opposite of what is meant, but merely less than what is meant. Though (1) is intuitively ironical, it does not communicate either (2a) or (2b), as the traditional definition of irony would suggest:

(2a)   You can't tell he's upset.
(2b)   You can tell he's not upset.

Or, take Mercutio's ironical comment on his death-wound:

(3)   No, 'tis not so deep as a well, nor so wide as a church door; but 'tis enough, 'twill serve.

(*Romeo and Juliet*)

Mercutio did not mean to convey that his wound was not deep enough, and would not serve. Ironical understatements thus fail to fit the traditional definition of irony.

IRONICAL QUOTATIONS

Imagine (4) as said in a cold, wet, windy English spring, or (5), as said in a rainy rush-hour traffic jam in London:

(4)   Oh to be in England
       Now that April's there. (Browning, "Home Thoughts From Abroad")
(5)   When a man is tired of London, he is tired of life.
                                                    (Boswell, *Life of Johnson*)

Either remark could be ironically intended. To succeed as irony, it must be recognized as a quotation, and not treated merely as communicating the opposite of what is literally said. What (4) would communicate when ironically intended is not—as the traditional definition suggests—a desire to be out of England now that April has arrived, but the idea that the English spring does not always live up to expectations, that the memory of home is not always accurate, that romantic thoughts do not always survive reality, and so on. The point of (5) would be not so much—as the traditional definition suggests—to deny the claim that when a man is tired of London he is tired of life, as to make fun of the sentiments that gave rise to it, the vision of London it was originally intended to convey. Ironical quotations thus fail to fit the traditional definition of irony.

Ironical Interjections

You have invited me to visit you in Tuscany. Tuscany in May, you write, is the most beautiful place on earth. I arrive in a freak cold spell, wind howling, rain lashing down. As you drive me home along flooded roads, I turn to you and exclaim the following:

(6)   Ah, Tuscany in May!

My exclamation would almost certainly be ironically intended. Ironical exclamations do not fit the traditional definition of irony. They do not express a complete proposition; hence, they cannot be true or false, and cannot usefully be analyzed as deliberate violations of a maxim of truthfulness. Moreover, it is hard to see what the opposite of the interjection "Ah, Tuscany in May!" would be. Yet verbal irony is clearly present here.

Nonironical Falsehoods

So far, we have considered three cases in which irony is present but the traditional definition is not satisfied. In a fourth case, the traditional definition appears to be satisfied, but irony is absent—which suggests that something is missing from the definition.

This example is taken from Grice (1978, p. 124). We are out for a stroll, and pass a car with a broken window. I turn to you and say the following:

(7)   Look, that car has all its windows intact.

When you ask me what on earth I mean, I explain that I was merely trying to draw your attention, in an ironical way, to the fact that the car has a broken window. My remark meets the traditional definition of irony. I have said something patently false, intending to communicate the opposite, namely (8):

(8)   That car has one of its windows broken.

Why do you not instantly leap to the conclusion that (8) is what I meant to convey? As Grice pointed out, though it fits the traditional definition, (7) cannot be understood as ironical in the circumstances. Clearly, something is missing from the definition.

The traditional definition of irony thus fails on the purely descriptive level: some ironical utterances do not communicate the opposite of what is literally said. But there is a more general problem. According to the traditional definition, an ironical utterance communicates a single determinate proposition which could, if necessary, have been conveyed by means of another, purely literal utterance. On this account, the ironical (9) should be pragmatically equivalent to the strictly literal (10):

(9)   What a wonderful party.
(10)   What an awful party.

Yet (9) and (10) clearly differ in their pragmatic effects. Intuitively, (9) expresses a certain attitude, creates a certain impression in the hearer. Thus even examples that fit the traditional definition are not adequately described by saying merely that they communicate the opposite of what was literally said. Yet one looks in vain, in either classical rhetoric or modern pragmatics, for attempts to deal with the obvious differences in effects achieved by ironical utterances and their strictly literal counterparts.

The traditional definition of irony raises another, more general problem. An adequate account of irony should provide not just descriptions but explanations. We need to know not just what verbal irony is, but why it exists, how it works, and what is its appeal. Now saying the opposite of what one means is, on the face of it, neither natural or rational. Traditional accounts of verbal irony thus suggest a certain sort of explanation: they suggest that irony is a deviation from the norm, that it should not arise spontaneously, that it is governed by arbitrary rhetorical rules or conventions, which may vary from culture to culture. We believe, on the contrary, that verbal irony is both natural and universal; that it can be expected to arise spontaneously, without having to be taught or learned. If this is so, then we need not only a different definition of verbal irony, but one that suggests a different explanation.

IRONY AS ECHOIC MENTION

In "Irony and the Use–Mention Distinction" (Sperber & Wilson, 1981), we outlined a new account of irony based on a distinction between *use* and *mention*. This distinction was originally developed to deal with the following sorts of contrasts:

(11a)   Natasha is a beautiful child.
(11b)   "Natasha" is a beautiful name.
(12a)   He deliberately provoked controversy.
(12b)   He deliberately mispronounced "controversy."

In (11a), the word "Natasha" is used to refer to a child; in (11b), it is used to refer to a word of English. In (12a), the word "controversy" is used to refer to a debate; in (12b), it is used to refer to a word. This self-referential use of words or other linguistic expressions is known in the philosophical literature as "mention." Thus, in (11a) and (12a), the words "Natasha" and "controversy" are *used*; in (11b) and (12b), they are *mentioned*.

In written English, as in the above examples, quotation marks are often used to mark off cases of mention. In the spoken language, such clues are rarely available. Sometimes, there is little room for doubt as to whether use or mention was intended: for instance, it is hard to see how a rational speaker could have intended "Natasha" in (11a) to refer to anything other than a child, or in (11b) to refer to anything other than a word. Sometimes, though, matters are less straightforward.

For instance, compare (14a) and (14b) as answers to the question in (13):

(13)   *Peter:* What did Susan say?
(14a)   *Mary:* I can't speak to you now.
(14b)   *Mary:* "I can't speak to you now."

In (14b), as in (11b) and (12b) above, quotation marks are used to distinguish mention from use. In (14a), the sentence "I can't speak to you now" is used to describe a certain state of affairs; in (14b), it is used to refer to a sentence of English—in other words, it is *mentioned*. Here, either (14a) or (14b) would, on the face of it, be an acceptable response to the question in (13), and in the spoken language some criterion for recognizing the intended interpretation is needed. Notice that, despite their linguistic similarities, the two utterances would be understood in very different ways: for example, in (14a) the referent of "I" is Mary, the referent of "you" is Peter, and the referent of "now" is the time of Mary's utterance; in (14b) the referent of "I" is Susan, the referent of "you" is the person Susan was speaking to, and the referent of "now" is the time of Susan's utterance. In order to understand Mary's reply, Peter must be able to recognize whether the sentence "I can't speak to you now" was being used or mentioned. A general criterion for resolving this and other linguistic indeterminacies is proposed later.

Utterance (14b) is, of course, a direct quotation. In direct quotations a sentence or other linguistic expression is mentioned. In "Irony and the Use–Mention Distinction" (Sperber & Wilson, 1981), we argued that indirect quotations could be analyzed as cases of mention too. Consider (15) as a possible reply to (13):

(15)   *Mary:* She couldn't speak to me then.

This utterance has two interpretations, closely paralleling those of (14a) and (14b). On one interpretation, Mary is not reporting what Susan said—Susan may not have said anything at all—but merely explaining why Susan did not speak. This interpretation parallels (14a) above: Mary uses the sentence "She couldn't speak to me then" to represent a certain state of affairs. On the other interpretation, paralleling (14b) above, Mary is reporting what Susan said. She is not directly quoting Susan's words: for example, Susan would have said "I," not "she," "can't," not "couldn't," and "now," not "then." On this interpretation, (15) is an indirect quotation, an attempt to reproduce not Susan's words but her meaning.

Now because (15), on this interpretation, is not a direct quotation, it cannot be analyzed as involving mention of the *sentence* Susan uttered. Hence, the contrast between the two interpretations of (15) cannot be analyzed in terms of a distinction between the use and mention of sentences. In "Irony and the Use–Mention Distinction" (Sperber & Wilson, 1981), we argued that it should be analyzed in terms of a distinction between the use and mention of *propositions*. On both interpretations of (15), we claimed, the sentence "She couldn't speak to me then" is used to express a proposition; the difference between the two interpretations lay in whether that proposition was itself mentioned or used. On the interpretation paralleling (14a), it was used to represent a certain state of affairs; on the interpretation paralleling (14b), it was mentioned—that is, used to represent itself. On this account, (14b), a direct quotation, mentions the sentence Susan spoke, whereas (15), an indirect quotation, mentions the proposition she expressed.

We went on to argue that verbal irony is a variety of indirect quotations, and thus crucially involves the mention of a proposition. The argument ran as follows. Note first that indirect quotations may be used for two rather different purposes—we called them *reporting* and *echoing*. A report of speech or thought merely gives information about the content of the original: in (15), for example, Mary may simply want to tell Peter what Susan said. An echoic utterance simultaneously expresses the speaker's attitude or reaction to what was said or thought: for example, Mary may use (15) to let Peter know not only what Susan said, but how she reacted to Susan's utterance, what she thought or felt about it. Irony, we argued, is a variety of echoic utterance, used to express the speaker's attitude to the opinion echoed.

Echoic utterances are used to express a very wide range of attitudes. Compare (16b) and (17b):

(16a)   *Peter:* Ah, the old songs are still the best.
(16b)   *Mary (fondly):* Still the best.

(17a)   *Peter:* Ah, the old songs are still the best.
(17b)   *Mary (contemptuously):* Still the best!

In both cases, Mary's utterance is echoic. In (16b), her attitude to the thought she is echoing is one of approval, from which it follows that she, like Peter, believes the old songs are best. In (17b), her attitude is one of disapproval. She dissociates herself from the thought she is echoing, perhaps indicating indirectly that she believes the old songs are *not* the best.

Verbal irony, we argue, invariably involves the expression of an attitude of disapproval, thus falling into the same broad category as (17b). The speaker echoes a thought she attributes to someone else, while dissociating herself from it with anything from mild ridicule to savage scorn. To illustrate, consider the following scenario. Mary has lent some money to Bill on the understanding that she will get it back the next day. She wonders aloud to Peter whether Bill will keep his word. Peter replies as in (18), thus reassuring her that Bill is trustworthy:

(18)   Bill is an officer and a gentleman.

The next day, Bill rudely denies all knowledge of his debt to Mary. After telling Peter what has happened, Mary comments as follows:

(19)   An officer and a gentleman, indeed.

This utterance is clearly ironical. Mary echoes Peter's earlier reassurance in order to indicate how ridiculous and misleading it turned out to be. To understand (19) as ironical, all that is needed is a realization that it is echoic, and a recognition of the type of attitude expressed.

Not all ironical echoes are as easily recognizable. The thought being echoed may not have been expressed in an utterance; it may not be attributable to any specific person, but merely to a type of person, or people in general; it may be merely a cultural aspiration or norm. For example, because the code of an officer and a gentleman is widely held up for admiration, a failure to live up to it is always open to ironical comment; hence (19) could be ironically uttered even in the absence of an explicit reassurance such as (18).

From both descriptive and explanatory points of view, the echoic account of irony compares favorably with the traditional account. On the descriptive level, it deals with the case where the speaker communicates the opposite of what she says, and with the various cases where she does not. What is common to all these cases is that the speaker echoes an implicitly attributed opinion, while simultaneously dissociating herself from it. What differ from case to case are the reasons for the dissociation.

Perhaps the most obvious reason for dissociating oneself from a certain opinion is that one believes it to be false; in that case, the speaker may implicate the opposite of what was literally said, and the utterance will satisfy the traditional definition of irony. However, as is shown by the ironical understatement in (1), a speaker may dissociate herself from an opinion echoed not because it is false but because it is too mild—because only someone dull-witted and imperceptive could put it forward in the circumstances. As is shown by the ironical quotations (4) and (5) and the ironical exclamation (6), she may dissociate herself from an opinion echoed not because it is false but because to hold it or express it in the circumstances would be patently absurd. The echoic account thus deals both with the examples that fit the traditional definition, and with those that do not.

The echoic account also sheds light on the problematic example (7) above, in which all the traditional conditions for irony are met but no irony is present. On the echoic account, what is wrong with this example is that no one's views are being echoed and made fun of. As soon as the missing condition is supplied, irony appears. Thus, consider the following scenario. As we set off for a stroll, I complain to you that my street is being used as a dumping ground for broken-down cars. You tell me I'm imagining things: the cars all look in perfect condition to you. Just then, we pass a car with a broken window, and I turn to you and say the following:

(7)   Look, that car has all its windows intact.

In the circumstances, this remark would certainly be ironical. I am echoing back to you the opinion you have just expressed, but in circumstances where it would clearly be ridiculous to maintain it. Thus, all that is needed to make (7) ironical is an echoic element and an associated attitude of mockery or disapproval.

Notice how inadequate it would be with this example to say that I was merely trying to communicate the opposite of what I had said. The main point of uttering (7) is to express my attitude to the opinion you have just expressed, and in doing so to imply that you were wrong to disagree with me, wrong to think the world is not going to the dogs, and so on. If I merely wanted to communicate (8) I would, of course, have expressed this proposition directly.

The echoic account of irony also differs from the traditional account in its explanation of irony. If irony is merely a variety of echoic utterances, then it should arise as naturally and spontaneously as echoic utterances in general, and require no separate rhetorical conventions or training. Since echoic utterances are not normally treated as departures from a norm, there is no reason to treat ironical utterances any differently. In fact, the existence of echoic utterances, and the ease with which they are understood, strongly suggest that there *is* no norm or maxim of literal truthfulness, as most modern pragmatists believe. *Any* utterance may be understood in two quite different ways: as expressing the speaker's own opinion, or as echoing or reporting an opinion attributed to someone else; it is up to the hearer to decide which interpretation was intended.

The echoic account of irony has considerable intuitive appeal. Indeed, it seems to accord with the intuitions of that expert ironist Jane Austen, who has Darcy say the following to that other expert ironist Elizabeth Bennet:

(20)   … you find great enjoyment in occasionally professing opinions which …
        are not your own.

                                                        (Austen, *Pride and Prejudice*)

However, we would like to modify one aspect of our original treatment. In the next
section, we will argue that the use–mention distinction is merely a special case of a
more general distinction, which is needed to account for the full range of echoic utterances, and of ironical utterances in particular.

IRONY AS ECHOIC INTERPRETATIONS

In "Irony and the Use–Mention Distinction" (Sperber & Wilson, 1981), we noted
that the traditional definition of irony fails to explain the very close links that exist
between irony and parody. The *Princeton Encyclopaedia of Poetry and Poetics*
(Preminger, 1974) defines parody as "the exaggerated imitation of a work of art."

> Like caricature, it is based on distortion, bringing into bolder relief the salient
> features of a writer's style or habit of mind. It belongs to the genus *satire* and thus
> performs the double-edged task of reform and ridicule. (p. 600)

If parody is exaggerated imitation, and irony is saying one thing and meaning the
opposite, it is hard to see what the two can have in common. On the echoic account
of irony, their similarities and differences can be brought out. Roughly speaking,
parody is to direct quotation what irony is to indirect quotation: both involve an
echoic allusion and a dissociative attitude, but in parody the echo is primarily of linguistic form; in irony, as we have seen, it is of content.

However, while both irony and parody intuitively involve echoic allusion, it is
hard to see how parody can strictly speaking be analyzed as a case of mention. Consider the following, from a parody of the later Henry James:

(21)   It was with the sense of a, for him, very memorable something that he
        peered now into the immediate future, and tried, not without compunc-
        tion, to take that period up where he had, prospectively, left it.

                                                        (Beerbohm, 1950, p. 3)

There are clear echoes here of James's style, but in what sense is (21) a *mention*?
Mention, we have seen, involves identical reproduction of an original; but (21) is not
a reproduction of anything James wrote: it merely *resembles* what he wrote. While
direct quotation involves mention in the strict sense—the exact words of the original
are reproduced—parody is typically based on looser forms of resemblance.

According to the *Princeton Encyclopaedia of Poetry and Poetics* (Preminger,
1974), parody may be directed not only at style, but also at content, or "habits of

mind." The following, from a parody of Galsworthy's (1922) *Forsyte Saga,* illustrates this aspect of parody:

(22)   Adrian Berridge paused on the threshold, as was his wont, with closed
         eyes and dilated nostrils, enjoying the aroma of complex freshness which
         the dining-room had at this hour ... Here were the immediate scents of dry
         toast, of China tea, of napery fresh from the wash, together with that
         vague, super-subtle scent which boiled eggs give out through their unbro-
         ken shells. And as a permanent base to these there was the scent of much-
         polished Chippendale, and of bees' waxed parquet, and of Persian rugs ...
             Just at that moment, heralded by a slight fragrance of old lace and of
         that peculiar, almost unseizable odour that uncut turquoises have, Mrs
         Berridge appeared.

                                                   (Beerbohm, 1950, pp. 110–111)

Clearly, there are echoes here of both form and content: of the sort of thing
Galsworthy said and the way he said it; but in what sense is (22) a mention? It is not
an identical reproduction of anything Galsworthy wrote: it merely resembles what
he wrote. Strictly speaking, then, neither parody of form nor parody of content can
be analyzed in terms of mention.

    In parody, as the *Princeton Encyclopaedia of Poetry and Poetics* (Preminger,
1974) said, an element of exaggeration is often involved. The same is true in many
standard examples of verbal irony. One such example is treated in Paola Fanutza's
(1985) excellent dissertation "Irony in Jane Austen's *Emma,*" in which a wide variety of ironical utterances are insightfully discussed. Emma is playing with her sister's child. Mr. Knightley comments as follows:

    If you were as much guided by nature in your estimate of men and women, and
    as little under the power of fancy and whim in your dealings with them, as you
    are where these children are concerned, we might always think alike. (Fanutza,
    1985)

To which Emma replies as follows:

    To be sure—our discordancies must always arise from my being in the wrong.
                                                   (Fanutza, 1985, pp. 47–48)

What Emma ironically echoes back to Mr. Knightley is a caricature of the opinions
he has just expressed. If mention involves identical reproduction of an original,
then where irony involves an element of exaggeration or caricature, an analysis in
terms of mention is too narrow.

    In fact, what is true of ironical echoes is true of all indirect quotations. Reports of
speech are not always identical reproductions of the content of the original: they may
be paraphrases or summaries; they may be elaborations, spelling out some assumptions or implications that the original speaker took for granted, or that struck the

hearer as particularly relevant. In such cases, the content of the indirect speech report resembles the content of the original without, however, being an identical reproduction of it; and the analysis of indirect speech in terms of mention is too restrictive.

In our book *Relevance* (Sperber & Wilson, 1986, chapter 4, sections 7 & 9), we therefore replaced the notion of mention by a notion of *interpretive resemblance,* or resemblance of content. In the appropriate circumstances, we argued, any object in the world can be used to represent any other object it resembles. A uniformed doll can be used to represent a soldier, an arrangement of cutlery and glasses can be used to represent a road accident, a set of vertical lines to represent the heights of students in a class. Such representations are used in communication for two main purposes: to inform an audience about the properties of an original, and for the expression of attitude. I may show you a uniformed doll so that you can recognize a soldier when you see one; I may communicate my attitude to soldiers by, say, kicking the doll.

Utterances, like other objects, enter into a variety of resemblance relations. It is not surprising, therefore, to find these resemblances exploited, and for just the same purposes, in verbal communication. Onomatopoeia is based on resemblances in sound, verbal mimicry on resemblances in phonetic and phonological form, direct quotation and parody on resemblances in syntactic and lexical form, translation on resemblances in propositional content. Where resemblance of propositional content is involved, we talk of *interpretive resemblance;* we reanalyze echoic utterances as echoic *interpretations* of an attributed thought or utterance, and verbal irony as a variety of echoic interpretation. In other respects, the account of verbal irony developed in "Irony and the Use–Mention Distinction" (Sperber & Wilson, 1981) remains unchanged.

What does it mean to say that one thought or utterance interpretively resembles another? Resemblance in general involves a sharing of properties: the more shared properties, the greater the resemblance. Interpretive resemblance, or resemblance in propositional content, we argue, is best analyzed as a sharing of logical and contextual implications: the more shared implications, the greater the interpretive resemblance. It is possible for two propositions to share all their implications; when one of these is interpretively used to represent the other, we say that it is a *literal* interpretation of that other proposition. On this account, literalness is just a special case of interpretive resemblance. However, one representation may interpretively resemble another when the two merely have implications in common.

Let us illustrate these ideas with an example. Mary says the following to Peter:

(23)   (a) I met an agent last night. (b) He can make me rich and famous.

As we have seen, an utterance such as (23b) has two possible interpretations, (24a) and (24b):

(24a)   He can make me rich and famous, I believe.
(24b)   He can make me rich and famous, he says.

On interpretation (24a), Mary's utterance is a straightforward assertion. On interpretation (24b), it is either an echoic utterance or a report of speech, and must therefore bear some degree of interpretive resemblance to what the agent said.

Suppose that what the agent said was actually (25):

(25)   I can make you rich and famous.

Then Mary's utterance would be a literal interpretation of what the agent said: the propositions expressed by the two utterances would be identical, and hence share all their implications in every context. In that case, it is quite reasonable to see Mary as having *mentioned* the proposition the agent originally expressed.

Suppose, however, that what the agent said was actually (26):

(26)   I can do for you what Michael Caine's agent did for him.

Then Mary's utterance would be a less than literal interpretation of what the agent said, and it would not be reasonable to claim that Mary had mentioned the proposition the agent originally expressed. It may be common knowledge, though, that Michael Caine's agent made him very, very rich and famous. In a context containing this assumption, (26) would contextually imply (23b). The report in (23b) thus interpretively resembles the agent's utterance in (26): the propositions expressed by the two utterances have implications in common. Many reports of speech, and many echoic utterances, are based on this looser form of resemblance.

We propose, then, to analyze indirect speech reports, echoic utterances and irony not as literal interpretations (i.e. mentions) of an attributed thought or utterance, but simply as interpretations, literal or nonliteral, of an attributed thought or utterance. This change corrects an over-restrictive feature of our earlier account.

THE RECOGNITION OF IRONY

Wayne Booth tells of a puzzling encounter with a graduate student, a sophisticated reader who was arguing that the whole of *Pride and Prejudice* is ironic. This student expressed a dislike of Mr. Bennet, and when asked to explain said, "Well, for one thing, he's really quite stupid, in spite of his claims to cleverness, because he says towards the end that Wickham is his favourite son-in-law." Booth commented as follows:

> He retracted in embarrassment, of course, as soon as we had looked at the passage together: "'I admire all my three sons-in-law highly,' said he. 'Wickham, perhaps, is my favourite; but I think I shall like *your* husband [Darcy] quite as well as Jane's.'" How could he have missed Mr. Bennet's ironic joke when he was in fact working hard to find evidence that the author was *always* ironic?'
>
> (Booth, 1974, p. 1)

Such failures, even in sophisticated readers, are quite common. Walter Scott, for example, is notorious for having missed the irony in Elizabeth Bennet's remark that she began to appreciate Darcy when she first set eyes on his magnificent estate at Pemberley (see Southam, 1976, pp. 155, 159, 165, footnote 8). The subtler the irony, the greater the risks.

There is no such thing as a fail-safe diagnostic of irony. All communication takes place at a risk. The communicator's intentions cannot be decoded or deduced, but must be inferred by a fallible process of hypothesis formation and evaluation; even the best hypothesis may turn out to be wrong. The standard works on irony (e.g., Booth, 1974, Muecke, 1969) provide good surveys of the sort of clues that put alert readers or hearers on the track of irony; but the clues themselves have to interact with more general interpretation procedures. In our book *Relevance* (Sperber & Wilson, 1986), we outline a general criterion for the resolution of linguistic indeterminacies which, we suggest, is used in every aspect of utterance interpretation, including the recognition of irony. This criterion is justified by some basic assumptions about the nature of relevance and its role in communication and cognition, which we can do no more than sketch briefly here. (For further details, see Sperber & Wilson, 1986; for summary and discussion, see Sperber & Wilson 1987.)

Human information processing, we argue, requires some mental effort and achieves some cognitive effect. Some effort of attention, memory, and reasoning is required. Some effect is achieved in terms of alterations to the individual's beliefs: the addition of contextual implications, the cancellation of existing assumptions, or the strengthening of existing assumptions. Such effects we call *contextual effects*. We characterize a comparative notion of *relevance* in terms of effect and effort as follows:

Relevance

(a)   Other things being equal, the greater the contextual effect achieved by the processing of a given piece of information, the greater its relevance for the individual who processes it.

(b)   Other things being equal, the greater the effort involved in the processing of a given piece of information, the smaller its relevance for the individual who processes it.

We claim that humans automatically aim at maximal relevance: that is, maximal contextual effect for minimal processing effort. This is the single general factor which determines the course of human information processing. It determines which information is attended to, which background assumptions are retrieved from memory and used as context, which inferences are drawn.

To communicate is, among other things, to claim someone's attention, and hence to demand some expenditure of effort. People will not pay attention unless they expect to obtain information that is rich enough in contextual effects to be relevant to them. Hence, to communicate is to imply that the stimulus used (for example, the utterance) is worth the audience's attention. Any utterance addressed to someone automatically conveys a presumption of its own relevance. This fact, we call the *principle of relevance.*

The principle of relevance differs from every other principle, maxim, convention, or presumption proposed in modern pragmatics in that it is not something that people have to know, let alone learn, in order to communicate effectively; it is not something that they obey or might disobey: it is an exceptionless generalization about human communicative behavior. What people do have to know, and always do know when they recognize an utterance as addressed to them, is that the speaker intends that particular utterance to seem relevant enough to them to be worth their attention. In other words, what people have to recognize is not the principle of relevance in its general form, but the particular instantiations of it that they encounter.

Speakers may try hard or not at all to be relevant to their audience; they may succeed or fail; they still convey a presumption of relevance: that is, they convey that they have done what was necessary to produce an adequately relevant utterance.

Relevance, we said, is a matter of contextual effect and processing effort. On the effect side, it is in the interest of hearers that speakers offer the most relevant information they have. However, speakers have their own legitimate aims, and as a result may choose to offer some other information which is less than maximally relevant. Even so, to be worth the hearer's attention, this information must yield at least adequate effects, and the speaker manifestly intends the hearer to assume that this is so. On the effort side, there may be different ways of achieving the intended effects, all equally easy for the speaker to produce, but requiring different amounts of processing effort from the hearer. Here, a rational speaker will choose the formulation that is easiest for the hearer to process, and manifestly intends the hearer to assume that this is so. In other words, the presumption of relevance has two parts: a presumption of adequate effect on the one hand, and a presumption of minimally necessary effort on the other.

As we have seen, the linguistic form of an utterance grossly underdetermines its interpretation. Direct quotations, indirect quotations, echoic utterances, and irony are not recognizable from their linguistic form alone. Various pragmatic theories appeal to complex sets of rules, maxims, or conventions to explain how this linguistic indeterminacy is contextually overcome. We claim that the principle of relevance is enough on its own to explain how linguistic form and background knowledge interact to determine verbal comprehension.

In a nutshell, for an utterance to be understood, it must have one and only one interpretation consistent with the principle of relevance—one and only one interpretation, that is, on which a rational speaker might have thought it would have enough effects to be worth the hearer's attention, and put the hearer to no gratuitous effort in obtaining the intended effects. The speaker's task is to see to it that the intended interpretation is consistent with the principle of relevance; otherwise, she runs the risk of not being properly understood. The hearer's task is to find the interpretation which is consistent with the principle of relevance; otherwise, he runs the risk of misunderstanding it, or not understanding it at all.

To illustrate these ideas, consider how Peter might set about interpreting Mary's remark in (19) above:

(19)   An officer and a gentleman, indeed.

As we have seen, this remark has two possible interpretations, (27a) and (27b), corresponding to what we originally called use and mention of the proposition expressed:

(27a)   Bill is an officer and a gentleman, I believe.
(27b)   Bill is an officer and a gentleman, you said.

Suppose that interpretation (27a) is the first to occur to Peter, and thus the first to be tested for consistency with the principle of relevance. To be consistent with the principle of relevance, an interpretation must achieve adequate contextual effects, or at least have been rationally expected to do so. To achieve contextual effects, an interpretation must either have contextual implications, strengthen an existing assumption, or contradict and eliminate an existing assumption. Now the hypothesis that, in the circumstances described, Mary might genuinely believe that Bill is an officer and a gentleman contradicts known facts; rather than eliminating existing assumptions, it is likely itself to be rejected. In the circumstances, Mary could not rationally have expected her utterance, on this interpretation, to achieve adequate contextual effects, and interpretation (27a) must be rejected as inconsistent with the principle of relevance.

Now consider (27b). This could be understood as either a report of speech or an echoic interpretation of an attributed thought or utterance. Suppose Peter decides to test the hypothesis that it is a straightforward report of speech. To be consistent with the principle of relevance on this interpretation, Mary's utterance must achieve adequate contextual effects—for example, by adding contextual implications, or by strengthening an existing assumption—or must at least have been rationally expected to do so. But, unless Peter's memory is defective, he will be able to remember his earlier remark, and will need no reminding of it. Hence, the hypothesis that Mary's utterance was intended as a report of speech is inconsistent with the principle of relevance.

The only remaining possibility is that Mary's utterance was intended as echoic: that is, she was echoing Peter's earlier utterance in order to express her attitude to it. What attitude was she intending to express? The hypothesis that her attitude was one of approval can be ruled out for reasons already given: in the circumstances, the idea that Mary could genuinely believe that Bill is an officer and a gentleman contradicts known facts. Hence, the only possible hypothesis is that Mary was echoing Peter's utterance in order to dissociate herself from the opinion it expressed.

Is Mary's utterance, on this interpretation, consistent with the principle of relevance? Would it achieve adequate contextual effects for the minimum necessary effort, in a way that Mary could manifestly have foreseen? It is easy to see how it might achieve adequate contextual effects: for example, it draws Peter's attention to the various ways in which Bill's behavior has fallen short of the ideal, and to the fact that he has made a mistake, is possibly responsible for Mary's loss of money, is unlikely to be trusted so readily again in his assessment of character, and so on; moreover, these are effects that Mary might easily have foreseen. As long as no other utterance would have achieved these effects more economically, this interpretation would also be satisfactory on the effort side, and would therefore be consistent with the principle of relevance.

In *Relevance* (Sperber & Wilson, 1986), we show that having found an interpretation consistent with the principle of relevance, the hearer need look no further: there is never more than one. The first interpretation tested and found consistent with the principle of relevance is the *only* interpretation consistent with the principle of relevance, and is the one the hearer should choose.

THE COMMUNICATION OF IMPRESSIONS AND ATTITUDES

What do ironical utterances communicate? While rejecting the traditional claim that they invariably communicate the opposite of what was literally said, we have, as yet, offered no alternative account. Ironical utterances, we said, communicate a certain attitude, create a certain impression in the hearer; but how are attitudes and impressions to be dealt with in a theory of communication?

At the end of "Irony and the Use—Mention Distinction" (Sperber & Wilson, 1981), we were rather skeptical about the possibility of dealing with the communication of impressions and attitudes within the framework of what we called "logical pragmatics," in which utterance interpretation was seen primarily as an inferential process involving the construction and manipulation of propositional (conceptual) representations:

> An ironical utterance carries suggestions of attitude ... which cannot be made entirely explicit in propositional form. In this respect, a logical-pragmatic model does not provide a better description ... than a semantic model. On the other hand, our analysis of irony ... crucially involves the evocation of an attitude—that of the speaker to the proposition mentioned. This attitude may imply a number of propositions, but it is not reducible to a set of propositions. Our analysis thus suggests that a logical-pragmatic theory dealing with the interpretation of utterances as an inferential process must be supplemented by what could be called a "rhetorical-pragmatic" or "rhetorical" theory dealing with evocation.
> (Sperber & Wilson, 1981, p. 317)

The suggestion was that the representational and computational resources of "logical pragmatics" would not be adequate to deal with expressions of attitude, which would have to be handled by entirely different mechanisms.

We would not now draw such a sharp distinction between logical and rhetorical pragmatics. We believe that the communication of impressions and attitudes can be handled in much the same terms as the communication of more standard implicatures. In this section, we will suggest how this might be done.

In *Relevance* (Sperber & Wilson, 1986, chapter 1), we argued that communication involves an intention to modify the audience's *cognitive environment*. The cognitive environment of an individual is a set of assumptions that are *manifest* to him; an assumption is manifest to an individual at a given time if and only if he is capable at that time of representing it conceptually and accepting that representation as true or probably true. Manifest assumptions may differ in their degree of manifestness: the more likely they are to be entertained, the more strongly manifest they are. To modify the cognitive environment of an audience is to make a certain set of assumptions manifest, or more manifest, to him. The intention to modify the cognitive environment of an audience we called the *informative intention*.

Consider now how utterance (28) might be handled in this framework:

(28)   *Mary, to Peter:* I can't stay to dinner tonight.

Mary's utterance modifies Peter's cognitive environment by making manifest to him a variety of assumptions. Peter's task, in interpreting (28), is to recognize Mary's informative intention: that is, to decide which set of assumptions she *intended* to make manifest, or more manifest, to him. In recognizing Mary's informative intention, he is guided by the criterion of consistency with the principle of relevance: that is, he looks for an interpretation on which (28) might rationally have been expected to achieve adequate contextual effects for the minimum necessary effort.

Among the assumptions made strongly manifest to Peter by Mary's utterance will be (29):

(29)   Mary has said to Peter that she can't stay to dinner that night.

It is easy to see how (29) might achieve contextual effects in a context easily accessible to Peter. For example, by assuming that Mary is a trustworthy communicator, Peter can infer that she is unable to stay to dinner; from this, together with other assumptions, he can infer that some of his plans for the evening will have to be abandoned; depending on the relationship between them, the effort he has gone to in preparing the meal, and the reason for her refusal, further implications would follow. In recognizing Mary's informative intention, Peter is entitled to assume that she intended to make manifest, or more manifest, to him enough of these implications to make her utterance worth his attention. These will be the *implicatures* of her utterance.

Manifestness, we said, is a matter of degree. Among the assumptions made manifest to Peter by Mary's utterance, some will be more strongly manifest than others; moreover, Mary's intentions concerning these assumptions will be more strongly manifest in some cases than in others. In the case of (28), for example, it is hard to see how Mary could have expected her utterance to be relevant enough to be worth Peter's attention if it did not make assumption (29) manifest to him. Let us say that when a communicator makes strongly manifest her intention to make a certain assumption strongly manifest, then that assumption is *strongly communicated.* Then in the circumstances described, (29) will be strongly communicated by (28).

However, not all the speaker's intentions are so easily pinned down. It may be clear, for example, that in saying (28), Mary intended to make manifest to Peter that she couldn't stay to dinner, and fairly clear that she intended him to infer from this that he would have to change his plans for the evening—by inviting someone else, say, by preparing less food, or by abandoning the meal and going out. It may not be so clear, however, that she expected him to follow any particular one of these courses of action, or to carry out the chosen course of action in any particular way. Thus, a wide array of assumptions is made marginally more manifest by Mary's utterance; as the chains of inference grow longer, and the set of possible conclusions wider, Mary's informative intentions become correspondingly less manifest, to the point where they are no longer manifest at all. We might describe this quite standard situation by saying that strong communication shades off into something less determinate, where the hearer is encouraged to think along certain lines, without being forced to any definite conclusion.

Let us say that when the communicator's intention is to increase simultaneously the manifestness of a wide range of assumptions, so that her intention concerning each of these assumptions is itself weakly manifest, each of these assumptions is *weakly implicated.* Then, by saying (28), Mary might weakly implicate a range of assumptions having to do with changes in Peter's plans for the evening, changes in her relationship to Peter, and so on. The less strongly manifest her intentions concerning such assumptions, the weaker will be the communication.

Most recent approaches to pragmatics have concentrated on strong communication. One of the advantages of verbal communication is that it allows the strongest possible form of communication to take place: it enables the hearer to pin down the speaker's intentions about the explicit content of her utterance to a single, strongly manifest candidate, with no alternative worth considering at all. On the other hand, what is implicitly conveyed in verbal communication is generally weakly communicated. Because all communication has been seen as strong communication, the vagueness of most implicatures and of nonliteral forms of expression has been idealized away, and the communication of feelings, attitudes, and impressions has been largely ignored. The approach just sketched, by contrast, provides a way of giving a precise description and explanation of the weaker effects of communication.

Suppose, for example, that in saying (28) Mary speaks sadly, thus making manifest to Peter assumption (30):

(30)   Mary has spoken sadly.

The effects thus created can be analyzed as weak implicatures. Assumption (30) makes manifest, or more manifest, to Peter a wide array of further assumptions. Why is Mary sad? Is it because she can't stay to dinner? Does Peter want her to be sad? How sad is she? Would she cheer up if he invited her for another evening? Would she stay if he cooked dinner immediately? Would she stay if he offered to drive her home afterwards, or if he lit a fire, or if he served fish instead of meat? By processing (30) in a context obtained by answering these and other questions, Peter can increase the contextual effects of (28). On the assumption that Mary intended to make (30) manifest to him, Peter is entitled to conclude that she also intended to make manifest to him enough of these effects to make (30) worth processing.

What we are suggesting is that the assumptions made manifest to Peter by Mary's utterance include not only the contextual effects of the proposition she has expressed, but also those of various descriptions of her utterance—her tone of voice, facial expression, accompanying gestures, and so on. Some subset of these may form part of the *intended* interpretation of her utterance, this subset being selected, as usual, by the criterion of consistency with the principle of relevance. The resulting communication will, of course, be weak, but it will not be different in kind from the communication of quite standard implicatures. In either case, the interpretation process will involve the inferential processing of newly presented information in the context of assumptions supplied by the hearer. What makes communication weak is merely the fact that a very wide array of assumptions is made manifest, or more manifest, so that, in forming hypotheses about the speaker's informative intentions, the hearer has a very wide range of contexts and contextual effects from which to choose.

Let us return, in the light of this suggestion, to our original example: the magazine cover with the caption "The Common Market—The Great Debate" printed across a photograph of spectators asleep at a village cricket match. How should this cover be understood?

The caption and photograph would, between them, have made a variety of assumptions manifest to contemporary readers. The caption would give them access to encyclopaedic information about the Common Market, including the information that a referendum on Britain's entry to it was shortly to be held, and that the referendum issue had been repeatedly referred to by politicians and journalists as the "Great Debate;" the photograph would give them access to a range of assumptions about the length and uneventfulness of village cricket matches, the lack of excitement normally felt by spectators, and so on. What set of assumptions was this cover *intended* to make manifest to contemporary readers? That is, on what interpretation might it have been intended to achieve adequate contextual effects for the minimum necessary effort?

Here, some hypotheses can be automatically eliminated as inconsistent with the principle of relevance. These would include the hypothesis that the designers of the cover merely intended to make manifest, or more manifest, the assumption that the debate on the Common Market would be exciting, together with some subset of its contextual effects. A communicator who merely wanted to achieve these effects could have achieved them without putting readers to the unnecessary effort of processing information about village cricket matches: hence, the use of this cover to achieve these effects would be inconsistent with the principle of relevance.

Consider now the hypothesis that the description "The Great Debate" was echoically used—a hypothesis that would have come easily to contemporary readers. Clearly, for reasons just given, the attitude being expressed to the opinion echoed cannot have been one of approval. By contrast, the hypothesis that it was one of dissociation or disapproval is strongly confirmed by the accompanying photograph. This photograph conveys an impression of stupefying boredom. On the assumption that the Common Market debate resembles the village cricket match in relevant respects, readers can infer that this debate too is one of stupefying boredom; that to call it a "Great Debate" is ridiculous; that it is not, in fact, a great debate. On the assumption that the cover designers intended to make these assumptions manifest to the audience, their behavior would be consistent with the principle of relevance. This is the interpretation, then, that the audience should choose.

On this account, the magazine cover would achieve a combination of strong and weak communication. It would strongly communicate that it was ridiculous to call the Common Market debate a "Great Debate," that this debate was very boring, and that it was not, in fact, a great debate. It would weakly implicate a wide array of contextual effects derivable from these assumptions, in terms of which readers would be able to create for themselves an impression of just how ridiculous the media descriptions were, and just how boring the debate was likely to be.

CONCLUDING REMARK

In this paper, we have analyzed irony as a variety of echoic interpretive use, in which the communicator dissociates herself from the opinion echoed with accompanying ridicule or scorn. The recognition of verbal irony, and of what it communicates, depends on an interaction between the linguistic form of the utterance, the shared cognitive environment of communicator and audience, and the criterion of consistency with the principle of relevance. This approach to irony, which appears to offer both better descriptions and better explanations than traditional accounts, has one surprising consequence which is perhaps worth mentioning here.

It is tempting, in interpreting a literary text from an author one respects, to look further and further for hidden implications. Having found an interpretation consistent with the principle of relevance—an interpretation (which may itself be very rich and very vague) which the writer might have thought of as adequate repayment for the reader's effort—why not go on and look for ever richer implications and reverberations? If we are right, and considerations of relevance lie at the heart of verbal communication, such searches go beyond the domain of communication proper. Though the writer might have *wished* to communicate more than the first interpretation tested and found consistent with the principle of relevance, she cannot rationally have *intended* to. Relevance theory thus explains how irony is (fallibly) recognized, and sets an upper limit to what the ironist can rationally expect to achieve.

ACKNOWLEDGMENTS

Deirdre Wilson is grateful to the British Council, the Associazione Italiana di Anglistica, and the University of Turin for their hospitality at the AIA conference on Le Forme Del Comico, October 1985, at which an earlier version of this paper was presented.

REFERENCES

Beerbohm, M. (1950). *A Christmas garland.* London: Heinemann.
Booth, W. (1974). *A rhetoric of irony.* Chicago: University of Chicago Press.
Fanutza, P. (1985). *Irony in Jane Austen's Emma. Tesi di Laurea* (Lingue e Letterature Straniere). Italy: Universita Degli Studi Di Cagliari.
Grice, H. P. (1975). Logic and conversation. In P. Cole & J. Morgan (Eds.), *Syntax and semantics* (Vol. 3: Speech acts; pp. 41–58). New York: Academic.
Grice, H. P. (1978). Further notes on logic and conversation. In P. Cole (Ed.), *Syntax and semantics* (Vol. 9: Pragmatics; pp. 113–128). New York: Academic.
Muecke, D. (1969). *The compass of irony.* London: Methuen.
Preminger, A. (Ed.). (1974). *Princeton encyclopaedia of poetry and poetics.* London: Macmillan.
Southam, B.C. (1976). *Sense and sensibility, pride and prejudice and Mansfield park: A casebook.* London: Macmillan.
Sperber, D., & Wilson, D. (1981). Irony and the use–mention distinction. In P. Cole (Ed.), *Radical pragmatics* (pp. 295–318). New York: Academic.
Sperber, D., & Wilson, D. (1986). *Relevance: Communication and cognition.* Oxford, England: Blackwell: Cambridge, MA: Harvard University Press.
Sperber, D., & Wilson, D. (1987). 'A precis of Relevance,' and 'Presumptions of relevance.' *Behavioral and Brain Sciences, 10,* 697–754.

CHAPTER 4

How About Another Piece of Pie:
The Allusional Pretense Theory
of Discourse Irony

Sachi Kumon-Nakamura
Sam Glucksberg
Mary Brown
Princeton University

The allusional pretense theory claims that ironic remarks have their effects by alluding to a failed expectation. In normal conversation, this is accomplished by violating pragmatic rules of discourse, usually the maxim of sincerity. Such violations simultaneously draw a listener's attention to the failed expectation and express the speaker's attitude (normally but not necessarily negative) toward the failed expectation. Using a variety of utterance types, 3 experiments tested the theory. The 1st experiment, using 4 speech act types, showed that both insincerity and allusion were perceived far more frequently in ironically intended utterances than in literally intended ones. The 2nd experiment demonstrated that the negative attitudes frequently expressed with ironic utterances are a function of the relative frequency of positive versus negative expectations and not an intrinsic characteristic of discourse irony per se. The 3rd experiment found that over-polite requests are more likely to be used ironically than under-polite ones, presumably because the former can serve a speaker's politeness considerations while simultaneously conveying both an intended request and the speaker's attitude. It was concluded that irony is used primarily to express a speaker's attitude toward the referent of the ironic utterance, while simultaneously fulfilling other goals as well, such as to be humorous, to make a situation less face threatening, and to serve politeness considerations.

This chapter was previously published as "How about another piece of pie: The allusional pretense theory of discourse irony" (S. Kumon-Nakamura, S. Glucksberg, & M. Brown) in the *Journal of Experimental Psychology: General, 124*, 3–21. Copyright © [1995] by the American Psychological Association. Reprinted with permission.

In a recent novel by a contemporary novelist, a woman enters a police station and asks the guard at the desk where she can find a certain police detective. The guard telephones for the information, and the following interchange is then described:

> "Three five one," the guard repeated slowly. "Third floor.
> Think you can make it on your own?"
> "Just about, I should think, thank you very much."
> Her attempt at irony did not make the slightest impression on the man's fatuous complacency. You couldn't beat them at their own game, of course.
>
> (Didbin, 1988, p. 249)

Three distinct instances of discourse irony are described here. The woman's answer "just about" is irony in the form of understatement. Her expression of gratitude "thank you very much" is irony in the form of over-politeness. And, as indicated by her observation that one couldn't beat them at their own game, the guard's initial question "think you can make it on your own?" is irony in the form of an insincere question: The guard does not really expect an answer to his question. Instead, his utterance is intended as an ironic barb.

What is interesting about these three clear instances of discourse irony is that not one of them is accounted for by any of the theories of irony that have been proposed thus far (cf. Grice, 1975, 1978; Jorgensen, Miller, & Sperber, 1984; Kreuz & Glucksberg, 1989; Sperber & Wilson, 1981, 1986). In this article we will review those theories, in particular those that have been submitted to empirical test. We then present a new theory of discourse irony that is intended to account for the entire range of ironic utterance types, along with some experimental tests of the theory.

Why do people use ironic expressions, and how are ironic expressions recognized? We can distinguish between two general kinds of irony: situational irony and discourse irony. Situations are ironic when an expectation is violated or otherwise invalidated in specific ways (Lucariello, 1994; Muecke, 1969). O. Henry's short story, *The Gift of the Magi* (Porter, 1912), contains a classic example of situational irony. An impoverished husband and wife each make sacrifices that render one another's gifts useless. He sells his gold pocket-watch to buy her a tortoise-shell brooch for her hair; she cuts off her hair and sells it so that she can buy a gold fob for his watch. The double irony lies in the particular way that their expectations were foiled. Note that it is the specific connection between what a person does and the violated expectation that produces the irony in this case. If, for example, someone had decided to trade in his pocket-watch for a wristwatch and then received a watch fob as a gift, we would not necessarily characterize the situation as ironic. As Lucariello pointed out, unexpectedness is a central property of ironic events. Such events can be referred to literally (e.g., "You bought a watch fob for me ... how ironic!"), or they can serve as an occasion for ironic remarks (e.g., "What a wonderful gift ... just what I needed!").

Just as situational irony does not necessitate ironic language, ironic language does not require situational irony. Like situational irony, however, ironic language also involves failed expectations of one kind or another. Consider a situation in which two people approach a door. The first person to reach the door opens it and lets it swing shut behind her. The second person, carrying a heavy box, says, (1) "Don't hold the door open;" I'll just say "open sesame; " or (2) "Thanks for holding the door." Both (1) and (2) are ironic.[1] Each expresses the speaker's displeasure or disapproval at having a door slammed in her face, and each is patently insincere. Further, both utterances allude to the expectation that doors will be held open for people who are burdened and cannot open doors for themselves. And, like our opening examples, both utterances also pose serious problems for the traditional pragmatic theory of discourse irony.

According to pragmatic theory (Grice, 1975, 1978; Searle, 1979), participants in conversation implicitly observe the cooperative principle, which includes following the maxims to be truthful and to be relevant in conversation. When a speaker says something that is obviously false, such as "What lovely weather" during a downpour, a listener must reject the literal meaning as the intended meaning and infer that the speaker means the opposite of what was said. This account is problematic for at least two reasons. First, it fails to provide the motivation for saying the opposite of what one means. Second, it is not clear that expressions such as (1) and (2) above are literally the opposite of what was intended. What, for example, might be the opposite of "Thanks for holding the door?" Because the notion of opposite meanings is applicable only to declarative assertions—assertions that can be judged as either true or false—the traditional pragmatic theory fails to account for the ironic uses of other types of expressions, such as requests, offers, or expressions of thanks, among others. The pragmatic theory also fails in those cases where the assertion is true but is nonetheless intended ironically, as when an annoyed listener says "You sure know a lot" to someone who is arrogantly and offensively showing off knowledge.

More recent accounts of irony abandon the concept of opposite meaning and focus instead on the concept of echoing. When using irony, a speaker is said to echo either someone's thoughts or feelings, or conventional wisdom, expectations, or preferences. Sperber and Wilson (1981, 1986), for example, proposed that irony involves echoic interpretation. When someone utters "what lovely weather" during a rainstorm, the intent is not to inform anyone about the state of the weather, but instead to express an attitude. The attitude is expressed in this case by echoing conventional preference for good weather. Sperber and Wilson also suggested that irony is generally used to express disapproval. For example, expressions such as "what terrible weather" uttered when the weather is actually gorgeous would normally be considered anomalous because there is no prior expectation or preference that the weather should be terrible. However, saying "what terrible weather" on a beautiful day can communicate irony when both speaker and listener share knowledge of a relevant antecedent event, such as someone's faulty prediction that the weather would be terrible (Kreuz & Glucksberg, 1989). In such cases, the irony can serve to remind the listener of that prediction and thus call attention to the discrepancy between what was expected and the actual state of affairs. More generally, Kreuz and Glucksberg (1989) proposed that irony is used to remind of antecedent

Irony is not just negative attitude

events, social norms, or shared expectations in order to call attention to a discrepancy between what is and what should have been.

Calling attention to a discrepancy between what is and what should have been implies that an important function of discourse irony is to express negative attitudes, often disappointment. However, although people generally do use irony to express negative attitudes such as disappointment, negativity may not be an intrinsic property of the ironic form. Kreuz and Long (1991) and Long and Kreuz (1991) have argued that irony can be used to accomplish a variety of communication goals. In one of their studies, subjects listed the goals that could be fulfilled by using irony in discourse. The most frequently listed goal was to emphasize a point, followed by to be humorous; being derogatory was the third most frequently listed goal. Other goals, in order of frequency, were to express emotion, to alleviate personal/social discomfort, to provoke a reaction, to get attention, to manage the conversation, and to dissemble. Because the relative frequency of these goals depends upon the sample of items chosen for the experiment, these frequency data need not reflect relative frequency of use in natural settings. However, these data clearly indicate that expressing a negative attitude is not a necessary property of irony.

What are the necessary properties of irony in discourse? The echo theories, outlined above, claim that irony must always echo some prior event or expectation. In cases such as a faulty weather prediction, echoing seems an apt term for the speaker's utterance. In many other cases, it is not immediately apparent that the speaker is echoing any specific utterance or even any specific unspoken thought. This problem is apparent when we consider the various ways that irony can be expressed. In addition to the counterfactual assertive, irony can be communicated in at least four other ways: (a) true assertions, such as "You sure know a lot" to someone who is arrogantly showing off their knowledge; (b) questions, such as "How old did you say you were?" to someone acting inappropriately for his or her age; (c) offerings, such as "How about another small slice of pizza?" to someone who has just gobbled up the whole pie; and (d) over-polite requests, such as "Would you mind very much if I asked you to consider cleaning up your room some time this year?" to an inconsiderate and slovenly housemate.

With the possible exception of (a), which could be construed as an echoic interpretation of the offensive person's view of himself or herself, the question, offering, and request examples do not seem to be echoic, although in rare instances they could be. Instead, they seem to be allusive: All four examples allude to expectations or norms that have been violated. The allusion can be direct, as in utterances that explicitly echo a prior utterance, or they can be indirect, as in examples (b) through (d) above. Because echoic utterances can be subsumed under the more general rubric of allusion, we propose that echoic interpretation is not a necessary property of discourse irony. Instead, the more general claim is that an allusion to some prior prediction, expectation, preference, or norm is a necessary property of discourse irony. More specifically, a necessary property of discourse irony is an allusion to some prediction, expectation, preference, or norm that has been violated. Thus, the allusional function of irony is not simply a type of topical reference or cohesion, but refers specifically to a discrepancy between what is expected (what should be) and what actually is.

A second characteristic of discourse irony is also apparent in these as well as other examples, namely, insincerity. In the paradigmatic case where people use a counterfactual assertion in order to communicate irony, the speaker does not sincerely intend to inform the listener about a state of the world. Saying that the weather is wonderful when in fact it is terrible is an insincere description of the weather. In such cases, people can be insincere by uttering a false statement. However, people can also be insincere yet utter a true statement. Saying "you know a lot," as in example (a) above, is true, but is also insincere as a compliment. The speaker in this case expresses a negative attitude toward the recipient of the remark. Example (b) above also involves insincerity. The speaker asks a question, but does not want to know the answer, presumably because the answer is already known. Instead, the speaker asks the question in order to rebuke the addressee. Similarly, in offering more pizza to a glutton who has polished off everything in sight, one neither wants nor expects the offer to be accepted, and so it is an insincere offer. Finally, using over-polite language when asking someone to do something that should have been done as a matter of routine also involves insincerity. The person making the request does not intend the excessive politeness, but instead uses over-polite language in order to express an attitude of irritation toward the recipient of the request. We suggest that all ironically intended utterances involve *pragmatic insincerity,* in that they violate one or more of the felicity conditions for well-formed speech acts.

Felicity conditions were originally described by Austin (1962), and then elaborated on by Searle (1969, 1979), as conditions that every utterance should satisfy in order to be a well-formed, smoothly functioning speech act. Felicity conditions concern (a) the propositional content of an utterance, (b) the status of both the speaker and the hearer of the utterance, (c) the sincerity of the psychological state expressed or implied by the utterance, and (d) the perception of the speaker's sincerity by the hearer. Pragmatic insincerity occurs when a speaker is perceived as intentionally violating felicity conditions for at least one of these aspects of an utterance. For example, declarative assertions should be true, compliments should be true and taken as compliments rather than rebukes, questions should be asked only when an answer is desired, offers should be made only when acceptance is desirable, and politeness levels should be appropriate to the situation. Whenever conventions such as these are violated, a speaker may be perceived as being intentionally insincere.

Insincerity thus may be a necessary condition for discourse irony, but it is certainly not a sufficient condition. When a speaker is perceived as lying, for example, irony would not be communicated. The insincerity must be at the pragmatic, not at the substantive, level. In addition to pragmatic insincerity, ironic utterances must also allude to some prior expectation, norm, or convention that has been violated in one way or another. These two prerequisites for ironically intended utterances are not inconsistent with the echo theories discussed above, but instead are more general statements of those theories. Because the hypothesis involves both allusion and pragmatic insincerity, we will refer to it as the allusional pretense theory of irony.[2]

The theory makes two major claims:

1. Ironic utterances are intended to be allusive in that they are intended to call the listener's attention to some expectation that has been violated in some way. Ironic remarks that are echoic accomplish this kind of allusion by either explicitly or implicitly echoing some prior utterance or some prior thought (cf. Jorgensen et al., 1984; Sperber & Wilson, 1981, 1986), but we propose that echoing or echoic interpretation are not the only ways that allusion to unfulfilled expectations is accomplished in ordinary discourse.

2. Pragmatic insincerity is a criterial feature of ironic utterances. The standard pragmatic theory (Grice, 1975, 1978; Searle, 1979) considered only one type of insincerity, semantic or propositional insincerity, namely, uttering false assertions. In standard pragmatic theory, a necessary condition for verbal irony is saying the opposite of what one means, in short, making a counterfactual statement. This formulation is too restrictive because there are a variety of utterance types that cannot be counterfactual because the criterion of truth is simply not applicable. Among such utterance types are compliments, questions, and requests. Such utterance types are neither true nor false, but they can be sincere or insincere. The construct of pragmatic insincerity rather than truth is thus the more general because it is the more inclusive.

Echo and reminder theories, although not explicitly limited to utterances that can be either true or false, have nevertheless been exclusively focused on this one utterance type, assertives. With respect to these theories, the allusional pretense theory claims to be the more general and inclusive.

We report three experiments that examine some of the empirical implications of the allusional pretense theory. Experiment 1 examines whether people perceive both allusion to failed expectations and insincerity in ironically intended utterances.

Experiment 2 addresses the issue of asymmetry in irony. Generally, irony can be communicated by using positive statements in the context of negative events, as when one says "thank you very much" to someone who has just stepped on one's toes. Kreuz and Glucksberg (1989) demonstrated that irony could be communicated by using negative statements in the context of positive events, provided that the ironist could allude to an explicit antecedent event, such as saying "what terrible weather" on a beautiful day to refer to a faulty forecast of rain. In Experiment 2 we extend this finding to the case where there are implicit rather than explicit antecedent conditions: (a) when people's expectations are negative and are then disconfirmed by a positive event, and (b) when there are expectations of appropriate quantity that are disconfirmed in either direction. The reminder theory of Kreuz and Glucksberg was limited to explicit antecedent events of which people could be reminded. The allusional pretense theory makes the more general claim that reminding per se is not a necessary condition for irony. Instead, calling attention to any expectation that has been violated is the more general condition for interpreting an utterance as ironic.

Experiment 3 examines another asymmetry in discourse irony, the use of over-polite requests rather than under-polite requests to communicate irony. As indicated above, Grice's (1975) pragmatic theory did not address this issue at all, focusing exclusively on assertions that could be judged either true or false. As such, it does not address the ironic use of requests. The echo and reminder theories also do not address the issue of why over- rather than under-polite requests communicate irony. The allusional pretense theory accounts for this asymmetry in terms of the joint operation of allusion to a violated expectation and the intentional use of pragmatic insincerity.

EXPERIMENT 1: PRAGMATIC INSINCERITY AND ALLUSIONAL FUNCTION

According to the allusional pretense theory, utterances will be perceived as ironic if they are perceived as insincere and if they are also perceived as alluding to a discrepancy between an expectation and reality. Because the theory was developed to account for counterfactual assertions and for the entire range of ironic forms, this experiment sampled a variety of utterance types from four major speech act categories: assertives, directives, commissives, and expressives. Assertives are utterances that purport to describe some state of the world. Examples of the kinds of assertives that we sampled are as follows:

i. Counterfactual statements.
   a. Positive surface form, such as "This certainly is beautiful weather" when the weather is actually terrible.
   b. Negative surface form, such as "You certainly don't know how to cook," addressed to a cook who had claimed incompetence in the kitchen yet had prepared a superb dinner.
   c. Neutral surface form, such as "This is a long paper," addressed to someone who had written a very short paper.
ii. True statements, such as "You sure know a lot," addressed to someone who is indeed knowledgeable but is being obnoxious about it.

Directives are statements that are intended to get someone to do something. The directives that we sampled included (a) questions, such as "How old are you?" addressed to an adult who is behaving childishly; and (b) over-polite requests, such as "I'm sorry to bother you but I'm just wondering if it is at all possible for you to maybe consider turning the music down a little bit?" addressed to a noisy neighbor late at night.

Commissives are statements that commit the speaker to an action, such as an offering. An example would be to say "Would you like to have another small slice of pizza?" to someone who has eaten a large pizza by himself. Expressives are statements that directly communicate a speaker's feelings, such as "Thank you for your concern," addressed to someone who has shown no concern at all.

Experiment 1a served as a pilot study and pretest for the materials of Experiment 1b. Participants in Experiment 1a were given a set of stories to read and asked to describe speakers' intentions in uttering potentially ironic statements and also to judge the degree of irony intended by speakers. Experiment 1a also served as a preliminary test of whether utterances perceived as ironic were also perceived as alluding to a failed expectation and as insincere. Experiment 1b tested these hypotheses directly, using the materials provided by Experiment 1a.

EXPERIMENT 1A: DOES IRONY INVOLVE ALLUSION AND INSINCERITY?

Method

Participants. Thirty undergraduate students at Princeton University participated in this study for pay. All were native English speakers, and none had participated in a similar experiment before.

Materials and Design. Fifty-two short stories were written in which two or three people have a brief interaction and at the end one of them makes a remark to another. Some of the stories were adapted from Gibbs (1986), Jorgensen et al. (1984), Kreuz and Glucksberg (1989), and Kreuz and Long (1991); the rest were prepared specifically for this study. Of the 52 stories, 26 were nonliteral. Twenty-two of the nonliteral stories contained a critical sentence that was potentially ironic, two contained a remark with a metaphoric intention, and two contained a conventional indirect request. The stories with metaphors and conventional indirect requests were included as fillers and also as checks to ensure that participants did not perceive just any nonliteral utterance as ironic, insincere, or allusive.

Of the 22 irony stories, ten contained assertives (four positive counterfactual statements, two negative counterfactual statements, one neutral counterfactual statement, and three factual statements), nine contained directives (four requests and five questions), one contained a commissive (offering), and two contained expressives (thanking). We chose this set of items because we wanted a diverse sample of ironic utterance types. The remaining 26 stories were literal. Table 4.1 presents an example of an irony story and a literal story with the same critical utterance. The stories had a mean length of 67 words.

Two sets of booklets were constructed, each of which contained thirteen nonliteral stories (eleven with potentially ironic remarks, one with a metaphoric remark, and one with a conventional indirect request) and thirteen literal stories. Story type (literal vs. nonliteral) was counterbalanced between the two sets such that the literal and the nonliteral versions of the same story did not appear together in one set. The presentation order of the stories was randomized for each booklet.

TABLE 4.1

Examples of Stories Used for Experiment

Knowledgeable Danny

Irony version

During the precept, Danny was dominating the discussion. He certainly seemed to be familiar with the subject, but he was obnoxious in the way he showed off his knowledge. Jesse, one of Danny's classmates, said, "You sure know a lot."

Literal version

Danny was helping Jesse with his calculus homework. Jesse was very bad at calculus and he had no clue about what he was supposed to do. However, Danny explained, starting from the basics, and finally Jesse managed to finish his homework. Jesse said to Danny, "Thank you. You sure know a lot."

Note. Subjects were asked to judge how ironic the character's final remark seemed to them.

Procedure. Participants were tested individually and were randomly assigned to one of the two sets of booklets. Participants began the experiment by reading the following instructions printed on the first page of their booklets:

I am interested in how people use language to communicate ideas to one another. As you know, people can accomplish this in a variety of ways. In the following pages you will read a number of short stories. In each story, two or three characters will have a brief interaction, and at the end, one of the characters will say something to another character.

For each short story, there will be two questions about the character's final remark. Please answer those questions in a few sentences. After answering the questions, please judge how ironic the character's final remark (shown in bold type) seems to you, if at all. There will be a rating scale on which to indicate your judgment. The scale will be 1 to 7, where 1 means "not at all ironic," 4 means "somewhat ironic," and 7 means "definitely ironic."

Before you begin, please look over a few of the stories. This will give you a general feel for the types of stories you will be seeing. If you occasionally find yourself unsure about your response, just use your best judgment. Remember, there are no right or wrong answers: I am simply interested in your intuitions. Please be sure to provide answers and ratings for all the stories. Thank you very much for your participation.

The participants then read the stories and answered three questions for each story: (a) "What do you think [the character] is trying to get across?" (b) "Why do you think [the character] said '[the critical utterance]' in order to convey what you mentioned above?" and (c) "How would you rate [the character's] final comment? Please circle the number that corresponds to your choice." Participants answered by indicating their responses on the 7-point scale described above. The participants took about 35 min to complete the booklets.

Results and Discussion

The primary purpose of this pilot study was to obtain items to be used in Experiment 1b, thus our initial concern was with the irony ratings for items in ironic and nonironic story contexts. Our criterion for considering an item as suitably ironic was whether or not it was rated as significantly more ironic in ironic contexts than in literal contexts. Only one item failed to meet this criterion, a true assertive, and so it was dropped from the sample of irony items. Excluding the two metaphor and two indirect request stories, the mean irony ratings for the remaining literal and nonliteral irony stories were 2.35 and 5.61, respectively. This difference is reliable, $t(21) = 11.11$, $p < .001$. With respect to utterance types, one might have expected that assertives would receive the highest irony ratings because they have been the focus of virtually all prior studies of irony and have generally been considered prototypical of ironic utterances. This was not the case. The mean irony rating for assertives was 5.95, not reliably different from the mean irony rating of 5.36 for the other utterance types combined. Indeed, the highest mean irony rating (6.10) was given to expressives (insincere thanks), with directives (mean rating = 5.14) and commissives (mean rating = 5.87) in between. In any case, these differences among utterance types are not reliable.

We turn now to the responses for each story as a function of story context—literal versus nonliteral. The responses for each story were compiled and rated by two independent judges for how explicitly the factors of interest appeared. The responses were examined in terms of the following: (a) explicit mention of the speaker being insincere (e.g., the speaker didn't mean what was said or the speaker intended the opposite of what was literally said), and (b) explicit mention that the utterance was allusive (e.g., the speaker was trying to draw the listener's attention to some aspect of the situation). The responses were also examined in terms of what attitude was explicitly expressed: positive, negative, or neutral. For example, funny, witty, humorous, compliment, light-hearted, and so forth were considered to indicate positive attitudes; anger, annoyance, irritation, and so forth indicated negative attitudes. When no specific attitude was mentioned, it was scored as neutral. Although not blind to the hypotheses, the judges were blind to the story contexts as well as to the type of target sentence (ironic and literal) when coding responses.

Table 4.2 presents the proportions of responses that included explicit mention of insincerity, allusion, and attitude. The percentages of agreement between the two judges for their scoring of insincerity, allusion, and attitude were 95.6%, 94.7%, and 97.9%, respectively. For the stories with potentially ironic utterances, participants explicitly mentioned that the speaker (a) did not sincerely intend what was said 69% of the time, and (b) was trying to draw the listener's attention to some aspect of the situation 36% of the time. In contrast, for the literal counterparts of these stories, insincerity was mentioned only 4% of the time and allusion 11% of the time. One-way analyses of variance[3] revealed that the proportions of reported insincerity and allusion were significantly higher for irony stories than for their corresponding literal stories: for insincerity, $F_1(1, 29) = 493.72$, $MS_e = .01$, $p < .001$;

TABLE 4.2

Proportion of Responses With Explicit Mention of Insincerity, Allusion, and Speaker's Attitude

			Attitude		
Story type	*Insincerity*	*Allusion*	*Pos.*	*Neg.*	*Neut.*
Irony	.69	.36	.11	.18	.71
Literal	.04	.11	.23	.06	.71
Metaphor	0	.03	.13	.10	.77
Literal	0	.06	.27	.07	.66
Indirect request	0	.03	.03	0	.97
Literal	0	.26	.03	0	.97

Note. Pos. = positive; Neg. = negative; Neut. = neutral.

$F_2(1, 21) = 86.61, MS_e = .05, p < .001$; for allusion, $F_1(1, 29) = 69.16, MS_e = .02, p < .001$; $F_2(1, 21) = 26.50, MS_e = .03, p < .001$. These data confirm our expectation that participants would perceive insincerity and allusion more often in ironic utterances than in literal ones.

With respect to attitudes, positive attitudes were explicitly mentioned 11% of the time for irony stories and 23% for literal stories, whereas negative attitudes were explicitly mentioned 18% of the time for irony stories and 6% for literal stories. These data were subjected to a 2 (Story type: Literal vs. Irony) × 2 (Attitude type: Positive vs. Negative) repeated measures analysis of variance (ANOVA). The F values for the main effect of story type were less than 1.0. The main effect of attitude was reliable when participants was treated as a random factor, $F(1, 29) = 6.32$, $MS_e = .01, p < .02$, but not with items as a random factor. More importantly, the interaction of story type with attitude was reliable, $F_1(1, 29) = 52.48, MS_e = .01, p < .001$, and $F_2(1, 21) = 5.60, MS_e = .06, p < .05$. For literal stories, more positive attitudes were expressed than negative ones, whereas the reverse was true for the irony stories. Although speakers may use either literal or ironic expressions to express attitudes, irony seems to be used more frequently to express a negative attitude, whereas the reverse seems to be true for literally intended utterances.

Among the nonliteral stories, participants never indicated that speakers in the metaphor and the indirect request stories were being insincere in any way. Similarly, participants rarely indicated that speakers in the metaphor or the indirect request stories were trying to draw the listener's attention to some aspect of the situation. These data suggest that the participants' responses to the irony stories were not just responses to nonliteral language per se, but instead were specific to ironic intentions. Although the data for metaphoric expressions and indirect requests cannot be generalized because of the small number of items (two stories each), they do provide an important manipulation check for nonliteral language in this pilot study. All four of the nonironic but nonliteral expressions were described by a majority of the participants as "sincere," "honest," "direct," "genuine," "exactly what the speaker means," and so forth. These responses contrast sharply with those for ironically intended utterances, which were largely characterized as insincere. These data strongly suggest that what makes an expression ironic is not whether it is nonliteral, but rather whether it is intended sincerely.

Similar conclusions can be drawn from a comparison between ironic and literal uses of expressions such as "You sure know a lot." When this was uttered in a literal context, a majority of participants indicated that not only did the speaker sincerely mean that the person was knowledgeable, but also that the speaker sincerely admired the person. In contrast, when the same sentence was uttered in an ironic context, many participants indicated that the speaker was annoyed by the obnoxiousness of the person while at the same time admitting that the person was knowledgeable.

Another example of insincerity at the pragmatic level can be seen in the use of over-polite requests. Participants frequently pointed out that the speaker was being overly polite (such as "He acted as polite as possible, yet it wasn't sincere"), while acknowledging a real desire for the listener to fulfill the request. Although the speaker is sincerely making a request, he or she does not sincerely intend to express respect toward the listener. These observations suggest that the kind of insincerity involved in ironic utterances is not at the semantic or propositional level, but rather is at the pragmatic level.

Utterances in everyday discourse thus can simultaneously convey the propositional contents of an utterance along with the speaker's communicative intention(s), such as to convey appreciation, admiration, approval, criticism, respect, sympathy, anger, and so forth. What makes an utterance ironic is not merely whether or not a speaker sincerely means what is literally said at the propositional level, but rather whether or not a speaker sincerely intends to convey the pragmatic communicative intention(s) that the utterance would ordinarily convey.

In addition to pragmatic insincerity, the allusive function of ironic utterances is also important. Allusion was mentioned about one third of the time. Considering that the only responses scored as referring to allusion were those that explicitly stated that the utterance drew the listener's attention to some aspect of the situation that violated an expectation, this is a reasonably high rate. Examples of responses that were judged as explicitly mentioning the allusive function of utterances are "… she [the speaker] mentions the opposite to draw attention to how ugly it really is" as a comment on "This certainly is beautiful weather"; "To bring Bill's attention to the late hour" for "What time is it now?" and "She's tactfully getting Vicky to notice her speed" for "Aren't you going too slow?" uttered when the driver is speeding.

The results of Experiment 1a, then, are compatible with the hypothesis that utterances convey irony when they are perceived as pragmatically insincere and as alluding to some failed expectation or norm. To test these hypotheses more specifically, we used a more constrained experimental task to assess the degree to which pragmatic insincerity and allusion are perceived in ironically intended utterances.

By using a more constrained experimental task, we hope to have a more sensitive test of the hypothesis that pragmatic insincerity and allusion to an expectation are criterial features of ironic utterances. Accordingly, an independent group of participants was asked to read both ironically intended and literally intended utterances in contexts and to indicate directly (a) whether speakers were sincerely trying to convey the pragmatic communicative intention of the critical utterance in each story and (b) whether the critical utterances drew listeners' attention to certain expectations.

EXPERIMENT 1B: IRONIC INSINCERITY AND ALLUSIONAL FUNCTION

Method

Participants.   Thirty Princeton undergraduates participated for pay. All were native English speakers, and none had previously participated in an experiment involving irony.

Materials and Task.   Seventeen nonliteral stories, all rated as being ironic in Experiment 1a, and their literal story counterparts were used as materials. For each story, two statements were generated to correspond with the two conditions, allusion and pretense (or pragmatic insincerity). The statements for each story were derived from participants' responses in Experiment 1a, based on the felicity conditions of each critical utterance. For example, the following statements were provided for the story shown in Table 4.1: "Jesse is trying to draw Danny's attention to the way Danny's acting" and "Jesse is sincerely admiring Danny for his knowledge." Participants were asked to indicate their agreement or disagreement with each of these statements. An analogous set of two statements each was provided for the irony and literal versions of each story.

Design and Procedure.   Two sets of booklets were constructed. One contained eight irony stories and nine literal stories, and the other contained eight literal stories and nine irony stories. Story type (literal vs. irony) was the only factor in this design and was counterbalanced between the two sets such that the same critical sentence never appeared twice in one set. The presentation order of the stories was randomized for each booklet.

Participants were tested individually and were randomly assigned to one of the two booklets. Participants were given instructions that were identical, except for the second paragraph, to the instructions given for Experiment 1a. The second paragraph of those instructions was replaced with the following:

> For each short story, two statements about the character's final remark (shown in bold type) will be provided. Please indicate whether you agree or disagree with each statement. Next, please rate the character's final comment in terms of the

following three aspects: (1) whether the remark is negative or positive; (2) whether the remark is derogatory or not; and (3) whether the remark is humorous or not. There will be rating scales on which to indicate your judgment.

The 7-point scales provided were (a) how positive or negative is [the character]'s final remark, with 1 indicating *extremely negative* and 7 indicating *extremely positive;* (b) how derogatory is [the character]'s final remark, with 1 indicating *not at all derogatory;* and (c) how humorous is [the character]'s final remark, with 1 indicating *not at all humorous.*

Results and Discussion

The mean proportions of agreement with each statement for the irony and literal stories are shown in Figure 4.1. For the irony stories, participants perceived allusion 97% of the time, compared with 56% of the time in the literal stories. In contrast, participants agreed that speakers were sincere 4% of the time in irony stories, compared with 87% of the time in literal stories. A 2 × 2 (Story Type: Irony vs. Literal × Statement Type: Allusional vs. Sincere) repeated measures ANOVA applied to these data yielded a main effect of story type, $F_1(1, 29) = 99.50$, $MS_e = .013$, $p < .001$, and $F_2(1, 16) = 19.20$, $MS_e = .04$, $p < .001$, as well as a main effect of statement type, $F_1(1, 29) = 209.66$, $MS_e = 0.01$, $p < .001$, and $F_2(1, 16) = 54.00$, $MS_e = .03$, $p < .001$. The finding of primary interest is the reliable interaction between the two factors, $F_1(1, 29) = 775.83$, $MS_e = 0.02$, $p < .001$ and $F_2(1, 16) = 246.89$, $MS_e = .03$, $p < .001$. This interaction reflects the agreement among participants that the critical utterance alludes to some expectation more frequently for irony stories than for literal stories, whereas the speaker is almost never sincere in irony stories but is sincere in most literal stories.

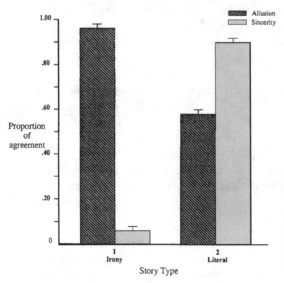

Figure 4.1. Mean proportion of subjects agreeing that (1) speakers intended to allude to some expectations and that (2) speakers intended to make the utterances sincerely.

These data indicate that perceived allusion and speaker insincerity differentiate ironically intended utterances from literal ones. The rather high proportion of participants perceiving allusion in literal utterances (.56) is not inconsistent with this conclusion because literal utterances, too, can allude to what has been said previously (e.g., when a lecture was boring and someone says "It was tedious, wasn't it?"). The important finding is that allusion is almost invariably perceived in ironically intended utterances, supporting the hypothesis that allusion is central to irony. The hypothesis concerning sincerity was also supported. Virtually all ironically intended utterances were perceived as insincere, whereas the majority of these same utterances in literally intended contexts were perceived as sincere. As predicted, then, ironic utterances were characterized as both allusive and insincere.

With respect to the degree to which ironic and literal utterances were positive or negative, derogatory, and humorous, the ratings are consistent with the view in the literature. Ironically intended utterances were rated as more negative, more derogatory, and more humorous than were those same utterances when literally intended. The mean ratings on these scales for ironic and literal utterances are shown in Table 4.3. These data were analyzed using a repeated measures multivariate analysis of variance (MANOVA)—with participants as a random variable—with the three rating scales (positive—negative, derogatory—not derogatory, and humorous—not humorous) as dependent variables and the two story types (irony vs. literal) as independent variables. The analysis yielded reliable effects for rating scale, story type, and the interaction of rating scale and story type, $F(2, 40) = 7.30$, $MS_e = 1.22$, $p < .002 < .01$, $F(1, 20) = 31.98$, $MS_e = .40$, $p < .001$, and $F(2, 40) = 28.49$, $MS_e = 1.96$, $p < .001$, respectively. These effects are interpreted via univariate ANOVAs as reported below.

A repeated measures ANOVA reveals that ironic utterances were rated as less positive than literal utterances. Ironically intended utterances received a mean rating of 2.33, whereas these same utterances in literal contexts received a mean rating of 4.76, $F_1(1, 29) = 523.81$, $MS_e = 0.17$, $p < .001$, and $F_2(1, 16) = 24.40$, $MS_e = 2.05$, $p < .001$. Ironic utterances ($M = 4.52$) were also rated as more derogatory than literal utterances ($M = 1.88$), $F_1(1, 29) = 178.11$, $MS_e = 0.56$, $p < .001$, and $F_2(1, 16) =$

TABLE 4.3

Mean Ratings on Positive—Negative, Derogatory, and Humorous Scales (SDs)

| Story type | Scale | | |
	Positive—Negative	Derogatory	Humorous
Ironic	2.33	4.52	3.77
	(0.98)	(1.23)	(1.08)
Literal	4.76	1.88	1.88
	(1.37)	(0.90)	(0.89)

Note. On a 7-point scale: 1 = extremely negative, 7 = extremely positive.

40.08, $MS_e = 1.47$, $p < .001$. Finally, ironic utterances ($M = 3.77$) were rated as more humorous than literal utterances ($M = 1.88$), $F_1(1, 29) = 86.93$, $MS_e = 0.61$, $p < .001$, and $F_2(1, 16) = 56.36$, $MS_e = 0.53$, $p < .001$. It is worth noting that on all three scales, ironically intended utterances were rated as more extreme than were those same utterances in literal contexts. The positive—negative rating for literal utterances was close to 4.0, the neutral point of the scale, and close to the neutral points of the other two scales, where a rating of 1.0 indicated *not at all derogatory/humorous*. These data support the long-standing view that irony is used to express a negative or positive attitude or intention (i.e., when a speaker is not affectively neutral about a topic).

As expected, the derogatory ratings and positive—negative ratings were correlated (the more positive, the less derogatory; $r = -.62$, $p < .001$), suggesting that participants were using the scales appropriately. There was no reliable correlation between positive–negative ratings and humorousness ratings, but we did obtain a reliable correlation between the derogatory ratings and the humorous ratings, $r = .58$, $p < .001$, suggesting that people tend to be humorous when being derogatory. To the extent that humor is intended, irony may serve multiple goals: expressing attitudes (generally negative) and derision, as well as humor.

The relative degrees of speaker attitudes obtained in this study, of course, are entirely a function of the materials that we used, and thus we cannot generalize to natural discourse situations. To the extent that our sample is representative of irony in natural settings, the data strongly suggest that irony involves pragmatic insincerity and allusion to some expectations, and that speakers' attitudes expressed in irony can include negativity, derision, and humor.

EXPERIMENT 2: IMPLICIT SOCIAL NORMS AND THE ASYMMETRY OF DISCOURSE IRONY

Theorists of irony agree that a major purpose for using ironic expressions is to communicate an ironist's attitude rather than to communicate specific propositional content. In principle, there are no restrictions to the kinds of attitudes that an ironist can express. Nevertheless, Sperber and Wilson contended that "irony is primarily designed to ridicule ..." (1981, p. 241). The traditional pragmatic theory also claimed that the most usual purpose of irony is to express a negative, derogatory feeling, attitude, or evaluation. The asymmetry in how counterfactual statements can be used ironically reflects the generalization that negative attitudes are the default condition. People can almost always express irony by using a positive assertion, such as "This is a terrific performance" when in fact the performance in question is terrible. The reverse, using a negative statement such as "This is a terrible performance" when the performance is actually quite good, seems anomalous.

Sperber and Wilson (1981) suggested that the asymmetry of irony may be attributable to the general prevalence of positive norms and expectations. If norms and expectations are usually positive, then most failed expectations would be negative events, making insincere positive statements generally appropriate for expressing irony. This hypothesis implies that if an expectation were to be negative, then a negative statement in the context of a positive event that disconfirmed that expectation would convey irony. Kreuz and Glucksberg (1989) confirmed this hypothesis for sarcastic irony. They reasoned that if an explicit negative expectation is available to both a speaker and a listener, then a negative statement uttered in a positive context could convey irony. When explicit negative expectations were provided, as when someone had incorrectly predicted rain and the day turned out to be sunny, then negative statements were perceived appropriately as ironic, such as "what terrible weather" uttered on a gorgeous day.

Kreuz and Glucksberg (1989) restricted their analysis to explicit antecedents, consistent with their notion of echoic reminding. The allusional pretense theory posits the more general mechanism of allusion, which can be accomplished via an explicit reminder, or via implicit reference to shared norms or expectations. If allusions can be made without explicit echoing or reminding, then explicit negative antecedents should not be necessary for negative utterances to communicate irony. All that should be necessary is any deviation from an expectation or norm, whether that expectation be explicit or implicit. To test this hypothesis, we used two kinds of situations. The first involved situations where expectations were negative, such as the state of subway cars in New York City. People generally expect New York subways to be dirty, so if one encounters a clean train, the remark "New York subways are certainly dirty" should communicate irony. The second kind of situation involves expectations of appropriate quantity. In such situations, a remark about a departure from expectation in either direction (too much or too little) should communicate irony. If a term paper, for example, were too short, then the comment "what a long paper" should communicate irony, and vice versa.

In both of these kinds of situations, there should be no asymmetry, but asymmetry still needs to be accounted for. Where specific expectations are negative, remarks in positive contexts should be able to communicate irony. Furthermore, because positive norms and expectations are the general default condition, positive remarks in negative contexts should also communicate irony even when specific expectations are negative, as in the New York subway situation. If the subways are in fact dirty, then saying "New York subways are certainly clean" should communicate irony on the basis of the general norm that passenger trains should be clean. Similarly, deviations from an appropriate quantity in either direction should not produce asymmetry: A remark about any deviation from expectation should be able to communicate irony. Experiment 2 tests these predictions in the context of situations for which people have negative expectations and for situations involving expectations of appropriate quantity.

Method

Participants. Forty Princeton undergraduates participated in the study for pay. An additional 26 students provided normative ratings (see below). All were native English speakers, and none had participated earlier in any related studies.

Materials. We first prepared a set of 10 candidate statements that we judged to express negative expectations that people would generally hold (e.g., "The air in Los Angeles is dirty"). We also prepared a set of 10 candidate statements about appropriate quantity (e.g., "A room's temperature should not be too hot, nor too cold"). Twenty filler statements were added to this set of 20 candidate experimental items, and 26 Princeton undergraduate students rated the extent to which they agreed with each statement, using a 7-point scale. The candidate statements that received mean agreement ratings of 5.0 or higher were selected for use in this experiment: nine statements of negative expectations and seven of appropriate medium quantity.

Sixteen pairs of test sentences were then presented in test booklets as follows. Half of the sentences were either negative statements, such as "New York subways are certainly dirty," or statements about too much quantity vis-à-vis a norm, such as "What a long concert that was!" The other half of the test sentences were direct opposites of the corresponding sentences: that is, either positive statements, such as "New York subways are certainly clean," or statements about too little quantity vis-à-vis a norm, such as "What a short concert that was!" For each pair of these test sentences, two kinds of contexts were constructed: positive or negative contexts (or, for those statements about quantity expectations, too-much or too-little). Examples of these contexts are shown in Table 4.4.

For the Positive–Negative contrast, four types of short stories were generated by factorially crossing Context Type (Positive or Negative) with Sentence Type (Positive or Negative). Similarly, four types of short stories were generated for the Too-Much/Too-Little contrast, by factorially crossing Context Type (Too-Much or Too-Little) with Sentence Type (Too-Much or Too-Little). Sixty-four short stories (four combinations for each of 16 story frames) were thus generated altogether. The stories had a mean length of six lines.

Design and Procedure. A 2×2 within-participants design was used. The factors Context Type (Positive vs. Negative or Too-Much vs. Too-Little) and Sentence Type (Positive vs. Negative or Too-Much vs. Too-Little) yielded four story types. Four sets of booklets were constructed, each containing 16 stories. The booklets were counterbalanced for type of story (Context Type × Sentence Type) with each story appearing only once in a booklet. The presentation order of the stories was randomized for each booklet.

Forty participants were randomly assigned to one of four sets of booklets. They were instructed to rate how ironic/sarcastic, if at all, the character's final remark seemed to them. Seven-point rating scales were provided for each story, where 1 indicated *Not at all ironic/sarcastic,* 4 indicated *Moderately ironic/sarcastic,* and 7 indicated *Extremely ironic/sarcastic.*

Results and Discussion

We present the data and analyses for the negative and the quantity expectations separately.

TABLE 4.4
Examples of Story Contexts and Target Sentences in Experiment 2

Story About a Negative Expectation: New York Subway

Positive Context

Pamela and Emily were visiting New York City for the first time. They took a subway and found it was sparkling clean. Surprisingly, they also found no graffiti at all on the train. As they were leaving the platform, Pamela whispered to Emily, "New York subways are certainly clean!" (*Positive statement*)

Or

"New York subways are certainly dirty!" (*Negative statement*)

Negative Context

Pamela and Emily were visiting New York City for the first time. They took a subway and found it was terribly dirty. They also found graffiti written all over the train. As they were leaving the platform, Pamela whispered to Emily, "New York subways are certainly clean!" (*Positive statement*)

Or

"New York subways are certainly dirty!" (*Negative statement*)

Story About an Appropriate Medium Quantity Expectation: The Term Paper

---

Too-Much Context

Greg was enrolled in psychology 200 this semester, along with several humanities courses. Although all of them required term papers, he put special effort into the psychology paper, because he enjoyed that class so much. Greg found an interesting topic and did a lot of library research. Despite the fact that the paper was to be between 15 to 20 pages in length, his paper turned out to be more than 50 pages. He tried to cut it down, but he couldn't. Feeling terrible, he submitted it to his instructor, Matt. As he flipped through the long paper, Matt commented, "This is a very long paper!" (*Too-Much Statement*)

Or

"This is a very short paper!" (*Too-Little Statement*)

Too-Little Context

Greg was enrolled in psychology 200 this semester, along with several humanities courses. To his dismay, all of them required term papers. The night before the psychology paper was due, Greg was still thinking about the topic. By the morning, he managed to write five pages, despite the fact that the paper was to be between 15 to 20 pages in length. Feeling terrible, he submitted it to his instructor, Matt. As he flipped through the short paper, Matt commented, "This is a very long paper!" (*Too-Much Statement*)

Or

"This is a very short paper!" (*Too-Little Statement*)

Note. Subjects were asked to rate how ironic/sarcastic the character's final remark seemed to them.

Negative Expectations. As expected, the mean irony ratings for counterfactual statements were higher than for true statements, 5.6 and 2.2, respectively. More interesting, negative statements in positive contexts were rated as quite ironic

(5.0 on a scale where 4.0 indicates *moderately ironic* and 7.0 is *maximally ironic*). As predicted, when a negative expectation is disconfirmed (e.g., New York subways turn out to be clean), then the negative statement "New York subways are certainly dirty" can allude to that expectation and communicate irony. Also as predicted, because the default condition is a positive expectation, a positive statement such as "New York subways are certainly clean" can also communicate irony when the subways are in fact dirty. The mean irony ratings as a function of statement and context polarity are shown in Figure 4.2. A 2 × 2 repeated measures ANOVA was applied to these data.

There was no main effect of context, $F_1(1, 39) = 1.52$, $MS_e = .66$, $p > .05$; $F_2(1, 8) = 1.36$, $MS_e = .27$, $p > .05$. The main effect of sentence polarity was reliable. Positive statements were rated as more ironic than negative, regardless of context polarity, $F_1(1, 39) = 35.40$, $MS_e = 1.04$, $p < .001$, and $F_2(1, 8) = 8.48$, $MS_e = .80$, $p < .02$, indicating that positive statements, in general, are rated as more ironic than negative statements. More important, the interaction between sentence and context polarities was also highly reliable, $F_1(1, 39) = 231.33$, $MS_e = 1.92$, $p < .001$, and $F_2(1, 8) = 221.37$, $MS_e = .46$, $p < .001$, reflecting the higher irony ratings for counterfactual over factual statements.

A *t* test with items as a random factor revealed that the difference between the mean irony ratings for positive and negative statements in positive contexts (2.53 vs. 5.02) was highly reliable, $t(8) = 10.27$, $p < .001$. This result confirms the hypothesis that when there is a negative expectation, a negative statement uttered in a positive context can be used ironically without an explicit negative antecedent.

When the context was negative, positive statements were more likely to be used ironically than negative statements, $t(8) = 21.07$, $p < .001$, despite the existence of specific but implicit negative expectations. This result confirms the prediction that, even when there are specific negative expectations, counterfactual positive statements can still be used ironically because of general positive expectations or norms,

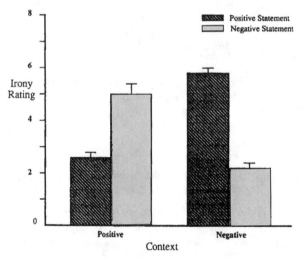

Figure 4.2.   Mean irony ratings for sentences about negative expectations in positive and negative contexts.

such as "things should be kept clean." Corresponding *t* tests with participants as a random factor yielded equivalent results.

Taken together, these results support the implicit social norm hypothesis. Ironic expressions can generally allude to implicit social norms and expectations. Therefore, when negative expectations are available, negative statements regarding positive situations can be used ironically. Positive statements regarding negative situations can be used ironically whether or not there exists a specific negative expectation, because positive statements can always allude to general positive expectations or norms.

Over and above the implicit social norm hypothesis, these data also support the allusional pretense theory. Counterfactual statements convey irony more than do factual statements, supporting the notion that pragmatic insincerity is a necessary condition for irony. And, although the default condition is that positive statements can always be used ironically, negative statements can also be used ironically when implicit expectations or norms are negative, supporting the claim that allusion is also a necessary condition for communicating irony.

Quantity Expectations. As expected, insincere remarks about quantity were judged as more ironic than sincere remarks. Insincere remarks (e.g., commenting on how short a paper was when it was patently too long and vice versa) received a mean irony rating of 6.22, whereas sincere remarks received a mean rating of 1.72. Also as expected, the direction of deviation from expectation made no difference: insincere comments about too much were rated as ironic as insincere comments about too little, mean ratings 6.05 and 6.38, respectively. These data are shown in Figure 4.3. A 2 × 2 repeated measures ANOVA applied to these data revealed no main effects for either context (deviation from expectation in one direction vs. the other) or statement type (too-much vs. too-little). For the context contrast, $F_1(1, 39) = 1.50, MS_e = .88, p > .05$, and $F_2(1, 6) = 3.22, MS_e = .05, p > .05$. For the statement

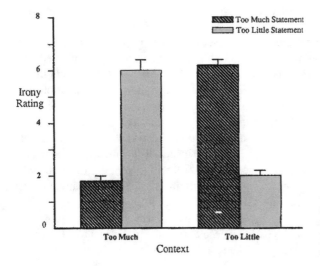

Figure 4.3. Mean irony ratings for sentences about medium quantity expectations in Too-Much and Too-Little contexts.

contrast, both F values were less than 1. There was, as expected, a reliable interaction between context and statement type, reflecting the higher irony ratings for insincere statements, $F_1(1, 39) = 1022.44$, $MS_e = .79$, $p < .001$, and $F_2(1, 8) = 5487.10$, $MS_e = .03$, $p < .001$. Too-much statements were perceived as ironic only when they were uttered in Too-little contexts, and Too-little statements were interpreted as ironic only when they were uttered in Too-much contexts.

These data provide further support for the hypothesis that any violation of norms or expectations can be alluded to ironically and that such allusions communicate irony when they are insincere. In the case of assertives in general, positive counterfactual statements serve this purpose, but negative counterfactual statements require either explicit or implicit negative expectations. In the case of comments about quantity, counterfactuals work in the same way, but there is no default condition vis-à-vis exceeding or falling short of a norm or expectation. The necessary condition is simply any deviation from an expectation, combined with an insincere allusion to that expectation.

EXPERIMENT 3: USING OVER-POLITE REQUESTS TO COMMUNICATE IRONY

There are two kinds of public self-image, or "face," that members of a society want to claim for themselves (Brown & Levinson, 1987; Goffman, 1967). One is the image of being desirable and acceptable to others, and the other is the image of one's actions being unimpeded by others. The use of irony, either sarcastic or nonsarcastic, may serve to maintain one's own face, as well as the face of others, particularly when things have gone awry or are unexpected and when commenting directly on such situations may be face threatening. Brown and Levinson (1987) argued that when a person, assumed to be a rational agent, has to engage in a potentially face-threatening act, such as giving a negative evaluation, or mentioning an embarrassing or unpleasant topic, that person would try to use some strategy to minimize the threat. Irony is one of the available strategies.

Although ironic expressions are often used to avoid being directly face threatening, they can still be used to insult others. When an utterance is accompanied with cues that suggest irony, such as obvious insincerity, a listener will interpret the utterance ironically. The speaker's face-threatening communicative intention then becomes apparent and the utterance can be insulting. However, because the speaker did not commit to any particular intention to insult, at least on the surface, the speaker can always offer the defense that no impolite act was committed. Being excessively polite could have this effect, that is, to insult a listener without making the speaker appear to be rude (cf. Becker, Kimmel, & Bevill, 1989; Blum-Kulka, 1987; Holtgraves, 1986). Ironic expressions could thus allow a speaker to maintain outer face, while effectively conveying a negative attitude.

A common occasion for using irony in this way is when one has to make a request when no request should have been necessary in the first place. Consider a situation in which a college student, Jill, had asked her roommate to keep the windows closed because she was often cold. Her roommate, however, is forgetful and does not fulfill the request. This situation provides an occasion for irony: An expectation has been disconfirmed, and Jill is now disappointed and perhaps annoyed or irritated. She now has at least two intentions to communicate: (a) her disappointment and irritation that her earlier request had been ignored, and (b) a repeated request that the windows be kept closed. She can communicate both of these intentions simultaneously by using an over-polite request such as "Would you mind if I asked you to keep the windows closed, please?" Such unexpectedly over-polite utterances are often interpreted as ironic. Interestingly, unexpectedly under-polite requests that could communicate the same two intentions of expressing irritation and repeating a request are likely to be interpreted as rude, but not ironic (Becker et al., 1989; Blum-Kulka, 1987; Holtgraves, 1986).

Why should over-polite utterances communicate irony more than under-polite utterances? Both over-polite and under-polite utterances can allude to a failed expectation or norm, but only over-polite utterances are likely to be perceived as insincere. When a speaker is unexpectedly over-polite, listeners may well doubt the speaker's sincerity in being so polite. In contrast, when a speaker is under-polite, listeners are quite likely to perceive intentional or unintentional rudeness, but not insincerity. A speaker's choice of politeness level should thus be guided by the intentions to be communicated and also by politeness considerations. If speakers wish to avoid being rude, then they should avoid direct confrontations. If, at the same time, a speaker wishes to express irritation, then it can be done by being over-polite. If insincerity is perceived by an addressee, then irony should be communicated, and the addressee would understand both the intended request and the speaker's displeasure. If insincerity is not perceived, then the speaker avoids being considered rude but still succeeds in conveying a request. Experiment 3 examines the relations between perceived insincerity, rudeness, insultingness, and irony, using comprehension and rating measures.

Are over-polite requests perceived as insincere and ironic? According to the allusional pretense theory of irony, over-polite requests should communicate irony, whereas under-polite requests should not. One reason for this asymmetry is that the former would be perceived as insincere, but the latter would not. Both under- and over-polite requests should communicate a request and should also communicate the speaker's displeasure, but the under-polite request, because it is perceived as sincerely under-polite, should also be perceived as rude. In contrast, over-polite requests avoid a direct confrontation, but do communicate a speaker's displeasure and so could be perceived as insulting, but not rude.

To test these hypotheses, we asked participants to read short stories in which a protagonist is annoyed or irritated and then makes a request that is over-polite, appropriately polite, or under-polite. The participants then rated the extent to which the request was (a) sincerely polite/impolite, (b) ironic, (c) rude, and (d) insulting to the addressee. Table 4.5 provides an example of the stories that were used.

We expected that over-polite requests would be rated as more ironic than either appropriately polite or under-polite requests. More specifically, over-polite re-

TABLE 4.5

Example of the Materials Used in Experiment 3

Jill asked her roommate to keep the windows of their room closed, explaining that she was often cold. Jill had to repeat this request several times. Still, her roommate left the windows open again. Jill says to her roommate,

Over-polite

"Would you mind if I asked you to keep the windows closed, please?"

Appropriately polite

"Would you keep the windows closed?"

Under-polite

"Keep the windows closed."

---

quests that are judged to be insincerely over-polite should be rated as more ironic than their corresponding under-polite requests, but they should be just as insulting as under-polite requests. Over-polite requests that are perceived as sincere should be perceived as no more ironic than their corresponding appropriately polite or under-polite requests. Finally, over-polite requests, whether perceived as ironic or not, should be less rude than their under-polite counterparts.

Method

Participants.　　Forty-five Princeton undergraduates participated in this study for pay. All were native English speakers, and none had participated in any other experiments involving irony. Thirty of these participants participated in the experiment proper; the other 15 provided ratings of materials for the experiment.

Materials.　　The experimental design required requests at three levels of politeness: over-, appropriately, and under-polite. Fifteen participants were given a booklet of 18 stories. Each story involved an annoyed protagonist and was followed by five different forms of requests. The participants were asked to rate each request form in terms of its politeness level. A 7-point scale, where –3 indicated *under-polite,* 0 indicated *appropriate,* and 3 indicated *over-polite,* was provided for each request form. The five forms of requests were (a) an imperative, such as "Keep the windows closed"; (b) an imperative "please," such as "Please keep the windows closed"; (c) a conventional indirect request, such as "Would you keep the windows closed?" (d) an elaborated indirect request, such as "Would you mind if I asked you to keep the windows closed, please?" and (e) a hint, such as "You have opened the windows again." The presentation orders of the stories were randomized for each participant, but the presentation order of the five request forms were kept constant for all the stories.

Mean politeness ratings were calculated for each request form of each story. For each story, three request forms—the most over-polite, the most under-polite, and the most appropriately polite—were selected, according to their mean politeness ratings. When there were more than two request forms that received the same politeness rating, one of them was randomly chosen.

For all of the stories, elaborated indirect requests were the most over-polite, with a mean rating of 1.48. For the appropriately polite requests, imperatives plus "please" were chosen for eight stories, conventional indirect requests were chosen for nine stories, and hints were chosen for one of the stories. The mean rating for this politeness level was –0.18. For the least polite (under-polite) requests, imperatives were chosen for 15 stories and hints were chosen for 3 stories. The mean rating for this request form was –1.62.

The ratings procedure described above provided the materials for Experiment 3: 18 short stories in which a speaker makes a request of another person who has irritated or annoyed that speaker. The critical request sentences were at one of three levels of politeness, as described above. Three sets of booklets with instructions and the 18 stories were constructed. Level of politeness was the only factor in the experimental design, and requests at each level were counterbalanced such that the same story appeared only once in each booklet. In addition, presentation order of the stories was randomized for each booklet.

Procedure. Participants were randomly assigned to one of the three booklets and were then individually tested. Each participant read the following instructions printed on the booklet's first page:

> I am interested in how people use language to communicate ideas to one another. As you know, people can accomplish this in a variety of ways. People can be more or less polite in a conversation. Sometimes, people will use irony or sarcasm to get a point across. People will even be rude or insulting on occasion—sometimes intentionally, sometimes unintentionally.
>
> In the following pages you will read a number of short stories. In each story, two characters have a brief interaction, and at the end, one of the characters says something to the other character.
>
> I would like you to rate the character's final remark (shown in bold type) with respect to the following four aspects: (a) how sincerely you think the character intends to be polite or impolite, (b) how ironic/sarcastic the character's remark sounds, (c) how rude/ill-mannered you think the character is, and (d) how insulting you think the character's remark is. The four scales on which you should indicate your ratings will be given with each story.
>
> Before you begin, please look over a few of the stories. This will give you a general feel for the types of stories you will be seeing. If you occasionally find yourself unsure about your rating, just use your best judgment. Remember, there are no right or wrong answers: I am simply interested in your intuitions. Please be sure to provide a rating for all the stories. Thank you very much for your participation.

The participants then read the stories and provided their ratings. The first scale was for the speaker's sincerity to be polite or impolite: For stories with appropriately polite and over-polite requests, participants were asked "Do you think [the character] intends to be polite?" and for the stories with an under-polite request, "Do you think [the character] intends to be impolite?" The second question was "How ironic/sarcastic do you think [the character's] request sounds?" and the third was "How rude or ill-mannered do you think [the character] is?" The participants indicated their ratings on a 7-point scale, where 1 meant *not at all,* 4 meant *not sure,* and 7 meant *very much.* The last question was "How insulting do you think [the character]'s remark is?" The participants again indicated their ratings on a 7-point scale, where 1 meant *not at all insulting,* 4 meant *neutral,* and 7 meant *very much insulting.* Participants took about 25 min to complete the booklets.

Results and Discussion

Table 4.6 presents the mean ratings of irony, sincerity, rudeness, and insultingness as a function of politeness level. A repeated measures multivariate ANOVA—with participants as a random variable—and the four rating scales (irony, sincerity, rudeness, and insult) as dependent variables and three levels of politeness (over-, appropriately, and under-) as independent variables yielded reliable effects for Rating Scale, Politeness Level, and the interaction of Rating Scale × Politeness Level, $F(3, 27) = 28.46$, $F(2, 28) = 22.52$, and $F(6, 24) = 35.01$, respectively, $ps < .001$. These effects are interpreted via univariate ANOVAs as follows:

The mean irony ratings were 3.85 for over-polite requests, 2.23 for appropriately polite requests, and 1.98 for under-polite requests. A repeated measures ANOVA yielded a reliable effect of politeness level, $F_1(2, 58) = 40.16$, $MS_e = .77$, $p < .001$, and $F_2(2, 34) = 21.71$, $MS_e = .86$, $p < .001$. Post hoc single degree-of-difference contrast analyses showed that over-polite requests were rated reliably more

TABLE 4.6
Mean Ratings of Sincerity, Degree of Irony, Rudeness, and Insultingness As a Function of Politeness Level (*SDs*)

Rating Scale	Politeness Level		
	Over-Polite	*Appropriate*	*Under-Polite*
Irony	3.85	2.23	1.98
	(1.27)	(0.91)	(0.89)
Rudeness	2.31	2.33	4.49
	(1.30)	(0.98)	(0.76)
Insultingness	3.50	3.04	4.17
	(0.87)	(0.77)	(0.76)
Sincerity	4.22	4.81	4.15
	(1.20)	(1.05)	(1.05)

Note. Politeness based on a 7-point scale: 1 = *not polite at all,* 4 = *unsure,* 7 = *very polite.* Insultingness based on a 7-point scale: 1 = *not at all insulting,* 4 = *neutral,* 7 = *very insulting.*

ironic than appropriately polite ones, $F_1(1, 29) = 42.72, MS_e = 1.84, p < .001$, and $F_2(1, 17) = 19.25, MS_e = 2.44, p < .001$, and more ironic than under-polite requests, $F_1(1, 29) = 48.03, MS_e = 2.19, p < .001$, and $F_2(1, 17) = 31.89, MS_e = 1.98, p < .001$. As expected, appropriately polite and under-polite requests did not differ in perceived irony, $F_1(1, 29) = 3.29, MS_e = .60, p > .05$, and $F_2(1, 17) = 1.67, MS_e = .71, p > .05$. These results indicate that over-polite requests were more likely to be taken ironically than either appropriately polite or under-polite requests.

As expected, under-polite requests were rated as most rude, with a mean rating of 4.62, compared to mean ratings of 2.31 and 2.39 for over-polite and appropriately polite requests, respectively. These differences were reliable, with participants as a random variable, as indicated by a main effect of politeness level, $F(2, 58) = 94.36, MS_e = 1.09, p < .001$. Post hoc single degree-of-difference contrast analyses indicated that under-polite requests were rated as reliably more rude than either appropriately polite or over-polite requests, $F(1, 29) = 125.92, MS_e = 4.75, p < .001$, and $F(1, 29) = 129.89, MS_e = 4.95, p < .001$, respectively, whereas ratings for the latter two politeness levels did not differ from one another ($F < 1$). These data are consistent with the hypothesis that over-polite requests can communicate irony without the risk of appearing rude.

However, the mean rudeness ratings of the over-polite requests may have been artifactually depressed because, overall, the irony ratings were fairly low (3.85 on a 7-point scale where 4.0 is the midpoint and was labeled as "not sure" vis-à-vis ironic). To address this problem, the over-polite items were divided into two categories, those with mean irony ratings 4.0 and higher and those with ratings below 4.0. This procedure yielded 10 stories in which an over-polite request was rated as ironic and 8 in which an over-polite request was rated as not ironic. The mean rudeness ratings for high- and low-irony stories as a function of politeness level are presented in Table 4.7 (along with insultingness ratings, as discussed below).

As expected, under-polite requests were considered more rude than either their over- or appropriately polite counterparts, with a mean rating of 4.10 compared with ratings of 2.51 and 2.14, respectively. A two-way repeated measures ANOVA of these data—with participants as a random variable—revealed a main effect of politeness level, $F(2, 28) = 94.36, MS_e = 1.10, p < .001$. Contrast analyses showed that under-polite requests differed reliably from over-polite and appropriate requests, $F(1, 29) = 129.89, MS_e = 4.95, p < .001$, and $F1 = 125.92, MS_e = 4.75, p < .001$, respectively, whereas over-polite and appropriate requests did not differ reliably ($F < 1$).

An analogous analysis of the insultingness ratings revealed the expected pattern of results. Over-polite requests that were considered ironic were rated as insulting as their under-polite counterparts, with mean ratings of 4.0 and 4.1, respectively. Over-polite requests that were not considered to be ironic were not rated as insulting at all. The mean rating of 2.88 for nonironic over-polite requests is not reliably different from the insultingness rating for appropriately polite requests, 3.27. A two-way repeated measures ANOVA applied to these data, again with participants as a random variable, revealed that under-polite requests differed reliably from the

TABLE 4.7a

Mean Rudeness Ratings as a Function of Irony and Politeness Levels (SDs)

	Politeness Level		
Irony Level	Over-Polite	Appropriate	Under-Polite
High	2.51	2.14	4.10
	(0.51)	(0.41)	(0.95)
	n = 10	n = 10	n = 10
Low	2.05	2.61	4.98
	(0.38)	(1.03)	(0.68)
	n = 8	n = 8	n = 8

Note. n denotes number of stories in each cell.

TABLE 4.7b

Mean Insultingness Ratings As a Function of Irony and Politeness Levels (SDs)

	Politeness Level		
Irony Level	Over-Polite	Appropriate	Under-Polite
High	4.02	2.90	4.08
	(0.72)	(0.53)	(0.82)
	n = 10	n = 10	n = 10
Low	2.85	3.26	4.31
	(0.86)	(1.20)	(0.98)
	n = 8	n = 8	n = 8

Note. n denotes number of stories in each cell.

other two forms of request, $F(2, 58) = 14.67$, $MS_e = 1.36$, $p < .001$, whereas there was no effect of level of irony ($p < .20$). However, there was a reliable interaction between irony level and insultingness, $F(2, 58) = 8.63$, $MS_e = 1.13$, $p < .001$, reflecting the high insultingness rating of over-polite requests that were perceived as ironic (3.96), as compared with the low insultingness ratings of such requests that were not perceived as ironic (2.88). These results, along with the rudeness results, support the notion that communicating irony via over-politeness serves to communicate negative attitudes without appearing rude. At the same time, when over-politeness is not perceived as ironic, then neither rudeness nor insult is perceived, permitting a speaker to avoid losing face.

We now turn to the relationship between pragmatic insincerity and irony. Over-polite utterances, according to our hypothesis, should be considered as ironic whenever the speaker is perceived as being insincere, that is, did not intend to be as polite as the utterance might suggest. We have already noted that the overall ratings of irony were rather low, below the scale midpoint of 4.0 (see Table 4.6). In order to assess whether perceived insincerity is related to perceived irony, we partitioned each request type into two categories, those that received mean insincerity ratings of 4.0 or greater and those that received mean ratings of less than 4.0 (the scale midpoint, where 1.0 is *maximally sincere* and 7.0 is *maximally insincere*). Twelve over-polite stories, 16 appropriately polite stories, and 11 under-polite stories were rated as sincere, and 6 over-polite stories, 2 appropriately polite stories, and 7 under-polite stories were rated as insincere. Accordingly, only participant analyses were performed on these data because of the unequal *ns* in each cell, as well as the few items in some cells (e.g., only two appropriately polite stories were rated as insincere).

Over-polite requests that were rated as insincerely polite received a mean irony rating of 5.2, whereas over-polite requests that were seen as sincerely polite were not rated as ironic, with a mean rating of 3.0 (see Fig. 4.4). In contrast, under-polite requests were not rated as ironic, whether they were rated as sincere or not (2.2 and 1.8, respectively). Appropriately polite requests were rated as not ironic, whether sincere or not (2.4 and 2.1, respectively).

A 3×2 repeated measures ANOVA of these data, with participants as a random variable, confirmed these interpretations. There was a main effect of politeness level, $F(2, 58) = 34.77, MS_e = 2.32, p < .001$, and of sincerity, $F(1, 29) = 9.41, MS_e = 1.15, p < .005$, as well as a reliable interaction between sincerity and politeness level, $F(2, 58) = 21.56, MS_e = 1.42, p < .001$. A single degree-of-difference contrast analysis revealed that over-polite requests differed reliably from appropriately and under-polite forms, $F(1, 29) = 53.43, MS_e = 10.3, p < .001$. In addition, the difference between insincere and sincere appropriately polite requests was also reliable, $F(1, 29) = 9.41, MS_e = 6.92, p < .005$.

One puzzling question remains: Why were the insincere under-polite requests not perceived as ironic? Although we have no data with which to directly address

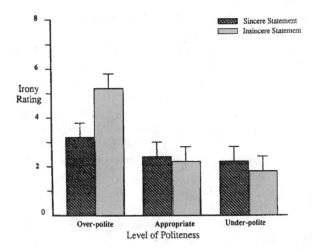

Figure 4.4.   Mean irony ratings as a function of politeness level and perceived sincerity.

this question, we can offer a plausible hypothesis. Recall that participants were asked to rate the degree to which over-polite and appropriately polite requests were intended as polite. In contrast, for under-polite requests, participants rated the degree to which the speaker "intends to be impolite." One possibility is that for over-polite and appropriately polite requests, participants rated pragmatic insincerity, the degree to which speakers were pretending to be polite. For under-polite requests, participants could have based their ratings on the degree to which speakers were seen as intentionally being rude. If impolite requests are rated as sincere, then this carries the clear implication that the speaker intended to be rude. Conversely, if impolite requests are rated as insincere, then this would imply that the speaker was unintentionally rude. In other words, participants may have viewed under-polite requests as unintentional rudeness, essentially a kind of social gaffe. This, of course, is quite different from the pragmatic insincerity that is involved when someone pretends to be polite. The rudeness and insultingness ratings for over- and under-polite requests are consistent with this interpretation: Under-polite requests were rated as much ruder than over-polite requests. At the same time, insincere and hence ironic over-polite requests were rated as insulting as under-polite requests. On this interpretation, speakers may very well intend to be insulting, but it would be rare for speakers to intend to be rude.

Although this account seems plausible and consistent with the data and with our general account of irony, additional data are needed to settle the question. The overall pattern of results, however, do support the allusional pretense theory. Irony was perceived when speakers were perceived as both allusive and pragmatically insincere, namely, when using over-polite and appropriately polite requests that were perceived as insincerely polite. The relations between perceived insincerity, irony, rudeness, and insultingness are also consistent with the notion that irony can be used to serve politeness considerations. Ironic utterances were perceived as insulting but not rude, in contrast to under-polite utterances that were seen as nonironic, and not only insulting, but also rude.

This interpretation is consistent with the results of a correlational analysis of the rating data. The intercorrelations among politeness levels and scale ratings are presented in Table 4.8. As would be expected, irony ratings and politeness levels were positively related: the more polite, the greater the degree of rated irony. Also as expected, irony and sincerity were negatively correlated: the less sincere, the greater the degree of rated irony. Irony was significantly related to rudeness, but the strength of this relation was rather low ($r = .12$). The relation between irony and insultingness was much stronger ($r = .48$): the greater the degree of rated insultingness, the higher the irony ratings.

The results of a multiple regression analysis with irony as the dependent variable confirmed the interpretation offered above. Consistent with the allusional pretense theory, politeness level, sincerity, and insultingness were reliable predictors of irony ($p < .001$ in all three cases). Also, as should be expected from our hypothesis that irony can serve politeness considerations, rudeness and irony were not reliably related to one another when politeness level and sincerity are partialed out.

TABLE 4.8

Intercorrelation of Politeness Levels and Scale Ratings

	Irony	Sincerity	Rudeness	Insultingness
Politeness	.37***	.01	−.49***	−.14***
Irony	—	−.54***	.12**	.48***
Sincerity		—	−.23***	−.41***
Rudeness			—	.58***

p < .01.*p < .001.

The overall pattern of results is thus consistent with the allusional pretense theory and clearly supports the argument that perceived pragmatic insincerity is a necessary condition for irony. Over-polite requests that were perceived as sincere were not seen as ironic, whereas those that were perceived as insincerely polite were seen as ironic. That ironic utterances were perceived as insulting but not rude supports the suggestion that irony can be used to communicate negative affect and even to insult others while still protecting the speaker's face, thus serving politeness considerations.

GENERAL DISCUSSION

The allusional pretense theory provides a coherent account of conversational irony. Utterances that allude to a failed expectation and that are pragmatically insincere can communicate irony. The strong claim is that these two conditions are necessary if irony is to be perceived. This is a significant extension and elaboration of prior theories of discourse irony. First, the mechanism of allusion replaces the narrower mechanisms of echoic mention (Sperber & Wilson, 1981), echoic interpretation (Sperber & Wilson, 1986), and echoic reminder (Kreuz & Glucksberg, 1989), because these are, by definition, special cases of allusion. Second, the concept of pragmatic insincerity extends the theory of discourse irony to speech acts other than assertives, to include such utterance types as offers, requests, and questions, among others (see below).

Consider, first, the concept of echoic mention. Sperber and Wilson (1981) pointed out the distinction between use and mention in the context of irony. An expression is used when it retains its illocutionary force, such as the request "Open the window for me, would you?" An expression is mentioned when it refers to its former illocutionary act, such as the retort "Open the window for me, would you? Just whom do you think you are talking to?" Sperber and Wilson (1981) argued that it is possible to mention not only words and sentences but also their meanings. Consider the following exchange between George and Mary.

George: "Wouldn't a cool breeze feel nice?"
Mary: "Wouldn't a cool breeze feel nice? I guess you expect me to open the
window for you. Well expect again!"

In the first part of Mary's retort, she echoes or mentions George's comment
about a breeze, which she interpreted as an indirect request to open a window. In the
second part of her retort, she echoes or mentions what she believes is George's intended meaning. Sperber and Wilson (1981) referred to this kind of mention of a
meaning or proposition as echoic mention and then argued that ironic utterances are
cases of echoic mention. By repeating (echoing) what was said, the ironist does not
intend to inform the listener of the contents of the utterance, but rather to show that
she had heard and understood the utterance and is now expressing her attitude toward the proposition she is echoing. Empirical support for this specific hypothesis
was provided in an experiment reported by Jorgensen et al. (1984). To account for
instances of irony where there is no specific utterance to be echoed, there are various types and degrees of implicit mention that are considered echoic, as when a
speaker can echo what may have been implied, or even popular wisdom or opinion
such as widely shared social norms.

Sperber and Wilson (1981) had originally argued that all ironic utterances can be
interpreted as cases of echoic mention. They later acknowledged that "the notion of
mention does not really stretch to cover the full range of cases [of ironic utterances]
we are now proposing to handle" (Sperber & Wilson, 1986, p. 264). They abandoned
the concept of mention in favor of the more general concept of interpretation, with
mention now a special case of interpretation. In echoic interpretation theory, Sperber
and Wilson argued that every utterance is an interpretive expression of a thought of
the ironist and that irony involves an interpretive relation between the ironist's
thought and the ironist's interpretation of another's thoughts or utterances. By interpreting another person's thought or a popular wisdom, the ironist informs the hearer
that he or she has in mind what was said and has a certain attitude toward it.

The act of echoing, be it via mention or interpretation, is necessarily an act of allusion. By alluding to someone else's explicit or implicit thoughts, beliefs, or actions, a speaker can call a listener's attention to those thoughts, beliefs, or actions.
Similarly, Kreuz and Glucksberg's (1989) concept of echoic reminder is also necessarily a special case of allusion. Kreuz and Glucksberg argued that echoic interpretation theories did not address the issue of why an ironist says something
different from what is really meant in the first place. They proposed that ironists use
echoic mention or interpretation as a way of reminding a listener of a failed expectation or norm and also pointed out that such reminding can be accomplished without necessarily echoing a prior utterance or thought. Ironic utterances are used to
remind a listener of antecedent events, social norms, or shared expectations, as well
as of a discrepancy between what is and what should be. By reminding listeners of
such a discrepancy, the ironist expresses his or her attitude toward that discrepancy.

Speakers can allude to an expectation or norm by explicitly echoing a prior utterance or by echoing someone's implicit thoughts, but speakers can also allude to ex-

pectations or norms without necessarily echoing anything. Similarly, a speaker can allude to an expectation or norm by reminding someone of that expectation or norm. However, a speaker can also make such allusions without reminding at all: There are certainly cases where both speaker and addressee are fully aware of a failed expectation, and thus no reminding is necessary (or even possible, given that the target of the allusion is already in mind). Thus, echoic mention, interpretation, and reminding are, by definition, special cases of allusion, where a listener's attention is directed toward some prior event or expectation. Restricting a theory of irony to allusion via echoic interpretation or reminding severely is unnecessarily restrictive because such a theory cannot account for the range of ironic utterance types that we have explored in the experiments reported here.

Similarly, the concept of pragmatic insincerity is a generalization of one particular condition for irony, that is, saying the opposite of what is meant. Saying the opposite of what is meant is an appropriate if imprecise way to characterize counterfactual assertions, as when someone says "what lovely weather" when it is raining. However, as we noted earlier, the notion of opposite meaning is not applicable to such speech acts as thanking, requesting, offering, or questioning. Pragmatic insincerity, of course, includes the kind of semantic or propositional insincerity that is involved when speakers use counterfactual assertions (cf. Grice, 1975, 1978), but it also includes any other type of utterance where a speaker intends something other than what is usually intended by use of a particular utterance form. Thus, a pragmatically insincere utterance from any of the five major speech act categories may, if it is used to allude to a failed expectation or norm, convey irony.

Recall that there are five such major speech act categories: assertives, directives, commissives, expressives, and declarations. We consider examples of each of these speech act categories to illustrate the utility of the allusional pretense theory, where the two principles—allusion and pragmatic insincerity—help to account for the major phenomenon of irony in conversation.

Assertives

Positive Counterfactuals.   When an utterance has the surface form of an assertion, then a counterfactual statement such as saying "what great weather" when it is raining will communicate irony. Such statements allude to the failed expectation of good weather and violate a felicity condition for assertives, namely, that people should not assert something that they believe to be untrue.

Negative Counterfactuals.   Positive counterfactual statements can generally be used to express irony, whereas negative counterfactual statements cannot. For example, saying "what terrible weather" on a fine sunny day would most likely be taken as anomalous. According to the allusional pretense theory, such statements fail to communicate irony because there is no norm or expectation that can be alluded to. However, if there is an explicit antecedent that can be alluded to, such as a failed prediction of bad weather, then such negative statements do communicate irony (Kreuz & Glucksberg, 1989). Furthermore, when people's expectations about a state of affairs are negative, explicit antecedents are not necessary for negative statements to communicate irony. As we found in Experiment 2, negative counterfactuals that alluded to negative expectations are understood as ironic, such as, saying "New York subways are certainly dirty" in the context of encountering a clean subway train. Such statements communicate irony because they are both allusive and pragmatically insincere.

Counterfactuals About Norm Violations.   When there is an expectation of appropriate amount or quantity, then a counterfactual assertion about a deviation from the norm can communicate irony, as shown in Experiment 2. If, for example, a student's paper is shorter than expected, then saying "this is a long paper" communicates irony. Similarly, if the paper were longer than expected, then saying "this is a short paper" also communicates irony.

True Assertions.   True assertions, when pragmatically insincere, can also communicate irony. Assertions can be used to express attitudes, and when the attitude expressed is counter to the surface form of the assertion, then the assertion can be interpreted as ironic. Consider the utterance "You sure know a lot." This may be a true assertion, but when uttered to someone who is obnoxiously showing off their knowledge, it may be viewed as an insincere compliment and so communicate a negative attitude toward that person via sarcastic irony (Experiment 1). Similarly, when a driver comments "I just love people who signal when turning" when the car ahead abruptly turns left, irony is communicated via the joint operation of allusion and pragmatic insincerity. The speaker in this case alludes to the social norm that drivers should signal before turning and is simultaneously being insincere by pretending to compliment the errant driver for something that wasn't done, namely, signaling. This last case has been problematic for both the traditional pragmatic theory and the more recent echo theories because none of these theories recognized the central roles of allusion and pragmatic insincerity.

Other Speech Acts That Communicate Irony

Directives.   Directives are statements that are intended to prompt someone to do something. These include questions such as "How old are you?" A speaker is insincere in asking such a question when no answer is really desired. When a pragmatically insincere question also alludes to a failed expectation or norm, then irony can be communicated. As we found in Experiment 1, when this question is uttered in the context of someone not acting his age, then the utterance is perceived as ironic because it alludes to the norm of people acting their age, and it is pragmatically insincere in that the speaker has no interest in the listener's exact age.

Requests are another type of directive, and these too can communicate irony when they allude to a failed expectation and convey pragmatic insincerity. One way to be pragmatically insincere is to be overly polite and so violate the felicity condition that requests should be made at an appropriate level of politeness. As we found in Experiment 3, over-polite requests in contexts where a speaker has been disappointed or when a norm has been violated can convey irony. For example, when a parent says "Would you mind if I asked you perhaps to consider turning off the TV?" to a teenager who is watching a very loud television program while the parent is trying to concentrate on an important piece of work, irony would be conveyed. Under-polite requests, in contrast, do not convey irony, but instead convey rudeness, even when the speaker is seen as not intending to be impolite, but has instead committed a social gaffe.

Commissives.   Commissives are utterances that commit a speaker to some action. These include promises, resolutions, and offers. Here too, the combination of allusion and pragmatic insincerity jointly permit irony to be communicated. For example, two of the felicity conditions for making an offer are as follows: (a) the person making the offer intends and expects that the offer will be accepted, and (b) he or she is also prepared to fulfill the offer. When, however, a norm or expectation has been violated, as when someone has eaten an entire pizza and left nothing for anyone else, an offer of another slice of pizza simultaneously alludes to the norm violation and is pragmatically insincere. In such circumstances, irony is communicated (Experiment 1).

Expressives.   Expressives are utterances that explicitly communicate a speaker's feelings. When expressives allude to a norm or expectation that has been violated and are pragmatically insincere, then they can communicate irony, usually sarcastic irony. Saying "thanks a lot" when someone has just stepped on your toes is a common everyday example, as is "thank you for your concern" when someone has shown no concern at all (Experiment 1).

Declarations.   Declarations are utterances that, simply by being uttered, accomplish something. For example, when a religious or legal official says "I now pronounce you man and wife," the utterance itself accomplishes the act of marrying. Although we did not sample any utterances from this speech act category, ironic uses of declarations can readily be accommodated in terms of the allusional pretense theory. When a declaration alludes to a violated norm or expectation and when it violates the felicity condition that a declaration can only be made by someone with the authority to make it, then a declaration may communicate irony. Consider, for example, a situation in which a young man ostentatiously throws his coat on the ground to permit the young woman that he's with to avoid getting her shoes wet. A bystander who then says "I dub thee Sir Galahad" would communicate irony because the statement (a) alludes to the act itself which, in contemporary society, is excessively polite and gallant, and (b) is pragmatically insincere in that the speaker does not have the authority to confer knighthood on anyone.

In each of the cases that we considered, allusion to a discrepancy between what should be and what actually is, combined with pragmatic insincerity, were important and perhaps necessary conditions for communicating irony. They are, however, not sufficient. In addition to these two factors, a number of other conditions must be satisfied if irony is to be communicated. An exhaustive enumeration of such conditions is beyond the scope of this paper, but two can be suggested. The first is the communication of the speaker's attitude toward the object of the ironic remark. In every case that we have considered so far, the speaker seemed to care one way or another about the failed expectation. If the speaker in fact doesn't care, and is perceived as not caring, then irony should not be communicated. For example, someone might comment "That's a real shiny pebble" upon picking up a dull stone on the beach, after a conversation in which both speaker and listener had mentioned that there were many shiny pebbles on that particular beach. Unless anyone cared about whether or not they had correctly anticipated shiny pebbles, or whether the pebbles on the beach were shiny or not, the remark would not be perceived as ironic, even though it alluded to their prior expectation and was also pragmatically insincere.

The example suggests a second precondition for irony. As Clark and Gerrig (1984) pointed out in their critique of echoic mention theory, participants in a conversation must share the failed expectation or the violated norm. Otherwise, irony would not be perceived even when a speaker might intend it. For example, when a speaker has the expectation that New York subways would be dirty and says "New York subways are certainly dirty" upon entering a clean subway car, irony would be communicated only if the listener shared that expectation. If the listener had not expected the subway to be dirty, then the remark about dirty subways would appear odd, not ironic.

What do ironic utterances accomplish by alluding to a disconfirmed expectation or violated norm? One purpose would be to bring such events into linguistic co-presence. Clark and Marshall (1981) argued that mutual knowledge is an important element in conversation. Participants in a conversation must explicitly or implicitly agree upon what they have in common (mutual knowledge) and what they do not. Mutual knowledge can be established in several ways, including community membership (e.g., everyone in the military knows who the commander-in-chief is) and physical co-presence (e.g., everyone on the beach at this moment knows that the sun is hidden behind clouds). Mutual knowledge can also be established by linguistic co-presence. When a teacher says "I expected this paper to be no more than 10 pages" to a student who has just turned in a 50-page opus, mutual knowledge of the teacher's expectation is established directly. When, in contrast, a teacher says "This sure is a short paper," an allusion is being made regarding the expected appropriate length of the paper. In so doing, the ironist indirectly brings the expectation into linguistic co-presence for the two people involved. Note that the expectation alluded to should have already been available in the listener's mind, whether or not the listener is aware of it when the ironist alludes to that expectation. By the allusion, the expectation that was available to both speaker and listener becomes accessible and manifest to them. Because it is now manifest to the speaker and listener, the speaker can convey his or her attitude toward the expectation and the discrepancy between the expectation and reality. The process of establishing mutual knowledge during discourse itself is not, of course, specific to irony. What is specific is that a disconfirmed thought, expectation, or norm is brought into linguistic co-presence.

Because irony is but one means of establishing mutual knowledge, what specifically motivates people to be ironic? There is general agreement that irony is used to express attitudes (Kreuz & Glucksberg, 1989; Muecke, 1969; Sperber & Wilson, 1981). These attitudes are usually negative, but not necessarily so (as the results of Experiment 1 suggest). In addition to this primary function, which can be served by a variety of communicative devices other than irony, ironic utterances seem uniquely suited to those situations that occasion the use of irony in the first place, namely, situations where something has unexpectedly gone awry (Lucariello, 1994). In such situations, people may experience discomfort, uneasiness, perhaps embarrassment, and perhaps disappointment.

Speaking ironically in such situations would be a face-saving way to express one's feelings about what has gone awry, whether the situation is mildly comical or the stuff of tragedy. As the writer Luc Sante (1993) said in a recent essay on the epidemic of gunshot-related deaths in America, "There is no defense against freakish tragedy, only the kind of internal preparation—equal parts fatalism, imagination, humor and an understanding of probability … available to [humans]" (p. 27). Irony provides one way to deal interpersonally with situations that threaten social relations by providing a way to express (usually) negative attitudes with humor, with imagination, yet still with some point.

ACKNOWLEDGMENTS

We are grateful for the financial support provided by the Public Health Service Grant HD25826. The research reported here was performed as a doctoral dissertation submitted to Princeton University by Sachi Kumon-Nakamura.

We thank Roger Kreuz for providing us with materials, and Boaz Keysar, Susan Fussell, Phillip Johnson-Laird, Deanna Manfredi, Matthew McGlone, and Deborah Prentice for their valuable comments on earlier drafts of this article.

Correspondence concerning this article should be addressed to Sam Glucksberg, Department of Psychology, Princeton University, Princeton, NJ 08544–1010. E-mail may be sent to samg@pucc.princeton.edu

ENDNOTES

1. Some of the expressions that we examine are examples of ironic sarcasm, whereas others are ironic but not sarcastic. Sarcastic irony is used to express a negative attitude as well as to insult or hurt to some degree. Nonsarcastic irony can be used to express either negative or positive attitudes, but in neither case is intended to hurt or insult any particular person. We deal with both types of irony in this paper.
2. We use the term *pretense* to refer to pragmatic insincerity. The same term was used by Clark and Gerrig (1984) to refer to an ironist who is "pretending to be an injudicious person speaking to an uninitiated audience" (p. 121). Their use of the pretense concept is

confined to the use of propositions, in the tradition of Grice (1975). If such pretense is extended to the full range of speech acts, it becomes equivalent to our concept of pragmatic insincerity.

3. Here and throughout the article, analyses were computed, when appropriate, with both subjects and items as random factors. The F values for subjects will be denoted by F, for items, by F.

REFERENCES

Austin, J. L. (1962). *How to do things with words.* Oxford, England: Oxford University Press.

Becker, J. A., Kimmel, H. D., & Bevill, M. J. (1989). The interactive effects of request form and speaker status on judgments of requests. *Journal of Psycholinguistic Research, 18,* 521–531.

Blum-Kulka, S. (1987). Indirectness and politeness in requests: Same or different? *Journal of Pragmatics, 11,* 131–146.

Brown, P., & Levinson, S. (1987). *Politeness: Some universals in language usage.* Cambridge, England: Cambridge University Press.

Clark, H. H., & Gerrig, R. J. (1984). On the pretense theory of irony. *Journal of Experimental Psychology: General, 113,* 121–126.

Clark, H. H., & Marshall, C. R. (1981). Definite reference and mutual knowledge. In A. K. Joshi, B. L. Weber, & I. A. Sag (Eds.), *Elements of discourse understanding* (pp. 10–63). Cambridge, England: Cambridge University Press.

Didbin, M. (1988). *Ratking.* London: Faber & Faber.

Gibbs, R. W., Jr. (1986). On the psycholinguistics of sarcasm. *Journal of Experimental Psychology: General, 115,* 3–15.

Goffman, E. (1967). *Interaction ritual: Essays on face-to-face behavior.* Garden City, NY: Doubleday.

Grice, H. P. (1975). Logic and conversation. In P. Cole & J. L. Morgan (Eds.), *Syntax and semantics: Vol. 3. Speech acts* (pp. 41–58). New York: Academic.

Grice, H. P. (1978). Further notes on logic and conversation. In P. Cole (Ed.), *Syntax and semantics: Vol. 9. Pragmatics* (pp. 113–127). New York: Academic.

Holtgraves, T. (1986). Language structure in social interaction: Perceptions of direct and indirect speech acts and interactants who use them. *Journal of Personality and Social Psychology, 51,* 305–313.

Jorgensen, J., Miller, G. A., & Sperber, D. (1984). Test of the mention theory of irony. *Journal of Experimental Psychology: General, 113,* 112–120.

Kreuz, R., & Glucksberg, S. (1989). How to be sarcastic: The reminder theory of verbal irony. *Journal of Experimental Psychology: General, 118,* 347–386.

Kreuz, R., & Long, D. (1991, April). *New approaches to the study of verbal irony:* Paper presented at the 71st Annual Convention of the Western Psychological Association, San Francisco.

Long, D., & Kreuz, R. (1991, August). *The influence of discourse function on perceived verbal irony.* Paper presented at the 99th Annual Convention of the American Psychological Association, San Francisco.

Lucariello, J. (1994). Situational irony. *Journal of Experimental Psychology: General, 123,* 129–145.

Muecke, D. C. (1969). *The compass of irony.* London: Methuen.

Porter, W. S. (1912). The complete works of O. Henry. Garden City, NY: Doubleday.

Sante, L. (1993, November 11). Where to hide? *The New York Times,* p. 27.

Searle, J. R. (1969). *Speech acts: An essay in the philosophy of language.* Cambridge, England: Cambridge University Press.

Searle, J. R. (1979). Literal meaning. In J. Searle (Ed.), *Expression and meaning: Studies in the theory of speech acts* (pp. 117–136). Cambridge, England: Cambridge University Press.

Sperber, D., & Wilson, D. (1981). Irony and the use-mention distinction. In P. Cole (Ed.), *Radical pragmatics* (pp. 295–318). New York: Academic.

Sperber, D., & Wilson, D. (1986) *Relevance: Communication and cognition.* Cambridge, MA: Harvard University Press.

CHAPTER 5

On Necessary Conditions
for Verbal Irony Comprehension

Herbert L. Colston
University of Wisconsin–Parkside

The conditions for verbal irony comprehension implicitly or directly claimed as necessary by all of the recent philosophic, linguistic, and psycholinguistic theories of verbal irony (Clark & Gerrig, 1984; Kreuz & Glucksberg, 1989; Kumon-Nakamura, Glucksberg, & Brown, 1995; Sperber & Wilson, 1981, 1986) were experimentally tested. Allusion to a violation of expectations, predictions, desires, preferences, social norms, etc., was confirmed as a necessary condition, but pragmatic insincerity was not. Pragmatically sincere comments can be comprehended ironically. A revised set of conditions was proposed, involving intentional violation of Gricean conversational maxims and the portrayal of a contrast between expectations and reality. A cautionary note was made, however, regarding the viability of a single account of verbal irony comprehension.

The purpose of this article is to evaluate claims about how people comprehend ironic comments in conversation, such as saying "Nice hair" to mean "Bad hair," or "What terrific news" to mean "What terrible news." Comments such as these, or verbal irony, are distinguishable from other forms of irony in that verbal irony involves an inconsistency between a verbal expression and a situation. For instance, the above comments contradict their referent situations. Other forms or irony might involve a contradiction within a situation itself, as in situational irony, or between a spectator and a participant in a situation, as is seen in dramatic or tragic irony (see Lucariello, 1994, or Preminger & Brogan, 1993, for discussions of different forms of irony).

Verbal irony has been of interest to philosophers, linguists, and cognitive psychologists because of the challenge it poses for theories of language comprehension. For example, consider a man who was asked by his girlfriend to help move her

This chapter was previously published as "On necessary conditions for verbal irony comprehension" (H. L. Colston) in *Pragmatics and Cognition, 8*, 277–324. Copyright © [2000]. Reprinted with kind permission by John Benjamins Publishing Company, Philadelphia.

belongings to a new apartment. Suppose the man said he could not assist because he wanted to watch television instead. Upon hearing this, the girlfriend might reply, "Well, that's very nice of you." This comment would be interpreted as sarcastically disparaging the boyfriend's selfishness rather than expressing that his act was genuinely "nice." Given, though, that the intended meaning, or the "speaker meaning," of the comment does not match the meaning of the words used, or the "utterance meaning" (Dascal, 1983, 1987, 1989), how do people understand such comments?

Each of the various linguistic and psycholinguistic theories that have offered explanations for verbal irony comprehension either implicitly or directly make claims about necessary conditions for such comprehension to succeed. The recently proposed "How About Another Piece of Pie? The Allusional Pretense Theory of Discourse Irony" (Kumon-Nakamura, Glucksberg, & Brown 1995) distills these claims into two conditions argued to be necessary for verbal irony comprehension. The first condition, *allusion to violated expectations,* is that a speaker must allude to a prediction, expectation, preference, previously made comment, or norm that was violated by ensuing events. The second condition is that an ironic comment must violate the felicity conditions for well-formed speech acts (Grice, 1975) or that the comment is *pragmatically insincere.* For instance, the ironic meaning of the woman's comment in the above example is understandable because it fulfills these two conditions. The comment alludes to the woman's expectation that her boyfriend should have been "nice" and helped her move—based upon the common courtesy that friends should help one another—that was violated by the boyfriend's actual behavior. The utterance meaning of the comment—statement of praise—is also inconsistent with the woman's intended meaning—to criticize her boyfriend's act—making the comment pragmatically insincere.

Although these conditions of allusion to violated expectations and pragmatic insincerity appear in various forms in most theories of verbal irony comprehension, and do seem to apply to many instances of verbal irony, it remains unclear as to whether comments that *do not* allude to violated expectations or that are pragmatically *sincere* could still be comprehended ironically. This brings into question whether these conditions should be considered necessary for verbal irony comprehension.[1]

In this article, the prevalence of these two conditions in the recent theories of verbal irony comprehension will be demonstrated and their necessity will then be experimentally tested. As will be seen, the results of the experiments call for a revision in the claim that pragmatic insincerity is a necessary condition for verbal irony comprehension. In order to account for the current results, I present a revised set of necessary conditions and I discuss the implications for theories of verbal irony comprehension.

ALLUSION TO VIOLATED EXPECTATIONS

What does it mean for a comment to allude to violated expectations? One possibility is that a speaker directly refers to prior statements, predictions, expectations, or desires in the midst of the current situation that violates those statements, etc. Two "echoic" accounts of verbal irony comprehension have this pattern. In one form, "echoic mention" (Sperber & Wilson 1981, 1986; Jorgensen, Miller, & Sperber 1984), a speaker directly mentions another speaker's previous comment that has turned out to be inaccurate. For instance, a speaker can mention another person's (or their own) inaccurate prediction about an event (e.g., if a weather reporter predicts "clear blue skies" for a given day but the weather is cloudy and rainy instead, a speaker could say, "Yup, 'clear blue skies' today"), or a speaker can repeat another person's description that turned out to be incorrect (e.g., repeating a person's earlier comment about how "very well behaved" a kitten is after the kitten has shredded a curtain, "Yes, a 'very well behaved' kitten indeed!").

Rather than directly mentioning another person's comments, a speaker can mention generally accepted beliefs about a situation, like a social norm, to remind the addressee of those beliefs when they have not held up in the ensuing situation (e.g., a speaker can say, "Thanks, you've been very polite" to a surly store clerk). Here the speaker echoes the social norm of politeness when a person has been rude. This echo of social norms or other common beliefs has been called "echoic reminder" (Kreuz & Glucksberg 1989, Colston 1997b). Note that in both types of echo—mention and reminder—the speaker refers to an expected or desired state of affairs that has not reached fruition.

A third form that allusion to violated expectations can take is to elicit expectations or desires in the mind of the addressee without direct reference, again when those expectations were violated by ensuing events. Kumon-Nakamura et al. (1995, pp. 4–5) discussed three ways that verbal irony takes this form:

(b)   Questions, like "How old did you say you were?" to someone acting inappropriately for their age.

(c)   Offerings, like "How about another small slice of pizza?" to someone who just gobbled up the whole pie.

(d)   Over-polite requests, like "Would you mind very much if I asked you to consider cleaning up your room some time this year?" to an inconsiderate and slovenly housemate.

Each of these comment types are not strict cases of echo because they are neither rementions of previous predictions or descriptions, nor statements reflecting common beliefs. These cases thus cannot be explained by explicit echoic theories unless one allows for echo of imagined comments. But since the comments nevertheless involve the speaker eliciting expectations or desires in the mind of the addressee that have not been met, the comments are understood as being ironic.

The fourth way in which a comment can allude to violated expectations is to directly mention a portion of the expected situation that actually has occurred, when the remaining portion of the expected situation has been violated. Kumon-Nakamura et al. (1995, p. 4) also discussed comments that have this pattern:

(a)   True assertions, such as "You sure know a lot" to someone arrogantly
        showing off his knowledge.

Here, part of the expected or desired state of affairs is that the addressee is knowledgeable. But the addressee might also be expected to not arrogantly show off this
knowledge. The actual state of affairs is thus a partial match with this expectation—the addressee *is* knowledgeable—but he is also unexpectedly or undesir-
ably being arrogant by showing off this knowledge. The speaker then mentions
only the portion of the expectations that has been met and allows the unexpected
or undesirable portion of the situation to be realized by the addressees. This comment type is also not strictly echoic since, although it does refer to something that
was expected, that referred-to portion of the expectation was not violated—it is
part of the ensuing situation. But since the comment nevertheless indicates some
other portion of the expectation or desire that has not reached fruition, it is understood as ironic.

The fifth and final source of the claim of allusion to violated expectations comes
from the Pretense account of verbal irony comprehension (Clark & Gerrig, 1984).
This account states that allusion to violated expectations is not so much a direct reference to, or elicitation of, expected events (or a combination of the two as in
Kumon-Nakamura et al.'s [1995] true assertions), although it often accomplishes
these, but rather that this allusion is achieved via transparent mimicry. For instance,
Pretense claims that a speaker is "pretending to be an injudicious person speaking
to an uninitiated audience; the speaker intends the addressees of the irony to discover the pretense and thereby see his or her attitude toward the speaker, the audience, and the comment" (Clark & Gerrig 1984, p. 121). For example, a speaker
could make the comment, "I just love all these commercials," perhaps with mocking intonation, to poke fun at that pretend assertion—a favorable attitude towards
an excessive number of television commercials—at a fictitious (or real) person who
might actually enjoy the interruptions, and at people who would believe the speaker
genuinely enjoys commercial interruptions. In doing this, the speaker expresses her
negative attitude towards these hypothetical or real people and their beliefs. Since
the speaker has a negative or derogatory attitude toward the ensuing events, it is apparent that those ensuing events are not as the speaker would have desired,
preferred, expected, etc. Thus, the speaker is understood to actually be ironically
complaining about the commercials.

All of these mechanisms of achieving verbal irony; echoic mention, echoic reminder, elicitation, true assertion and pretense, have the common denominator of
pointing out some expectation, desire, social norm, etc., that was violated. Since
they do not all rely upon the same mechanisms for doing so, the broad term
"allusional pretense" was used by Kumon-Nakamura et al. (1995, p. 5) to describe reference to violated expectations. Thus, according to the Allusional
Pretense Theory of Discourse Irony, all ironic comments have the necessary characteristic of allusion to a discrepancy between what occurs and what should have
occurred.

PRAGMATIC INSINCERITY

The second necessary condition found in theories of verbal irony comprehension—pragmatic insincerity—derives generally from the myriad of claims that verbal irony involves a "contradictory," "opposite," "non-veridical," "counterfactual," "insincere," or "contrary" relationship between what is uttered and what is ironically intended (Clark & Gerrig, 1984; Gibbs, 1986a; Grice, 1975, 1978; Kreuz & Glucksberg, 1989; Kumon-Nakamura et al., 1995; Searle, 1978; Sperber & Wilson, 1981). These terms come from many different theories of verbal irony comprehension including the Pretense, Allusional Pretense, and, arguably, Echoic Mention/Reminder theories thus far discussed.

But what does it mean for a comment to be pragmatically insincere? The intention of Kumon-Nakamura et al. (1995, p. 5) in creating the term *pragmatic insincerity* was to account for comments that are not insincere on a propositional level, but that instead are insincere on a speech act level. For instance, the example comments from Kumon-Nakamura et al. reported above are either propositionally true, or they are not assertions. In example (a), when the speaker says, "You sure know a lot," to someone arrogantly showing off his knowledge, she is uttering a true proposition—the speaker *is* knowledgeable. In examples (b) through (d), the comments are not assertions. In example (b), the speaker inquires something about the addressee, in (c) the speaker offers something to the addressee, and in (d) the speaker requests something from the addressee. Thus, these comments cannot be insincere on a propositional level. The comments instead achieve their irony via insincerity at the speech act level, or via their insincere illocutionary force (Haverkate, 1990). In (a), the speaker uses the comment to insincerely compliment the person and ironically express that the person's arrogance is in fact not praiseworthy. In (b) through (d), the speaker insincerely inquires, offers, and requests something from the addressee, respectively, when she never genuinely wants those directives followed. Since these speech acts do not achieve their irony at a propositional level, Kumon-Nakamura et al. created the construct of pragmatic insincerity that allows for these broader types of insincerity.

But how do comments achieve this pragmatic insincerity? To illustrate, note how each of the theories of verbal irony comprehension makes the claim of pragmatic insincerity. Consider the scenario and possible ironic comments depicted in Table 5.1.

The expected or desired outcome of the scenario in Table 5.1 is that the boy would receive an attractive haircut. The ensuing situation, however, is that the boy's haircut is ugly. The girl who makes the ironic comment in this scenario could use any of the methods of alluding to this violated expectation discussed in the previous section to make an ironic comment. She could echoically mention the boy's term for the barber's work, "That sure is a 'terrific 'do'" (1). She could echoically remind her audience of the common expectation or desire for haircuts to be attractive, "Nice hair" (2). She could elicit the expected or desired situation from her addressees, "When are you going to get a haircut?" (3). She could mention the portion of

TABLE 5.1

Forms of Verbal Irony

Scenario: A boy in junior high school goes to a barber for a haircut. The boy had been bragging at school about the "terrific 'do'" this barber gives. The barber actually does a horrible job on the boy's hair though, and it looks terrible. The next day, the boy goes to school, dreading the reaction he is going to get from the students in his class. When he walks in the room, the girl he sits next to, who is known for being arrogant and cruel, says to the boy ...

Expected situation: An attractive haircut

Ensuing situation: An ugly haircut

Possible Ironic Comments	Allusional Mechanism	Type of Insincerity
1. "That Sure is a terrific 'do'"	*Echoic Mention:* mentions explicit expectation	semantic
2. "Nice hair"	*Echoic Reminder:* reminds addressee(s) of implicit expectation	semantic
3. "When are you going to get a haircut?"	*Elicitation:* elicits expectation from addressee(s)	pragmatic
4. "You sure did get a haircut"	*True Assertion:* mentions portion of expectation that occurred	pragmatic
5a. "This barber gives a terrific 'do'"	*Pretense:* mentions expectation while imitating the boy's voice	semantic
5b. "That really is a terrific 'do'"	*Pretense:* mentions expectation in a mocking voice	semantic
6. "I really like guys with nice haircuts"	mentions opinion of expectation	?

the expectation that did actually occur but leave out the portion that was violated, "You sure did get a haircut" (4). Or, she could pretend to be the boy making his earlier prediction that the barber would give a good haircut, "This barber gives a terrific 'do'" (5a) or someone who incorrectly believes this prediction, "That really is a terrific 'do' (5b). I will return to the sixth possible ironic comment in the next section.

The first two of these comments demonstrate that, as mentioned earlier, the claim of pragmatic insincerity is inherently made by the echoic accounts of verbal irony. Since the echoic accounts rest upon the use–mention distinction (Sperber & Wilson, 1981, 1986) concerning the purpose of an ironic comment, the accounts allow speakers to not directly say what they mean, or put differently, they allow speakers to be pragmatically insincere. These accounts thus claim that pragmatic insincerity is a necessary condition of verbal irony comprehension.

The third and fourth examples demonstrate Kumon-Nakamura et al.'s (1995) notion of pragmatic insincerity where a speaker can make an insincere inquiry (or insincere request or insincere offering) or make a true but incomplete assertion and be pragmatically insincere.

The pragmatic insincerity claim can also be found in the Pretense account of verbal irony comprehension (Clark & Gerrig, 1984) as demonstrated in examples (5a) and (b). Since, according to Pretense, the success of an ironic interpretation relies upon the speaker making the pretend nature of her assertion obvious to the intended addressee, or, that the speaker makes it clear that she does not sincerely mean what she says (e.g., by mimicking the boy's voice or using a mocking tone), Pretense also is inherently consistent with the notion of pragmatic insincerity.[2]

The claim of pragmatic insincerity is also inherently made by another theory of verbal irony comprehension, proposed to account for many forms of non-literal language, the Standard Pragmatic Model (Grice, 1975, 1978; Searle, 1978). The Model argues that speakers normally follow a "cooperative principle," whereby they adhere to a set of rules or maxims when they converse. A Maxim of Quality, for example, states that comments that are known to be false by the speaker are improper. For example, when a person makes a comment (e.g., "What lovely weather!") that is inconsistent with the current situation (the weather is terrible), she violates that maxim. According to the Model, a speaker intentionally violates or "flouts" one of the maxims to set up a conversational implicature, i.e., an inference authorized by the speaker to be made by the addressee, that something different from the utterance meaning is actually meant by using the comment. The speaker may for example have actually meant that the weather is terrible. The process of conversational implicature is straightforward; it is detrimental to a conversation to violate maxims. If a maxim therefore *is* violated, the speaker is either being uncooperative or intends something other than the utterance meaning of her comment. Since the speaker is participating in the conversation, it is unlikely that she would mean to be uncooperative. She must therefore mean something else. Moreover, the speaker will likely select an indirect meaning that the addressee is capable of deriving from the comment, given the common ground (Clark & Carlson, 1981) between the interlocutors. Otherwise, again, the speaker would be uncooperative. The addressee, in realizing this, selects an interpretation that fits with the common ground (suppose the obvious fact that the weather is terrible) and that adheres to what he thinks the speaker would find him capable and likely of deriving. In this fashion, an interpretation of a comment is made that does not correspond with the utterance meaning of that comment.

In verbal irony, speakers may stimulate a conversational implicature by violating the Maxim of Quality since ironic expressions are generally untrue when taken at their utterance meaning level. An ironic comment would then set up a conversational implicature that the speaker intends for her comment to be taken ironically.

The Standard Pragmatic Model, in requiring that correct ironic interpretation depend upon intentionally violated or flouted conversational maxims, thus is also inherently consistent with the claim that an ironic comment must be pragmatically insincere.

As all of these cases of verbal irony—whether based upon echoic mechanisms, insincere non-assertions/true but incomplete assertions, Pretense, or the Standard Pragmatic Model—demonstrate the characteristic that some level of the speakers' meaning is insincere, the Allusional Pretense Theory of Discourse Irony (Kumon-Nakamura et al., 1995) also argues that all ironic comments have the necessary condition of pragmatic insincerity.

In the five accounts of verbal irony comprehension reviewed here—Echoic Mention (Sperber and Wilson 1981, 1986), Echoic Reminder (Kreuz & Glucksberg, 1989), Allusional Pretense (Kumon-Nakamura et al., 1995), Pretense (Clark & Gerrig, 1984), and the Standard Pragmatic Model (Grice, 1975, 1978; Searle, 1978)—one or both of the necessary conditions for verbal irony comprehension discussed by the Allusional Pretense Theory of Discourse Irony is explicitly or inherently claimed. As will be demonstrated in the next section, however, there are cases of verbal irony that may not meet the allusion to violated expectations or pragmatic insincerity conditions. In order to answer whether these conditions are necessary for verbal irony comprehension, allusion to violated expectations and pragmatic insincerity were put to experimental test.

AN EXPERIMENTAL TEST OF ALLUSION AND PRAGMATIC INSINCERITY

In order to evaluate allusion to violated expectations and pragmatic insincerity, comments that meet one of the following two criteria must be tested to see if they are interpreted ironically: (1) the comments do *not* allude to violated expectations, or (2) the comments are pragmatically *sincere*. If comments that fulfill these criteria are interpreted ironically, then the claim that allusion to violated expectations and pragmatic insincerity are necessary conditions for verbal irony comprehension will require revision.

Criterion 1: Verbal Irony That Does not Make Reference to Violated Expectations

The speech form that comes closest to fitting the first criterion are negative jests—operationally defined for the present study as negative assertions about positive situations where no explicit statements concerning the speaker's expectations precede the situations. For example, a speaker could use the negative jest, "Well that person was incredibly rude," to remark about someone who has been extremely polite and helpful.

We know from previous work that negative jests are interpreted ironically (Kreuz & Glucksberg, 1989). The question for the present research thus becomes whether negative jests allude to violated expectations.

Since negative jests are negative assertions about positive situations, and are not preceded by statements of the speaker's expectations, they neither echoically remind addressees about social norms, which are generally positive (Brown & Levinson, 1978; Kreuz & Glucksberg, 1989), nor echoically mention previous expectations. Negative jests can thus be considered non-echoic in that they are not using echoic mechanisms to allude to violated expectations. With positive assertions about negative situations (e.g., saying "Well, that person was incredibly polite" to someone who was very rude), speakers *are* echoically reminding addressees of commonly recognized, positive social norms that have not been followed in the actual situation. Speakers can also express violated expectations with negative assertions about positive situations when those situations follow explicit statements of negative expectations. For instance, had a companion of the first speaker above initially predicted that a person would be rude (e.g., by saying, "Don't bother asking this guy for directions, people in this town are always incredibly rude"), after which the person was actually very helpful and the speaker said, "Well that person was 'incredibly rude,'" the comment would be a simple case of echoic mention of an explicit expectation that has not reached fruition.

Since negative jests are also assertions about the current situation, they would not make use of the allusional mechanisms noted by Kumon-Nakamura et al. (1995, p. 4) for non-assertive speech acts (see examples b–d).

Negative jests are also not "true assertions" of the sort described by Kumon-Nakamura et al. (1995, p. 4, see example a), so they could not make use of allusional mechanisms based upon those forms to indicate violated expectations.

The mechanism that would seem to explain the comprehension of negative jests is pretense. The use of pretense in negative jests, however, does not necessarily involve an allusion to violated expectations as it would for other kinds of comments. It is possible that in making a negative jest, a speaker posits some *merely alternative* description of current events that is obviously inconsistent with those events, and makes the pretense of this assertion obvious (e.g., saying with an expression of ridicule and mocking intonation, "Oh, what awful weather," during beautiful weather).

In making this display, the speaker could certainly demonstrate the irrationality or foolishness of the purported viewpoint (e.g., actually thinking that the current weather is awful), and anyone who would genuinely propose or believe it, given that that viewpoint is obviously wrong. In so doing, the speaker could also express his actual and accurate opinion of the current events—that the weather in fact is beautiful. In these ways, pretense on negative jests *is* similar to pretense on other kinds of comments.

It is not clear, though, that the alternative events a speaker of negative jests pretends to advocate are expectations, desires, or the like. In this way, pretense on negative jests *is not* similar to pretense on other kinds of comments. Speakers could simply be joking about the current events without finding them unexpected, undesirable, etc. As argued earlier, since a speaker using pretense is "expressing a negative attitude," his desires or preferences would not seem to have been fulfilled by the current state of affairs. With negative jests, however, this may not be the case. Speakers could simply be joking about the current events without finding them unexpected, undesirable, etc.

To illustrate, return again to the example of the woman and her selfish boyfriend. Imagine a different context in which the boyfriend not only helped his girlfriend move, but also freely gave her a lot of furniture. Here, had the woman said, "Well, that's very selfish of you," she would not be echoing a social norm because there is no negative social norm that people should be selfish to their friends. The comment also does not echo an expectation or desire that was said earlier because the comment is not preceded with such a statement. Since the comment is a false assertion, it cannot make use of allusional mechanisms based upon true assertions or non-assertions. We know from previous research, however, that this type of comment is interpreted ironically (Kreuz & Glucksberg, 1989). The only remaining explanation is that the comment is interpreted via noting the pretense of the speaker—the woman pretending to find her boyfriend's act selfish and in doing so, mocking that assertion and anyone who would genuinely propose or believe it. Yet, it is not necessary that the events the speaker pretends to advocate (e.g., the boyfriend being selfish) were expectations, desires, predictions, norms, etc. It may be that the woman simply refers to an alternative event that is not expected, desired, etc., to make a joke. For instance, the woman may be poking fun at her boyfriend perhaps as an expression of affection, without finding his generosity unexpected.

These observations suggest that the interpretation of negative jests may not involve allusion to a violation of expectations, desires, preferences, norms, etc., which calls into question whether this allusion should be a necessary condition of verbal irony comprehension.

There is, however, one other possibility. Negative jests might involve an allusion to expectations after all, but in a way that is different from all of the mechanisms discussed thus far. Negative jests might involve an *inference* on the part of the interpreter that the speaker actually held *negative* expectations. In this roundabout way, one can consider negative jests echoic, with the speaker directly mentioning what he or she expected. The difference with negative jests, though, is that those expectations were not explicitly mentioned before, are not commonly held by most people, and therefore must be *inferred* by the interpreter.

The question addressed by the first set of experiments below is thus whether the ironic interpretation of negative jests involves an inference of violated negative expectations on the part of the interpreter. If violated negative expectations are not inferred, then the claim that verbal irony comprehension must involve allusion to violated expectations will require revision.

Criterion 2: Verbal Irony That Is Pragmatically Sincere

A speech form that fits the second criterion are pragmatically sincere comments used in situations where a speaker's expectations have been violated. For example, return to Table 5.1 and consider the sixth possible ironic comment that the speaker could make, "I really like guys with nice haircuts." This comment is made in a context where expectations or desires about the world have been violated—the boy that the girl is talking about had publicly expected an attractive haircut but received an ugly one instead. The comment is not, however, pragmatically insincere because the speaker genuinely means what she says and what she implies. The girl earnestly wishes to be interpreted as appreciating boys who have nice haircuts. The girl may also intend to imply more than the utterance meaning of her comment, but this additional implied meaning is not inconsistent with, and indeed is dependent upon, comprehending the utterance meaning of the comment. For instance, the girl may also mean to insult the boy, but this meaning does not contradict the interpretation that the girl appreciates boys with nice haircuts—these interpretations can coexist. Moreover, the former interpretation is dependent upon the latter—in order to ascertain that the girl does not like the boy's ugly haircut, one must know that the girl genuinely appreciates boys with attractive haircuts.[3]

If pragmatically sincere comments like these are interpreted ironically, then the claim that verbal irony comprehension must involve pragmatic insincerity will require revision. Thus, the question posed by Experiment 2 is whether pragmatically sincere comments are interpreted ironically.

In the following experiments, negative jests and pragmatically sincere assertions were presented to participants for interpretation. Experiments 1a through 1d test the necessity of allusion to violated expectations and Experiment 2 tests the necessity of pragmatic insincerity. To refer ahead, the third experiment tests for another necessary condition of verbal irony comprehension—violation of Gricean maxims.

Allusion

Experiment 1a

Is allusion to violated expectations a necessary condition of verbal irony comprehension? [Are negative jests interpreted ironically?]

This experiment sought to establish whether the negative jests to be used in subsequent experiments are interpreted ironically as was originally reported by Kreuz and Glucksberg (1989). It can thus be considered a replication test of the Kreuz and Glucksberg study with a new set of experimental items. This finding must be established first in order to then evaluate whether negative jests involve allusion to violated expectations. People were asked to rate the degree of sarcasm (a common term used to describe an expression of verbal irony) they interpreted from negative jests along with echoic and earnest comments. Following Kreuz and Glucksberg's (1989) findings, negative jests were predicted to be interpreted as sarcastic, but not to the same degree as echoic comments. Both negative jests and echoic comments were predicted to be interpreted as more sarcastic than earnest comments.

In general, the materials and procedures used in the experiments were similar. Therefore, the methods described here can serve as a model for the other experiments. Only exceptions to the methods used in the present experiment will be mentioned for the other experiments.

Participants.   Twenty-four University of California undergraduates participated for a course requirement. All were native English speakers. None of the people participated in the other experiments.

Materials and Design.   Twenty scenarios described situations where a person makes a comment as if spoken directly to the reader about a situation the speaker encounters. The scenarios were adaptations of actual comments overheard by the author and research assistants.[4] Each scenario had four versions. One described a negative situation about which the speaker made an earnest negative comment (earnest negative). Another described a negative situation with the speaker making a comment that echoed a positive social norm (echoic). The third version described a positive situation with the speaker making a negative jest (negative jest). The final version described a positive situation with the speaker making an earnest positive comment (earnest positive). The situations were described with a minimum of context to prevent the possibility of the negative jests inadvertently echoing some information in the description. Example scenarios are presented in Table 5.2.

Four sets of scenarios were created with each set containing a different version of each scenario. For example, set one would contain the earnest negative version of the first scenario, where set two would contain the echoic version of that scenario, set three would contain the negative jest version of that scenario, and set four would contain the earnest positive version of that scenario. Set one would then also contain the echoic version of the second scenario, the negative jest version of the third scenario, the earnest positive version of the fourth scenario, and so on, so that five instances of each version were represented. The order of scenarios in each set was

TABLE 5.2

Example Scenarios Used in Experiments 1a Through 1d

Comment Type	Example Scenarios
Earnest negative	You and Julie want to go to a concert but neither of you have enough money for the ticket. She says, "This sucks." You tell your housemate Marilyn that the person moving in with you two was kicked out of his previous home. She says, "That sure is frightening." Your housemate Joel tells you that he got invited to a party by people you know he hates. He says, "This party sounds awful."
Echoic	You and Julie want to go to a concert but neither of you have enough money for the ticket. She says, "This is great." You tell your housemate Marilyn that the person moving in with you two was kicked out of his previous home. She says, "That sure is comforting." Your housemate Joel tells you that he got invited to a party by people you know he hates. He says, "This party sounds like fun."
Negative jest	You and Julie want to go to a concert and you both have enough money for the ticket. She says, "This sucks." You tell your housemate Marilyn that the person moving in with you two was adored at his previous home. She says, "That sure is frightening." Your housemate Joel tells you that he got invited to a party by people you know he likes. He says, "This party sounds awful."
Earnest positive	You and Julie want to go to a concert and you both have enough money for the ticket. She says, "This is great." You tell your housemate Marilyn that the person moving in with you two was adored at his previous home. She says, "That sure is comforting." Your housemate Joel tells you that he got invited to a party by people you know he likes. He says, "This party sounds like fun."

random, and each set was presented to an equal number of participants, resulting in counterbalancing of the scenarios and comment types across participants. Each scenario was presented with a 7-point rating scale ranging from 1 (*not at all sarcastic*) to 7 (*extremely sarcastic*).

Each participant received all levels of the independent variable—comment type (earnest negative, echoic, negative jest, and earnest positive), making a one factor, within-participants design. Considering items as a random factor, the design is also one factor, within-participants.

Procedure. Participants were told they would complete a task involving their interpretations about what people say. They were then presented with the 20 scenarios in a booklet with instructions on the cover. The instructions told the participants to read each scenario and decide how sarcastic they thought the speaker was being with his or her comment. Participants were told to indicate their decisions by marking the rating scales. When participants had completed this task, they were debriefed and dismissed.

Results and Discussion. A brief comment on how the data in this and the other experiments were analyzed and reported is in order. All analyses of variance (ANOVAs) were conducted in two ways—one treating participants as the random factor and the other treating items as the random factor. Conducting analyses this way allows for generalization of significant effects across both participant and item populations. ANOVAs treating participants as the random factor are referred to with *F1,* and analyses treating items as a random factor are referred to with *F2.*

The mean sarcasm ratings for the four comment types are presented in Table 5.3. A one-way ANOVA revealed a significant difference in the degree to which participants found the comments sarcastic, $F1(3, 69) = 118.23$, $p < .001$, $F2(3, 57) = 147.17$, $p < .001$.

TABLE 5.3
Degree of Sarcasm As a Function of Comment Type: Experiment 1a

Comment Type	Degree of Sarcasm	
Earnest negative	Mean	1.69
	SD	0.92
Echoic	Mean	5.62
	SD	0.91
Negative jest	Mean	5.11
	SD	1.23
Earnest positive	Mean	1.58
	SD	0.57

Note. The rating scale ranged from 1 (*not at all sarcastic*) to 7 (*extremely sarcastic*).

Pairwise comparisons revealed that echoic comments were considered more sarcastic than both earnest negative, $F1(1, 23) = 144.89$, $p < .001$, $F2(1, 19) = 262.61$, $p < .001$, and earnest positive comments, $F1(1, 23) = 222.91$, $p < .001$, $F2(1, 19) = 402.19$, $p < .001$. No difference was found between the two kinds of earnest comments. This result is not surprising as echoic comments are sarcastic by definition and earnest comments are not. This finding does, however, demonstrate the sensitivity of the rating scale to perceived differences in the degree of sarcasm.

Echoic comments were also rated as more sarcastic than negative jests, $F1(1, 23) = 7.77$, $p < .01$, $F2(1, 19) = 6.63$, $p < .01$ (note that, although reliable, the difference was small). This finding replicates previous results of asymmetry in verbal irony where positive comments about negative situations were considered more sarcastic than negative comments about positive situations (Kreuz & Glucksberg, 1989), and further demonstrates the sensitivity of the rating scale.

Most interesting for present purposes, however, was the additional finding that negative jests were rated as significantly more sarcastic than both earnest negative, $F1(1, 23) = 88.64$, $p < .001$, $F2(1, 19) = 136.54$, $p < .001$, and earnest positive comments, $F1(1, 23) = 132.03$, $p < .001$, $F2(1, 19) = 146.45$, $p < .001$. The interpretation of verbal irony is presumed to rely upon allusion to violated expectations. Positive assertions about negative situations achieve this allusion because they echo commonly recognized positive social norms when things have turned out negatively. That is why echoic comments were rated as more sarcastic than earnest comments. The finding that negative jests were also interpreted ironically is more difficult to explain, however, because it is not clear that these comments allude to violated expectations. Negative jests do not echo common expectations like social norms. They also do not refer to explicit prior expectations because no statements concerning the speaker's expectations were made prior to the negative jest. Moreover, since the negative jests are false assertions, they cannot rely upon allusive mechanisms that occur with non-assertive comments like inquires, offerings, and requests, or with true assertions (Kumon-Nakamura et al., 1995). The only remaining mechanism by which the negative jests could allude to violated expectations is pretense. But it is not clear that the pretense used in the negative jests involves an allusion to violated expectations. Speakers of negative jests could simply state some alternative events that are inconsistent with the current situation to make a joke.

These results suggest that allusion to violated expectations may not be a necessary condition for verbal irony comprehension. Before testing this possibility further, however, an alternative explanation of the current results must first be evaluated. It is possible that participants in the present experiment did not interpret negative jests ironically but instead interpreted them through inference chains that rendered the comments' utterance meanings consistent with the speakers' intended meanings. Participants could have then rated the comments as sarcastic simply because the comments were negative. For instance, when reading the scenario, "Your housemate Joel tells you that he got invited to a party by people you know he likes. He says, 'This party sounds awful,'" participants could infer that other people who Joel despises were also invited to the party so that the comment's utterance meaning is what Joel intended—that the party will be awful. Even though this information is not provided in the scenario, it is possible that participants assumed it in order to comprehend the comment. Participants would then have used the term *sarcasm,* which traditionally has been considered a negative, bitter, or caustic form of speech (Urdang, 1972, p. 1169), to indicate that the comment was negative.

To address this possibility, a second experiment (Experiment 1b) presented the same items as Experiment 1a with a rating scale that ranged from "literal" to "non-literal."[5] This scale was designed to detect if negative jests are interpreted at their utterance meaning level and then rated sarcastic only because they are negative statements.

Experiment 1b

Is allusion to violated expectations a necessary condition of verbal irony comprehension? [Are negative jests interpreted literally?]

This experiment was designed to test the alternative explanation that negative jests were considered sarcastic in Experiment 1a because the comments were interpreted at their utterance meaning level and only labeled sarcastic because the comments were negative. In the present experiment, participants were presented with the same items as in Experiment 1a with a literalness rather than a sarcasm rating scale.

Participants.   Twenty-four University of California undergraduates participated for a course requirement. All were native English speakers. None of the people participated in the other experiments.

Materials and Design.   The same 20 scenarios used in Experiment 1a were used in this experiment. Each scenario was presented with a 7-point rating scale ranging from 1 (*literal*) to 7 (*non-literal*). The same design as that used in Experiment 1a was used in the present experiment.

Procedure.   The same procedure as that used in Experiment 1a was also used in the present experiment except for the instructions given for using the rating scales. Participants were told to read each scenario and decide how literal or non-literal they thought the speaker was being with his or her comment.

Results and Discussion.   The mean literalness ratings for the four comment types are presented in Table 5.4. A one-way ANOVA revealed a significant difference in the degree to which participants found the comments non-literal, $F1(3, 69) = 310{:}60, p < .001, F2(3, 57) = 89.19, p < .001$.

Pairwise comparisons revealed that echoic comments were rated as more non-literal than negative jests $F1(1, 23) = 28.39, p < .001, F2(1, 19) = 15.78, p < .01$. Negative jests were rated as significantly more non-literal than earnest negative comments, $F1(1, 23) = 244.86, p < .001, F2(1, 19) = 34.3, p < .001$, and no difference was found between the two kinds of earnest comments.

TABLE 5.4
Degree of Non-Literalness As a Function of Comment Type: Experiment 1b

Comment Type	Degree of Non-Literalness	
Earnest negative	Mean	1.94
	SD	0.71
Echoic	Mean	6.53
	SD	0.46
Negative jest	Mean	5.29
	SD	1.09
Earnest positive	Mean	1.78
	SD	0.55

Note. The rating scale ranged from 1 (*literal*) to 7 (*non-literal*).

The results replicate those of Experiment 1a with a literalness rating scale. This supports the conclusion that negative jests are interpreted ironically, rather than being interpreted at their utterance meaning level and reported as sarcastic because they are negative statements.

It still remains unclear, though, whether this ironic interpretation involves allusion to violated expectations. In order to make this determination, one must test if speakers of negative jests are pretending to find the positive situations they encounter to be negative only as a joke, or if the speakers mean to indicate that their expectations have been violated. If the former is true, then speakers of negative jests would not find the situations they encounter to be in violation of what they expected. Also, since the situations encountered by speakers of negative jests are positive by definition, then the speakers should not have expected something negative relative to what they encountered. In the following two experiments (Experiments 1c and 1d), these predictions were tested.

Experiment 1c

Is allusion to violated expectations a necessary condition of verbal irony comprehension? [Do negative jests indicate violated expectations?]

This experiment was designed to test whether negative jests, which according to Experiments 1a and 1b are interpreted ironically, indicate violated expectations. If negative jests reflect that a speaker's expectations have been violated, then those speakers should not have expected the positive situations they encountered. Speakers in the same situations who make earnest comments, however, should have expected those positive situations. But, if people do not think speakers making negative jests have experienced violated expectations, then no difference should be found in what was expected by those speakers versus speakers making earnest positive comments.

To test these possibilities, participants received the same items as in the previous experiments with the instruction to rate the degree to which the speakers expected the situations they encountered.

Participants.   Twenty-four University of California undergraduates participated for a course requirement. All were native English speakers. None of the people participated in the other experiments.

Materials and Design.   The same 20 scenarios used in the previous experiments were used in this experiment. Each scenario was presented with a 7-point rating scale designed to assess participants' intuitions about the expectations of the speakers in the scenarios. It ranged from 1 (*not at all expected*) to 7 (*completely expected*). The same design as that used in Experiment 1a was used in the present experiment.

Procedure.   The same procedure as that used in Experiment 1a was also used in the present experiment except for the instructions given for using the expectancy rating scales. Participants were told to determine how much the speakers in the scenarios expected the situations they encountered, based upon what the speakers said, and to then indicate those assessments on the expectancy rating scales.

Results and Discussion.   The mean expectancy ratings are presented in Table 5.5. A one-way ANOVA conducted on these ratings revealed an overall difference in how much the speakers expected the situations they encountered, $F1(3, 69) = 5.61, p < .01, F2(3, 57) = 4.43, p < .01$.

Pairwise comparisons revealed that when speakers made either type of comment about a negative situation (earnest negative or echoic), they did not expect those situations relative to making an earnest positive comment about a positive situation, $F1(1, 23) = 6.71, p < .01, F2(1, 19) = 3.73, p = .06$, for earnest positive versus earnest negative, and $F1(1, 23) = 23.81, p < .001, F2(1, 19) = 12.13, p < .01$, for earnest positive versus echoic. This finding makes sense given the claim that people have generally positive expectations or desires about the world as reflected in social norms (Kreuz & Glucksberg, 1989). When people are in negative situations and comment either earnestly or echoically about those situations, other people think the speakers are relatively surprised. The speakers in each case were seen as simply not expecting to be in those negative situations.

Interestingly, a comparison of negative jests and earnest positive comments revealed that negative jests also express more surprise on the part of the speaker than earnest positive comments. The degree to which people making negative jests expected the situations they encountered was rated as significantly lower than that for people making earnest positive comments, even though in both cases the positive situations were the same, $F1(1, 23) = 9.04, p < .01, F2(1, 19) = 10.79, p < .01$.

TABLE 5.5

Degree of Expectedness As a Function of Comment Type: Experiment 1c

Comment Type	Degree of Expectedness	
Earnest negative	Mean	4.07
	SD	1.24
Echoic	Mean	3.80
	SD	1.09
Negative jest	Mean	3.77
	SD	1.38
Earnest positive	Mean	4.80
	SD	1.20

Note. The rating scale ranged from 1 (not at all expected) to 7 (extremely expected).

These results are interpreted as supporting the claim that speakers of negative jests have in fact had their expectations violated. The next experiment tests if negative jests indicate that the speakers actually expected something negative.

Experiment 1d

Is allusion to violated expectations a necessary condition of verbal irony comprehension? [Do negative jests indicate negative expectations?]

Experiment 1c demonstrated that negative jests—which by operational definition are made when speakers have encountered positive situations—reveal a violation of the speaker's expectations. This suggests that speakers of negative jests expected situations relatively worse than the ones they encountered. Experiment 1d was designed to test this prediction.

If negative jests are thought to reveal expectations of relatively negative situations, then people should think that the situations expected by speakers of negative jests are more negative than the situations expected by speakers of earnest positive comments. If no negative expectations are inferred, then the quality of the situations that were expected should not differ between the two groups of speakers.

Participants.   Twenty-four University of California undergraduates participated for a course requirement. All were native English speakers. None of the people participated in the other experiments.

Materials and Design.   Two copies of the scenarios used in the previous experiments were prepared. One omitted the comments made by the speakers and the other did not. The copies were otherwise identical. Both sets of scenarios were presented with a 7-point rating scale ranging from 1 (*very bad*) to 7 (*very good*). The same design as that used in Experiment 1a was used in the present experiment.

Procedure. Participants were first presented with the 20 scenarios without the comments, in a booklet with instructions on the cover. The instructions told participants to read each scenario and decide how good or bad they thought were the situations described in the scenarios. Participants were told to indicate their decisions by marking the rating scales. Next, participants were presented with the 20 scenarios with the comments, along with instructions to read each scenario and imagine the situations that speakers expected. Participants were asked to rate the quality of those situations on the quality rating scales.

Results and Discussion. The mean quality ratings given for the encountered and expected situations along with the differences between those ratings are presented in Table 5.6. The results of the ratings of the encountered situations were straightforward. A one-way ANOVA revealed a significant difference in the quality ratings, $F1(3, 69) = 17.32, p < .001, F2(3, 57) = 17.38, p < .001$.

A pairwise comparison revealed a significant difference between negative and positive situations, $F1(1, 23) = 448.47, p < .001, F2(1, 19) = 177.59, p < .001$. Further pairwise comparisons revealed no differences between the negative situations that were later commented on earnestly versus those that were later commented on with echoic comments. There also was no difference between the positive situations that were later commented on earnestly versus those that were later commented on with negative jests.

The results of the quality of the expected situations were also straightforward. A one-way ANOVA revealed a significant difference in the quality ratings, $F1(3, 69)$

TABLE 5.6

Degree of Quality for Encountered and Expected Situations As a Function of Comment Type: Experiment 1d

Comment Type		Degree of Quality		Difference
		Encountered Situation[a]	*Expected Situation*	
Earnest negative	Mean	2.88	3.70	0.82
	SD	0.58	1.22	
Echoic	Mean	2.83	3.73	0.9
	SD	0.64	1.12	
Negative jest	Mean	5.88	3.80	—2.08
	SD	0.55	1.04	
Earnest positive	Mean	5.92	5.52	—0.40
	SD	0.67	1.04	

[a]No comments were present when these rating were made, only the situations were presented.
Note. The rating scale ranged from 1 (*very bad*) to 7 (*very good*).

$= 13.78, p < .001, F2(3, 57) = 22.58, p < .001$, with pairwise comparisons revealing that speakers making negative jests expected situations significantly worse than speakers in the same situations who spoke earnestly, $F1(1, 23) = 24.50, p < .001$, $F2(1, 19) = 53.12, p < .001$. No concurrent difference was found between speakers making echoic versus earnest negative comments.

Differences were computed between the quality ratings given for the encountered and expected situations. A one-way ANOVA revealed that these differences were significantly different across the four speech forms, $F1(1, 23) = 24.27, p < .001, F2(1, 19) = 29.58, p < .001$.

Pairwise comparisons revealed that earnest positive comments expressed the least difference between what was expected and what ensued and things were expected to turn out slightly worse than they did. Both kinds of comments made in negative situations (earnest negative and echoic) expressed a greater difference between what was expected and what ensued than earnest positive comments and were not different from each other. Here, events were expected to turn out better than they did, $F1(1, 23) = 7.28, p < .05, F2(1, 19) = 12.04, p < .01$, for earnest positive versus earnest negative, and $F1(1, 23) = 5.73, p < .05, F2(1, 19) = 9.01, p < .01$, for earnest positive versus echoic irony. Finally, negative jests expressed the greatest difference between what was expected and what ensued, this time with events having been expected to turn out relatively *much worse* than they did. When compared to either echoic, $F1(1, 23) = 12.72, p < .01, F2(1, 19) = 8.99, p < .01$, or earnest negative comments, $F1(1, 23) = 5.43, p < .05, F2(1, 19) = 6.20, p < .05$, negative jests expressed a greater difference between what was expected and what ensued. These results are consistent with the claim that speakers of negative jests are interpreted as having expected relatively negative situations.

It thus appears that allusion to violated expectation *is* in fact a necessary condition for verbal irony comprehension. Even when ironic comments do not *obviously* allude to violated expectations, the people interpreting those comments will *infer* that the speakers' expectations have been violated. The comments do not make use of the clearly allusional and most frequently used mechanisms found in verbal irony and they need not necessarily involve a reference to expected events. Nonetheless, interpreters of the comments think the speaker is alluding to his or her violated expectations.

In the next experiment, the claim that pragmatic insincerity is also a necessary condition for verbal irony comprehension was tested.

Pragmatic Insincerity

Experiment 2

Is pragmatic insincerity a necessary condition of verbal irony comprehension? [Are pragmatically sincere assertions interpreted ironically?]

In this experiment, the possibility that pragmatically *sincere* comments would be interpreted ironically was tested. People were asked to rate the degree of sarcasm they perceived in pragmatically insincere, pragmatically sincere, and earnest comments.

Participants.   Twenty-four University of California undergraduates participated for a course requirement. All were native English speakers. None of the people participated in the other experiments.

Materials and Design.   Sixteen scenarios described situations about which a
person in the situation makes a comment as if spoken directly to the reader. Each
scenario had four versions. All of the versions described a negative situation of
which the speaker was known to genuinely disapprove. The speaker could refer to
the current, disapproved-of situation, or to an alternative, approved-of situation,
and the speaker could make this reference either sincerely or insincerely. Example
scenarios are presented in Table 5.7.

TABLE 5.7

Example Scenarios Used in Experiment 2

Comment Type	Example Scenarios
Earnest	Michael was a very safe driver. He always used his turn signals and thought all drivers should also use their turn signals. One day you are riding in Michael's car when a driver of another car makes a sudden turn without signaling. Michael hits his brakes and says, "I just hate when people don't use their turn signals." Margaret was a very prim and proper person and she appreciated good table manners. You and her were having lunch once, when a man at an adjacent table let out a very loud belch. Margaret said to the man, "I hate when people belch at the table."
Pragmatically sincere	Michael was a very safe driver. He always used his turn signals and thought all drivers should also use their turn signals. One day you are riding in Michael's car when a driver of another car makes a sudden turn without signaling. Michael hits his brakes and says, "I just love when people use their turn signals." Margaret was a very prim and proper person and she appreciated good table manners. You and her were having lunch once, when a man at an adjacent table let out a very loud belch. Margaret said to the man, "I love when people don't belch at the table."
Pragmatically insincere approval	Michael was a very safe driver. He always used his turn signals and thought all drivers should also use their turn signals. One day you are riding in Michael's car when a driver of another car makes a sudden turn without signaling. Michael hits his brakes and says, "I just love when people don't use their turn signals." Margaret was a very prim and proper person and she appreciated good table manners. You and her were having lunch once, when a man at an adjacent table let out a very loud belch. Margaret said to the man, "I love when people belch at the table."
Pragmatically insincere disapproval	Michael was a very safe driver. He always used his turn signals and thought all drivers should also use their turn signals. One day you are riding in Michael's car when a driver of another car makes a sudden turn without signaling. Michael hits his brakes and says, "I just hate when people use their turn signals." Margaret was a very prim and proper person and she appreciated good table manners. You and her were having lunch once, when a man at an adjacent table let out a very loud belch. Margaret said to the man, "I hate when people don't belch at the table."

For instance, in one version, the speaker sincerely expresses his disapproval of the current situation (earnest), e.g., "I hate when X happens." In another version, the speaker sincerely expresses his approval of the alternative situation (pragmatically sincere), e.g., "I love when X does not happen." In the two remaining versions, the speaker insincerely expresses her opinion of the current situation (pragmatically insincere approval), e.g., "I love when X happens," or the alternative situation (pragmatically insincere disapproval), e.g., "I hate when X does not happen." Half of the scenarios described situations where the presence of a behavior would be approved of (e.g., a driver using her turn signal before making a turn), and the remainder of the scenarios depicted an absence of a behavior that would be approved of (e.g., a person not belching at the dinner table).

Four sets of scenarios were created with each set containing a different version of each scenario. For example, set one would contain the earnest version of the first scenario, whereas set two would contain the pragmatically sincere version of that scenario, set three would contain the pragmatically insincere approval version, and set four would contain the pragmatically insincere disapproval version of that scenario. Set one would then also contain the pragmatically sincere version of the second scenario, the pragmatically insincere approval version of the third scenario, the pragmatically insincere disapproval version of the fourth scenario, and so on, so that four instances of each version were represented. The order of scenarios in each set was random, and each set was presented to an equal number of participants, resulting in counterbalancing of the scenarios and comment types across participants. Each scenario was presented with a 7-point rating scale ranging from 1 (*not at all sarcastic*) to 7 (*extremely sarcastic*).

Each participant received all levels of the independent variable—comment type (earnest, pragmatically sincere, pragmatically insincere approval, and pragmatically insincere disapproval)—making a one factor, within-participants design. Considering items as a random factor, the design is also one factor, within-participants.

Procedure. Participants were told they would complete a task involving their perceptions about what people say. They were then presented with the 16 scenarios in a booklet with instructions on the cover. The instructions told the participants to read each scenario and decide how sarcastic they thought the speaker was being with his or her comment. Participants were told to indicate their decisions by marking the rating scales. When participants had completed this task, they were debriefed and dismissed.

Results and Discussion. The mean sarcasm ratings for the four comment types are presented in Table 5.8. A one-way ANOVA revealed a significant difference in the degree to which participants found the comments sarcastic, $F1(3, 69) = 165.74, p < .001, F2(3, 45) = 197.10, p < .001$.

Pairwise comparisons revealed that pragmatically sincere and both types of pragmatically insincere comments were rated as more sarcastic than earnest comments, $F1(1, 23) = 216.67, p < .001, F2(1, 15) = 173.39, p < .001$, for pragmatically

TABLE 5.8

Degree of Sarcasm As a Function of Comment Type: Experiment 2

Comment Type	Degree Of Sarcasm	
Earnest	Mean	1.41
	SD	0.58
Pragmatically sincere	Mean	5.89
	SD	1.37
Pragmatically insincere disapproval	Mean	6.16
	SD	1.36
Pragmatically insincere approval	Mean	6.76
	SD	0.90

Note. The rating scale ranged from 1 (*not at all sarcastic*) to 7 (*extremely sarcastic*).

sincere versus earnest, $F1(1, 23) = 242.42$, $p < .001$, $F2(1, 15) = 601.67$, $p < .001$, for pragmatically insincere disapproval versus earnest, and, $F1(1, 23) = 481.50$, $p < .001$, $F2(1, 15) = 1632.18$, $p < .001$, for pragmatically insincere approval versus earnest. No difference was found between pragmatically sincere and pragmatically insincere disapproval comments, but they were each less sarcastic than pragmatically insincere approval, $F1(1, 23) = 12.57$, $p < .01$, $F2(1, 15) = 8.86$, $p < .01$, for pragmatically sincere versus pragmatically insincere approval, and, $F1(1, 23) = 12.41$, $p < .001$, $F2(1, 15) = 12.94$, $p < .01$, for pragmatically sincere disapproval versus pragmatically insincere approval.

These results indicate that pragmatic insincerity may actually *not* be a necessary condition for verbal irony comprehension. Although pragmatic insincerity does result in ironic interpretations of comments, other comments that are pragmatically sincere are also interpreted ironically.

If pragmatic insincerity is not necessary for a comment to be interpreted ironically then what is? A concept similar to pragmatic insincerity (Kumon-Nakamura et al., 1995) is needed to account for all of the instances of verbal irony that are pragmatically insincere. But a concept that is somewhat broader in scope than pragmatic insincerity is needed to account for the ironic comprehension of the pragmatically sincere comments used in the present experiment. I wish to propose à la Myers (1974, pp. 128–129) that an intentional violation or flouting of Gricean conversational maxims rather than pragmatic insincerity is the second necessary condition of verbal irony comprehension.

A flouting of Gricean conversational maxims would account for the comprehension of pragmatically insincere and pragmatically sincere comments. Pragmatic insincerity is itself a flouting of Gricean conversational maxims. When a speaker makes a comment that she does not sincerely believe to be true, then she is flouting the Gricean Maxim of Quality. A flouting of a Gricean conversational maxim also appears to account for the ironic interpretation of the current study's pragmatically sincere comments. Consider the following item:

> Michael was a very safe driver. He always used his turn signals and thought all drivers should also use their turn signals. One day you are riding in Michael's car when a driver of another car makes a sudden turn without signaling. Michael hits his brakes and says, "I just love when people use their turn signals."

The speaker in this situation earnestly means what he says, he genuinely wishes to express his appreciation of drivers who use their turn signals, so the comment is pragmatically sincere—it is a declarative assertive that is true. But the comment nevertheless flouts the Gricean conversational Maxim of Relevance. The comment refers to a situation *other than the one that occurred.* The driver in the current situation *did not* use his turn signal, but the man refers to his opinion of when people *do* use their turn signals. This flouting then sets up the conversational implicature that the speaker wishes the addressee to form an ironic interpretation of the comment—namely that the speaker disapproves of the driver in the current situation who did not use his turn signal.

In order to test if this flouting of conversational maxims underlies the ironic interpretation of pragmatically sincere comments, the next experiment presented participants with similar items as Experiment 2, but this time the pragmatically sincere comments no longer violated conversational maxims.

Maxim Flouting

Experiment 3

Is conversational maxim flouting a necessary condition of verbal irony comprehension? [Are maxim-flouting comments interpreted ironically?]

In this experiment, I tested the possibility that pragmatically sincere (and insincere) comments are interpreted ironically because they involve floutings of conversational maxims. To illustrate this explanation, consider the following situation. A woman and a visitor are standing in the woman's kitchen on opposite sides of a table. The woman is bragging about how well-behaved is her kitten. She says that she has never had to chase her kitten off the table, where the kitten is not allowed. At that moment, the woman turns her back to the table so that she can no longer see it, and the kitten jumps and lands right in the middle of the table. Imagine that the woman's visitor then says, "The kitten is on the table." Although this situation is somewhat ironic—as soon as the woman finishes bragging that her kitten stays off the table, the kitten jumps on the table—the speaker's comment would probably not be considered ironic. The comment does point out a situational irony, but it is not ironic by itself. However, imagine the same situation with the kitten's owner not turning her back before the kitten jumps on the table and the two people staring for a moment at the kitten. If the other person said the same comment in this situation, "The kitten is on the table," the comment probably would be interpreted as being ironic. The reason for why the same comment would be more ironic in the latter situation is that the comment violates the maxim of quantity in the latter situation but it does not violate that maxim in the first situation. In the first situation, the comment is informative because the addressee had her back turned and would not know that the kitten is on the table. In the latter situation, the woman does not have her back turned and can therefore readily see that the kitten is on the table. When the speaker makes the comment while the woman is looking, he provides information that the woman already has and he thus violates the conversational maxim of quantity.

In order to test this explanation, people were asked to rate the degree of sarcasm they perceived in the same pragmatically insincere, pragmatically sincere, and earnest comments used in Experiment 2, but this time the "pragmatically sincere" comments did not violate conversational maxims and the "earnest" comments did.

This alteration was accomplished via the use of conterfactuals. The scenarios used in the previous experiment were reworded so that they were now counterfactual statements about the speakers' opinions. For instance, in the previous experiment, the speakers made direct statements about their opinions, (e.g., "I hate when X happens," "I love when X happens," "I hate when X does not happen," and "I love when X does not happen"). In the current experiment, the comments were reworded to be counterfactual statements, (e.g., "I would hate if X happened," "I would love if X happened," "I would hate if X did not happen," and "I would love if X did not happen").

This change alters which comments flout conversational maxims. For example, in Experiment 2, the "earnest" comment, spoken in a situation where a driver did not use his turn signal, did not flout a maxim (e.g., "I just hate when people don't use their turn signals"), whereas the "pragmatically sincere" comment did (e.g., "I just love when people use their turn signals"). The pragmatically sincere comment referred to an irrelevant situation and the earnest comment referred to the current, relevant situation.

In the current experiment, however, the counterfactual "earnest" comment now *does* flout a maxim (e.g., "I would hate if people didn't use their turn signals"), whereas the counterfactual "pragmatically sincere" comment now *does not* (e.g., "I would love if people used their turn signals"). The counterfactual "earnest" comment flouts the maxim of quality. The speaker is essentially saying something he knows to be untrue. He says that *if* X happened, he would have a certain reaction. This comment presupposes that X *did not* happen. But since X actually *did* happen, the speaker is saying something that is not true. The counterfactual "pragmatically sincere" comment, however, implies that Y did not happen when in fact, Y did not happen.

In both the previous and present experiments, both types of pragmatically insincere comments violate conversational maxims, so they did not change. Thus, the design of the current experimental items allows us to determine whether or not a violation of conversational maxims is the underlying necessary factor in verbal irony comprehension.

Participants.   Twenty-four University of California undergraduates participated for a course requirement. All were native English speakers. None of the people participated in the other experiments.

Materials and Design.   The same 16 scenarios used in the previous experiment were used in the present experiment with each comment being reworded into
a counterfactual statement. Each scenario had four versions. All of the versions
described a negative situation of which the speaker was known to genuinely disapprove. The speaker could make counterfactual reference to the current, disapproved-of situation, or to an alternative, approved-of situation, and this reference
could be pragmatically sincere or insincere. Example scenarios are presented in
Table 5.9.

In one version of the scenarios, the speaker counterfactually mentions a disapproving opinion of the current situation (labeled *earnest*), e.g., "I would hate if X
happened." In another version, the speaker counterfactually expresses an approving opinion of the alternative situation (labeled *pragmatically sincere*), e.g., "I
would love if X did not happen." In the two remaining versions, the speaker insincerely expresses an opinion with a counterfactual comment about the current situation (labeled *pragmatically insincere approval*), e.g., "I would love if X happened,"
or the alternative situation (labeled *pragmatically insincere disapproval*), e.g., "I
would hate if X did not happen." Half of the scenarios described situations where
the presence of a behavior would be approved of (e.g., a person using her turn signal), and the remainder of the scenarios depicted an absence of a behavior that
would be approved of (e.g., a person not belching at the table). The same design
used in Experiment 2 was used in the current experiment.

Procedure.   The same procedure as that used in Experiment 2 was also used in
this experiment.

Results and Discussion.   The mean sarcasm ratings for the four comment
types are presented in Table 5.10. A one-way ANOVA revealed a significant difference in the degree to which participants found the comments sarcastic, $F1(3, 69) =
96.46$, $p < .001$, $F2(3, 45) = 83.44$, $p < .001$.

Pairwise comparisons revealed that earnest and both types of pragmatically insincere comments were rated as more sarcastic than pragmatically sincere comments, $F1(1, 23) = 96.13$, $p < .001$, $F2(1, 15) = 52.57$, $p < .001$, for earnest versus
pragmatically sincere, $F1(1, 23) = 130.41$, $p < .001$, $F2(1, 15) = 233.18$, $p < .001$,
for pragmatically insincere disapproval versus pragmatically sincere, and, $F1(1,
23) = 182.30$, $p < .001$, $F2(1, 15) = 180.50$, $p < .001$, for pragmatically insincere ap-
proval versus pragmatically sincere. No difference was found between pragmatically insincere disapproval and pragmatically insincere approval comments, but
they were each more sarcastic than earnest, $F1(1, 23) = 21.18$, $p < .001$, $F2(1, 15) =
22.28$, $p < .001$, for pragmatically insincere disapproval versus earnest, and, $F1(1,
23) = 27.54$, $p < .001$, $F2(1, 15) = 16.55$, $p < .01$, for pragmatically insincere
approval versus earnest.

TABLE 5.9

Example Scenarios Used in Experiment 3

Counterfactual[a]	Example Scenarios
"Earnest"	Michael was a very safe driver. He always used his turn signals and thought all drivers should also use their turn signals. One day you are riding in Michael's car when a driver of another car makes a sudden turn without signaling. Michael hits his brakes and says, "I would hate if people didn't use their turn signals." Margaret was a very prim and proper person and she appreciated good table manners. You and her were having lunch once, when a man at an adjacent table let out a very loud belch. Margaret said to the man, "I would hate if people belched at the table."
"Pragmatically sincere"	Michael was a very safe driver. He always used his turn signals and thought all drivers should also use their turn signals. One day you are riding in Michael's car when a driver of another car makes a sudden turn without signaling. Michael hits his brakes and says, "I would love if people used their turn signals." Margaret was a very prim and proper person and she appreciated good table manners. You and her were having lunch once, when a man at an adjacent table let out a very loud belch. Margaret said to the man, "I would love if people didn't belch at the table."
"Pragmatically insincere approval"	Michael was a very safe driver. He always used his turn signals and thought all drivers should also use their turn signals. One day you are riding in Michael's car when a driver of another car makes a sudden turn without signaling. Michael hits his brakes and says, "I would love if people didn't use their turn signals." Margaret was a very prim and proper person and she appreciated good table manners. You and her were having lunch once, when a man at an adjacent table let out a very loud belch. Margaret said to the man, "I would love if people belched at the table."
"Pragmatically insincere disapproval"	Michael was a very safe driver. He always used his turn signals and thought all drivers should also use their turn signals. One day you are riding in Michael's car when a driver of another car makes a sudden turn without signaling. Michael hits his brakes and says, "I would hate if people used their turn signals." Margaret was a very prim and proper person and she appreciated good table manners. You and her were having lunch once, when a man at an adjacent table let out a very loud belch. Margaret said to the man, "I would hate if people didn't belch at the table."

[a]To facilitate comparison of these items with the noncounterfactual items in Experiment 2 (from which these items were created), the same labels applied to the source items in Experiment 2 were used on these items.

These results demonstrate that a flouting of Gricean conversational maxims does appear to be the second necessary condition for verbal irony comprehension. Pragmatic insincerity is one way in which such violations are accomplished, but other comments that are pragmatically sincere and yet still violate a conversational maxim are also interpreted ironically.

TABLE 5.10

Degree of Sarcasm As a Function of Comment Type When Comments Are Counterfactual: Experiment 3

Comment Type	Degree of Sarcasm	
Counterfactual earnest	Mean	5.15
	SD	1.37
Counterfactual pragmatically sincere	Mean	1.98
	SD	1.20
Counterfactual pragmatically insincere disapproval	Mean	6.73
	SD	0.99
Counterfactual pragmatically insincere approval	Mean	6.67
	SD	0.82

Note. The rating scale ranged from 1 (*not at all sarcastic*) to 7 (*extremely sarcastic*).

GENERAL DISCUSSION

The results of the experiments presented here allow us to refine claims about necessary conditions for verbal irony comprehension. The first claim is that ironic comments must allude to violated expectations. Five different mechanisms for doing this have been proposed in the literature on verbal irony comprehension. These mechanisms claim that ironic comments allude to violated expectations via the following:

a. An echo of a previously stated inaccurate prediction about future events or an echo of a previously stated description that has been made inaccurate by ensuing events.

b. An echo of a commonly recognized expectation like a social norm that has not been observed.

c. An allusion to expected or desired events that have not reached fruition by eliciting them from the addressee via an ingenuine inquiry, request, or offering.

d. An allusion to expected or desired events via an ingenuinely intended yet true assertion.

e. Obviously pretending to be a person who is purporting something that does not correspond with reality to demonstrate a negative attitude toward that position and its proponents.

Although each of these mechanisms appears to involve an allusion to expected, desired, predicted, preferred, etc. events that have not reached fruition, it is not obvious that all comments which use these mechanisms involve violated expectations. The pretense mechanism (e), for example, *could* involve an allusion to an arbitrarily alternative set of events that, although they are discontinuous with the current events, are not expected, preferred, desired, etc. For instance, a person could say, "That's very selfish of you" to someone who had done something generous, simply to make a joke and not to hint at violated expectations. It is not clear that the speaker's expectations were violated for this type of comment to work. However, where comments such as these—which do not obviously point out violated expectations on the speaker's part—are interpreted ironically, interpreters nevertheless *infer* that the speaker's expectations were violated. The current study (Experiments 1a through 1d) thus in fact supports the claim that the interpretation of ironic comments necessarily involves an allusion to violated expectations.

Although allusion to violated expectations seems to be necessary for verbal irony comprehension, it does not appear to be sufficient. For instance, a speaker could allude to violated expectations with a comment that would not be interpreted ironically. Consider a person saying to a friend who is late, "You were supposed to be here at 5 p.m." Although this speaker is alluding to violated expectations, he would not be interpreted ironically. Some other condition must be met in order for an allusion to violated expectations to be ironic.

Kumon-Nakamura et al.'s (1995) proposal that this other condition is pragmatic insincerity is well motivated. The observation above demonstrates that a comment needs to somehow be non-literal in order to be interpreted ironically. Recall, though, that the basis for pragmatic insincerity involved the felicity conditions for well-formed speech acts. According to Kumon-Nakamura et al., these conditions

> … concern (a) the propositional content of a comment, (b) the status of both the speaker and the hearer of the comment, (c) the sincerity of the psychological state expressed or implied by the comment, and (d) the perception of the speaker's sincerity by the hearer. Pragmatic insincerity occurs when a speaker is perceived as intentionally violating felicity conditions for at least one of these aspects of a comment. For example, declarative assertions should be true, compliments should be true and taken as compliments rather than rebukes, questions should be asked only when an answer is desired, offers should be made only when acceptance is desirable, and politeness levels should be appropriate to the situation. Whenever conventions such as these are violated, a speaker may be perceived as being intentionally insincere. (p. 5)

As the results of Experiment 2 and 3 demonstrated, however, pragmatic insincerity is an insufficient description of the scope of this non-literality. Comments that are pragmatically sincere (e.g., that do not violate felicity conditions for well-formed speech acts) can also be interpreted ironically. Note that the comment "I just love when people use their turn signals" is a declarative assertion and is true. It is a statement of the speaker's opinion of people who use their turn signals and it genuinely reflects that speaker's opinion.

It therefore appears that a concept that captures the non-literal nature of a comment but that is broader than pragmatic insincerity must be the remaining necessary condition for verbal irony comprehension. I have proposed that flouting of Gricean conversational maxims is this other factor. Note also that the comment "I just love when people use their turn signals" *is* a violation of a Gricean Maxim for it is spoken in a situation where a person has *not* used his or her signal but it refers to situations where people *do* use their turn signals.

When one considers each of the ways in which a Gricean conversational maxim can be intentionally violated (flouted), it indeed appears that this is a more precise description of the second necessary condition for verbal irony comprehension than pragmatic insincerity. For instance, Grice argued that the four conversational maxims—quality, relevance, quantity, and manner—require respectively that comments be true, relevant, informative, and unambiguous (Grice 1975). An intentional violation of any of these maxims in a context where expectations, desires, social norms, etc. have not been met results in an ironic interpretation.

For instance, a flouting of the Maxim of Quality is synonymous with "pragmatically insincere" comments, (e.g., saying "Nice weather" during a terrible rainstorm). Here the speaker has said something that is patently untrue, and that is known to be untrue by the speaker, and hence he flouts the Maxim of Quality.

As the results of the second set of experiments reported here demonstrated, floutings of the Maxim of Relevance also result in ironic interpretations (e.g., saying "I just love when people use their turn signals" when someone has not used his or her signal). This comment does not flout the Maxim of Quality because it is a true statement that the speaker knows to be true. The comment can therefore be considered pragmatically sincere and in coherence with felicity conditions for well-formed speech acts. The comment does, however, flout the Maxim of Relevance because it refers to a situation that is not the one at hand. The speaker mentions his opinion about people who *do* use their turn signals, when the current situation is one where a person has not signaled.

Flouting the Maxim of Quantity would also result in an ironic interpretation. Consider comments that provide more information than what is required by the conversation, or, statements of obvious facts:

1. One morning, you and your friend Michael listened to the weather report that called for clear skies all day. A short while after hearing the report, you walk outside together and see that it is pouring down rain. As you both stand there getting soaked, Michael looks at you and says, "It's raining."

In this example, a speaker states something already known by the interlocutors by virtue of being in the common ground (Clark & Carlson, 1981). Because the speaker provides more information than is required by the context of the conversation, he flouts the Maxim of Quantity. Understatement, often considered a form of verbal irony, can also be argued to flout the Maxim of Quantity because it usually provides insufficient information to adequately describe the situation:[6]

2. You and your brother Elliot are driving in your car and you hear a traffic report on the car radio saying that route 17 is completely clear. Just as soon as the

reporter finishes; though, you turn onto route 17 and see that it is jammed completely shut with traffic. Elliot says to you, "It seems we have a tiny bit of traffic."

Finally, floutings of the Maxim of Manner would also result in ironic interpretations. Consider comments that provide ambiguous or obscure references:

3. You and your co-worker Anne are on a business trip. As soon as you get to the airport, you make your way to the rental car counter to collect your car. You take care of the business with the agent at the counter and walk toward the door leading to the lot with the rental cars. When you open the door onto the lot though, you see that every single car of the hundreds on the lot are red. Anne asks you which car is yours and you reply, "The red one."

These examples demonstrate how floutings of the Quality, Relevance, Quantity, or Manner Maxims, in tandem with the unexpected nature of the events, result in ironic interpretations of the comments.

It thus appears that allusion to violated expectations and floutings of Gricean conversational maxims are the two necessary conditions for verbal irony comprehension. But these conditions may still not be sufficient. Consider the following example:

4. Your son has finished basketball practice and walks outside to wait for you to pick him up. There is a huge clock on the wall right behind him, where he sees that it is 4 p.m., exactly the time you are supposed to arrive. He waits and waits, but you don't show. Finally after 2 hours, you drive up, get out of your car, and walk towards him. You both glance at the clock that obviously reads 6 p.m. When your son looks back at you, he says in a very angry voice, "It is six o'clock!"

This speaker would not be interpreted ironically even though he fulfills both conditions for verbal irony comprehension. He intentionally violates the Maxim of Quantity because he provides more information than is required by the conversation—it is obvious to both people that the time is 6 p.m. He is also alluding that the actual event—your arriving at 6 p.m.—is a violation of expectations—your arriving at 4 p.m. So why is this comment not ironic?

One possibility is that the comment does not involve a pretense (Clark & Gerrig, 1984) on the part of the speaker. The speaker is earnest in his expression of anger rather than pretending to have some other opinion in order to mock it. To illustrate, consider an identical situation with the same comment, but here the speaker's intonation feigns surprise at the lateness of the hour:

5. Your son has finished basketball practice and walks outside to wait for you to pick him up. There is a huge clock on the wall right behind him, where he sees that it is 4 p.m., exactly the time you are supposed to arrive. He waits and

waits, but you don't show. Finally after 2 hours, you drive up, get out of your car, and walk towards him. You both glance at the clock that obviously reads 6 p.m. When your son looks back at you, he gasps and says in a voice that feigns surprise at the later hour, "It is six o'clock!"

The comment spoken in this manner probably would be interpreted ironically because the speaker is pretending to find the late hour surprising—as if he did not realize how late it was—when in fact he is well aware that the hour is very late.

Although pretense does appear to account for why the same comment is interpreted ironically in one case but not ironically in another, it is, in fact, an insufficient explanation. Comments without pretense can also be interpreted ironically. For example, consider again the violations of the Maxim of Relevance used in Experiment 2:

> 6. A man is carrying an armload of packages towards an exit door. Another person exits in front of the man, but she does not hold the door open for him and it slams into him. The man turns to a companion and says, "I love when people hold doors open for others."

If this comment were spoken in the same angry tone as example 4, it also would not involve pretense. Since the intonation is consistent with the speaker's true feelings, the speaker is not using pretense. In both example 4 and example 6, the speaker is earnestly expressing his anger. Yet, example 6 would be interpreted ironically whereas example 4 would not.

The reason for this difference in interpretation is that, although the comment in example 4, which fulfills the two conditions but is not ironic, alludes to a violated expectation, it does not *portray a contrast* between that expectation and reality. The comment in example 6, which also fulfills the two conditions but is ironic, does portray such a contrast.

Pretense is one powerful way to portray this contrast, as example 5 demonstrates. But, as example 6 demonstrates, not all ironic comments use pretense. Perhaps it is better to consider what pretense achieves rather than the use of pretense per se. Pretense achieves a contrast between expected and ensuing events, but other mechanisms can also achieve this contrast, such as that used in example 6.

Do these observations mean that a third condition—portraying a contrast—is necessary in order to account for verbal irony comprehension? Probably not—the notions of portraying a contrast and allusion to violated expectations can be described in a single condition:

> Ironic comments must portray a contrast of expectations, desires, preferences, social norms or the like, against the actual events that have occurred. This contrast can be achieved by pretending to advocate or assert expected events in contrast with reality, but it can also be achieved by invoking those alternative events in the mind of the speaker while speaking earnestly.

This condition subsumes the claim that ironic comments must allude to violated expectations—things must have not turned out as expected and this discrepancy must be made salient by the comment. But, this condition also claims that mere allusion to the discrepancy is insufficient. The comment must present expectations and reality as if in contrast with one another. This condition also explains why intentional violation or flouting of Gricean conversational maxims is the second necessary condition of verbal irony comprehension. The flouting is necessary in order to portray a contrast of expectation with reality. These two conditions together then provide the basis for verbal irony comprehension.

Despite this article's conclusion that a flouting of Gricean maxims and a portrayal of a contrast between expectations and reality are the two necessary conditions for verbal irony comprehension, a cautionary note might be in order. I have become increasingly concerned in interpreting these results and in conversations with colleagues who have worked on irony, that, as is the case in many domains, the search for necessary conditions for irony comprehension may shroud the breadth of the phenomenon of verbal irony. Although I think the current study makes a fair case that the pragmatic insincerity condition proposed by Allusional Pretense is under-defined, and that my revised condition of Gricean maxim flouting is better, there are still cases of verbal irony that might put even this revised set of conditions to the test.

Consider instances of "collaborative irony" (Gibbs, 2000) where interlocutors mutually contribute a sequence of comments that collectively build up an ironic perspective on a situation. To use a personal example, I recently had an interaction with a colleague who gave me a brochure on autumn weekend vacation packages in the North Woods of Wisconsin, in an attempt to get me to take time off work. When she gave it to me I politely accepted her suggestions and said neutrally that I'd look at it and consider going there some weekend. After several days, I put the brochure in the person's office with a thank-you note, but I was unsure which desk was hers. So later, when I ran into the person, I inquired if she got the brochure back. She said she did, and then added "So, I'm sure you'll be going up several weekends now." I replied "Yeah, I even thought of going up *every* weekend." She then responded "Why don't you just go up permanently and do your classes via correspondence?" I said "Great idea, and I could hold all my meetings through teleconference." Effectively, we were sharing a collective feigned attitude that I was genuinely interested in going, with each of us progressively adding more preposterous expressions of this attitude. The interesting part is that each of us clearly knew that I had no plans of going. It is as if we were each very much aware of the shared conceptual reality of the situation, and then glibly portrayed various perspectives on that reality in order to demonstrate our knowledge of that situation. This mechanism appears to be very much like pretense, although it allows for more complexity with multiple speakers who deftly keep switching roles. It is interesting though, how these "roles" are created by using language that varies the degrees of contrast with the collectively understood truth of the situation.

Instances of verbal irony such as these do not seem to *easily* fit into *any* of the proposed necessary conditions for verbal irony comprehension, unless the conditions are interpreted fairly liberally. Gricean maxim violation does not appear to take place locally within the exchange—it is only through the global build-up of the untrue perspective that a violation occurs—the perspective might be said to violate the Quality maxim since it is not a true depiction of reality. It is also not clear where the precise violation of expectations is in this situation.

It might thus simply be the case that verbal irony involves a family of mechanisms, each of which might have a slightly different set of necessary conditions for success, that overlap on many instances but which leave some gaps—hence the proliferation of accounts and the difficulty in sifting them down into one.

One final issue concerning the use of Grice's idea of maxim flouting must be addressed. Grice's account of non-literal language comprehension has generally fallen upon disfavor. The primary basis for the dismissal is that Grice's model was interpreted as claiming that two stages are required for non-literal language, including verbal irony, comprehension. For instance, an interpreter must first derive the utterance meaning of an ironic comment in order to determine that the comment violated a conversational maxim. The interpreter would then derive the ironic, speaker-intended meaning of the comment from the context in which the comment is made. These two stages should take longer to complete than the one stage required to interpret a straightforward utterance meaning.

A large number of studies have been conducted to assess the time required to comprehend a variety of non-literal language forms, including verbal irony. The vast majority of these studies have shown that non-literal language comprehension does *not* take longer than "literal" language comprehension as a two-stage model would predict (Burt, 1992; Gibbs, 1979, 1980, 1983, 1986b; Gibbs & Gonzales, 1985; Gibbs, Nayak, & Cutting, 1989; Kemper, 1981; Swinney & Cutler, 1979). These results have been taken as evidence against a Gricean two-stage model of verbal irony and other non-literal forms of language comprehension.

Several recent studies, however, have begun to challenge this dismissal of two-stage models, as pertaining to verbal irony. Giora (1995; see also Giora, Fein, & Schwartz, 1998), for instance, claimed that both the "literal" and non-literal interpretations of an ironic comment are made by an interpreter so that the difference between the interpretations can be computed. This study was based upon some of the same data from previous studies that had seemingly shown no difference in the time required to comprehend "literal" and non-literal comments. The Giora (1995) study claimed, however, that the data actually showed that non-literal interpretation took longer.

Other studies have attempted to account for the pragmatic functions of verbal irony, including to dilute or "tinge" the degree of criticism of an ironic comment. These studies argue that the "literal" meaning of a comment must be interpreted to explain the decreased criticism in ironic as compared to "literal" comments. For instance, if someone says, "What a nice haircut," versus, "What a terrible haircut," to comment about a bad haircut, the positive utterance meaning of the former comment dilutes the degree of criticism that is expressed relative to the latter comment (Dews & Winner, 1995; Dews, Kaplan, & Winner, 1995; Jorgensen, 1996; although see Colston, 1997b, for a discussion of *increased* ironic as opposed to "literal" criticism).

These studies, although undertaken to address different phenomena concerning verbal irony, nevertheless suggest that some component of the utterance meaning of an ironic comment is processed (see also Chen, 1990; Winner, 1988).

Reconciliation of this issue is a very complicated matter and is beyond the intent and scope of this paper. However, in order to justify the use of Grice's model as an account of verbal irony comprehension given the seemingly opposing claims the model has generated—that the utterance meaning is not processed versus that it is processed—one might consider a general alternative interpretation of the Gricean model as applied to verbal irony comprehension; The interpretation of Grice's non-literal language comprehension model as requiring two stages, and the recent research demonstrating that both "literal" and non-literal interpretations of an ironic comment play a role in the final interpretation of that comment, are in fact reflective of a *one-stage* model of verbal irony comprehension that involves the contrast of utterance meaning and context. To illustrate, consider that before an interpretation of a comment is made—indeed before the comment is even spoken—the context of the situation is already available to the interpreter. This context serves as the conceptual backdrop to the comment's interpretation. The comment is then spoken, and is interpreted in light of that backdrop. If the comment coheres with that backdrop, then an interpretation of the speaker's intention in making that coherent comment in the midst of the contextual backdrop is made. This interpretation is the ultimate interpretation of the speaker's intention. This same process occurs with an ironic comment, except the comment in this case is inconsistent with the context (or put differently, it flouts a Gricean conversational maxim). But the speaker's intention in making that comment in the midst of the contextual backdrop is still derived by the interpreter, just as it is with consistent comments. In this fashion, "literal" interpretation and non-literal interpretation would take similar amounts of time, as previous research has shown, and moreover, non-literal interpretation would also incorporate aspects of the utterance meaning of a comment as recent studies have begun to demonstrate (Chen, 1990; Colston, 1997a, 1997b; Dews & Winner, 1995; Dews, Kaplan, & Winner, 1995; Giora, 1995; Winner, 1988).

Essentially then, one can retain the constructs of conversational maxim flouting while dropping the claim that non-literal, including ironic, language comprehension requires two stages of processing. This idea has been put forth previously where it has been argued that any interpretation of any comment involves the recovery of the speaker's intention in making a comment within the conversational context (Gibbs, 1994). Moreover, the idea that Grice's model can be interpreted as involving only one stage of processing has been proposed regarding the comprehension of indirect speech acts (Clark, 1979; Clark & Schunk, 1980; Gibbs, 1982, 1983), and idioms

(Estill & Kemper, 1982; Swinney & Cutler, 1979). The primary difference between the interpretation of ironic and "literal" comments is that the utterance meaning of the comment provides a contrast with the contextual backdrop in an ironic comment, but there is no contrast in a non-ironically intended comment.

ACKNOWLEDGMENTS

Support for this work was provided by a postdoctoral Research Associateship awarded to the author by the University of California, Santa Cruz, and a Faculty Professional Opportunity Grant from the University of Wisconsin–Parkside. I gratefully thank Raymond W. Gibbs, Jr., Sam Glucksberg, Roger Kreuz, and two anonymous reviewers for their helpful comments on an earlier version of the manuscript, and Shauna Keller and Mariah Kirk for their assistance in testing participants.

ENDNOTES

1. I use the term *comprehension* because most accounts of verbal irony that have the conditions I am testing also attempt to explain comprehension. It is entirely possible, however, that the conditions also apply to verbal irony "appreciation" or " interpretation"—a distinction also applied to metaphor.
2. If the speaker did not make her pretense obvious (and hence did not appear pragmatically insincere), it's possible that her addressee would not comprehend the ironic intention of the comment. Indeed, achieving the appropriate level of obviousness for addressees whom the speaker wishes to understand the comment but not for addressees the speaker wishes to be misled by the comment is an intricate skill (Gibbs, O'Brien, & Doolittle, 1995).
3. This kind of comment can be contrasted with the "true assertions" of Kumon-Nakamura et al. (1995, p. 4), e.g., a speaker saying, "You sure know a lot" to a braggart showing off his knowledge. Although the speaker does probably mean to genuinely assert that the other person is knowledgeable, the implied speech act meaning of this comment—a compliment—*is* contradictory to the speaker's intended ironic meaning—an insult—and thus violates the felicity conditions for well-formed speech acts. The comment, "I really like guys with nice haircuts," does fulfill these felicity conditions, however, since, as a declarative assertion of the speaker's opinion, it is true.
4. This was done to maintain the ecological validity while ensuring reasonable structural similarity between the items.
5. The rating scale used the terms *literal* and *non-literal* because it was felt that the participants would find these more familiar than other possible terms.
6. Note that violations of the other Gricean maxims might also apply here—the maxims need not be mutually exclusive.

REFERENCES

Brown, P., & Levinson, S. C. (1978). *Politeness: Some universals in language usage.* New York: Cambridge University Press.

Burt, J. (1992). Against the lexical representation of idioms. *Canadian Journal of Psychology, 46,* 582–605.

Chen, R. (1990). *Verbal irony as conversational implicature.* Unpublished doctoral dissertation, Ball State University, Muncie, IN.

Clark, H. H. (1979). Responding to indirect speech acts. *Cognitive Psychology, 11*, 430–477.

Clark, H. H., & Carlson, T. B. (1981). Context for comprehension. In J. Long & A. Baddeley (Eds.), *Attention and performance* (pp. 313–330). Hillsdale, NJ: Lawrence Erlbaum Associates.

Clark, H. H., & Gerrig, R. J. (1984). On the pretense theory of irony. *Journal of Experimental Psychology: General, 113*, 121–126.

Clark, H. H., & Schunk, D. (1980). Polite responses to polite requests. *Cognition, 8*, 111–143.

Colston, H. L. (1997a). I've never seen anything like it: Overstatement, understatement and irony. *Metaphor and Symbol, 12*, 43–58.

Colston, H. L. (1997b). Salting a wound or sugaring a pill: The pragmatic functions of ironic criticism. *Discourse Processes, 23*, 25–45.

Dascal, M. (1983). *Pragmatics and the philosophy of mind I: Thought in language.* Amsterdam: Benjamins.

Dascal, M. (1987). Defending literal meaning. *Cognitive Science, 11*, 259–281.

Dascal, M. (1989). On the roles of context and literal meaning in understanding. *Cognitive Science, 13*, 253–257.

Dews, S., Kaplan, J., & Winner, E. (1995). Why not say it directly? The social functions of irony. *Discourse Processes, 19*, 347–367.

Dews, S., & Winner, E. (1995). Muting the meaning: A social function of irony. *Metaphor and Symbolic Activity, 10*, 3–19.

Estill, R., & Kemper, S. (1982). Interpreting idioms. *Journal of Psycholinguistic Research, 11*, 559–568.

Gibbs, R. W. (1979). Contextual effects in understanding indirect requests. *Discourse Processes, 2*, 1–10.

Gibbs, R. W. (1980). Spilling the beans: On understanding and memory for idioms in conversation. *Memory and Cognition, 8*, 449–456.

Gibbs, R. W. (1982). A critical examination of the contribution of utterance meaning to understanding nonliteral discourse. *Text, 2*, 9–27.

Gibbs, R. W. (1983). Do people always process the utterance meanings of indirect requests? *Journal of Experimental Psychology: Learning, Memory, and Cognition, 9*, 524–533.

Gibbs, R. W. (1986a). On the psycholinguistics of sarcasm. *Journal of Experimental Psychology: General, 115*, 3–15.

Gibbs, R. W. (1986b). What makes some indirect speech acts conventional? *Journal of Memory and Language, 25*, 181–196.

Gibbs, R. W. (1994). *The poetics of mind: Figurative thought, language, and understanding.* New York: Cambridge University Press.

Gibbs, R. W. (2000). Irony in talk among friends? *Metaphor and Symbol, 15*, 5–27.

Gibbs, R. W., & Gonzales, G. (1985). Syntactic frozenness in processing and remembering idioms. *Cognition, 20*, 243–259.

Gibbs, R. W., Nayak, N., & Cutting, C. (1989). How to kick the bucket and not decompose: Analyzability and idiom processing. *Journal of Memory and Language, 28*, 576–593.

Gibbs, R. W., O'Brien, J. E., & Doolittle, S. (1995). Inferring meanings that are not intended: Speakers' intentions and irony comprehension. *Discourse Processes, 20*, 187–203.

Giora, R. (1995). On negation and irony. *Discourse Processes, 19*, 239–264.

Giora, R., Fein, O., & Schwartz, T. (1998). Irony: Graded salience and indirect negation. *Metaphor and Symbol, 13*, 83–101.

Grice, H. P. (1975). Logic and conversation. In P. Cole & J. L. Morgan (Eds.), *Syntax and semantics, volume 3: Speech acts* (pp. 41–58). New York: Academic.

Grice, H. P. (1978). Further notes on logic and conversation. In P. Cole (Ed.), *Syntax and semantics, Volume 9: Pragmatics* (pp. 113–127). New York: Academic.

Haverkate, H. (1990). A speech act analysis of irony. *Journal of Pragmatics, 14*, 77–109.

Jorgensen, J. (1996). The functions of sarcastic irony in speech. *Journal of Pragmatics, 26,* 613–634.

Jorgensen, J., Miller, G. A., & Sperber, D. (1984). Test of the mention theory of irony. *Journal of Experimental Psychology: General, 113,* 112–120.

Kemper, S. (1981). Comprehension and interpretation of proverbs. *Journal of Psycholinguistic Research, 10,* 179–198.

Kreuz, R. J., & Glucksberg, S. (1989). How to be sarcastic: The echoic reminder theory of verbal irony. *Journal of Experimental Psychology: General, 118,* 374–386.

Kumon-Nakamura, S., Glucksberg, S., & Brown, M. (1995). How about another piece of pie? The allusional pretense theory of discourse irony. *Journal of Experimental Psychology: General, 124,* 3–21.

Lucariello, J. (1994). Situational irony: A concept of events gone awry. *Journal of Experimental Psychology: General, 123,* 129–145.

Myers, A. R. (1974). Toward a definition of irony. In R. Fasold & R. Shuy (Eds.), *Studies in language variation* (pp. 171–183). Washington, DC: Georgetown University Press.

Preminger, A., & Brogan, T. V. F. (Eds.). (1993). *The new Princeton encyclopedia of poetry and poetics.* Princeton, NJ: Princeton University Press.

Searle, J. R. (1978). Utterance meaning. *Erkenntnis, 13,* 207–224.

Sperber, D., & Wilson, D. (1981). Irony and the use–mention distinction. In P. Cole (Ed.), *Radical pragmatics* (pp. 295–318). New York: Academic.

Sperber, D., & Wilson, D. (1986). *Relevance: Communication and cognition.* Cambridge, MA: Harvard University Press.

Swinney, D., & Cutler, A. (1979). The access and processing of idiomatic expressions. *Journal of Verbal Learning and Verbal Behavior, 18,* 523–534.

Urdang, L. (Ed.). (1972). *The Random House college dictionary.* New York: Random House.

Winner, E. (1988). *The point of words: Children's understanding of metaphor and irony.* Cambridge, MA: Harvard University Press.

CHAPTER 6

Irony as Relevant Inappropriateness

Salvatore Attardo
Youngstown State University

This article presents a theory of irony which claims that an ironical utterance is both inappropriate and relevant to its context. Extensive discussion of previous theories of irony is presented to justify the various aspects of the theory and in particular its two-stage processing approach and the vexing issue of the motivation for the speakers' use of irony.

This article deals with the pragmatics of irony. Its purposes are as follows:

1. To present a "new" approach to the analysis of irony.
2. To discuss critically the main currents in the analysis of irony.
3. To highlight the symmetries and differences within the general framework of (Neo-)Gricean pragmatic analyses.
4. To assess the impact of this discussion on the (Neo-)Gricean program for pragmatics revolving around the cooperative principle.

Many views of the nature of irony have been proposed. We will limit ourselves to the approaches to irony that are predominant within linguistics and deliberately ignore the vast literature on the literary and philosophical uses of irony (e.g., Kierkegaard, Romantic irony, etc.).

Two principal types of theories or approaches present themselves at first look. The first approach is essentially a rewording in linguistic terms of the traditional theory of irony as a trope (figure of speech). The second approach, presented as vastly different from the traditional theory, is based on the language/metalanguage distinction and is known as the theory of "irony as mention/pretense." The next sections will briefly review some central definitional issues, before turning to a review of some of the various theories of irony proposed in linguistics. Basically, I will discuss the (Neo-)Gricean approaches and their critiques, as well as

---

This chapter was previously published as "Irony as relevant inappropriateness" (S. Attardo) in the *Journal of Pragmatics, 32*, 793–826. Copyright © [2001] by Elsevier. Reprinted with permission.

the Relevance-theoretic and cognitive ones, reject the latter and significantly revise the former. A section will then present this author's proposal for a revision of
the irony-as-trope theory, based on the notion of simultaneous inappropriateness
and relevance.

DEFINITIONS

Irony has a very ancient tradition of studies and interpretations. Most of the research on irony has been done within the paradigm of literary studies, with all the
implied interest in its aesthetic and emotional value, and the corresponding lack of
formalization. Some issues are relatively well understood; for example, the clues
with which the ironist signals his or her ironical intention to the hearer have been
studied in some detail (see Attardo, in press). Others are left almost entirely unexplored, for instance why S[1] would prefer to use irony rather than a literal message.
As an introduction to the problematics of irony from the linguistic point of view, the
works of Muecke (1969, 1970, 1973, 1978a, 1978b), Booth (1974), Kerbrat-
Orecchioni (1976, 1980), Schaffer (1982: 1–24), Chen (1990), Gibbs (1994),
Barbe (1995), and Giora (in press) will provide a good starting point and useful
references.

Irony is defined by Webster as "the use of words to express something other than
and especially the opposite of the literal meaning." We will take this informal definition as operational, at least pre-theoretically. We turn now to a few definitional issues, best presented before the main body of critical analysis.

Verbal Versus Situational Irony

A basic distinction in the field of irony is that between verbal irony, which is a linguistic phenomenon, and situational irony (a.k.a. irony of fate; Muecke, 1970),
which is a state of the world which is perceived as ironical, e.g., the fire station
burning down to the ground. Most treatments of irony deliberately ignore situational irony (e.g., Kerbrat-Orecchioni, 1976: *ironie référentielle,* 1980; Holdcroft,
1983). Exceptions are Littman and Mey (1991), who, on the contrary, deal exclusively with situational irony; Lucariello (1994); and Shelley (in press). Some, e.g.,
Haverkate (1990, p. 78), distinguished further irony of fate and dramatic irony,
within the broader situational irony. Dramatic irony is the telling of an ironical
event. Kreuz and Roberts (1993) distinguished between four types of irony:

1. Socratic irony.
2. Dramatic irony.
3. Irony of fate.
4. Verbal irony.

Socratic irony is the pretense of ignorance of a given topic, for pedagogical purposes. Kreuz and Roberts defined dramatic irony as the situation where the audi-

ence knows something that the character of a play, novel, etc., ignores (e.g., the case of Oedipus). Irony of fate corresponds to situational irony. In this context, however, we will consider exclusively verbal irony.

Sarcasm

Sarcasm is an overtly aggressive type of irony, with clearer markers/cues and a clear target. There is no consensus on whether sarcasm and irony are essentially the same thing, with superficial differences, or if they differ significantly. Some authors (e.g., Muecke, 1969; Mizzau, 1984, p. 26); Gibbs & O'Brien, 1991; Kreuz & Roberts, 1993), including the present one, believe the former. Rundquist (1991) noted (ironically?) that "there does not appear to be a consensus on how to determine whether an utterance is ironic or sarcastic" (p. 26). Other scholars try to distinguish sarcasm from irony. Haiman (1990, 1998) claimed that irony does not require the intention of the speaker, whereas sarcasm does. Haiman (1998, p. 20) further noted that irony may be situational, whereas sarcasm may not. Sperber and Wilson (1981) distinguished between echoing one's own utterance (irony) and echoing another person's utterance (sarcasm). Schaffer (1982, pp. 76–77) reported different verbal clues for irony and sarcasm. Perhaps the strongest claim for the differentiation between irony and sarcasm is Brown (1980, pp. 111, 124n), who claimed that a teacher who writes "Nice cover–F" on a student's paper, in case he/she really likes the cover, is being sarcastic but not ironical; Kreuz and Glucksberg (1989, p. 374) concurred (with different examples).

Unintended Irony

Gibbs, O'Brien, & Doolittle (1995) introduced the concept of "unintentional irony." An instance of irony is unintentional if "the speaker did not intend the utterance to be understood this way" (Gibbs et al., 1995, p. 189). Gibbs et al. noted that this type of irony is a complex case which contains "elements of both verbal and situational irony" (p. 189). They also noted the similarity to Kreuz and Roberts's (1993) dramatic irony. While they make much of the distinction (Gibbs et al., 1995, p. 199), there seems to be no need to introduce the distinction at all: consider that to S, the unintentionally ironical utterance u is simply not ironical. On the other hand, u becomes ironical when H interprets it as such. Since H does so intentionally (after all, H has to recognize S's intention to be able to detect the ironical mismatch between S's intended utterance and u), it follows that all cases of irony involve intentionality, except that, contrary to common belief, it need not be S's. On Gibb's theory of irony, see also below.

The Attitude of Irony

Many influential scholars have claimed that irony implies necessarily a negative, critical attitude towards its object (Grice, 1978, 1989; Kerbrat-Orecchioni, 1976,

1980; Sperber & Wilson, 1981). This claim, however, seems to be refuted by the rhetorical figure called "asteism" as well as by numerous counter-examples.

Asteism is a rhetorical figure, described as "genteel irony" (OED) which Fontanier (1977; quoted in Mizzau, 1984, p. 19) defines as praising or flattering someone under pretense of blaming or criticizing.[2] Berrendonner (1981) also cited asteism as a counter-example of the claim that irony implies a negative attitude.

Holdcroft (1983, p. 496) claimed that irony does not involve necessarily a negative attitude and can be "playful and affectionate." Some examples of irony expressing a positive attitude in a negative mode can be found in Berrendonner (1981, p. 225), Brown (1980, p. 114), Mao (1991, pp. 179–189), Haverkate (1990, p. 90), and Glucksberg (1995, p. 53). Brown's (1980, p. 114) example is particularly good and deserves being repeated:

(1)   Sorry to keep bothering you like this. (Spoken by your stock broker on calling for the third time to announce unexpected dividends.)

I have also collected the following example:

(2)   These American-made cars that break down after 100,000 miles!

Haverkate (1990, p. 90) reported a convincing argument by Myers Roy (1977) as to why positive irony is much less frequent than negative irony: positive irony involves saying something negative that one does not believe; this is obviously more dangerous than saying something positive that one does not believe, since, if the intent of having one's insincere utterance be recognized fails, one is taken as having said something negative. Based on her reinterpretation of Gibbs's and associates' results (see below, section 4.4), Giora (1995, p. 255) noted also that negative irony is harder to process (if for no other reason, because it involves an explicit negation) and that alone could account for its relative rarity.

One-Stage Versus Two-Stage Theories

A very significant issue has emerged recently in the theory of irony, namely, whether irony presupposes a two-stage processing which would involve the processing of a meaning of the text, the rejection of this interpretation on pragmatic grounds, and a subsequent reinterpretation of the text. The opposing approach claims that the processing of irony is not distinct from that of "literal" meaning and that crucially, ironical meaning is arrived at directly, without the mediation of a first interpretation that is rejected. Grice; (and the rhetorical approach to irony as a trope) can be seen as the principal proponent of the two-stage approach to irony, while Sperber and Wilson's (1981) mention theory is the main proponent of the one-stage approach.

This issue has assumed a central role in the debate over irony in the last years, as Gibbs's work (1994) has purportedly provided empirical support for the one-stage approach and therefore against the two-stage approach. The one-stage/two-stage distinction parallels that between "equivalent" (one stage) and "sequential" processing (two stages) in Giora (1997).[3]

IRONY AS A FIGURE OF SPEECH

From the point of view of the traditional theory, echoed in the dictionary definition quoted above, irony may be defined as "saying something while meaning something else" or more formally, if S utters a sentence whose (literal) meaning is M, he/she intends to communicate non-M, i.e., the complementary meaning. Kaufer (1981) and Haverkate (1990) noted that the traditional theory, which sees irony as a trope (figure of speech), is too broad, since it does not differentiate between irony and other figures of speech such as metaphor, litotes, etc.

Irony As Negation

A refinement of the theory of irony as a figure of speech has been proposed suggesting that irony does not express *any* other meaning but a more specific "opposite" meaning (e.g., Brown & Levinson, 1978, p. 221). For example, Levin (1982, pp. 116–118) proposed to distinguish between irony as a trope, when irony is focused on a word, or as a figure of thought, when it is focused on a sentence. In the former case, the relationship is that of antonymy, in the latter of negation. Haverkate (1990, pp. 83–85) proposed the same distinction, arguing that irony may focus on the negation of a word or of a proposition.

Kaufer (1981, pp. 496–502) reviewed the problems involved in this approach: they essentially boil down to the fact that many sentences without truth conditions can be ironical (see below) and that the conditions under which an utterance should be recognized as ironical are not specified. Furthermore, when the irony revolves around non-truth functional aspects of meaning,[4] it is impossible to apply the negation to any of the sentences in the utterance and/or its constituents. For a further "negation" theory of irony.

Irony As Violation of Quality: Grice's Theory

As is well known, Grice (1975, 1989) listed irony as an example of implicature and showed how one can account for irony as a case of flouting the cooperative principle (CP), by violating the maxim of quality (Grice, 1989, p. 34). Grice later returned to the analysis of irony, but we will examine this revision separately in what follows.

Grice's theory of irony is not radically different from the traditional accounts (Sperber & Wilson, 1981). An analysis of Tanaka's (1973) and Cutler's (1974, p. 117) Gricean, or Muecke's (1973) and Booth's (1974) pre-Gricean accounts of irony does indeed confirm that assessment. Kaufer (1981, p. 499) also treated Grice's account of irony as essentially similar to the traditional accounts of irony, over which it constitutes a "significant advance" in that it allows for the determination of the conditions in which an utterance should be considered ironic (i.e., the violation of the maxim of quality) and it allows the reconstruction of the ironical intent even when irony revolves around non-truth conditional elements of the sentence. However, Grice's account is flawed insofar as the violation of other maxims can be shown to trigger irony, as shown by Sperber and Wilson (1981) in the case of understatement. Holdcroft (1983, p. 507) listed a number of examples in which irony involves no breach of a maxim and further argued that, in the absence of a target of the irony, it is unclear why a violation of the CP should lead one to look for ironical meanings as opposed to any other form of indirect meaning.

Kaufer (1981) further showed that the violation of any of the maxims can be ironical (pp. 500–501). He did, however, go on to argue that the violation of a maxim is not sufficient for the creation/perception of irony (p. 502), on the basis of the following apparent counterexample:

(3)   America's allies—always there when they need you.

Kaufer (1981, p. 501) claimed that this followed all the maxims. Kaufer immediately below noted that "the statement is undeniably crafted as irony because of its obvious contrast with a much more common slogan that conveys an attitude diametrically opposed" (p. 502) and that because of this, the statement achieves great relevance.[5]

I believe that Kaufer's analysis is incorrect, because it overlooks some of the dynamics of the intertextual allusion to the slogan "X: Always there when you need them" (which, if I am not mistaken, was once used by the British police). Because he or she has made the intertextual reference and inverted the subject and direct object of the embedded clause, the writer to *Time*[6] can no longer be said to be abiding by the maxim of manner, as (3) hardly avoids ambiguity. In fact, (3) is structurally built as a pun, the quintessential example of exploitation of ambiguity in language.

Interestingly, Mizzau (1984, p. 37) noted that Grice himself had used an example of ironical implicatures generated via the flouting of another maxim (manner):

(4)   Miss X produced a series of sounds that corresponded closely with the
        score of "Home Sweet Home" (Grice, 1989, p. 37).

However, Grice does not call this an irony.

Chen (1990) presented a theory of irony based on an "augmented" version of the CP.[7] Chen defined irony as a violation of the maxim of quality (p. 188) in its augmented version. This formulation is clearly in error, cf. Myers Roy (1977, 1981), Schaffer (1982, p. 12), and Sperber and Wilson's (1981, p. 300) example:

(5)   Two people [are] caught in a downpour ... "It seems to be raining."

Here, Sperber and Wilson pointed out, the speaker does not say the opposite of what he or she means, only *less*. There seems to be no doubt that the example does not violate the maxim of quality, but only the maxim of relevance (what is said is obvious, hence irrelevant) or quantity (the speaker is not saying enough).

Therefore, we conclude that Grice's theory suffers from a crucial flaw, i.e., it is too restricted, since the violation of any maxim, not just of quality, may trigger irony. We turn now to another account of irony, which, while Gricean in spirit, detaches itself from Grice's in significant ways.

Graded Salience Violation

An important contribution to the study of irony comes from the work of Giora (1995, 1997; Giora, Fein, & Schwartz, 1998; Giora & Fein, in press). Giora's theory is a two-stage theory, although she considerably revises Grice's approach. A discussion of Giora's refutation of the one-phase approach, exemplified by Gibbs's work, can be found in Giora (1995), Giora et al. (1998), and see section 4.4 for discussion.

Giora's theory revolves around the two concepts of "indirect negation" and "graded salience." We turn to both, in that order.

Indirect Negation

The basic concept of the indirect negation view is that irony involves the presence of both the literal and the implied meanings and that the relationship between the two is that of indirect (i.e., non-explicit) negation. As will be recalled, Grice's (and the traditional view's) approach postulates that the first meaning is discarded, and hence no longer available (Giora, 1995, pp. 241, 245). In this respect, irony is quite different from the process of disambiguation, in which rejected meanings are discarded and are no longer available to the speaker for processing, since irony *retains* both senses (Giora et al., 1998, p. 97). This point constitutes, then, a second flaw in Grice's theory.

Giora (1995) listed a number of differences between explicit/direct and indirect negation. Primarily, direct negation is subject to a number of implicatures (e.g., scalar implicatures; cf. Horn, 1989) which irony, being indirect, avoids (Giora, 1995, p. 242). Also, direct negation implies the opposite of what one negates, whereas indirect negation accommodates "more mitigated interpretations" (1995, p. 244), i.e., intermediate values on the negated axis.

The Graded Salience Hypothesis

The graded salience hypothesis (GSH), which has been developed and presented independently of the study of irony, consists in the idea that more salient meanings have priority in interpretation, i.e., when a polysemous item is encountered during processing, the speaker processes first its most salient meaning and then the other(s).

Needless to say, the definition of "salience" is a central issue. Salience is defined as a function of

1. A word's meaning conventionality (i.e., whether a word has that meaning by convention; in other words, if it is listed in the lexicon as having that meaning).
2. Familiarity (e.g., *freedom* is more familiar than *liberty*).
3. Frequency (i.e., more frequent meanings are more salient).
4. "Givenness status" in a linguistic co(n)text (Giora, 1997, p. 185).

Whereas the first three aspects of this definition, while not necessarily straightforward, are reasonably clear, the last one is more problematic, as the theme/rheme distinction has been found to be questionable (e.g., Levinson, 1983). This is not to say that a proposal based on the theme/rheme articulation should be automatically discounted; however, it should be kept in mind that there is a degree of vagueness in the present definition of the concept which may be problematic, since, for example, it precludes a quantification of the value of salience.

The processing of an utterance, from the standpoint of the GSH, looks as follows:

• Salient meanings have priority.
• Novel meanings are interpreted by accessing the salient meaning first, rejecting it as the intended meaning, and reinterpreting.
• Novel meanings are harder to process (Giora, 1997, p. 186).

In other words, Giora (1997) rejected the priority of literal meaning and instead postulated the priority of salient meanings (p. 197). Thus, Giora rejected the traditional and Gricean interpretations of irony (and of figurative language, as well, incidentally), which postulate the unquestioned priority of literal meaning, while retaining the two-stage model, since her processing of novel ironies requires backtracking and reinterpretation. Giora (1997) suggested that a revision of the "standard pragmatic model" along these lines would shield it from the psycholinguistic criticisms mentioned above (see further section 4.4).

The rejection of the primacy of the literal sense, in favor of the primacy of the salient sense (be it literal or figurative/indirect) constitutes then a third criticism of Grice's original model.

The GSH makes clear empirical predictions, which have been tested. These boil down to two principal claims:

1. Literal meanings should still be available after non-literal meanings have been activated (from the "indirect negation" aspect).
2. Ironical interpretations are less salient that literal readings, hence they should take longer to process.

These predictions have been empirically supported in experiments reported in Giora et al. (1998) and Giora and Fein (in press).

Conclusion: Critical Assessment of Grice's Theory

The following critiques have been leveled at Grice's model of irony:

1. Violation of any maxim (not just of that of quality) may trigger irony.
2. The non-ironical sense is not discarded, but is used to compute the ironical sense.
3. The priority of the literal meaning of the text is rejected in favor of the priority of the most salient text.
4. Irony implies an attitude towards its object (cf. Grice's own revision of the definition, below).

It should be kept in mind, however, that Grice is responsible for the basic two-stage model of irony, which will be defended in what follows.

IRONY AS AN (INSINCERE) SPEECH ACT

We turn now to four analyses of irony from within speech act theory. As such, these could well be considered as Gricean theories of irony as well.

Amante

Ironical speech acts are not performatives (Amante, 1981, p. 81), they are necessarily indirect speech acts, and must be insincere. Amante (1981) argued that in an ironical speech act, two propositions are predicated (or one is predicated and one implied). He claimed that the propositions must conflict[8] "$P \neq P'$" (p. 82), or in other words, that

> [They] must be in formal opposition to [one an]other through negation or through some opposing semantic relationship such as complementarity, antonymy, contradiction, or converseness. If no such formally negative relationship seems to exist between P and P', then there still must be a very discernible but perhaps non-polar difference [...]. (p. 82)

Amante (1981) insisted that clues to the irony be present (pp. 82–83); "*It is mandatory that some clue to irony be provided by the ironist*" (p. 83; emphasis in the original). However, he does not provide arguments for this position.

Finally, Amante (1981) argued that irony creates a "quasi-perlocutionary" force, called "affective force" (p. 88) which is a "blend of illocutionary and perlocutionary forces" (p. 88). The affective force of irony is, strangely, defined as drawing "attention to the language [of the irony] itself and focus[ing] on the message" (p. 92), i.e., it "causes the audience to reprocess the illocutionary act" (p. 92). No mention is made of the critical attitude often associated with irony.

Brown

A significant issue, highlighted by Brown (1980), is that irony is not limited to assertions, or in other words, that other speech acts can be ironical too. Brown (p. 114) provided examples of congratulations, thanking, requesting, and apologizing. Brown initially defined irony as the performance of a speech act with an attendant flaunting of the absence of the required sincerity conditions. A corollary is that speech acts that do not have sincerity conditions (such as greetings) cannot be performed ironically (p. 116). A possible counterexample to this claim could be comedian Jerry Seinfeld's famous "Hello Newman" ironical/sarcastic greeting, said with a sneer which clearly belies the greeting.

Further examination of speech acts that do not just involve statements leads Brown (1980) to revise the definition, broadening it to the utterance of a sentence which is "use[d] in a speech act with a necessary associated psychological state;" here, S intends H to understand that the "psychological state requirement [is] intentionally unfulfilled" (p. 120). The psychological states of which he speaks, following Searle (1979), are such things as believing something, regretting something, desiring something, etc.

An advantage of this approach, as Brown (1980) noted, is that it ties irony to the normal processing of speech acts, without requiring special modes of communication or other apparatus. Thus, the theory is very economical.

Haverkate

Haverkate (1990) started out by noting that irony can focus on predicates, on propositions, and on illocutionary force. He then expressed his adherence to the theory that "irony is the intentional expression of insincerity" (p. 104), which corresponds essentially to Brown's (see 3.2), whose work is, however, not quoted. It should be noted that Haverkate qualified his formulation, noting that S intends H to recognize his or her insincerity, in that it is "transparent" (p. 102), i.e., overt.

The article consists mostly of a discussion of various types of speech acts and how they can be employed ironically. It thus provides a valuable resource for the analysis of irony in speech acts other than assertives.

An important aspect of the speech act analyses of irony, which emerges powerfully in Haverkate's article, is their strong dependence on Gricean pragmatics. Essentially, one could recast the speech act theory of irony in a completely Gricean mold by calling it (as Haverkate does) an intentional and obvious violation (in this case, a flouting) of the maxim of quality.

Glucksberg

Glucksberg (1995) introduced the concept of "pragmatic insincerity" by which he meant that "the speaker has violated at least one of the felicity conditions of well-formed speech acts, usually the sincerity condition" (p. 52). He then went on to state that pragmatic insincerity is a necessary but not sufficient condition for the creation/perception of irony (p. 53). The other necessary condition is the allusion to "some prior expectation, norm, or convention that has been violated in one way or another" (p. 53).

Despite these discussions, one still finds the violation of the maxim of quality quoted as the necessary and sufficient condition for irony; cf. Kreuz and Glucksberg (1989), Kreuz and Roberts (1995, pp. 21–22): "nonveridicality is essential for the perception of irony."

IRONY AS MENTION

We now turn to a family of theories which claim to have introduced a substantial change in the analysis of irony. We will review the basic theory and then address its offshoots and the attempts at empirical verification.

The mention (or echoic mention) theories were first[9] presented in Sperber and Wilson's much quoted paper on irony as mention (1981) which has been somewhat revised in Sperber and Wilson (1986).[10] Specifically, Sperber and Wilson rejected the notion of "mention" as too limited and replace it with the notion of "interpretation," i.e., "the use of a propositonal form to represent not itself but some other propositional form it more or less closely resembles" (1986, p. 264n). They also pointed out that this terminological change does not substantially affect their account of irony.

The notion of *echoic* utterance is introduced as a case of interpretation of someone else's thought (e.g., reported speech). In the case of reported speech, the relevance of the utterance is arrived at on the basis of the fact that the speaker informs the hearer that someone has said X. In the case of echoic utterances, the speaker informs the hearer that he or she "has in mind" (Sperber & Wilson, 1986, p. 238) X and has "a certain attitude to it." Thus in the following example

(6) Peter: The Joneses aren't coming to the party.
     Mary: They aren't coming, hum. If that's true, we might invite the Smiths
     (Sperber & Wilson, 1986, p. 238).

Mary's reply is relevant not in virtue of informing Peter that he has just uttered the sentence "The Joneses aren't coming to the party" but because it informs Peter that Mary "has paid attention to his utterance and is weighing up its reliability and implications" (Sperber & Wilson, 1986, p. 238). Finally, echoic utterances must not necessarily be attributable to a given specific individual, as proverbs and sayings show.[11]

The speaker of an echoic utterance must necessarily have a certain attitude towards the echoic utterance itself. This attitude can be anything (positive, negative, neutral). Sperber and Wilson (1986) noted the following:

Sometimes, the speaker's attitude is left implicit, to be gathered only from tone of voice, context and other paralinguistic clues; at other times it may be made explicit. (p. 239)

This corresponds to the weak and strong versions of mention theory (Attardo, 1993), respectively.

Sperber and Wilson (1986) proceeded to expand their theory of irony on this basis. They argued that

[Irony] invariably involves the implicit expression of an attitude, and that the relevance of an ironical utterance invariably depends, at least in part, on the information it conveys about the speaker's attitude to the opinion echoed. (p. 239)

As to the attitude, they claimed that it is "invariably of the rejecting or disapproving kind" (p. 239), a claim falsified by numerous examples, as was seen above.

The implicatures of an ironical utterance, according to Sperber and Wilson (1986, p. 240), depend on the following factors:

1. "A recognition of the utterance as echoic."
2. "Identification of the source of the opinion echoed."
3. "Recognition that the speaker's attitude to the opinion echoed is one of rejection or disapproval."

Sperber and Wilson compared then their account of irony to the traditional account of irony (which is very close to Grice's, as we have seen). They found the biggest problem for the traditional account in the question of why the speaker should choose to express his or her meaning indirectly when he or she can do so directly. In their opinion, because irony is echoic and critical of the echoed utterance, it is used to ridicule the utterance echoed. In other words, the point of irony is to express one's attitude towards an utterance.[12]

There are several weak points in this account of irony, which will lead to its rejection. In fact, it can be shown that mentioning is neither a necessary nor sufficient condition of the ironical status of a text.

Mention is not a sufficient condition of irony (Kerbrat-Orecchioni, 1980, p. 122; Carston, 1981, p. 27; Schaffer, 1982, p. 16; Chen, 1990, p. 36). This can be seen clearly from the fact that not all mentioned sentences are ironical.

(7)   John said that Bob said X.

The sentence in (7) is not ironical. Thus, whatever the status of the mentioning itself, some other factor would have to be present for the mention theory to function.[13]

The second point parallels the rejection of mention theory for jokes (Attardo, 1993, pp. 277–286). One of the crucial claims of the echoic mention theory is that it must allow for implicit (i.e., nonsignaled) mention. Specifically, Berrendonner (1981, p. 217) noted that in irony there are no markers of mention. Explicit mention is set out by appropriate metalinguistic markers of the kind in (8)

(8)   As my uncle Bob used to say ...

Implicit mention may also be fairly easy to spot, such as when a speaker verbatim repeats the previous utterance of the hearer. It is, however, clear that one can utter sentences that merely resemble (e.g., paraphrase) other utterances. For example, the following is likely to be recognized as a mention by most people familiar with Shakespeare: "I wonder whether I should kill myself or not. Whether it would be better, as far as socially sanctioned behavior is concerned, to have patience, etc." Also, consider that one may echo no one in particular, but merely an hypothetical speaker. It follows that if one utters any sentence, one may be mentioning/echoing another utterance. This leads obviously to an infinite regression; how does H know that S is not mentioning someone else's mention of an utterance?

Even if infinite regression is somehow avoided, one is left with the problem of identifying an implicit echoic utterance (cf. Schaffer, 1982, p. 16; Chen, 1990, p. 38). In many cases, as Sperber and Wilson said, the intonation or kinesic factors will reveal that the speaker does not endorse the utterance. However, there exists a so-called "dead-pan" delivery, which consists precisely in *not* signaling that one's utterance is a joke/irony; or consider the case of a written ironical text, in which no intonational or kinesic clues mark off the utterance. In these cases, it is necessary to use contextual clues to decide if an utterance is echoic or not (as per Sperber and Wilson's list of factors). The only factor in the context of the utterance which can identify an utterance as echoic is that the utterance is somehow inappropriate either to the context or to the set of beliefs that the hearer knows the speaker to have. Suppose that I were to say

(9)   Only Italians can make good pasta.

Given knowledge of my background (namely that I am partly Italian), the sentence would be perfectly reasonable. H therefore has no reason to believe that I am echoing some unnamed chauvinistic Italian gourmet. On the other hand, suppose that I say

(10)   We should throw all these immigrants, legal or illegal, out of the U.S.

The knowledge of my background (namely that I am a legal alien residing in the United States) and the logical assumption that I would not want to advocate something that would be damaging to myself, will lead H to believe that I am echoing some unnamed American xenophobe.

As seen in the quote above, Sperber and Wilson's (1981) mention theory of irony explicitly allows for "implicit mention," i.e., mention of an utterance without any overt trace of the mentioning. This means that the mentioned status of an utterance has to be determined inferentially, since by definition there is no co-textual clue to the mentioned status of the utterance. How can this status be determined? Apparently, through contextual inappropriateness, i.e., if S utters a sentence that is patently inappropriate, H can decide that that sentence is being zero-mentioned in S's utterance. But if this account is valid, then the ulterior step of the mentioning is unnecessary, since I propose that purposeful inappropriateness is a necessary and sufficient cause of irony in an utterance (see below). Schaffer (1982, p. 16) pointed out that the same problem exists at the level of deciding whether a given mention of an utterance is a case of ironical mention or one of non-ironical mention. Schaffer believed that Sperber and Wilson are victims of circular reasoning: "[they] use the presence of mention to identify irony and irony to identify the presence of mention" (p. 16). In conclusion, mention is not a necessary condition for irony.

Thus, we have seen that mentioning is neither a sufficient condition for irony (there exist non-ironical mentions) nor a necessary one (one can account for irony more simply without introducing the concept of mention). Finally, both the identification of the source of the echoic utterance and the negative attitude are unnecessary (per Sperber and Wilson's own account) or incorrect (see above).

Let us now return to the traditional/Gricean account of irony. In this account too, one recognizes a given utterance as non-literal (i.e., having implicatures) on the basis of perceived incongruity between the utterance and its context and/or the set of beliefs ascribed to the utterer. An inferred meaning intended by the speaker is then looked for, using the CP (mostly relevance, probably). In particular, one assumes that if the speaker is bothering to be non-literal, he or she must want to convey some attitude towards some fact/object in the context. If we go on a picnic and it rains, the utterance of

(11)   What nice weather! (with sarcastic tone)

will be interpreted as conveying annoyance at the weather, rather than towards the innocent sentence.

If we compare the echoic mention theory and the traditional/Gricean view, we can easily see that their explanatory power is the same, but that the echoic mention theory involves some extra steps (labeling the utterance echoic and looking for a source of the utterance) which are unnecessary, since mere contextual inappropriateness is enough to trigger the assumption of implicature.[14] This is not to say that one cannot have cases of echoic irony, but only that all irony is not necessarily echoic.[15]

Empirical Verifications of the Mention Theory

An attempt has been made to test the claims of mention theory against empirical evidence (Jorgensen, Miller, & Sperber, 1984). The experiments consisted in reading tests, in which the subjects were presented with short stories ending in an ironical sentence which was either a mention of another sentence in the text or a sentence which did not echo anything in the text. This was obtained by omitting a sentence in the text which provided the first occurrence of the echo. The results were mixed: in two experiments, the echoic mention stories scored as well or barely better as the non-echoic stories. In the remaining four, while statistically significant higher numbers of subjects reported irony in the mentioned sentences, some subjects still reported irony. This seems to suggest, as Jorgensen et al. (1984) admitted, that mentioning barely reinforces the ironic intent. Jorgensen et al. rejected such a weakening of the mention theory (p. 118) and proposed alternative explanations (such as that the subjects may have imagined an antecedent of which the ironical sentence was a mention). Jorgensen et al.'s attempt at validating mention theory has been criticized on methodological grounds as well (Williams, 1984; Barbe, 1995, p. 46).

Gibbs (1994, pp. 109, 384) reported some experimental results that seem to show that mention may reinforce the ironic nature of an utterance: subjects rated echoic utterances as more ironical than non-echoic utterances and processed echoic ironical utterances faster than non-echoic ironical utterances. The same results were found for sarcastic utterances.

Irony As Pretense

Clark and Gerrig (1984) have presented a theory of irony as pretense. Essentially, the theory claims that when S is being ironical, he or she pretends to be S¢ speaking to H¢ (a pretend hearer,[16] who may or may not be real and/or present). Clark and Gerrig (1984, p. 122) followed Grice's (1978, 1989) point that the attitude of the ironist is critical towards what S¢ is saying. H¢ is meant to take S¢ seriously (i.e., not to perceive the irony), while H is assumed to be able to understand all the above: "the pretense, S¢'s injudiciousness, H¢'s ignorance, and hence S¢'s attitude toward S¢, H¢, and what S¢ said" (Clark & Gerrig, 1984, p. 122). See also Clark (1996, pp. 369–374) for the "joint pretense" version of this theory.

While the two theories claim to be substantially different (e.g., Sperber, 1984), it has been claimed that they are for all practical purposes notational variants of each other (Williams, 1984; Winner, 1988; Chen, 1990, pp. 39–42; Barbe, 1995, pp. 48–50). Winner (1988) has noted that they are both "substitution" theories. Furthermore, as Williams (1984, p. 129) noted, they both ultimately derive from the same traditional account of irony they seek to criticize.

While the above criticisms have their fair share of plausibility, I think that they end up throwing out the baby with the bath water: mention and pretense are indeed very similar concepts, but, as Clark and Gerrig (1984) noted, mention is a far more restricted concept than pretense. Thus, pretense theory can be shown to be able to handle some cases that mention theory would struggle with (e.g., Swift's *A Modest Proposal;* for an opposing view, see Sperber, 1984, p. 133n); moreover, pretense theory can be expanded very easily to cover dramatic and situational irony (Clark & Gerrig, 1984, p. 124) while mention theory cannot, in principle, handle these cases (it would not make sense to say that an event is a "mention" of another event). Furthermore, pretense theory does not fall victim as readily to the infinite regression that plagues mention theory. For example, it would be relatively easy to constrain pretense theory in such a way as to exclude cases in which the pretend nature of S's utterance is not somehow marked as such.

Reminder Theory

Kreuz and Glucksberg (1989) revised mention theory in their "echoic reminder theory." They admitted that not all ironies are echoic mentions (p. 375), and they claimed instead that an ironical utterance need only allude "to an antecedent event" (p. 375); such "events" may include expectations and implicit norms. The purpose of irony is, as in echoic mention theory, to express disapproval towards the situation. Kreuz and Glucksberg's (1989) results are "consistent with the notion of implicit reminding through positive social norms and expectations" (p. 383).

Kreuz and Glucksberg (1989) tested a number of predictions that they claimed follow from their theory, but do not follow from a traditional/Gricean account of irony. The most significant are as follows:

1. Positive statements are more readily interpreted as sarcastic.
2. Positive sarcastic utterances do not require explicit antecedents, while negative ones do.
3. In particular, the presence of a victim (i.e., a target for the sarcastic utterance) should provide an explicit antecedent (p. 376).

Unfortunately, as seen in section 1.4, there are other reasons, outside of reminder theory, that positive ironical statements are difficult to process and/or occur more rarely. This fact undermines the conceptual basis of the entire experimental set-up.

Kreuz and Glucksberg (1989) found that their results are consistent with their theory when "taken as a whole" (p. 383). Indeed, they found that the presence of an explicit antecedent and of a victim does increase the ratings of sarcasm and that positive statements are interpreted sarcastically more readily than negative ones (p. 379). However, when they consider all the data, Kreuz and Glucksberg arrived at some results that are incompatible with reminder theory:

- The subjects in their experiment 1 expressed "an attitude towards the object of sarcasm by expressing the opposite of that attitude" (p. 380). This, as Kreuz and Glucksberg noted, is what the standard theory predicts.
- There was no interaction between whether a statement was positive or negative and the presence or absence of a victim, therefore suggesting that "a blatantly counterfactual statement may be a sufficient condition for inferring sarcastic intent" (p. 381); this finding is also along the lines of a traditional theory of irony/sarcasm.

Kreuz and Glucksberg (1989) concluded that "when a statement is obviously counterfactual [...] this seems to be sufficient to prompt at least a suspicion of sarcastic intent" (p. 382), and also that "people are likely to judge a remark as sarcastic whenever it is obviously false to both speaker and listener, *even when that remark has no explicit victim*" (p. 382; my emphasis).

Overall, therefore, it seems clear that reminder theory fails to provide an alternative to mention theory, since per its proponents' own results, two out of three predictions are falsified by the data, and the third prediction can be explained by other means. Conversely, the results that Kreuz and Glucksberg (1989) reported show clearly that the central factor in the stimuli used was the counterfactual nature of the utterance, and that the positive value of the utterance and the presence of a victim were mere facilitators. I would speculate that this is because the presence of an obvious target makes it simpler to direct the critical attitude of irony and because a critical attitude is more logically expressed about a negative fact (and hence with a positive utterance).

Psycholinguistic Critiques of Pragmatic Approaches to Irony

Gibbs and his associates have presented a large body of results of empirical research which they claim invalidates the general approach of pragmatic and logical approaches to irony (e.g., Gibbs, 1986; Gibbs & O'Brien, 1991; Gibbs, 1994). For the purposes of this discussion, we can describe a "standard pragmatic model' (SPM) as a two-stage model which prescribes that the literal, non-figurative, direct meaning of the linguistic expression be processed first and the non-literal, indirect, figurative meaning be arrived at via implicature (or other inferential processing).

Basically, Gibbs and his associates have shown that the most straightforward prediction of the SPM can be shown to be incorrect: it does not take longer to process indirect, figurative language.

I have shown elsewhere (section 4.4.2 below and see Attardo, in press) that, while interesting and thought provoking, the results discussed only refute one of the several possible psychological models that can be derived from Gricean pragmatics, and that it is possible to design a theory of processing of indirect speech (including irony) which is consistent with Gibbs's results while retaining the basic two-stage model of implicature (see also section 4.4.2 below).

Other models have also been presented. For example, Mizzau (1984) argued the that

> A comment such as "Paul is smart," accompanied by an eloquent facial expression, produces simultaneously a characterization of the message as ironical and its antiphrastic translation. If the same sentence is said without any accompanying non-verbal indices, but everybody knows the obtuseness of the person referred to, the understanding of the irony seems to be somehow posterior to the discovery of the true meaning. (Only this second case represents the mental process hypothesized by Grice.) (p. 38; my translation)

We find here the same argument as that used by Gibbs, viz. that the context primes the ironical meaning directly without the need to access the literal/non-ironical meaning first. However, Mizzau (1984) acknowledged the possibility of all three paths of interpretation: i.e., ironical meaning first, literal first, and simultaneous interpretation (her first example in the quote above).

The "Computability" Problem

Furthermore, the one-stage model that Gibbs and associates (as well as relevance theoretic adherents) propose, runs into the logical problem of computability, which I discuss in Attardo (in press). Basically, the issue boils down to the fact that a one-stage model is logically incapable of accounting for novel input, since it will fail to differentiate between a semantically ill-formed sentence and a novel instance of metaphor, irony, or other indirect figure of speech.

The one-stage model cannot utilize a "fail-then-recover" strategy since, obviously enough, a fail-then-recover strategy is a two-stage model. A one-stage model is forced to succeed or fail in its interpretation at first try, so to speak. So, if faced with an utterance u whose meaning is ironical, a one-stage model would necessarily arrive at the intended meaning without considering the possibility of a different interpretation. To do so would *eo ipso* transform the one stage model into a two-stage model.

Consider now that it is known that Ss will backtrack and reanalyze a text fragment he or she has misprocessed (e.g., garden-path sentences); in other words, we know that fail-then-recover strategies are used by Ss/Hs. It follows that a two-stage model of processing must be admissible, at least in those cases. The question becomes now: If a two-stage processing model is possible, why isn't it used in irony, metaphor, etc.?

In fact, Sperber and Wilson's (1981) mention theory is a two-stage model: the recognition that u_1 is a mention of u_0 presupposes a metalinguistic distance between u_1 and u_0 which could be represented as in (12), where s_0 and s_1 are the original speaker and the mentioning speaker, respectively.

(12) $S_1 \vdash u_1 (S_0 \vdash u_0)$

To say that u_1 "echoes," "mirrors," etc. u_0, implies the recognition that $u_1 \neq u_0$ (note that the proposition p_1 asserted in the sentence of which u_1 is the utterance may in fact be equal to p_0). If $u_0 = u_1$, there is no mention, since u_0 cannot differ from u_1, as it would have to if u_1 were a mention of u_0, as per (12). Therefore, for S_n to recognize that $u_n \neq u_0$ and then to infer (12), there must be a two-stage process. Gibbs (1994) admitted to as much when he introduced the category of "product."

Let us examine the processing of a metaphor, for example. Suppose that a one-stage processing mechanism encounters a novel combination of attributes. It either discards as ill-formed a semantically "inappropriate" combination or it looks for a prior instance of the combination in its database. The search may fail, which would then lead the model to also discard the input, or it may succeed, with the possibility that either the novel input does match the older one (in which case it is not really a novel input) or it does not, in which case the model will fail to attribute the intended meaning to the novel input (it will analyze it in terms of the old input). A more sophisticated processor may perhaps realize that this novel input needs to be added to the database and do so. Thereafter, the processor will recognize the (now no longer novel) input and proceed accordingly. It remains, however, that the processor cannot, short of bootstrapping itself into a two-stage device, process the input as novel and anomalous, yet not to be discarded on first run.

Consider the following example, consisting of my saying

(13)   I love Heidegger.

Let us assume that no kinesic or suprasegmental cues are available (such as that S is busy ripping up a copy of *Being and Time* and feeding it to the flames). The only bit of information available is that I dislike phenomenological thought. The one-stage model, faced with (13), may either

1. Process the utterance at face value.
2. Process the utterance and reject it as incompatible with what is known about my system of beliefs.

Consider similarly what would happen if I uttered (14):

(14)   I am not Salvatore Attardo.

Here the only options available to a one-stage model are as follows:

1. To discard (14) as a contradiction.
2. To revise the database and delete the link between the speaker and the "Salvatore Attardo" identifier.

In other words, a one-stage model has no reason (or capacity) to look for a second, ulterior interpretation of the text, just because the first one it runs into is anomalous.[17]

A possible objection to this argument may go as follows: since H (or a model of H) has available as contextual information both (13) and the attending information in (15), and both (14) and (16), then from the combination of (13) and (15) H can infer that S does *not* in fact like Heidegger.

(15)   S dislikes phenomenology and Heidegger is a phenomenologist.
(16)   S is Salvatore Attardo.

However, this reasoning begs the following question: why shouldn't H rather conclude that S is being inconsistent or irrational? If H is to entertain and discard this hypothesis, then *eo ipso* we have no longer a one-stage model but a two-stage model. Then, how can H decide which of the two possible interpretations is to be preferred? The obvious answer is as follows: via the CP (or by appealing to relevance). But this does not solve the original problem: at some point in the processing (not necessarily as the first step), H will run into a second possible interpretation. At this point a choice will have to be made, presumably on the assumption of cooperation/relevance. However, the very fact that there is a choice entails that this is in fact a two-stage model. Note that the escape solution that H directly arrives at the antiphrastic meaning without *ever* considering the positive meaning is impossible, as shown by Giora's (1995) argument that the two meanings must coexist, since they need to be compared to compute the distance between them, which is the source of the value judgment implicit in irony.[18]

Consider further that from the combination of (14) and (16), S is somehow supposed to arrive at an interpretation, such as for example that S is joking, which is incompatible with a literal, CP abiding interpretation of the text. Since there is no available information in H's knowledge about ritual denials of identity or about playful memory loss, H is forced to do the following: (a) register his or her failure to assign (14) a satisfactory interpretation (given its clash with 16), and (b) look for a reinterpretation along novel lines, if possible.[19]

Empirical Studies Contradicting Gibbs's Conclusions

McDonald (1992) reported an empirical study with patients suffering from closed head injury. He found that while the patients can identify the literal meaning of sentences and the illocutionary force of an indirect speech act, they have considerable more difficulty rejecting the literal meaning when it is presented as an option. More significantly, the subjects who had suffered head injury failed to identify ironical/sarcastic statements. These results are interpreted as going against the one-stage mention theory account of irony and sarcasm. Dews and Winner (1995) reported results that go against Gibbs's theory, by showing that speakers must access the literal meaning of the ironical utterances, since the literal meaning affects the perception of the degree of aggressiveness of the utterance. Dews and Winner (1995) used assessment scales (instead of reaction times as does Gibbs) and argued that the difference in testing methodologies may be responsible for the different results.

Work done by Giora and her associates (Giora, 1995, 1997; Giora et al., 1998; Giora and Fein, in press) has shown that ironical utterances take longer to process (see section 2.3 above for discussion). Giora (1995) also demonstrated that Gibbs's results, in one representative study, can be reinterpreted as showing that the subjects are reacting more to the high informativeness of the ironical/sarcastic test sentences and the corresponding low informativeness of the literal sentences, than to the presence or absence of irony. By ingeniously comparing results from different examples and carefully reading Gibbs's own materials, Giora came to the conclusion that Gibbs's own data show that irony takes longer to process than equivalently informative literal sentences.

IRONY AND THE PRINCIPLE OF LEAST DISRUPTION

Having reviewed the literature on irony, we can now turn to the present discussion of irony, which is Gricean at the core, but includes several significant departures from Grice's own model. Let us start with the following points:

1. The ironic meaning is arrived at inferentially.
2. Hence, irony is entirely a pragmatic phenomenon.
3. The interpretation of the ironical meaning depends crucially on the active guidance of the CP.
4. Ergo, the CP needs to be immediately restored into functionality after having been violated. This I will call the "principle of least disruption."

The reconstruction of the ironist's intended meaning is supposed to be based on a set of shared presuppositions: H knows that S cannot mean M, and S knows that H knows that, and therefore S can count on the fact that H will not stop at S's literal meaning M, but rather look for a more suitable meaning among the infinite set of other meanings which may have been implicated by S.

How Does One Arrive at the Ironical Meaning Arrived?

The fact that irony does not necessarily implicate the opposite or the converse of the literal meaning is important. Schaffer (1982, p. 15) summed up the situation brilliantly:

> Recognition of irony rarely comes from the words themselves [...], but rather from cues in the conversational context or nonverbal communication of the speaker. The ironic implicatures resulting from such cues *merely point to the possibility that the speaker's meaning may be other than that of the literal content of the utterance;* other conversational implicatures and semantic considerations can then supply an alternative interpretation. (p. 15; my emphasis)

Therefore, it follows that irony is a completely pragmatic phenomenon, with no semantic correlates. As such, it is entirely dependent on context, including but not limited to, S's intentions and goals. The ironical meaning needs to be inferred, it is never "said" (in Grice's sense), i.e., found in the text itself.

This point is quite important and bears restating. There are two distinct phenomena at work: (1) the determination that a (part of) a text is ironical (the recognition of irony), and (2) the determination of the intended meaning of the irony (the interpretation of the value of the irony).

We turn first to the determination of the value of the irony and will return to the recognition of irony in a subsequent section.

Principle of Least Disruption

To be noted here is the fact that Grice's CP, momentarily suspended when an ironic utterance is first encountered—since H notes the violation of at least one maxim[20] —becomes fully operational again once the first step of rejecting the literal meaning has been taken, for example in (17):

(17)   S: "What nice weather." (Context: it is raining.)

H will assume that the utterance is relevant to the condition of the weather, and not to, say, the location of our cat.

There seems to be, to the best of my knowledge, a yet unnoticed principle of "smallest possible disruption"[21] of the CP at work here. As a first approximation to its formulation, it seems that the principle of smallest possible disruption warns S to limit his or her violation of the CP to the smallest possible conversational unit (one utterance, one conversational turn, one speech exchange), and to try to link the entire CP-violating unit to the rest of the interaction, for example by finding a certain appropriateness to the CP-violating unit.

Thus, in example (17) above, H, upon noticing the disruption of the CP, does not withdraw from the conversation (which would be a safe move, since his or her interlocutor has just given manifest proof of being untrustworthy), but assumes that the violation of the CP is the smallest possible, and, therefore, that the violation must somehow refer to the context, and be meaningful. Let us note that in principle, one might say

(18)   What nice weather.

with an ironical tone while it is raining, and upon the hearer's interpretation of utterance (18) as ironical say something along the lines of (19):

(19)   I was just kidding, as a matter of fact I love rain.

In other words, here S would be deceiving H about his or her intention to be ironical. There is no *a priori* reason for limiting the violation of the CP to the smallest possible context, except for the desire of the speakers to facilitate communication even when a violation is present or necessary. This means that there is another, broader communicative principle, that tolerates violations as long as they are kept as limited as possible. This issue is further developed in Attardo (in press).[22]

Grice (1989) remarked that irony was problematic in a straightforward implicational framework because "irony is intimately connected with the expression of a feeling, attitude, or evaluation" (p. 53). On the basis of the principle stated above, it is now easy to see how the expression of a speaker attitude towards the ironical referent would fit the descriptive framework, since the ironical utterance would be interpreted as referring, cooperatively, to some element of the context. It is necessary, however, to further specify the cooperative nature of the inferential process that determines the value of the irony. As we have seen, Grice himself realized that his original account left a significant gap in the description of irony, namely, that irony points to an evaluative aspect of S's intention (or intended meaning). I am here suggesting that two factors direct the inferential processing of the value of the irony:

1. The maxim of relevance.
2. The antiphrastic/antonymic assumption of irony (cf. Giora's "negation").

In other words, after having recognized (a part of) a text as ironical, H assumes that the maxim of relevance holds and that the relevance of the irony lies in the direction of an antiphrastic meaning (i.e., in the direction of the opposite of what S is saying) with a special emphasis on S's value judgments. Berrendonner (1981, p. 183) argued that an utterance can be used ironically only if it has an "argumentative value" (*valeur argumentative*), i.e., it can be seen as part of an axiological and/or teleological system from which it acquires its value. In other words, someone is trying to do something with the utterance, such as convince someone or argue for something; see also Braester (1992, pp. 84–85).

A Contextual-Appropriateness Theory of Irony

We have seen that irony is non-cooperative at first reading. In what respect does irony violate CP at that first moment? This is an interesting issue, since every ironical utterance seems to be literally false and/or not appropriate to its context. Let us consider a few examples, starting with the standard Gricean violation of quality.

(20) I love children so.

If one says "I love children so" while, in fact, disliking them, clearly, one is technically lying, but one's tone of voice or other signals may make it clear that one is deliberately and conspicuously violating the maxim of quality, and signaling to the hearer(s). Then one is not "really" lying (since one wants to be "outguessed"), but rather being ironical. This type of example can be readily explained as an implicature. Let us turn now to examples that would be problematic for a straightforward Gricean model.

(21)   This is the happiest night of my life (uttered during the middle of the day).

Katz and Fodor's (1963, reprinted in Rosenberg & Travis, 1971) famous example in (21)—which may well be the only well-known example of the seriously under-explored category of appropriateness[23]— is neither true or false (hence, it does not violate quality), when pronounced in daylight, but it is inappropriate, i.e., it violates the rules that determine the deictic anchoring of discourse in reality. In the appropriate context, (21) could also be ironical (if for instance pronounced in the early morning by a speaker well-known for his or her late-rising habit). Or consider the following situation:

(22)   Two farmers in a drought-stricken area are talking and farmer A says the following: "Don"t you just love a nice spring rain?"

While probably literally true (farmer A and B may like spring rains) and not (necessarily) a mention or an echo of another utterance, the utterance is contextually inappropriate because it is not raining.

The earlier example (17) uttered while it is raining, clearly belongs to the inappropriateness category of irony as well, but unlike (21), it also involves a literal non-truth. In other words, appropriateness and several other conditions and maxims can be violated in an ironic utterance, just as the violation of more than one maxim at a time in a joke is a common phenomenon (see Attardo, 1993, and references therein).

What examples (17), (21), and (22) have in common is that they would fail to be identified as ironical by a Gricean account of irony (they fail to violate a maxim); however, they all entail an inappropriate utterance, given the context in which they occur. Violation of a maxim, needless to say, creates an inappropriate utterance. Therefore, all examples of irony accounted for by implicature can be accounted for as inappropriate utterances as well. Consider again (20) above: if one does not like children, then it is inappropriate to say that one does.

It is possible to extrapolate these observations and define as ironical an utterance that, while maintaining relevance,[24] explicitly or implicitly violates the conditions for contextual appropriateness, either deictically or more broadly in terms of the knowledge by the participants of the opinions and belief systems of the speakers (see Searle, 1979, p. 113, for a brief mention of an account of irony in terms of inappropriateness).

Let us note also that we are introducing here an interesting exception to CP, since we are drawing an inference on the basis of a rule not included in it: "be contextually appropriate" (which is not the same as being relevant). We will return to the issue of the relationship between relevance and appropriateness in section 5.4. The most obvious consequence is that we are hereby extending Grice's CP.

In light of the previous discussion, we can state the theory of irony that we are proposing as follows: an utterance u is ironical if

1. u is contextually inappropriate.
2. u is (at the same time) relevant.
3. u is construed as having been uttered intentionally and with awareness of the contextual inappropriateness by S.
4. S intends that (part of) his or her audience recognizes points 1 to 3.
5. Unless H construes u as being unintentional irony, in which case 3 to 4 do not apply.

Usually, irony is used to express an evaluative judgment about a given event/ situation which is commonly, but not exclusively, negative.

I believe that most of the aspects of this proposal are fairly obvious (at least to those with some familiarity with Gricean pragmatics). Some theoretical issues are dealt with in more detail below, but a few relatively minor points are better addressed immediately. The proviso on point (4) that at least part of the audience recognizes the ironical intent of S, is meant to account for a situation in which, as Clark and Carlson (1982) pointed out, S addresses two different audiences at the same time, one who is essentially the "butt" of the irony and another audience who is "in" to the ironical intent and appreciates the irony (or at least appreciates the fact that S intends to be ironical; cf. Schaffer, 1982, p. 8). Consider for example, the situation in which a child is pestering his or her parents for ice cream and S, one of the parents, says to him or her

(23)   Are you sure you want ice cream?

intending the other parent to understand the ironical intent, but clearly aware that this will be lost on the child. Point (3) is thus meant to remind the reader of Grice's reflexive intention.

The following questions need now to be addressed:

- How is "appropriateness" defined, and is it necessary to introduce such a new concept? Couldn't we do just with Grice's four maxims, or Sperber and Wilson's principle of relevance? Is the role of appropriateness the same as that of "felicity conditions" for speech acts? Should/could appropriateness be replaced by the concept of graded salience (see section 2.3)?
- Does the proposed theory account for all the data and the speakers' intuitions about the phenomenon?

Appropriateness

Consider the following operational definition of appropriateness: an utterance u is contextually appropriate if all presuppositions of u are identical to or compatible with all the presuppositions of the context C in which u is uttered (cf. the notion of "common ground;" Clark, 1996), except for any feature explicitly thematized and denied in u.[25]

From this definition it follows that appropriateness is truth-sensitive, since if we change the truth-value of a proposition presupposed by an utterance, the utterance's appropriateness may change:

(24)   John should leave the room.
(25)   John is in the room.

The utterance in (24) presupposes (25). If (25) is false, then (24) becomes inappropriate.

Relevance, on the other hand, is not truth-sensitive. This is clearly established by Sperber and Wilson: "Our definition of the relevance of an assumption in a context takes no account of the objective truth or falsity of the assumption itself" (p. 263)[26]

Consider the sentence in (26), uttered as the answer to the question in (27):

(26)   The cat is on the mat.
(27)   Where is the cat?

Given a non-idiosyncratic context, we can readily assume that the sentence is a relevant answer to the question. Suppose now that we go to the next room and discover that the cat is in fact not on the mat; then (26) is false and hence the answer was false. This does not alter its relevance to (27). Hence the claim that relevance and truth are independent. Thus, lies can go undetected, as they are relevant but false (misleading) accounts of the state of affairs.[27]

On the other hand, a false utterance may be inappropriate because of its false-hood:

(28)   Father: "Did you eat the chocolate?"
         Daughter: "No" (her mouth is covered with chocolate).

In this example, which I collected personally during extensive fieldwork, the daughter's utterance is clearly inappropriate, because the factual evidence of the chocolate smears on her face belies her statement. Note that the daughter's utterance in (28) is inappropriate both as an (inept) lie (since H will inevitably fail to be misled, at least in face-to-face communication) and as a truthful statement (since the statement is contradicted by ostensive evidence). Note that as either speech act, the utterance would be relevant. Relevance and appropriateness are thus not coextensive, since relevance is truth-insensitive and appropriateness is truth-sensitive.

Katz and Fodor (1963, reprinted in Rosenberg & Travis, 1971) called example (21) a "token-oddity" because the presuppositions do not match the context ("setting") in which the sentence is uttered (daylight). The question to be asked in this context is as follows: is the sentence relevant? It may be; suppose the sentence is the answer to the question, "How are you feeling?" Although clearly inappropriate to the context, the sentence is relevant and would count as an answer. Better still, consider the following inappropriate question:

(29)   How is this night treating you? (Uttered in daylight.)

Here (21) is perfectly relevant, although still entirely inappropriate. Incidentally, I will readily admit that most frequently, the relevance of a sentence and its appropriateness go hand in hand, since saying something that is inappropriate will tend to render it irrelevant as well.

Cf. also Sperber and Wilson's (1986) example of Mary telling Peter, an Iris Murdoch fan, that her latest book is at the bookstore, while Peter already knows that. Sperber and Wilson commented as follows: "It may turn out that Peter already has this information in which case [it] will be irrelevant to him. However, it would still have been perfectly appropriate ... [for Mary to say that]" (p. 160).

Is Appropriateness Necessary?

Let us begin with the easy part of this question: since appropriateness has been shown not to be coextensive with relevance, it follows that both Gricean pragmatics and Relevance Theory would require the introduction of the concept.

The situation is more complex with regard to speech act theory, and in particular in relation to the concept of "felicity conditions." As is well known, the latter were introduced by Austin (1962) to account for the fact that some performatives may be performed "unhappily." Austin listed several such conditions, but we need focus only on the second sub-type of the first case: "the particular persons and circumstances in a given case must be appropriate for the invocation of the particular procedure invoked" (p. 15). An example of this "misfire" would be the performance of a wedding ceremony when one or both of the couple is already married, or the performance of the ceremony at sea by someone else other than the captain (p. 16). Other examples discussed by Austin are the naming of a ship by someone not entitled to do so, and the baptism of penguins by a saint (pp. 23–24).

Clearly, the notion of inappropriateness invoked above and Austin's (1962) use of the term are quite close, the biggest difference being that Austin's discussion, at this point in the text, is limited to performatives, while inappropriateness has been introduced as applying to all utterances. Appropriateness is also defined here much more technically than in Austin's work, but it seems fairly clear that the two concepts overlap significantly.

Returning to the original question, we can conclude that, while there is a significant overlap between appropriateness and one of Austin's (1962) felicity conditions, it is nevertheless necessary to introduce the concept alongside the CP, since the CP is merely a subset of the felicity conditions (and as was shown above, does not cover appropriateness).

Appropriateness and Pragmatic Insincerity/Allusion

Are pragmatic insincerity and appropriateness distinct? Or are they different formulations of the same concept? Since pragmatic insincerity is defined in terms of felicity conditions, it is clear that the discussion above also applies to this case. However, Glucksberg's (1995) emphasis on the allusion to a violated norm needs to be handled separately.

As we have seen, according to Glucksberg (1995), pragmatic insincerity is not a sufficient condition for irony; an allusion to an expectation or norm that has also been violated is necessary. The theory of appropriateness, however, conflates the two violations into one, since a violation of felicity conditions or Gricean maxims may subsist only on the background of societal norms and expectations. Returning to Austin's (1962) example of a saint baptizing penguins, the violation of felicity conditions is clearly dependent on the violation of the norm/expectation that penguins are not baptizable.

Moreover, as seen above, appropriateness includes deictic (in)appropriateness, which would not be subsumed under allusions to cultural norms (except, perhaps, as a norm governing the contextually appropriate, which begs the question).

Appropriateness and the Graded Salience Hypothesis

At first blush, it appears that the graded salience hypothesis (GSH) and appropriateness theory are incompatible: "According to the [GSH] the factor determining initial activation [i.e., the meaning first accessed by S] is neither literality *nor compatibility with context*, but, rather, the salience status of the verbal stimulus" (Giora & Fein; my emphasis). However, if we recall the definition of salience discussed above, it incorporates a metric of "givenness status" in a linguistic co(n)text (Giora, 1997, p. 185). Furthermore, when discussing the similarities between humor and irony, Giora (1995) noted that in both phenomena, "the passage from the least- to the most-informative message is abrupt and surprising" (p. 256).

It seems fairly clear that abrupt and surprising shifts in informativeness and contextual inappropriateness are very closely related concepts. In fact, I would argue that "contextual salience" may be triggered by contextual inappropriateness. From information theory, we know that the most appropriate element is also likely to be the least informative, since it will be the most predictable. The least appropriate element will tend to be the most informative. For example, research in jokes has shown that they tend to end in a punch-line (unexpected/inappropriate element) which is also the rheme of the last sentence of the text, and hence the most informative element (Attardo, Attardo, Baltes, & Petray, 1994).

I would therefore suggest that when we encounter a contextually inappropriate element in the text, that element becomes highly informative and hence salient. Needless to say, other factors may also determine saliency. My interest here is limited to establishing that contextual inappropriateness may trigger salience.

Let me note in passing that the second half of Giora's theory (indirect negation) is subsumed by the definition of inappropriateness: if A is a function which returns a boolean value v ($1 = $ *appropriate,* $0 = $ *inappropriate*) of appropriateness, given an utterance u and a context C

$$A(Cu) = v$$

then it follows that

$$A \left[(\neg\ C(u)) \ v \ (C\ (\neg\ u)) \right] = \neg\ v$$

Or, in other words, the notion of inappropriateness presupposes that of negation and furthermore, since this is achieved by flouting a maxim, it is done indirectly.[28]

Coverage of the Theory

Because of its general Gricean character, the (in)appropriateness theory is at least as powerful as any of the (Neo-) Gricean theories of irony. However, the inappropriateness theory is an expansion of the Gricean approach, and as such it is broader. Trivially, this is so because it encompasses the notion of appropriateness. Much more significantly, appropriateness is explicitly context-based, and as such it can elegantly handle contextual factors. Therefore, the approach proposed in this paper can handle not only all cases of irony derived from the violation of a Gricean maxim, but also those that derive from a violation of appropriateness conditions or felicity conditions; since felicity conditions encompass significantly more ground than the CP, this is a theoretical gain of some significance.

Let us note that the appropriateness theory accounts for Kaufer's (1981) "tension" between S's "subjective attitude" and the expectation sets of the utterance. In particular, it answers his principal objection to pragmatic and logical accounts of irony: "they try to explicate irony primarily through objective properties of ut[t]erances [sic] rather than through the interaction of these with expectation sets of utterances and the subjective attitudes of communicators" (p. 505).

In fact, by calling for relevant inappropriateness, the theory accounts for the *ethos* of irony and addresses Grice's concern that the function of irony is to express an attitude and/or a judgment. The stipulation that the inappropriate utterance must be nonetheless relevant provides an inferential path towards reconstructing S's intention (criticism, derision, etc.).

Furthermore, the inappropriateness theory makes a strong principled stand on the issue of one- vs. two-stage processing of irony, coming down on the side of the two stages. This is probably the most significant aspect of the discussion, although it is overshadowed by the fact that this has been common knowledge for a couple of millennia. Essentially, the neo-Gricean analyses of irony end up confirming the traditional analysis of irony as a trope and the present analysis is no different, in that respect. As far as the order of the processing of the ironical meanings goes, strictly speaking, the inappropriateness theory does not need to choose a given order of processing (literal first, salient first, or contextually imposed first, etc.); it is in principle compatible with any order of processing, provided that a two-stage model is used, which allows for the determination of the inappropriateness of the meaning accessed first. However, the work of Giora and her associates seems to point towards the answer that processing is done in order of salience.

Still, the aspect of the inappropriateness theory which strikes me as most interesting is the fact that it links inappropriateness and violation of the CP to the (perlocutionary) goals of S via the principle of least disruption. By doing so, the pragmatic function(s) of irony follow logically: if S is being inappropriate, he or she must have a goal for doing so, and this goal[29] may be arrived at inferentially via the Principle of Perlocutionary Cooperation (PCP; Attardo, 1997).[30] Therefore, the present treatment of irony may claim to have provided at least a good starting point to answer the vexing question of "why would S use irony?" (on which, see Attardo, in press).

CONSEQUENCES

The previous discussion has brought about a number of interesting conclusions and consequences. These include effects both for the theory of irony and for the CP:

1. The theory of irony.
   * The reconstruction of the intended meaning (value) of the irony is entirely inferential and abductive: it is totally indirect, no aspect of the meaning is given in the text, except the presumption of relevance (and not of quality, manner, or quantity); or, in other words, irony is a purely pragmatic phenomenon.
   * Irony is essentially an inappropriate utterance which is nonetheless relevant to the context.
   * Irony crucially involves a two-stage processing. The order in which the conflicting senses are accessed is (probably) determined by salience.
2. The CP.
   * We need to add a 5th maxim, "be appropriate," since appropriateness is not equal to relevance nor truth.
   * The graded salience specification needs to be added to the maxim of manner.
   * A super-principle of smallest possible disruption of the CP needs to be assumed as operational above and beyond the CP itself.

ENDNOTES

1. S is the speaker. Correspondingly, and for the rest of the article, H is the hearer. Speaker and hearer are here taken as generic terms, standing respectively as the producer of the communicative message and the receiver of the message. No speech-centrism should be read in this choice of terms.
2. It is not clear, however, if Mizzau (1984) does or does not believe that irony can have a positive meaning, as she claims, without explanation, that asteism has "a different function."
3. A broader discussion of Gibbs's critique of the "standard pragmatic model" is to be found in Attardo (in press).
4. Kaufer's (1981) example is the sentence "Johnny was deprived of his spinach last night" where "it is well known that Johnny has a passionate hatred for spinach" (p. 499). The use

of "deprived" presupposes that the patient wants what he or she was deprived of, but this fact is not truth-sensitive.

5. "Relevance" should be taken in Sperber and Wilson's relevance-theoretical sense; Kaufer has "impact," but is quoting from a manuscript of Sperber and Wilson's work.

6. The sentence appeared in a letter to *Time* on May 19, 1980, according to Kaufer (1981, p. 501).

7. The nature of this augmentation need not detain us in this context.

8. Actually, from the notation quoted in the text, merely that they must differ (but this is probably irrelevant).

9. Although Mizzau (1984, p. 15) found an anticipation of the mention theory in the work of Lausberg (1949/1969) who speaks of the use of the words of one's opponent (p. 128).

10. See also Wilson and Sperber (1992), Sperber and Wilson (1998), and the other essays in the symposium on irony, published as Carston and Uchida (1998).

11. Berrendonner (1981, p. 216) argued that irony is self-referential, besides being a mention.

12. It should be noted that Chen (1990, p. 38) directed essentially the same argument *against* the mention theory of irony, noting that the theory fails to explain why the ironist would choose mention and irony (indirectness) to express his or her feelings towards the situation. Needless to say, the irony of this counterattack is not lost to this author.

13. According to Kerbrat-Orecchioni), the extra element present is essentially the semantic opposition between what is said and what is implied, which corresponds to the traditional treatment of irony. Kerbrat-Orecchioni concluded that therefore the mention theory and the traditional approach are not incompatible. This author's conclusion is much stronger.

14. It should be noted that these extra steps contrast with mention theory's claim of being a "direct access" theory. See section 4.4.1 for a fuller discussion of why mention is necessarily a two-step theory.

15. Further discussion of mention theory can be found in Chen (1990, pp. 68–73) and Barbe (1995, pp. 44–48). An interesting issue, brought up by Glucksberg (1995: 54), is that the mention theory fails to recognize both the allusion to a violated norm and the violation of a felicity condition for the speech act performed in the utterance (cf. section 3). Further discussion of this issue is found in section 5.4.

16. I am standardizing the notation to the use adopted in this article, although I retain the numbering of Ss and Hs by primes.

17. Consider Sperber and Wilson (1986: 109 and passim), who list the following "contextual effects," besides inferences: adding, deleting, reinforcing, and weakening of assumptions. As we can see, there is no reinterpretation option available. I owe this point to Rachel Giora (personal communication).

18. The same argument can be made for humorous texts, such as jokes: the incompatible meanings (scripts) must coexist in the text (however playfully) if their opposition is to be ascertained. See Attardo (1994) for discussion.

19. Note that I deliberately leave the interpretation of the utterance open, to stress the fact that at this first stage there is no appropriate interpretation at all. It is only at the second stage, that is *after* a failure to accommodate the utterance (and its presuppositions) to the common ground, that a suitable interpretation will be generated out of contextual pressure and cooperative/relevance assumptions. Note also that a recourse to the relevance theoretical principle is *a priori* ruled out, since the speaker has clearly just violated it and hence the presumption of relevance is no longer available to generate implicatures. Admitting the violation of the CP, backtracking, and reinterpretation nullifies the claimed differences between mention theory and the Gricean interpretations. See, however, Curcó (1995, 1996) and Yus Ramos (1998) for two-stages relevance theoretic accounts of humor.

20. Actually, as will appear below, this is strictly not true, but as a beginning this wording will do.

21. Parts of this section were originally developed jointly with Victor Raskin as an appendix to Raskin and Attardo (1994). Editorial reasons led to the elimination of the discussion of irony from that paper. The text included in this section has been heavily revised, but I would like to acknowledge Raskin's contribution.

22. An interesting issue, brought to my attention by Rachel Giora, is the problem of how the principle of least disruption can be reconciled with entire texts, such as Swift's *A Modest Proposal,* which violate the CP. At one level, the issue is fairly simple: by advocating a practice the author finds abhorrent (cannibalism), he draws attention on the conditions of the Irish poor (via relevance); thus the text behaves according to the second part of the principle of least disruption. However, it remains that the text as a whole violates the CP in that it seems to fly in the face of the first requirement of the principle of least disruption. Possibly, texts such as this (and other) pamphlet(s) are seen as one utterance or conversational turn (however large). It is obvious that further work is needed here.

23. The notion of appropriateness explored in the text differs significantly from the one used incidentally in De Beaugrande and Dressler (1981), where it is only a stylistic element.

24. Note that as per Attardo's (1997) two-stage approach to implicatures, it is perfectly acceptable for S to violate the maxim of relevance in the first stage and then follow it in the second. Thus, the definition in the text should be understood as "maintaining relevance' in the second stage of processing.

25. The last clause is necessary to handle certain more or less metalinguistic utterances of the type "This table is not a Duncan Phyfe," which presuppose (roughly) that H has the belief that the table is a Duncan Phyfe.

26. Sperber and Wilson (pp. 263–266) went on to revise the original definition of relevance (by taking into account the truthfulness of utterances), when they recognized that Ss may be more interested in true statements than false ones. This idea is then incorporated in the revised definition of relevance under the label of "positive cognitive effect," i.e., "a cognitive effect that contributes positively to the fulfillment of cognitive functions or goals" (p. 265). This strikes me as both too little and too late: too little because it does not recognize the independence of the truthfulness of the utterance as a separate pragmatic principle, which needs to be assumed if communication is to take place; too late, because the essentially purposeful, goal-oriented nature of communication (e.g., Attardo, 1997) fails to be recognized and made a central tenet of the theory. Purposeful communication is invoked only to rescue the faltering definition of relevance.

27. In fact, the picture about lies is a lot more complex, but we simplify here for the sake of the argument; see Winner and Leekam (1991) and Winner and Gardner (1993) on the differences in understanding irony and lies. By and large, irony is much harder to understand than lies. Irony is also harder to understand than metaphor; see Winner (1988).

28. An interesting issue, discussed in some detail in Attardo (1997) in the context of humor, is related to the nature of the negative relationship between the two senses of the irony/humor. In Attardo, I showed how the concepts of salience and accessibility may be a good starting point to account for the intuitively richer notion of "negation" used in humor and irony. I believe that an account of antonymy, antiphrasis, etc., based on the concept of "conceptual axis" (p. 400) may in fact be necessary to account for these issues. The conceptual axis is, roughly speaking, what the words "married" and "unmarried" have in common. The negation of "married" is *not* "green," as would be acceptable to a purely set-theoretic account of negation. For a treatment of antonymy, contrast, etc., see Lyons (1977, pp. 270–290).

29. One of the anonymous reviewers noted (somewhat ironically?) that he or she found the claim "stunning." that the Principle of Perlocutionary Cooperation (PCP) can infer a specific goal. Obviously it all depends on what we mean by "specific." Clearly, the PCP cannot predict, outside of a given context, what the individual instance of irony is intended to achieve. However, in context, the PCP will guide S (and especially H) along their inferen-

tial paths towards a "best available educated guess" as to what that specific instance of irony's specific goal is.

30. It should be noted that I have deliberately avoided, as much as possible, wording the discussion of the inappropriateness theory in terms of the Principle of Perlocutionary Cooperation in order to make this treatment self-contained. It is a relatively trivial task to rephrase the above discussion in terms of locutionary and perlocutionary cooperation.

ACKNOWLEDGMENTS

I would like to thank Rachel Giora, Katherina Barbe, Victor Raskin, Cameron Shelley, and two anonymous referees for their help and suggestions. Needless to say, all errors are mine.

REFERENCES

Amante, D. J. (1981). The theory of ironic speech acts. *Poetics Today, 2,* 77–96.

Attardo, S. (1993). Violation of conversational maxims and cooperation: The case of jokes. *Journal of Pragmatics, 19,* 537–558.

Attardo, S. (1994). *Linguistic theory of humor.* Berlin, Germany: Mouton De Gruyter.

Attardo, S. (1997). The semantic foundations of cognitive theories of humor. *HUMOR: International Journal of Humor Research, 10,* 395–420.

Attardo, S. (in press). *Theoretical pragmatics.*

Attardo, S., Attardo, D. H., Baltes, P., & Petray, M. J. (1994). The linear organization of jokes: Analysis of two thousand texts. *HUMOR: International Journal of Humor Research, 7,* 27–54.

Austin, J. L. (1962). *How to do things with words.* Oxford, UK: Oxford University Press.

Barbe, K. (1995). *Irony in context.* Amsterdam: Benjamins.

Berrendonner, A. (1981). Éléments de pragmatique linguistique. Paris: Les éditions de minuit.

Booth, W. C. (1974). *A rhetoric of irony.* Chicago: University of Chicago Press.

Braester, M. (1992). Du "signe ironique" à l'énoncé ironique]. *Semiotica, 92,* 75–86.

Brown, P., & Levinson, S. C. (1978). *Politeness: Some universals in language usage* (2nd ed.). Cambridge, England: Cambridge University Press.

Brown, R. L. J. (1980). The pragmatics of verbal irony. In R. W. Shuy & A. Shnukal (Eds.), *Language use and the uses of language* (pp. 111–127). Washington, DC: Georgetown University Press.

Carston, R. (1981). Irony and parody and the use–mention distinction. *The Nottingham Linguistic Circular, 10,* 24–35.

Carston, R., & Uchida, S. (1998). *Relevance theory: Applications and implications.* Amsterdam: Benjamins.

Chen, R. (1990). *Verbal irony as implicature.* Unpublished doctoral dissertation, Ball State University, Muncie, IN.

Clark, H. H. (1996). *Using language.* Cambridge, England: Cambridge University Press.

Clark, H. H., & Carlson, T. B. (1982). Hearers and speech acts. *Language, 58,* 332–373.

Clark, H. H., & Gerrig, R. J. (1984). On the pretense of irony. *Journal of Experimental Psychology: General, 113,* 121–126.

Curcó, C. (1995). Some observations on the pragmatics of humorous interpretations: A relevance theoretic approach. UCL Working papers in Linguistics, 7, 27–47.

Curcó, C. (1996). The implicit expression of attitudes, mutual manifestness, and verbal humor. UCL Working papers in *Linguistics, 8,* 89–99.

Cutler, A. (1974). On saying what you mean without meaning what you say. In M. W. LaGaly, R. A. Fox, & A. Bruck (Eds.), *Papers from the Tenth Regional Meeting, Chicago Linguistic Society* (pp. 117–127). Chicago: Chicago Linguistic Society.

De Beaugrande, R-A., & Dressier, W. U. (1981). *Introduction to text linguistics.* London: Longman.

Dews, S., & Winner, E. (1995). Muting the meaning: A social function of irony. *Metaphor and Symbolic Activity, 10,* 3–19.

Fontanier, P. (1977/1830). *Les figures du discours.* Paris: Flammarion.

Gibbs, R. W. (1986). On the psycholinguistics of sarcasm. *Journal of Experimental Psychology: General, 115,* 3–15.

Gibbs, R. W. (1994). *The poetics of mind.* Cambridge, England: Cambridge University Press.

Gibbs, R. W., & O' Brien, J. E. (1991). Psychological aspects of irony understanding. *Journal of Pragmatics, 16,* 523–530.

Gibbs, R. W., O'Brien, J. E., & Doolittle, S. (1995). Inferring meanings that are not intended: Speakers' intentions and irony comprehension. *Discourse Processes, 20,* 187–203.

Giora, R. (1995). On irony and negation. *Discourse Processes, 19,* 239–264.

Giora, R. (1997). Understanding figurative and literal language: The graded salience hypothesis. *Cognitive Linguistics, 7,* 183–206.

Giora, R. (2000). Irony. In J. Verschueren, J.-O. Östman, J. Blommaert, & C. Bulcaen (Eds.), *Handbook of pragmatics.* Amsterdam, Netherlands: Benjamins.

Giora, R., & Fein, O. (1999). Irony: Context and salience. *Metaphor and Symbol, 14,* 241–257.

Giora, R., & Fein, O. (1999). Irony comprehension: The graded salience hypothesis. - *HUMOR: International Journal of Humor Research, 12,* 425–436.

Giora, R., & Fein, O., & Schwartz, T. (1998). Irony: Graded salience and indirect negation. *Metaphor and Symbol, 13,* 83–101.

Glucksberg, S. (1995). Commentary on nonliteral language: Processing and use. *Metaphor and Symbolic Activity, 10,* 47–57.

Grice, H. P. (1975). Logic and conversation. In P. Cole & J. L. Morgan (Eds.), *Speech acts* (Vol. 3, pp. 41–58). New York: Academic.

Grice, H. P. (1978). Further notes on logic and conversation. In P. Cole (Ed.), *Pragmatics* (Vol. 9, pp. 113–127). New York: Academic.

Grice, H. P. (1989). *Studies in the way of words.* Cambridge, MA: Harvard University Press.

Haiman, J. (1989). Alienation in grammar. *Studies in Language, 13,* 129–170.

Haiman, J. (1990). Sarcasm as theater. *Cognitive Linguistics, 1,* 181–205.

Haiman, J. (1998). *Talk is cheap: Sarcasm, alienation, and the evolution of language.* Oxford, UK: Oxford University Press.

Haverkate, H. (1990). A speech act analysis of irony. *Journal of Pragmatics, 14,* 77–109.

Holdcroft, D. (1983). Irony as a trope, and irony as discourse. *Poetics Today, 4,* 493–511.

Horn, L. R. (1989). *A natural history of negation.* Chicago: Chicago University Press.

Jorgensen, J., Miller, G. A., & Sperber, D. (1984). Test of the mention theory of irony. *Journal of Experimental Psychology: General, 113,* 112–120.

Kaufer, D. (1981). Understanding ironic communication. *Journal of Pragmatics, 5,* 495–510.

Kerbrat-Orecchioni, C. (1976). Problèmes de l'ironie. *Linguistique et sémiologie, 2,* 10–47.

Kerbrat-Orecchioni, C. (1980). L'ironie comme trope. *Poétique, 41,* 108–127.

Kreuz, R. J., & Glucksberg, S. (1989). How to be sarcastic: The echoic reminder theory of verbal irony. *Journal of Experimental Psychology: General, 118,* 374–386.

Kreuz, R. J., & Roberts, R. M. (1993). On satire and parody: The importance of being ironic. *Metaphor and Symbolic Activity, 8,* 97–109.

Kreuz, R. J., & Roberts, R. M. (1995). Two cues for verbal irony: Hyperbole and the ironic tone of voice. *Metaphor and Symbolic Activity, 10,* 21–31.

Lausberg, H. (1969). *Elemente der literarischen rhetorik* [Elements of Literary Rhetoric] (L. R. Santini, Trans.). München, Germany: Hueber. (Original work published 1949)

Levin, S. R. (1982). Are figures of thought figures of speech? In H. Byrnes (Ed.), *Contemporary perceptions of language: Interdisciplinary dimensions* (pp. 112–123). Washington, DC: Georgetown University Press.

Levinson, S. C. (1983). *Pragmatics.* New York: Cambridge University Press.

Littman, D. C., & Mey, J. L. (1991). The nature of irony: Toward a computational model of irony. *Journal of Pragmatics, 15,* 131–151.

Lucariello, J. (1994). Situational irony. *Journal of Experimental Psychology: General, 113,* 112–120.

Lyons, J. (1977). *Semantics.* Cambridge, England: Cambridge University Press.

Mao, L. R. (1991). *Pragmatic universals and their implications.* Unpublished doctoral dissertation, University of Minnesota.

McDonald, S. (1992). Differential pragmatic language loss after closed head injury: Ability to comprehend conversational implicature. *Applied Psycholinguistics, 13,* 295–312.

Mizzau, M. (1984). *L'ironia: La contraddizione consentita.* Milan: Feltrinelli.

Muecke, D. C. (1969). *The compass of irony.* London: Methuen.

Muecke, D. C. (1970). *Irony.* London: Methuen.

Muecke, D. C. (1973). The communication of verbal irony. *Journal of Literary Semantics, 2,* 35–42.

Muecke, D. C. (1978a). Irony markers. *Poetics, 7,* 363–375.

Muecke, D. C. (1978b). Analyses de l'ironie. *Poétique, 36,* 478–494.

Myers Roy, A. (1977). Towards a definition of irony. In R. W. Fasold & R. Shuy (Eds.), *Studies in language variation* (pp. 171–183). Washington, DC: Georgetown University Press.

Myers Roy, A. (1981). The function of irony in discourse. *Text, 1,* 407–423.

Raskin, V., & Attardo, S. (1994). Non-literalness and non-bona-fide in language: An approach to formal and computational treatments of humor. *Pragmatics and Cognition, 2,* 31–69.

Rosenberg, J. F., & Travis, C. (Eds.). (1971). *Readings in the philosophy of language.* Englewood Cliffs, NJ: Prentice Hall. (Reprinted from *Language, 31,* 170–210, by J. J. Katz & J. A. Fodor, 1963)

Rundquist, S. M. (1991). Flouting Grice's maxims: A study of gender-differentiated speech. Unpublished doctoral dissertation, University of Minnesota.

Schaffer, Rachel R. (1982). *Vocal clues for irony in English.* Unpublished Ph.D. dissertation, Ohio State University.

Searle, J. R. (1979). *Expression and meaning: Studies in the theory of speech acts.* Cambridge, England: Cambridge University Press.

Shelley, C. (in press). The bicoherence theory of situational irony. *Cognitive Science, 25,* 775–818.

Sperber, D. (1984). Verbal irony: Pretense or echoic mention? *Journal of Experimental Psychology: General, 113,* 130–136.

Sperber, D., & Wilson, D. (1981). Irony and the use-mention distinction. In P. Cole (Ed.), *Radical pragmatics* (pp. 295–318). New York: Academic.

Sperber, D., & Wilson, D. (1986). *Relevance: Communication and cognition.* Cambridge, MA: Harvard University Press.

Sperber, D., & Wilson, D. (1998). Irony and relevance: A reply to Seto, Hamamoto and Yamanashi. In R. Carston & S. Uchida (Eds.), *Relevance theory: Applications and implications* (pp. 283–293). Amsterdam: Benjamins.

Tanaka, R. (1973). The concept of irony: Theory and practice. *Journal of Literary Semantics, 2,* 43–56.

Williams, J. P. (1984). Does mention (or pretense) exhaust the concept of irony? *Journal of Experimental Psychology: General, 113,* 127–129.

Wilson, D., & Sperber, D. (1992). On verbal irony. *Lingua, 87,* 53–76.

Winner, E. (1988). *The points of words: Children's understanding of metaphor and irony.* Cambridge, MA: Harvard University Press.

Winner, E., & Gardner, H. (1993). Metaphor and irony: Two levels of understanding. In A. Ortony (Ed.), *Metaphor and thought* (2nd ed., pp. 425–443). Cambridge, England: Cambridge University Press.

Winner, E., & Leekam, S. (1991). Distinguishing irony from deception: Understanding the speaker's second-order intention. *The British Journal of Developmental Psychology, 9,* 257–270.

Yus Ramos, F. (1998). A decade of relevance theory. *Journal of Pragmatics, 30,* 305–345.

PART III

CONTEXT
IN IRONY COMPREHENSION

CHAPTER 7

On the Psycholinguistics of Sarcasm

Raymond W. Gibbs, Jr.
University of California, Santa Cruz

Results are reported of 6 experiments in which comprehension and memory for sarcastic statements in conversation are examined. Data from 3 reading-time studies indicate that people do not need to first process the literal meanings of sarcastic expressions, such as "You're a fine friend" (meaning "You're a bad friend"), before deriving their nonliteral, sarcastic interpretations. Subjects also comprehended instances of sarcasm based on an explicit echoic mention of some belief, societal norm, or previously stated opinion faster than they did instances in which the echo was only implicit. Three additional experiments examining memory for sarcasm showed that sarcasm was remembered much better than literal uses of the same expressions of nonsarcastic equivalents. Moreover, subjects recalled sarcasm that explicitly echoed a previously mentioned belief or societal norm more often that they remembered sarcasm that did not involve some explicit echo. Together, these experiments demonstrated that ease of processing and memory for sarcastic utterances depends crucially on how explicitly a speaker's statement echoes either the addressee or some other source's putative beliefs, opinions, or previous statement.

The purpose of this article is to examine how people comprehend and remember sarcastic utterances in conversation, such as "You're a fine friend," meaning "You are a bad friend;" or "He's a real genius," meaning "He's not very smart." It is difficult to define sarcasm, particularly because it is closely related to the concept of irony. The *Oxford English Dictionary* says that ironic utterances are generally thought to include "the use of words to express something other than and especially the opposite of the literal meaning of a sentence," whereas sarcasm depends for its effect on "bitter, caustic, and other ironic language that is usually directed against an individual." Thus, if a speaker says "You're a fine friend" to someone who has injured the speaker in some way, the utterance is sarcastic. But, if a speaker says "They tell me you're a slow runner" to someone who has just won a marathon race,

This chapter was previously published as "On the psycholinguistics of sarcasm" (R. W. Gibbs) in the *Journal of Experimental Psychology: General, 115,* 3–15. Copyright © [1986] by the American Psychological Association. Reprinted with permission.

the utterance is seen as ironic. Even though it is possible to make sarcastic remarks without being ironic, most sarcasm uses irony to get its bitter, caustic effect (see Fowler, 1965). Later in the article, I will present evidence that people often view ironic utterances as being sarcastic. The concern in this article is primarily on the psycholinguistics of sarcasm. However, given that sarcasm and irony are closely related, much of the following will include discussion of irony. My overall goal is to show that sarcastic utterances have special pragmatic properties, which affect how they are understood and remembered.

UNDERSTANDING SARCASM

There has been little experimental research in psychology investigating the underlying mechanisms used in understanding sarcastic utterances. Most of the interest in sarcasm and irony comes from linguistic, philosophical, and literary theorists, who have been primarily concerned with a rationalistic account of the factors involved in understanding sarcasm. The most traditional view, which I call the *Standard Pragmatic Model,* proposes that a hearer must first analyze an expression's complete literal interpretation before deriving its nonliteral, sarcastic meaning (Cutler, 1976; Grice, 1975, 1978; Searle, 1979a), similar to the way indirect requests, idioms, and metaphorical utterances are interpreted (see Bach & Harnish, 1979; Clark & Lucy, 1975; Gordon & Lakoff, 1971; Grice, 1975; Searle, 1975, 1979a). Specifically, these proposals have suggested that a sarcastic utterance, such as "You are a fine friend" (meaning "You are a bad friend"), is interpreted in three steps. A person must (a) compute the utterance's context-independent, literal meaning; (b) decide whether the literal meaning is the speaker's intended meaning; and (c) if the literal interpretation is inappropriate, compute the nonliteral meaning by assuming the opposite of the literal interpretation.

This Standard Pragmatic Model is suspect on a number of grounds. First, there is good evidence to suggest that people do not always analyze the literal meanings of other nonliteral expressions before their conveyed meanings are determined. If they did, then they should take longer to read indirect requests than literal sentences. Yet in earlier work (Gibbs, 1979, 1983a), I demonstrated that people take no longer to process indirect requests like, "Must you open the window?" (meaning "Do not open the window"), presented in story contexts, than to understand the same expressions when their literal interpretations were appropriate to context (meaning "Need you open the window?"). Moreover, subjects took no longer to process indirect requests than to comprehend direct ones (Gibbs, 1979). Taken together, these results suggested that people are able to comprehend indirect requests directly with appropriate context, without first analyzing and rejecting their literal interpretations. I have also shown that people do not analyze the literal meanings of idiomatic expressions like "You can let the cat out of the bag" before understanding their nonliteral, idiomatic interpretations (Gibbs, 1980, in press; and also see Ortony, Reynolds, Schallert, & Antos, 1978; Swinney & Cutler, 1979). It is misleading, then, to suppose in understanding nonliteral language that one type of meaning (literal) is automatically determined before the other (nonliteral; see Glucksberg, Gildea, & Bookin, 1982).

These conclusions suggest that the Standard Pragmatic Model may not be an accurate account of the processes involved in understanding sarcasm. In fact, the model has great difficulty in specifying exactly how hearers arrive at speakers' sarcastic intentions. For example, if you commit a grievous deed toward a good friend and he says to you "Thanks," the Standard Pragmatic Model suggests that taken literally the utterance is grossly inappropriate and you are forced to render it appropriate by determining in what way the sentence and speaker meanings differ. Although the sarcastic interpretation is usually assumed to be the opposite of the literal meaning, in many cases the opposite is not clear. The opposite of your friend's comment would be something like "No thanks" or "It is not the case that I'm thanking you." But this does not capture the true sarcastic intention in using this utterance, namely, "You have done something that I do not appreciate." The sarcastic meaning of "Thanks" denies one of this utterance's felicity, not truth, conditions: It is infelicitous to thank someone who deserves ingratitude. However, felicity conditions are pragmatically and not logically related to the use of a sarcastic utterance (cf. Kaufer, 1981).

Furthermore, in many cases, speakers actually do mean what they literally say but are still speaking sarcastically (Sperber & Wilson, 1981). For example, a driver can say to a passenger "I love people who signal," when another car has just cut in front without signaling and mean this sarcastically even though the statement is literally true.

These observations indicate that it is beyond the scope of the Standard Pragmatic Model to specify exactly how people actually comprehend sarcasm. In fact, this model is unable to explain the experimental results in Experiments 1, 2, and 3, which follow. There is, however, another theory that may be better able to capture what goes on psychologically in understanding sarcasm; namely the *Echoic Mention Theory* (Jorgensen, Miller, & Sperber, 1984; Sperber & Wilson, 1981; Wilson & Sperber, 1981). This theory proposes that irony involves the distinction between use and mention, rather than the distinction between literal and nonliteral meaning. The sentence "Please be quiet," for example, can be *used* to tell people to be quiet, but it is only *mentioned* in "The sign says '*Please be quiet.*'" This distinction is useful because the truth value of the mentioned expression is irrelevant to the truth of the proposition it specifies.

According to the Echoic Mention Theory, there is no nonliteral proposition that hearers must substitute for the literal proposition. Rather, the listener is *reminded* echoically of some familiar proposition (whose truth value is irrelevant) and of the speaker's attitude toward it. There are many different types and degrees of echoic mention, some of these are immediate echoes, and others are delayed; some have their sources in actual utterances, others in thoughts or opinions; some have real sources, others have imagined ones; some are traceable back to particular individuals, whereas others have a vague origin (Sperber & Wilson, 1981).

Consider this example: Al says to Bob, "You're a big help," when Bob has not assisted Al in doing some task. The sarcasm comes from the fact that Al has echoed some previously mentioned statement or belief, or perhaps some unspoken agreement between Al and Bob. That is, Bob might have earlier offered to help Al or it might be Bob's job to do so. When Al says, "You're a big help," he is in a sense quoting this previous statement or verbalizing a mutually shared belief that Bob is supposed to help Al as part of his job.

Jorgensen et al. (1984) have recently reported some preliminary empirical support for this approach to irony. They had subjects read short descriptions of episodes ending with a sentence that was intended as ironic. Some of the stories' final utterances echoed an earlier statement in the story; others did not. Subjects were asked to answer questions designed to test whether they perceived the intended, ironic meanings of the final utterances. The results showed that subjects generally viewed final utterances that contained explicit echoes as being ironic more often than they did final utterances with no echoed antecedents. Jorgensen et al. suggested that these data support the claim that people do not generally perceive utterances as ironic unless they echo previously mentioned beliefs, attitudes, or opinions.

Most of the hypotheses tested in the following experiments were derivative of either the Standard Pragmatic Model or the Echoic Mention Theory. My purpose was to investigate some of the factors that relate to how people interpret the meanings of sarcastic utterances. The first three experiments assessed the speed with which people comprehended sarcastic statements in written descriptions of conversations. Although this reading-time paradigm has been a valuable tool for testing various theories of sentence processing (see Gibbs, 1979, 1980), it is not necessarily sensitive to all of the on-line processes operating in language comprehension. Consequently, the results of the following studies should not be viewed as providing detailed constraints on a theory of sarcastic language comprehension. The results should, nonetheless, illustrate how different pragmatic conditions influence the interpretation of sarcastic utterances.

EXPERIMENT I

The purpose of Experiment 1 was to determine whether sarcastic utterances like, "You are a fine friend" (meaning "You are a bad friend") were more difficult to process than either literal uses of the same expressions or nonsarcastic remarks. Subjects read stories that ended in a sentence that was an evaluative remark. Half of the time the stories were negative evaluations; half of the time they were positive ones. For the negative stories, the final sentence was either a sarcastic remark like, "You are a fine friend," or a nonsarcastic remark like, "You are a bad friend." For the positive contexts, the final sentences were either literal uses of sarcastic statements such as, "You are a fine friend," or simple acknowledgements such as, "You are a good friend" After reading the last line of each story, subjects made a paraphrase judgment for the final sentence. The time it took subjects to read the last lines and to make the paraphrase judgments was recorded.

The results of this study should confirm the findings of earlier research that with appropriate context, nonliteral expressions do not necessarily take longer to process than literal utterances. If subjects actually take longer to read and make paraphrase judgments for sarcastic remarks than they do for either nonsarcastic targets or literal utterances, these results would support the predictions of the Standard Pragmatic Model. Such findings would also suggest, in terms of the Echoic Mention Theory, that locating the source of a speaker's echo in using sarcasm makes sarcastic expressions more difficult to interpret than literal utterances.

Method

Subjects.   Forty undergraduates from the University of California, Santa Cruz, served as subjects to satisfy a course requirement. All were native speakers of English.

Stimuli and Design.   Subjects were assigned to read one of four lists of stories. Each list contained 16 stories, 8 with negative contexts and 8 with positive ones. For the negative contexts, 4 of the stories ended in sarcastic remarks, ("You're a big help"), and 4 ended with nonsarcastic remarks ("You have not helped"). For the positive contexts, 4 stories ended with literal remarks that were identical to the sarcastic remarks used in the negative contexts but this time having literal, positive meanings ("You're a big help"). Four other positive stories ended with remarks that were simple acknowledgments ("Thanks for your help"). If a given story theme (e.g., Help) ended with a sarcastic remark in List A, it ended with a nonsarcastic remark in List B, a literal target in List C, and an acknowledgment in List D. The targets in each of the four lists had the same number of words. Across the four lists, equal numbers of subjects heard the four target types for each of the 16 stories. Table 7.1 presents an example of the positive and negative story contexts and their respective target sentences.

All of the experimental stories were followed by a sentence that was intended to be a true paraphrase of the target sentence. These paraphrases were "literal" translations of the target sentences. Thus, if subjects read a sarcastic target such as "You're a fine friend," they saw a sentence like "You're a bad friend" as its paraphrase. In a separate rating study completed by 16 undergraduate students, all paraphrases were rated as being equally appropriate for their respective targets. The paraphrases were included to ensure that subjects truly understood the meanings of the target sentences in the experimental task.

In addition to these 16 stories, 12 filler stories had target sentences whose paraphrases were false. These stories were not included in the data analysis. Each subject, therefore, saw 28 stories in the session along with 3 practice stories: one with a sarcastic target sentence, one with a literal target sentence, and one story with a false paraphrase. The stories had a mean length of seven lines, target sentences and

TABLE 7.1

Example of Story Contexts and Their Target Sentences for Experiment 1

Negative context

Harry was building an addition to his house. He was working real hard putting in the foundation. His younger brother was supposed to help. But he never showed up. At the end of a long day,December 21, 2006 Harry's brother finally appeared. Harry was a bit upset with him. Harry said to his brother, [Sarcastic target] "You're a big help." [Nonsarcastic target] "You're not helping me."

Positive context

Greg was having trouble with calculus. He had a big exam coming up and he was in trouble. Fortunately, his roommate tutored him on some of the basics. When they were done, Greg felt he'd learned a lot. "Well," he said to his roommate, [Literal target] "You're a big help." [Compliment target] "Thanks for your help."

---

paraphrases averaged a little less than four words in length. For a given story context, all target sentences had the same number of words. Thus, no reading-time difference between target sentence and paraphrase can be attributed to difference in the length of the targets.

A rating study was performed to ensure that the last lines of these stories were interpreted as they were intended to be. Sixteen subjects participated in the study. For each story theme, 4 people saw the version ending with sarcastic remarks, 4 saw nonsarcastic remarks, 4 saw literal targets, and 4 saw stories ending with acknowledgments. Subjects made judgments as to whether each target was sarcastic, nonsarcastic, literal, or an acknowledgment in its context. They also rated, on a 5-point scale, the degree to which the final sentence of each story related to its context. Results showed agreement on a sarcastic, nonsarcastic, literal, or acknowledgment interpretation 96%, 98%, 97%, and 98% of the time, respectively, for each of the four story types. An analysis of variance performed on the ratings showed no significant differences between the effectiveness of the sarcastic (4.34), nonsarcastic (4.54), literal (4.44), and acknowledgment (4.47) stories in conveying the appropriate meanings of the targets.

Procedure. The stimuli were presented in a different random order for each subject on a computer terminal screen under the control of a PDP–11/23 computer. The computer controlled the response keyboard and recorded the latencies of the comprehension and paraphrase responses. Subjects pushed a button to get the first sentence of the first story, read the sentence, and pushed a button as soon as they understood what it meant. The first sentence was then replaced by the second sentence of the story. Subjects read and gave a comprehension response for each sentence of the story. After their response to the last sentence (the target), subjects heard a tone, and a possible paraphrase of the previous sentence appeared. The tone signified that the subjects were to make a true–false paraphrase judgment on a designated part of the keyboard as quickly as possible; then the trial was over. To get the first sentence for the next trial, subjects could push the comprehension response button. Subjects were always timed from the onset of the display to the instant the response button was pushed. The instructions emphasized that the subjects should try to understand exactly what each sentence said before they pushed the comprehension response button or the true–false paraphrase buttons.

Results and Discussion

Only targets that were followed by a correct paraphrase judgment were included in the data analysis. Reading times longer than 7 sec (less than 1% of all responses) were eliminated from the analysis. These outliers represented cases in which experimental instructions could not have been followed, as when subjects' attention wandered from the task. Means were calculated by averaging across subjects. Each analysis was performed twice: once treating subjects as a random factor while collapsing over sentences ($F1$), and once treating sentences as the random factor while collapsing over subjects ($F2$). Note that subjects assigned to different lists read different assortments of targets. This means that the analysis of variance (ANOVA) with targets as a random factor is confounded by subjects and vice versa. F'_{min} was also calculated as recommended by Clark (1973). I have placed greatest reliance on effects that were significant by F'_{min}, but results achieving significance by subjects and items should also be seriously considered.[1]

Comprehension Times for the Target Sentences. Table 7.2 presents the response times for understanding the target sentences. An ANOVA revealed that subjects took different amounts of time to read the four kinds of target sentences, $F1(3, 117) = 8.56, p < .001, F2(3, 45) = 4.34, p < .001, F'_{min}(3, 93) = 2.88, p < .05$. Further analysis on the individual means showed that subjects took less time to read sarcastic remarks than nonsarcastic equivalent sentences ($p < .05$ across subjects and items). The difference between the reading times for sarcastic and literal sentences was not significant. These data indicate that people do not take any longer to process sarcastic sentences than they do literal ones, and as such do not support the predictions of the Standard Pragmatic Model. It also appears that locating the source of a speaker's echo in using sarcasm does not increase the difficulty of understanding these nonliteral utterances as compared to comprehending literal sentences. This issue is explored in more detail in Experiments 2 and 3.

Interestingly, subjects also took longer to read literal sentences than acknowledgments ($p < .01$ across subjects, $p < .05$ across items). These findings suggest that conventional acknowledgments, such as "Thanks for your help," are understood more rapidly than literal sentences, like "You're a big help." Acknowledgment targets also took less time to process than sarcastic remarks ($p < .05$ across subjects, $p < .10$ across items). This suggests that positively intended evaluative remarks are processed more quickly than negatively evaluative remarks, although it

TABLE 7.2

Mean Response Times (in Milliseconds)

	Context			
	Negative		Positive	
Comprehension Measure	Sarcastic	Nonsarcastic	Literal	Acknowledgment
Target sentences	1,503	1,643	1,525	1,361
Paraphrase judgments	1,634	1,812	1,813	1,724
Error rate	(.08)	(.07)	(.12)	(.06)
Combined RT	3,149	3,395	3,334	3,056

Note. RT = response time. Error rates are shown in parentheses.

could simply mean that conventional phrases within the acknowledgments, such as "thank you," facilitated processing for these targets. Nevertheless, the time it took subjects to make the paraphrase judgments for the acknowledgments was actually longer than for the sarcastic remarks.

Paraphrase Judgments and Error Rates.   Much work on sentence comprehension and use has demonstrated the need for some secondary task, like a sentence verification paradigm, to measure the comprehension criteria subjects use in understanding sentences (Carpenter & Just, 1975; Glushko & Cooper, 1978). Although the reaction times for the target sentences are a good indicator of understanding, it is also important to examine the reaction times for making the paraphrase judgments.

An ANOVA on the time it took subjects to make the paraphrase judgments showed a significant effect of sentence type, $F1(3, 117) = 6.70, p < .001, F2(3, 45) = 3.56, p < .025, F'_{min}(3, 95) = 2.32, p < .10$. Closer analysis showed that subjects took less time to make paraphrase judgments for sarcastic remarks than for both nonsarcastic equivalents or literal uses of the same expressions ($p < .01$ across both subjects and items for both comparisons). Subjects also took somewhat longer to make paraphrase judgments for literal sentences than they did for acknowledgments, but this difference was not statistically reliable.

An examination of the error rates showed that the difference in error rates was statistically reliable, $F1(3, 117) = 4.64, p < .025, F2(3, 45) = 3.21, p < .05, F'_{min}(3, 109) = 1.90, p > .10$. Further analysis indicated that subjects made more errors in accepting literal targets than for the acknowledgments ($p < .05$ across subjects, $p < .10$ across items).

A more conservative measure of comprehension time for the target sentences is to add together the response time to make the paraphrase judgment and that to understand the preceding target sentence. This measure is useful because a subject may push the comprehension button for the target without fully understanding its meaning. If the subject does understand the target sentence when he or she pushes the comprehension button, then the subsequent paraphrase judgment should be made quickly. Adding the paraphrase judgment reaction time to that for the target sentence ensures a more accurate measure of comprehension. This seems particularly important given that the sarcastic targets may severely deviate from their "literal" meanings.

This analysis revealed a significant effect of sentence type, $F1(3, 117) = 8.68$, $p < .01$, $F2(3, 45) = 5.81$, $p < .01$, $F'_{min}(3, 107) = 3.48$, $p < .025$. Newman-Keuls tests showed, once again, that subjects were much faster at understanding and making paraphrase judgments for sarcastic utterances than for both nonsarcastic equivalents ($p < .01$ across subjects and items) and literal sentences ($p < .01$ across subjects, $p < .05$ across items). Subjects were also much faster at reading and making paraphrase judgments for acknowledgment sentences than for literal ones ($p < .01$ across subjects and items).

The data from each of the three measures of comprehension in Experiment 1 provide strong support for the idea that people can understand sarcastic utterances without having to *first* analyze the literal meanings of these expressions. Given adequate information about the speaker's intentions, understanders can comprehend the meanings of sarcastic utterances more or less directly. This conclusion is consistent with previous research on understanding nonliteral language (Gibbs, 1979, 1980, 1983a; Ortony et al., 1978). The results are also consistent with the notion that locating the source of a speaker's echo in using sarcasm does not make these utterances more difficult to process than more "literal" statements.

One alternative interpretation of the present study merits consideration. One could argue that the processing-time differences were not due to whether or not the literal meanings of sarcastic remarks were examined but were primarily influenced by the naturalness of the target sentences given their preceding story contexts. Thus, sarcastic remarks might have been processed quickly simply because these targets were more "natural" extensions of their contexts than were either nonsarcastic targets or literal utterances in their respective stories. The rating study showed that people did not view the sarcastic targets as being more related to their contexts; nonetheless, this rating study may not have adequately addressed the "naturalness" issue. Consequently, the following control study was conducted.

A group of 16 University of California, Santa Cruz, undergraduates read the experimental materials and rated each target on a 5-point scale as to how "natural" an ending it was for its preceding story. If sarcastic targets were more natural endings for their story contexts than were nonsarcastic remarks (stated in identical stories) or literal targets, then subjects should give higher ratings to the sarcastic utterances. Sarcastic targets received a rating of 3.70, nonsarcastic targets 3.89, literal targets 3.72, and acknowledgments 3.86. An ANOVA and planned comparison tests showed that these means did not differ reliably. Consequently, it seems even less likely that the reading-time differences observed in Experiment 1 were due to any discourse conventions relating to the "naturalness" or "consistency" of the target sentences in their given contexts.

EXPERIMENT 2

Jorgensen et al. (1984) found that people often judge sarcastic utterances that have explicit echoic mentions earlier in a story as being ironic, whereas they are usually just puzzled by sarcastic statements that do not have such mention. The purpose of Experiment 2 was to see whether people understand sarcasm based on an explicit echo faster than they process sarcastic expressions in which the echoes are less explicit or even nonexistent.

Subjects in Experiment 2 read stories which ended in sarcastic remarks, such as "This sure is an exciting life" (meaning "This is very boring"). In one case, the story context contained an explicit mention of some idea or belief that the subsequent sarcastic expression explicitly echoed. Other story contexts contained no such antecedent. I predicted that people would understand sarcasm based on explicit echoes (explicit contexts) faster than they would comprehend sarcastic expressions for which echoes were not easily available (implicit contexts). The reading times for the literal uses of these sentence should be about equal and there should be evidence of an interaction of Type of Sarcasm (explicit echoes vs. implicit echoes) × Type of Sentence (sarcastic vs. literal).

Method

Subjects.   Forty undergraduates from the University of California, Santa Cruz, served as subjects to fulfill a course requirement.

Stimuli and Design.   Subjects were assigned to read one of two lists of stories. Each list contained 28 stories—12 filler stories and 16 stories that ended in sarcastic remarks. Half of the sarcastic remarks echoed some attitude or opinion that was previously mentioned in the story, and half of the stories contained no such echo. If a given story ended with a sarcastic remark that echoed an earlier stated belief in List A, it ended with the same sarcastic remark in List B, but it no longer echoed something mentioned earlier in the story. Thus, the final sentences were identical in both lists.[2] The explicit stories were written so that the final target sentences did not repeat the same words as the echo but referred to them using different words. Across the two lists, equal numbers of subjects read the two target types (explicit vs. implicit echoes). Table 7.3 presents an example of the two-story contexts for one particular sarcastic target.

A rating study was performed to ensure that the last lines of these stories were interpreted as they were intended to be. Twelve subjects participated in the study. For each target utterance, six people saw the story that contained an explicit echo, and six saw stories that contained implicit or nonexistent echoes. Subjects received the following instructions:

TABLE 7.3

Examples of Story Contexts and Target Sentences for Experiment 2

Echoic story

Gus just graduated from high school and he didn't know what to do. One day he saw an ad about the Navy. It said that the Navy was not just a job, but an adventure. So, Gus joined up. Soon he was aboard a ship doing all sorts of boring things. One day as he was peeling potatoes he said to his buddy, "This sure is an exciting life."

Nonechoic story

Gus just graduated from high school and he didn't know what to do. So, Gus went out and joined the Navy. Soon he was aboard a ship doing all sorts of boring things. One day as he was peeling potatoes he said to his buddy, "This sure is an exciting life."

The purpose of this study is to examine people's perceptions of sarcasm. Presented below are a number of brief stories that contain conversation. Your task is to read each story and make a judgment as to whether or not the last sentence of each story should be interpreted as having a sarcastic interpretation. Sarcasm is generally thought to be instances of speech where the speaker's intended meaning differs from what his or her utterance literally means. In many cases, the speaker's meaning is the opposite of the sentence's literal interpretation. Read each story and indicate in the space next to the last line whether you think it should be interpreted sarcastically or not. For those final sentences you view as sarcastic, I want you to also rate on a 6-point scale, with 6 meaning *very sarcastic* and 1 meaning *just a little sarcastic,* the degree to which each sentence is sarcastic.

Results showed that subjects saw both the explicit and implicit stories as ending in sarcastic expressions, 89% of the time for the implicit stories, and 92% for the explicit story contexts. An analysis of the ratings showed, however, that subjects gave higher sarcastic ratings for the stories with explicit echoes (5.89) than they did for the stories with implicit echoes (4.96), $F(1, 11) = 5.24, p < .05$. These data indicate that subjects saw the target sentences in both contexts as being sarcastic, but that sarcasm based on explicit echoes were rated as being more sarcastic than were the instances based on implicit or nonexistent echoes.[3] This latter result supports the general findings of Jorgensen et al. (1984).

Procedure. The procedure was identical to that used in Experiment 1.

Results and Discussion

The data were analyzed in the same way as described in Experiment 1.

Comprehension Times for Target Sentences. An ANOVA on the latencies to read the target sentences showed that subjects took less time to understand sarcastic remarks made in contexts with explicit echoes (1,763 msec) than they did to process sarcastic remarks made in contexts in which the echo was only implicit (1,913 msec), $F1(1, 39) = 5.45, p < .05, F2(1, 19) = 4.23, p < .10, F'_{min}(1, 58) = 2.40, p > .10$.

Paraphrase Judgments and Error Rates.   Preliminary analyses revealed a significant main effect of groups in the analysis across subjects, $F(3, 36) = 3.51, p < .025$, suggesting that there were differences in the subsets of items subjects read. An ANOVA on the latencies to make the paraphrase judgments indicated that subjects took less time to make paraphrase judgments for sarcastic utterances in contexts with explicit echoes (1,757 msec) than in contexts in which the echo is only implicit (1,957 msec), $F1(1, 39) = 6.21, p < .025, F2(1, 19) = 4.43, p < .05, F'_{min}(1, 58) = 2.58, p > .10$. A similar difference is found for the combined analysis. Here, subjects took less time to read and made paraphrase judgments for sarcastic utterances that had explicit echoes (3,554 msec) than for sarcastic utterances read in contexts where the echoes were implicit (3,804 msec), $F1(1, 39) = 6.76, p < .01, F2(1, 19) = 4.80, p < .05. F'_{min}(1, 58) = 2.87, p < .10$. An ANOVA on the error rates revealed no significant differences in the errors subjects made to the paraphrase judgments (8% for the explicit echoic contexts and 10% when subjects read stories with implicit echoes).

This study showed that people understood sarcastic utterances more easily in contexts that echo some putative belief or opinion than when no such echo was explicit. Such findings strongly support the idea that understanding sarcasm is based at least partly on locating the source of a speakers' echo.

EXPERIMENT 3

The asymmetric nature of sarcasm poses an interesting problem for how it is understood. Why does it seem permissible to say "You are a fine friend," meaning "You are a bad friend," but not "You are a terrible friend," meaning "You are a good friend?" The main difference between these two utterances lies in the extent to which they echo social norms. Sperber and Wilson's (1981) theory proposed that it is always possible to make ironic mention of a norm. Societal norms for politeness, for example, are that people should only compliment others ("If you don't have anything nice to say, don't say anything"). When speakers echo an addressee's beliefs about this norm, they intend their comment to be taken sarcastically.

This idea, which I will refer to as the *Social Norm Model,* suggests that sarcasm based on a mention of some social norm should be easier to comprehend than instances not based on such a mention. In the present study, then, the sarcastic comments made in the normative contexts involved mention of a norm, whereas sarcastic remarks in the non-normative stories did not involve this kind of echoic mention. The Social Norm Model predicts that subjects should take less time to read and make paraphrase judgments for sarcastic targets in normative contexts than in non-normative stories. Moreover, this model suggests that people should take longer to read sarcastic targets than nonsarcastic ones in non-normative stories. Overall, then, there should be an interaction between context and sentence type. These results would provide support for the idea that understanding sarcasm is based at least partly on discovering the norm that is being echoically mentioned in an utterance, as proposed by Sperber and Wilson (1981).

Method

Subjects. Forty students from the University of California, Santa Cruz, served as subjects to fulfill a course requirement.

Stimuli and Design. Subjects were randomly assigned to read one of four lists of stories. Each list contained 32 stories—12 filler stories and 20 experimental stories. For the experimental stories, 10 appeared in normative contexts and 10 in non-normative ones. For the normative contexts, 5 of the stories ended in sarcastic remarks ("You are a fine friend"), and 5 ended in nonsarcastic remarks ("You are a terrible friend"). For the non-normative contexts, 5 stories ended with sarcastic remarks ("You are a terrible friend"), and 5 ended in nonsarcastic comments ("You are a fine friend"). If a given story theme (e.g., Friend) ended with a sarcastic remark in a normative context in List A, it ended with a nonsarcastic remark in a normative context in List B, a sarcastic remark in a non-normative context in List C, and a nonsarcastic comment in a non-normative context in List D. The targets in each of the four groups had the same number of words. Across the four groups, equal numbers of subjects heard the four target types for each of the 20 stories. Table 7.4 presents an example of the normative and non-normative story contexts and their respective target sentences.

A rating study was performed to ensure that the last lines of these stories were interpreted as they were intended to be. The subjects were the same ones used in the rating study for Experiment 2 and followed the identical instructions. For each story theme, three people saw the normative contexts ending with sarcastic remarks, three people saw normative contexts ending with nonsarcastic comments,

TABLE 7.4

Example of Story Contexts and Target Sentences for Experiment 3

Normative (negative) context

Billy and Joe were long-time pals. But one time when Billy was away on a business trip, Joe slept with Billy's wife, Lynn. When Billy found out about it afterwards, he was upset. He confronted Joe and said to him, [Sarcastic target] "You're a fine friend." [Nonsarcastic target] "You're a terrible friend."

Non-normative (positive) context

Billy and Joe were long-time pals. One time Billy was in desperate need of money. His car had broken down and he needed $300 to fix it. So, he asked Joe for a loan. Joe said he could lend Billy the money. This made Billy happy and he said to Joe, [Sarcastic target] "You're a terrible help." [Nonsarcastic target] "You're a fine friend."

three saw non-normative contexts ending with sarcastic remarks, and three saw non-normative stories ending with nonsarcastic utterances. Results showed agreement that the sarcastic-normative (95%), nonsarcastic-normative (93%), sarcastic-non-normative (90%), and nonsarcastic-non-normative (93%) had either sarcastic or nonsarcastic meanings as they were supposed to. An analysis of the sarcastic ratings showed that sarcastic sentences in normative stories were seen as being more sarcastic (5.68) than those that were present in non-normative contexts (4.87). Therefore, although subjects viewed the final sarcastic sentences as being sarcastic in both the normative and non-normative contexts, they rated the ones in the normative contexts as being more sarcastic.

Procedure.   The procedure was identical to that used in Experiments 1 and 2.

Results and Discussion

The data were analyzed in the same manner as described in the first two studies.

Comprehension of the Target Sentences.   The times to comprehend the targets sentences are shown in Table 7.5.

ANOVAs revealed a significant main effect of context (normative vs. non-normative), $F1(1, 39) = 12.33, p < .001, F2(1, 19) = 11.04, p < .001, F'_{min}(1, 55) = 5.82, p < .025$, and a reliable interaction of Context × Sentence Type (sarcastic vs. nonsarcastic), $F1(1, 39) = 19.70, p < .0001, F2(1, 19) = 13.98, p < .001, F'_{min}(1, 58) = 8.19, p < .01$. Newman-Keuls tests indicated that subjects took less time to read sarcastic remarks in normative contexts than they did in non-normative contexts ($p < .01$ across subjects, $p < .05$ across items). Moreover, subjects took *longer* to read sarcastic remarks than nonsarcastic ones in non-normative contexts ($p < .01$ across subjects, $p < .05$ across items). This finding supports the predictions of the social norm model and demonstrates that understanding sarcasm is facilitated when these utterances echo some sort of social norm.

TABLE 7.5
Mean Response Time (in Milliseconds)

	Context			
	Normative		Non-Normative	
	Sarcastic	Nonsarcastic	Sarcastic	Nonsarcastic
Target sentences	1,716	1,721	1,987	1,554
Paraphrase judgments	1,767	1,901	1,908	1,807
Error rate	(.09)	(.08)	(.14)	(.08)
Combined RT	3,471	3,622	3,889	3,360

Note. RT = response time. Error rates are shown in parentheses.

Interestingly, subjects took longer to read sarcastic remarks in normative contexts than they did to process literal uses of the same sentences when they were presented in non-normative contexts ($p < .05$ across subjects and items). Similarly, subjects were faster at reading nonsarcastic targets in non-normative contexts than in normative ones ($p < .05$ across subjects and items). It appears that literally saying something nice about someone is understood more rapidly than sarcastically saying something nice and more rapidly than saying something negative, whether literally or sarcastically.

Paraphrase Judgments and Error Rates. A preliminary ANOVA on the time to make the paraphrase judgments revealed a statistically reliable main effect of list, $F(3, 36) = 3.51, p < .025$, and a significant interaction of List × Context, $F(3, 36) = 3.01, p < .05$. This indicates that there was some difference among the items that effected subjects' reaction times to make the paraphrase judgments. ANOVAs performed when lists was dropped as a factor revealed some evidence of a significant interaction of Context × Sentence Type when subjects were a random variable, $F1(1, 39) = 3.99, p < .05$, but again it is clear that this effect is not as strong when items are a random factor, $F2(1, 23) = 3.10, p < .10, F'_{min}(1, 57) = 1.74, p > .10$. Further analysis showed that subjects took less time to make paraphrase judgments for sarcastic remarks in normative contexts than to make these same judgments for sarcastic utterances in non-normative contexts ($p < .05$ across subjects, $p < .10$ across items). Subjects were also slightly faster at making paraphrase judgments for sarcastic remarks than for nonsarcastic targets in normative contexts, but this difference did not approach significance.

An analysis of the errors to make the paraphrase judgments showed that subjects made more errors when they read non-normative contexts than when they read normative contexts. This difference, however, was only statistically reliable in the ANOVA across subjects, $F1(1, 39) = 4.42, p < .05$. There was also a reliable main effect of list in the preliminary ANOVA, $F(1, 36) = 4.47, p < .05$, but this factor did not interact with any other variable.

The analysis of the combined latencies to read the target sentences and make the paraphrase judgments indicated a reliable main effect of context in the subject analysis, $F1(1, 39) = 4.48, p < .05$, although this effect was not statistically significant in either the item analysis or by F'_{min}. There was, however, a significant interaction of Context × Sentence Type, $F1(1, 39) = 16.57, p < .0001, F2(1, 19) = 9.03, p < .01$, $F'_{min}(1, 61) = 5.84, p < .025$. Newman-Keuls tests on the individual means showed that subjects took much less time to read and make paraphrase judgments for sarcastic utterances in normative stories than in non-normative contexts ($p < .01$ across subjects and items). Subjects were also somewhat faster at undemanding the sarcastic statements than nonsarcastic remarks when they read these expressions in normative contexts ($p < .05$ across subjects, $p < .10$ in the item analysis). Moreover, subjects took longer to read and make paraphrase judgments for sarcastic remarks than non-sarcastic utterances in the non-normative stories ($p < .01$ across both subjects and items).

In summary, the results of Experiment 3 indicated that subjects more easily understood sarcastic remarks made in contexts with explicit echoes about some societal norm than they did sarcastic statements made in situations in which such echoes were not explicitly stated. These data support the findings of Experiment 2 and suggest that ease of understanding sarcasm depends on how difficult it is to locate the source of the proposition or attitude which the speaker's comment echoes.

MEMORY FOR SARCASM

The results of the first three studies illustrate the importance of certain pragmatic information, which must be shared between speakers and understanders, in interpreting sarcastic utterances. If sarcasm has special pragmatic properties associated with it, then these utterances may be particularly memorable. Experiments 4 through 6 were conducted to test this idea.

Previous research has shown that how well people remember the exact surface forms of utterances in everyday conversation depends on four general factors: (a) Whether the surface form is unique to the context in which it occurs (Kintsch & Bates, 1977), (b) whether the forms are unusual or nonconventional in manner (Gibbs, 1981), (c) how important a form is pragmatically to the discourse topic (Bates, Kintsch, Fletcher, & Giuliani, 1980; Bates, Masling, & Kintsch, 1978), and (d) the degree to which a form involves the speaker's intentions, beliefs, and knowledge of and attitude toward the hearer (Keenan, MacWhinney, & Mayhew, 1977). Keenan et al. (1977) demonstrated that memory for the surface forms and meanings of sentences high in such "interactive content" was superior to memory for sentences with similar propositional content that were of low "interactive value." MacWhinney, Keenan, and Reinke (1982) have gone on to show that superior memory for sentences with high "interactive content" is not simply due to arousal.

These studies illustrate the importance of interpersonal information in memory for sentences in conversation. None of this work, however, focuses on the specific pragmatic properties that make sentences more or less memorable. Memory for sarcastic expressions should be particularly interesting because of sarcasm's special role of relating speakers and hearers by the mention of a previously stated belief or attitude. Although other studies have shown that an utterance's pragmatic function affects its memorability, none have examined exactly how the effects are achieved. The point of the following studies was to extend the findings of the first three studies into the domain of memory. These memory experiments attempt to show not only that sarcasm is more memorable because it plays an important pragmatic role in discourse but also that sarcasm is memorable *precisely* because it is an instance of echoic mention. Experiment 4 tested whether people remembered sarcastic expressions better than nonsarcastic expressions that are similar in meaning. Experiments 5 and 6 investigated whether people better recall sarcasm that is based on a speaker's echoing of some norm than sarcastic utterances that do not explicitly echo any such norm.

EXPERIMENT 4

In this study, subjects were visually presented with the stories used as stimuli in Experiment 1. Subjects read the stories without any auditory information to control for the possibility that memory for sarcasm is due mostly to any special tone of voice that could accompany sarcastic expressions. Following this, subjects read a set of unrelated stories for 15 min and then were given a multiple-choice recognition test for the target sentences. They were also asked to give confidence ratings for their recognition judgments.

Following the premise that sarcasm relates speakers and hearers in a special way, via the mention of a previously stated belief or attitude, it was predicted that subjects would better recognize the verbatim forms of sarcastic remarks than they would nonsarcastic utterances that were equivalent in meaning. This should be so even though nonsarcastic remarks are often judged as being more direct attacks upon the hearer and consequently may be thought of as more distinctive and memorable. In fact, one could even predict that nonsarcastic remarks and literal targets should be best remembered, since subjects spend more time processing these expressions as shown by the reading-time results in Experiment 1. Other research has demonstrated that people often remember utterances in conversation when they spend more time processing them (Gibbs, 1980, 1981), and a similar finding could be predicted here for nonsarcastic remarks and literal targets.

However, as Craik and Tulving (1975) suggested, the amount of time spent processing verbal material does not always correlate with memorability for these items. What matters most is the kind of processing that takes place on an item when first encountered. I predicted that the special pragmatic properties associated with sarcasm should make these expressions most memorable because of the unique manner in which they relate speakers and hearers, via the echoing of a familiar proposition or attitude by the speaker. Sarcastic comments should also be recognized better than literal uses of the same expressions in different circumstances. This finding would further demonstrate that the surface form of an utterance by itself does not make a particular expression more or less memorable. Rather, it is the specific purpose an utterance plays in conversation that determines how well it is remembered (Bates et al., 1978; Gibbs, 1981; Jarvella & Collas, 1974; Keenan et al., 1977).

Method

Subjects.   Forty-eight undergraduates at the University of California, Santa Cruz, served as subjects to satisfy a course requirement. All the subjects were native speakers of English.

Stimuli and Design.   The stimuli and design employed were identical to those of Experiment 1. Each of the four groups of subjects read the 16 stories in a different random order. In addition, two filler scenes were included, one at the beginning and one at the end of each series, to prevent primacy and recency effects from occurring in the subsequent memory testing.

For the recognition phase of the experiment, subjects were given a test containing 16 multiple-choice items. Subjects also saw a title for each item indicating the scene in which the target sentence had appeared. This title was simply one key word from each of the target sentences (e.g., *help*), and for any story theme (e.g., Help) the same title was used for each type of target. Three distractor sentences were constructed to correspond to each of the 16 target sentences. The distractors for the sarcastic targets were (a) a paraphrase of the target that could also be seen as a sarcastic remit given the specific scene, (b) a nonsarcastic remark that had the same intended meaning as the sarcastic one and was a target in another group of stories, and (c) a distractor that paraphrased the second distractor. For example, for the target sentence, "You're a big help," the distractors were (a) "Thanks for your help," (b) "You're not helping me," and (c) "You've not helped much."

The distractors for the nonsarcastic, literal, and acknowledgment targets were (a) a paraphrase that maintained the same meaning as the target, (b) a sarcastic remark that was actually the target for this same scene in a different group, and (c) a distractor whose meaning was the opposite of the target's intended interpretation.

Procedure. Subjects were randomly assigned to read one of the four story groups. Each was instructed to read the stories carefully because they would be asked some questions about them afterwards. The subjects then read the stories at their own pace. When they had finished, subjects were presented with another booklet containing some unrelated stories that they read for approximately 15 min. Immediately after this, subjects were given a booklet containing the recognition test. For each multiple-choice item, the subjects circled the letter next to the sentence they heard earlier. In addition, subjects also gave a rating on a scale of 1 to 6 of their confidence that their choice was correct (1 represented *guess* and 6 indicated very *confident*). They were given as much time as they needed to complete the recognition task.

Results and Discussion

The top half of Table 7.6 presents the proportion of subjects' correct recognition of the target sentences for each context condition.

People were generally quite good at recognizing the exact target sentences they originally heard, being 69% accurate overall. False alarms to the distractor items on the recognition test were relatively low and were evenly distributed across the alternatives. These false recognitions are not discussed further because of their low frequency, especially in the item analyses.

An ANOVA on subjects' correct recognitions of the targets revealed a significant effect of target type, $F1(3, 117) = 13.24$, $p < .001$, $F2(3, 45) = 6.93$, $p < .001$, $F'_{min}(3, 94) = 4.55$, $p < .01$. Individual comparisons using Newman-Keuls tests revealed that subjects recognized sarcastic remarks better than they did either

TABLE 7.6

Proportion of Target Sentences Correctly Recognized and Their Mean Confidence Ratings for Experiment 4

Sentence Type	Proportion Recognized	Confidence Ratings
Sarcastic	.83	3.38
Nonsarcastic	.60	1.68
Literal	.65	2.08
Compliment	.69	2.46

nonsarcastic ones ($p < .01$ across both subjects and items), literal utterances ($p < .01$ across both subjects and items), or acknowledgements ($p < .01$ across subjects, $p < .05$ across items). No other differences approached significance.

Subjects' confidence ratings were converted into a single recognition score in the following manner (cf. Bransford & Franks, 1971). Correct recognition of a target sentence was given a positive value of the confidence rating. If subjects incorrectly chose a distractor item, their confidence rating was given a negative value. Thus, a 12-point rating scale emerged, ranging from plus 6 to minus 6 (excluding 0). The mean confidence ratings are presented in the far right-hand column of Table 7.6.

These ratings showed patterns very similar to the target recognition data. Subjects were generally much more confident in their recognition judgments for sarcastic remarks than for the other target sentences. An ANOVA revealed a significant effect of target type, $F1(3, 117) = 9.35, p < .01, F2(3, 45) = 4.50, p < .05$, $F'_{min}(3, 91) = 3.04, p < .05$. Newman-Keuls tests showed that subjects had higher confidence scores for sarcastic remarks than for any of the other target sentences ($p < .01$ across both subjects and items for all comparisons). Subjects also had higher confidence scores for acknowledgements than for nonsarcastic remarks ($p < .05$ across both subjects and items). No other comparisons were significant.

Both the recognition scores and the confidence ratings are consistent with the hypothesis that sarcastic expressions like "You're a fine friend" and "You're a big help" are more memorable than nonsarcastic equivalents not simply because of how much they involve the speaker and addressee but because they do so in a particular way. In these cases, the speaker's sarcastic remark is a mention of a hearer's or some known source's putative belief. Explicit mention of this belief in the context of contradictory evidence makes these expressions sarcastic. Recognition of this by the addressee or other hearers makes these expressions quite distinctive and more memorable than nonsarcastic utterances just as high in "interactive content."

The superiority of memory for sarcastic comments over literal uses of the same expressions demonstrates that it is not simply the surface form of an utterance by itself that makes a particular expression more or less memorable. Rather it is the specific purpose the utterance plays in the conversation that determines how well it is remembered (Bates et al., 1978; Gibbs, 1981; Keenan et al., 1977). In particular, sarcasm plays a very special pragmatic role in conversation, since it interrelates the speaker and hearer in a unique way in that it is an instance of echoic mention.

The memory advantage for the sarcastic remarks cannot be attributed to the supposition that these targets were more "natural" in their contexts than the other target sentences were in their respective stories (as shown in the follow-up to Experiment 1). However, another potential response bias may have influenced subjects' performance on the recognition test. In particular, the alternatives on the recognition test may be of poorer quality for the sarcastic remarks than for the other targets.

To eliminate this possibility, 20 undergraduates from the University of California, Santa Cruz, were given the recognition test to complete without having first read the stories used as stimuli in Experiment 4. The subjects were instructed to read the title with each set of alternatives (e.g., Help) and to circle the sentence that was most likely to occur in a conversation with that title name. All subjects were told that one of the statements in each set of alternatives had actually occurred in the conversation indicated by the title. The data for this study are shown in Table 7.7.

There were two results of interest. First, subjects were no more likely to choose the sarcastic target over its distractors than they were to choose any of the other targets over their distractors. Second, subjects were no more likely to pick any of the targets over any of their other alternatives. An ANOVA confirmed that there were no main effects of target type or alternative ($Fs < 1$), although the interaction between these factors was significant, $F(3, 930) = 2.83, p < .025$. These results clearly indicate that there was nothing peculiar about the alternatives on the recognition test used in Experiment 4 that could have influenced the results.

Another rival explanation of the results of Experiment 4 is that sarcasm was best remembered because these utterances tended to have very frozen surface forms. It is true that there are many sentence forms that are conventionally used sarcastically, such as "A fine friend you are" and "I bet." However, care was taken in the preparation of the stimulus materials not to include many of these kind of sentences, although some expressions like "You're a big help" are somewhat common in everyday usage. But, even if such sentence forms were used, this

TABLE 7.7

Proportion of Targets and Distractors Selected As "Most Likely to Occur" in a Story With a Specific Title

	Alternative on Recognition Test			
Sentence Type	Target	Paraphrase	Opposite	Distractor
Sarcastic	.24	.29	.20	.27
Nonsarcastic	.28	.19	.28	.25
Literal	.26	.27	.23	.24
Compliment	.24	.23	.30	.23

would not necessarily mean that they would be best recognized. In other research on memory for idiomatic expressions, I found that people recalled literal uses of expressions such as "You can let the cat out of the bag" more often than when these sentences were used idiomatically (Gibbs, 1980). If memory for sarcasm depended simply on the frozenness of these expressions' surface forms, then one would expect that literal, and to some extent uncoventional, uses of the sentences would be best recognized. This was not the case, however, given that subjects remembered sarcastic uses of expressions like "You're a big help" better than literal uses of the same sentences. Thus, the surface form of an utterance has less to do with how well it is remembered than does the primary communicative function that an utterance has in some discourse situation.

One other explanation of the data from Experiment 4 is that subjects recreated the proper intonation covertly for the sarcastic utterances after they had understood them as instances of sarcasm. Sarcastic utterances are often thought to have special intonation properties (nasalization, exaggeratedly slow speaking rate, very heavy stress; see Cutler, 1974, 1976). Although there was no intonation information that could have helped subjects comprehend these expressions' sarcastic meanings in Experiment 4, subjects' recreation of what the intonation might have been could have led to the memory differences observed. To assess this idea, an additional 14 subjects read the stories used in the present study and then completed the recognition test. Afterwards, these subjects were informally asked whether they imagined any of the speakers' voices as they read the stories. Only four subjects said they did so consistently, and of these, each one reported recreating the speakers' voices for all of the target utterances, not just the sarcastic ones. Interestingly, two of these subjects did *not* better recognize the sarcastic targets on the memory test during the recognition test, which could have led to the memory differences observed. It seems unlikely, then, that the observed memory superiority for sarcastic expressions could have been caused solely by subjects consistently imagining any special tone of voice for the sarcastic remarks.

In summary, the results of Experiment 4 showed that sarcasm is well remembered and that this finding cannot be explained by other alternative hypotheses. The hypothesis that best accounts for these results is that sarcasm is best remembered because it is an instance of echoic mention. Nevertheless, the results of Experiment 4 do not, per se, support the idea, and so two studies more were conducted. In order to ensure that the effects found in Experiment 4 examining recognition would generalize to other measures of memory performance, Experiments 5 and 6 both tested subjects' recall of sarcastic statements.

EXPERIMENT 5

Experiment 5 examined whether people remember sarcasm for which there is an explicit echo better than sarcasm for which no echo is explicitly mentioned. The main hypothesis tested was that memory for sarcasm is primarily affected by hearers' recognition of the echo involved. If memory for sarcasm is dependent on hearers' recognition of the echo, subjects should better remember sarcastic expressions that echo a previously mentioned belief than they would remember sarcastic remarks for which the echo was implicit or nonexistent. An alternative hypothesis would be that the two instances of sarcasm should be remembered equally well, given that they both are counterfactual uses of language.

Method

Subjects. Forty undergraduates at the University of California, Santa Cruz, served as subjects to satisfy a course requirement. All the subjects were native speakers of English.

Stimuli and Design. The stimuli and design were identical to those of Experiment 2. Table 7.3 presents an example of the explicit and implicit story contexts used as stimuli in this study.

The present study employed a cued-recall paradigm. In the acquisition part of the study, each of two groups heard the 28 stories in a different random order. In addition to these contexts, one filler story at the beginning of each group of stories and one at the end were included to prevent primacy and recency effects in the subsequent recall test. For the recall phase of the experiment, subjects were given a list of 16 cues, each of which was one key word in the target. For the stories shown in Table 7.3, for example, subjects were given the cue *life.*

Procedure. Subjects were randomly assigned to one of the two story groups. Each was instructed to pay close attention to the materials presented because they would be asked some questions about them afterwards. The tape containing the stories was then played to the subjects. Following this, subjects read some unrelated stories for approximately 15 min. Immediately afterwards, subjects were given an answer sheet containing the 16 recall cues. They were asked to look at the cues and to write down the sentences that corresponded to the cues. Subjects were informed that they were only being tested on the last line of each story they heard. They were given approximately 15 min to complete the memory task.

Results and Discussion

A sentence was scored as correct if it was a verbatim replication of the utterance presented. Subjects recalled more instances of sarcasm based on explicit echoes (61%) than they did sarcastic utterances based on implicit echoes (45%), $F1(1, 39) = 20.75, p < .0001, F2(1, 15) = 11.57, p < .01, F'_{min}(1, 61) = 7.43, p < .01$. This is particularly interesting given that both the explicit and implicit echoic utterances were identical and seen as being sarcastic, as shown in the Method section of Experiment 2. These results support the hypothesis that sarcasm is well remembered because it involves the speaker echoing some putative belief of the addressee or some other source.

EXPERIMENT 6

Experiment 6 tested to see whether there are memory differences between sarcastic expressions like "You are a fine friend" and "You are a bad friend." The results of Experiment 3 showed that people understood expressions like "You are a fine friend" more quickly than "You are a bad friend" because the former utterance ech- oes a social norm that one should say nice things to other people. Recognition of this by hearers facilitated the understanding of expressions like "You are a fine friend" as having sarcastic meanings.

Two alternative hypotheses were examined here. One could hypothesize that people will recall expressions, such as "You are a bad friend," *meaning* "You are a good friend," particularly well, since they are unusual instances of sarcasm, al- though they are known to occur in everyday speech. My hypothesis was that people should recall instances of sarcasm that are based on a mention of some social norm, like "You are a fine friend," more often than instances of sarcasm that are not based on any such mention, despite the fact that non-normative instances seem slightly unusual. The effect of the echo should make sarcasm based on mention of a norm particularly memorable. In the present example, then, people should recall "You are a fine friend," much more often than "You are a terrible friend," said in the same story context, and they should correctly recall "You are a fine friend" more often than "You are a terrible friend" (*meaning* "You are a good friend"). Overall, then, there should be evidence of an interaction of Context (normative or negative vs. non-normative or positive) H Sentence Type (sarcastic vs. nonsarcastic).

Method

Subjects.   Forty-eight students from the University of California, Santa Cruz, served as subjects to fulfill a course requirement. All subjects were native speakers of English.

Stimuli, Design, and Procedure.   The stimuli and design were identical to those used in Experiment 3. The procedure was identical to that used in the previous study, with the exception that subjects were now randomly assigned to one of four story groups. Table 7.4 above presents examples of these stories and their target sentences.

Results and Discussion

Sentences were scored as being correctly recalled according to the same criteria used in the previous study. The mean proportion of sentences correctly recalled is shown in Table 7.8. Overall, subjects correctly recalled sarcastic expressions in normative contexts better than they recalled any other target type. ANOVAs re- vealed reliable main effects of context (normative vs. non-normative), $F1 (1, 47) =$

TABLE 7.8
Proportion of Target Sentences Correctly Recalled for Experiment 6

| | Sentence Type | |
Context	Sarcastic	Nonsarcastic
Normative (negative)	.56	.27
Non-normative (positive)	.27	.32

$15.93, p < .001$, $F2(1, 19) = 9.33, p < .01$, $F'_{min}(1, 60) = 5.88, p < .025$; and sentence type (sarcastic vs. nonsarcastic), $F1(1, 47) = 18.89, p < .001$, $F2(1, 19) = 8.59, p < .01$; $F'_{min}(1, 64) = 5.90, p < .025$. The interaction of Context × Sentence Type was also significant, $F1(1, 47) = 52.41, p < .0001$, $F2(1, 19) = 21.40, p < .0001$, $F'_{min}(1, 63) = 15.20, p < .001$. Newman-Keuls tests indicated that subjects recalled sarcastic remarks in normative contexts more often than they did any other target ($p < .01$ across subjects and items for each comparison). These data, once again, support the idea that memory for sarcasm is determined by whether or not it is seen as an instance of echoic mention. Sarcasm that does not involve such a mention, or does so to a lesser extent, is not as memorable despite that it too is an instance of nonliteral language.

GENERAL DISCUSSION

A fundamental issue in the study of natural language understanding concerns the role of pragmatic information in comprehending what speakers mean by what they say. This is a particularly important problem for metaphoric language, in which sentence and speaker meanings are thought to differ. A speaker who says sarcastically to an addressee "You're a fine friend" assumes that the hearer shares enough pragmatic knowledge concerning the contextual setting and the speaker's beliefs and attitudes to interpret the utterance. Most traditional analyses of irony and sarcasm have supposed that pragmatic information is evaluated only after some analysis of the literal meanings of these sentences is completed. It is commonly assumed that the speaker's tone of voice then acts as a cue to sarcastic intentions (Grice, 1978; Searle, 1979b). Specifically, the tone of voice is thought to cue the listener to compute the opposite of the sentence's literal meaning to get to its sarcastic interpretation.

However, the present studies have shown that people appear to use pragmatic information, as presented in the story contexts, very early in understanding what speakers mean in using sarcasm. People do not take any longer to process sarcastic utterances than literal ones even without auditory information. This doesn't necessarily mean that prosody plays no role in the interpretation of sarcasm. Sperber and Wilson (1981) provided a convincing argument that prosodic cues function to help hearers recognize the echoic mention involved by a speaker's use of sarcasm or irony. Nevertheless, the results of the present studies indicate that prosody does not by itself make sarcastic expressions particularly memorable or easy to understand. The fact that speakers can comprehend sarcastic remarks as fast as, if not faster than, literal utterances suggests that computation of the context-in-dependent, literal meanings of sarcastic expressions is *not* necessary before their nonliteral, sarcastic interpretations can be derived.

This may, at first, seem like a startling conclusion. After all, to understand what a speaker means when uttering "You're a fine friend" will at the very least have to take into account that he or she uttered the words "You're a fine friend" and meant them literally, even if it is then argued that the speaker intends the hearer to set aside the literal meaning for one that is sarcastic. Another possibility, though, espoused by the Echoic Mention Theory, is that in being sarcastic a speaker is mentioning, rather than using, the literal meaning of his or her utterance. Understanding sarcasm, according to this view, depends on identifying the mentioned material and the speaker's attitude toward it. Certainly, the results of Experiments 2 and 3, examining reading time, and Experiments 5 and 6, examining recall, strongly demonstrated that people comprehend sarcastic utterances much more easily, and remember them better, if these expressions mention some putative belief or attitude held by the addressee (which are presented as antecedent information in the story contexts).

Nevertheless, it may not be the case that recognition of the sarcastic utterance as an instance of mention involves understanding these expressions' literal, context-independent meanings. Many sarcastic remarks do not even possess well-defined literal meanings, such as "You are the cream in my coffee" (meaning something like "You are a burden to me"). Moreover, there are instances of sarcasm in which the literal meaning has nothing whatsoever to do with the speaker's intentions. The literal meaning of the sarcastic indirect request "Why don't you take your time getting the ball?" (meaning "Hurry up and get the ball") is just a simple literal question and is not related to the speaker's intention to use this utterance sarcastically as a request (Gibbs, 1983b).

The assumption that any utterance has a fixed, context-independent meaning may not be true (see Gibbs, 1984, for details). The literal meaning of any utterance will depend, from the first moment, on the different assumptions people have about the circumstances of its production. This suggests, then, that the literal meaning of a sentence is no more stable than the eventual interpretation that it supposedly yields. Literal meaning, rather than being independent of interpretation, is a product of it. Because literal meanings are interpretive, and not given by the putative semantics of the sentence in a null context, they cannot be the indisputable ground on which subsequent interpretation rests (see Fish, 1980, 1983; Gibbs, 1982, 1984).

This alternative view proposes that understanding sarcasm involves figuring out the literal meaning of the utterance, but more specifically, the literal meaning of the utterance as interpreted in light of the pragmatic information shared by speakers and hearers. In understanding sarcasm, or irony (see Jorgensen et al., 1984; Clark &

Gerrig, 1984; Sperber, 1984; Williams, 1984), hearers must see how the speaker's utterance is relevant to the common ground—the mutual beliefs, knowledge, and suppositions—already established between speakers and addressees. On this account, the interpretation of sarcasm lies in the difficulty of determining *which* literal meaning the speaker is referring to by his or her *mention* of an utterance, such as "You're a fine friend." The fact that speakers and hearers recognize that they mutually share certain pragmatic information makes the use of sarcasm possible and easy to comprehend and remember.

ACKNOWLEDGMENTS

This research was supported by a Faculty Research Grant from the University of California, Santa Cruz.

I wish to thank Keith Brittany for his assistance in testing subjects and Gayle Gonzales and Rachel Mueller for their comments on an earlier draft of this article.

Correspondence concerning this article should be addressed to Raymond W. Gibbs, Jr., Program in Experimental Psychology, Clark Kerr Hall, University of California, Santa Cruz, CA 95064.

ENDNOTES

1. In the present experiment, and for each of the following studies, analyses of variance (ANOVAs) were initially performed with list (subsets of items) as a between-subjects variable. Because a number of subjects were assigned to receive a given list of items, the ANOVA treats both subjects within-list and Sentence Type × Subjects within-list as random effects. If the effect of list does not interact with other variables, this suggests that the individual items are behaving alike. Some researchers have argued that the statistical tests performed with lists as a factor are generalizable to the larger population of subjects and materials (see Clark, 1973, p. 348; Clark, Cohen, Smith, & Keppel, 1976, pp. 264–265). Nevertheless, because it is not entirely clear how many lists are needed and because such generalizations would depend on accepting the null hypothesis, I have chosen to report the conservative F'_{min} statistic. Consequently, I will discuss the list factor only when the main effect or interaction of list with other variables is significant. Otherwise, list will be dropped as a factor in the analyses presented throughout the article.
2. The people echoed in this study were obviously not the hearers whose comprehension was assessed. That is, subjects were not actively involved in the conversation, but participated as overhearers (see Clark & Carlson, 1982, for a discussion of overhearers and their effect on conversation). Consequently, the narratives accompanying the conversations were constructed so that the overhearers or subjects would know the beliefs of the hearer being echoed. This was done to ensure that the subjects would be able to comprehend the source of the sarcastic remark.
3. The fact that subjects viewed the final sentences in the nonechoic contexts as sarcastic is interesting. This result suggested that there may be some very implicit echoes operating in the nonechoic contexts, perhaps echoes of some vague cultural or social norms. This possibility will be further explored in Experiment 3.

REFERENCES

Bach, K., & Harnish, S. (1979). *Linguistic communication and speech acts*. Cambridge, MA: MIT Press.

Bates, E., Kintsch, W., Fletcher, C., & Giuliani, V. (1980). The role of pronominalization and ellipsis in texts: Some memory experiments. *Journal of Experimental Psychology: Human Learning and Memory, 6*, 676–691.

Bates, E., Masling, M., & Kintsch, W. (1978). Recognition memory for aspects of dialogue. *Journal of Experimental Psychology: Human Learning and Memory, 3*, 187–197.

Bransford, J., & Franks, J. (1971). The abstraction of linguistic ideas. *Cognitive Psychology, 2*, 331–350.

Carpenter, P., & Just, M. (1975). Sentence comprehension: A psycholinguistic processing model of verification. *Psychological Review, 82*, 45–73.

Clark, H. (1973). Language-as-a-fixed-effect-fallacy: A critique of language statistics in psychological research. *Journal of Verbal Learning and Verbal Behavior, 12*, 335–359.

Clark, H., & Carlson, T. (1982). Hearers' beliefs and speech acts. *Language, 58*, 332–373.

Clark, H., Cohen, J., Smith, K., & Keppel, G. (1976). Discussion of Wike and Church's comments. *Journal of Verbal Learning and Verbal Behavior, 15*, 257–266.

Clark, H., & Gerrig, R. (1984). On the pretense theory of irony. *Journal of Experimental Psychology: General, 113*, 121–126.

Clark, H., & Lucy, P. (1975). Understanding what is meant from what is said: A study in conversationally conveyed requests. *Journal of Verbal Learning and Verbal Behavior, 14*, 430–477.

Craik, F. I. M., & Tulving, E. (1975). Depth of processing and the retention of words in episodic memory. *Journal of Experimental Psychology: General, 104*, 268–294.

Cutler, A. (1974). On meaning what you say without saying what you mean. In *Papers from the Tenth Regional Meeting, Chicago Linguistic Society* (pp. 117–127). Chicago: Chicago Linguistic Society.

Cutler, A. (1976). Beyond parsing and lexical look-up: An enriched description of auditory sentence comprehension. In R. Wales & E. Walker (Eds.), *New approaches to language mechanisms* (pp. 133–150). Amsterdam: North-Holland.

Fish, S. (1980). Normal circumstances, literal language, direct speech acts, the ordinary, the everyday, the obvious, what goes without saying, and other special cases. In S. Fish (Ed.), *Is there a text in this class?* (pp. 268–292). Cambridge, MA: Harvard University Press.

Fish, S. (1983). Short people got no reason to live: Reading irony. *Daedalus, 112*, 175–191.

Fowler, H. (1965). *A dictionary of modern English usage* (2nd ed.). Oxford, UK: Oxford University Press.

Gibbs, R. (1979). Contextual effects in understanding indirect requests. *Discourse Processes, 2*, 1–10.

Gibbs, R. (1980). Spilling the beans on understanding and memory for idioms in conversation. *Memory & Cognition, 8*, 449–456.

Gibbs, R. (1981). Memory for requests in conversation. *Journal of Verbal Learning and Verbal Behavior, 20*, 630–640.

Gibbs, R. (1982). A critical examination of the contribution of literal meaning to understanding nonliteral discourse. *Text, 2*, 9–27.

Gibbs, R. (1983a). Do people always process the literal meanings of indirect requests? *Journal of Experimental Psychology: Learning, Memory and Cognition, 9*, 524–533.

Gibbs, R. (1983b, August). Understanding sarcasm and irony. In R. Hoffman (Chair), *Recent research on metaphor*. Symposium conducted at the annual meeting of the American Psychological Association, Anaheim, CA.

Gibbs, R. (1984). Literal meaning and psychological theory. *Cognitive Science, 8*, 275–304.

Gibbs, R. (1986). Skating on thin ice: Literal meaning and understanding idioms in conversation. *Discourse Processes, 9,* 17–30.

Glucksberg, S., Gildea, P., & Bookin, H. (1982). On understanding non-literal speech: Can people ignore metaphor? *Journal of Verbal Learning and Verbal Behavior, 21,* 85–98.

Glushko, R., & Cooper, L. (1978). Spatial comprehension and comparison processes in verification tasks. *Cognitive Psychology, 10,* 391–421.

Gordon, D., & Lakoff, G. (1971). Conversational postulates. *Papers from the Seventh Regional Meeting, Chicago Linguistic Society* (pp. 63–84).

Grice, H. P. (1975). Logic and conversation. In P. Cole & J. Morgan (Eds.), *Syntax and semantics 3: Speech acts* (pp. 41–58). New York: Academic.

Grice, H. P. (1978). Some further notes on logic and conversation. In P. Cole (Ed.), *Syntax and semantics 9: Pragmatics* (pp. 113–128). New York: Academic.

Jarvella, R., & Collas, J. (1974). Memory for the intentions of sentences. *Memory & Cognition, 2,* 185–188.

Jorgensen, J., Miller, G., & Sperber, D. (1984). A test of the mention theory of irony. *Journal of Experimental Psychology: General, 10,* 1–9.

Kaufer, D. (1981). Understanding ironic communication. *Journal of Pragmatics, 5,* 495–510.

Keenan, J., MacWhinney, B., & Mayhew, D. (1977). Pragmatics in memory: A study of natural conversation. *Journal of Verbal Learning and Verbal Behavior, 16,* 549–560.

Kintsch, W., & Bates, E. (1977). Recognition memory for statements from a classroom lecture. *Journal of Experimental Psychology: Human Learning and Memory, 3,* 150–168.

MacWhinney, B., Keenan, J., & Reinke, P. (1982). The role of arousal in memory for conversation. *Memory & Cognition, 10,* 308–317.

Ortony, A., Reynolds, R., Schallert, D., & Antos, S. (1978). Interpreting metaphors and idioms: Some effects of context on comprehension. *Journal of Verbal Learning and Verbal Behavior, 17,* 465–477.

Searle, J. (1975). Indirect speech acts. In P. Cole & J. Morgan (Eds.), *Syntax and semantics 3: Speech acts* (pp. 59–82). New York: Academic.

Searle, J. (1979a). Literal meaning. In J. Searle (Ed.), *Expression and meaning* (pp. 117–136). Cambridge, UK: Cambridge University Press.

Searle, J. (1979b). Metaphor. In A. Ortony (Ed.), *Metaphor and thought* (pp. 92–123). Cambridge, UK: Cambridge University Press.

Sperber, D. (1984). Verbal irony: Pretense or echoic mention? *Journal of Experimental Psychology: General, 113,* 130–136.

Sperber, D., & Wilson, D. (1981). Irony and the use-mention distinction. In P. Cole (Ed.), *Radical pragmatics* (pp. 295–318). New York: Academic.

Swinney, D., & Cutler, A. (1979). Access and processing of idiomatic expressions. *Journal of Verbal Learning and Verbal Behavior, 18,* 523–534.

Williams, J. (1984). Does mention (or pretense) exhaust the concept of irony? *Journal of Experimental Psychology: General, 113,* 127–129.

Wilson, D., & Sperber, D. (1981). On Grice's theory of conversation. In P. Werth (Ed.), *Conversation and discourse* (pp. 155–178). New York: St. Martin's Press.

CHAPTER 8

Irony: Context and Salience

Rachel Giora
Tel Aviv University

Ofer Fein
Princeton University

Two experiments test a graded salience account of irony processing (Giora, Fein, & Schwartz, 1998). Experiment 1 shows that, as predicted, less familiar targets embedded in ironically biasing contexts facilitate only the salient literal meaning initially: 150 msec after their offset. However, 1,000 msec after their offset, the less salient ironic meaning becomes available and the literal meaning is still as active. In contrast, familiar ironies facilitate both their salient literal and ironic meanings initially: 150 msec after their offset. Results do not change significantly after a 1,000-msec delay. In the literally biasing contexts, less familiar ironies facilitate only the salient literal meaning. In contrast, familiar ironies facilitate both their salient literal and ironic meanings under both interstimulus interval conditions, as predicted. Experiment 2 confirms that these findings were affected by the target sentences rather than by the contexts themselves. In Experiment 2, the contexts were presented without the targets, inducing no difference in response patterns.

Irony comprehension is believed to rely heavily on context (cf. Katz & Lee, 1993). Researchers, however, fail to agree on the temporal stage at which context affects irony comprehension. Some studies report results consistent with the interactive, direct access view (e.g., Gibbs, 1986a, 1986b, 1994; Gibbs, O'Brien, & Doolittle, 1995; see Sperber & Wilson, 1986/1995, p. 239 for similar assumptions) that assumes that contextual information affects comprehension very early on. They question the traditional assumptions often known as the Standard Pragmatic Model (Grice, 1987; Searle, 1979; see Temple & Honeck, 1999, for recent findings regarding proverb comprehension) that posit the precedence of the compositional interpretation of the sentence over its nonliteral interpretation. The claim is that in a rich

This chapter was previously published as "Irony: context and salience" (R. Giora & O. Fein) in *Metaphor and Symbol, 14,* 241–257. Copyright © [1999] by Lawrence Erlbaum Associates. Reprinted with permission.

201

and supportive context, irony is comprehended more or less directly, bypassing the contextually incompatible literal interpretation of the ironic utterance. According to the direct access view, then, appropriate contexts should enhance activation of the contextually appropriate meaning, so that only that meaning becomes available for comprehension. Embedded in appropriate contexts, then, ironic and literal interpretations should involve equivalent processes (see also Kumon-Nakamura, Glucksberg, & Brown, 1995). Evidence supporting the direct access view of irony comes from equal reading times of ironic and nonironic utterances (Gibbs, 1986a, 1986b; Gibbs et al., 1995; see Giora, 1995, and Dews & Winner, 1997, for a critique of some of the findings).

In contrast, some studies are consistent with some aspects of the modular view (Dews & Winner, 1997, 1999; Giora, 1995; Grice, 1975; Searle, 1979) that assumes that the lexical processes involved at the initial stage of comprehension should not be affected by nonlexical information. Rather, they are automatic and autonomous, and impervious to context effects (cf. Fodor, 1983). The initial stage of irony comprehension must, therefore, be literal. Contextual information should affect irony comprehension only at a later stage and should trigger revisitation of the contextually incompatible literal meaning. On this view, irony comprehension should involve more complex inferential processes than literal interpretation. Findings consistent with a modular-based view of irony comprehension show that utterances took longer to read in ironically than in literally biased contexts (Giora, 1999a; Giora, Fein, & Schwartz, 1998; Schwoebel, Dews, Winner, & Srinivas, 1999) and longer to be judged as positive or negative relative to their literal counterparts (Dews & Winner, 1997). They further show that irony comprehension involved longer response times to ironically than to literally related probes (Giora et al., 1998).

The different views and findings may be reconciled by a more general principle of salience. According to the graded salience hypothesis (Giora, 1997, 1999a, 1999b; Giora et al., 1998; Giora & Fein, in press; see also Goldvarg & Glucksberg, 1998), the factor determining initial activation is neither literality nor compatibility with context, but rather the salience of the verbal stimulus: Salient meanings of words and expressions should always be accessed and always first. A meaning of a word or an expression is salient if it is coded in the mental lexicon. Salience, however, admits degrees. Factors affecting degree of salience are, for example, conventionality, frequency, familiarity, or prototypicality. For instance, both meanings of *bank* (i.e., the "financial institution" and the "river edge" meanings) are listed in the mental lexicon. However, for those of us from urban communities, in which rivers are less common than financial institutions, the commercial sense of *bank* is foremost (i.e., salient). By the same token, the riverside sense is less salient. In contrast, inferences computed on the fly are nonsalient because they are not coded in the mental lexicon.

Although prior context may enhance a word's meaning, it is relatively ineffective in inhibiting activation of salient meanings. For example, in *I needed money, so I went to the bank,* the prior occurrence of the word *money* may speed up activation of the financial institution meaning of *bank*. In *Standing on the riverbank I saw some fish,* the word *river* may facilitate activation of the riverside meaning of *bank*. However, although "river" in *riverbank* may enhance the less salient riverside meaning of *bank,* it may not prevent activation of its more salient, financial institution meaning on its encounter: The salient, financial institution meaning would pop up in spite of contextual misfit. The major claim of the graded salience hypothesis, then, is that salient meanings of words and collocations are always accessed initially (although not necessarily solely), irrespective of contextual information or bias (see also Rayner, Pacht, & Duffy, 1994; for a more detailed discussion, see Giora, 1997, 1999a; see Vu, Kellas, & Paul, 1998, for a different view).

According to the graded salience hypothesis, then, the salient meaning of a word or an expression is accessed directly. When it is contextually compatible, no more processes are required. However, when a less salient meaning has to be activated to make sense of an utterance (as in the case of the literal meaning of conventional idioms or the ironic interpretation of familiar metaphors), comprehension should involve an ordered access: The more salient, albeit inappropriate meaning should be processed initially, before the less salient, appropriate meaning can be retrieved. Indeed, participants took longer to read idioms in a literally than in an idiomatically biased context (Gibbs, 1980, 1986c), and their literal paraphrases took longer to be judged as meaningful than their nonliteral interpretations, regardless of contextual bias (Gibbs, 1986c). In this connection, we should introduce a cautionary note about possible confounds. Appropriate paraphrases for literal utterances are always problematic. Although idioms may have a nonliteral interpretation at their disposal, which is different from their literal compositional meaning, literal utterances do not. Whereas *"Kick the bucket"* has a coded interpretation that can be computed directly from the mental lexicon ("die"), its literal interpretation (kick the bucket, literally) does not have a ready-made literal paraphrase that can be similarly computed (e.g., "tip the pail"). Consequently, literal paraphrases tend to be made up of a lot less salient or frequent words. Consider the commonality of the interpretation of the nonliteral meaning of the idiom *"He kept it under his hat"* ("He did not tell anyone") as opposed to the oddity and scarcity of its literal interpretation and words ("It is beneath his cap"). This could be one reason why literal targets took longer to read in Gibbs (1986c). In Pexman, Ferretti, and Katz (1999), participants took longer to read ironic than metaphoric interpretations of familiar (but also less familiar) metaphors.

In the same vein, when two or more meanings are salient, they should be accessed in parallel. Thus, conventional metaphors whose figurative and literal meanings are similarly salient should be processed directly both literally and metaphorically (as shown by Blasko & Connine, 1993; see Giora, 1999a, for a critique; see also Williams, 1992, regarding metaphorically based polysemies). Consequently, they should take equally long to read in literally and metaphorically biasing contexts (Giora & Fein, 1999; see Turner & Katz, 1997, for similar findings regarding familiar proverbs).

The graded salience hypothesis (Giora, 1997, 1999a, 1999b; see also Récanati, 1995, and Turner & Katz, 1997, for somewhat similar views) is thus consistent with an ordered access account (see Gorfein, 1989; Hogaboam & Perfetti, 1975; Kawamoto, 1993; Rayner et al., 1994; Simpson & Burgess, 1985), which maintains that lexical processes are autonomous but sensitive to frequency. It holds that the factor relevant to comprehension is not literality (or nonliterality), but the degree of salience of the utterance processed. It predicts that less familiar ironies would be initially processed only literally, in both literally and ironically biasing contexts, because less familiar ironies have only one salient meaning—the literal meaning (made up, among other things, of the salient, literal meanings of the lexical components). Ironically biasing contexts should affect their processing only at a later stage, in which the ironic meaning may be inferred. In contrast, familiar ironies, whose ironic (utterance) meaning and literal (lexical) meanings are coded in the lexicon, would be processed in parallel in both types of contexts.

EXPERIMENT I

In Experiment 1, 48 students were shown both familiar and less familiar ironies, embedded in contexts biasing their interpretation either toward a literal or an ironic meaning. Having read the texts, the participants had to make a lexical decision as to whether a letter string was a word or a nonword. The critical manipulations were the type of word—which was either related to the ironic or the literal interpretation of the irony—and the interval between the display of the irony and the display of the letter string. This enabled us to assess the activation of both the literal and ironic meanings in both types of ironies after two different intervals (150 msec and 1,000 msec).

Method

Design.   A $2 \times 2 \times 2 \times 2 \times 2$ factorial design was used with interstimulus interval (ISI; 150 msec and 1,000 msec) as a between-subjects factor, and irony type (less familiar and familiar), context type (ironically and literally biased), word type (ironically and literally related), and stimulus type (word and nonword) as within-subjects factor.

Participants.   Forty-eight undergraduate students (23 women and 25 men) of Tel Aviv University, ranging from 22 to 30 years old, served as paid participants. They were all native speakers of Hebrew.

Texts.   Thirty-two ironies ("target sentences") were selected for Experiment 1 and presented in Hebrew. Sixteen were familiar ironies, and 16 were less familiar ironies. The ironies were classified as "familiar" and "less familiar" on the basis of a familiarity pretest. In the familiarity pretest, 24 undergraduates, all of whom are native speakers of Hebrew, were presented 40 contextless sentences. They participated in the test as part of their class assignments. They were asked to write down the coded meaning or meanings of the sentences. A sentence that received an ironic interpretation from more than half of the tested population was classified as "a familiar irony." Sentences not reaching that threshold were classified as "less familiar ironies." Sixty-four contexts, three to four sentences long, were created, two for each target sentence. One biased the last clause—the target sentence—toward the ironic interpretation (e.g., 1a and 2a translated from Hebrew; see also the Appendix), and the other biased it toward the literal interpretation (e.g., 1b and 2b translated from Hebrew; see also the Appendix):

Familiar irony:
(1a)   Iris was walking on her own in the dark alley, when all of a sudden a hand was laid on her back. Startled, she turned around to find out that the hand was her young brother's who sneaked behind her to frighten her. She said to him, "Very funny."
(1b)   Tal and Ortal, the twins, wanted to go to the movies. Their mother recommended a movie she had seen shortly before. When they came home, she was eager to know how they found the movie. They both agreed, "Very funny."
        Ironically related test word: *annoying*
        Literally related test word: *amusing*

Less familiar irony:
(2a)   After he had finished eating pizza, falafel, ice cream, wafers, and half of the cream cake his mother had baked for his brother Benjamin's birthday party, Moshe started eating coated peanuts. His mother said to him, "Moshe, I think you should eat something."
(2b)   At two o'clock in the afternoon, Moshe started doing his homework and getting prepared for his Bible test. When his mother came home from work at eight p.m., Moshe was still seated at his desk, looking pale. His mother said to him, "Moshe, I think you should eat something."
        Ironically related test word: *stop*
        Literally related test word: *little*

Apparatus.   Stimuli presentation and response collection were controlled by an IBM-compatible 386 PC, using a Pascal program. Each of the 32 target sentences was followed by one of four (Hebrew) stimuli:

   a. A word related to the literal meaning of the target sentence (e.g., *amusing;* see 1b).
   b. A word related to the ironic meaning of the target sentence (e.g., *annoying;* see 1a).
   c. A nonword created by a rearrangement of the letters of 1a (e.g., *uamsing*).
   d. A nonword created by a rearrangement of the letters of 1b (e.g., *oyignnan*).

The combination of two context types and four stimulus types created eight conditions. Two familiar and two less familiar ironies were assigned to each condition, in an 8 × 8 Latin square design, in which each row was assigned to six participants. All texts were arranged randomly and presented in a different order for each participant.

Procedure.   Participants were tested individually. They were each seated in front of a computer and were instructed as follows:

> During the experiment, you will have to assess whether a letter string that will be displayed on the screen is a word (e.g., *table*) or a nonword (e.g., *latbe*). You will be presented with short stories that will be displayed sentence by sentence, which you will have to read. After the last sentence of each story, the letter string will be displayed. You will have to press the "l" key if the string makes up a word, and the "a" key if it is a nonword. You have to press the key as fast as possible, but make sure that you do not make mistakes. Now you will be presented with 3 trial texts for training. Please put your right finger on the "l" key and the left finger on the "a" key and press one of them to start the training.

The texts were presented line by line. Each line, mostly corresponding to a sentence, appeared in the center of the screen for 3 sec. It then disappeared, and the next line was displayed. The last line—the target sentence—was displayed for a length of time that was determined by its score in a pretest. This pretest, which included 10 participants, measured the average reading time of each sentence out of context. After the target sentence was displayed for as long as it had scored in the pretest, the screen went blank for an ISI of either 150 msec or 1,000 msec. For half of the participants (three of each group of six participants assigned to each Latin square row), the ISI was 150 msec, and for half it was 1,000 msec. After the ISI, the test word (either a word or a nonword) was displayed in the center of the screen, and the participant had to respond by pressing one of two ("l" or "a") keys. The latency between the onset of the word–nonword and the pressing of the key was measured by the computer and served as response time (RT). A 2-sec blank screen followed the response, and then the first line of the next text was displayed. The presentation of the 32 trials began after three training trials and was preceded by two buffer trials.

Results

Both participant and item analyses were conducted. For the participant analyses, we averaged the RT of the two trials in each condition. For the item analyses, we averaged the RT of the three trials in each condition. RT outliers above or below 2 standard deviations from either the participants' or the items' mean (about 7%) were excluded from the analysis. In addition, five participants who had means 2 standard deviations above the overall mean were replaced. In both the participant and item analyses, only the responses to word stimuli were of interest, and only they were subjected to four-way analyses of variance (ANOVAs). Means and standard deviations for all conditions are presented in Table 8.1. The participant ANOVA included one between-subjects variable (ISI: 150 msec or 1000 msec) and three within-subjects factors: irony type (less familiar and familiar), context type (ironically and literally biased), and word type (compatible and incompatible with context). This ANOVA showed only two significant effects. First, there was a significant Context Type × Word Type interaction, $F(1, 44) = 4.28, p < .05$. However, this effect results primarily from the three-way Irony Type × Context Type × Word Type interaction, $F(1, 44) = 6.31, p < .05$. The equivalent item ANOVA showed only a significant effect of ISI, $F(1, 30) = 11.45, p < .005$. To test more precisely the different predictions about Context Type × Word Type interactions, four separate ANOVAs were performed, two for less familiar ironies (one for an ISI of 150 msec and another for an ISI of 1,000 msec) and two for familiar ironies (for both ISIs). Each 2 × 2 ANOVA included two within-subjects factors, context type (ironically and literally biased) and word type (compatible and incompatible with context).

Less Familiar Ironies. For less familiar ironies ("*Moshe, I think you should eat something*"), the participant ANOVA for the 150 msec ISI revealed no main effects (all *F*s < 1), but a significant Context Type × Word Type interaction, $F(1, 22) = 5.07, p < .05$, as illustrated in Figure 8.1 (top panel). The same interaction in the corresponding item analysis was almost significant, $F(1, 15) = 4.38, p = .054$. As predicted by the graded salience hypothesis, participants were faster to respond to the salient than to the less salient test word. In the literally biasing context (2b), it was the contextually compatible (i.e., literally related) test word (*little*) rather than the contextually incompatible (i.e., ironically related) test word (*stop*) that was responded to faster. In the ironically biasing context (2a), however, it was the contextually incompatible (i.e., literally related) test word (*little*) rather than the contextually compatible (i.e., ironically related) test word (*stop*) that was responded to faster. At this early stage of processing, participants always

TABLE 8-1

Mean Response Times (in Milliseconds) to Words Compatible or Incompatible With Context–Experiment 1

	150 msec				1,000 msec			
	Ironic Text		Literal Text		Ironic Text		Literal Text	
Word	M	SD	M	SD	M	SD	M	SD
Less familiar ironies								
Compatible	1,099	253	993	232	937	313	920	261
Incompatible	1,055	259	1,099	373	934	278	1078	321
Familiar ironies								
Compatible	1,053	252	1,063	320	877	239	964	281
Incompatible	1,031	327	1,094	293	932	255	963	346

responded faster to the salient (literally related) test word, irrespective of contextual compatibility.

The participant ANOVA for the 1,000 msec ISI produced different results. This time there was a significant context type effect, $F(1, 22) = 5.65$, $p < .05$, which can be explained by the significant Context Type × Word Type interaction, $F(1,22) = 8.30$, $p < .01$. The pattern of this interaction is quite different from the pattern of the previous (150 msec ISI) interaction, as the bottom panel of Figure 8.1 illustrates. As predicted by the graded salience hypothesis, after a 1,000-msec delay, contextual information affected comprehension of less familiar irony, and participants no longer responded faster to the salient, contextually incompatible, literally related (*lit-*

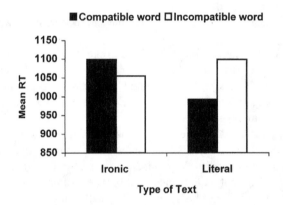

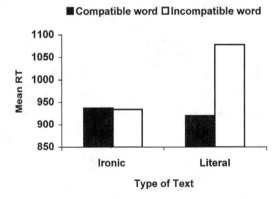

Figure 8.1.   Mean response time (in milliseconds) to compatible and incompatible words related to less familiar ironies embedded in ironically and literally biasing contexts, for interstimulus intervals of 150 msec (top panel) and 1,000 msec (bottom panel).

tle) test word in these contexts. This was confirmed by the lack of significant effect when comparing the compatible and the incompatible responses in the ironically biasing context alone, $F(1, 22) < 1$. In contrast, the same comparison performed on results obtained from the literally biasing context reveals a significant word type effect, $F(1, 22) = 15.90$, $p < .001$, reflecting the fact that in this context, literally related test words were still processed faster than ironically related test words. The item analysis, however, failed to show any significant effect (all $ps > .15$). These results show that after a long delay, less salient but contextually compatible meanings no longer lag behind salient meanings.

Familiar Ironies. For familiar ironies, all ANOVAs (for the 150 msec and 1,000 msec ISIs, both across participants and items) indicate no significant effect (all $ps > .20$), as predicted. According to the graded salience hypothesis, given the coded, salient status of both the literal and the ironic meanings of familiar ironies, they should both be activated initially, regardless of context.

Discussion

Our findings show that salient meanings are always processed initially, regardless of contextual information. The salient literal meaning of both familiar and less familiar ironies was swiftly available in the ironically biased context, even though it was incompatible with contextual information. Furthermore, familiar ironies facilitated their salient albeit contextually incompatible ironic meaning in the literally biasing contexts. These findings are consistent with the view that contextual information does not affect initial access (cf. Fodor, 1983; Swinney, 1979): At the early stage of comprehension, context neither availed the meaning compatible with it, nor did it block the meaning incompatible with it. Salient information was accessed directly and automatically. When it did not reach contextual fit, it was adjusted to contextual information. This adjustment stage occurred at a later moment of comprehension—1,000 msec after the offset of the target sentence. When it did, as in the case of familiar ironies, search for the appropriate meaning was stopped. Direct access, then, is not necessarily a function of context monitoring access of appropriate meanings (see Gibbs, 1994; Glucksberg, Kreuz, & Rho 1986). Rather, direct access may be a function of meaning salience (for a similar view of comprehension, see Gibbs, 1980, 1982, 1983, 1986c; for recent research, see Horton & Keysar, 1996; Keysar, Barr, Balin, & Paek, 1998; Keysar, Barr, & Horton, 1998).

EXPERIMENT 2

A number of alternative explanations for the results obtained in Experiment 1 may come to mind. It is plausible that word frequency of the probes affected our results. It is also possible that the context itself, rather than the target sentences, induced the pattern of results achieved under the short ISI condition in Experiment 1. To control for these confounds, we repeated the 150 msec condition, where we found differ-

ences, with one exception. We simply presented participants with the contexts
without the target sentences. We assumed that if the results of Experiment 1 were
replicated in the absence of the target sentences, this would suggest that these results were not determined by the degree of salience of the targets, but rather by either word frequency or contextual information. However, if no differences ensue,
this would support our claim that the early moments of comprehension are impervious to context effects, yet sensitive to degree of salience.

Method

Design.   A $2 \times 2 \times 2 \times 2$ factorial design was used with context type (ironically
and literally biased), word type (ironically and literally related), irony type (familiar
and less familiar), and stimulus type (word and nonword) as within-subjects factors.

Participants.   Twenty-four undergraduate students (14 women, 10 men) of
Tel Aviv University, ranging in age from 21 to 24 years old, served as paid participants. They were all native speakers of Hebrew. They did not participate in Experiment 1.

Texts.   As in Experiment 1, except for the target sentences, which were left out.

Procedure.   As in Experiment 1, except for the ISI, which this time was only
150 msec.

Results and Discussion

The data were analyzed in the same way as in Experiment 1: 5.5% of the RTs that
were outliers were excluded from the analyses. Means and standard deviations for
all conditions are presented in Table 8.2. Overall, three-way participant and item
ANOVAs did not produce any significant result (all $ps > .15$). Even when the data
were analyzed separately for familiar and less familiar ironies, both ANOVAs indicated no significant effect (all $ps > .15$) either across participants or across items.

TABLE 8-2

Mean Response Times (in Milliseconds) to Words Compatible or Incompatible With Context,
in the Absence of Targets–Experiment 2

| | Less Familiar Ironies (150 msec) | | | | Familiar Ironies (150 msec) | | | |
| | Ironic Text | | Literal Text | | Ironic Text | | Literal Text | |
Word	M	SD	M	SD	M	SD	M	SD
Compatible	1,213	304	1,183	289	1,207	363	1,237	294
Incompatible	1,200	301	1,200	330	1,286	440	1,265	340

Experiment 2 served as a control. The results show that when no target sentences (i.e., ironies) were presented, test words were responded to with similar RTs (although with higher latencies than in Experiment 1). Neither test words' saliency and frequency nor contextual information (which, if anything, was slightly, though insignificantly, biased toward the ironic interpretation) can account for the results of Experiment 1. Such results, then, have to be attributed to the effect of the target sentences themselves (albeit in context).

GENERAL DISCUSSION

Our findings support a salient-first comprehension model (Giora, 1997, 1999a, 1999b; Giora et al., 1998). Salient meanings were processed initially, regardless of contextual information. They were always responded to faster at the initial comprehension stage, irrespective of contextual information. For instance, in the ironically biasing contexts, familiar and less familiar ironies were processed literally initially, in spite of contextual incompatibility. Similarly, in the literally biasing contexts, familiar ironies were processed ironically initially, regardless of contextual bias (see Experiment 1).

Experiment 2 further demonstrates that the various patterns of response exhibited in Experiment 1 were not a result of context effects or (test) word frequency. The targetless contexts in Experiment 2 did not result in different response pattern to the test words, as did the same contexts when followed by the target sentences (see Experiment 1). Taken together, these findings suggest that salient meanings, both literal and nonliteral, are initially processed alike. In contrast, utterances diverging in salience (e.g., less salient ironic interpretation and more salient literal interpretations of less familiar ironies) behave differently.

Because the intended ironic meaning of less familiar irony is not salient, it requires extra processing time to be retrieved, as shown. The literal interpretation of the same utterances, however, did not benefit from extra processing time, because in the literally biasing context, salient (literal) meaning and contextual information accidentally matched. These findings contest a direct access view of irony comprehension that assumes that context constrains comprehension even at the initial stage of comprehension so that only contextually compatible meanings reach sufficient levels of activation. They also contest a literal-first model of comprehension (cf. Grice, 1975; Searle, 1979). They show, instead, that it is salient rather than either literal or contextually compatible meaning that is activated initially.

However, it could be argued that, although there is no doubt that it is the target sentences rather than the contexts that primed the test words, our probes were not, in fact, tailored to distinguish word from message level meanings. Thus, literally related test words could be primed by words, whereas ironically related test words could only be primed by the sentence (ironic) interpretation. For instance, whereas *funny* in "Very funny" (see Example 1) could prime *amusing* (the literally related test word), interpreting the utterance "Very funny" was required before *annoying* (the ironically related test word) could be primed, because *annoying* taps the message level meaning. If this is the case, then, the version of the direct access view that argues against the priority of the utterance's literal interpretation over the utterance's ironic interpretation (Gibbs, 1986b, 1994; Kumon-Nakamura et al., 1995) cannot be rejected.

Note, however, that it was not always the case that the literally related test words were responded to faster. Rather, it was salience-related test words that were responded to fastest, regardless of literality and nonliterality. These findings do not stand in isolation, but are corroborated by previous findings, which include reading times of whole sentences. In Giora et al. (1998), we measured the reading times of the set of unfamiliar stimuli used here. We found that these targets took longer to read in the ironically than in the literally biasing contexts, suggesting that non-salient (ironic) utterances took longer to comprehend than their more salient (literal) interpretations. Recall that the contexts were not found to be more heavily biased in favor of the literal interpretations (see Experiment 2). Such findings, then, suggest that participants analyzed the salient literal meanings of sentences before deriving their nonsalient ironic interpretation.

Longer reading times for less salient (ironic) interpretations than for more salient (literal) interpretations were also found by Schwoebel et al. (1999), in which participants advanced the text phrase by phrase across the screen by pressing a key. Pexman et al. (1999) also presented evidence in favor of a salient-first model of comprehension. They used self-paced moving windows in which participants advanced a text word by word, reflecting the moment by moment processing that occurs naturally. Their findings showed that utterances took longer to read when embedded in contexts biasing their interpretation toward the nonsalient ironic meaning than when embedded in contexts biasing their interpretation toward the salient (conventional metaphoric) meaning. Such findings support the graded salience hypothesis. They go beyond lexical decision tasks and help tease apart word-level, sentence-level, and message-level effects.

Our findings replicate previous findings. In Giora et al. (1998), lexical decision tasks induced similar patterns to those found in this article, only emerging more slowly. In Giora et al., the salient literal meaning was facilitated immediately in both types of context, as found in this article, but it was also the only one available after an ISI of 1,000 msec. Less salient ironic meanings were facilitated later than a 1,000-msec delay and were available 2,000 msec after the offset of the target sentence. We speculate that this change in speed of response is a matter of fatigue. In Giora et al., participants were presented with three times as many texts as in this article, a load that may have affected the participants' alertness.

In sum, our findings show that the processes involved in irony comprehension are a function of their salience. Less familiar ironies, whose literal but not ironic meaning is coded in the mental lexicon, were processed literally first, and consequently took longer to comprehend (ironically) than their literally intended counterparts. Processing more familiar ironies, however, involved accessing both their literal and ironic interpretations initially, because both these meanings are coded in the mental lexicon. Such ironies did not take longer to process than their literal counterparts, because their intended ironic meaning was accessed directly, in parallel with the unintended literal meaning. Direct access, then, may be a function of meaning salience, rather than of context effects. According to the graded salience hypothesis, more salient ironies than the Hebrew set tested in this article may, like idioms, be processed ironically first and literally second. Future research will show whether this is true of conventional English ironies, which are more common and frequent than Hebrew conventional ironies.

ACKNOWLEDGMENTS

Support for this research was provided to Rachel Giora by grants from The Israel Science Foundation and Lion Foundation.

We thank Lior Noy and Olga Zeigelman for preparing the software for the experiment, Shay Michaely for preparing the materials, Noga Balaban and Naama Har'el for their help in administering the experiments, and Ray Gibbs, Albert Katz, Ken McRae, and two anonymous referees for very helpful comments.

REFERENCES

Blasko, G. D., & Connine, C. (1993). Effects of familiarity and aptness on meta processing. *Journal of Experimental Psychology: Learning, Memory, and Cognition, 19,* 295–308.

Dews, S., & Winner, E. (1997). Attributing meaning to deliberately false utterances: The case of irony. In C. Mandell & A. McCabe (Eds.), *The problem of meaning: Behavioral and cognitive perspectives* (pp. 377–414). Amsterdam: Elsevier.

Fodor, J. (1983). *The modularity of mind.* Cambridge, MA: MIT Press.

Gerrig, R. J. (1989). The time course of sense creation. *Memory & Cognition, 17,* 194–207.

Gibbs, R. W., Jr. (1980). Spilling the bean on understanding and memory for idioms in conversation. *Memory & Cognition, 8,* 449–456.

Gibbs, R. W., Jr. (1986a). Comprehension and memory for nonliteral utterances: The problem of sarcastic indirect requests. *Acta Psychologica, 62,* 41–57.

Gibbs, R. W., Jr. (1986b). On the psycholinguistics of sarcasm. *Journal of Experimental Psychology: General, 115,* 3–15.

Gibbs, R. W., Jr. (1986c). Skating on thin ice: Literal meaning and understanding idioms in conversation. *Discourse Processes, 9,* 17–30.

Gibbs, R. W., Jr. (1994). *The poetics of mind.* Cambridge, England: Cambridge University Press.

Gibbs, R. W., Jr., O'Brien, J. E., & Doolittle, S. (1995). Inferring meanings that are not intended: Speakers' intentions and irony comprehension. *Discourse Processes, 20,* 187–203.

Giora, R. (1995). On irony and negation. *Discourse Processes, 19,* 239–264.

Giora, R. (1997). Understanding figurative and literal language: The graded salience hypothesis. *Cognitive Linguistics, 7,* 183–206.

Giora, R. (1999a). *On our mind: Salience, context, and figurative language.* Manuscript in preparation.

Giora, R. (1999b). On the priority of salient meanings: Studies of literal and figurative language. *Journal of Pragmatics, 31,* 919–929.

Giora, R., & Fein, O. (1999). On understanding familiar and less-familiar figurative language. *Journal of Pragmatics, 31,* 1601–1618.

Giora, R., & Fein, O. (1999). Irony comprehension: The graded salience hypothesis. *Humor: International Journal of Humor Research, 12,* 425–436.

Giora, R., Fein, O., & Schwartz, T. (1998). Irony: Graded salience and indirect negation. *Metaphor and Symbol, 13,* 83–101.

Glucksberg, S., Kreuz, R., & Rho, S. H. (1986). Context can constrain lexical access: Implications for models of language comprehension. *Journal of Experimental Psychology: Learning, Memory, and Cognition, 12,* 323–335.

Goldvarg, Y., & Glucksberg, S. (1998). Conceptual combinations: The role of similarity. *Metaphor and Symbol, 13,* 243–255.

Gorfein, S. D. (Ed.). (1989). *Resolving semantic ambiguity.* New York: Springer-Verlag.

Grice, P. H. (1975). Logic and conversation. In P. Cole & J. Morgan (Eds.), *Speech acts: Syntax and semantics* (Vol. 3, pp. 41–58). New York: Academic.

Hogaboam, T. W., & Perfetti, C. A. (1975). Lexical ambiguity and sentence comprehension. *Journal of Verbal Learning and Verbal Behavior, 14,* 265–174.

Horton, W. S., & Keysar, B. (1996). When do speakers take into account common ground? *Cognition, 59,* 91–117.

Katz, A., & Lee, C. J. (1993). The role of authorial intent in determining verbal irony and metaphor. *Metaphor and Symbolic Activity, 8,* 257–279.

Kawamoto, A. H. (1993). Nonlinear dynamics in the resolution of lexical ambiguity: A parallel distributed processing account. *Journal of Memory and Language, 32,* 474–516.

Keysar, B., Barr, D. J., Balin, J. A., & Paek, T. S. (1998). Definite reference and mutual knowledge: Process models of common ground in comprehension. *Journal of Memory and Language, 39,* 1–20.

Keysar, B., Barr, D. J., & Horton, W. S. (1998). The egocentric basis of language use: Insights from a processing approach. *Current Directions in Psychological Sciences, 7,* 46–50.

Kumon-Nakamura, S., Glucksberg, S., & Brown, M. (1995). How about another piece of the pie: The allusional pretense theory of discourse irony. *Journal of Experimental Psychology: General, 124,* 3–21.

Pexman, P., Ferretti, T., & Katz, A. (1999). *Discourse factors that influence irony detection during on-line reading.* Manuscript submitted for publication.

Rayner, K., Pacht, J. M., & Duffy, S. A. (1994). Effects of prior encounter and global discourse bias on the processing of lexically ambiguous words: Evidence from eye fixations. *Journal of Memory and Language, 33,* 527–544.

Récanati, F. (1995). The alleged priority of literal meaning. *Cognitive Science, 19,* 207–232.

Schwoebel, J., Dews, S., Winner, E., & Srinivas, K. (1999). *Obligatory processing of the literal meaning of ironic utterances: Further evidence.* Manuscript submitted for publication.

Simpson, G. B., & Burgess, C. (1985). Activation and selection processes in the recognition of ambiguous words. *Journal of Experimental Psychology: Human Perception and Performance, 11,* 28–39.

Sperber, D., & Wilson, D. (1995). *Relevance: Communication and cognition.* Oxford, England: Blackwell. (Original work published 1986)

Swinney, D. A. (1979). Lexical access during sentence comprehension: (Re)consideration of context effects. *Journal of Verbal Learning and Verbal Behavior, 18,* 645–659.

Temple, J. G., & Honeck, R. P. (1999). Proverb comprehension: The primacy of literal meaning. *Journal of Psycholinguistic Research, 28,* 41–70.

Turner, N. E., & Katz, A. (1997). Evidence for the availability of conventional and of literal meaning during the comprehension of proverbs. *Pragmatics and Cognition, 5,* 203–237.

Vu, H., Kellas, G., & Paul, S. T. (1998). Sources of sentence constraint on lexical ambiguity resolution. *Memory & Cognition, 26,* 979–1001.

Williams, J. N. (1992). Processing polysemous words in context. Evidence from interrelated meanings. *Journal of Psycholinguistic Research, 21,* 193–218.

APPENDIX

Examples of Test Stimuli

Translated sample items include the following: (a) versions are ironically biasing contexts, (b) versions are literally biasing contexts.

Familiar Ironies

Example 1

(1a)   Iris was walking on her own in the dark alley, when all of a sudden a hand was laid on her back. Startled, she turned around to find out that the hand was her young brother's who sneaked behind her to frighten her. She said to him, "Very funny."

(1b)   Tal and Ortal, the twins, wanted to go to the movies. Their mother recommended a movie she had seen shortly before. When they came home, she was eager to know how they found the movie. They both agreed, "Very funny."

Ironically related test word: *annoying*
Literally related test word: *amusing*

Example 2

(2a)   Ziv visited his friend, Ran, in New York. Ran advised him to use the subway, but Ziv insisted on renting a car. Three days later, Ziv gave up and told Ran: I have had enough. The traffic jam here is incredible. Ran said: "Tell me about it."

(2b)   In the middle of the night Royi woke up and started crying. His mother heard him and went up to his room. "What happened?" she asked. Royi said that he had had a nightmarish dream. His mother said, "Tell me about it."

Ironically related test word: *known*
Literally related test word: *disclosing*

Example 3

(3a)   At dinner Erez was talking to his family, bragging about how he beat all the neighborhood kids at chess. After his parents expressed their admiration, he admitted that actually all the competitors were at least four years younger than him. His sister retorted, "Very smart."

(3b)   Two year old Galit played with the new Lego pieces she had just received. Trying hard, she finally managed to build a nice and big Lego house. Her mother said, "Very smart."

Ironically related test word: *simple*
Literally related test word: *cleverness*

Less Familiar Ironies

Example 4

(4a)   After he had finished eating pizza, falafel, ice cream, wafers, and half of
        the cream cake his mother had baked for his brother Benjamin's birthday
        party, Moshe started eating coated peanuts. His mother said to him,
        "Moshe, I think you should eat something."

(4b)   At two o'clock in the afternoon, Moshe started doing his homework and
        getting prepared for his Bible test. When his mother came home from
        work at eight p.m., Moshe was still seated at his desk, looking pale. His
        mother said to him, "Moshe, I think you should eat something."
        Ironically related test word: *stop*
        Literally related test word: *little*

Example 5

(5a)   Just how far have women risen in the film community?
        According to M. P., who was at a Woman in Film luncheon recently in Los
        Angeles, it has actually been a very good year for women. Demi Moore
        was sold to Robert Redford for $1 million in the movie Indecent Proposal
        … Uma Thurman went for $40,000 to Robert De Niro in the recent movie,
        Mad Dog and Glory. "Just three years ago, in Pretty Woman, Richard Gere
        bought Julia Roberts for—what was it? $3,000?"
        "I'd say women have had real progress."

(5b)   Just how far have women risen in the film community?
        According to M. P., who was at a Woman in Film luncheon recently in Los
        Angeles, it has actually been a very good year for women: Demi Moore
        earned $10 million in the movie Indecent Proposal … Uma Thurman
        made $400,000 in the recent movie, Mad Dog and Glory. "Just three years
        ago, in Pretty Woman, Julia Roberts earned—what was it? $130,000?"
        "I'd say women have had real progress."
        Ironically related test word: *regress*
        Literally related test word: *success*

Example 6

(6a)   Tom was building an addition to his house. He was working real hard putt-
        ing in the foundation. His younger brother was supposed to help. But he
        never showed up. At the end of a long day, when Tom's brother finally ap-
        peared, Tom said to his brother,
        "Thanks for your help."

(6b)   Tom was building an addition to his house. He was working real hard putt-
        ing in the foundation. Suddenly his younger brother showed up and
        started to work too. At first Tom was afraid his brother would just be a nui-
        sance. But at the end of a long day, Tom said to his brother,
        "Thanks for your help."
        Ironically related test word: *angry*
        Literally related test word: *useful*

CHAPTER 9

Neuropsychological Studies of Sarcasm

Skye McDonald
University of New South Wales

Discussions concerning the processes underlying the comprehension of sarcasm
can be facilitated by research into brain-damaged participants. Acquired brain
damage impairs certain cognitive processes, leaving others intact. The finding
that patients with damage to the right hemisphere (RH) and patients with traumatic brain injury (TBI) affecting frontal lobe function both find it difficult to
comprehend sarcasm provides the opportunity to determine what aspects of the
process they find difficult and what inferences are particularly problematic. RH
patients have trouble processing information about the emotional state, intentions, and beliefs of the speaker. TBI patients' ability to understand sarcasm is
independent of their ability to comprehend emotional state. They also find
counterfactual inferences relatively straightforward. In contrast, they, too, appear to have trouble interpreting a speaker's intentions. The implications of these
findings for theoretical discussions of the comprehension of sarcasm are briefly
discussed.

When a speaker makes a sarcastic comment, this is frequently in the form of an assertion that contradicts the true state of affairs. Sarcastic comments are also normally associated with an attitude of derision or scorn toward the recipient of the
comment. The pragmatic inferences generated by sarcasm, and the process by
which this occurs, have been discussed frequently in the linguistic literature. Empirical research to validate various theoretical positions has been generally scanty,
although recent years have seen an upsurge of interest in this area (Gibbs, 1986a,
1986b; Gibbs, O'Brien, & DoLittle, 1995; Jorgenson, Miller, & Sperber, 1984;
Kruez & Glucksberg, 1989; Slugoski & Turnbull, 1988). Study of normal speakers
can be facilitated by parallel research into deficits in sarcasm comprehension following brain injury. Some forms of brain injury (e.g., damage to the left hemisphere
[LH]) lead to primary disorders of language (aphasia). On the other hand, damage
that occurs outside these primary language zones (e.g., localized damage to the

---

This chapter was previously published as "Neuropsychological studies of sarcasm" (S. McDonald)
in *Metaphor and Symbol, 15,* 85–98. Copyright © [2000] by Lawrence Erlbaum Associates. Reprinted
with permission.

right hemisphere [RH] as a result of a cerebrovascular accident or damage to the frontal lobes of the brain as a result of trauma) does not disrupt basic language abilities but may impair the ability to use language to communicate effectively. Research into these populations provides a unique perspective on the kinds of processes that contribute to competent comprehension of pragmatic inferences. This article separately reviews the nature of cognitive impairments seen in RH damage and traumatic brain injury (TBI), including common deficits in communication skills. Following this, specific investigations into the comprehension of sarcasm are outlined, including possible explanations for deficits in this area in terms of cognitive function. What these studies tell us in terms of the type of inferences generated in sarcasm and the cognitive processes necessary to decode them shall then be considered.

RH BRAIN DAMAGE

The RH has classically been viewed as nondominant for language. This has been repeatedly demonstrated in so-called split brain research. In specialized situations, participants have the connections between their cerebral hemispheres dissected and are asked to respond to stimuli when they can only use their RH. Under these conditions, the RH has been found to have only limited "automatic speech," such as emotional expletives, pause fillers, and overlearned phrases, and only relatively better comprehension of verbal material at the level of concrete nouns and some verbs and adjectives (Gazzaniga & Sperry, 1967; Sperry, Gazzaniga, & Boden, 1969; Zaidel, 1977, 1978). The RH's ability to understand simple verbal commands appears to be very limited, and it is particularly poor on syntax comprehension (Gazzaniga & Hillyard, 1971).

In contrast, the RH has been considered to have a specialized role in mediating a wide variety of visuospatial and other nonverbal functions. Lesions in the RH are frequently associated with a profound failure to perceive and attend to information on the left side (unilateral spatial neglect), problems making constructions that are spatially sound (visuoconstructional apraxia), topographical disorientation, impaired visuospatial learning, disturbances in facial recognition, emotional indifference, and inappropriateness (Cicone, Wapner, & Gardner, 1980; DeRenzi, 1982; Gainotti, 1972; Goldstein, 1948; Hecaen & Angelergues, 1962; Milner, 1965; Ratcliff, 1982).

There has also been a growing interest in the observation that patients with damage to the RH appear impaired in their communication skills. First, it has been well established that the RH has a specific role in the acoustic modulation of spoken language. Patients with RH lesions have been reported to lose control over prosodic variation in verbal expression and suffer a loss of sensitivity to prosody in comprehension tasks (Heilman, Scholes, & Watson, 1975; Ross & Mesulam, 1979). In addition, there are an increasing number of empirical studies that attribute RH lesions to deficits in broader aspects of pragmatic language skills. The verbose and tangential nature of speech in RH lesion cases has been described frequently. Patients have been found either to produce less information than normal speakers with the same amount of output or to produce more speech than normal including tangential and confabulatory intrusions (Diggs & Basili, 1987; Gardner, 1975; Hecaen, 1978; Wapner, Hamby, & Gardner, 1981).

RH patients have also been investigated for their capacity to comprehend inferential aspects of language. They have been reported to have problems interpreting metaphors, proverbs, and idiomatic phrases and have difficulty recognizing abstract relations between words and appreciating the punch line of jokes (Bihrle, Brownell, Powelson, & Gardner, 1986; Brownell, Potter, Michelow, & Gardner, 1984; Burgess & Chiarello, 1996; Hier & Kaplan, 1986; Myers, Linebaugh, & Mackisack-Morin, 1985; Van Lancker & Kempler, 1987; Winner & Gardner, 1977).

A range of tasks assessing the capacity to understand pragmatic inferences has been used in RH research, including some studies specifically investigating sarcasm. Tompkins and Mateer (1985) investigated RH temporal lobectomy candidates and non-brain-damaged matched controls on a sarcasm task where they listened to pairs of vignettes, one of which implied a very positive mood and the other a very negative mood. Both ended with the identical, positive comment from one of the story characters. This would be interpreted as sincere in the positive vignette and as incongruent and therefore sarcastic in the negative vignette. Participants listened to the final comment, which was spoken in a tone of voice that was either consistent with that expected (sarcastic or sincere) or inconsistent. They were required to make judgments about the appropriateness or otherwise of the tone of voice in the given context. They were also asked to answer questions about factual and inferential information contained within the vignettes. As would be expected, the RH patients had difficulty judging whether the tone of voice used was appropriate. This is consistent with known deficits in the comprehension of prosodic information in this group. But, over and above this, these patients had difficulty integrating the incongruent final comments into their understanding of the negative vignettes as evidenced by their inability to answer inferential questions about them. Tompkins and Mateer interpreted this as reflecting a difficulty understanding the emotional mood developed in the incongruent vignettes. The congruent vignettes, they argued, contained lexical referents to a positive general mood that was reinforced throughout. The inconsistent items, on the other hand, were ambiguous because the lexical content of the final comment contradicted the mood that had been established by the preceding context. It may have been the case that impaired RH functioning caused problems in this area by rendering the patients less able to process complex emotional inferences.

A similar interpretation may be offered for the findings of Kaplan, Brownell, Jacobs, and Gardner (1990). Kaplan et al. investigated RH-damaged patients using a similar story format to Tompkins and Mateer (1985), but asked specific questions regarding the speaker's intentions and the effects on the listener. Once again, RH patients were indistinguishable from controls when interpreting literally consistent end comments and evaluating the emotional impact of such comments on the listener. In contrast, when faced with counter-factual end comments, they were less inclined to use information about the affective relationship between speakers to assist their interpretation (Kaplan et al., 1990). In a related study (Brownell, Carroll, Rehak, & Wingfield, 1992), it was again found that RH participants were less likely to use the mood of speakers as an indicator of whether a remark was sarcastic or meant as a joke.

The notion that RH patients have difficulty interpreting sarcastic remarks because of a loss of sensitivity to subtle emotional cues is plausible. It is commonly accepted that sarcasm is intimately associated with particular negative affective states (e.g., scorn and contempt), and empirical data on normal speakers have provided support for this position (Kaplan et al., 1990; Slugoski & Turnbull, 1988). Furthermore, observations and research have attributed the RH with a specialized role in the regulation of emotional behavior. Whereas LH patients often appear to experience a catastrophic reaction to their brain injury, RH patients are often euphoric or indifferent to their disabilities, suggesting impaired emotional responsivity (Gainotti, 1991). *Anasognosia,* or denial of illness, is also a common consequence of right- rather than left-brain damage (Heilman, Bowers, & Valenstein, 1993). Such patients have also been found to be poor at discriminating emotion in faces, have been found to lose their ability to laugh and cry, and be prone to socially inappropriate humor and behavior (Cicone et al., 1980; DeKosky, Heilman, Bowers, & Valenstein, 1978; Ross & Mesulum, 1979). There are also the previously mentioned difficulties with interpreting tone of voice that render the patients impaired in the processing of emotion expressed via this medium (Ruckdeschel-Hibbard, Gordon, & Diller, 1984; Tucker, Watson, & Heilman, 1977). In addition, there is evidence for impaired processing of emotional information conveyed via verbal material using independent experimental paradigms. For example, it has been reported that RH patients attribute incorrect emotions to characters in narratives and have difficulty recalling emotionally charged verbal material (Cicone et al., 1980; Wapner et al., 1981; Wechsler, 1973).

In sum, there is a prima facie case to suggest that disturbances in emotional processing may account for some of the difficulties RH patients have when interpreting sarcasm. Nevertheless, this is unlikely to be a sufficient explanation for their performance because there are other aspects of sarcasm that are independent of emotion that have also proven difficult for RH participants. In a study by Winner, Brownell, Happe, Blum, and Pincus (1998), RH patients were presented with vignettes similar to Tompkins and Mateer (1986) and Kaplan et al. (1990). In this case, emotional factors were not explicitly controlled. Rather, Winner et al. were interested in investigating whether RH participants could infer what each of the protagonists in the story was thinking—that is, whether they were able to accurately appraise what each character knew or did not know. This manipulation is important because a particular counterfactual response may be a sarcastic comment if both speaker and listener are aware of the true state of affairs or a lie if the speaker believes that the listener is not aware of the truth. Winner et al. found that RH patients were less able than controls to determine whether a comment was a lie or a sarcastic joke and that this was significantly related to their ability to make accurate judgments about what each of the protagonists actually knew about the situation. This pattern of performance was also suggested in qualitative observations made of the participants in Kaplan's study where it was noted that control participants were able to reason from the perspective of the speaker (i.e., his intentions) or the listener (his knowledge of the speaker's intentions), whereas RH patients did not seem to be aware that the hearer could impute the speaker's intentions and were more inclined to believe that the listener would take a sarcastic comment at face value. These results suggest that RH patients were unable to form a theory of what another person was thinking ("theory of mind") in the sarcasm vignettes and were therefore restricted to a more superficial consideration of the meaning of utterances.

There is little independent evidence that the RH has a specific role in the imputation of mental states, although one study of "mentalizing" ability has suggested that this is a specific deficit associated with RH damage rather than brain damage in general (Happe, Brownell, & Winner, 1997, as cited in Winner et al., 1998). On the other hand, there is a growing literature which suggests that RH patients have difficulty with a variety of verbal inferences that may well include inferences about mental state. In this regard, there has been a certain amount of speculation as to the role the RH may play in inference processing. It has been hypothesized on the basis of visuoperceptual studies that

> the right hemisphere attends to the overall configuration of the stimulus situation, synthesizing fragmentary chunks of perceptual data received from the sensory surround into a meaningful percept of the environment. The right hemisphere is thus viewed as giving a spatial context to the major hemisphere. (Nebes, 1974, p. 156)

This model of visuospatial processing has been extended to explain language deficits. Consequently, it has been suggested that the RH is instrumental for the integration of verbal information in a verbal analogy of visuospatial synthesis that includes integration of new with prior knowledge and integration of linguistic and extralinguistic elements to construct a mental model of the world (Benowitz, Moya, & Levine, 1990; Brownell et al., 1992; Grzybek, 1993; Schneiderman, Murasugi, & Saddy, 1992; Weylman, Brownell, Roman, & Gardner, 1988). Such mental models would make it possible to assume varied perspectives (Gardner, Ling, Flamm, & Silverman, 1975) and would assist the process of imputing the mental state of others. Whether the RH does actually process and synthesize information in this manner is yet to be established, and evidence to the contrary has been found (McDonald, 1999).

In summary, RH damage seems to retard the ability to interpret sarcastic comments. Many RH patients are impaired in their capacity to use prosodic cues when listening to the speaker's tone of voice, so they are unable to benefit from this source of information concerning the speaker's attitude and intention. Nor it seems are they as able to infer the emotional state of various speakers on the basis of verbal cues to this effect. In addition, it appears that RH patients have some difficulty inferring what is on another's mind, and this incapacity to assume another perspective seems to also impede their ability to interpret a comment as sarcastic. It is important not to overstate the degree of impairment experienced by RH participants. In each of the studies mentioned, the RH patients were poor *relative* to non-brain-damaged participants with whom they were compared. On the whole, however, they demonstrated that they were able to consider sarcasm as a feasible explanation for many of the comments they were asked to interpret, and they could discriminate sarcasm from other kinds of speech acts (such as joking, lying, sincere responding, nonsensible, etc.). Their interpretations of counterfactual end comments were also influenced by exactly the same contextual parameters as the non-brain-damaged control participants, but to a smaller extent. It is therefore possible that the relative loss of competence on these tasks simply reflected a loss of efficiency as a result of the general effects of brain impairment (Kaplan et al., 1990).

TBI

The other brain-injured population in which sarcasm has been examined in detail is that of TBI. TBI in the Western world is most frequently a result of motor vehicle accidents. Patients experience bruising and laceration of the brain that, in severe cases, results in permanent disability in both sensorimotor and cognitive functions. Although TBI is very heterogeneous in its effects, there are certain constellations of impairments that are common, reflecting damage to the temporal and frontal lobes of the brain. Memory impairments occur secondary to damage to the temporal lobes and are very disabling. However, even more devastating are impairments to the frontal lobes of the brain leading to dysfunction of the executive control systems that coordinate and regulate all other cognitive activity. The frontal lobes of the brain constitute a very large area of brain tissue, and damage in this area is both variable and various. Nevertheless, in general terms, impairments to frontal function are known to disrupt the capacity of the individual to behave in an adaptive fashion, causing a loss of conceptual and problem-solving skills and impaired ability to regulate behavior to meet internally generated goals (Lezak, 1995).

As with RH lesions, primary loss of language abilities (aphasia) is infrequent in severe TBI. On the other hand, loss of communication skills is relatively frequent. Unlike many patients with a primary loss of language who are observed to communicate better than they can talk, TBI patients appear to have problems in the reverse (Holland, 1984).

First, they have been described as overtalkative but inefficient, drifting from topic to topic while making tangential and irrelevant comments (Hagan, 1984; Hartley & Jensen, 1992; Prigatano, Roueche, & Fordyce, 1986; Snow et al., 1986). Alternatively, some patients are impoverished in the amount and variety of language produced, their conversational style characterized by slow, frequently incomplete responses, numerous pauses, a reliance on set expressions, and difficulty following long or complex utterances (Hartley & Jenson, 1991, 1992; Thomsen,

1975). In addition, conversational style may fail to acknowledge important social requirements as suggested by insensitivity to others, self-focused conversation without interest in other people, immature or inappropriate humor, frequent interruptions, blunt manner, overly familiar and disinhibited remarks, or advances and inappropriate levels of self-disclosure (Crossen, 1987; Flanagan, McDonald, & Togher, 1995).

In general terms, there appear to be a number of features of communication disturbances after TBI that reflect executive dysfunction as previously defined. There appears to be a disruption to the regulation of language activity and a failure to use it adaptively to meet social communicative goals. In terms of comprehension, such patients are frequently stimulus bound when interpreting incoming information. They respond to the most concrete, superficial aspect of their environment and are unable to process information beyond its most salient, literal meaning. This type of deficit may underscore their difficulty coping with the social or pragmatic dimensions of conversation.

Several studies have been conducted by myself and colleagues to investigate the capacity of TBI patients to understand sarcasm (Flanagan, McDonald, Rollins, & Hodgkinson, 1997; McDonald, 1992, in press; McDonald & Pearce,1996). In several of these, TBI patients were asked to interpret written pairs of sentences that represented two kinds of conversational exchanges. In the first, the exchange was sincere, such as the following:

1. Mark: *"What a great football game."*
   Wayne: *"So you are glad I asked you."*

In the second, the meaning of one member of the pair was reversed so as to represent a literally contradictory exchange:

2. Mark: "What a great football game."
   Wayne: *"Sorry I made you come."*

Normal speakers usually interpreted the second type of exchange as encompassing a sarcastic comment, meaning that the game was actually poor. It was predicted that TBI participants would have trouble with this task because they would be transfixed by the superficial meaning of the sentence and would be unable to reinterpret it to make conversational sense. As expected, all participants were able to interpret the meaning of the first type of exchange (example 1) without difficulty. In contrast, a proportion of the TBI participants had greater difficulty interpreting the second type of exchange (example 2) as sarcastic compared to matched non-brain-damaged control participants. Interestingly, performance did not improve when the same material was presented in an auditory form—that is, participants listened to the items presented via an audiotape that had been prepared using professional actors (McDonald & Pearce, 1996). The proportion of participants performing in the normal range (i.e., within 2 standard deviations of the average of the normal control group) on the written versus audio presentations are shown in Table 9.1.

Admittedly, a number of TBI participants were subsequently shown to have difficulties discerning emotional tone of voice. But interesting, this was independent of their capacity to interpret inconsistent remarks as sarcastic. For example, one participant was shown to have above-average abilities in the recognition of emotional tone of voice, but was markedly impaired when interpreting sarcasm in both the written and audio versions. Conversely, some participants were inept at discriminating emotion via auditory channels and yet were similar to non-brain-injured participants in the accuracy with which they interpreted sarcastic comments. In sum, in this population, the ability to recognize and interpret emotional information did not guarantee success in the interpretation of sarcasm. This reinforces the findings from the RH research that recognition of emotional parameters in sarcasm may facilitate comprehension, but is not, on its own, sufficient or even necessary.

Moreover, performance on the sarcasm task was significantly associated with performance on a neuropsychological test of abstract reasoning, concept formation, and flexibility of thought in all TBI patients. The combined results of these studies suggest that poor comprehension of sarcasm is not primarily due to a failure to recognize the literal meaning of the utterance, because all participants managed the sincere exchanges adequately. Nor was it necessarily due to a failure to recognize the attitude or emotional state of the speaker (although in some there were definitely problems in the recognition of this type of information). But more generally apparent was a failure in inferential reasoning regarding the possible meaning behind a counterfactual comment.

Interestingly, it appears that not all forms of sarcasm are equally difficult for TBI participants. There was a single case (AJ) reported in a larger series (McDonald & Pearce, 1996) who was unable to interpret accurately a contradictory exchange such as example 2, even though he was provided with prosodic information and was

TABLE 9.1
Proportion of Nine TBI Patients Who Performed Normally on the Written and Audio Versions of the Sarcasm Items

	Proportion of Participants With Normal Performance
Written version	
Consistent items	9/9
Inconsistent items	5/9
Audio version	
Consistent items	6/9
Inconsistent items	4/9

Note. TBI = traumatic brain injury.

known to be competent in detecting emotion in auditory and visual channels (Flanagan et al., 1997; McDonald & Pearce, 1996). In contrast, he could detect sarcasm in videotaped vignettes when the speaker's demeanor was the salient cue that the sarcastic comment was insincerely meant—that is, the same script. For example, see the following:

3.   *"Oh you have been a great help."*

This example could be enacted sincerely or sarcastically (Flanagan et al., 1997). The difference between these paradigms lies in the mode within which the inconsistency was found. In the first task (example 2), there was a contradiction within the content of the utterances themselves. In the second task (example 3), the contradiction was between what was said and other contextual information (paralinguistic or circumstantial). Bara, Tirassa, and Zettin (1997) reported a similar finding using video-taped vignettes where the literal meaning of the sarcastic comment contradicted the outcome of an activity rather than other verbal information. Their 13 TBI participants did not, on average, have difficulty registering sarcasm in these simple vignettes. It appears that the juggling of two speakers' contradictory utterances poses particular difficulty for some TBI participants. Although it is difficult to generalize across TBI participants due to the heterogeneity in the extent and nature of brain injury in this population, these findings suggest that different types of contextual information may be differentially difficult for brain-injured speakers to process.

It has been argued that there are a spectrum of inferences that may be generated by a sarcastic comment, the counterfactual inference being merely one (Sperber & Wilson, 1986). Although TBI patients are often deficient on tasks of inferential reasoning, it is less clear whether certain kinds of inferences are more difficult than others. Interestingly, another study (McDonald, in press) used a similar paradigm to McDonald (1992; McDonald & Pearce, 1995; examples 1 and 2 mentioned earlier) but encompassed a different set of exemplars of sarcastic exchanges such as the following:

4.   Tom: *"That's a big dog."*
     Monica: *"Yes, it's a miniature poodle."*

In this case, no impairment was apparent in the TBI group. Consideration of the differences between the sets of stimuli provides some interesting insights into the kinds of inferences that are required for competent comprehension of sarcasm. In example 4, the response (by Monica) was a direct contradiction of the factual information provided in the initial remark (by Tom). This exchange differed from the previous example of a sarcastic exchange (example 2) because in that case, the response (by Wayne) is not simply a refutation of the factual status of the original comment, but also alludes to the first speaker (Mark's) reaction to that state of affairs.

There are two possible reasons for the improved performance of the TBI participants on the modified version (example 4). First, the necessary inferential process required to unravel the nonliteral meanings in the original version may have been longer and therefore more difficult for the TBI participants. In example 2, the participants had to infer that the first speaker was being critical because the second speaker was apologizing. They then had to make a subsequent inference that the first speaker thought the opposite to what they stated. Thus, there were at least two necessary steps to the inferential process. In example 4, the only inference necessary was that the first premise was being responded to as if it meant the opposite to that literally asserted.

An alternative explanation for this difference in performance lies in the difference in the nature of the inferences in the two tasks. It may be that counterfactual inferences are so obvious (Bara et al., 1997) that they pose little difficulty for TBI individuals. Just as participants with executive dysfunction may not be fazed when interpreting simple proverbs or conventional indirect speech acts (McDonald & van Sommers, 1993; Shallice & Burgess, 1991), they may have little difficulty inferring an opposite meaning from blatantly false statements. However, the original task (example 2) not only required counterfactual inferences to be made, but also required the participants to infer something about the first speaker's intentions—to insult, joke, and so forth. Thus, although the counterfactual nature of sarcastic comments may be recognized by brain-injured participants, this may leave them with only a partial understanding of the illocutionary force of the utterance because what is implied in terms of the speaker's intention is more problematic for them to grasp. This aspect of inferential reasoning is similar to the poor mentalizing ability attributed to patients with RH damage. Furthermore, independent studies have also attributed TBI patients with poor ability to infer mental states. Although TBI participants are not impaired when inferring the mental state of another in a simple "theory of mind" task (e.g., asking the participant what a naive observer would expect to find in a Smarties packet that is, in fact, full of pencils; Bara et al., 1997), a proportion of moderate to severely TBI participants do experience difficulty when considering the perspectives of a number of protagonists in stories of conflict and deceit and have more difficulty than matched controls when answering personality questionnaires "as if they were someone else" (Bara et al., 1997; Levine, Van Horn, & Curtis, 1993; Santoro & Spiers, 1994; Spiers, Pouk, & Santoro, 1994; Van Horne, Levine, & Curtis, 1992). As mentioned, TBI patients frequently suffer executive dysfunction characterized by concrete and inert response modes hampering their ability to think flexibly and at a level of abstraction. These executive deficits are thought to underlie a range of communicative deficiencies such as egocentricity and reduced sensitivity to others. The idea that mental state inferences may be particularly problematic for adults with brain injury is promising but requires further work. It also suggests that any adequate model of sarcasm comprehension needs to address the notion that not all inferences are equally accessible.

CONCLUSION

Dissociations in cognitive abilities that occur as a result of specific brain pathology provide insights into the processes that underlie the competent interpretation of pragmatically laden conversational remarks such as sarcasm. As this review suggests, accurate appraisal of the emotional state of the speaker facilitates the comprehension of sarcasm, but is neither necessary nor sufficient for the full pragmatic force of the sarcastic comment to be detected. On the other hand, abilities to think flexibly and conceptually appear to be important prerequisites for drawing inferences from sarcastic comments. Having said this, recognition of the counterfactual inference generated by the sarcastic remark appears relatively straightforward for some brain-injured patients who, nevertheless, have difficulty with less transparent versions of sarcasm. The problem in such cases seems to lie in a failure to understand what is on the speaker's mind and to infer the intention behind the sarcastic comment.

REFERENCES

Bara, B. G., Tirassa, M., & Zettin, M. (1997). Neuropragmatics: Neuropsychological constraints on formal theories of dialogue. *Brain and Language, 59,* 7–14.

Benowitz, L. I., Moya, K. L., & Levine, D. N. (1990). Impaired verbal reasoning and constructional apraxia in subjects with right hemisphere damage. *Neuropsychologia, 28,* 231–241.

Bihrle, A. M., Brownell, H. H., Powelson, J. A., & Gardner, H. (1986). Comprehension of humorous and nonhumorous materials by left and right brain-damaged patients. *Brain and Cognition, 5,* 399–411.

Brownell, H. H., Carroll, J. J., Rehak, A., & Wingfield, A. (1992). The use of pronoun anaphora and speaker mood in the interpretation of conversational utterances by right hemisphere brain-damaged patients. *Brain and Language, 43,* 121–147.

Brownell, H. H., Potter, H., Michelow, D., & Gardner, H. (1984). Sensitivity to lexical denotation and connotation in brain damaged patients: A double dissolution? *Brain and Language, 22,* 253–265.

Burgess, C., & Chiarello, C. (1996). Neurocognitive mechanisms underlying metaphor comprehension and other figurative language. *Metaphor and Symbolic Activity, 11,* 67–84.

Cicone, M., Wapner, W., & Gardner, H. (1980). Sensitivity to emotional expressions and situations in organic patients. *Cortex, 16,* 145–158.

Crossen, B. (1987). Treatment of interpersonal deficits for head-trauma patients in inpatient rehabilitation settings. *The Clinical Neuropsychologist, 1,* 335–352.

DeKosky, S. T., Heilman, K. M., Bowers, D., & Valenstein, E. (1980). Recognition and discrimination of emotional faces and pictures. *Brain and Language, 9,* 206–214.

DeRenzi, E. (1982). *Disorders of space exploration and cognition.* Chichester, England: Wiley.

Diggs, C. C., & Basili, A. (1987). Verbal expression of right cerebrovascular accident patients: Convergent and divergent language. *Brain and Language, 30,* 130–146.

Flanagan, S., McDonald, S., Rollins, J., & Hodgkinson, A. (1997). Social perception ability following traumatic brain injury. *Proceedings of the 21st Annual Brain Impairment Conference, Brisbane, Australia, 59.*

Flanagan, S., McDonald, S., & Togher, L. (1995). Evaluation of the BRISS as a measure of social skills in the traumatically brain injured. *Brain Injury, 9,* 321–338.

Gainotti, G. (1972). Emotional behaviour and hemispheric side of lesion. *Cortex, 8,* 41–55.

Gainotti, G. (1991). Disorders of emotion after unilateral brain damage. In F. Boller & J. Grafman (Eds.), *Handbook of neuropsychology* (Vol. 3, pp. 345–362). Amsterdam: Elsevier.

Gardner, H. (1975). *The shattered mind: The person after brain damage.* London: Routledge & Kegan Paul.

Gardner, H., Ling, K., Flamm, L., & Silverman, J. (1975). Comprehension and appreciation of humour in brain damaged patients. *Brain, 98,* 399–412.

Gazzaniga, M., & Hillyard, S. (1971). Language and speech capacity of the right hemisphere. *Neuropsychologia, 9,* 273–280.

Gazzaniga, M., & Sperry, R. (1967). Language after section of the cerebral commissures. *Brain, 90,* 131–148.

Gibbs, R. W. (1986a). Comprehension and memory for nonliteral utterances: The problem of sarcastic indirect requests. *Acta Psychologia, 62,* 41–57.

Gibbs, R. W. (1986b). On the psycholinguistics of sarcasm. *Journal of Experimental Psychology, 115,* 3–15.

Gibbs, R. W., O'Brien, J. E., & DoLittle, S. (1995). Inferring meanings that are not intended: Speakers' intentions and irony comprehension. *Discourse Processes, 20,* 187–203.

Goldstein, K. (1948). *Language and language disturbances.* New York: Grune & Stratton.

Grzybek, P. (1993). A neurosemiotic perspective on text processing. In H. H. Brownell & Y. Joanette (Eds.), *Narrative discourse in neurologically impaired and normal aging adults* (pp. 47–76). San Diego, CA: Singular.

Hagan, C. (1984). Language disorders in head trauma. In A. Holland (Ed.), *Language disorders in adults* (pp. 245–281). San Diego, CA: College-Hill.

Hartley, L. L., & Jenson, P. J. (1991). Narrative and procedural discourse after closed head injury. *Brain Injury, 5,* 267–285.

Hartley, L. L., & Jenson, P. J. (1992). Three discourse profiles of closed-head-injured speakers: Theoretical and clinical implications. *Brain Injury, 6,* 271–382.

Hecaen, H. (1978). Right hemisphere contribution to language. In P. A. Buser & A. Rouget-Buser (Eds.), *Cerebral correlates of conscious experience.* North-Holland.

Hecaen, H., & Angelergues, R. (1962). Agnosia for faces (proposagnosia). *Archives of Neurology, 7,* 92–100.

Heilman, K. M., Bowers, D., Speedie, L., & Coslett, H. B. (1984). Comprehension of affective and nonaffective prosody. *Neurology, 34,* 917–921.

Heilman, K. M., Bowers, D., & Valenstein, E. (1993). Emotional disorders associated with neurological diseases. In K. M. Heilman & E. Valenstein (Eds.), *Clinical neuropsychology* (3rd ed., pp. 461–498). New York: Oxford University Press.

Heilman, K. M., Scholes, R., & Watson, R. T. (1975). Auditory affective agnosia. *Journal of Neurology, Neurosurgery and Psychiatry, 38,* 69–82.

Hier, D. B., & Kaplan, J. (1980). Verbal comprehension deficits after right hemisphere damage. *Applied Psycholinguistics, 1,* 279–294.

Holland, A. L. (1984). When is aphasia aphasia? The problem of closed head injury. In R. W. Brookshire (Ed.), *Clinical aphasiology* (Vol. 14, pp. 345–349). Minneapolis, MN: BRK.

Jorgenson, J., Miller, G., & Sperber, D. (1984). Test of the mention theory of irony. *Journal of Experimental Psychology: General, 113,* 112–120.

Kaplan, J. A., Brownell, H. H., Jacobs, J. R., & Gardner, H. (1990). The effects of right hemisphere brain damage on the pragmatic interpretation of conversational remarks. *Brain and Language, 38,* 315–333.

Kruez, R. J., & Glucksberg, S. (1989). How to be sarcastic: The echoic reminder theory of verbal irony. *Journal of Experimental Psychology: General, 118*, 374–386.

Levine, M. J., Van Horn, K. R., & Curtis, A. B. (1993). Developmental models of social cognition in assessing psychosocial adjustments in head injury. *Brain Injury, 7,* 153–167.

Lezak, M. (1995). *Neuropsychological assessment* (3rd ed.). New York: Oxford University Press.

McDonald, S. (1992). Pragmatic language skills after closed head injury: Ability to comprehend conversational implicature. Applied Psycholinguistics, 13, 295–312.

McDonald, S. (1999a). *Exploring the cognitive basis of right hemisphere language disorders.* Manuscript submitted for publication.

McDonald, S. (1999b). Exploring the process and nature of inference generation in sarcasm: A review of normal and clinical studies. *Brain and Language, 68*, 486–506.

McDonald, S., & Pearce, S. (1996). Clinical insights into pragmatic language theory: The case of sarcasm. *Brain and Language, 53,* 81–104.

McDonald, S., & van Sommers, P. (1993). Differential pragmatic language loss following closed head injury: Ability to negotiate requests. *Cognitive Neuropsychology, 10,* 297–315.

Milner, B. (1965). Visually guided maze learning in man: Effects of bilateral hippocampal, bilateral frontal, and unilateral cerebral lesions. *Neuropsychologia, 3,* 317–338.

Myers, P. S., Linebaugh, C. W., & Mackisack-Morin, L. (1985). Extracting implicit meaning: Right versus left hemisphere damage. In R. J. Brookshire (Ed.), *Clinical aphasiology* (Vol. 15, pp. 72–80). Minneapolis, MN: BRK.

Nebes, R. D. (1974). Dominance of the minor hemisphere for the perception of part–whole relationships. In M. Kinsbourne & W. Lynn Smith (Eds.), *Hemispheric disconnection and cerebral function* (pp. 155–164). Springfield, IL: Thomas.

Pearce, S., McDonald, S., & Coltheart, M. (1998). Ability to process ambiguous advertisements after frontal lobe damage. Brain and Cognition, 38, 150–164.

Prigatano, G. P., Roueche, J. R., & Fordyce, D. J. (1986). *Neuropsychological rehabilitation after brain injury.* Baltimore: Johns Hopkins University Press.

Ratcliff, G. (1982). Disturbances of spatial orientation associated with cerebral lesions. In M. Potegal (Ed.). New York: Academic.

Ross, E. D., & Mesulam, M. (1979). Dominant language functions of the right hemisphere? Prosody and emotional gesturing. Archives of Neurology, 36, 144–148.

Ruckdeschel-Hibbard, M., Gordon, W. A., & Diller, L. (1984). Affective disturbances associated with brain damage. In S. Filskov & T. Boll (Eds.), *Handbook of neuropsychology* (Vol. 2, pp. 305–337). New York: Wiley.

Santoro, J., & Spiers, M. (1994). Social cognitive factors in brain-injury associated with personality change. *Brain Injury, 8,* 265–276.

Schneiderman, E. I., Murasugi, K. G., & Saddy, J. D. (1992). Story arrangement ability in right brain damaged patients. *Brain and Language, 43,* 107–120.

Shallice, T., & Burgess, P. W. (1991). Deficits in strategy application following frontal lobe damage in man. *Brain, 114,* 727–741.

Slugoski, B. R., & Turnbull, W. (1988). Cruel to be kind and kind to be cruel: Sarcasm, banter and social relations. Language and Society, 7, 101–121.

Snow, P., Lambier, J., Parson, C., Mooney, L., Couch, D., & Russell, J. (1986). Conversational skills following closed head injury: Some preliminary findings. In C. Field, A. Kneebone, & M. W. Reid (Eds.), *Brain impairment: Proceedings of the Eleventh Annual Brain Impairment Conference.*

Sperber, D., & Wilson, D. (1986). *Relevance: Communication and cognition.* Oxford, England: Blackwell.

Sperry, R. W., Gazzaniga, M. S., & Boden, J. (1969). Interhemispheric relationships: The neocortical commissures; syndromes of hemispheric disconnection. In P. J. Vinkin & G.

W. Bruyn (Eds.), *Handbook of clinical neurology* (Vol. 4, pp. 273–290). Amsterdam: New Holland.

Spiers, M. V., Pouk, J. A., & Santoro, J. M. (1994). Examining perspective taking in the severely head injured. *Brain Injury, 8,* 463–473.

Thomsen, I. V. (1975). Evaluation and outcome of aphasia in patients with severe closed head trauma. *Journal of Neurology, Neurosurgery and Psychiatry, 38,* 713–718.

Tompkins, C. A., & Mateer, C. A. (1985). Right hemisphere appreciation of prosodic and linguistic indications of implicit attitude. *Brain and Language, 24,* 185–203.

Tucker, D. M., Watson, R. T., & Heilman, K. M. (1977). Discrimination and evocation of affectively toned speech in patients with right parietal disease. *Neurology, 27,* 947–950.

Van Horn, K. R., Levine, M. J., & Curtis, C. L. (1992). Developmental levels of social cognition in head injury patients *Brain Injury, 6,* 15–28.

Van Lancker, D. R., & Kempler, D. (1987). Comprehension of familiar phrases by left but not right hemisphere damaged patients. Brain and Language, 32, 265–277.

Wapner, W., Hamby, S., & Gardner, H. (1981). The role of the right hemisphere in the apprehension of complex linguistic materials. *Brain and Language, 14,* 15–32.

Wechsler, A. F. (1973). The effect of organic brain disease on recall of emotionally charged material versus neutral narrational texts. Neurology, 23, 130–135.

Weylman, S. T., Brownell, H. H., Roman, M., & Gardner, H. (1989). Appreciation of indirect requests by left and right damaged patients: The effects of verbal context and conventionality of wording. *Brain and Language, 36,* 580–591.

Winner, E., Brownell, H., Happe, F., Blum, A., & Pincus, D. (1998). Distinguishing lies from jokes: Theory of mind deficits and discourse interpretation in right hemisphere brain damaged patients. *Brain and Language, 62,* 89–106.

Winner, E., & Gardner, H. (1977). Comprehension of metaphor in brain damaged patients. *Brain, 100,* 719–727.

Zaidel, E. (1977). Unilateral auditory language comprehension on the Token Test following cerebral commissurotomy and hemispherectomy. *Neuropsychologia, 15,* 1–13.

Zaidel, E. (1978). Lexical organisation of the right hemisphere. In P. A. Buser & A. Roget-Buser (Eds.), *Cerebral correlates of conscious experience* (pp. 263–284). North-Holland.

CHAPTER 10

Discourse Factors That Influence Online Reading of Metaphor and Irony

Penny M. Pexman
University of Calgary

Todd R. Ferretti
Albert N. Katz
The University of Western Ontario

Statements such as "children are precious gems" can be interpreted as either a metaphor (children are valuable) or as a sarcastic comment on the metaphor (children are a burden). Katz and Pexman (1997) identified several constraints that biased readers toward either the metaphoric or the sarcastic-ironic interpretation: nature (occupation) of the person making the statement, whether the statement was counterfactual to information in the preceding discourse context, and whether the root metaphor instantiated in the statement was familiar. In this experiment, we investigated whether these constraints would be used online during normal reading. In a moving-window reading task, results showed that readers used the constraints early in processing the target statement and took longer to resolve the ironic (relative to the metaphoric) sense of the target statement. Also, data from the online reading measures were strongly correlated with ratings and memory data obtained by Katz and Pexman.

A statement can be ambiguous with respect to the meaning intended by its speaker. Consider the statement, "children are precious gems" (1), in which the speaker is using a metaphor. It might be the positive metaphoric claim that children are valuable. However, one can easily imagine that the speaker is using the metaphor to be sarcastically ironic, namely to convey a negative evaluation, such as the claim that children are a burden. Thus, the same nonliteral statement can be interpreted as either metaphor or irony.[1] The online comprehension of these types of statements is the focus of this study.

This chapter was previously published as "Discourse factors that influence on-line reading of metaphor and irony" (P. Pexman, T. Ferretti, & A. Katz) in *Discourse Processes, 29,* 201–222. Copyright © [2000] by Lawrence Erlbaum Associates. Reprinted with permission.

The interpretation given to statements such as (1) depends on many factors. It has been shown that irony and sarcasm interpretations are invited by quite a few context-based conditions including, but not limited to, echoic mention or reminding (Kreuz & Glucksberg, 1989), use of exaggeration (Kreuz, 1996), pragmatic insincerity (Kumon-Nakamura, Glucksberg, & Brown, 1995), presence of a privileged audience (Katz & Lee, 1993), and social knowledge and conventions (Katz & Lee, 1993). These have been studies involving either *ratings* or *memory* data, or both. Ratings data provide insights into the nature of the underlying processes by asking readers to make judgments about the meaning of nonliteral statements, as occurs when utterances are rated along psychologically relevant dimensions, such as whether in a given context a sentence is perceived as ironic (e.g., Jorgensen, Miller, & Sperber, 1984; Katz & Lee, 1993). In memory studies, episodic memory data are employed, such as when statements rated as ironic subsequently are remembered better than those rated as not ironic (e.g., Kreuz, Long, & Church, 1991). In this latter case, the memorial data are taken as indirect evidence for differences that occurred somewhere in the comprehension process.

Although ratings and memory-based studies have shown the importance of context in determining judgments of irony, differences in discourse contexts have not been systematically studied in online studies of metaphor and irony comprehension. It should be noted that there have been, however, a small number of studies of irony involving online measures, with the main aim being to determine if the intended (ironic) message is processed as rapidly as the expressed (literal) message (e.g., Gibbs, 1986; Giora, Fein, & Schwartz, 1998). The aim of this study is not, however, to contrast literal and nonliteral interpretation of irony. Instead, we focus here on the interpretive processes involved in understanding metaphor and irony. As such, there are important questions about nonliteral processing that could be addressed in online studies. Consider, for instance, the various factors shown in memory-based studies to influence irony judgments (i.e., echoic mention, exaggeration, etc.). In principle, each of these factors might play separable roles in inviting a person to perceive a comment as sarcastic irony. Some might play their role quickly online whereas others might only be a factor at some much later processing stage.

To address such questions, the strategy employed in this study was to explicitly manipulate cues shown by Katz and Pexman (1997) to have an effect in ratings and memory-based measures and to see whether these cues to metaphoric or ironic intent have their influence at the very earliest stages of comprehension, in an online reading study. Katz and Pexman tested three cues they believed might be used to constrain the interpretation, and hence, help disambiguate the intended meaning of statements such as (1). In their study, participants read a series of short passages in which one of the characters uttered a statement of the form "A is (does) a B." The three potential cues were selected, based on previous findings in the literature: First, the target statement was either highly familiar or not, as based on norming data, because familiar statements may be more easily understood as either metaphor or irony. Second, each statement was made by a person from an occupation previously rated as likely to use sarcastic irony (e.g., army sergeant, cab driver) or likely to use metaphor (e.g., scientist, clergyman), because occupation is an indicator of the speaker's social status, which has been shown to affect the interpretation given to figurative statements (Kemper & Thissen, 1981; see also Holtgraves, 1994, Experiment 1). Speaker occupation is also a variable that conveys the speaker's social knowledge, which Katz and Lee (1993) showed was an important factor in ironic intent. Third, because Katz and his colleagues (e.g., Katz & Lee, 1993; see Katz, 1996, for a review) have repeatedly shown that a statement of the form "A is (does) a B," which is counterfactual to the discourse, is taken as irony whereas the same statement that is factually consistent with respect to the preceding discourse is taken as metaphor, each target statement was placed in an irony-inviting counterfactual context, a metaphor-inviting factually consistent context, or a context that was neutral with respect to counterfactuality. These three cues were factorially manipulated.

Following each passage, participants answered several questions about speakers' intentions along 7-point rating scales (such as the degree to which the speaker was mocking someone or the degree to which the speaker was being sarcastic). After reading the complete set of passages, participants were also administered an unexpected recall test of the target statements. Evidence for the effectiveness of the three hypothesized cues to speakers' intentions was found in both the memory and the ratings data. For instance, overall, a given statement was more likely to be recalled if uttered by a person from a high-irony (low metaphor) rather than a high-metaphor (low irony) occupation. Also, in the rating data, there was clear evidence that a statement placed in a counterfactual context was perceived as especially sarcastic, relative to both a neutral context and the metaphor-inviting factually consistent context. Moreover, the effects of both counterfactuality of discourse context and nature (occupation) of speaker interacted with statement familiarity. Familiar statements were perceived as especially sarcastic when uttered in the counterfactual irony-inviting context or when uttered by a member of a high-irony occupation.

Taken together, these data indicated the studied cues were employed in disambiguating speakers' intentions to be metaphoric or sarcastic, sometimes interactively. An unresolved issue is whether, by asking participants to rate speaker intent, Katz and Pexman (1997) induced a strategy to use the manipulated factors in the experimental task or whether, during normal online reading, these cues would be used to resolve the ambiguity and determine speaker intent. In this study, we examine whether the factors studied by Katz and Pexman act online, using a moving-window procedure.

In this study, we address two basic questions. First, we examine whether certain cues to metaphoric and ironic intent act online. In particular, we examine the effects of three such cues: the counterfactuality of the discourse context with an ambiguous target statement, the familiarity of the target statement, and the nature (occupation) of the person who utters the target statement. Second, we examine whether there is a significant relation between online measures and ratings, and memory measures of metaphor and irony processing. To the extent that memory measures reflect processes that occur during the act of comprehension, one would expect that online indexes should correlate well with subsequent memory measures. There is a clear relation between the comprehension of and subsequent memory for linguistic input: For instance, the amount of information remembered increases with comprehension (e.g., Marschark & Hunt, 1985) and with the extent to which meaning is elaborated (e.g., Noice, 1992). It is less clear why ratings measures should correlate with online measures; that is, it is probable that the processing that leads to an interpretation (rating) of a statement as ironic might be different than the processing of a statement that is interpreted as metaphor, and it is possible those differences in processing might show up in online measures. It is also possible, however, that the processing involved in making ratings of irony occurs after online processing has been completed. There is as yet no evidence to distinguish between these possibilities, but this study addresses this issue. To our knowledge, no one has yet directly compared online processing with memory-based data and ratings data for the same set of potentially ironic stimuli. The items we employed in the online study were also employed in Katz and Pexman (1997), and so we were able to make that direct comparison. Specifically, we identify differences in the ratings and memory-based data that are coordinated with differences in the online data. Observing coordinated differences indicates that the ratings and memory-based data are sensitive to processes that take place online, when the stimulus is first encountered.

In this study, we examine online processing with a "moving-window" procedure (Just, Carpenter, & Woolley, 1982), in which readers advance a text word by word at their own pace. This ensures that reading latencies are not contaminated by spurious strategies adopted by readers forced to read at an uncomfortable pace. Another advantage of employing this procedure is that it permits the computation of reading latencies for each word in a text. This is especially important for this study as we were interested in contextual influences on a target statement. Employing this procedure allowed us to determine when the contextual manipulations exerted their influence on the target statement. Indeed, this procedure has proven useful to many researchers in psycholinguistics because it has allowed them to detect more precisely when different sources of information (e.g., syntactic, semantic, pragmatic, etc.) exert their influence during online comprehension (e.g., Garnsey, Pearlmutter, Myers, & Lotocky, 1997; McRae, Spivey-Knowlton, & Tanenhaus, 1998; Trueswell, 1996).

There are predictions one can make concerning when the contextual manipulations may have an influence on processing of the target statement. The first interesting possibility involves the structure of the target statements that we employed and the increase in reading time (RT) that occurs typically at the end of sentences (i.e., so-called wrap-up effect). The sentence wrap-up effect is taken as an index of the integration of a number of different sources of information, both those internal and external to the sentence itself (e.g., Just & Carpenter, 1980; Kintsch, 1988; Rayner & Sereno, 1994). For example, sentence wrap-up effects have been shown to result from "a search for referents that have not been assigned, the construction of inter-clause relations ... and an attempt to handle any inconsistencies that could not be resolved within the sentence" (Just & Carpenter, 1980, p. 345). Recall that the target sentences used in this study are all metaphoric statements of the following form: "A is (does) a B." Both theoretical claims (see Katz, 1996, for a review) and experimental priming studies (e.g., Paivio & Clark, 1986) put the processing load for comprehension on the metaphoric vehicle (i.e., the "B" term). Consequently, if the resolution and integration of metaphor meaning occurs online, one should expect variability in the reading time for the final word in the statement depending on how readily the word can be integrated into the representation of the text. There is by now a fairly extensive literature (see Gibbs, 1994, for a review) that indicates that the processing of metaphor in context occurs directly, and, as such, one might expect that the resolution of any ambiguity would be completed with the statement itself and not spill over to RTs taken downstream. This downstream spillover would be evidenced by either increased time taken after the target statement before one goes onto the next sentence or increased RTs for the following sentence, or both.

Second, one can examine whether processing of a statement is the same when the statement is used as a metaphor or as sarcasm. If one took a direct access, context-driven explanation of nonliteral sentence processing, then one would suggest that the context sets up an interpretative framework and therefore both the metaphor and sarcastic uses could demonstrate the same pattern of reading: an expected increase in RT for the last item in the statement. A difference in RT between the item used metaphorically or sarcastically is somewhat difficult to interpret. For instance, an increase in RT for the last word in the target statement when that statement is used sarcastically (relative to the same item when used metaphorically) could suggest that the comprehension of a statement used metaphorically involves only resolving the metaphor, whereas the same item used sarcastically involves resolving both the metaphor and making an attribution about it. Alternatively, any such difference might just reflect differences in the contexts themselves wherein it is easier to constrain for a metaphoric relative to an ironic interpretation.

Third, one can assess whether mentioning speaker occupation by itself is processed online. The relevant contrast here is between the three neutral context conditions: In one condition, a person from a high-metaphor occupation is identified as the speaker of the target statement; in a second condition, the speaker is from a high-irony occupation; and in the third, the occupation of speaker is not provided. If the manipulation of speaker occupation affects RTs for words in the target statement, then that would be evidence that general knowledge about people in different occupations is accessed quite early in the comprehension process.

Finally, we can examine the individual and interactive effects of statement familiarity, speaker occupation, and discourse context counterfactuality. For instance, if the cues manipulated here influence online language comprehension then we should observe differences in RTs as a function of statement familiarity, context counterfactuality, and speaker occupation. The locus of the effects, if they do arise, should indicate whether the cues work to constrain interpretation within the statement or further downstream, such as the space after the statement or even into the reading of a later sentence. This is the main focus of this study.

METHOD

Participants

Fifty-two English-speaking psychology undergraduates from the University of Western Ontario received partial course credit in an introductory psychology course or $6 for their participation. Three participants were replaced due to scoring lower than 60% on the recognition task described in the following section.

Materials and Design

Key Passages. Participants read 10 practice and 80 experimental passages. Sixteen of the experimental passages were the key trials in this experiment.[2] These were slightly extended versions of the passages used in Katz and Pexman (1997, Experiment 1), involving target statements that were ambiguous as to speakers' intent. The key passages were constructed such that the target statement was uttered by a person from an occupation rated as likely to use irony or from an occupation rated as likely to use metaphor (or, in the control condition, was uttered by a person for whom no occupation was given). High-irony and high-metaphor occupations were selected based on normative ratings (see Katz & Pexman, 1997). In the Katz and Pexman study, 50 participants rated the likelihood that a person in a particular occupation would use irony, and, separately, metaphor in their conversation. Six high-irony occupations were chosen for inclusion in the study, using the criterion that irony-use ratings were significantly greater than were the metaphor-use ratings, $M = 4.86, SD = 0.87$ vs. $M = 3.81, SD = 1.05; t(5) = 9.72, p < .001$. These occupations were army sergeant, cab driver, comedian, factory worker, police officer, and truck driver. A set of six high-metaphor occupations were analogously chosen; metaphor-use ratings were $M = 5.08, SD = 0.94$, and irony-use ratings were $M = 3.52, SD = 0.81, t(5) = 7.52, p < .001$. These occupations were artist, clergyman, doctor, nurse, scientist, and teacher. Most important, the irony use and metaphor use ratings provided for each type of occupation were statistically unrelated ($r = .13$), with a shared variance of less than 2%.

The target statement was always a nonliteral sentence in the form "A is (does) a B"; in half of the statements the item was a familiar instantiation of a conceptual metaphor and in the other half a less familiar instantiation. Familiarity was also based on normative data (see Katz & Pexman, 1997). From the norming data, the eight least familiar statements ($M = 1.97, SD = 0.39$) and the eight most familiar statements ($M = 4.93, SD = 0.87$) were selected. Familiar statements were rated significantly more familiar than less familiar statements, $t(14) = 8.74, p < .001$.

Finally, each target statement was placed in one of four discourse contexts. For irony-inviting contexts, the meaning of the discourse in the paragraph was counterfactual (i.e., incongruent) with the metaphoric interpretation of the statement. For metaphor-inviting contexts, the meaning of the discourse was congruent with the metaphoric interpretation of the statement. A neutral context condition was created by limiting the amount of information provided in the context for the target statement, and thus the context was neither congruent nor incongruent with the target. Finally, a no-occupation neutral context condition was created, which was the same as the neutral-context condition except that the occupation of the speaker was not provided. The no-occupation context served as a control condition for the manipulation of speaker occupation.

As noted earlier, there was one slight modification from the passages employed in Katz and Pexman (1997). In this study, an extra sentence followed the target statements. This added sentence allowed us to measure effects that occurred after the statement had been read, such as increased RT for the space after the target statement or into the next sentence. Such spillover effects would indicate that the resolution and integration processes for the target were not completed by statement end. Thus, spillover effects are a measure of the increased difficulty in the comprehension of these statements (relative to statements that do not exhibit spillover). Also, the key trials were constructed so that the beginning and end of the statements were not located at the beginning or end of lines in the paragraphs when they were presented on the computer screen. This avoided variability in RTs for target statements caused by moving from one line to the next in the paragraphs.

In summary, each target statement was, across participants, uttered by a person from a high-irony occupation, a high-metaphor occupation, or for whom no occupation information was provided. Moreover, each target statement was presented in a discourse context that was irony inviting, metaphor inviting, or neutral (with little context provided). Finally, each target statement was either familiar or unfamiliar.

Here are three sample passages:

(1)   A truck driver and a friend, Robin, were talking about a comment that Robin had made to her boss that day. Robin's comment had been scornfully rejected by her boss. The truck driver said the following: "That comment hit the bull's eye." Robin nodded in response to her friend's comment.

In the aforementioned sample passage, the speaker is from a high-irony occupation, the context is irony inviting (because the boss scornfully rejected the comment), and the statement itself (presented in quotation marks) is familiar. The comprehension question that followed this passage was "Did Robin make a comment to her boss?"

(2)   While Andrew and a nurse were having coffee at an outdoor cafe, a man was panhandling in the street nearby. The panhandler smiled at everyone he asked for money. He seemed to be getting a lot of money from the people he asked. The nurse commented that, "his smiles are can openers." Andrew sipped his coffee.

In this sample passage, the speaker is from a high-metaphor occupation, the context is metaphor inviting (because the panhandler was getting a lot of money), and the statement is unfamiliar. The comprehension question that followed this passage was the following:"Was Andrew at a cafe?"

(3)   Casey and a friend had both received Christmas cards from an acquaintance. Referring to the acquaintance, Casey's friend said the following: "His Christmas cards are progress charts." Casey and his friend then talked about their Christmas plans.

In this sample passage, there is no speaker (the no-occupation control condition), the context is neutral, and the statement is unfamiliar. The comprehension question that followed the passage was the following: "Did Casey receive a Christmas card?"

Filler Passages.   Sixty-four filler paragraphs that were approximately the same length as the key trials were also constructed. Sixteen of these paragraphs closely resembled the key trials except that the filler statements were literal instead of figurative. These trials ensured that the figurative statements and at least some of the literal filler statements were presented in the same way, and thus the form of presentation alone did not cue a nonliteral interpretation.

Manipulation Checks.   There were two checks to ensure that participants were reading the material attentively. First, following every paragraph, participants answered a simple yes or no comprehension question. Second, after all the passages had been read, participants completed a short recognition task that consisted of a list of 64 statements, including the 16 key statements and the 16 literal fillers mentioned previously. The remaining 32 statements were additional statements that had not been presented during the reading phase. Half of these distracters were literal, and half were figurative statements. The distracter statements were constructed so that the information provided in them was not similar to statements that actually were presented in the online task. The participants' task was to identify the statements they read during the online procedure.

Basic Design of Experiment.   The primary dependent measure was RTs, and the design of this experiment was a factorial combination of 3 Contexts (irony inviting, metaphor inviting, neutral) × 2 Types of Speaker Occupation (high irony vs. high metaphor) × 2 Types of Statements (familiar vs. unfamiliar). An additional context was considered: the neutral, no-occupation condition. This was a control condition, separate from the basic factorial design.

Procedure

Online Reading Task.   Paragraphs were displayed on a 14-in. Sony Trinitron monitor controlled by a Macintosh LCIII and presented using PsyScope (Cohen, MacWhinney, Flatt, & Provost, 1993) in a one-word-at-a-time moving-window format. Thus, paragraphs were initially presented on the screen with each non-space character replaced by a dash. Participants pressed a button to reveal the first word of the paragraph. Each subsequent button press revealed the next word and replaced the previous word with dashes. It should be noted that after each sentence in a passage there was a space, and the time taken to pause at this space was recorded. Participants read each paragraph in this manner and then answered a yes or no comprehension question. Testing sessions began with 10 practice passages. Participants then completed the remaining 80 experimental trials, taking a break after 40 trials. Participants were instructed to read at a pace that resembled how they would typically read a magazine or newspaper. One-word-at-a-time reading latencies were recorded with millisecond accuracy via a PsyScope button box, measured as the time interval between successive button presses. After completing the reading task, participants completed the recognition task. The testing sessions lasted approximately 40 min.

RESULTS AND DISCUSSION

RT Data

To ascertain whether participants were reading the passages attentively, we examined performance on the comprehension questions asked immediately after reading each passage and performance on the later recognition memory task. Accuracy in both tasks was high. Erroneous responses on the comprehension questions occurred on average for only 2.15 of the 80 trials. All key trials in which comprehension errors occurred were excluded from the analyses of RTs. We also identified outliers, eliminating from analysis any RT that was more than 3 standard deviations from the overall mean for a particular condition: This occurred only 12 times in 832 key trials (1.4% key trials). Finally, we used the recognition memory task as a second index to determine if participants were paying attention during the reading task. The data here also indicated a high level of attentive reading: Recognition accuracy for the key trials was near ceiling (88% correct). Only 3 participants had recognition accuracy of less than 60%, and these participants were replaced by 3 additional participants.

Data Analyses. We examined RTs for each word on the key trials. First, as expected, examination of RTs indicated that the most obvious effects were found for the last word in the target statement (i.e., the metaphoric vehicle, or the B term) in the "A is (does) a B" sentence. Initial analyses indicated little systematic variability in RT for words leading up to the B term and that the average RT for these words (312 msec) was not significantly different from the time taken to read the first word of the sentence that followed the target statement (332 msec). Also, the target statements differed somewhat in length, and some target statements had modifiers before the B term (e.g., "Her mind is an active volcano") whereas others did not (e.g., "His standards are at the ceiling"). This variability in stimulus characteristics (along with the aforementioned lack of variability in reading times across the first words in the statements) led us to believe it would be best to look at the average RTs for the first words in the target statements and to look at subsequent words in terms of individual RTs. Consequently, for expositional purposes, we calculated four RTs for each key passage: (a) an average RT for the words in the target statement leading up to the B term, (b) an RT for the last (B) word in the target statement, (c) an RT for the space following the last word in the target statement, and (d) an RT for the first word in the next sentence following the target statement. The measures of the time taken at the space after the target statement and time to read the first word of the next sentence were taken to see if, after the statement had been read, the effects of cues spilled over and influenced processing downstream.

The analyses are described in four main sections: (a) the effect of mentioning speakers' occupation; (b) the effects of discourse context counterfactuality, speaker occupation, and statement familiarity; (c) an analysis of the recognition memory data; and (d) a correlational analysis of the online RTs with the ratings and memory data from Katz and Pexman (1997). Where relevant, analyses are conducted with participants, and, separately, items treated as random factors.[3]

Effect of Occupation Mention.   We manipulated the occupation of the person who uttered the target statement: The speaker (a) was from a high-irony occupation, (b) was from a high-metaphor occupation, or (c) did not have an occupation mentioned. Thus, this analysis permitted examination of the online effects of just mentioning occupation. This analysis involved 4 Reading Locations (first part of target statement, last word in target statement, space after target statement, or first word next sentence) × 3 Occupation Conditions (high irony, high metaphor, or no occupation) × 2 Levels of Target Familiarity (familiar vs. unfamiliar).

Figure 10.1 represents the mean RTs for the three speaker occupation conditions as a function of reading location and statement familiarity. There are two main effects: (a) for occupation mention, with longer RTs for the two conditions in which an occupation was mentioned, $F_1(2, 50) = 12.34, p < .001; F_2(2, 13) = 1.36, p > .05$; and (b) for location, with longer RTs for the last word in the target statement relative to the other locations, $F_1(3, 49) = 20.44, F_2(3, 12) = 3.58, p < .05$.

The highest level significant interaction was Location × Occupation, $F_1(6, 46) = 4.43, p < .001; F_2(6, 9) = 0.80, p > .05$. The nature of this interaction was that the occupational effects were most evident at the last word in the target statement. Thus, participants were sensitive to the mention of speakers' occupation and were taking that source of information into account as they were reading the target statement.

Although statement familiarity did not significantly modify the two-way interaction of Location × Occupation, visual inspection of mean RTs suggests that the Location × Occupation effect is most evident for unfamiliar statements at the last word in the target statement. Post hoc examination of this possibility is consistent with the contention. For unfamiliar statements, RTs of the last word were significantly longer when the speaker was a member of a high-irony occupation, compared to trials when no occupation was mentioned, $t_1(51) = 2.14, p < .05; t_2(7) = 1.25, p > .05$. RTs were marginally longer when the speaker was a member of a

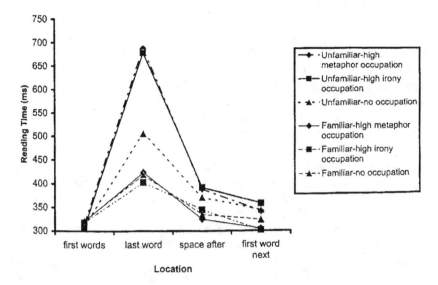

Figure 10.1.   Mean reading time as a function of statement familiarity, speaker occupation, and reading location.

high-metaphor occupation, compared to trials when no occupation was mentioned, $t_1(51) = 1.94$, $p = .06$; $t_2(7) = 1.21$, $p > .05$. However, for familiar statements, these comparisons did not approach significance.

Taken together, these data indicate that mentioning occupation alone influences processing of the target statement while that statement is being read. Thus, these data support the contention that a world-knowledge pragmatic cue to sarcastic intent is available at an early stage of statement processing. The occupation mention effect seems most apparent when the statement is relatively unfamiliar, suggesting that at the earliest stages of processing the cue is mainly useful in the comprehension of unfamiliar statements, presumably those without a well-established canonical meaning. As such, these data are consistent with interactive models of language comprehension in which the comprehension system continuously integrates all available and relevant information to compute the best interpretation (e.g., Mac-Donald, Pearlmutter, & Seidenberg, 1994; McClelland, 1987; McClelland, St. John, & Taraban, 1989; McRae et al., 1998).

Effects of Discourse Context, Speaker Occupation, and Statement Familiarity. This analysis involved 3 Discourse Contexts (metaphor inviting, irony inviting, neutral) × 2 Levels of Statement Familiarity (familiar vs. unfamiliar) × 2 speaker occupations (high metaphor vs. high irony) × 4 Reading Locations (first words in target statement, last word in target statement, space after target statement, first word of next sentence). The RTs for all of these conditions are presented in Table

10.1. In this analysis, there were main effects of location, $F_1(3, 49) = 24.51$, $F_2(3, 12) = 6.87$, $ps < .01$; target statement familiarity, $F_1 (1, 51) = 48.58$, $F_2(1, 14) = 7.09$, $ps < .05$; and discourse context, $F_1(2, 50) = 3.48$, $p < .05$; $F_2(2, 13) = 1.11$, $p > .05$.

The familiarity effect indicated that familiar target statements were read more rapidly than more unfamiliar statements. The context effect indicated that when the target statement (which one should recall is an "A is [does] a B" metaphor) was consistent with the preceding discourse (i.e., it was metaphor inviting), participants read the statement more rapidly relative to the neutral control. These data are consistent with earlier findings (see Katz, 1996, for a review) that show when a metaphor is placed in context its meaning is available quite rapidly, a finding that has been taken as support for the context-driven, direct-access view of metaphor comprehension, at least when the contrast has been made to the availability of the expressed literal sense of the metaphor.

The nature of the main effect of location was that average RT was fast for the first words in the target statements (312 msec) and very slow for the last words in the target statements (488 msec). This confirms our speculation that the vehicle (the B term) plays the critical role in resolving metaphor meaning. RT was still somewhat slow at the space after the statement (366 msec), indicating a spillover effect that lasted after the last word in the statement had been read but that was fading by the time the first word of the next sentence was read (332 msec).

There were several interactive effects involving location. There was a Location × Context interaction, $F_1(6, 46) = 3.16$, $p < .05$; $F_2(6, 9) = 1.37$, $p > .05$. The nature of this interaction was that targets in a metaphor-inviting context produced less pronounced spillover to locations downstream. Further, targets in the irony-inviting context were initially read at the same rate as in the neutral condition, but, at the last word in the target statement, were read at a speed similar to that found in the metaphor-inviting condition. This suggests that, regardless of the nature of the two elaborated contexts, a nonliteral metaphoric interpretation of the key statement was largely completed by statements' end. Marked differences were observed, however, for the time taken at the space after the statement. At this location, the RT for items in the irony-inviting condition was significantly slower than that found in the metaphor-inviting conditions by 54 msec, $t_1(51) = 2.68$, $p < .05$; $t_2(15) = 1.95$, $p = .08$. That is, although the metaphoric content of the statement might be available very rapidly, it takes additional time to resolve the sarcastic evaluation of the metaphor being used ironically. The resolution of sarcastic intent is completed by the time one commences reading the next sentence: Reading of the first word in the sentence following the target used ironically was only 12 msec slower than observed in the neutral condition.

There was also an interaction of Location × Statement Familiarity, $F_1(3, 49) = 16.90$, $p < .01$; $F_2(3, 12) = 3.49$, $p < .05$. The nature of this interaction was that familiar statements showed much faster RTs for the last word and at the space following the statement than did unfamiliar statements, indicated by main effects of familiarity at those locations, $F_1(1, 51) = 43.57$, $p < .001$; $F_2(1, 14) = 8.06$, $p < .05$, and $F_1(1, 51) = 3.57$, $p < .06$; $F_2(1, 14) = 2.14$, $p < .05$, for the last word in target statement and space

TABLE 10-1

Mean Reading Times for Four Locations as a Function of Speaker Occupation, Statement Familiarity, and Discourse Context Counterfactuality

| | High-Metaphor Occupation | | | | | | High-Irony Occupation | | | | | | No Occupation | |
| | Neutral Context | | Metaphor-Inviting Context | | Irony-Inviting Context | | Neutral Context | | Metaphor-Inviting Context | | Irony-Inviting Context | | Neutral Context | |
Statement Familiarity	M	SD	M	SD	M	SD	M	SD	M	SD	M	SD	M	SD
First word in statement														
Unfamiliar	316	98	326	109	327	140	307	110	321	102	218	88	311	108
Familiar	320	113	313	115	306	106	318	116	324	129	342	149	321	105
Last word in statement														
Unfamiliar	687	650	564	569	496	301	678	501	528	384	504	382	506	334
Familiar	424	367	346	242	396	296	403	357	383	174	445	281	419	401
Space after statement														
Unfamiliar	389	200	361	133	353	142	392	194	345	140	437	244	371	145
Familiar	325	107	338	251	357	133	345	127	315	83	429	404	335	137
First word in next sentence														
Unfamiliar	342	104	326	108	327	95	359	100	363	258	346	85	345	100
Familiar	305	106	279	83	346	257	302	97	355	345	338	182	324	138

Note. Times are in milliseconds.

243

after target statement locations, respectively. This finding suggests that unfamiliar statements cause more "unfinished" processing than do familiar statements.

There was also an interaction of Statement Familiarity × Context, $F_1(2, 50) = 5.29, p < .01; F_2(2, 13) = 1.12, p > .05$. This interaction of Familiarity × Context indicated that, whereas familiar statements were read more rapidly than unfamiliar statements in the neutral, by 91 msec, $t_1(51) = 5.48, p < .001; t_2(14) = 1.99, p = .07$, and metaphor-inviting contexts, by 60 msec, $t_1(51) = 4.31, p < .001; t_2(14) = 3.58, p < .005$, the familiar and unfamiliar statements did not differ in RT when placed in the irony-inviting context, 6 msec, $t_1(51) = 1.33; t_2(14) = 1.23, ps > .05$.

Finally, there was a three-way interaction of Location × Familiarity × Context, $F_1(6, 49) = 2.28, p = .05; F_2(6, 9) = 1.13, p > .05$. This interaction indicated that the locus of the familiarity effects differed for the irony- and metaphor-inviting contexts. With familiar statements, RTs were similar at all locations in the neutral and metaphor-inviting conditions, except at the last-word position where, when a metaphoric context was given, RTs were faster by 49 msec, $t_1(51) = 1.83, p = .09; t_2(7) = 0.66, p > .05$, although the effect only approached significance. In contrast, for the irony-inviting and neutral conditions, RTs were similar at both the initial and final-word locations but differed at the space after the statement and at the first word from the next sentence: At these two latter locations, reading was slower in the irony-inviting context than in the neutral condition, by 58 and 38 msec, $t_1(51) = 1.72, p = .09; t_2(27) = 1.17, p > .05$, and, $t_1(51) = 2.08, p < .05; t_2(7) = 1.22, p > .05$, respectively. These data indicate that providing a metaphor-inviting context facilitates the comprehension of the metaphoric content of a familiar comparison (relative to a neutral context) whereas the item placed in a counterfactual, irony-inviting context requires a noticeably longer period in which the sarcastic intent of the metaphor is understood.

A different pattern was seen when the target statement was unfamiliar. With these statements, both the metaphor-inviting and irony-inviting contexts exhibited a similar pattern of results: Faster RT at the last-word location compared to the RT observed in the neutral condition, by 137 and 183 msec, $t_1(51) = 2.15, p < .05; t_1(7) = 1.13, p > .05$, and, $t_1(51) = 3.02, p < .005; t_2(7) = 1.31, p > .05$, for the metaphor-inviting and irony-inviting contexts, respectively. At the space after the target, the RT in the metaphor-inviting condition was 38 msec faster than the neutral condition and 42 msec faster than the irony-inviting condition, $t_1(51) = 1.76, p = .08; t_2(7) = 1.83, p = .11$, and, $t_1(51) = 2.18, p < .05; t_2(7) = 1.43, p > .05$, respectively. Thus, whereas there is evidence that more processing time is required for the irony-inviting condition than the metaphor-inviting condition, in general, for unfamiliar statements, both metaphor and sarcastic irony exhibit similar patterns of reading: Both exhibit reduced RT at the last word of the target statement (relative to the neutral context condition) and spillover effects at the later locations, albeit reduced spillover in the metaphor-inviting condition.

There was one additional three-way interaction: Location × Context × Occupation, $F_1(6, 49) = 1.96, p = .09; F_2(6, 9) = 3.39, p < .05$. The nature of this interaction was that in the case in which the target statement was uttered by a person from a high-metaphor occupation, RTs were remarkably similar for all three contexts across all four locations. The exception was at the time taken to read the last word in the statement: In the neutral context condition, RTs were substantially slower than observed in the metaphor-inviting condition, by 101 msec, $t_1(51) = 1.92$, $p = .06$; $t_2(15) = 1.20$, $p > .05$, and the irony-inviting condition, by 110 msec, $t_1(51) = 1.96$, $p = .06$; $t_2(15) = 1.43$, $p > .05$. Thus, at least when spoken by a person from a high-metaphor occupation, there is much less ambiguity to resolve for a nonliteral statement of the form "A is (does) a B" when it is situated in either a metaphor-inviting or irony-inviting context, relative to a context that is not biased toward either nonliteral interpretation.

Consider next when the same statements are uttered by a person from a high-irony occupation. Once again RT for the last word in the statement was faster in the metaphor-inviting, by 86 msec, $t_1(51) = 2.11$, $p < .05$; $t_2(15) = 0.94$, $p > .05$, and irony-inviting context, 66 msec, $t_1(51) = 1.72$, $p = .10$; $t_2(15) = 0.75$, $p > .05$, relative to that observed in the neutral context. However, when the speaker was from a high-irony occupation (unlike the aforementioned case, when the speaker was associated with metaphoric speech), differences in RTs were found beyond the statement itself. Quite different effects were observed at the space after the last word in the target statement: Relative to the neutral condition, the time spent at the space was 39 msec faster in the metaphor-inviting context, $t_1(51) = 2.32$, $p < .05$; $t_2(15) = 1.84$, $p = .08$, but 64 msec slower in the irony-inviting context, $t_1(51) = 1.98$, $p = .06$; $t_2(15) = 1.30$, $p > .05$. This pattern is consistent with an interaction of speaker knowledge and discourse content in which discourse interacts with the nature of the speaker in resolving speakers' intent. A metaphor-inviting context is sufficient in clarifying the metaphoric content of the "A is (does) a B" statement, even if uttered by a person associated with ironic usage. When uttered by a person associated with ironic usage in a context that is biased toward the ironic interpretation, more time is required to resolve the speaker's intent. Indeed, the time spent at the space after the statement is 103 msec longer in the irony-inviting context than in the metaphor-inviting condition, $t_1(51) = 3.10$, $p < .005$; $t_2(15) = 2.64$, $p < .05$. There is a suggestion of a partial reversal when RT is assessed at the first word of the following sentence; now in the metaphor-inviting condition, RTs are 28 msec longer than found in the neutral condition, although this difference was not significant, $t_1(51) = 1.18$, $p > .05$; $t_2(15) = 0.99$, $p > .05$. It is as if there is a delayed or "sleeper" effect in which the incongruity of the nature of the speaker (high irony) and nature of the discourse context (inviting a metaphoric interpretation) becomes apparent.

The interaction of location, occupation of speaker, and discourse context suggests that providing a more elaborated context leads to some resolution of meaning by the last word of the nonliteral statement. Given that all the statements were of the form, "A is (does) a B," it is reasonable to assume that the metaphoric content is understood when sufficient context is provided. When the speaker is associated with metaphoric usage, further analysis of the statement does not appear to occur, even when the statement is embedded in an irony-inviting context. When the speaker is associated with ironic usage, however, additional processing occurs downstream, most immediately when the discourse invites an ironic interpretation and more slowly when the discourse invites a metaphoric interpretation. These findings suggest that (a) when the discourse context is consistent with a sarcastic-ironic interpretation, the sarcastic nature of the speaker is being assessed early, and aids in the integration of a target statement's meaning very shortly after that target has been read; and (b) the incongruity between the sarcastic nature of the speaker and a context inviting a nonsarcastic reading is initially ignored but appears to be noted by the beginning of the next sentence.

Recognition Memory for the Target Statements

Recall that immediately following the reading of all the passages, participants were asked to complete a recognition memory task in which they had to identify the statements they read during the experiment. We discussed these aforementioned data as a means of assessing whether our participants read the stimuli attentively. Here we discuss a substantive and not methodological aspect of these data.

Recall also that, in addition to the 16 key figurative statements, we presented for recognition 16 literal statements that had been presented during the reading phase of the study and that took the same "A is (does) a B" form as the figurative statements. Thus it was possible to examine directly recognition memory for a set of literal and nonliteral statements of the same form, presented in the same manner. The data are clear: Mean accuracy is reliably greater for the nonliteral statements ($M =$ 88% for nonliteral, $M = 72$% for the literal counterparts). The difference is significant across both participants, $t_1(51) = 7.79$, and items, $t_2(31) = 3.31$, $ps < .05$. These data are consistent with others that suggest a memory advantage for nonliteral stimuli (e.g., Katz & Pexman, 1997; Kreuz et al., 1991).

Correlation of Online Data With Ratings and Memory Data

Recall that in Katz and Pexman (1997), participants were presented with the same 16 statements for rating and subsequent memory testing that were employed here as our key items. Two of the rating measures were particularly relevant to sarcasm. In the Katz and Pexman study we obtained ratings of the degree to which each of the 16 items was perceived as sarcastic and also the degree to which each item was perceived to be mocking a character in the passage. To test whether the ratings and memory findings reported in the earlier study were coordinated with the RTs reported here, we correlated the RTs from the matrix created for each location measured (first words, last word, space after, first word next sentence) in our 2 (speaker occupation) × 3 (discourse context counterfactuality) × 2 (statement familiarity) design with the corresponding cells in Katz and Pexman (in which the numbers represented mean ratings or mean percentage recall). The resulting correlation matrix is presented in Table 10.2.

As illustrated in Table 10.2, the time taken in this study to read the last word in the statement was positively and significantly correlated with the time taken at the

TABLE 10-2

Correlations of Reading Times From Four Locations in This Study With Mocking Ratings, Sarcasm Ratings, and Recall Percentages From Katz and Pexman (1997, Experiment 1)

	1	2	3	4	5	6	7
1. First words in statement	—						
2. Last word in statement	−.10	—					
3. Space after statement	**−.49***	**.47***	—				
4. First word next sentence	−.16	**.52***	.35	—			
5. Mocking	−.29	.29	**.68***	.34	—		
6. Sarcasm	−.19	.15	**.65***	.33	**.95***	—	
7. Recall	.39	.10	−.09	**.51***	.22	.29	—

Note. Coefficients in boldface are significant at $p < .05$; *$p < .05$.

space after the statement ($r = .47$) and the time taken to read the first word of the next sentence ($r = .52$). Thus, the various indexes of comprehension measured on-line were associated with one another. It is interesting to note that RTs for the initial words in the target statement were negatively correlated with the time taken at the space after the statement ($r = .49$), but not with the RTs for the last word or RTs for the first word of the following sentence. Although these data are correlational and causation cannot be inferred, it appears that, for the statements employed here, superficial processing of the initial words in the statement reduces the likelihood of capturing the nuances of the metaphor in context and hence increases the likelihood that an elaborated analysis of sentence meaning will be required later on in the processing sequence.

The more critical findings for our purposes can be found in the correlations of the RT measures with the ratings and memory measures taken from Katz and Pexman (1997). As can be seen, about 45% of the variance in the ratings of sarcasm and mocking can be predicted by the time taken at the space after the statement had been read. The recall of the statements are also predicted by measures taken during our reading task. One can predict about 25% of the variance in the memory test by knowing how long one spent reading the first word in the sentence following the target statement.

There are several implications of these findings. First and foremost, the strong coordination of online and memory-based measures gives additional support to the argument that ratings and memory indexes (albeit indirect) can be used to make inferences about the initial processing of sarcasm. The degree of sarcasm or mocking in this case appears to be related to processes that occur within about 2,300 msec from the time when participants start processing the statement (an estimate based on the average complete statement reading time of 1,938 msec plus the time taken at the space after the statement, another 366 msec). These times are most certainly long enough to incorporate a number of different processes: syntactic analysis, lexical access for the component words, finding of referents, interclause integration, and various inferences needed to resolve inconsistencies. Further work is required to identify how each of these processes work in the comprehension of sarcasm.

Second, the online RTs by themselves do not shed direct light on the nature of the processes that occur, although they constrain the types of explanations that are reasonable. The correlations shown here indicate that whatever these processes might be, they are directly related to the phenomenological experience of sarcasm.

Third, the findings that different online loci are associated with rating measures (space after the statement) and with memory measures (time to read first word of next sentence) suggest that separable aspects of processing affect how we perceive a sentence and how we subsequently remember it, with the processes especially important for memory taking an additional 332 msec, on average, to complete (estimated on the time taken to read the first word of the following sentence). We are not making the separate-process argument that a sense of sarcasm is necessary before one can process it for memory accessibility—merely that whatever processing occurs (and it might just be one process), information becomes available for use in making judgments about the degree of sarcasm earlier than that useful for subsequent memory access.

SUMMARY AND CONCLUSIONS

There were two questions addressed in this study. The first question was whether three cues expected to convey sarcastic versus metaphoric intent played a role during online language comprehension. Second, were online measures of sarcasm coordinated with ratings and memory measures for the same set of statements? The data indicate that the answer to both questions is yes.

In the online reading task, all three of the cues demonstrated some early effects, sometimes interactively and usually at the end of the statement or slightly later downstream, at the space after the statement or during reading of the first word following the statement. These effects are usually taken as a measure of the settling of inconsistencies and comprehension issues that have not been completed earlier in the processing sequence. Later effects should not be a surprise because the comprehension of sarcasm is based on understanding both the meaning of a statement and the social implications that arise from its use. Indeed, one could argue that a person who goes to the effort of using sarcasm to make a point that could be made in some more direct fashion wants the listener—reader to consider both the expressed message and the indirect intended message.

In general, the findings were that the "A is (does) a B" items employed here were read initially as metaphors but that the nature of the speaker or counterfactuality of the statement and preceding discourse context came into play quite rapidly, slowing processing at the space following the statement or during reading of the first word of the sentence following the target statement. We observed as well that the nature (occupation) of the speaker was noted early, and, at least in the stimuli used here, was available for use during the reading of the metaphoric vehicle. Higher order interactions of this variable with context indicate that knowledge about the nature of the speaker is not as powerful a factor in comprehension as is the nature of the discourse leading to the nonliteral target, but it still plays a role: Knowing that a speaker is associated with ironic use slows down reading of the first word of the sentence following the target statement if the discourse leads one to expect a metaphoric usage and acts more immediately, at the space after the target, if the context invites a sarcastically ironic reading. The reason that occupation has an effect is probably because of the social information it conveys. Certain occupations, in this case those that tend to be blue-collar occupations, are associated with ironic speech, whereas others (those that tend to be white-collar occupations) are associated with metaphoric speech. These associations likely stem from social stereotypes.

These data give additional support to the findings of Katz and Pexman (1997) and suggest that the social identity of the person making the comment (operationalized here by occupation), the familiarity of the statement itself, and the counterfactuality of the discourse context in which the statement is placed all have effects that occur early in processing and were not merely an artifact created by their ratings task. Moreover, the interactive nature of these effects suggests that, even for as highly an inferential aspect of comprehension as sarcasm, multiple sources of information are being evaluated and integrated continuously (cf. McRae et al., 1998).

In terms of theoretical implications, some linguistic theories (e.g., Relevance Theory; Sperber & Wilson, 1986, 1995) might hold that the contextual cues constrain the relevant meanings of these statements so that only intended meanings are accessed: the metaphoric meaning for the metaphor-inviting cues and the sarcastic meaning for the irony-inviting cues. Giora, on the other hand (e.g., Giora et al., 1998), would likely argue that the salient meaning would be accessed that, for the familiar items in this study, would be the metaphoric meaning. For our results, both positions have validity because cues to speaker intent were accessed immediately (suggesting that readers settled on either the metaphoric or ironic interpretation very quickly), but ironic usage led to spillover effects in processing (suggesting that the ironic interpretation required additional processing).

The correlations of the online measures taken here with the memory-based measures available from Katz and Pexman (1997) indicate that the two types of measures are well coordinated. One can predict how sarcastic or mocking the statement is perceived to be by the amount of time a reader pauses after the statement has been read, before moving on to the next sentence. Also, the likelihood that the statement will be subsequently remembered is predicted by the amount of time a reader spends looking at the first word of the next sentence. These data indicate, first, that ratings and memory indexes are related to mental activities that occur fairly early in the processing sequence, and, second, that the online differences we observed at sentence wrap-up can be directly related to a consciously felt sense of sarcasm.

ACKNOWLEDGMENTS

This research was supported by a grant from the University of Calgary Research Grants Committee to Penny M. Pexman, a Natural Sciences and Engineering Research Council of Canada (NSERC) postgraduate scholarship to Todd R. Ferretti, and NSERC operating Grant 06P007040 to Albert N. Katz. Portions of this article were presented in August 1998 at the American Psychological Association Convention in San Francisco, CA. We thank Rachel Giora for her helpful comments on an earlier draft of this article.

ENDNOTES

1. We use the terms *ironic* or *irony* to refer to the form of verbal irony that is perceived as sarcasm.
2. These stimuli can be obtained from Penny M. Pexman.
3. Analyses were conducted with both participants, and, separately, items treated as random factors. These analyses are reported as F_1 and F_2 (or t_1 and t_2), respectively. It should be noted that our aim of directly comparing performance in the online reading task with the memory-based data available in Katz and Pexman (1997) constrained the number of items that we could present here, and consequently, the degrees of freedom in the items' analyses were very small. Thus, in drawing conclusions, we place more weight on the analyses by participants, although in some cases effects are also significant by items.

REFERENCES

Cohen, J. D., MacWhinney, B., Flatt, M., & Provost, J. (1993). PsyScope: An interactive graphic system for designing and controlling experiments in the psychology laboratory using Macintosh computers. *Behavior Research Methods, Instruments, and Computers, 25,* 257–71.

Garnsey, S. M., Pearlmutter, N. J., Myers, E., & Lotocky, M. A. (1997). The contributions of verb bias and plausibility to the comprehension of temporarily ambiguous sentences. *Journal of Memory and Language, 37,* 58–93.

Gibbs, R. W. (1986). On the psycholinguistics of sarcasm. *Journal of Experimental Psychology: General, 115,* 3–15.

Gibbs, R. W. (1994). *The poetics of mind.* Cambridge, England: Cambridge University Press.

Giora, R., Fein, O., & Schwartz, T. (1998). Irony: Graded salience and indirect negation. *Metaphor and Symbol, 13,* 83–101.

Holtgraves, T. (1994). Communication in context: Effects of speaker status on the comprehension of indirect requests. *Journal of Experimental Psychology: Learning, Memory, and Cognition, 20,* 1205–1218.

Jorgensen, J., Miller, G. A., & Sperber, D. (1984). Test of the mention theory of irony, *Journal of Experimental Psychology: General, 113,* 112–120.

Just, M. A., & Carpenter, P. A. (1980). A theory of reading: From eye fixation to comprehension. *Psychological Review, 87,* 329–354.

Just, M. A., Carpenter, P. A., & Woolley, J. D. (1982). Paradigms and processes in reading comprehension. *Journal of Experimental Psychology: General, 111,* 228–238.

Katz, A. N. (1996). On interpreting statements as metaphor or irony: Contextual heuristics and cognitive consequences. In J. S. Mio & A. N. Katz (Eds.), *Metaphor: Implications and applications* (pp. 1–22). Mahwah, NJ: Lawrence Erlbaum Associates.

Katz, A. N., & Lee, C. J. (1993). The role of authorial intent in determining verbal irony and metaphor. *Metaphor and Symbolic Activity, 8,* 257–279.

Katz, A. N., & Pexman, P. M. (1997). Interpreting figurative statements: Speaker occupation can change metaphor to irony. *Metaphor and Symbol, 12,* 19–41.

Kemper, S., & Thissen, D. (1981). Memory for dimensions of requests. *Journal of Verbal Learning and Verbal Behavior, 20,* 552–563.

Kintsch, W. (1988). The role of knowledge in discourse comprehension: A construction integration model. *Psychological Review, 95,* 163–182.

Kreuz, R. J. (1996). The use of verbal irony: Cues and constraints. In J. S. Mio & A. N. Katz (Eds.), *Metaphor: Implications and applications* (pp. 23–38). Mahwah, NJ: Lawrence Erlbaum Associates.

Kreuz, R. J., & Glucksberg, S. (1989). How to be sarcastic: The echoic reminder theory of verbal irony. *Journal of Experimental Psychology: General, 118,* 374–386.

Kreuz, R. J., Long, D. L., & Church, M. B. (1991). On being ironic: Pragmatic and mnemonic implications. *Metaphor and Symbolic Activity, 6,* 149–162.

Kumon-Nakamura, S., Glucksberg, S., & Brown, M. (1995). How about another piece of pie: The illusional pretense theory of discourse irony. *Journal of Experimental Psychology: General, 124,* 3–21.

MacDonald, M. C., Pearlmutter, N. J., & Seidenberg, M. S. (1994). The lexical nature of syntactic ambiguity resolution. *Psychological Review, 101,* 676–703.

Marschark, M., & Hunt, R. (1985). On memory for metaphor. *Memory and Cognition, 13,* 193–201.

McClelland, J. L. (1987). The case for interactions in language processing. In M. Coltheart (Ed.), *Attention and performance XII: The psychology of reading* (pp. 3–36). Hillsdale, NJ: Lawrence Erlbaum Associates.

McClelland, J. L., St. John, M., & Taraban, R. (1989). Sentence comprehension: A parallel distributed processing approach. *Language and Cognitive Processes, 4,* 287–336.

McRae, K., Spivey-Knowlton, M. J., & Tanenhaus, M. K. (1998). Modeling the influence of thematic fit (and other constraints) in online sentence comprehension. *Journal of Memory and Language, 38,* 283–312.

Noice, H. (1992). Elaborative memory strategies of professional actors. *Applied Cognitive Psychology, 6,* 417–427.

Paivio, A., & Clark, J. M. (1986). The role of topic and vehicle imagery in metaphor comprehension. *Communication and Cognition, 19,* 367–387.

Rayner, K., & Sereno, S. C. (1994). Eye movements in reading: Psycholinguistic studies. In M. A. Gernsbacher (Ed.), *Handbook of psycholinguistics* (pp. 57–81). San Diego, CA: Academic.

Sperber, D., & Wilson, D. (1986). *Relevance: Communication and cognition* (1st ed.). Oxford, England: Blackwell.

Sperber, D., & Wilson, D. (1995). *Relevance: Communication and cognition* (2nd ed.). Oxford, England: Blackwell.

Trueswell, J. C. (1996). The role of lexical frequency in syntactic ambiguity resolution. *Journal of Memory and Language, 35,* 566–585.

CHAPTER 11

Obligatory Processing of the Literal Meaning of Ironic Utterances: Further Evidence

John Schwoebel
Moss Rehabilitation Research Institute, Philadelphia

Shelly Dews
Boston College

Ellen Winner
Boston College and Harvard Project Zero

Kavitha Srinivas
Boston College

We tested the hypotheses that the literal meaning of an ironic utterance is activated during comprehension and (a) slows the processing of the key ironic portion of the utterance (literal activation hypothesis), and (b) slows the processing of the literal portion of the utterance that follows (the spillover hypothesis). Forty-eight stories, each ending in an ironic comment, were constructed. Half of the ironic comments were ironic criticism (positive literal meaning, negative ironic meaning), half were ironic praise (negative literal meaning, positive ironic meaning). Final utterances were divided into 3 phrases: Phrase 1 gave no indication of irony, Phrase 2 contained the key word that made the utterance ironic, and Phrase 3 gave no indication of irony. Each story was then altered by 1 phrase so that the final comment became literal. One version of each of the stories was presented to each of 48 college undergraduates. Stories were presented 1 sentence at a time, but the final utterances were presented in 3 consecutive phrases. Participants pressed the space bar as soon as they understood the sentence or phrase presented. For ironic criticism, participants took longer to process the key phrases in an irony- than a literal-biasing context, but they took longer to process the final (literal) phrase following irony only when the analysis was performed for item rather than participant variability. For ironic praise, participants again took longer to process the key

This chapter was previously published as "Obligatory processing of literal meaning of ironic utterances: Further evidence" (J. Schwoebel, S. Dews, E. Winner, & K. Srinivas) in *Metaphor and Symbol, 15,* 47–61. Copyright © [2000] by Lawrence Erlbaum Associates. Reprinted with permission.

phrases in an irony- than a literal-biasing context, but this difference did not reach significance, and they did not take any longer to process the final phrase following irony. Thus, results support the literal activation hypothesis in the case of ironic criticism but not ironic praise, and provide no clear support for the spillover hypothesis.

Both everyday as well as literary uses of language are riddled with verbal irony (Booth, 1974; Dews, Winner, Nicolaides, & Hunt, 1994; Muecke, 1969). No one has yet demonstrated the existence of a language or culture that does not make use of verbal irony. Although we do not know precisely what the incidence of irony is, some attempts at estimates have been made. For example, on contemporary popular American television shows we noted an average of four instances of verbal irony every half hour. Simple calculation leads to the conclusion that a person who watches 2 hr of popular television per day hears about 5,800 instances of irony a year. Most of the instances of irony on television that we observed were in the most prototypical form of irony, the form we refer to as ironic criticism, in which a positively worded utterance conveys a negative message (e.g., saying "That's just great" to convey that someone has done something undesirable). Less common, but still heard, were instances of what we refer to as ironic praise, in which a negatively worded utterance conveys a positive message (e.g., saying "You have a hard life" to a friend going off to the Caribbean for an all-expense-paid vacation). Ironic praise, while less common, is readily understood when it echoes a previously stated belief (Gibbs, 1986b; Kreuz & Glucksberg, 1989) and when it alludes to some prior expectation, norm, or convention (Kumon-Nakamura, 1993). In the aforementioned example, the utterance could be echoing (and countering) the culturally held belief that life is hard.

Another estimate of the frequency of irony comes from studies of contemporary American literature. Kreuz, Roberts, Johnson, and Bertus (1996) showed that readers of such literature are exposed to approximately one instance of irony every four pages. And of course we know that verbal irony crops up frequently in everyday conversation. In short, there is no denying the prevalence of irony in our linguistic environment.

Because irony is ubiquitous, this form of language must be accounted for in any theory of language use and understanding. We must understand how irony is processed, and whether the mechanisms for understanding irony are the same as, or different from, those used to process literal language. And in addition, we must understand why speakers use irony at all. What social and communicative functions does irony serve that would lead speakers to choose irony rather than to phrase what they intend to convey in direct and literal speech? In our research, we have tried to develop a theory of the functions served by irony to constrain theories about how irony is processed.

We propose the "Tinge Hypothesis" to account for why irony is used (Dews, Kaplan, & Winner, 1995; Dews & Winner, 1995). We show that irony is perceived as muting the underlying evaluative message. Although ironic criticism (or sarcasm) is commonly assumed to be a particularly biting form of criticism, we showed that in fact ironic criticism is perceived as less negative and confrontational than is literal criticism. In parallel fashion, we show that ironic praise is perceived as less positive and complimentary than is literal praise. Thus, speakers may choose to use ironic criticism in place of literal criticism when they wish to criticize in a muted and less confrontational way. To say to someone who arrives an hour late to a dinner party that he is "on time, as usual" is less hostile than to announce that he is "late, as usual." The ironic comment is light, mildly humorous, and provides a face-saving out for the late person, who can counter with, "Yes, I am very punctual, aren't I?" Similarly, speakers may choose to use ironic praise in place of literal praise when they wish to praise but also sting. Suppose you see your fashionably slim friend staring at herself in the mirror worrying that she has gained a pound. You might choose to use irony and say, "Oh, you're just so fat." Or you might choose to speak literally and say, "Oh, you're just so thin." The ironic version conveys the message that not only is the person thin, but also that her concerns about being fat are silly. There is the sting. The literal version conveys the positive evaluation of thinness without any added sting.

This muting effect could occur only if the literal meaning of the ironic utterance is processed at some level. The evaluative tone of the literal meaning of ironic utterances must "color" the hearer's perception of the intended meaning. We have argued that the literal meaning of an ironic utterance is accessed when we read or hear such an utterance, and that traces of the literal meaning color the listener's interpretation of the intended meaning. In the case of ironic criticism, the positive literal meaning "tinges" the negative intended meaning, resulting in a less critical evaluation. Conversely, in the case of ironic praise, the negative literal meaning tinges the positive intended meaning, resulting in a more critical evaluation.

The claim that the literal meaning of irony is accessed and processed is a controversial one. In the 1970s, the linguist Grice (1975) and the philosopher Searle (1993) proposed that we make sense of nonliteral utterances in three sequential steps: (a) We begin by accessing the literal meaning; (b) we test the literal meaning against the context, recognize that it does not make sense, and thus reject it; and (c) finally, we try out a nonliteral meaning. This "three-stage hypothesis" of nonliteral language comprehension was further developed by Clark and Lucy (1975). According to this model, there is nothing problematic about the notion of accessing the literal meaning of a nonliteral utterance. And according to this model, comprehending nonliteral language differs from comprehending literal language because it involves an extra inferential step—inferring the nonliteral meaning from the relation between the literal meaning and the context.

This traditional view was challenged in the 1980s and 1990s by cognitive psychologists, who rejected the notion that there was any kind of principled difference between literal and nonliteral language (Gibbs, 1989; Rumelhart, 1993). They also argued and presented evidence for the claim that comprehension of nonliteral language is no different in underlying process from comprehension of literal language (Gibbs, 1994; Gibbs & Gerrig, 1989; Gildea & Glucksberg, 1983; Glucksberg, Gildea, & Booking, 1982; Keysar, 1989; Ortony, Schallert, Reynolds, & Antos,

1978; Sperber & Wilson, 1986). According to this view, the nonliteral meaning of an ironic utterance is automatically derived from its context, and the literal meaning need never be accessed (Gibbs, 1982). Thus, understanding irony is no different from understanding literal language: In both cases, the hearer accesses the speaker's intended message directly. The fact that the ironic speaker has said something different from what was intended does not matter, because the hearer goes directly to what was intended through the use of the context. We refer to this view, in Giora, Fein, and Schwartz's (1998) terms, as the "processing equivalence hypothesis."

Yet a third view, the "graded salience hypothesis," was put forward by Giora (1997). She argued that when we confront an ironic utterance, we initially access the most salient meaning. Except for the most conventionalized forms of irony, the most salient meaning is the literal one. Less salient meanings are accessed later, and these are the nonliteral meanings. (For a similar argument with respect to metaphor, see Blasko & Connine, 1993.) This view differs from the three-stage hypothesis because if the most salient meaning of a nonliteral utterance is nonliteral, the nonliteral meaning will be accessed first. This might occur in the case of conventionalized idioms (e.g., to "spill the beans"), or conventionalized irony (e.g., "Yeah, right"), but would not occur in the case of most forms of irony. Only in cases in which the nonliteral meaning of a nonliteral utterance is less salient than the literal meaning does the graded salience hypothesis make the same predictions as does the three-stage model.

Giora (1995) distinguished her view of irony from the traditional three-stage hypothesis in another key respect. According to the three-stage hypothesis, once the literal meaning is recognized to be wrong, it is rejected. According to Giora's "indirect negation" view of irony, even though the hearer recognizes the literal meaning to be the wrong interpretation, the literal meaning is retained, not suppressed. The literal meaning plays a role in irony comprehension because it contrasts sharply with the ironic meaning, and this contrast is part of the speaker's message. If it were not, the speaker might as well have uttered the literal paraphrase of his or her irony. The claim of the indirect negation view that the rejected literal meaning is still retained for its contrast effect is entirely consistent with the claim of the tinge hypothesis. For if the literal meaning were fully suppressed once the utterance was recognized as ironic, there would be no way for the literal meaning to tinge the evaluative tone of the speaker's conveyed message.

These conflicting views of how nonliteral language is processed can be tested using reaction time measures to access processing time. The three-stage model predicts that comprehension of the nonliteral meaning of irony should take longer than comprehension of the literal meaning of literal utterances, because the former involves three stages, whereas the latter involves only one. In contrast, the processing equivalence hypothesis predicts that the nonliteral meaning of irony should take no longer than comprehension of the literal meaning of literal utterances. The graded salience hypothesis makes the same prediction as the three-stage hypothesis as long as the ironic utterances are not overly conventionalized: Therefore, ironic utterances should take longer to understand than literal ones.

What is the evidence? Gibbs (1986a, 1986b) compared the time taken to comprehend sarcasm versus "equivalent" literal paraphrases, or versus the same comments used literally. He showed that people take less time to process sarcasm than literal paraphrases (e.g., "You're a big help" vs. "You have not helped;" Gibbs, 1986b, Experiment 1) and thus argued for the equivalence of processing of ironic and literal language. However, when he compared time to comprehend identical utterances in literal versus ironic contexts, different results emerged. In one study, participants understood the sarcastic versions more rapidly (e.g., "Sure is nice and warm in here;" Gibbs, 1986a, Experiment 1). But in two others, participants understood the two versions in an equally rapid amount of time (Gibbs, 1986b, Experiment 1) or took longer for the sarcastic ones (Gibbs, 1986b, Experiment 3). When Giora (1995) reanalyzed Gibbs's (1986) results, she found that the identical utterances took longer when in ironic contexts, but reported that the same comparison did not reach significance in Gibbs, O'Brien, and Doolittle (1995). We conclude from this that Gibbs's results have not ruled out the possibility that some aspects of the literal meaning of nonliteral utterances are indeed processed.

Several studies have tested comprehension of identical utterances in ironic versus literal contexts and have found evidence that the literal meaning of ironic utterances is processed. It takes longer to read sentences on a computer screen when these sentences follow an irony-biasing context rather than one that biases the hearer toward the literal meaning (Giora et al., 1998). Processing unfamiliar ironic utterances facilitates the literal meaning instantly and facilitates the nonliteral meaning only 1,000 msec after offset, but not at the cost of suppressing the salient literal meaning. In contrast, familiar ironies facilitate both meanings right after offset (Giora & Fein, 1998b; see also Giora, in press). And both the literal and ironic meanings of ironies are activated for children (9- to 10-year-olds; Giora & Fein, 1998a).

Consistent with the findings of Giora et al. (1998), we have also shown that it takes longer to process utterances in an irony-biasing than a literal-biasing context (Dews & Winner, 1999). We presented participants with instances of ironic praise and criticism on a computer screen and asked them to press a key as quickly as possible to indicate whether the speaker was intending to convey something positive or negative. Along with the irony, we presented the identical utterances used literally. Thus, each sentence appeared as both ironic praise and literal criticism, or as ironic criticism and literal praise, but no individual heard the same sentence in both an ironic and a literal context.

If hearers process the literal meaning, then the evaluative tone of the literal meaning should interfere with judging the evaluative tone of the nonliteral (speaker's) meaning and slow down responses to the ironic utterances. And this is precisely what we found. People took significantly longer to judge ironic criticism as negative (e.g., "Good move" to a person whose has just done something foolish) than to judge the identical utterance used literally as positive (e.g., "Good move" to a person whose has just done something clever). We also found that people took longer to judge ironic praise as positive (e.g., "We never do anything fun" to a companion on a dream vacation) than to judge the identical phrase used literally as negative (e.g., "We never do anything fun" to a roommate who has been studying hard for finals). We argued that these results demonstrate that the positive literal meaning of the ironic utterance conflicts with the negative intended meaning, and that the negative literal meaning of the ironic utterance conflicts with the positive intended meaning. This kind of conflict could, of course, occur only if the literal meaning of irony is accessed prior to (or simultaneously with) the nonliteral meaning, and if the literal meaning is retained along with the nonliteral meaning.

In this study, we sought to pinpoint the precise point in the ironic sentence at which the processing is slowed. Studies of metaphor and idiom processing have demonstrated that processing is slowed "online" as the sentence is being read (Blasko & Connine, 1993; Cacciari & Tabossi, 1988; Janus & Bever, 1985). We hypothesized that the slowing effect would be the greatest at the precise point at which the word or words appear that render the utterance ironic rather than literal. We also hypothesized that this slowing effect would carry over into the final phrase of the utterance. Such a finding would be consistent with one of the findings reported by Giora et al. (1998, Experiment 3). These researchers found that after hearing ironic utterances, people responded faster to a literally than an ironically related word when it was presented 1,000 msec after the utterance, indicating that the literal meaning was still more highly activated than the ironic meaning. In contrast, people responded just as quickly to the ironically related word when it was presented 2,000 msec after the utterance, indicating that by this point, both meanings were equally activated. These results suggest that it takes a while for the ironic interpretation of irony to consolidate. Hence, we hypothesized that we would be able to detect some slowing of processing even after the key ironic word had been processed: The consolidation of the ironic interpretation should slow processing of the final part of the utterance even if that final part were entirely literal.

We presented participants with ironic utterances following a context of three or four sentences. Ironic utterances were broken into three phrases, and phrases were presented one at a time. Phrase 1 alone gave no indication of irony, Phrase 2 contained the key word that revealed that the utterance was ironic, and Phrase 3 again gave no indication of irony. We hypothesized that both Phrase 2 and Phrase 3 would be delayed in the ironic as compared to the literal version, but that the delay in Phrase 3 would be smaller than that in Phrase 2. We refer to this hypothesis as the "spillover" hypothesis, because we are suggesting that the processing of the ironic word(s) spills over and interferes with the processing of literal words that follow immediately after the ironic words.

METHOD

Participants

Twenty college undergraduates participated in the item development phase of this study as part of a course requirement. Later, 48 college undergraduates, who were paid $10 for their participation, served as the experimental participants. There were

44 female and 4 male participants. This uneven ratio was not intentional, but because we were not investigating sex differences, we did not attempt to rectify this ratio.

Materials and Procedure

Forty-eight 3- to 5-sentence stories, each ending in an ironic comment by a character, were first constructed. We refer to these as "ironic" stories, and to the final comment as the "target" sentence. Each ironic story was then altered by one phrase so that the target statement was clearly intended literally. In the following example, the irony-biasing and literal-biasing contexts are in italics:

> A new professor was hired to teach philosophy. The professor was supposed to be really sharp. When Allen asked several questions, the professor offered *naive and ignorant/incisive and knowledgeable* answers. Allen said: That guy is brilliant at answering questions.

(The first italic phrase appeared in the ironic version; the second italic phrase appeared in the literal version.)

Half of the ironic versions ended in ironic criticism, in which a literally positive utterance conveys a critical, negative meaning, as in the aforementioned example. In their literal versions, ironic criticism stories ended in literal praise, in which a literally positive utterance conveys a praising, positive meaning. Thus, Allen criticizes the poor professor (behind his back) in the ironic version by referring to him as brilliant and praises the good professor (again behind his back) in the literal version.

The remaining half of the ironic stories ended in ironic praise. In their literal versions, ironic praise stories ended in literal criticism, in which a literally critical utterance conveys a critical, negative meaning. See the following, for example:

> Maryellen expected to rough it when she went camping on a remote island off the coast of Maine. When she arrived, she found camping grounds with *running water and hot showers/no running water and no showers*. Maryellen said: Life is going to be primitive on this vacation.

Thus, in the ironic version, Maryellen praises the unexpectedly good conditions by calling them primitive and thus conveys a positive evaluation. And in the literal version, she makes a negative evaluation of the bad conditions by calling them, correctly, primitive. (We refer to a positive evaluation as a form of praise, and a negative evaluation as a form of criticism.)

During item development, the 20 participants were asked to read printed copies of the stories and (a) decide whether the final sentence was ironic or literal, and (b) underline the word or words in the final sentence that made the final sentence either ironic or literal. Ten of the participants read and responded to one version of each of the 48 stories, whereas the remaining 10 participants read and responded to the other version of the 48 stories. Of the 48 stories read by each participant, 12 ended with ironic praise, 12 with literal criticism, 12 with ironic criticism, and 12 with literal praise. None of the ironies were highly conventionalized. The stories were presented in random order.

In general, participants agreed on whether the final sentences of each story were ironic or literal: At least 90% agreement was observed for all but 4 of the 48 stories. Similarly, participants agreed on which word(s) indicated whether the final sentence was literal or ironic: At least 90% agreement was observed for all but 14 of the stories.

Both versions of the stories that yielded less than 90% agreement for either irony judgments or the critical word(s) judgments were revised and then repiloted with a different set of 20 participants. After revision, all of the stories yielded at least 90% agreement. Both versions of each of the 48 stories described earlier then served as test stories that were presented one sentence or phrase at a time on a Macintosh Quadra computer. The sentences/phrases appeared centered on the computer screen as black 12-point Times font against a white background. The main body of each story appeared one sentence at a time. The final (target) sentence of each story appeared one phrase or word at a time, such that each final sentence appeared across three consecutively presented phrases. The first phrase appeared before the critical word(s) indicating the intended meaning of the final sentence (i.e., before the word or words identified during item development as making the sentence either ironic or literal). The second phrase ended with the key word(s) identified during item development as indicating that the sentence was either literal or ironic. The third phrase appeared after the key word(s) and completed the final sentence. Thus, for the ironic criticism example cited earlier, the phrases seen in the ironic version were as follows: That guy/is brilliant/at answering questions. And for the ironic praise example cited earlier, the phrases were as follows: Life/is going to be primitive/on this vacation.

Two versions of a true/false question were also created for each story to assess participants' comprehension of the intended meaning of the target sentence (e.g., Allen thinks the professor is smart/stupid; Maryellen thinks the camping facilities are good/poor). Comprehension questions were included so that we could rule out processing time responses to items that participants did not understand.

Four practice stories, ending with one of each of the four final sentence types (i.e., ironic criticism, literal praise, ironic praise, or a literal criticism), were constructed along with 24 distracter stories, consisting of 12 stories ending with literal criticism and 12 stories ending with literal praise. The distracter stories were included along with the test stories so that there were more literal than ironic statements, and so that we would thus more closely approximate the relative frequency of ironic and literal statements in everyday language usage. Both practice and distracter stories were presented as described earlier for test stories. The first four stories participants received were practice stories.

Thus, out of 72 stories (not counting the 4 practice stories), participants were presented with 48 (24 distracters, 24 test stories) ending in literal statements and 24 ending in ironic statements. Even though this ratio of ironic to literal utterances overrepresents the ratio heard in natural speech, participants did hear twice as many literal as ironic statements. Thus, they were unlikely to get into a mode of expecting irony.

A single factor (Target Sentence Type: Ironic Praise, Literal Criticism, Ironic Criticism, and Literal Praise) within-subject design was used. One version of each of the 48 test stories and each of the 24 distracter stories was presented to each participant. Counterbalancing ensured that each version of each story was presented along with each version of each comprehension question equally, often across participants. A random order of story presentation was determined by the computer for each participant.

Participants were tested individually. They were told to press the space bar when they were ready to begin reading each story and "immediately after you have read and understood each sentence or phrase that appears on the screen." Participants were also instructed to use their preferred hand to press the space bar. Each sentence/phrase remained on the screen until a participant pressed the space bar. When the space bar was pressed, the sentence/phrase appearing on the screen was replaced by the next sentence/phrase in a story. Each story was immediately followed by a true/false question concerning the intended meaning of the final sentence of the story. Each true/false question appeared on the screen along with a prompt for participants to press the "t" key if they thought the statement was true and the "f" key if they thought the statement was false. The correct answer to half of the true/false questions was "true" and for the other half the correct answer was "false."

PsychLab software was used to present stimuli, record latencies to press the space bar after each of the three phrases of the final sentence of each story, and record accuracy data for the true/false questions (Gum, 1998).

RESULTS

To test the hypothesis that ironic utterances take longer to process than do literal ones, comparisons were restricted to identical statements in irony-biasing versus literal-biasing contexts. Two repeated measures analyses of variance (ANOVAs) were performed. One analysis compared latencies for ironic criticism and literal praise and the other analysis compared latencies for ironic praise and literal criticism. These two analyses were conducted three times, first for latencies to process the first phrase, which appeared before the key word(s) indicating the intended meaning of the target sentence; second for latencies to process the phrase that ended with the key word(s); and finally for latencies to process the third phrase, which appeared after the key word(s).

Only latency data for stories in which the true/false question was answered correctly were included in analyses. Thirteen participants, who answered fewer than 70% of the true/false questions correctly, were excluded from analyses of the latency data because their low accuracy rates indicated that they did not understand or were not attending to the experimental task. These relatively high error rates probably occurred because participants had to judge nonconventionalized irony given very little context.

Latencies greater than 3,000 msec were considered outliers and were also not included in analyses. Prior to analyses, each participant's latency data were transformed into z scores to reduce variability (Srinivas, 1995). The z scores were calculated for each participant by subtracting each latency from a participant's mean latency and dividing the resulting value by the participant's standard deviation. All reported comparisons include analyses by participant (F1) and item (F2) variability.

Ironic Criticism and Literal Praise

The mean percentages of correct responses to the true/false comprehension questions following stories ending with ironic criticism and literal praise were 84% and 94%, respectively, indicating that both types of utterance were understood most of the time. (These percentages, as well as those following for ironic praise/literal criticism, were calculated after eliminating the 13 individuals who scored less than 70% correct.)

Figure 11.1 represents mean latencies (in msec) for Phrases 1, 2, and 3 of ironic criticism and literal praise target sentences. As can be seen, participants took about the same amount of time to process the first phrase of the matched ironic ($M = 606$, $SD = 194$) and literal comments ($M = 612$, $SD = 180$). ANOVAs indicated no reliable difference between these two response times, $F1(1, 34) = 0.11$, $MSE = .12$, $p < .75$; $F2(1, 23) = 0.36$, $MSE = .02$, $p < .56$. Figure 11.1 also shows longer latencies to process the target phrase when that phrase appeared after an irony-biasing context ($M = 653$, $SD = 244$) than when it appeared after a literal-biasing context ($M = 609$,

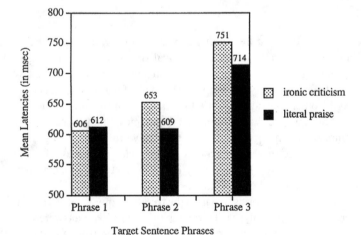

Figure 11.1.   Mean latencies (in msec) to comprehend Phrases 1, 2, and 3 of ironic criticism and literal praise target sentences.

$SD = 200$). ANOVAs indicated that this difference was significant, $F1(1, 34) = 5.53$, $MSE = .08$, $p < .03$; $F2(1, 23) = 7.62$, $MSE = .03$, $p < .02$. The longer processing time for the ironic phrase supports Giora's graded salience hypothesis and is consistent with the view that both the literal and intended meaning of ironic statements are processed.

The spillover hypothesis was not supported. Figure 11.1 shows that indeed participants took longer to process the final phrase in the irony-biasing context ($M = 751$, $SD = 295$) than in the literal-biasing context ($M = 714$, $SD = 272$). The analysis by item variability indicated that mean latencies at Phrase 3 were reliably longer when that phrase followed an ironic-biasing rather than a literal-biasing context, $F2(1, 23) = 4.95$, $MSE = .03$, $p < .04$. However, when the analysis was performed by participant variability, the difference did not reach significance, $F1(1, 34) = 2.35$, $MSE = .08$, $p < .14$. Thus, there was no consistent support for the spillover hypothesis that listeners are still processing ironic criticism after the key phrase, which then slows down the processing of the final part of the utterance.

Ironic Praise and Literal Criticism

The mean percentages of correct responses to the true/false comprehension questions following stories ending with ironic praise and literal criticism were 81% and 96%, respectively, indicating that both types of utterance were understood most of the time. Figure 11.2 represents mean latencies (in msec) for Phrases 1, 2, and 3 of ironic praise and literal criticism.

As shown in Figure 11.2, participants took longer to process the first phrase in the literal-biasing context ($M = 555$, $SD = 157$) than in the irony-biasing context ($M = 519$, $SD = 158$). This difference approached but did not quite reach significance,

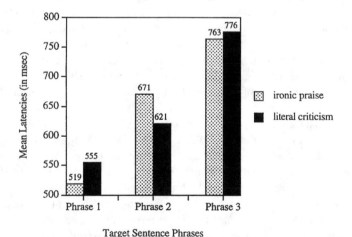

Figure 11.2.   Mean latencies (in msec) to comprehend Phrases 1, 2, and 3 of ironic praise and literal criticism target sentences.

$F1(1, 34) = 4.16, MSE = .07, p < .05; F2(1, 23) = 4.24, MSE = .03, p < .06$. Because the two phrases being compared were identical, and because they were the first sentences and thus did not differ in preceding context, we cannot explain this effect and suggest that it is possibly spurious. Note also that the longer latencies were for the sentences in the literal contexts. This is the opposite pattern found for the second phrase containing the key word. As shown in Figure 11.2, participants took longer to process the ironic ($M = 671, SD = 282$) than the literal ($M = 621, SD = 233$) target phrases. Although this result is consistent with the graded salience hypothesis, the difference in latencies did not reach significance, $F1(1, 34) = 1.99, MSE = .21, p < .17; F2(1, 23) = 1.95, MSE = .07, p < .18$. Despite the fact that the difference between the latency to understand the literal and ironic phrases was about the same for both types of irony, the variability in response times was considerably greater in the case of ironic praise ($SD = 282$) than ironic criticism ($SD = 244$). This may well reflect the fact that ironic praise is a less common form of irony than is ironic criticism.

Again, no support was found for the spillover hypothesis. As shown in Figure 11.2, there was almost no difference in latencies to process the third phrase in the ironic context ($M = 763, SD = 273$) than in the literal context ($M = 776, SD = 297$). These two latencies did not differ at the level of participant variability, $F1(1, 34) = 0.02, MSE = .08, p < .89$. However, this difference approached significance at the level of item variability, $F2(1, 23) = 3.06, MSE = .03, p < .10$, and this difference was in the opposite direction from that predicted by the spillover hypothesis.

DISCUSSION

This study replicates and extends the results of Dews and Winner (1999) and is consistent with the results reported by Giora et al. (1998). An utterance intended ironically takes longer to process than that same utterance intended literally, if the irony takes the prototypical form of ironic criticism. Although irony in the less typical form of ironic praise also took longer, this difference did not reach significance. We can only speculate here that our failure to demonstrate reliably longer processing time for the atypical form of irony was due to the high variability in response due to the oddity of ironic praise.

The fact that the prototypical form of irony took longer to process than the identical utterances in literal contexts indicates clearly that the literal meaning of the irony must be processed at some level. This result is also consistent with the tinge hypothesis, according to which the underlying message conveyed by irony is muted or tinged by the evaluative tone of the literal meaning.

No support was shown for the spillover hypothesis. Only in the case of ironic criticism, and only when the analysis was performed at the level of item variability, did we demonstrate slower processing time for the phrase following the ironic key phrase. We conclude, thus, that processing of the literal meaning of the ironically intended words slows momentarily the processing of the ironic meaning. However, the consolidation of the ironic meaning does not spill over into the final phrase and disrupt or slow the processing of the literal meaning that follows.

The lack of support for the spillover hypothesis is consistent with studies showing that the literal meaning of metaphors and idioms is processed and completed online during comprehension of the critical word (or words; Blasko & Connine, 1993; Cacciari & Tabossi, 1988; Janus & Bever, 1985). In general, then, it seems likely that obligatory processing of the literal meaning of ironic statements occurs during the comprehension of the word(s) critical to the intended meaning of a sentence, with little or no enduring processing costs occurring after comprehension of the critical word(s).

The finding that understanding irony takes longer than understanding literal language shows that to make sense of irony we must recognize (whether consciously or unconsciously) the discrepancy between the evaluation implied by the literal meaning and the evaluation intended (as also argued by Giora, 1995, in her indirect negation view of irony). Hearers who only recognize the intended meaning of an ironic utterance, without noting at some level what was said literally, have not fully understood the irony. Such hearers are not perceiving a difference between an ironic utterance and its literal equivalent. Full understanding of nonliteral language involves, in Olson's (1988) words, a recognition that the utterance is not "just plain talk" (p. 218). Hence, deriving both the intended meaning and aspects of the literal meaning are obligatory for fully interpreting a speaker's ironic intent. Irony is not equivalent to its literal paraphrase. If it were, there would be no need to speak ironically, and irony would not be such a ubiquitous linguistic phenomenon.

ACKNOWLEDGMENT

This research was supported by a Boston College Faculty Research Grant to Ellen Winner. The complete set of items is available on request.

REFERENCES

Blasko, D. G., & Connine, C. M. (1993). Effects of familiarity and aptness on metaphor processing. *Journal of Experimental Psychology: Learning, Memory and Cognition, 19,* 295–308.

Booth, W. (1974). *A rhetoric of irony.* Chicago: University of Chicago Press.

Cacciari, C., & Tabossi, P. (1988). The comprehension of idioms. *Journal of Memory and Language, 27,* 668–683.

Clark, H. H., & Lucy, P. (1975). Understanding what is meant from what is said: A study in conversationally conveyed requests. *Journal of Verbal Learning and Verbal Behavior, 14,* 56–72.

Dews, S., Kaplan, J., & Winner, E. (1995). Why not say it directly? The social functions of irony. *Discourse Processes, 19,* 347–367.

Dews, S., & Winner, E. (1995). Muting the meaning: A social function of irony. *Metaphor and Symbolic Activity, 10,* 3–19.

Dews, S., & Winner, E. (1999). Obligatory processing of literal and nonliteral meanings in verbal irony. *Journal of Pragmatics, 31,* 1579–1599.

Dews, S., Winner, E., Nicolaides, N., & Hunt, M. (1994). [Irony use in natural discourse: An analysis of the forms and functions.] Unpublished raw data.

Gibbs, R. W. (1982). A critical examination of the contribution of literal meaning to understanding nonliteral discourse. *Text, 2,* 9–27.

Gibbs, R. W. (1984). Literal meaning and psychological theory. *Cognitive Science, 8,* 275–304.

Gibbs, R. W. (1986a). Comprehension and memory for nonliteral utterances: The problem of sarcastic indirect requests. *Acta Psychologica, 62,* 41–57.

Gibbs, R. W. (1986b). On the psycholinguistics of sarcasm. *Journal of Experimental Psychology: General, 115,* 3–15.

Gibbs, R. W. (1989). Understanding and literal meaning. *Cognitive Science, 13,* 243–251.

Gibbs, R. W. (1994). *The poetics of mind.* Cambridge, England: Cambridge University Press.

Gibbs, R. W., & Gerrig, R. J. (1989). How context makes metaphor comprehension seem special. *Metaphor and Symbolic Activity, 3,* 145–158.

Gibbs, R. W., O'Brien, J. E., & Doolittle, S. (1995). Inferring meanings that are not intended: Speakers? intentions and irony comprehension. *Discourse Processes, 20,* 187–203.

Gildea, P., & Glucksberg, S. (1983). On understanding metaphor: The role of context. *Journal of Verbal Learning and Verbal Behavior, 22,* 577–590.

Giora, R. (1995). On irony and negation. *Discourse Processes, 19,* 239–264.

Giora, R. (1997). Understanding figurative and literal language: The graded salience hypothesis. *Cognitive Linguistics, 7,* 182–206.

Giora, R. (1999). On understanding familiar and less familiar figurative language. *Journal of Pragmatics, 31,* 12.

Giora, R., & Fein, O. (1999a). *Irony comprehension: The graded salience hypothesis.* Unpublished manuscript.

Giora, R., & Fein, O. (1999b). *Irony: Salience and context.* Manuscript submitted for publication.

Giora, R., Fein, O., & Schwartz, T. (1998). Irony: Graded salience and indirect negation. *Metaphor and Symbol, 13,* 83–102.

Glucksberg, S., Gildea, P., & Bookin, H. B. (1982). On understanding nonliteral speech: Can people ignore metaphors? *Journal of Verbal Learning and Verbal Behavior, 21,* 85–98.

Grice, P. H. (1975). *Logic and conversation.* Cambridge, MA: Harvard University Press.

Gum, T. (1998). *PsychLab Version Two: Macintosh software application program* [Computer software]. Montreal, Canada.

Janus, R. A., & Bever, T. G. (1985). Processing of metaphoric language: An investigation of the three-stage model of metaphor comprehension. *Journal of Psycholinguistic Research, 14,* 473–487.

Keysar, B. (1989). On the functional equivalence of literal and metaphorical interpretations in discourse. *Journal of Memory and Language, 28,* 375–385.

Kreuz, R. J., & Glucksberg, S. (1989). How to be sarcastic: The echoic reminder theory of verbal irony. *Journal of Experimental Psychology: General, 118,* 374–386.

Kreuz, R. J., Roberts, R. M., Johnson, B. K., & Bertus, E. L. (1996). Figurative language occurrence and co-occurrence in contemporary literature. In R. J. Kreuz & M. S. MacNealy (Eds.), *Empirical approaches to literature and aesthetics* (pp. 83–97). Norwood, NJ: Ablex.

Kumon-Nakamura, S. (1993). *What makes an utterance ironic: The allusional pretense theory of verbal irony.* Unpublished doctoral dissertation, Princeton University, Princeton, NJ.

Muecke, D. C. (1969). *The compass of irony.* London: Methuen.

Olson, D. (1988). On what's a metaphor for? *Metaphor and Symbolic Activity, 3,* 215–222.

Ortony, A., Schallert, D. L., Reynolds, R. E., & Antos, S. J. (1978). Interpreting metaphors and idioms: Some effects of context on comprehension. *Journal of Verbal Learning and Verbal Behavior, 17,* 465–477.

Rumelhart, D. E. (1993). Some problems with the notion of literal meanings. In A. Ortony (Ed.), *Metaphor and thought* (2nd ed., pp. 71–82). Cambridge, England: Cambridge University Press.

Searle, J. R. (1993). Metaphor. In A. Ortony (Ed.), *Metaphor and thought* (2nd ed., pp. 83–111). Cambridge, England: Cambridge University Press.

Sperber, D., & Wilson, D. (1986). *Relevance: Communication and cognition.* Oxford, England: Blackwell.

Srinivas, K. (1995). Representation of rotated objects in explicit and implicit memory. *Journal of Experimental Psychology: Learning, Memory, and Cognition, 21,* 1019–1036.

CHAPTER 12

Irony: Negation, Echo, and Metarepresentation

Carmen Curcó
Universidad Nacional Autónoma de Mèxico

There is a current debate on the nature of verbal irony. On one view, held by
Sperber and Wilson (1981, 1986; Wilson & Sperber, 1992), verbal irony is a subtype of echoic use of language. On another view, advocated by Giora (1995;
Giora & Fein, 1998), verbal irony is a form of indirect negation. This paper compares both approaches and looks at their predictions with regard to the cognitive
abilities that the processing of verbal irony should demand. In particular, it con-
centrates on the degree of higher order mental representations that interpreters of
verbal irony should be able to manipulate. The results of the analysis favor the
framework proposed by Sperber and Wilson.

The literature on irony and its interpretation is very extensive. In this paper, I concentrate on two current views on the pragmatic nature of verbal irony: one that sees
irony as a subtype of echoic use of language (Sperber & Wilson, 1981, 1986;
Wilson & Sperber, 1992), and one that suggests irony is a form of indirect negation
(Giora, 1995). I contrast them looking both at their descriptive and their explanatory power. I offer some critical thoughts about the analysis of irony as negation, in
particular, with regard to the implications it would have for the processing of verbal
irony and the manipulation of mental metarepresentations, and I make an attempt to
clarify the similarities and differences between the two approaches.

THE GENERAL PICTURE

Giora (1995) has recently suggested that irony is a form of indirect negation. The
idea that negation is somehow involved in irony is not particularly new. The rhetorical tradition always treated irony as the figure of speech in which the figurative
meaning is the opposite of the literal meaning, so that an ironist's primary intention
is to communicate the opposite of what he says, and hence, in a way, to deny the

---

This chapter was previously published as "Irony: Negation, echo, and metarepresentation" (C.
Curco) in *Lingua, 110,* 257–280. Copyright © [2000] by Elsevier. Reprinted with permission.

proposition expressed by his utterance.[1] Modern Gricean pragmatic theory has not departed radically from this view. While it has offered an account of how the speaker's intended meaning can be recognized, a question not addressed by the rhetorical tradition, it has adhered to the belief that the speaker's intended meaning is the opposite of what his utterance says. What in classical rhetoric was treated as figurative meaning is, in Gricean terms, an implicature, but the link between irony and negation is preserved. More recently, Martin (1992) has claimed that negation is always involved in irony, although not in the way authors in the rhetorical tradition, Grice and Searle, originally thought. Martin pointed out that an ironist often says something false in order to suggest something true, and that even when an ironic speaker tells the truth, in being ironic he says something true in order to reveal something false. In all cases, he argued, there is some reversal of meaning which justifies the parallel drawn between irony and negation.[2] In this general picture, what is new, then, about Giora's suggestion?

First, she has added some precision to the common association between irony and negation by attempting to spell out the exact type of negation involved in irony. She denied, along with Martin, that ironic utterances necessarily communicate the opposite of what they say. What they do, Giora suggested, is to indirectly negate the prepositional content expressed.[3] Second, Giora has tried to work out the consequences of viewing irony as an indirect form of negation for our understanding of how ironic discourse is processed, and she has conducted experimental research to support her approach (Giora & Fein, 1998). On the issue of processing, she reacted against Grice (1975) and Clark and Gerrig (1984) because she saw their proposals as leading to the conclusion that interpreting irony involves abandoning the proposition expressed by the utterance. In other words, the interpreter is seen as canceling what she called the indirectly negated message and replacing it with the implicated one. Instead, she argued that in interpreting verbal irony, the literal meaning of an ironic utterance is retained, and suggested that "irony understanding involves processing both the negated and implicated messages so that the difference between them may be computed" (Giora, 1995, p. 239). Third, Giora has revived the notion of negation to explain irony after such a tendency seemed almost gone, at least within the fields of linguistics, psychology, and philosophy of language.[4] Views of irony as a form of negation were popular before alternative accounts were put forward. But in the 1980s, however, Sperber and Wilson (1981, 1986) proposed to treat irony as a variety of implicit echoic use, while Clark and Gerrig suggested viewing verbal irony as a mode of pretense, and Kreuz and Glucksberg (1989) analyzed it as an echoic reminder. Whether or not the pretense and the echoic reminder views of irony are substantially different from the relevance theoretic approach (Sperber & Wilson, 1981, 1986; Wilson & Sperber, 1992) is a separate issue.[5] The point is that approaches based on the notion of negation became less popular after such developments.[6] Giora also attempted to show that Sperber and Wilson's approach is inadequate. She claimed that verbal irony is not necessarily echoic, and also that several utterances that do fit Sperber and Wilson's description of irony fail to be ironic, hence she concluded that Sperber and Wilson's conditions on irony are not sufficient to characterize it either. If it is true that the views proposed by Clark and Gerrig and Kreuz and Glucksberg are very close to Sperber and Wilson's framework, then Giora's attack would affect the whole spectrum of proposals denying the parallel between irony and negation. The three reasons I have mentioned raise an interest in looking at her approach in detail.

Let me first describe how Giora places her account within current research on irony and irony comprehension. On her general characterization of irony, Giora sees herself keeping company with Grice (1975), Searle (1979), and Martin (1992): they all view irony as involving some form of negation. So, as already mentioned, she rejects alternative accounts, in particular, the one proposed within relevance theory which suggests that irony is a variety of implicit echoic interpretive use, in which the communicator dissociates herself from the opinion echoed (Wilson & Sperber, 1992).

At the level of processing, and with regard to the time course of understanding irony, Giora sees current research as falling within one of two positions, each of which, she argues, holds three tenets: (a) understanding that irony is a one-stage process, it shouldn't be any more difficult to process than literal language, and it shouldn't take longer to understand; and (b) understanding that irony is a two-stage process, that it is more difficult to process than literal language, and it takes longer to understand.

Under the first position, she places pragmatists such as Sperber and Wilson (1986; Wilson & Sperber, 1992), apparently because they have argued that the process of understanding literal and nonliteral language is ruled by one single principle: the search for an interpretation consistent with the Principle of Relevance, and, therefore, they maintain that figurative language does not deviate from standard communicative norms. Cognitive psychologists such as Gibbs (1986a, 1986b, 1994), Gibbs and Gerrig (1989), and Gibbs and O'Brien (1991) are also seen by Giora as belonging to this tradition because their experiments have shown that irony does not take longer to understand than nonironic statements, and they have hence concluded that irony is no more difficult to understand than nonironic expressions. Jorgensen, Miller, and Sperber (1984) are also included here because in their experiments, they have adopted Sperber and Wilson's view, which denies that "to speak ironically is to express a figurative meaning that is the opposite of the literal meaning" and that to "to comprehend any irony consists in retrieving such a figurative meaning" (Jorgensen et al., 1984, p. 112).[7] However, I will argue below that Giora's placing of these authors under the first heading is unjustified, since the conclusions she draws do not necessarily follow from their work.

She sees the second position represented mainly by Searle (1979) and Grice (1975). Because for Gricean pragmatists verbal irony involves a breach of the maxim of quality, and the overt violation makes the addressee cancel the literal meaning and generate an implicature, it gives rise to a "two-stage comprehension process," she claims. Giora also thinks understanding irony is essentially a two-stage process, where the speaker violates a communicative norm (in this case, her "graded informativeness requirement"; Giora, 1988, 1995, and not the Gricean maxim of truthfulness), and the hearer derives an "implicated message" (Giora, 1995). However, while Grice and Searle maintain that the literal meaning expressed by an utterance is the opposite of what a speaker intends to convey by using it, according to Giora (1995), the "implicated message is more attenuated or mitigated than 'the opposite of what is said'" (p. 261). A further difference, she added, is that Grice and Searle claim that the literal meaning is rejected, canceled, and replaced with another implicated one. For Giora, the activated literal meaning should be retained rather than suppressed, and it is functional in deriving the intended interpretation (Giora, 1998, pp. 5–6).

ON THE CHARACTERIZATION OF IRONY: ECHO OR NEGATION?

As mentioned above, Giora attempted to show that the relevance theoretic view of irony is inadequate. Sperber and Wilson's proposal is that irony is characterized by three defining features: (a) it is a variety of interpretive use in which the proposition expressed by the utterance represents a belief implicitly attributed by the speaker to someone other than herself at the time of utterance,[8] (b) it is echoic (i.e., it implicitly expresses the speaker's attitude to the beliefs being represented),[9] and (c) the attitude involved in the echo is one of dissociation from the thoughts echoed. Giora argued that these features are neither necessary to produce verbal irony, nor sufficient, and hence concluded that they are inadequate to define verbal irony.

It seems to me that Giora's arguments do not fully consider some features of the relevance-theoretic account of irony, and that once these are taken into account, her objections lose force. Let me go through her points in detail.

As examples of "nonechoic" ironies, she offers the following (Giora, 1995, p. 246):

(1)   I think the washing hasn't dried (said on a very rainy day).
(2)   "Do you know any G.M.?" my friend asks.
        "Rings a bell," I reply (when the person in question is well known to the speakers).

She claimed that neither (1) nor (2) are echoic because they "need not be attributed to another speaker" (Giora, 1995, p. 246). Perhaps she's right. However, nothing in the definition of echoic use (and hence of irony) imposes the requirement that an echoic ironic utterance should represent a belief attributed to *another* speaker. Echoic utterances are those that achieve relevance by informing the hearer that the speaker is entertaining a certain attributable thought and that the speaker simultaneously holds an attitude to it. Echoic utterances, therefore, include those cases where the speaker attributes a thought or an utterance to *herself at a time different from the time of utterance,* precisely what the first condition on verbal irony proposed by Sperber and Wilson requires. Nothing in the definition of echoic, nor of interpretive use, rules out this possibility. In fact, it is this displacement from the "here and now" which demands a sophisticated cognitive machinery to handle verbal irony, a point to which I will return later. A different issue is whether (1) and (2) are actually echoic, or under what conditions they would be echoic.

Let us take the example in (1). In circumstances where the speaker may legitimately and reasonably wonder whether the washing has dried (e.g., the washing is drying in a partially covered shelter, the rain has just started), and uses (1) to indicate it, (1) would be descriptively used, given that it would be used to represent a state of affairs in the world because its propositional form is true of that state of affairs.[10] In this case, the utterance may be naive, but not ironic. Interpretive and descriptive uses are mutually exclusive categories, and an utterance that is descriptively used cannot, by definition, be an instance of irony. In this case, (1) is not a counterexample.

(1) can only be ironic if it is not put forward as a description of a state of affairs, but as an interpretation of an attributed thought or utterance, and if the speaker simultaneously and implicitly expresses towards it a dissociative attitude (which makes it echoic). In such a case, the speaker may attribute the thought or utterance to someone else, or to himself at another time. For instance, imagine that the speaker is just coming back home. Before leaving, he instructed his son to get the washing in when it dried or before, if it started to rain. As he returns, it is raining, and he notices the washing hanging outside. He utters (1), attributing it to his son or to himself in a different situation (one in which it is not raining), with an implicit attitude of dissociation. In such circumstances, (1) can only be ironic. Giora's example, as it stands, can still be ironic, but only if a dissociative attitude is implicitly expressed simultaneously. All that is needed is to view the utterance as echoing a potential utterance that the speaker could have produced in a situation where the assumption that it has been raining all day was not part of the context of interpretation.

The example in (2) works in a similar way. If the speaker uses it interpretively, she must be attributing it to someone other than herself at the time of the utterance. This leaves two possibilities: she attributes it to someone else, or to herself at a different time. The content of the utterance, "Rings a bell," is attributable to the speaker in a situation in which it is not mutually known to speaker and hearer that G.M. is someone very well known to the speaker—contrary to the conditions pertaining at the time of utterance in Giora's example. Under these circumstances, (2) would be interpreted as ironic.

So, the point that an utterance cannot be echoic whenever the thought it interprets cannot be attributed to someone else is based on a misinterpretation of the relevance theoretic notion of interpretive use, and all examples built upon it fail to be counterexamples at all. Sperber and Wilson characterize verbal irony as instances of implicit echoic use in which the proposition expressed by an utterance represents an actual or potential thought or utterance attributable to *someone other than the speaker at the time of utterance*. To produce a real counterexample to Sperber and Wilson's view, one would need to show a case of verbal irony where the thought represented by the ironic utterance can only be attributed to the speaker *at the time of utterance.*

Giora also argued that there are cases of implicit echoic use where the attitude involved is one of dissociation and yet such utterances fail to be ironic. So, not only would there be ironic utterances that are not echoic, as her previous examples attempt to show, but also utterances that fulfill Sperber and Wilson's characterization and are not ironic. As an example of this, she proposed (3):

(3)   Dina: I missed the last news broadcast. What did the Prime Minister say about the Palestinians?
       Mira: (with ridiculing aversion) That we should deport them (Giora, 1995, p. 248).

Her point is that Mira's utterance is echoic in that it simultaneously reports a content and expresses the speaker's attitude to what is reported, and still it doesn't come across as ironic.

However, Mira's reply in (3) is elliptical, so that the proposition expressed by her utterance can be represented by (4):

(4)   The Prime Minister of Israel said that we should deport the Palestinians.

Now, this is a clear case of descriptive use. Mira is using her utterance to represent a state of affairs in the world because the proposition it expresses is true of it (namely, the actual state of affairs where the Prime Minister of Israel has said that the Palestinians should be deported). Sperber and Wilson's claim is that ironies are cases of interpretive use, and their prediction, then, is exactly the same as Giora's: there is no reason why (3) should come across as ironic. Though the utterance in (3) *contains* an interpretation of the Prime Minister's discourse, (3) is not an in interpretation itself. Moreover, the attitude of dissociation expressed by the speaker is directed to the embedded interpretation "we should deport them." Mira is not dissociating herself from the proposition expressed by her utterance. Rather on the contrary, she's endorsing it *qua* description of a state of affairs in the world. She is using her utterance to describe a state of affairs in the world in virtue of its propositional form being true of it. It would be very strange for a theory to predict that any case of reported speech combined with the implicit expression of a dissociative attitude on the part of the speaker would produce an instance of verbal irony, and certainly this is not what Sperber and Wilson's characterization of irony does.

It therefore seems that Giora's objections to the relevance theoretic approach to irony are unfounded. In another paper, I have provided a few examples which, I think, refute Giora's characterization of irony at a descriptive level (Curcó, 1999). Because here I want to concentrate on the issue of how irony is processed, let us assume that both views account equally for the data and turn to this point.

ON THE PSYCHOLINGUISTIC PROCESSING
OF VERBAL IRONY

The past twenty years have seen a considerable number of experiments looking at the psycholinguistic processing of figurative language. Giora has grouped some of this research as endorsing what she called the "processing-equivalence hypothesis" (Giora, 1998, p. 3). These experiments, she argued, have attempted to show that "understanding literal and nonliteral language require equivalent processes" (1998, p. 3).[11] She saw them as presenting an alternative view to "traditional theorists," such as Grice (1975) and Searle (1979), who, in her view, "assumed that understanding nonliteral language requires a sequential, multiple-stage process, involving first a literal interpretation which is then revisited" (1998, p. 3).[12] Giora's proposal is put forward as an alternative to both positions: she suggested that it is not literal or nonliteral meaning that determines the type of processing followed, but her notion of "meaning salience."[13]

First, I would like to suggest that the picture she draws for this area is not fully justified. I argue that Sperber and Wilson's characterization of verbal irony does not lead to a "processing-equivalence hypothesis." In particular, it does not predict a one-stage process in the interpretation of verbal irony, and it does not suggest that irony should be as easy to understand as literal language. Rather on the contrary, it allows for a "multiple-stage processing" for both literal and non literal language, and it points towards the hypothesis that verbal irony should in general be more difficult to understand than literal language. Given the features used by Sperber and Wilson to define verbal irony, it follows in fact that irony should require a more complex set of cognitive abilities than comprehending literal discourse, whether or not this is reflected directly in the length of time each takes to process.[14]

Second, I look into the role of negation in the frameworks proposed both by Giora and by Sperber and Wilson, and contrast the consequences each view would have for the process of comprehending verbal irony in terms of the ability to manipulate mental metarepresentations of different orders.

In what follows, I take Giora's claims about the relevance-theoretic approach to irony one by one.

On the Stages of Comprehension in Verbal Irony

Contrary to what Giora concluded, relevance theory does not suggest a one-stage interpretation process for any kind of discourse, much less for ironic utterances. What Sperber and Wilson did say is that figurative language is not a deviation from standard norms of language, and that no special principles of interpretation are required to understand it. They claim that, as with any other instance of utterance interpretation, a hearer who processes an ironic utterance is trying to select amongst the set of all possible interpretations of an utterance the one that was intended by the speaker, exactly as he does in processing all kinds of discourse, whether ironically intended or not. In so doing, the hearer's process is guided by the search for optimal relevance, that is, the search for an interpretation consistent with the Communicative Principle of Relevance (CPR, also called Second Principle of Relevance [SPR]; Sperber & Wilson, 1995).[15] Sperber and Wilson's claim is that the first interpretation *tested* and found consistent with the CPR will be selected as the one intended by the speaker. But they made no claims as to how many potential interpretations a hearer will need to test before hitting on the one he will finally attribute to the speaker. In fact, it is most likely that on several occasions—not necessarily involving figurative language—candidate interpretations will be considered and abandoned before a hearer recovers the one attributed to the speaker. Clearly, this allows for a multistage process of interpretation in a large number of cases. Consider for instance the case of puns, or the case of short-lived misunderstandings self-corrected by the hearer, to name but a few. It is one thing to maintain that understanding natural language is a cognitive task constrained by one single principle, regardless of the type of discourse encountered. It is quite another to claim that the precise process, including the stages, the type of mental representations at work, and complexity of their manipulation will be identical in all occasions of discourse interpretation. As far as I can see, only the first claim can be attributed to relevance theory, and not the second. It seems then that relevance theory is perfectly compatible with, and indeed predicts, a several-stage process of comprehension on a number of occasions, which may well include figurative utterances.

There is, however, a genuine issue about whether a hearer computes candidate interpretations serially or in parallel.[16] As far as I know, this point is not fully settled, but it seems to me that the assumptions of the relevance theoretic account do not lead to a view of a one-stage process of interpretation for verbal irony.

Let us go further into the reasons that led Giora to suppose that relevance theory does not predict several stages of interpretation for verbal irony, nor a more complex interpretation process than it does for literal language. She said the following: "The echoic-mention theory assumes that irony does not involve a two-stage procedure, because no norm is violated and therefore no implicature is generated. As a result, irony is as easy to understand as nonironic language" (1995, p. 261). However, the fact that no norm is violated on Sperber and Wilson's account of irony is merely a result of their general framework, where no communicative norms are stipulated, but where the existence of implicatures is, of course, fully acknowledged. The idea that no implicature is generated in understanding verbal irony is simply not part of Sperber and Wilson's proposal. Besides, there seems to be no reason to conclude that *because* no norm is violated, "irony is as easy to understand as nonironic language." Causes for processing difficulty in the interpretation of verbal irony, as I will argue below, may come from several different sources, and certainly, not only—and not even necessarily—from rule or maxim violations.

Undoubtedly, Sperber and Wilson claim that the notion of a "figurative meaning" is not needed *theoretically* to account for irony and metaphor.[17] They also insist that all that is *encoded* (as opposed to *conveyed*) by ironic utterances is their "literal meaning." Hence, according to Sperber and Wilson, hearers need not go through two stages of interpretation where first a literal meaning is computed and then a figurative meaning is recovered, because there is nothing like a "figurative meaning."[18] However, this doesn't mean that the whole process of interpretation should be over after the proposition expressed by an utterance has been computed, nor that the ironic interpretation is recovered at this point.[19] Hearers may well need to go through several stages until they finally hit on the intended ironic in interpretation.

According to Sperber and Wilson, the literal meaning is not used by an ironic speaker to convey her own thoughts. Rather, the proposition expressed by an utterance is used interpretively as a representation of an object of contempt, ridicule, or disapproval (Jorgensen et al., 1984, p. 112).[20] It doesn't follow from this either that "irony does not involve a two-stage processing and is as easy to understand as literal language," as Giora concluded (1995, p. 240). After the proposition expressed by an utterance has been retrieved, hearers still need to recognize that it represents a thought the speaker is entertaining and attributing to someone other than himself at the time of utterance, and they need to distinguish the implicit expression of the speaker's dissociative attitude from this thought. Nothing has been said about "stages" in which this might occur, but the task need not be cognitively simple, even if carried out fast. Besides, stages and difficulty of comprehension are two variables not necessarily connected in a simple way. It is possible to conceive of a very complex single stage, so that even if irony comprehension should take place in one single stage (as it probably does at times, for instance, in the cases of conventional— hence salient—irony studied by Giora and Fein [1999]), it is not a necessary conclusion that it is as easy to interpret as nonfigurative language. Let us then turn to the issue of the relative difficulty of interpreting literal and nonliteral language.

ON THE RELATIVE DIFFICULTY OF INTERPRETING LITERAL AND NONLITERAL LANGUAGE

Sperber and Wilson have in fact made very few comments on the issue of irony understanding. However, Jorgensen et al. (1984) made a crucial point which seems to suggest a relevance theoretic answer to this question: "the task of the hearer is to reconstruct both the literal meaning of the utterance *and the attitude of the speaker toward that meaning*" (1984, pp. 112–113, my emphasis). They made no claims, however, as to the processes involved in this, nor about the difficulty attached to the recovery of the ironic interpretation.[21]

The idea is that an ironist interpretively uses an utterance while he implicitly expresses his own attitude of dissociation from its literal meaning. But there is no reason to suppose that a hearer jumps to the final interpretation at the same speed and at no extra cost than he would if the same utterance were literally intended. fact, the prediction of relevance theory is quite the opposite.

On Sperber and Wilson's account, irony need not be as easy to understand as literal language, as Giora takes them to propose. In fact, the issue of the relative difficulty of both types of interpretation boils down to asking whether attributing to the speaker a thought about an attributed thought, as well as an attitude of dissociation from it which he does not communicate explicitly, is as easy a task as interpreting an utterance literally or not. The answer suggested by the work of Happé (1993) and Curcó (1995, 1997) and by the evidence found by Smith and Tsimpli (1995) is that it is not.

Recognizing Attribution

What is involved then in retrieving an interpretation? Since Grice characterized meaning and communication in terms of the communicator's intentions, there have been extensive discussions about what intention it is that the hearer must recognize in verbal communication. Humans have a remarkable ability to attribute intentions to others. In fact, if confronted with a situation where the behavior of humans is observed, other humans tend to prefer explanations given in terms of the intentions of the agents involved over other kinds of explanation. Communication merely exploits this fact. Participants in a conversation are constantly representing the mental states of speakers as they interpret their utterances. Not only do they compute the propositional content of utterances and relate it to the propositional content of thoughts attributed to the communicator, but they attach to this propositional content certain attitudes. In other words, it is not enough for an interpreter to compute the propositional content of an utterance of "I'll come tomorrow." In the process of retrieving the interpretation intended by the speaker, he will need to attribute to the speaker also some propositional attitude of belief, hope, etc., to that propositional content.

The view within relevance theory is that communication involves producing a certain stimulus intending thereby to inform the audience of something (what Sperber and Wilson called the *informative intention*) and to inform the audience of one's informative intention (known in the framework of relevance theory as the *communicative intention*). Notice that the communicative intention is a second-order informative intention (an intention about an intention; Sperber & Wilson, 1986, p. 29). Communication demands then, not only an ability to represent facts and basic thoughts, but also an ability to represent primary representations, sometimes referred to as an ability to metarepresent. To interpret a piece of discourse as an act of ostensive communication, a hearer must recognize the speaker's communicative intention, even if the informative intention is not fulfilled. On the other hand, an ability to decode does not require the ability to attribute intentions to others.

In computing the propositional form of an utterance, a competent hearer needs to be able to recognize the relationship between it and a thought of the speaker's, and also the relationship that holds between that thought and what the thought itself represents. So, what is it for an utterance to be literal in Sperber and Wilson's terms?

[A]n utterance, in its role as an interpretive expression of a speaker's thought, is strictly literal if it has the same propositional form as that thought. (Sperber & Wilson, 1986, p. 233)

A hearer of a literally intended utterance will compute the propositional form of an utterance, will attribute to the speaker a thought having the same propositional form, and will assess whether the speaker might reasonably have expected it to be (or to seem) optimally relevant to the hearer on that interpretation.[22]

The next question I would like to raise concerns the representational level that is required to perform this operation. Let us refer to the propositional content of the utterance as *p*. For the sake of exposition, we can simplify things a bit and use the following diagram to illustrate the level of representation involved:

S intends
   me to know that
     S thinks that
       p

When an utterance is ironically intended, a competent hearer will somehow recognize that the speaker could not reasonably have expected it to be (or to seem) optimally relevant to the hearer on a literal interpretation, so the process will not stop here. But what is needed to detect an ironic intent? This time, the hearer will need to attribute to the hearer not the thought interpreted by his utterance (a first-order metarepresentation), but a thought about a thought attributed to someone other than the speaker at the time of utterance (a second-order metarepresentation), illustrated as follows, where S' is different from S at the time of the utterance:

S intends
   me to know that
     S thinks that
       S' thinks that
         p

Clearly, mentally representing this is a more complex operation, involving as it does entertaining a metarepresentation of a higher order. This shows that relevance theory cannot be taken to predict that there will be the same cognitive complexity involved in interpreting literal and ironic language. Now, what empirical evidence is there in support of this view?

Leslie (1987, 1988) has suggested that pretending and representing certain mental states requires metarepresentation, that is, an ability to entertain not only mental representations, but also mental representations of basic representations. Even attributing a first-order false belief (e.g., John doesn't know that p) is not a simple cognitive task. It is known that children develop this capacity only at about 3.5 years, and that most autistic subjects never do. So, the ability to metarepresent can be impaired, and it is now recognized that such impairment can appear in different degrees.

Understanding second-order intentions (intentions about other's mental states) is of course more complex than understanding first-order intentions.[23] There is some evidence that a minority of autistic subjects develop some metarepresentational abilities and succeed in understanding first-order intentions, but cannot attribute a second-order false belief of the type "John doesn't know that Peter knows ..." (Baron-Cohen, 1989). Interestingly, the different levels of impairment seem to correlate with specific cognitive difficulties, such as those involved in interpreting similes, metaphors, and ironies.

Happé (1993) studied individuals with different levels of impairment in their ability to metarepresent, and hence, to attribute mental states to others. Her hypothesis, based on the claims of relevance theory, was that

> if most autistic individuals cannot represent a speaker's intention, then communication should break down most noticeably where the speaker's attitude must be taken into account in modifying the literal meaning of the utterance ... In the face of the puzzle that ostensive communication must pose them, they may have no choice but to adopt a rigid interpretation—a default value of the propositional form of the utterance. (p. 103)[24]

I showed above how the characterization of irony made within relevance theory makes it clear that understanding irony requires an understanding of a higher order metarepresentation: a thought about an attributed thought. What Happé found was a direct relation between degree of metarepresentational ability and degree of communicative ability. Autistic subjects who failed all the metarepresentation tests were only able to interpret language literally, while autistic subjects who passed first-order metarepresentation tests were able to comprehend metaphors, but not irony. Only those autistic subjects who passed second-order metarepresentation tests displayed the ability to understand the whole spectrum of utterances, including irony.[25]

Along the same lines, in their study of Christopher, an autistic individual with remarkable linguistic abilities, Smith and Tsimpli (1995) found that he is invariably truthful, seems incapable of lying and to handle irony and metaphor, and has general trouble with any pragmatic task demanding metarepresentational abilities.

These results suggest the need to analyze the processing of nonliteral language exploring in detail the type of mental metarepresentations involved in understanding it.

Understanding Dissociation

Sperber and Wilson did not go into details about what is involved in retrieving a dissociative attitude in the process of reaching a final ironic interpretation. However, as I have attempted to show (Curcó, 1995), the identification of a dissociative attitude can be explained in terms of the CPR in the following way. According to the CPR, the hearer is entitled to assume that the utterance yields enough cognitive effects for no unjustifiable processing cost. Given this principle, the existence of a contradiction between the propositional content of a contextual assumption and the content of some assumption conveyed by the utterance may lead the hearer to attribute an attitude of dissociation to the speaker. In this way, a clash between context and the propositional content of the utterance may act as a cue for the attribution of a dissociative attitude. This is not, of course, to say that communicative devices such as tone of voice, raising of eyebrows, gestures, etc., do not play a role in triggering the recognition of an attitude of dissociation. However, such devices might be said to direct the hearer toward the sort of clash I have described.

Since it might be felt that this account does not differ from that of Giora's, let me spell it out in more detail. First-order clashing of propositional contents of the type mentioned are entertained in a number of cases where irony is not intended. Consider, for instance, repairs in discourse, occasions when a hearer decides that a speaker is mistaken, or lying, or expressing disagreement, or trying to convince the hearer of something he is reluctant to accept. In some of these cases, there may be intended or unintended falsehood, in others, the question is not one of truth, but merely of conflicting propositional forms, regardless of their truth value. I would like to argue that the difference between irony, on the one hand, and any of the other cases where a propositional clash is encountered (mistakes, lies, arguments, deception), on the other, is also associated with the order of the metarepresentations in which the clashing propositions become embedded.

Take the case of an utterance of (5):

(5)   Mr. Z is a president concerned about his people.

Imagine that this is uttered in a context where it is highly salient to me that Mr. Z is *not* a president concerned about his people. What we have here is a clash of first-order propositional contents. Of course, there is no contradiction in a system of beliefs that holds both $\neg p$ and *Peter says that p*. However, an interpreter will want to know why Peter says that p when it is so salient to him that $\neg p$. My point is that in cases like this, a hearer will embed the clashing propositional forms in metarepresentations in such a way that no contradiction arises, and there are a number of ways in which this can be done. The more specific claim I want to make is that the order of the metarepresentation in which p and $\rangle p$ are embedded in the inferential process of understanding an utterance is crucial for the recognition of an ironic intent.

There are a number of different possible ways in which a hearer might approach the utterance in (5). In the inferential processes that are illustrated below, the first premise is always the same, and it is what allows the hearer to recognize the speaker's communicative intention. The second premise is a metarepresentation containing the contextual assumption that clashes with the propositional content of the utterance. Notice how its order affects the resulting interpretation.

Case 1. The Hearer Concludes That the Speaker Is Mistaken

Embedding the clashing contextual assumption in a first-order metarepresentation will lead to the conclusion that the speaker is mistaken. That is, the capacity to attribute a false belief to the speaker rests on the hearer's ability to manipulate a first-order metarepresentation.

Premises

(1)   The speaker intends
                the hearer to know
                        that the speaker intends
                                the hearer to believe
                                        that Mr. Z is a president concerned about his people.
(2)   The hearer believes that
                Mr. Z is not a president concerned about his people.

Conclusion: The Hearer Concludes That the Speaker Is Mistaken.

Case 2. The Hearer Concludes That the Speaker Is Lying

Recognizing a deliberate nontruthful contribution requires the capacity to embed the clashing assumption in a second-order metarepresentation, and to manipulate it in an inference as follows.

Premises

(1)   The speaker intends
                the hearer to know
                        that the speaker intends
                                the hearer to believe
                                        that Mr. Z is a president concerned about his people.
(2)   The hearer believes that
                the speaker believes that
                        Mr. Z is not a president concerned about his people.

Conclusion: The Hearer Concludes That the Speaker Is Lying.

Case 3. The Hearer Concludes That the Speaker Is Trying to Convince Her That P, or Arguing that P

Of course, engaging in an argument, or recognizing an attempt to convince a hearer of something, involves representing not only the beliefs of the speaker, but also the beliefs of the speaker about the beliefs of the hearer, something that clearly demands a more complex representational capacity.

Premises

(1)   The speaker intends
                the hearer to know
                        that the speaker intends

> the hearer to believe
>> that Mr. Z is a president concerned about his people.

(2)   The hearer believes that
>   the speaker believes that
>> the hearer believes that
>>> Mr. Z is not a president concerned about his people.

Conclusion: The Hearer Believes That the Speaker Is Arguing Against Him, or Trying to Convince him of Something the Hearer Doesn't Believe.

Case 4. The Hearer Concludes That the Speaker Is Being Ironic

The recognition of an ironic intent demands embedding the clashing contextual assumption in a metarepresentation of at least fourth order.

Premises

(1)   The speaker intends
>   the hearer to know
>> that the speaker intends
>>> the hearer to believe
>>>> that Mr. Z is a president concerned about his people.

(2)   The hearer believes that
>   the speaker believes that
>> the hearer believes that
>>> the speaker believes that
>>>> Mr. Z is not a president concerned about his people.

Conclusion: The Hearer Believes That the Speaker Is Ironic.

INDIRECT NEGATION AND DISSOCIATION

On the surface, indirectly negating a propositional form and dissociating oneself from it might seem like two fairly connected actions. Let me explain how Giora conceives of indirect negation in her approach to irony.

It seems Giora (1995) assumed that, at least for irony, indirect negation amounts to a computation of the difference between the literal meaning of an utterance and a representation of the ironicized situation:

> The view of irony I present here suggests that irony is a form of negation that does not make use of an explicit negation marker. An affirmative (more often than a negative) expression is used to implicate that a specific state of affairs is different or far from the taken-for-granted, expected (or more desirable) state of affairs, explicitly indicated by the same affirmative expression. Such a view suggests that irony does not cancel the indirectly negated message, as suggested by the tra-

ditional and pretense accounts. Nor does it necessarily implicate its opposite as contended by the traditional view. Rather, it entertains both the explicit and the implicated messages so that the dissimilarity between them may be computed. By saying "What a lovely party!" in the middle of a lousy party, the ironist points out that the party fails (standard) expectations and is far from being lovely. In the act of processing the utterance, then, the surface meaning is involved. The product is, therefore, and interpretation close to "how far it is from being the expected lovely party." (p. 241)

It would seem that attributing to the speaker a thought along the lines of "how far it is from being the expected lovely party" (Giora's view) is fairly similar to attributing to the speaker the intention to let the hearer know that he has in mind a potential, attributable thought with the propositional content that the party is lovely, while at the same time implicitly attempting to convey that it is absurd to entertain such thought given the circumstances (Sperber and Wilson's view), only Sperber and Wilson's formulation of the issue is more complicated than Giora's. But is this an accident? Is this a mere question of simplicity in stating a position or is there something else that makes the two approaches differ? In order to compare them along the same parameters, let me try to recast Giora's proposal in terms of the metarepresentational demands imposed on the hearer, as I did with Sperber and Wilson's above.

Let us take the example in (5). If I understand her correctly, the ironic utterance would receive an interpretation along the lines of "how far is Mr. Z from being the expected president concerned about his people?" The interpretation would be recovered via some process where an indirect negation of the explicit content of the utterance would be contrasted with it. The interpretation, I take it, would result from "computing the difference between the explicit and the implicated messages" (Giora, 1995, p. 241), where perhaps the "implicated message" is the fact, salient to speaker and hearer, that Mr. Z is not a president concerned about his people at all, as suggested by the following quotations:

> [I]rony is viewed as a mode of indirect negation. Based on this view, interpreting irony does not involve canceling the indirectly negated message and replacing it with the implicated one ... Rather, irony understanding involves processing both the negated and implicated messages, so that the difference between them may be computed. (Giora, 1995, p. 239)

> According to the indirect negation view, the literal meaning of an ironic utterance is functional in irony comprehension, because it enables the comprehender to compute the difference between the literal meaning (usually pertaining to a desirable state of affairs) and the ironicized (less desirable) situation or object. (Giora & Fein, 1998, p. 5)

Notice that Giora and Fein (1998) made use of the notion of desirability. If we accept, along with Sperber and Wilson, that beliefs are the only primary representations, desires would have to be represented as second-order representations (first-order metarepresentations):

Let us assume that there is a basic memory store with the following property: that any representation stored in it is treated by the mind as true description of the actual world, a fact. What this means is that a fundamental propositional attitude of belief or assumption is pre-wired into the very architecture of the mind ... , desires could play a cognitive role only by being represented in factual assumptions of the form *I desire that p.* (Sperber & Wilson, 1986, p. 74)

Let us now think of the assumptions a hearer would need to manipulate according to Giora's account.[26] Upon hearing (5), a hearer would perform an inference involving (a), (b), and (c) as premises, whereby he would compute the difference between (a) and (c).[27]

Premises

a. Mr. Z is not a president concerned about his people.
b. The speaker says that
      Mr. Z is a president concerned about his people.
c. It is desirable that
      Mr. Z is a president concerned about his people.

Conclusion.   It Is Far From Being the Case That Mr. Z Is a President Concerned About His People.

The prediction of Giora's characterization of verbal irony is then that comprehending irony would not demand the very sophisticated metarepresentational capacity I have suggested it does. It will be enough with being able to entertain first-order metarepresentations. But if this is so, how can one explain the findings of Happé (1993), which, as already mentioned, show that autistic subjects without second-order metarepresentational capacity fail to interpret irony? In this respect, Giora's view seems to be more in line with Grice's since it doesn't predict a difference in the processing difficulty of metaphor and irony. The empirical evidence I have mentioned, however, speaks against this particular consequence of both approaches, and supports the characterization of metaphor and irony made within relevance theory.

Happé herself (1993) pointed out how relevance theory can help explain why similes, metaphors, and ironies are increasingly difficult to comprehend. Similes can be understood at a purely decoding level. Of course, a competent hearer will need some inference to fully understand something like "She is like a rainbow," since he will have to establish where the similarity between "she" and "a rainbow" lies, but the decoding process indicates explicitly that this comparison must be made, exactly as in the case of interpreting "She is like her sister." In any case, for someone without a theory of mind, a default interpretation resulting from mere decoding would do. However, if we accept the relevance theoretic view that metaphor is a form of loose talk, someone who interprets "She is a rainbow" has to realize that the proposition expressed by the utterance is only a loose interpretation of the speaker's thought. A hearer will need to attribute to the speaker the intention to communicate a thought that interpretively resembles the proposition expressed by his utterance.[28] Happé made clear that this task is very close to that of attributing a false belief to another person, which requires a first-order theory of mind. Understanding irony, as we have seen, is more complex, demanding as it does the possession of a second-order theory of mind.

Let us now consider the empirical evidence in support of Giora's approach. To test the view of irony as a form of indirect negation, Giora and her colleagues conducted an experimental study where they showed that the literal meaning of an ironically interpreted utterance is activated and retained (Giora & Fein, 1998, 1999), thereby contradicting the assumptions of Grice and Searle, who believed that the literal meaning was rejected and suppressed during interpretation. This is taken as evidence in support of the indirect negation view of irony, because it means that the literal meaning of an ironic utterance is functional in irony comprehension.[29]

Nonetheless, it seems to me that while indeed Giora and Fein have provided evidence that the propositions expressed by ironically intended utterances are computed and retained in the process of understanding irony, they have only thereby shown that (something close to) the literal meaning of an utterance is functional in deriving an ironic interpretation. Their finding is important in that it constitutes evidence against the rhetoric and the Gricean approaches to the interpretation of irony, which assume that the literal meaning is rejected. It doesn't, however, provide strong direct evidence in favor of the indirect negation view of irony. The findings of Giora and Fein are equally compatible with the idea that irony is a variety of implicit interpretive use of language, where the hearer echoes an attributed thought and simultaneously expresses an implicit dissociative attitude from it. The proposition expressed by the utterance is also functional in this view. It is the object of the propositional attitude of dissociation, and therefore, it cannot be said to play no role in the interpretation process, or be "rejected," as Giora put it.

NEGATION AND DISSOCIATION AGAIN

Before drawing this paper to a close, let me add a few remarks about Sperber and Wilson's proposal. Recall that they claimed that one of the three characteristic features of verbal irony is that it is a variety of interpretive use in which the *proposition expressed by the utterance* (my emphasis) represents a belief implicitly attributed by the speaker to someone other than the speaker at the time of utterance.

There is a type of irony, frequently overlooked in the literature, in which the speaker is ironic even though he means what he says (i.e., he endorses the content of the proposition expressed by her utterance). Consider, for instance, (6), uttered in a context where the speaker is trying to say something to the hearer and the hearer's attention is clearly somewhere else:

(6)   I love it when you pay attention to me.

Although the utterance is ironic, it just does not seem to be the case that the speaker is implicitly dissociating herself from the belief represented by *the proposition expressed* by her utterance. In (6), the proposition expressed represents a belief the speaker endorses. Because of this, Giora (1995) has argued that similar cases cannot be accounted for by the echoic view, "because the speaker does not dissociate herself from the opinion echoed" (p. 247).

I don't think that this type of example (also considered by Gibbs and O'Brien, 1991, and Curcó, 1995) proves the echoic view of irony wrong, but such cases certainly show that it needs some reformulation so that its claims are made clearer and more specific.

Imagine that it is a habit of the hearer to get distracted when the speaker addresses him, or to dismiss his opinions. Suppose as well that, to the speaker's surprise, on this specific occasion the hearer has been particularly attentive to what the speaker has to say and has even replied "I think you're right. Let's do as you suggest." In such a scenario, a speaker uttering (6) endorses the proposition expressed by her utterance and *also* all the strong implicatures to which it gives rise, for instance, the implicated conclusion that the speaker is now pleased that the hearer has paid attention to him, represented by (7):

(7)   The speaker is now pleased by the attention the hearer has paid her.

Normally, (7) would have been derived from the utterance and the contextual assumption in (8):

(8)   The hearer is paying attention to what the speaker is saying.

Imagine, however, a different scenario: one where the speaker is trying to get a point across and the hearer is overtly concentrating on something else. The speaker utters (6). This time, the utterance does not carry the implicature in (7). For one thing, (8) is not manifest in the context of interpretation.

I would like to argue that the difference between situations where (6) is ironic and situations where it is not hinges on two related factors: (a) whether the speaker dissociates himself not from the content of the proposition expressed, but from the implicatures to which the utterance would normally give rise, and (b) the kind of contextual assumptions that are at stake in interpreting the utterance.

The view of irony where the target of the echo is taken to be the opinion directly represented by the proposition expressed by the utterance is too narrow. Nonetheless, this is not what the requirements on irony proposed by Sperber and Wilson necessarily demand. They do not claim that the target of the echo (that from which the speaker dissociates) should be the proposition expressed, but only that the proposition expressed by the utterance should interpretively resemble a thought of the someone other than the speaker at the time of utterance. From this it does not follow that the target of the implicit dissociation should be *the content of the proposition expressed itself,* as the requirement is often interpreted. An ironic speaker who uses an utterance interpretively can be expressing an attitude of dissociation from the range of assumptions that the utterance makes strongly mutually manifest, not only, and not necessarily, from the proposition expressed by his utterance. Whether a hearer will search for the implicit expression of such an attitude depends crucially on the type of assumptions that are mutually manifest to the speaker and the audience. Finding some contradiction is, of course, a significant factor in this process.

So, the echoic view would benefit from a slight modification to acknowledge that the opinions echoed by the utterance need not be those represented by the content of the proposition it expresses. It can have as its target the propositional content of one or more of its implicatures, and even the propositional content of an assumption that the utterance makes strongly mutually manifest.

CONCLUDING REMARKS

I have argued that some of Giora's qualms about the relevance-theoretic approach to irony are, to a large extent, unfounded. I have also tried to trace the main differences and similarities between her view of irony as an indirect form of negation and Sperber and Wilson's idea that it is a variety of implicit echoic use, with a resulting picture that differs at several points from her own.

With regard to a number of issues concerning processing, such as the stages involved in the interpretation of verbal irony, I have suggested that the two views may have more in common than Giora originally thought. Concerning the relative difficulty of processing ironic and literal language, I have tried to show that not only does relevance theory not differ from Giora's suggestion in that it does not claim that figurative language is as easy to understand as literal language, but it goes further than Giora herself in predicting a very complex process of interpretation for ironic discourse. I haven't dwelled much on the issue of the length of time it takes to process literal and nonliteral language first because I see no obvious prediction of the relevance theoretic account in this respect, and second because I am not sure that complexity and length of time of processing will always correlate. Finally, my own way of interpreting the relevance theoretic framework when analyzing irony has led me to notice that very often during the process of interpreting ironic utterances, contradictions are encountered. This may be linked, of course, to some vaguely defined notion of negation. However, I think that what is characteristic of the comprehension of verbal irony is not whether or not some propositional content is computed along with its negation, but the way in which the contradiction encountered is manipulated. What distinguishes irony from other communicative acts is, I believe, the degree of the metarepresentations involved in handling it.

ENDNOTES

1. For an interesting view about the rhetorical model and its influence on contemporary work on irony, see Stringfellow (1994) and references therein.

2. Martin (1992) stressed that the type of negation at stake in irony is often contrary negation and not necessarily contradictory negation.

3. Giora found support for her view in a number of similarities between irony and indirect negation. Indirect negation avoids some of the effects of direct negation. For instance, she argued, consider the direct negation of a scalar term. When a member of a set is directly negated, the rest can take over (so that "not hot" means "less than hot," rather than "cold;" and "not warm" may mean "hot" or "cold" or "neither warm nor cool"). She believes this effect does not take place in verbal irony. Consider a situation in which we go to a beach on holiday, looking forward to a week of hot weather by the sea. In fact, we find hurricanes and bad weather all along. Someone says ironically "It's hot." If all possible interpretations are placed on a scale and we think of the proposition expressed as being indirectly negated, then it is not the most distant interpretation on the scale that is suggested by the use of irony, but neither is an approximate one. The meaning conveyed, she would argue, is not "It's less than hot." Also, indirect negation avoids the psychologically marked nature of direct negation, revealed by the processing difficulty induced by explicit negation, and an alleged "unpleasant hedonic value" usually attached to overt negation (Wason & Jones, 1963, cited by Giora, 1995).

4. However, see Stringfellow (1994) and Dubois (1981) for an account of how Group m has brought up the Freudian concept of "negation" in its discussion of irony and related tropes.

5. It can be argued that Clark and Gerrig and Kreuz and Glucksberg have simply recast Sperber and Wilson's ideas, but this issue is beyond the scope of this paper.

6. But see Martin (1992) for an attempt to fit irony, characterized as a form of negation, within a semantico-logical framework based on universes of belief.

7. Giora unjustifiedly attributed to Sperber and Wilson a number of assumptions. What Sperber and Wilson did suggest is that the notion of a "literal meaning" is simply not needed theoretically to account for irony and metaphor. They did claim that utterances used ironically encode merely their "literal meaning." This lateral meaning, however, is not used by an ironic speaker to convey her own thoughts, rather it is mentioned as a representation of an object of contempt, ridicule, or disapproval (Jorgensen et al., 1984, p. 112). It doesn't follow from this that "irony does not involve a two-stage processing and is as easy to understand as literal language," as Giora (1995, p. 240) concluded. Sperber and Wilson have made few comments on the issue of irony understanding, but a hint about their view was indeed explicit on the paper by Jorgensen et al. (1984): "the task of the hearer is to reconstruct both the literal meaning of the utterance *and the attitude of the speaker toward that meaning*" (pp. 112–113). They made no claims, however, as to the processes involved in this, nor the stages that the interpretation process undergoes.

8. Sperber and Wilson (1986, pp. 228–229) distinguished two dimensions of language that are derived from the observation that any utterance can be used to represent things in any of two ways. It can represent some state of affairs because its propositional form is true of that state of affairs, or it can represent some other representation with a propositional content (e.g., a thought, another utterance, etc.) because of a resemblance between the two propositional forms. In the first case, they say that the utterance is used as a *description,* in the second, they call the utterance an *interpretation.* Of course, these is a sense in which all utterances are interpretations of a thought of the speaker. So, an utterance is descriptively used when this thought is a description, and interpretively used when the thought is itself an interpretation.

9. An echoic utterance is one that achieves relevance by informing the hearer of the fact that the speaker has in mind some representation and also that the speaker has a certain attitude to it (Sperber & Wilson, 1986, p. 238).

10. The state of affairs here being a mental state of limited conviction "I think."

11. This experimental research would fall within position (a) mentioned earlier, to which Giora attributed the idea that understanding irony is a one-stage process, the idea that irony shouldn't be any more difficult to understand than literal language, and the idea that irony shouldn't take longer to understand than literal language.

12. Research that would fit in position (b), holding the ideas that irony comprehension involves a two-stage process, that it is more difficult to understand than literal language, and that it should take longer to understand than literal language.

13. Giora (1998) defined salience as follows: "The meaning of a linguistic expression is considered salient in case its interpretation can be directly computed from lexical meanings automatically associated with entries before any extra inferences based on contextual assumptions have been derived" (p. 3). According to the graded salience hypothesis (Giora, 1997, in press), for information to be salient, i.e., to be foremost on one's mind, it needs to be stored or coded in the mental lexicon. Salience, however, is not an either-or notion in her view. Rather, it admits of degrees. The more familiar, frequent, conventional, or prototypical the information, the more salient it is. A full discussion of Giora's notion of salience is beyond the scope of this paper.

14. In fact, Sperber and Wilson's theory allows precise predictions about the type of cognitive abilities that an adequate handling of verbal irony demands and the kind of cognitive deficits that should impair the capacity to engage in figurative language, something Happé (1993) has already pointed out and provided evidence for.

15. The Second Principle of Relevance (SPR) is a communicative principle (as opposed to the First Principle of Relevance [FPR], which is a broader principle pertaining to cognition in general). The FPR states that the human cognitive system is looking for relevant information, and the more relevant, the better. The SPR establishes that every utterance creates a presumption of its own optimal relevance, where it is understood that an utterance, on a given interpretation, is optimally relevant if and only if (a) it has enough contextual effects to be worth the hearer's attention, and (b) it puts the hearer to no unjustifiable effort in achieving those effects. Sperber and Wilson proposed that hearers have at their disposal a pragmatic criterion that allows them to choose amongst the set of all possible interpretations one that can be attributed to the speaker. This criterion is called the *criterion of consistency with the principle of relevance* and is stated as follows: An utterance, on a given interpretation, is consistent with the principle of relevance if and only if the speaker might reasonably have expected it to be (or to seem) optimally relevant to the hearer on that interpretation (Sperber & Wilson, 1995). In interpreting utterances, according to Sperber and Wilson's (1995) proposal, listeners look for an interpretation that is consistent with this criterion, and the first interpretation to meet it is the one selected.

16. On the issue of serial versus parallel processing, see Bezuidenhout, Morris, and Cutting (1999), where an important contribution to the question of the role of literal meaning in understanding utterances also is found.

17. More recently, the idea that there should be a theoretical notion of "literal meaning" has also been challenged within relevance theory (see Carston, 1999).

18. In fact, relevance theorists would now be more precise about the notion of "literal meaning" as a theoretical construct. An utterance encodes a certain linguistic meaning (logical form and other encoded instructions), and it communicates a set of propositional forms, which are derived by pragmatic inference even at the level of "what is said." As Carston (1999) has argued, a "literal meaning" in the Gricean sense of "what is said" (encoded linguistic meaning, disambiguated and with referents assigned) is probably not a representational level at all in utterance interpretation. Inferential processes through which linguistically encoded concepts get enriched or loosened are taken to be at work at very early stages during interpretation. Hence, the standard view within relevance theory is that minimal propositions obtained from linguistic

decoding, ambiguity resolution, and reference assignment, which are not communicated, are unlikely to be computed at all, not even as the vehicle by means of which the communicated assumptions are recovered. There are, however, other assumptions which do help recover the intended interpretation (i.e. implicated premises, contextual assumptions) and these are probably entertained in the process of understanding. The above remarks suggest that an analysis of irony is possible and fruitful without any reference to notions such as "literal meaning" and "figurative meaning" as theoretical constructs.

19. Notice that Sperber and Wilson's contention is against "classical accounts of irony (which) assume a specialized mechanism of meaning invention that does not seem to govern any other mental process"(Jorgensen, Miller, & Sperber, 1984, p. 112), as opposed to standard accounts of metaphor, where it is discussed in terms of mental processes such as the ability to perceive similarities, to construct or appreciate analogies, to condense verbal expressions, which apply to other domains as well.

20. This is the first version of the echoic view of irony talks of "mention" of a linguistic expression, and not of interpretive use, but the essence of the account is the same.

21. Giora (1995, pp. 239–240) also attributed to Jorgensen, Miller, and Sperber (1984) and Jorgenson, Miller, & Sperber (1984) the idea that "irony has only one interpretation and involves processing only one meaning." Distinguishing between the notions of interpretation and meaning should be of help at this point. By "meaning," Sperber and Wilson referred to the literal meaning encoded by the utterance, but such meaning cannot be the final interpretation an ironic utterance will receive if at all understood as such by its hearer. To recognize an utterance as ironically intended, the proposition it expresses should be recognized as an interpretation of an attributed thought, and the speaker's attitude to it needs to be recovered. As in all cases of utterance comprehension, the material linguistically encoded by the utterance, which gives rise to a representation close to the folk notion of "literal meaning," is just an element to retrieve the "final interpretation," which will be identified as that intended by the speaker.

22. Someone with a deficit in his ability to attribute mental states to others would be able to handle only coded communication, and hence, his interpretations would be literal most of the time. It is important to notice, though, that even when the final interpretations coincide, the processes undergone by normal competent hearers, and by subjects with an impaired "theory of mind," will be different, even if their observable behavior is the same in terms of the interpretation they give to an utterance literally intended.

23. In fact, between a cognitive organism with an ability to represent mentally only basic representations and a cognitive organism with the ability to form representations of representations, there seems to be a crucial evolutionary step (see Sperber, 1994, 1996, in press).

24. It must be remarked that even when the observable behavior of normal and impaired subjects coincides in interpreting literally intended utterances, the processes followed by each group of people are substantially different. For autistic people, a literal interpretation is a default option, arising from their intact ability to decode. For normal individuals, the literal interpretation represents a thought attributed to the speaker, as well as an interpretation consistent with the Second Principle of Relevance.

25. Notice that a Gricean view of what is involved in the interpretation of figurative language (i.e., computing the literal meaning, finding that it does not fit the context, and accessing the opposite meaning for irony, and a related meaning for metaphor) would not predict these results: understanding irony would not call for any ability that understanding metaphor does not also require; irony and metaphor would both be as easy or as difficult to interpret.

26. For sure, this is but a free paraphrase of her view, and I alone am responsible for any misconception or misrendering of Giora's proposal.

27. I have excluded from this pattern the metarepresentational premises needed to recognize a communicative intention, in the terms of Sperber and Wilson (1986), simply because this notion is not part of Giora's approach to verbal communication. Another reason why the metarepresentational demands predicted by Giora are much lower than those resulting from Sperber and Wilson's view is that Giora's characterization completely omits talking about *attribution* and about *propositional attitudes.* The crucial role of these two notions in the relevance-theoretic proposal clearly accounts for the complex metarepresentational resulting picture.

28. The notion of interpretive resemblance between two propositional forms is defined in terms of the logical and contextual implications they share. The more implications they share, the closer their interpretive resemblance (Sperber & Wilson, 1986).

29. According to Gernsbacher and Faust, meanings relevant to comprehension are retained, while information that is no longer functional in comprehension is suppressed (Gernsbacher, 1990; Gernsbacher & Faust, 1990, 1991, cited by Giora, 1998).

ACKNOWLEDGMENTS

I am grateful to Marilyn Buck and an anonymous reviewer for their very valuable comments on a previous version of this paper.

REFERENCES

Baron-Cohen, S., (1989). The autistic child's theory of mind: A case of specific developmental delay. *Journal of Child Psychology and Psychiatry 30,* 285–297.

Bezuidenhout, A., Morris, R., & Cutting, C. (1999, June). *The role of literal meaning in the understanding of utterances.* Paper presented at the International Pragmatics Conferences on Pragmatics and Negotiation PRAGMA 99, Tel Aviv University, Israel.

Carston, R. (1999, June). *Linguistic meaning and literal meaning.* Paper presented at the International Pragmatics Conference on Pragmatics and Negotiation PRAGMA 99, Tel Aviv University, Israel.

Clark, H., & Gerrig, R. (1984). On the pretense theory of irony. *Journal of Experimental Psychology: General, 113,* 121–126.

Curcó, C. (1995). Some observations on the pragmatics of humorous interpretations: A relevance-theoretic account. *UCL Working Papers in Linguistics, 7,* 27–47.

Curcó, C. (1997). *The pragmatics of humorous inte*rpretations: A relevance theoretic account. Doctoral dissertation, University of London, UK.

Curcó, C. (1999). Lenguaje figurado y teoría de la mente. *Estudios de Lingüística Aplicada, 29,* X.

Dubois, J. (1981). *A general rhetoric* (P. B. Burrell & E. M. Slotkin, Trans.). Baltimore: John Hopkins University Press.

Gernsbacher, M. (1990). *Language comprehension as structure building.* Hillsdale, NJ: Lawrence Erlbaum Associates.

Gernsbacher, M., & Faust, M. (1990). The role of suppression in sentence comprehension. In G. Simpson (Ed.), *Understanding word and sentence* (pp. 97–128). Amsterdam: North-Holland.

Gernsbacher, M., & Faust, M. (1991). The mechanism of suppression: A component of general comprehension skill. *Journal of Experimental Psychology: Learning, Memory and Cognition 17,* 194–207.

Gibbs, R. (1986a). On the psycholinguistics of sarcasm. *Journal of Experimental Psychology: General, 115,* 3–15.

Gibbs, R. (1986b). Comprehension and memory for nonliteral utterances: The problem of sarcastic indirect requests. *Acta psychological, 62,* 41–57.

Gibbs, R. (1994). *The poetics of mind.* Cambridge, England: Cambridge University Press.

Gibbs, R., & Gerrig, R. (1989). How context makes metaphor comprehension seem "special." *Metaphor and Symbolic Activity, 4,* 143–158.

Gibbs, R., & O'Brien, J. (1991). Psychological aspects of irony understanding. *Journal of Pragmatics, 16,* 523–530.

Giora, R. (1988). On the informativeness requirement. *Journal of Pragmatics, 12,* 547–565.

Giora, R. (1995). On irony and negation. *Discourse Processes, 19,* 239–264.

Giora, R. (1997). Understanding figurative and literal language: The graded salience hypothesis. *Cognitive Linguistics, 7/1,* 183–206.

Giora, R. (2003). *On our mind: Salience, context and figurative language.* New York: Oxford University Press.

Giora, R., & Fein, O. (1998). Irony: Graded salience and indirect negation. *Metaphor and Symbol, 13,* 83–101.

Grice, P. (1975). Logic and conversation. In: P. Cole & J. Morgan (Eds.), *Speech acts (Syntax and semantics 3)* (pp. 41–58). New York: Academic.

Happé, F. (1993). Communicative competence and theory of mind in autism: A test of relevance theory. *Cognition, 48,* 101–119.

Jorgensen, J., Miller, G., & Sperber, D. (1984). Test of the mention theory of irony. *Journal of Experimental Psychology: General, 113,* 112–120.

Kreuz, R., & Glucksberg, S. (1989). How to be sarcastic: The echoic reminder theory of verbal irony. *Journal of Experimental Psychology: General, 118,* 112–120.

Leslie, A. (1987). Pretence and representation: The origins of "theory of mind." *Psychological Review, 94,* 412–426.

Leslie, A. (1988). Some implications of pretence for mechanisms underlying the child's theory of mind. In J. Astington, P. Harris, & D. Olson (Eds.), *Developing theories of mind* (pp. 19–46). New York: Cambridge University Press.

Martin, R. (1992). Irony and universe of belief. *Lingua, 87,* 77–90.

Searle, J. (1979). *Expression and meaning.* Cambridge, England: Cambridge University Press.

Smith, N., & Tsimpli, I. (1995). *The mind of a savant.* Oxford, England: Blackwell.

Sperber, D. (1994). Understanding verbal understanding. In J. Khalfa (Ed.), *What is intelligence?* (pp. 179–198). Cambridge, England: Cambridge University Press.

Sperber, D. (1996). *Explaining culture. A naturalistic approach.* Oxford, England: Blackwell.

Sperber, D. (in press). Metarepresentations in an evolutionary perspective. In D. Sperber (Ed.), *Metarepresentations.* Oxford, UK: Oxford University Press.

Sperber, D., & Wilson, D. (1981). Irony and the use-mention distinction. In P. Cole (Ed.), *Radical pragmatics* (pp. 295–318). New York: Academic.

Sperber, D., & Wilson, D. (1986). *Relevance: Communication and cognition.* Oxford, England: Blackwell.

Stringfellow, F. (1994). *The meaning of irony: A psychoanalytic investigation.* New York: Sunny.

Wason, P., & Jones, S. (1963). Negation: Denotation and connotation. *British Journal of Psychology, 54,* 299–307.

Wilson, D., & Sperber, D. (1992). On verbal irony. *Lingua, 87,* 53–76.

PART IV

THE SOCIAL FUNCTIONS OF IRONY

CHAPTER 13

Why Not Say It Directly?
The Social Functions of Irony

Shelly Dews
Massachusetts General Hospital

Joan Kaplan
University of California, Berkeley

Ellen Winner
Boston College and Harvard Project Zero

In three experiments, we investigated the social payoffs of speaking ironically. In Experiment 1, participants rated videotaped ironic remarks (criticisms and compliments) as funnier than literal remarks, but no more or less status enhancing. In Experiment 2, participants listened to audiotaped ironic criticisms and compliments. Ironic compliments were rated as *more* insulting than literal compliments, but ironic criticisms were found to be *less* insulting than literal criticisms. In Experiment 3, participants read literal or ironic criticisms. Ironic comments were rated as more amusing than literal ones. When irony was directed at the addressee's poor performance, it served to protect the addressee's face by softening the criticism. When irony was directed at the addressee's offensive behavior, it served to protect the speaker's face by showing the speaker as less angry and more in control. In addition, irony damaged the speaker–addressee relationship less than did literal criticism. Taken together, these studies suggest that speakers choose irony over literal language in order to be funny, to soften the edge of an insult, to show themselves to be in control of their emotions, and to avoid damaging their relationship with the addressee.

Much of the meaning people intend to convey when they speak goes beyond the literal meaning of the words they utter. Often, people do not say what they mean. Irony is a widely used form of nonliteral language in which the speaker means

---

This chapter was previously published as "Why not say it directly? The social functions of irony" (S. Dews, J. Kaplan, & E. Winner) in *Discourse Processes, 19,* 347–367. Copyright © [1995] by Lawrence Erlbaum Associates. Reprinted with permission.

much more than he or she says. Irony is characterized by opposition between two levels of meaning: The speaker's literal meaning is evaluatively the (approximate) opposite of the speaker's intended meaning (Booth, 1974; Muecke, 1969).

The most commonly used form of irony is one in which the speaker says something positive to convey a negative attitude (e.g., "Great game" after a losing game). This type of ironic remark is referred to here as an *ironic criticism*. Irony can also take the form of a negative statement used to convey a positive evaluation (e.g., "Terrible game" after a winning game). This form is referred to here as an *ironic compliment*. Sarcasm is a form of ironic criticism that targets an individual and is intended to chastise (Long & Graesser, 1988).

Although research has investigated how ironic utterances are processed (Gibbs, 1986a, 1986b), very little is known about *why* people use irony. We know little about why speakers do not say what they mean directly, but rather cloak their meanings in the indirect form of irony. A theory of irony must include not only how irony is processed, but also the conditions under which irony is used and the effects of using irony rather than literal language.

Irony has traditionally been considered a form of meaning substitution in which the speaker says one thing to convey something else. Searle (1979) argued that, with literal language, speakers mean what they say and more, whereas with nonliteral language, speakers do not mean what is said but instead mean something else. In our view, however, defining irony simply as a substitution for literal language hinders our understanding of why people choose to use irony instead of literal language: There would be no motivation to use nonliteral language if literal language could be used instead. Thus, it must be that irony is not equivalent to its literal paraphrase, however close is that paraphrase.

A number of theories of irony have recently been put forth (Clark & Gerrig, 1984; Kreuz & Glucksberg, 1989; Kumon-Nakamura, Glucksberg, & Brown, 1995; Sperber, 1984). The major thrust of these theories has been to capture the defining characteristics of irony. These theories have only informally addressed the question of the functions of irony, that is, why irony might by used in place of literal discourse. The goal of these studies was to investigate directly the functions of irony.

SOCIAL FUNCTIONS OF IRONY

We investigated four possible functions of irony: humor, status elevation, aggression, and emotional control. These four social functions were posited to be those most often associated with irony.

Humor

It may be useful for speakers to be funny when they are also being critical. In an experiment comparing communication goals of ironic and literal remarks, Kreuz, Long, and Church (1991) found that subjects were more likely to identify humor as a communication goal of irony than of literal language. Irony may be funnier than literal language because of the surprise yielded by the disparity between what is said and what is meant (Long & Graesser, 1988; Suls, 1977).

Status Elevation

A speaker who delivers a criticism elevates his or her own status and/or puts down the status of the person being criticized. An ironic criticism may be even *more* status elevating than a literal criticism because the speaker implies how the victim should have behaved in contrast to how he or she did behave. Alternatively, an ironic criticism may be *less* status elevating than a literal one because the ironic speaker may be perceived as joking.

In contrast, complimenting another seems to diminish the speaker's status relative to the addressee. However, this may only be true of literal compliments. Ironic compliments render the compliment ambiguous by putting it in negative terms, leaving the addressee to wonder whether the speaker intended praise or put-down. Hence, an ironic compliment may elevate the speaker's status, while a literal compliment may diminish it.

Aggression

It is often assumed that irony is an especially nasty form of criticism, more insulting than a directly negative statement. Irony has been described as a way of mocking and thereby humiliating the "victim" of the irony (e.g., *Merriam-Webster Dictionary*, 1974). Perhaps irony is assumed to be harsher than literal language because of the contrast between what is said (positive) and what is meant (negative). This contrast may emphasize how far off the behavior is from what is expected. Consistent with this hypothesis, Brownell, Jacobs, Gardner, and Gianoulis (1990) found that people rated ironic criticism as "meaner" than literal criticism, and Kreuz et al. (1991) found that subjects chose "mocking" as a communication goal fulfilled by irony.

However, it is equally plausible to suggest that ironic criticism is *less* aggressive than literal criticism. Brown and Levinson (1987) have argued that because it is indirect, ironic criticism can be used to convey criticism in a less face-threatening way than literal criticism. The term *face,* here, refers to a universal desire to be unimpeded by others and to be approved of by others. A speaker can insult or criticize another off-the-record, using irony, and therefore provide the addressee with more than one possible interpretation. As a result, it is left up to the addressee to decide how to interpret the utterance, and the speaker is left free of responsibility. If the addressee appears to disapprove, the speaker can withdraw the remark and suggest that the addressee has misinterpreted it or can simply make a joke of it. In a similar point, Leech (1983) argued that ironic criticism is less likely than literal criticism to lead to further conflict because the ironist pays lip service to politeness. Hence, it is more difficult for the addressee of an ironic remark to respond impolitely.

Lessening the threat to face and reducing the likelihood of further conflict seem plausible functions of irony. However, such functions may account for the use of irony to criticize another person directly, but cannot account for the use of irony to comment on a situation (when there is no face to lose) or to criticize someone not present. A more general hypothesis, one that we suggest may account for all forms of irony, is that the positive, literal meaning of an ironic criticism colors the interpretation of the speaker's intended meaning, resulting in a decreased negative tone.

A similar argument applies in the case of ironic compliments. Ironic compliments may allow the speaker to appear to present a compliment, but actually to convey negative intent as well. The negative sentence meaning may overwhelm the positive speaker meaning and leave the addressee feeling as if he or she did something that warranted criticism. However, it is also possible that ironic compliments are perceived as more positive than literal compliments. Perhaps the contrast between what is said and what is meant increases the degree of praise conveyed by the utterance.

Emotional Control

A fourth, potentially important function of irony, as yet unexplored, is a demonstration of emotional control. The ironist displays some measure of self-control by virtue of having made a "joking," literally positive remark (J. Levy, personal communication, April, 1993).

If, as hypothesized, ironic remarks are perceived as funnier than literal remarks, and if ironic remarks yield less status discrepancy, are less critical, and show more self-control than literal remarks, it follows that irony should leave addressees feeling less defensive and insulted. It also follows that irony should prove less detrimental to the speaker–addressee relationship. These hypotheses were tested in the following three experiments.

EXPERIMENT I

In Experiment 1, we tested two of the hypotheses set forth in the previous section. First, we tested the hypothesis that ironic criticisms and compliments are perceived as funnier than their literal equivalents. We predicted; however, that the humor differential between ironic and literal criticisms should be greater than that between ironic and literal compliments. The reason for this is that an ironic criticism puts down someone who has committed a clear offense and thus deserves to be put down, whereas an ironic compliment puts down someone whose only "offense" has been to excel on some dimension, but in so doing may have inspired envy. Because an ironic compliment violates the social norm of praising positive behavior, it may sound jealous, petulant, and thus, less funny.

Second, we tested the hypothesis that ironic criticisms and compliments leave less of a status disparity between speaker and addressee than do literal forms. When a speaker criticizes someone, the speaker puts down the other. Hence, the speaker's status is elevated with respect to the addressee. However, we hypothesized that if irony is perceived as joking, then ironic criticisms should elevate the speaker's status *less* than do literal criticisms. When a speaker compliments someone, the speaker elevates the other. Hence, the speaker's status is diminished with respect to the addressee. However, we hypothesized that if an ironic compliment is perceived as ambivalent, then ironic compliments should diminish the speaker's status less than do literal compliments.

Method

Participants. Twelve college undergraduates recruited from an introductory psychology class participated in the experiment. The sample comprised approximately equal numbers of men and women.

Materials and Procedure. Sixteen brief, one- to three-sentence scenes each involving 2 people were videotaped. Each scene showed two characters interacting in some way and ended with the speaker commenting to the addressee about some action or characteristic of the addressee. There were four types of final utterances: *ironic criticism, literal criticism, ironic compliment,* and *literal compliment.* Ironic utterances and literal criticisms were spoken in a negative, mocking intonation. Literal compliments were spoken in a sincere, positive intonation. Table 13.1 presents a sample story of each type.

The scenes were performed by student actors. The order was randomized before taping. To constrain the types of relationships that subjects might infer existed between the two performers, the speaker and addressee in each scene were of similar age and of the same sex and race.

Participants were seen in groups of 4. At the end of each episode, the tape was stopped and participants rated the speaker's final remark on two 5-point scales. Ratings were made first on the humor of the remark: Utterances could be evaluated from *not funny, does not evoke a smile* (–2) to *slightly funny* (0) to *funny, evokes a chuckle* (+2). Ratings were then made on the speaker's status relative to the ad-

TABLE 13.1
Experiment 1: Sample Items

Criticism
(Speaker 1 plays violin very badly, making a screeching noise. Speaker 2 enters.)
Speaker 1: What do you think of my playing? I've been practicing all day.
Speaker 2: Sounds terrific. (Irony)
      or
Speaker 2: Sounds horrible. (Literal)

Compliment
Speaker 1: I don't know who to go to the dance with. Mike, Tom, and Jeff *all* asked me.
Speaker 2: You sure aren't very popular. (Irony)
      or
Speaker 2: You sure are popular. (Literal)

dressee on a scale from *inferior* (−2) to *equal* (0) to *superior* (+2). Participants were instructed to base their evaluations on the speakers' utterances and not on any other features of the scene (e.g., subject matter or characters' appearances).

Before viewing the videotape, participants were asked to respond to a written sample item to familiarize them with the task. On the sample item, the ending was ironic, but the irony was a comment about fate (the weather) rather than a criticism or compliment. During testing, participants could request to view a scene a second time, but such a request was rarely made.

Results and Discussion

Ratings were recorded as scores between −2 and +2. Remarks were rated as *not funny* if the remark received a score of −1 or lower. For status, negative ratings indicated that the speaker was perceived as lower in status than the addressee, whereas positive ratings indicated that the speaker was perceived as higher. Two one-way analyses of variance (ANOVAs) were performed on the humor and status ratings, respectively, with utterance type (4) as the repeated measures factor.

Humor. There was a main effect of utterance type on humor ratings, $F(3, 33) = 32.31$, $MSE = .25$, $p < .001$. Tukey honestly significant difference (HSD) tests showed that ironic criticisms were perceived as funnier than their literal counterparts (HSD = .68, $p < .01$; $M = .58$ vs. −1.0), and ironic compliments were perceived as funnier than literal compliments (HSD = .54, $p < .05$; $M = −.59$ vs. −1.25). As predicted, the difference between ironic and literal criticisms was greater than that between ironic and literal compliments, and ironic criticisms were rated as funnier than ironic compliments (HSD = .68, $p < .01$; $M = .58$ vs. −.59). Hence, the choice of irony lends humor, and it does so more when the speaker comments on something overtly negative (ironic criticism) than on something overtly positive (ironic compliment).

Status. There was a main effect of utterance type on status ratings, $F(3, 33) = 23.87$, $MSE = .35$, $p < .001$. Speakers who insulted the addressee, either ironically or literally, were seen as having higher status than the addressee. Speakers who complimented the addressee, either ironically or literally, had slightly lower status than the addressee. These results could be due to one of three factors: a perceived change in the speaker's status, the listener's status, or both. Our measure as designed did not discriminate among these possibilities. Tukey tests revealed no difference in status elevation between ironic versus literal criticisms ($M = 1.08$ vs. 1.23) or between ironic versus literal compliments ($M = −.01$ vs. −.51). Thus, contrary to our prediction, the choice of irony over literal language did not increase the speaker's status.

These results show that ironic remarks, whether intended as criticisms or compliments, are perceived as funnier than their literal counterparts, and that ironic criticisms are perceived as funnier than ironic compliments. It seems likely that the humor of irony comes from its surprise value. The speaker says the opposite of what one would expect. The contrast between what is said and what is clearly meant creates tension and surprise, which is perceived as funny.

Why should an ironic criticism be perceived as funnier than an ironic compliment? As mentioned earlier, an ironic criticism puts down someone who has committed some offense and thus in some sense deserves to be put down. In contrast, an ironic compliment puts down someone who has committed no clear offense. One may feel more inclined to laugh at aggression when it is perceived as deserved than when it is felt to be gratuitous. These results also show that, contrary to prediction, the use of irony rather than literal discourse did not affect the perceived status of the speaker.

EXPERIMENT 2

In Experiment 2, we compared ironic remarks (criticisms and compliments) to their literal counterparts to test whether irony *sharpens* or *mutes* the level of aggression conveyed by the literal equivalent. We expected to find that irony mutes the message, and hence, that ironic criticisms are less aggressive than literal criticisms, and ironic compliments are more aggressive than literal compliments.

Of course, the context also matters. One contextual variable that is relevant here is the prior relation between the speaker and the addressee. In an experiment comparing ironic criticisms and compliments, subjects rated ironic utterances produced by speakers who liked the addressees as more complimentary than those produced by speakers who disliked the addressees (Slugoski & Turnbull, 1988). To the extent that speaker and addressee are friends, both ironic criticisms and ironic compliments may be perceived as light jokes, as forms of "laughing with." To the extent that the speaker and addressee are only casual acquaintances, or even enemies or rivals, both kinds of irony may be heard as mockery, as forms of "laughing at."

We tested the hypothesis that the relationship between speaker and addressee would more strongly affect the interpretation of irony than literal language. In particular, ironic utterances between friends, whether compliments or criticisms, were expected to be perceived as more positive than such utterances between casual acquaintances. In contrast, the perceived message of a literal criticism or compliment should be less affected by the relationship between speaker and addressee. The justification for this is that irony is inherently ambiguous. We often cannot decide just how negative or positive the ironist is trying to be, and thus we fall back on what we already know about the speaker's attitude toward us. Literal comments are not ambiguous, and hence should be less vulnerable to this kind of contextual information.

Method

Participants. Thirty college undergraduates were recruited from an introductory psychology class to participate in the experiment. Approximately equal numbers of men and women participated. None of these subjects had participated in Experiment 1.

Materials and Procedure.   Sixteen brief, four- to five-sentence stories were constructed. Each story described a situation involving two characters, and each ended with one, the speaker, commenting on the actions of the other, the addressee. The same four types of final utterances, spoken in the same types of intonation, were used as in Experiment 1. There were four stories ending with each of the four possible utterance types on each tape. The stories were recorded in random order onto two audiotapes.

Each story was written in two versions. In one version, the speaker was described as a friend of the addressee, and in the other, the speaker was simply described as "someone," indicating no special relation between speaker and addressee. On each tape, half of the scenes for each type of final utterance involved characters who were friends, and the other half involved characters who were casual acquaintances. (For example, of the four stories ending in an ironic criticism, two were about friends, and two were about casual acquaintances.) Each story that was recorded in the "friends" version on Tape A was recorded on Tape B in the "acquaintance" version. See Table 13.2 for sample stories and endings.

TABLE 13.2
Experiment 2: Sample Items

Ironic criticism

Sebastian did not regularly attend his classes, and when he did he was always disruptive. He
    stormed into class for the first time in a month. His friend/someone turned to him and said the
    following:

"It's always so nice to have you in class."

Literal criticism

Dexter was preparing himself for his senior portrait. He spent hours choosing the right tie and
    jacket.

He chose a purple plaid shirt and a bright green polka dot tie. A friend/someone said the following:

"You're going to look awful in your picture."

Ironic compliment

Gertie was the star of the track team. She had just gotten first place in her fifth consecutive meet.
    Her friend/someone said the following to her:

"It's too bad you have no talent as a runner."

Literal compliment

Kathy was the best dancer in the company. She had the solo part in the performance which she did
    perfectly. Everyone clapped and her friend/someone said the following to her:

"You sure know how to dance."

Participants were randomly assigned to either Tape A or B and were seen individually. They were asked to rate, on a 5-point scale from *very, very insulting* (–2) to *neutral* (0) to *very, very complimentary* (+2) the degree of insult perceived in the final comment of the story. Stories were occasionally played again upon request.

Results and Discussion

A two-way ANOVA, with utterance type (4) and familiarity (2) as repeated measures, was performed on aggression ratings. The two tapes were used to control for story effects, so the effect of tape was not analyzed.

There was a significant effect of utterance type, $F(3, 87) = 149.08$, $MSE = .89$, $p < .0001$. Tukey tests showed that ironic criticisms were rated as *less* negative than literal criticisms (HSD = .78, $p < .01$; $M = -.55$ vs. -1.63). In contrast, ironic compliments were rated as *more* negative than literal compliments (HSD = .78, $p < .01$; $M = -.82$ vs. 1.83).

There was no main effect of familiarity, nor was there an interaction. The fact that a main effect of familiarity was not found may be due to the simple labels used to describe the speaker–addressee relationship. It may be that more information, such as an historical rationale (as used in Slugoski & Turnbull, 1988), is needed for subjects to develop a schema that represents the relationship and allows it to be taken into account when rating literal and ironic remarks.

These results demonstrate that irony serves to mute the message that would have been conveyed by a literal paraphrase. If one intends to criticize another, irony is less negative than a literal, direct confrontation; if one intends to compliment someone, irony is less positive than a literal, direct form of praise. Thus, irony makes criticism gentler, just as it renders praise more ambivalent. We suggest that the same mechanism may account for both of these effects. The evaluative tone of the literal sentence meaning may color the perceived tone of the speaker's meaning. Thus, the positive tone of the literal meaning of an ironic criticism may decrease the negative tone of the speaker's meaning. Similarly, the negative tone of the literal meaning of an ironic compliment may decrease the positive tone of the speaker's meaning.

There may also be an additional factor operating in the case of ironic compliments. The perceived hostility of the comment may be due to the fact that the speaker violates the social convention which dictates that one be courteous and considerate when someone has done a job well.

EXPERIMENT 3

In Experiment 3, we tested the hypothesis that a person who criticizes ironically displays some measure of self-control and thus is perceived as less critical and less angry than a person who expresses anger literally. As a result, the addressee should feel less strongly attacked and thus less defensive and less insulted than if a literal criticism had been delivered. Though criticism in general may have a negative effect on the speaker–addressee relationship, irony should have a less negative impact than literal language because the speaker has "muted" the criticism, made light of the situation, and remained in control. In addition, we examined the effect of the "topic" of the remark (whether the remark was about an offense, a poor performance, or a situation where no one is to blame) on the perceived impact of irony.

Participants rated how *critical,* how *angry,* and how *in control* was the speaker. The first dependent measure allowed us to attempt to replicate our finding from Experiment 2 that ironic criticisms are perceived as less critical than are literal criticisms. We predicted that irony would be perceived as less critical than literal language. We also predicted that the ironic speaker would be perceived as less angry and more in control than a literal speaker because irony is both indirect and witty—two qualities that people are unlikely to convey when emotionally distraught.

Participants also rated how *insulted,* how *defensive,* and how *amused* was the addressee. The amount of criticism and anger conveyed by the speaker should be related to how insulted and defensive the addressee feels. The less critical and angry the speaker is, the less insulted and defensive the addressee should feel in response. Hence, we predicted that recipients of ironic criticisms should be less insulted and less defensive than recipients of literal criticisms. We also predicted that recipients of ironic remarks should be more amused than recipients of literal remarks, as Experiment 1 and other research has demonstrated (Kreuz et al., 1991; Long & Graesser, 1988).

Finally, participants rated the *impact* (positive or negative) the remark would have on the relationship. We reasoned that irony serves to bond the speaker and addressee by giving them a way to laugh about criticism or about an unpleasant situation. Thus, we expected subjects to rate irony as having a less negative impact on the speaker–addressee relationship than does literal language. We say "less negative" rather than positive because any criticism, literal or ironic, may have a negative impact on relationships.

One open-ended question was used to explore the notion that irony reduces the likelihood of further aggression by the addressee (Leech, 1983). Participants were asked to describe how the addressee would respond to the literal and ironic criticisms. We predicted that, in comparison to literal language, addressees would respond to irony in a negative manner less often and that they would respond with amusement and ironic remarks more often.

Method

Participants.   Thirty native English-speaking Boston College undergraduates volunteered to participate in the study as fulfillment of a requirement for introductory psychology and statistics courses. Twenty-two subjects were women and 8 were men.

Materials and Procedure.   Thirty brief vignettes were written describing an interaction between two people. In each of 10 vignettes, the object of the speaker's remark was either the addressee's performance, the addressee's offensive behavior, or the situation. In the *performance* vignettes, one character performed poorly on an activity or task in the presence of the other character (e.g., failed an exam, lost a tennis match). Each of these vignettes ended with the speaker commenting on the addressee's poor performance (e.g., "You really showed her a thing or two, didn't you?"). In the *offense* vignettes, one character did something to offend the other (e.g., failed to introduce the other to someone on the street, arrived late for a meeting). Each of these vignettes ended with the offended character commenting on the offense (e.g., "You're right on time, Gene"). In the *situation* vignettes, the characters were together in an unfavorable situation for which neither was to blame and by which both were inconvenienced (e.g., a traffic jam, a boring lecture). Each of these vignettes ended with one character commenting to the other about the situation (e.g. "Great lecture, isn't it?").

Half of each type of vignette featured two male characters, and the other half featured two female characters. The structure of the stories was held constant. The remarks that ended each vignette were designed to be as natural sounding as possible given the constraint that each vignette had to have a matched literal and ironic ending. One third of the remarks from each type of vignette ended with either a tag phrase such as "isn't it?" or the addressee's name. Half of the remarks were complete sentences (e.g., "The traffic is really moving today"), and half were incomplete sentences (e.g., "What great workmanship").

Stimulus Pretesting. Eighteen native English-speaking subjects (9 men, 9 women) rated the seriousness of the 30 vignettes just described, as well as 12 distractor vignettes. The vignettes were rated without the final utterances, as these might influence seriousness ratings. The distractor vignettes were written with the same specifications as the other vignettes except that the situations described were either serious (e.g., an usher being late for a wedding) or trivial (e.g., playing marbles poorly). Seriousness was rated on a scale from *not at all* (1) to *somewhat* (2) to *very* (3) to *extremely* (4).

The same raters also judged whether the final remark was literal or ironic. The final remark was presented on a separate page, following each vignette and its seriousness rating scale. The presentation of items was counterbalanced so that half of the remarks subjects saw were literal, and half were ironic.

Ten vignettes had to be revised. Ten additional participants (from the same population) rated the seriousness of these revised vignettes and classified the remarks as literal or ironic. Two of these participants incorrectly classified over 30% of the final utterances. Given that all except 1 of the remaining 26 participants were incorrect on less than 15% of these judgments (the one exception was a participant who was incorrect on 26% of the judgments), it seemed that these 2 participants either did not understand the task or were not attending to it. Thus, they were replaced by 2 more participants. These participants correctly classified over 95% of the final utterances.

The results from the seriousness ratings and the literal/ironic judgments were used to select the final 24 vignettes. The vignettes selected had been rated by participants as somewhat serious (seriousness ratings ranged from 1.5–215, $M = 2.1$, $SD = 1.7$). A repeated measures ANOVA showed there were no significant differences in seriousness ratings for the three types of vignettes. The remarks of all but one vignette selected had been incorrectly classified by no more than 1 participant. The one exception was a literal remark that 2 participants out of 14 identified as ironic. The result was 13 stories with male characters, and 11 stories with female characters. Samples of the vignettes and final remarks are included in Table 13.3.

Participants were presented with booklets that consisted of eight of each of the three vignette types. The design was completely within subjects and counter-balanced such that each participant read eight stories of each type, half of which ended with literal, and half of which ended with ironic remarks. The order in which the vignettes were presented was randomly determined and counter-balanced across participants.

Each vignette was followed by one open-ended question and seven rating scales. The open-ended question asked subjects to describe how the addressee would respond ("How will [addressee's name] respond?"). The seven scales focused on three

TABLE 13.3

Experiment 3: Sample Items

Topic of remark is a poor performance

Hal and Mark were amateur golfers who often played golf together. Mark entered a tournament in which he expected to do well. Hal watched the tournament and saw that Mark played very badly and kept missing easy shots. Afterwards, Hal said the following to Mark:

"What a great game, Mark." (Irony)

"What a lousy game, Mark." (Literal)

Topic of remark is offensive behavior

Harry and Joe both considered themselves handymen and often helped one another with household projects. Harry was renovating one wing of his house and he asked Joe to help him hang wallpaper. Joe agreed and said he'd be over the next morning. Harry started working by himself and had almost finished wallpapering by the time Joe arrived around noon. He said the following to Joe:

"You're just in time to help." (Irony)

"You're too late to help." (Literal)

Topic of remark is the situation

Karen and Sandra were going to the movie theater to see a movie premiere when the bus they were on got stuck in traffic. They got there a few minutes late and the movie was nearly sold out. There were only a few seats left so they had to sit in the back row and could hardly see a thing. Karen leaned over and said the following to Sandra:

"These are the best seats in the house." (Irony)

"These are the worst seats in the house." (Literal)

issues: the speaker's motivation, the addressee's feelings, and the impact of the remark on the relationship. Participants rated the speaker's motivation on three 6-point scales: How critical was the speaker (0 = *not at all*, 1 = *somewhat critical*, 3 = *critical*, and 5 = *very critical*), how angry was the speaker (0 = *not at all*, 1 = *somewhat angry*, 3 = *angry*, and 5 = *very angry*), and how much in control was the speaker (0 = *not at all*, 1 = *somewhat in control*, 3 = *in control*, and 5 = *very in control*).

Participants rated how the addressee would feel as a result of the speaker's remark on three similar 6-point scales: How insulted was the addressee (0 = *not at all*, 1 = *somewhat insulted*, 3 = *insulted*, and 5 = *very insulted*), how amused was the addressee (0 = *not at all*, 1 = *somewhat amused*, 3 = *amused*, and 5 = *very amused*), and how defensive was the addressee (0 = *not at all*, 1 = *somewhat defensive*, 3 = *defensive*, and 5 = *very defensive*).

Participants rated the impact the speaker's remark would have on the relationship with the addressee on a bipolar scale ranging from very positive to very negative (1 = *very positive*, 2 = *somewhat positive*, 3 = *neutral*, 4 = *somewhat negative*, 5 = *very negative*).

Participants were asked to read the instructions to themselves as the experimenter read them aloud. The instructions asked them to read the stories and indicate on a series of scales what they thought the speaker meant by the remark and how the addressee would feel as a result of the remark on the rating scales. Participants were asked to choose the item *not at all* only as a last resort, to avoid floor effects. Participants were also told that their answers to the open-ended question might include verbal responses, descriptions of how the addressee felt or thought, or other nonverbal responses. Participants were debriefed at the end of the session. The testing session lasted approximately 1 hr.

Results and Discussion

Data were analyzed from two perspectives. Following Clark (1973), we assessed whether the results could be generalized both to new participants (reported as *t1*) and to new items (reported as *t2*). For both subject and item analyses, a series of paired *t* tests analyzing the effect of remark (literal, ironic) was performed on each dependent variable. The effect of topic was not included in this analysis because it does not inform us about irony per se. Rather, the results of interest were how ironic remarks were perceived differently from literal remarks in each context. Thus, in addition to *t* tests for the overall effects, we carried out a set of similar *t* tests to analyze the effect of remark type for each topic of remark. One-tailed *t* tests were used based on the a priori prediction that irony "mutes" criticism in comparison to literal language. One-tail probability levels of less than .10 are considered significant.

How Critical Was the Speaker? A paired *t* test performed on ratings of speaker criticalness showed that the ironic speaker was rated as less critical than the literal speaker, $t1(29) = 2.19, p < .025; t2(23) = 1.38, p < .09$. Planned comparisons revealed that ironic remarks were less critical than literal ones only when the topic of the remark was a poor performance, $t1(29) = 2.66, p < .01; t2(7) = 1.42, p < .10$. Together, these results provide support for the prediction that ironic remarks are perceived as less critical than literal remarks. Means for this, and for all other dependent measures, are reported in Table 13.4.

How Angry Was the Speaker?   A paired t test performed on ratings of speaker anger showed that the ironic speaker was seen as less angry than the literal speaker, $t1(29) = 2.32, p < .025; t2(23) = 1.51, p < .07$. Planned comparisons showed this to be true only when the topic of the remark was offensive behavior, $t1(29) = 1.92, p < .05; t2(7) = 2.59, p < .025$.

How In Control Is the Speaker?   A paired t test on speaker control ratings showed no effect of remark. However, planned comparisons revealed that ironic speakers were perceived as more in control than literal speakers when commenting on offensive behavior, $t1(29) = 2.93, p < .01; t2(1, 21) = 2.29, p < .05$.

How Insulted Is the Addressee?   Ratings for how insulted the addressee felt were at floor levels for both types of remarks in the situation context ($M = .22$), because a remark about the situation was not a criticism of the addressee. Thus, only ratings of remarks about performances and offensive behaviors were analyzed. The effect of remark was significant, $t1(29) = 2.79, p < .01; t2(15) = 1.69, p < .06$. The addressee was rated as less insulted by ironic than literal criticism. Planned comparisons revealed that this occurred when the object of the criticism was the addressee's offensive behavior, $t1(29) = 2.56, p < .01; t2(7) = 1.50, p < .09$. The fact that addressees were perceived as less insulted by ironic than literal criticism is consistent with the finding that the ironic speaker is perceived as less critical than the literal speaker.

TABLE 13.4
Experiment 3: Means for Irony and Literal by Topic of Remark

	Performance		Offense		Situation	
	Irony	Literal	Irony	Literal	Irony	Literal
Speaker criticalness	3.06	3.57	3.38	3.55	2.92	2.83
Speaker anger	1.33	1.29	2.84	3.28	2.28	2.51
Speaker control	2.88	2.77	2.73	2.34	3.19	3.22
Addressee insult	2.80	3.26	2.23	2.55	0.23	0.21
Addressee defensiveness	2.68	3.13	2.53	2.80	0.37	0.34
Addressee amusement	1.14	0.73	0.98	0.70	2.17	1.13
Impact on relationship	3.53	3.81	3.63	3.87	2.77	2.87

How Defensive Is the Addressee?   Ratings for addressee defensiveness were at floor levels for both types of remarks about the situation ($M = .36$). Thus, only remarks about performances and offenses were analyzed. The effect of remark was significant, $t1(29) = 2.78, p < .01; t2(15) = 1.73, p < .05$. Addressees were less defensive when the speaker commented ironically than literally. However, defensiveness ratings did not differ significantly for any one topic.

How Amused Is the Addressee?   A paired t test on ratings of speaker amusement showed that the addressee was more amused by irony than by literal language, $t1(29) = 6.46, p < .001; t2(23) = 4.25, p < .001$. Planned comparisons revealed that addressees of ironic remarks were more amused in all three contexts than were addressees of literal remarks, but were most amused by remarks about the situation, $t1(29) = 5.51, p < .001; t2(7) = 4.95, p < .001$. The differential was less pronounced when remarks were about a performance, $t1(29) = 2.63, p < .01; t2(7) = 1.82, p < .06$, or offense, $t1(29) = 2.53, p < .025; t2(7) = 1.40, p < .10$.

What Kind of Impact Will the Remark Have on the Relationship?   A paired t test on ratings of the impact of the remarks on the speaker–addressee relationship revealed an effect of remark, $t1(29) = 3.13, p < .01; t2(23) = 2.32, p < .01$. Ironic criticism was rated as having a less negative impact on the relationship than literal criticism. Planned comparisons showed that, in comparison to literal remarks, ironic criticisms had a less negative impact on the relationship when the topic of the remark was offensive behavior, $t1(29) = 1.89, p < .05; t2(7) = 1.48, p < .09$, or the situation, $t1(29) = 1.30, p < .10; t2(7) = 2.31, p < .05$.

How Will the Addressee Respond?   When asked how the addressee would respond, participants gave hypothetical verbal responses and action responses. Most responses fell into the following categories: addressee would be amused, addressee would respond with irony, addressee would feel bad, addressee would express regret, addressee would indicate agreement, addressee would explain, and addressee would express negative feelings about the speaker. Participants' responses were coded by two coders working independently. On a sample of 30% of the responses, intercoder reliability was 90%.

The analyses used here are the same as those described previously, except that two-tailed t tests are used. One participant did not provide any hypothetical responses. As a result, these data are based on the responses of 29 subjects.

As predicted, participants' responses more often included an indication of amusement (e.g., laughter, smiles, joking) in response to irony than to literal language, $t1(28) = 4.50, p < .0001; t2(23) = 4.58, p < .0001$. However, this was true only for remarks about poor performances, $t1(28) = 3.74, p < .001; t2(7) = 3.37, p < .01$, and unfavorable situations, $t1(28) = 3.49, p < .001; t2(7) = 4.94, p < .001$.

Irony was used more often in response to ironic than to literal remarks, $t1(28) = 2.16, p < .05; t2(23) = 1.73, p < .10$. However, most of the ironic responses were as a result of ironic comments about the situation, $t1(28) = 3.39, p < .01; t2(7) = 2.98, p$

< .025. Participants did not respond to comments about offensive behavior with irony, and they responded to approximately equal numbers of literal and ironic remarks about poor performances with irony.

Participants were more likely to include a form of agreement (e.g., "yes" or "in agreement") in their responses to literal remarks than to ironic remarks, $t1(28) = 5.15, p < .001; t2(23) = 3.60, p < .001$, suggesting that they were replying to the literal meanings of remarks. This was true only for remarks about the addressee's performance, $t1(28) = 2.92, p < .01; t2(7) = 2.19, p < .06$, or the situation, $t1(28) = 4.02, p < .001; t2(7) = 2.72, p < .05$.

Participants responded to approximately equal numbers of literal and ironic remarks with expressions of regret (e.g., "I'm sorry"), explanation (e.g., "I forgot"), and negative feelings about the speaker (e.g., anger, name-calling).

Though there were some identifiable differences between responses to ironic and literal remarks, our findings do not provide clear support for the hypothesis that the use of irony reduces the likelihood of further aggression (Leech, 1983). However, participants were told they could write verbal responses, nonverbal responses, or descriptions of how the addressee felt after hearing the remarks. This resulted in a wide variety of responses. Perhaps if participants were given a more constrained task with a limited number of responses from which to choose, differences between responses to ironic versus literal remarks would emerge. Table 13.6 summarizes the findings from Experiment 3.

GENERAL DISCUSSION

Consistent with previous research on the social functions of irony (Brownell et al., 1990; Kreuz et al., 1991; Long & Graesser, 1988), our results demonstrate that ironic criticisms convey information different from that conveyed by literal criti-

TABLE 13.5

Experiment 3: Percentages of Each Type of Hypothetical Response by Addressee to Literal and Ironic Criticisms

	Performance		Offense		Situation	
	Irony	Literal	Irony	Literal	Irony	Literal
Amusement	23	5	3	3	34	11
Irony	5	7	0	0	15	0
Feeling bad	21	30	17	18	2	3
Agreement	12	30	1	6	55	83
Explain	23	30	61	70	5	7
Regret	3	3	53	57	1	1
Negative feelings	38	34	4	7	18	17

TABLE 13.6

Experiment 3: Payoffs of Using Ironic Criticism Versus Literal Criticism

	Performance	*Offense*	*Situation*
Speaker	Less critical	Less angry More in control	No difference between literal and ironic remarks
Addressee	More amused	More amused Less insulted	More amused
Relationship	No difference between literal and ironic remarks	Less negative	Less negative

cisms. This finding demonstrates the inadequacy of a substitution theory of irony: Ironic remarks function quite differently from their closest literal paraphrases.

Experiment 1 demonstrated that both ironic criticisms and ironic compliments are funnier than their literal counterparts. Experiment 2 demonstrated that irony mutes the message conveyed by literal language: Ironic criticisms are *less* aggressive than literal criticisms, and ironic compliments are *more* aggressive than literal compliments. Experiment 3 demonstrated that the functions and effects of ironic criticisms are in part determined by the topic of the remark. Of the functions of irony examined in this study, only one characterized irony across the three topics: humor. The other functions examined must be considered as a function of the topic of the remarks.

In the studies reported here, participants were not the direct addressees of the ironic or literal remarks. Instead, they were, in effect, "overhearers" of the remarks. It is possible that overhearers perceive remarks differently from direct addressees. For example, Schober and Clark (1989) found that the opportunity to interact with the speaker allowed a more accurate understanding on the part of the addressee in contrast to an overhearer. However, in these studies, neither addressee nor overhearer had the opportunity to interact with the speaker. Thus, the two were equally informed. Another reason why addressees might perceive irony differently from overhearers is that an ironic remark might be intended literally to an addressee but ironically to an overhearer, or vice versa. The speaker might intend to deceive the addressee while winking ironically at the overhearer, or to do the reverse. However, the ironic remarks in these studies were not set up this way. in all cases, the remarks were intended to be taken ironically by both the addressee and the overhearer. Thus, given the design of our items, the distinction between addressee and overhearer is not a critical one. However, future research might examine this distinction when addressees have the opportunity to interact with speakers, and when remarks are intended to be taken one way by addressees and another by overhearers.

In what follows, we highlight our major findings. Some of the results discussed here were marginally significant in the item analysis. However, we consider these results to be worthy of discussion, because in each case, the analysis by item revealed a result in the predicted direction. Had we had as many items as participants, it is likely that the analyses by item would have been strengthened.

Ironic Criticism About Performances: Irony As Face Saving

When people make comments about how another person has performed, the social payoffs seem to benefit the addressee. The speaker is seen as less critical when stating the criticism ironically. Probably as a result of this, the addressee is seen as more amused by an ironic criticism than by a literal one.

These findings suggest that ironic criticisms about a person's performance may serve to mute the level of criticism conveyed by the remark in order for the addressee to save face. In uttering an ironic remark about poor performance, the speaker jokes about a sensitive subject. In doing so, speakers may succeed in minimizing the poverty of the performance, and thus, in reducing the addressee's embarrassment. Given this, it is somewhat surprising that the addressees were not rated as less insulted and less defensive following ironic criticisms.

The ironic speaker who criticizes another's performance was rated as neither less angry nor more in control than was the literal speaker. Even though this finding was contrary to prediction, it can be understood if one considers that speakers in this context have no reason to be angry, and thus, no need to control their anger, because the addressee's performance does no harm to the speaker.

In summary, our results suggest that speakers whose goal is to criticize without provocation are better off couching their criticism in indirect language. They are perceived as being less critical and their addressees are more amused.

Ironic Criticism About Offensive Behavior: Irony As Face Saving

When people make comments about another person's offensive behavior, the payoffs seem to benefit the speaker and the addressee equally. When speakers remark about the addressee's offensive behavior, the ironic speaker is seen as no less critical, but as less angry and more in control than the literal speaker. Addressees are just as defensive as when criticized literally, but are less insulted and more amused by the ironic remark. Finally, the relationship is less negatively affected when the criticism is couched ironically rather than literally.

Thus, in this case, irony provides a way for a person who has been wronged to criticize the offender in a way that reflects well on the speaker, and renders the addressee as less insulted than the recipient of a literal insult. It is socially desirable not to appear to be too angry (even given just cause) and to appear to be in control of one's emotions. Thus, this type of irony may serve a social control function by allowing speakers to sanction addressees without having this reflect negatively on themselves.

Because the speakers of ironic and literal criticisms in this context were perceived as equally critical, it is not surprising that the addressees were perceived as equally defensive. It may be that literal and ironic criticisms that are warranted are seen as equally critical simply because they are deserved. There is no reason for speakers to diminish their criticism, nor is there reason for the addressees to expect a softened blow. The fact that the relationship was affected in a less negative manner when speakers spoke ironically may be because ironic speakers are perceived as being less angry and more funny than literal speakers.

Ironic Criticism About the Situation: Irony As Humor

When people make comments about unpleasant situations that are out of their control, the payoffs found here for commenting ironically were that the remark is perceived as humorous and it has a less negative impact on the speaker–hearer relationship. Two of our measures of how addressees perceived the remarks (how insulted and how defensive) were not applicable in the situation context because the object of the speaker's remark was not the addressee. Addressees have no reason to feel insulted or defensive as a result of remarks about situations that are not their responsibility. Subject ratings confirmed this.

The impact of ironic remarks on the speaker–addressee relationship was more positive than that of literal remarks. It makes sense that an ironic remark about an unfavorable situation would bond the speaker and addressee by pointing out that they share feelings about the situation and can make light of it. It also seems reasonable to assume that a literal remark would be perceived negatively because the speaker is complaining and may be seen as "bringing down" the mood of the addressee. Although both ironic and literal remarks are complaints in this context, the ironic complaint makes light of the situation and the literal complaint does not.

The fact that irony had a relatively small effect on the speaker–addressee relationship may be due to the vignettes used. One ironic remark may have little effect on the relationship between speaker and addressee when these two parties are already friends. However, an ironic remark about a mutual situation may have more of a bonding effect when speaker and addressee are strangers or newly acquainted, and the remark can thus shape their future interactions. Ironic remarks may also have a greater positive effect on the speaker–addressee relationship in extremely stressful situations. In such situations, humorous ironic complaints may relieve the addressee's anxiety, whereas literal complaints may increase his or her anxiety.

It was somewhat surprising that speakers of ironic remarks in this context were not perceived as less critical, less angry, or more in control than speakers of literal remarks. After all, if people can joke about bad situations, they ought to seem less angry and more in control.

Our central hypothesis was that irony conveys a different level of aggression than literal language, and that this quality of softened criticism (in the case of ironic criticism) leads to social payoffs for both the speaker and the addressee.

These predictions were partially confirmed, although the topic of the criticism was found to affect interpretations of the remarks. The results of these experiments replicate Brownell et al.'s (1990) finding that ironic compliments are perceived as more negative than literal compliments, but contradict the finding by Brownell et al. that ironic criticisms are also perceived as more negative. However, an important difference in these studies is whether the remark is about the addressee, as in these studies, or is about a third person, as in the Brownell study. Ironic remarks that are about the addressee may be perceived as less critical than literal remarks because they offer the addressee a number of ways to respond that may soften the negative impact of the remark. Ironic remarks about a third person may be seen as more critical than literal remarks because they allow the speaker and addressee to laugh *at* the third person and to align themselves as insiders against the outsider. When ironic criticisms are directed to the victims, the victims have the opportunity to deflect the criticism. It may be the availability of this opportunity that determines how critical the ironic criticism is perceived to be.

One important variable suggested by this research is how deserved is the criticism. It appears that when criticism is not merited, as here when the speaker commented on another person's poor performance, ironic criticism is less harsh than direct literal criticism. But when criticism is merited (either of a person or a situation), ironic criticism is no less harsh than literal criticism. Irony diminishes the negative effects of unwarranted criticism, and makes the speaker who has justification to be angry and out of control seem less angry and more in control. This suggests that when criticism is warranted, and when that criticism is of another person, the phrasing of the criticism is not so important to addressees, but that the phrasing is important when the criticism is not warranted. However, when the criticism is warranted, speakers are seen as speaking in a more socially acceptable manner (i.e., they are less angry and more in control) when they speak ironically, and their remarks are judged as having less negative impacts on their relationships with addressees.

These experiments demonstrate that the social functions of irony differ from those of literal language. Although many of the differences found here between literal and ironic remarks were small, they were significant. Our results suggest that irony has subtle effects that are small but consistent.

The functions identified here for ironic discourse were not predicted by any of the major definitional theories of irony. Thus, for example, the finding that ironic criticism is less critical than literal criticism is equally consistent with a view of irony as pretense (Clark & Gerrig, 1984) and irony as echoic mention (Sperber, 1984). We suggest that theories of irony need to focus not only on the structural properties of irony, but also on the functions of irony. Any definitional theory of irony must take into account, and be able to predict, the two overarching functions of irony uncovered here—to save face and to be funny.

ACKNOWLEDGMENT

This research was supported by the National Institutes of Health Grant No. 1 ROI NS27894.

REFERENCES

Booth, W. (1974). *A rhetoric of irony.* Chicago: University of Chicago Press.

Brown, P., & Levinson, S. C. (1987). *Politeness: Some universals in language usage.* New York: Cambridge University Press.

Brownell, H. H., Jacobs, J. R., Gardner, H., & Gianoulis, D. (1990). *Conditions for sarcasm.* Unpublished manuscript, Boston College, Department of Psychology, Chestnut Hill, MA.

Clark, H. H., & Gerrig, R. I. (1984). On the pretense theory of irony. *Journal of Experimental Psychology: General, 113,* 121–126.

Gibbs, R. W. (1986a). Comprehension and memory for nonliteral utterances: The problem of sarcastic indirect requests. *Acta Psychologica, 62,* 41–57.

Gibbs, R. W. (1986b). On the psycholinguistics of sarcasm. *Journal of Experimental Psychology: General, 115,* 3–15.

Kreuz, R. J., & Glucksberg, S. (1989). How to be sarcastic: The echoic reminder theory of verbal irony. *Journal of Experimental Psychology: General, 118,* 374–386.

Kreuz, R. J., Long, D. L., & Church, M. B. (1991). On being ironic: Pragmatic and mnemonic implications. *Metaphor and Symbolic Activity, 6,* 149–162.

Kumon-Nakamura, S., Glucksberg, S., & Brown, M. (1995). How about another piece of pie: The allusional pretense theory of discourse irony. *Journal of Experimental Psychology: General, 124,* 3–21.

Leech, G. N. (1983). *Principles of pragmatics.* New York: Longman.

Longman, D. L., & Graesser, A. C. (1988), Wit and humor in discourse processing. *Discourse Processes, 11,* 35–60.

Merriam-Webster dictionary. (1974). New York: Pocket Books.

Muecke, D. C. (1969). *The compass of irony.* London: Methuen.

Schober, M. F., & Clark, H. H. (1989). Understanding by addressees and overhearers. *Cognitive Psychology, 21,* 211–232.

Searle, J. R. (1979). Metaphor. In A. Ortony (Ed.), *Metaphor and thought.* Cambridge, England: Cambridge University Press.

Slugoski, B. R., & Turnbull, W. (1988). Cruel to be kind and kind to be cruel: Sarcasm, banter, and social relations. *Journal of Language and Social Psychology, 7,* 101–121.

Sperber, D. (1984). Verbal irony: Pretense or echoic mention? *Journal of Experimental Psychology. General, 113,* 130–136.

Suls, J. M. (1977). Cognitive and disparagement theories of humor: A theoretical and empirical synthesis. In A. J. Chapman & H. C. Foot (Eds.), *It's a funny thing, humor.* Oxford, UK: Pergamon.

CHAPTER 14

Salting a Wound or Sugaring a Pill:
The Pragmatic Functions of Ironic Criticism

Herbert L. Colston
University of Wisconsin–Parkside

Recent investigations of the pragmatic functions of ironic criticism (e.g., saying "Nice shot" to condemn a fellow player for missing a free throw and losing a basketball game) have argued that ironic criticism is used to dilute condemnation. Dews and Winner (1995) and Dews, Kaplan, and Winner (1995) showed that, relative to literal criticism (e.g., "Terrible shot"), ironic criticism expresses less condemnation. This article reports the results of four experiments to show that ironic criticism in many cases is used for just the opposite reason—to *enhance* rather than to dilute condemnation. These findings have significant implications for both pragmatic and processing theories of verbal irony.

Verbal irony is often used to criticize a person or a situation when events have not turned out as expected or desired. For example, if a woman expects her boyfriend to pick her up promptly at 7 p.m., but he does not arrive until 8 p.m., the woman might say to him, "Thanks for being on time."

Speech such as this is considered nonliteral because the words used do not correspond with the meaning intended by the speaker. Indeed, the words often mean something quite different from and even the opposite of what is meant. Verbal irony can thus at times have multiple meanings that can invite the possibility for misunderstanding. Children in particular often misunderstand verbal irony (Demorest, Silberstein, Gardner, & Winner, 1983; Winner, 1988).

But according to Grice (1975), we seek to communicate with one another without being misleading. To do so we operate according to a cooperative principle whereby we exchange meaning with participants in conversation in the most clear and concise means possible. Why then would we use this indirect form of speech—verbal irony—to criticize or condemn someone instead of directly stating what we

This chapter was previously published as "Salting a wound or sugaring a pill: The pragmatic functions of ironic criticism" (H. L. Colston) in *Discourse Processes, 23,* 24–53. Copyright © [1997] by Lawrence Erlbaum Associates. Reprinted with permission.

mean? Wouldn't the indirect nature of verbal irony invite misunderstanding? Returning to the example, wouldn't the woman risk being misunderstood by literally thanking her boyfriend for being punctual instead of literally saying that she was disappointed in or angry with him for being late?

The likely explanation is that speakers achieve certain pragmatic goals with the indirectness of verbal irony that warrant its use. These goals may be reflected in the reasons people give for using verbal irony. Several recent studies have investigated these reasons. Roberts and Kreuz (1994) listed a host of discourse goals reported by people for using many kinds of indirect speech, including verbal irony. Among these are to be humorous, to protect oneself, and to show positive emotion. Verbal irony is also used, often in conjunction with hyperbole, to express surprise (Colston, in press; see also Colston & Keller, 1996). Brown and Levinson (1987) argued that verbal irony is used to reduce threat and to emphasize shared knowledge and common attitudes among the interlocutors.

All of these reasons appear to suggest that ironic criticism serves the general pragmatic function of reducing or somehow *diluting* the degree of condemnation of a critical remark. Dews and Winner (1995) tested if ironic criticism performs this function. They proposed a Tinge Hypothesis that ironic criticism automatically reduces the amount of condemnation that is interpreted. By stating literally positive words in an ironic criticism, the speaker forces the addressee's interpretation to be tinged toward the positive. In this way, a speaker can criticize someone but do so in a less offensive way (sugaring a pill). For instance, because the woman in the example literally says something positive, she causes the boyfriend to unavoidably interpret her remark less negatively than had she spoken literally negative words; even though in both cases the intended meaning of her remark is negative. Dews and Winner (1995; see also Dews et al., 1995) found evidence to support this hypothesis in that ironic criticism was interpreted less negatively than literal criticism.

Others, however, have argued that verbal irony, particularly sarcastic irony, is used to express intensely negative feelings such as sardonic or biting criticism (Cutler, 1974; Gibbs, 1986b; Grice, 1978; Kreuz & Glucksberg, 1989; Perret, 1976; see also Muecke, 1980). Kreuz, Long, and Church (1991) listed mocking as a discourse goal of verbal irony. Brownell, Jacobs, Gardner, and Gianoulis (1990) found that people find ironic criticisms to be meaner than literal criticisms, and indeed several entire theories for how verbal irony is comprehended are based on the idea that it is used to ridicule a person or a point of view (see Clark & Gerrig, 1984, p. 122; Kumon-Nakamura, Glucksberg, & Brown, 1995; Sperber & Wilson, 1981). Moreover, many dictionary definitions of sarcasm describe it as being particularly negative (Fowler, 1965; *Webster's Ninth New Collegiate Dictionary,* 1988). These reasons suggest that people might use verbal irony to condemn someone because it *enhances* the condemnation that is expressed relative to literal criticism. By stating the more desirable state of affairs that did not occur, the speaker creates a contrast with the current situation, making the current situation look worse by comparison. In this way, a speaker can not only criticize someone, but do so with added emphasis (salting a wound).

The previous research thus appears to suggest that ironic criticism serves opposing pragmatic goals—to dilute and to enhance condemnation. How is this possible? If each function can be achieved by ironic criticism, when is one function achieved but not the other? What factors affect when one function is performed and not the other? Or, is it the case that ironic criticism only performs one of these functions? The following study provides some evidence bearing on these issues.

If ironic criticism can perform each of these pragmatic functions, one should be able to identify factors that would affect whether ironic criticism enhances or dilutes condemnation. For instance, a speaker would probably wish to enhance his condemnation of someone if that person were guilty of causing the situation that the speaker is complaining about compared to the person not being directly responsible. To illustrate, if the woman in the example knew her boyfriend was late because he had been dawdling, she may be more willing to enhance her condemnation than if her boyfriend was late because of poor weather. In the first case, the boyfriend's lateness is his fault and therefore may be correctable in the future. Enhanced condemnation may achieve this goal. In the second case, the lateness is not the boyfriend's fault, and thus enhanced condemnation would be inappropriate.

Another factor that should affect whether ironic criticism dilutes or enhances condemnation is whether or not the speaker is guilty of what she criticizes. For instance, a speaker would probably wish to dilute her condemnation of a person engaging in behavior that might be construed as negative or otherwise in violation of some norm or ideal, if the speaker herself were guilty of that behavior relative to being innocent. If the woman in the example were guilty herself of frequently being late, for instance, she may wish to dilute her condemnation of her boyfriend's lateness more than if she were always punctual. Otherwise, she may invite an accusation of hypocrisy.

In four experiments, the pragmatic functions of ironic criticism were put to test under circumstances such as these. As will become clear, ironic criticism does not appear to dilute the degree of condemnation expressed by a speaker under any circumstances. Indeed, the results of the experiments demonstrate that the Tinge Hypothesis fails to account for the amount of condemnation expressed by ironic criticism. Even in circumstances where ironic utterances should reduce the level of condemnation that is expressed, ironic criticism expresses more condemnation than literal criticism.

EXPERIMENT I

This experiment was conducted to test the degree to which ironic criticism condemns an addressee for a negative situation depending on whether or not the addressee is at fault for the negative situation. The Tinge Hypothesis (Dews & Winner, 1995) predicts that ironic criticism would dilute the degree of condemnation whether or not the addressee of that remark caused the situation that the ironic remark was about. Instead, if the degree of condemnation of ironic criticism is affected by whether or not the addressee is responsible for the negative situation, then ironic criticism should enhance and dilute condemnation accordingly. Finally, if ironic criticism does not dilute the amount of condemnation that is expressed, then it should express more condemnation than literal criticism under all conditions. To test these predictions, participants were asked to rate the degree of condemnation they perceived in literal and ironic criticism under circumstances where the addressee either was or was not the cause of the negative situation.

Method

In general, the materials and procedures used in the experiments were similar. Therefore, the method described in this experiment can serve as a model for the others. Only exceptions to the method used in this experiment will be provided for the other experiments.

Participants.   Thirty-two University of California undergraduates participated for a course requirement. All were native English speakers. None of them participated in the other experiments.

Materials and Design.   Twelve scenarios described situations where something negative happens, and a person makes a comment about the situation to an addressee who is also in the situation. Each scenario had four versions. Two of the versions described the addressee as the cause of the problem in the situation, and the other two described some other cause. For one of the versions where the addressee was at fault, a speaker made a literal comment that was negative to the addressee. For the other version, the speaker made an ironic comment that echoed the expected or desired outcome of the situation. The same held for the versions where the addressee was not at fault. Other than the differences just described, the versions of the scenarios were identical. See the following, for example:

> Manuel was the star player on the soccer team, but he could not play in the city championship game because he partied too much and was extremely sick. When the team captain heard about this he said, "We'll never win the championship now."
> (*addressee's fault, literal comment*)
>
> Manuel was the star player on the soccer team, but he could not play in the city championship game because he partied too much and was extremely sick. When the team captain heard about this he said, "We'll win the championship for sure now."
> (*addressee's fault, ironic comment*)
>
> Manuel was the star player on the soccer team, but he could not play in the city championship game because he caught the flu and was extremely sick. When the team captain heard about this he said, "We'll never win the championship now."
> (*not addressee's fault, literal comment*)

Manuel was the star player on the soccer team, but he could not play in the city championship game because he caught the flu and was extremely sick. When the team captain heard about this he said, "We'll win the championship for sure now."
(*not addressee's fault, ironic comment*)

Four sets of scenarios were created with each set containing a different version of each scenario. For example, Set 1 would contain the *addressee's fault, literal comment* version of the first scenario; Set 2 would contain the *addressee's fault, ironic comment* version of that scenario; Set 3 would contain the *not addressee's fault, literal comment* version; and Set 4 would contain the *not addressee's fault, ironic comment* version. Set 1 would then also contain the *addressee's fault, ironic comment* version of the second scenario; the *not addressee's fault, literal comment* version of the third scenario; the *not addressee's fault, ironic comment* version of the fourth scenario; and so on, so that three instances of each version were represented. The order of scenarios in each set was random, and each set was presented to an equal number of participants. Each scenario was presented with a 7-point rating scale ranging from 1 (*not at all condemning*) to 7 (*very condemning*). Example items used in this and the other experiments are provided in the Appendix.

Each participant received all levels of the independent variables—cause of the negative situation (*addressee, not addressee*) and comment type (*literal, ironic*)—making a 2 – 2 within-participants design. Considering items as a random factor, the design is also 2 – 2 within-participants.

Procedure.   Participants were told they would complete a task involving their perceptions about what people say. They were then presented with the 12 scenarios in a booklet with instructions on the cover. Participants followed along as the experimenter read the instructions aloud. The instructions told the participants to read each scenario and decide how condemning of the addressee they thought the comments were. They were told to indicate their decisions by marking the rating scales. When participants had completed this task they were asked to return to the scenarios and write down a number from 1 to 7 to represent how sarcastic they thought the comments were. A 7-point rating scale was drawn on a chalkboard for the participants to use as a reminder. The scale resembled those in the booklets. The endpoints of the scale were labeled *not at all sarcastic* (1) and *very sarcastic* (7). The sarcasm rating scales were not printed in the booklets because I did not want participants to know they would be rating how sarcastic the comments were until the other ratings had been completed. When participants had finished, they were debriefed about the experiment and dismissed.

Results and Discussion

A brief comment on how the data in this and the other experiments were analyzed and reported is in order. Following Clark (1973), all analyses of variance

(ANOVAs) were conducted in two ways—one treating participants as the random factor, and the other treating items as the random factor. Conducting analyses this way allows for generalization of significant effects across participant and item populations. ANOVAs treating participants as the random factor are referred to with F_1, and analyses treating items as a random factor are referred to with F_2.

The mean condemnation and sarcasm ratings are presented in Table 14.1. Two-way ANOVAs on the condemnation ratings revealed significant main effects of comment type, $F_1(1, 31) = 5.47, p < .05; F_2(1, 11) = 2.60, p = .13$, and cause of the negative situation, $F_1(1, 31) = 20.76, p < .001; F_2(1, 11) = 32.24, p < .001$, but no significant interaction.

Analysis of the sarcasm ratings also revealed significant main effects of comment type, $F_1(1, 31) = 112.46, p < .001; F_2(1, 11) = 53.97, p < .001$, but no effect of cause of the negative situation or an interaction.

The results of the sarcasm ratings are straightforward. Ironic criticisms are rated as more sarcastic than literal criticisms whether or not the addressee of the criticism is at fault for the negative situation that the interlocutors encounter.

The results of the condemnation ratings are rather intriguing. Regardless of whether or not the negative situation was the fault of the addressee, ironic criticism was more condemning of the addressee than literal criticism. For example, if a soccer team will lose an important game because the star player is sick, ironic remarks like, "We'll win the championship for sure now," are more condemning of the player than literal remarks like, "We'll never win the championship now," even if it is not the player's fault that he or she is sick. Notice that this difference between literal and ironic criticism holds even though overall the comments express less condemnation when the situation is not the addressee's fault.

These results suggest that the Tinge Hypothesis (Dews & Winner, 1995) does not account for the degree of condemnation expressed by ironic criticism. The re-

TABLE 14.1
Condemnation and Sarcasm Ratings for Literal and Ironic Criticisms: Experiment 1

Cause of Negative Situation	Condemnation Ratings: Comment Type		Sarcasm Ratings: Comment Type	
	Literal	Ironic	Literal	Ironic
Addressee				
M	4.92	5.24	2.55	5.41
SD	0.78	1.01	1.50	0.86
Not addressee				
M	3.86	4.29	2.44	5.67
SD	1.14	1.35	1.42	1.07

Note. The rating scales ranged from 1 (not at all condemning) to 7 (very condemning) and from 1 (not at all sarcastic) to 7 (very sarcastic).

sults do demonstrate that the amount of condemnation expressed is affected by whether or not the addressee is responsible for the negative situation, but this effect holds for both literal and ironic criticism. Ironic criticism does not dilute in one case and enhance in the other; it always enhances criticism.

It may be, however, that other conditions exist where the Tinge Hypothesis is correct, and ironic criticism is less condemning than literal criticism. Experiment 2 was conducted to test whether a speaker being guilty of the thing she or he criticizes affects the degree of condemnation interpreted from literal and ironic criticism.

EXPERIMENT 2

If a speaker who criticizes someone else's behavior, smoking cigarettes for example, is guilty of that behavior himself, it is possible that ironic criticism would dilute the condemnation compared to the speaker not engaging in that behavior. Imagine for instance that two friends who both know that they both smoke meet in a bar. One might say to the other as she lights a cigarette, "That's really good for your lungs." Because the speaker is also guilty of the behavior—that is, he is also a smoker, this ironic criticism may be interpreted as less condemning than if the speaker spoke literally. This experiment was designed to test this possibility.

The Tinge Hypothesis again predicts that ironic criticism should always express less condemnation than literal criticism. Instead, if the degree of condemnation of ironic criticism is affected by whether or not the speaker is guilty of what she criticizes, then ironic criticism should enhance and dilute condemnation accordingly. Finally, if ironic criticism does not dilute the amount of condemnation that is expressed, then it should express more condemnation than literal criticism under all conditions. To test these predictions, participants were asked to rate the degree of condemnation they perceived in literal and ironic criticism under circumstances where the speaker either was or was not guilty of the thing she criticizes.

Method

Participants.   Thirty-two University of California undergraduates participated for a course requirement. All were native English speakers. None of them participated in the other experiments.

Materials and Design.   Twelve scenarios described situations where a person is doing something that could be construed as negative behavior and another person makes a comment about the situation to the first person. Each scenario had four versions. Two of the versions described the addressee as also being guilty of the negative behavior, and the other two described the addressee as not having engaged in the behavior. For one of the versions where the speaker is also guilty of the behavior, the speaker made a literal comment to the addressee that was negative. For the other version, the speaker made an ironic comment that echoed a more positive form of behavior. The same held for the versions where the speaker was not guilty of the behavior. Other than these differences, the versions of the scenarios were identical. See the following, for example:

> Ellen despised smoking cigarettes. Ellen saw her boyfriend smoking and said, "I see you don't have a healthy concern for your lungs."
> (*speaker doesn't do negative behavior, literal comment*)

> Ellen despised smoking cigarettes. Ellen saw her boyfriend smoking and said, "I see you have a healthy concern for your lungs."
> (*speaker doesn't do negative behavior, ironic comment*)

> Ellen enjoyed smoking cigarettes. Ellen saw her boyfriend smoking and said, "I see you don't have a healthy concern for your lungs."
> (*speaker does negative behavior, literal comment*)

> Ellen enjoyed smoking cigarettes. Ellen saw her boyfriend smoking and said, "I see you have a healthy concern for your lungs."
> (*speaker does negative behavior, ironic comment*)

The same design used in Experiment 1 was used in this experiment. Each scenario was presented with a 7-point rating scale ranging from 1 (*not at all condemning*) to 7 (*very condemning*).

Procedure.   The same procedure used in Experiment 1 was also used in this experiment.

Results and Discussion

The mean condemnation and sarcasm ratings are presented in Table 14.2. Two-way ANOVAs on the condemnation ratings revealed significant main effects of comment type, $F_1(1, 31) = 4.45, p < .05; F_2(1, 11) = 9.92, p < .01$, and speaker's conduct regarding the negative behavior, $F_1(1, 31) = 46.01, p < .001; F_2(1, 11) = 76.78, p < .001$, along with a significant interaction, $F_1 (1, 31) = 4.43, p < .05; F_2 (1, 11) = 6.34, p < .05$.

Analysis of the sarcasm ratings revealed the same pattern as Experiment 1 for ironic utterances but a different pattern for literal comments. Significant main effects for comment type, $F_1(1, 31) = 177.12, p < .001; F_2(1, 11) = 194.27, p < .001$, and speaker's conduct regarding the negative behavior, $F_1(1, 31) = 15.87, p < .001; F_2(1, 11) = 41.44, p < .001$, were found along with a significant interaction, $F_1(1, 31) = 31.77, p < .001; F_2 (1, 11) = 42.11, p < .001$.

The results of the sarcasm ratings, although different from those in Experiment 1, are nevertheless also straightforward. Ironic criticism is overall more sarcastic than literal criticism, and literal criticism is also more sarcastic when the speaker is guilty of what he or she is criticizing than when he or she is not.

The first result follows from the nature of the items—ironic criticism is sarcastic by definition—and the latter result makes sense given that a speaker is making a

TABLE 14.2
TABLE 14.2
Condemnation and Sarcasm Ratings for Literal and Ironic Criticisms: Experiment 2

Speaker's Conduct Regarding Negative Behavior	Condemnation Ratings: Comment Type		Sarcasm Ratings: Comment Type	
	Literal	Ironic	Literal	Ironic
Engages in behavior				
M	3.66	3.79	3.63	6.08
SD	1.52	1.71	1.93	0.56
Does not engage in behavior				
M	5.47	6.16	1.68	6.31
SD	1.30	0.75	1.66	0.77

Note. The rating scales ranged from 1 (*not at all condemning*) to 7 (*very condemning*) and from 1 (*not at all sarcastic*) to 7 (*very sarcastic*).

nonveridical comment when he or she criticizes that which he or she is also guilty of. Nonveridicality is a necessary and at times sufficient (Colston, 1996) condition for the perception of sarcasm.

The results of the condemnation ratings replicate those of Experiment 1. Ironic comments were rated overall as more condemning than literal comments. This difference was most pronounced when the speaker was not guilty of the negative behavior of the addressee. When the speaker is guilty of the negative behavior, the difference nearly goes away, but ironic criticism is clearly not less condemning than literal criticism.

These results again demonstrate that the speaker's guilt with respect to the behavior she or he criticizes affects the degree of condemnation expressed, and this effect holds for both literal and ironic criticism. Ironic criticism does not dilute in one case and enhance in the other—it either condemns as much as (e.g., when the speaker is guilty of the behavior) or more than (e.g., when the speaker is not guilty of the behavior) literal criticism.

These results, along with those of Experiment 1, seem to suggest that the Tinge Hypothesis is incorrect. Under four different conditions—a speaker criticizes an addressee who is the direct cause of a negative situation, a speaker criticizes an addressee who is not the direct cause of a negative situation, a speaker criticizes a negative behavior that he himself does not do, and a speaker criticizes a negative behavior that he himself does do—ironic criticism is never less criticizing than literal criticism. Moreover, in three of these four conditions, ironic criticism is significantly more criticizing than literal criticism.

To be fair, the possibility remains that this study evaluates the condemnation expressed by ironic and literal criticism differently than the Dews and Winner (1995) study that supported the Tinge Hypothesis. In Dews and Winner, the rating scale ranged from *strong criticism* to *strong praise.* This scale, in having an endpoint that is positive, may test for the more positive aspects of ironic criticism rather than simply the negative ones. For instance, recall that Brown and Levinson (1987) argued how verbal irony can stress the shared knowledge or common attitudes between interlocutors; a rather positive pragmatic goal. Because the study presented here has thus far made use of a rating scale that does not have a positive endpoint, it is possible that it has not been a fair test of the Tinge Hypothesis. The study presented here may only have tapped into the negative pragmatic functions performed by ironic criticism.

To address this possibility, a third experiment presented the same items used in Experiment 1 to a new group of participants. This time a different rating scale that ranged from 1 (*not at all sympathetic*) to 7 (*very sympathetic*) was used. If ironic criticism performs more positive pragmatic functions than literal criticism, such as to indicate that the interlocutors share a common unfortunate fate, as a means of bonding or increasing camaraderie, then the use of this scale with positive endpoints should detect this function.

If ironic criticism dilutes condemnation to perform this positive pragmatic function, then it should express more sympathy than literal criticism, particularly when the negative situation is not the addressee's fault. If ironic criticism does not perform this function, then it should always express less sympathy than literal criticism.

EXPERIMENT 3

Method

Participants.   Thirty-two University of California undergraduates participated for a course requirement. All were native English speakers. None of them participated in the other experiments.

Materials and Design.   The same 12 scenarios used in Experiment 1 were used in this experiment. Each scenario was presented with a 7-point rating scale ranging from 1 (*not at all sympathetic*) to 7 (*very sympathetic*). The same design used in Experiment 1 was used in this experiment.

Procedure.   The same procedure used in Experiment 1 was also used in this experiment, except for the instruction given for using the sympathy rating scales. Participants were told to read each scenario and decide how sympathetic of the addressee they thought the comments were.

Results and Discussion

The mean sympathy and sarcasm ratings are presented in Table 14.3. Two-way ANOVAs on the sympathy ratings revealed an exact reversal in the pattern of results found in Experiment 1. Significant main effects of comment type, $F_1(1, 31) = 7.38$, $p < .01$; $F_2(1, 11) = 4.95$, $p < .05$, and problem cause, $F_1(1, 31) = 4.67$, $p < .05$; $F_2(1, 11) = 6.51$, $p < .05$, were found with no significant interaction. Ironic comments were universally rated as less sympathetic than literal comments.

Analysis of the sarcasm ratings revealed an identical pattern as Experiment 1—significant main effects of comment type, $F_1(1, 31) = 136.79$, $p < .001$; $F_2(1, 11) = 79.95$, $p < .001$, with no effect of the cause of the negative situation or interaction.

Again, the results with the sarcasm ratings are straightforward. Ironic criticism is more sarcastic than literal criticism regardless of the cause of the negative situation.

The results of the sympathy ratings corroborate those of Experiments 1 and 2. Under all circumstances, ironic criticism is less sympathetic than literal criticism. Even when the interlocutors are fellow victims of a negative situation that was caused by someone or something other than the addressee, an ironic remark expresses less sympathy than a literal one. Note again that this difference between ironic and literal criticism holds even though, overall, the comments express more sympathy when the situation was caused by some external factor.

EXPERIMENT 4

One final account for the failure to find support for the Tinge Hypothesis concerns the type of items and the instructions given in the previous experiments. The items were written to provide a variety of situations where a speaker could enhance or dilute her or his condemnation of another person. This was done purposefully to pose a strong test for the generalizability of any significant effects across the item population. This strategy, however, may have inadvertently introduced other factors that in turn might have affected the results. For instance, in some of the items, speakers

TABLE 14.3
Sympathy and Sarcasm Ratings for Literal and Ironic Criticisms: Experiment 3

Cause of Negative Situation	Sympathy Ratings: Comment Type		Sarcasm Ratings: Comment Type	
	Literal	Ironic	Literal	Ironic
Addressee				
M	3.34	2.70	2.32	5.49
SD	1.07	1.46	1.32	1.15
Not addressee				
M	3.89	3.26	2.41	5.67
SD	1.71	1.31	1.35	1.16

Note. The rating scale ranged from 1 (*not at all sympathetic*) to 7 (*very sympathetic*) and from 1 (*not at all sarcastic*) to 7 (*very sarcastic*).

might have appeared to not speak directly to the person they were criticizing. Items may also have seemed to indirectly refer to the topic of the criticism. For instance, the item

> Manuel was the star player on the soccer team, but he could not play in the city championship game because he partied too much and was extremely sick. When the team captain heard about this he said, "We'll win the championship for sure now."

may not seem to be spoken directly to the person being criticized. Manuel is ill and thus probably not present to hear the remark. The comment is also indirectly related to the topic of condemnation. The speaker ironically refers to an outcome of Manuel's act, losing the championship game, rather than the act itself, Manuel's self-induced illness.

It is possible that the instructions given to participants also affected the results. Participants were told that they could imagine the tone of voice of the speakers if that helped to rate the degree of condemnation of the remarks. This instruction may have overemphasized the ironic remarks, which often are spoken with unusual intonation, and thus increased the condemnation attributed to those remarks above that attributed to literal remarks.

To evaluate these other possible factors, a fourth experiment was conducted that explicitly manipulated three factors in addition to the comment type (ironic vs. literal). These factors were the addressee of the remark (either the person being criticized or a bystander), the directness of the remark (either a statement about the behavior being criticized or a statement about the outcome of that behavior), and the instructions for imagining the speakers' intonation (either to imagine the intonation or no mention being made of intonation).

Method

Participants. Thirty-two University of California undergraduates participated for a course requirement. All were native English speakers. None of them participated in the other experiments.

Materials and Design. The same 12 scenarios used in Experiment 1 were used in this experiment, along with four additional scenarios, for a total of 16. Only the versions from Experiment 1 where the addressee was at fault for the situation were used. The new scenarios also depicted situations where the addressee was at fault. Eight versions of each scenario were created. Half of them had the speaker talking directly to the person being criticized; the other half were spoken to a bystander. Half of the items were also direct references to the person's behavior; the other half were indirect references to the outcome of the person's behavior. Finally, half of the remarks made by the speaker were ironic, and half were literal. Example items are provided in the Appendix.

These three factors were crossed along with a factor of imagining the intonation of the speaker. Half of the participants were explicitly instructed to imagine the speaker's tone of voice, and half were not. This created a $2 \times 2 \times 2 \times 2$ mixed design. The intonation factor was necessarily between-participants, and the other factors were within-participants. Each scenario was presented with a 7-point rating scale ranging from 1 (*not at all condemning*) to 7 (*very condemning*).

Procedure. The same procedure used in Experiment 1 was also used in this experiment, except for the instruction given for imagining the tone of voice of the speakers. Half of the participants were explicitly told to imagine the speakers' tone of voice, and half were not. Also, no sarcasm ratings were collected because the previous experiments had already established that the literal items were not thought to be sarcastic and the ironic items were.

Results and Discussion

The mean condemnation ratings are presented in Tables 14.4, 14.5, and 14.6. ANOVAs on the condemnation ratings revealed significant main effects of comment type, $F_1(1, 30) = 4.79, p < .05; F_2(1, 15) = 13.21, p < .01$, and directness, $F_1(1, 30) = 11.96, p < .01; F_2(1, 15) = 4.63, p < .05$, with no significant interaction between the two factors. Ironic remarks were considered more condemning than literal remarks, and direct remarks were considered more condemning than indirect ones, but these effects were independent and did not influence one another. It thus appears that although the directness of a remark does play a role in the condemnation attributed to that remark and may have played a role in the previous experiments, it does not affect the finding that irony is more condemning than literal criticism. The claim of the Tinge Hypothesis that literal criticism should be more condemning remains incorrect.

TABLE 14.4

Condemnation Ratings for Literal and Ironic Criticisms As a Function of Directness: Experiment 4

| | Condemnation Ratings: Comment Type | |
Directness	Literal	Ironic
Direct		
M	4.98	5.74
SD	1.38	1.42
Indirect		
M	4.69	4.99
SD	1.25	1.53

Note. The rating scale ranged from 1 (*not at all condemning*) to 7 (very condemning).

TABLE 14.5

Condemnation Ratings for Literal and Ironic Criticisms as a Function of Addressee: Experiment 4

Addressee	Condemnation Ratings: Comment Type	
	Literal	Ironic
Target of criticism		
M	4.88	5.42
SD	1.26	1.46
Bystander		
M	4.79	5.31
SD	1.35	1.59

Note. The rating scale ranged from 1 *(not at all condemning)* to 7 *(very condemning)*.

TABLE 14.6

Condemnation Ratings for Literal and Ironic Criticisms as a Function of Intonational Cues: Experiment 4

Instruction Regarding Intonational Cues	Condemnation Ratings: Comment Type	
	Literal	Ironic
Imagine them		
M	4.67	5.65
SD	1.30	1.49
No mention		
M	4.99	5.07
SD	1.29	1.50

Note. The rating scale ranged from 1 *(not at all condemning)* to 7 *(very condemning)*.

No other factors were reliable.

The results of this experiment eliminate two possible alternative factors for the failure to find support for the Tinge Hypothesis. Speaking a condemning remark directly to the person being condemned does not affect the degree of condemnation attributed to the remark, relative to speaking to someone other than the person being condemned. Nor does instructing participants to imagine the tone of voice that speakers might use when uttering the remarks appear to influence the results compared to not instructing participants to imagine intonational cues.

The failure to find evidence for these two factors probably stems from the structure of the rating task and the nature of interpreting written verbal irony. The rating task did not ask how much condemnation would be interpreted by the person targeted by the criticism. Had that been the case, then a significant effect of the "addressee" factor would have been likely. It is not considered interesting that a person would not find a remark condemning if he or she had never heard the remark. The task was instead oriented to test how people understand what is meant by a speaker's nonliteral, ironic utterance and thus evaluated the degree of condemnation intended by the speaker of the remark. Here, it is perhaps interesting that equivalent levels of condemnation were perceived when a remark is made behind the target's back versus directly to the target. Apparently the intention by the speaker in both cases is to condemn. The only difference is to whom the speaker is expressing her or his condemnation.

Regarding the intonation factor, it is quite possible that people naturally infer or imagine intonational cues when interpreting verbal irony and thus do not require instructions to do so. This would explain the lack of a difference found with that factor.

GENERAL DISCUSSION

The results of the four experiments reveal that ironic criticism is used to enhance the amount of condemnation aimed at the addressee of the criticism. This finding does not support the Tinge Hypothesis (Dews & Winner, 1995) that ironic criticism is used to reduce the amount of condemnation expressed. Why were the current results different from other studies that have shown ironic criticism to be less condemning than literal criticism (Dews & Winner, 1995; Dews et al., 1995)?

First, consider the Dews and Winner (1995) study. Although there are minor methodological differences between Dews and Winner and the study presented here having to do with the measures used, these are probably not responsible for the difference in the results. For instance, Dews and Winner used a 5-point rating scale ranging from *strong criticism* to *strong praise,* whereas the study presented here used a 7-point rating scale ranging from *very condemning* to *not at all condemning.* Because only half of the Dews and Winner scale involves criticism, it is effectively a condemnation scale with a range of 2.5 units, compared to this study's condemnation scale with a range of 7 units. This would tend to make the Dews and Winner condemnation ratings more crowded and reduce the standard deviations, leading to very small differences being significant (particularly with a large group of participants; Dews and Winner used 80). Dews and Winner noted this as a characteristic of their findings. Although this accounts for the significance of the very small differences Dews and Winner found, it does not explain the direction of the results—literal criticism was found to be more condemning than ironic criticism.

This difference in the direction of the results between Dews and Winner (1995) and the study presented here probably results from the format in which the items were presented. Dews and Winner used an auditory recording of a voice speaking their items with systematic intonation, whereas the study presented here allowed participants to read the items. Dews and Winner thus fixed the intonation and other prosodic cues: "Literal insults were spoken in an angry intonation and ironic insults were spoken in a nasal, mocking, sarcastic intonation, in either a male or a female voice" (p. 9), whereas the study presented here allowed participants to infer these cues on their own: "Please feel free to imagine the tone of voice that the speaker might use if it helps you with your ratings" (instructions given to participants in Experiments 1, 2, and 3). Moreover, the failure to find a difference between conditions where participants were explicitly instructed to imagine intonation versus where no mention of intonation was made (Experiment 4) suggests that participants probably normally imagine intonational cues on their own when those cues are not available.

Intonation and other prosodic cues have traditionally been thought of as not being strictly necessary for the interpretation of verbal irony (Kreuz & Roberts, 1995)—people can interpret verbal irony without intonational cues (Gibbs & O'Brien, 1991). The cues may be helpful in the interpretation of verbal irony—they could make the ironic intonation more obvious and thus easier to process. They may also reduce the possibility for confusion—taking an ironic remark seriously, for example. But they are not necessary.

This study, in conjunction with Dews and Winner (1995), thus suggests that, although prosody is not necessary, it still greatly impacts the particular interpretation of an ironic utterance. When certain intonational cues are held constant, as was done by Dews and Winner, ironic criticism is consistently thought to dilute condemnation. When these cues are allowed to vary, as in the study presented here, both when participants are explicitly told to imagine the cues or when they are allowed to naturally imagine them on their own, irony is consistently thought to enhance criticism. The particulars of how the variance in the intonational cues affects the interpretation of verbal irony await further research. For instance, if the intonational cues used by Dews and Winner with ironic criticism were too rigid or did not appear strong enough to participants, the utterances may have been stilted or may not have expressed the ironic nature of the criticism and thus may have been rated as less condemning. Such research is certainly warranted because intonational cues may play a greater role in the interpretation of verbal irony than previously suspected.

As was the case with Dews and Winner (1995), the difference in the condemnation of ironic and literal criticism found in the study presented here also is most likely not due to differences in the ironic and literal items. Other than changes in wording required to make the items either literal or ironic—in many cases the use of opposites (e.g., *"I see you have a healthy concern for your lungs," "I see you don't have a healthy concern for your lungs"*)—the literal and ironic items were identical.

Dews and Winner (1995) also argued that their results speak to the debate surrounding how ironic and other nonliteral language is processed. In finding that ironic criticism was interpreted as less condemning than literal criticism, Dews and Winner supported the argument that the literal meaning of ironic utterances is processed along with the figurative meaning. Because this literal meaning is positive, the ironic remarks were interpreted as less condemning. This argument opposes earlier work (Gibbs, 1986a, 1986b) that the literal meaning of ironic utterances is not processed and instead that the intended ironic meaning is interpreted directly.

The study presented here in turn would then seem to support the earlier work by Gibbs on the processing of verbal irony. In finding that ironic criticism is more condemning than literal criticism, it appears that the literally positive meaning of the ironic criticism is not processed.

Dews and Winner (1995) acknowledged that their evidence against this earlier work is indirect, because the earlier work was based on reading time measures, whereas the Dews and Winner study used off-line ratings. I must make a similar claim. The study presented here was motivated by the phenomenon of opposing pragmatic functions performed by ironic criticism recently addressed by Dews and Winner (1995) and Dews et al. (1995). As these studies made use of ratings rather than reading times, the study presented here used a similar measure. Clearly, although the processing debate might be informed by measures of this kind, it should be addressed primarily with reading time measures.

Next, consider the Dews et al. (1995) study. This study used a 6-point condemnation rating scale ranging from *not at all critical* to *very critical* and also allowed speakers to read the items (Experiment 3). This study is thus much more similar to the current study methodologically. Despite these similarities, however, Dews et al. also found ironic criticism to be less condemning than literal criticism, but only when the topic of the speaker's remarks was poor performance on the addressee's behalf that did not affect the speaker. When the topic was some offensive behavior on the part of the addressee that did affect the speaker, or a negative situation in general that affected the speaker, no significant difference was found.

It thus appears that, in addition to intonational cues, another important factor in whether ironic criticism enhances or dilutes condemnation is the involvement of the speaker. If the topic of the criticism is something that affects the speaker, it appears that in lieu of other factors, ironic criticism is more likely to enhance than dilute criticism.

Although one may consider this study as evidence that ironic criticism is almost exclusively more condemning or critical than literal criticism, this is not the conclusion I wish to advocate. There are cases where it appears likely that ironic criticism can lighten up a situation and deliver a criticism less negatively than literal criticism, as Dews and Winner (1995) and Dews et al. (1995) demonstrated, and perhaps future research should continue to identify these instances. Indeed, one can imagine that softening or diluting condemnation would make the criticism more pragmatically successful. A person is probably more likely to accept and act on an appropriate level of criticism if the criticism is delivered in as inoffensive a means as possible. The point I wish to make is that ironic criticism is also not inherently less condemning than literal criticism, as the Tinge Hypothesis claims. In many instances, ironic criticism is used precisely because it is particularly negative and critical.

ACKNOWLEDGMENTS

Support for this work was provided by postdoctoral positions awarded to Herbert L. Colston by the University of California, Santa Cruz, and Interval Research Corporation. I thank Julie Holloway for her assistance in testing participants.

REFERENCES

Brown, P., & Levinson, S. C. (1987). *Politeness: Some universals in language usage.* New York: Cambridge University Press.

Brownell, H. H., Jacobs, J. R., Gardner, H., & Gianoulis, D. (1990). *Conditions for sarcasm.* Unpublished manuscript, Boston College, Department of Psychology, Chestnut Hill, MA.

Clark, H. H. (1973). Language-as-a-fixed-effect-fallacy: A critique of language statistics in psychological research. *Journal of Verbal Learning and Verbal Behavior, 12,* 335–359.

Clark, H. H., & Gerrig, R. J. (1984). On the pretense theory of irony. *Journal of Experimental Psychology: General, 113,* 121–126.

Colston, H. L. (1996). *Understanding non-echoic verbal irony.* Manuscript in preparation.

Colston, H. L. (1997). I've never seen anything like it: Overstatement, understatement and irony. *Metaphor and Symbol, 12*(1), 43–58.

Colston, H. L., & Keller, S. B. (1996). *You'll never believe this: Irony and hyperbole in expressing surprise.* Manuscript submitted for publication.

Cutler, A. (1974). On meaning what you say without saying what you mean. In *Papers from the Tenth Regional Meeting, Chicago Linguistic Society* (pp. 117–127). Chicago: Chicago Linguistic Society.

Demorest, A., Silberstein, L., Gardner, H., & Winner, E. (1983). Telling it as it isn't: Children's understanding of figurative language. *British Journal of Developmental Psychology, 1,* 121–134.

Dews, S., Kaplan, J., & Winner, E. (1995). Why not say it directly? The social functions of irony. *Discourse Processes, 19,* 347–367.

Dews, S., & Winner, E. (1995). Muting the meaning: A social function of irony. *Metaphor and Symbolic Activity, 10,* 3–19.

Fowler, H. (1965). *A dictionary of modern English usage* (2nd ed.). Oxford, England: Oxford University Press.

Gibbs, R. W. (1986a). Comprehension and memory for nonliteral utterances: The problem of sarcastic indirect requests. *Acta Psychologica, 62,* 41–57.

Gibbs, R. W. (1986b). On the psycholinguistics of sarcasm. *Journal of Experimental Psychology: General, 115,* 3–15.

Gibbs, R. W., & O'Brien, J. (1991). Psychological aspects of irony understanding. *Journal of Pragmatics, 16,* 523–530.

Grice, H. P. (1975). *Logic and conversation.* Cambridge, MA: Harvard University Press.

Grice, H. P. (1978). Further notes on logic and conversation. In P. Cole (Ed.), *Syntax and semantics: Vol. 9. Pragmatics* (pp. 113–128). New York: Academic.

Kreuz, R. J., & Glucksberg, S. (1989). How to be sarcastic: The echoic reminder theory of verbal irony. *Journal of Experimental Psychology: General, 118,* 374–386.

Kreuz, R. J., Long, D., & Church, M. (1991). On being ironic: Pragmatic and mnemonic implications. *Metaphor and Symbolic Activity, 10,* 21–31.

Kreuz, R. J., & Roberts, R. M. (1995). Two cues for verbal irony: Hyperbole and the ironic tone of voice. *Metaphor and Symbolic Activity, 6,* 149–162.

Kumon-Nakamura, S., Glucksberg, S., & Brown, M. (1995). How about another piece of pie: The allusional pretense theory of discourse irony. *Journal of Experimental Psychology: General, 124,* 3–21.

Muecke, D. C. (1980). *The compass of irony.* London: Methuen.

Perret, D. (1976). *On irony* (Pragmatics Microfiche 1.7:D3). University of Cambridge, Department of Linguistics.

Roberts, R. M., & Kreuz, R. J. (1994). Why do people use figurative language? *Psychological Science, 5,* 159–163.

Sperber, D., & Wilson, D. (1981). Irony and the use–mention distinction. In P. Cole (Ed.), *Radical pragmatics* (pp. 295–318). New York: Academic.

Sperber, D., & Wilson, D. (1986). *Relevance: Communication and cognition.* Cambridge, MA: Harvard University Press.

Webster's ninth new collegiate dictionary. (1988). Springfield, MA: Merriam.

Winner, E. (1988). *The point of words: Children's understanding of metaphor and irony.* Cambridge, MA: Harvard University Press.

APPENDIX

Example Items Used in the Experiments

Example Items Used in Experiments 1 and 3

Addressee's Fault, Literal Comment

Mary was about to unlock the door so her and her boyfriend Carlos could get in from the cold. When she looked in her purse, she discovered that she had left her keys at the restaurant. Carlos said, "We'll be freezing cold soon."

Addressee's Fault, Ironic Comment

Mary was about to unlock the door so her and her boyfriend Carlos could get in from the cold. When she looked in her purse, she discovered that she had left her keys at the restaurant. Carlos said, "We'll be nice and warm soon."

Not Addressee's Fault, Literal Comment

Mary was about to unlock the door so her and her boyfriend Carlos could get in from the cold. When she looked in her purse, she discovered that her sister had taken her keys. Carlos said, "We'll be freezing cold soon."

Not Addressee's Fault, Ironic Comment

Mary was about to unlock the door so her and her boyfriend Carlos could get in from the cold. When she looked in her purse, she discovered that her sister had taken her keys. Carlos said, "We'll be nice and warm soon."

Example Items Used in Experiment 2

Speaker Doesn't Do Negative Behavior, Literal Comment

Maria did not approve of going out and drinking. When she saw a bunch of her friends drinking and having a good time, Maria said, "I see none of you are health conscious."

Speaker Doesn't Do Negative Behavior, Ironic Comment

Maria did not approve of going out and drinking. When she saw a bunch of her friends drinking and having a good time, Maria said, "I see all of you are health conscious."

Speaker Does Negative Behavior, Literal Comment

Maria loved going out and drinking. When she saw a bunch of her friends drinking and having a good time, Maria said, "I see none of you are health conscious."

Speaker Does Negative Behavior, Ironic Comment
Maria loved going out and drinking. When she saw a bunch of her friends drinking and having a good time, Maria said, "I see all of you are health conscious."

Example Items Used in Experiment 4

Ironic, Direct Remark Spoken to Addressee
Mark was supposed to drive five people to go camping, but when they all got in the car it wouldn't start because Mark didn't buy gas when he used the car last. One of the campers in the car said out loud, "Nice move."

Ironic, Direct Remark Spoken to Bystander
Mark was supposed to drive five people to go camping, but when they all got in the car it wouldn't start because Mark didn't buy gas when he used the car last. One of the campers in the car whispered privately to another, "Nice move."

Ironic, Indirect Remark Spoken to Addressee
Mark was supposed to drive five people to go camping, but when they all got in the car it wouldn't start because Mark didn't buy gas when he used the car last. One of the campers in the car said out loud, "People can sure be reliable."

Ironic, Indirect Remark Spoken to Bystander
Mark was supposed to drive five people to go camping, but when they all got in the car it wouldn't start because Mark didn't buy gas when he used the car last. One of the campers in the car whispered privately to another, "People can sure be reliable."

Literal, Direct Remark Spoken to Addressee
Mark was supposed to drive five people to go camping, but when they all got in the car it wouldn't start because Mark didn't buy gas when he used the car last. One of the campers in the car said out loud, "Bad move."

Literal, Direct Remark Spoken to Bystander
Mark was supposed to drive five people to go camping, but when they all got in the car it wouldn't start because Mark didn't buy gas when he used the car last. One of the campers in the car whispered privately to another, "Bad move."

Literal, Indirect Remark Spoken to Addressee
Mark was supposed to drive five people to go camping, but when they all got in the car it wouldn't start because Mark didn't buy gas when he used the car last. One of the campers in the car said out loud, "People can sure be unreliable."

Literal, Indirect Remark Spoken to Bystander
Mark was supposed to drive five people to go camping, but when they all got in the car it wouldn't start because Mark didn't buy gas when he used the car last. One of the campers in the car whispered privately to another, "People can sure be unreliable."

CHAPTER 15

Irony in Talk Among Friends

Raymond W. Gibbs, Jr.
University of California, Santa Cruz

This article reports the findings of a single study examining irony in talk among friends. Sixty-two 10-min conversations between college students and their friends were recorded and analyzed. Five main types of irony were found: jocularity, sarcasm, hyperbole, rhetorical questions, and understatements. These different forms of ironic language were part of 8% of all conversational turns. Analysis of these utterances revealed varying linguistic and social patterns, and suggested several constraints on how and why people achieve ironic meaning. The implications of this conclusion for psychological theories of irony are discussed.

The 19th-century philosopher Soren Kierkegaard (1965) once wrote the following: "As philosophers claim that no true philosophy is possible without doubt, by the same token, one may claim that no authentic human life is possible without irony" (p. 378). Kierkegaard's comment holds true as much now as it did over 100 years ago, especially in this postmodern age where irony is often seen as the master trope, replacing metaphor as the king of all figurative language. A brief look at both everyday speech and various written texts illustrates the prominence of different forms of irony in the ways people talk about themselves, their addressees, and the world around them.

Consider the following exchange between two college students. This conversation occurred in their apartment and focused on some visitors who were staying with them at the invitation of another roommate:

Anne:	By the way, were our wonderful guests still here when you came out and ate lunch?
Dana:	I had a sandwich and ...
Anne:	Isn't it so nice to have guests here?
Dana:	Totally!

This chapter was previously published as "Irony in talk among friends" (R. W. Gibbs) in *Metaphor and Symbol, 15,* 5–27. Copyright © [2000] by Lawrence Erlbaum Associates. Reprinted with permission.

Anne: I just love it, you know, our housemates. They bring in the most
             wonderful guests in the world and they can totally relate to us.
Dana: Yes, they do.
Anne: (laughs) Like I would just love to have them here more often
             (laughs) so I can cook for them, I can prepare (laughs) …
Dana: To make them feel welcome?
Anne: Yeah, isn't this great, Dana? Like today I was feeling all de-
             pressed and I came out and I saw the guests and they totally
             lightened up my mood. I was like the happiest person on earth.
Dana: Uh huh.
Anne: I just welcome them so much, you know, ask them if they want
             anything to drink or eat (laughs).

This conversation reveals how irony may be one of our most powerful weapons in everyday speech. Anne and Dana each employ different forms of ironic language (e.g., sarcasm, jocularity, rhetorical questions, hyperbole) to indirectly convey their mutual displeasure about the people staying as guests in their apartment. Much of the irony here is humorous, despite its implied criticism of the visitors (and the roommate who invited them). Moreover, none of these speakers' ironic meanings can be easily derived by simply assuming the opposite of what they literally said.

In recent years, psychologists, linguists, and philosophers have proposed various theories to explain how people use and understand irony. These theories focus on widely different cognitive, linguistic, and social aspects of ironic language use, even though each theory claims to provide a single umbrella for capturing the essence of irony. For example, some theorists maintain that irony is a type of echoic mention, in which speakers echo, or repeat, a previously stated utterance or belief, which in context is recognized as conveying ironic meaning (Sperber & Wilson, 1995; Wilson & Sperber, 1992). By contrast, pretense, not echoic mention, is seen as the key to irony by other researchers (Clark, 1996; Clark & Gerrig, 1984). Under this view, speakers of irony pretend to be some other person or persona and pretend also to be speaking, in some cases, to some person other than the listener. Other researchers argue that ironic utterances mostly accomplish their communicative intent by reminding listeners of some antecedent event, even if not all such reminders are echoic or refer to actual or implied utterances (Kreuz & Glucksberg, 1989). Many ironic remarks merely remind listeners of the attitudes and expectations that they might share with speakers. The allusional pretense theory combines features of both the echoic mention and pretense view by proposing that ironic utterances convey pragmatic meaning by alluding to failed expectations, which is usually achieved by violating the maxim that speakers should be sincere in what they say (Kumon-Nakamura, Glucksberg, & Brown, 1995). Some scholars have alternatively proposed that irony is special because it mutes the usually negative meaning communicated by an ironic statement (Dews, Kaplan, & Winner, 1995) and appears less rude, especially when expressing trivial criticism (Jorgensen, 1996), although other research suggests that irony can be more critical in many situations than literal statements (Colston, 1997b). Finally, various scholars suggest that different forms of irony often have different communicative functions (Kreuz, Long, & Church, 1991; Lee & Katz, 1998; Roberts & Kreuz, 1994) and evoke different emotional responses in listeners (Leggitt & Gibbs, in press).

These competing ideas about irony may not be mutually exclusive, as each proposal may contribute to a comprehensive theory of ironic language use. Sociolinguistic studies, in fact, suggest that ironic talk can serve multiple communicative purposes, each requiring different psychological mechanisms. For instance, some forms of irony are affiliative, whereas others are sources of estrangement between individuals (Coer, 1959; Seckman & Couch, 1989). Irony is routinely used in the ongoing flow of conversation between group members to affirm their solidarity by directing comments at individuals who are not group members and not deemed worthy of group membership. Some forms of irony, like sarcasm, may promote group solidarity, indicate the boundaries of acceptable behavior, and "reign in" normative transgressions (Ducharme, 1994). Sarcasm, in particular, is often used to vent frustration when an individual finds some situation or object offensive or sees a group's normative standards violated. A good illustration of this venting is seen in the aforementioned conversation between the two roommates. Sarcastic comments may also be self-directed and thus affirm the speaker's allegiance to the group and the prescribed behavioral norms.

Most studies of irony generally assume that sarcasm is the most typical instance of ironic discourse. The psycholinguistic literature has traditionally studied irony as cases where speakers utter sarcastic comments with negative, critical intent. But a good deal of ironic language enables speakers to bond together through their disparagement of some other person (e.g., the conversation between Anne and Dana) or a speaker's mockful teasing of the addressee. Consider the following conversation between a group of college students, which took place outside a campus coffee shop:

Kayla:	How are you doing?
Cherie:	Um … good. We're going to study Latin but the coffee shop is just packed.
David:	It's rockin'.
Sarah:	… study Latin … Latin language?
Kayla:	It's wet out here.
Sarah:	You guys are taking Latin? (laughs).
Cherie:	Yeah … (laughs).
Kayla:	(whiny tone of voice) But that's a dead language (everyone laughs). I'm just kidding. Is that not what everyone tells you?
Cherie:	It's true and we don't really know how to pronounce everything.
David:	It's really hard.
Cherie:	Yeah, but it's only a year-long program.
David:	So, you're fluent in Latin after a year (everyone laughs).
Kayla:	Right … right.

David:	It's true (everyone laughs).
Sarah:	You read all those ancient texts, that's cool (laughs).
Cherie:	Why you guys dissin' on Latin?
David:	(mocking tone) What, wo-ah, you're dissin' my Latin.
Kayla:	Actually, Latin helps because, doesn't it, it helps with etymology, it helps with words, breaking words down.
David:	Totally … yeah, yeah, she got it … yeah.
Cherie:	Structure, parts of speech, yeah.
David:	I'm a changed person since the last couple of weeks of Latin.

Sarcastic exchanges such as seen here have been called "humorous aggression," "humorous derision," "banter," "jocularity" (Coser, 1959; Pogrebin & Poole, 1989; Seckman & Couch, 1989; Slugoski & Turnbull, 1988), or "teasing" (Drew, 1987). Empirical studies show that teasing frequently occurs in talk between parents and children (Dunn & Brown, 1994; Reddy, 1991), friends (Drew, 1987; Keltner, Young, Heerey, Oeming, & Monach, 1998; Mooney, Cresser, & Blatchford, 1991), romantic partners (Baxter, 1992), and even psychotherapists and clients (Ruvelson, 1988). Teasing and jocularity offer gentler, indirect ways of pointing out people's deviation from social standards and is central to socialization practices between parents and children, friends, and romantic partners. Teasing also allows individuals to enhance their bonds through the indirect expression of affection, shared laughter, and the messages that the act of teasing communicates—namely, that the individuals are close enough to tease without harming the relationship (Baxter, 1992). Although teasing can have a dark side, in which people begin to outright bully one another, teasing generally allows individuals to learn about, negotiate, and assume social identities.

This brief discussion about the diverse ways that irony can be used in conversation poses an important challenge for cognitive science theories of irony. Is it necessarily the case that a single theory will account for the multiple forms and functions of irony in ordinary speech? One of the difficulties in forming hypotheses about ironic language understanding is the continued failure to recognize the diversity of ways that irony is used in conversation. This article reports the findings of an exploratory study on irony in talk among friends. There are numerous experimental studies on different aspects of irony comprehension (see Gibbs, 1994; Katz, 1996a, for reviews), and many theories of ironic language use (Gibbs, 1994). Yet there are few systematic, quantitative investigations of the ways irony is used in ordinary conversation. My goal was to examine the ways people use ironic language and to show how this work constrains contemporary theoretical accounts of irony in cognitive science.

I collected and analyzed, with the assistance of many others, sixty-two 5- to 10-min conversations between college students and their friends in natural environments. My first interest was to discover how often students use irony when talking with one another. The only quantitative analysis of irony in speech, which focused on a single, extended conversation among adults in their 20s and 30s, revealed that irony is used in 7% of all conversational turns (Tannen, 1984). Although my analysis is limited to young adults speaking in familiar, often intimate, circumstances, my initial expectation was that irony would not be a rare occurrence and should be found in almost every conversation studied.

I did not analyze the nonironic utterances in the students' conversations. In principle, this would have been good to do, especially to compare people's use and reactions to irony against nonironic speech. But it does not make much sense to lump together all the nonironic utterances because there are many types of language subsumed here, including metaphor, metonymy, various idioms, and a wide range of utterances that might be referred to as "literal." Although most psycholinguistic studies compare people's interpretation of ironic and literal utterances in the same contexts, the reality of ordinary conversations makes these kinds of comparisons difficult to systematically investigate.

A second aim was to examine the different forms of irony used in these conversations. As noted earlier, most psycholinguistic studies assume that sarcastic remarks (e.g., "You're a fine friend," *meaning* "You're a bad friend") are the norm in ironic discourse. Yet my expectations were, following the empirical studies from psychology and sociolinguistics, that the most frequent form of irony would be where students spoke in a jocular, mocking, or teasing manner. Sarcasm with the intent to severely criticize something or somebody should be less frequent than jocularity, even in these conversations where speakers should feel fairly free to criticize others. At the same time, other forms of irony should also occur with some frequency, such as hyperbole, rhetorical questions, and understatement. Although a few studies have examined these related forms of irony (Colston, 1997a; Colston & Keller, 1998; Kreuz, 1996; Kreuz & Roberts, 1995), no study has investigated how frequently each type of irony is found in ordinary conversation (see Kreuz, Roberts, Johnson, & Bertus, 1996, for one analysis of some aspects of irony in written discourse). My general interest here was to discover patterns of ironic language use in conveying different propositional and affective meaning.

A third concern was to discover how frequently men and women use different forms of irony. For example, are men more sarcastic in their speech than women? Some research shows that men tend to be more aggressive than women in their style of speaking (Harris & Knight-Bohnhoff, 1996), but does this extend to irony? Are women more playful when speaking and tease more than men do? Finally, do men and women address their various ironic comments to each other differentially?

My fourth interest concerned the topics of irony. Do people speak ironically more about specific topics, more about people who are absent as opposed to present, more about things previously said in the conversation, and do speakers ever direct ironic comments at themselves? Several scholars have commented that irony, as opposed to metaphor, is especially useful for indirectly commenting on human topics (Katz, 1996b). In fact, the presence of an identifiable person who serves as the victim of irony, sarcasm, or both is seen as one important heuristic in the interpretation of irony (Katz, 1996b; Kreuz & Glucksberg, 1989). The data presented in this article should provide some additional information on the idea that irony mostly focuses on human topics.

The next attributes of irony analyzed were whether speakers' remarks were echoic, involved pretense, and employed specific intonational cues. There are several debates, as suggested earlier, over whether irony is best characterized as instances of echoic mention or pretense. I have previously argued that neither view necessarily captures all aspects of irony (Gibbs, 1994), and this study provides a test of that idea. Nonetheless, my expectation was that a significant portion of speakers' utterances would be based on pretense, and echoic mention to a lesser extent. I was especially interested to see whether this pattern for pretense and echoic mention varied across different forms of irony. Echoic mention may be more prevalent in jocularity than in sarcasm because people often repeat what others say when teasing them. Related to this concern was the analysis of the particular tone of voice speakers used when uttering their different ironic comments. There is debate over whether ironic language necessarily includes a special tone of voice (e.g., nasalization, slow speaking rate, exaggerated stress on certain words), with some scholars arguing that this prosodic cue is essential to inferring what speakers mean (Cutler, 1974; Grice, 1989), and others suggesting that these properties are not obligatory (Gibbs, 1986a, 1986b, 1994; Kreuz, 1996; Kreuz & Roberts, 1995). The data collected here allowed me to distinguish between these competing claims.

To what extent were the students' ironic comments perceived as mocking, critical, or humorous? Once again, the answer to this question depends on the type of ironic statement produced. As illustrated in the two conversations described earlier, much of students' irony is nonserious and jocular (e.g., the conversation about studying Latin). Yet even with humorous ironic remarks (e.g., the exchange about the visitors), there is an undertone of negativity and criticism toward the topic (or topics; e.g., the guests and the roommate who invited them). In some cases, then, ironic comments can be both humorous and negative, precisely because people find amusement in disliked targets being disparaged (Graesser, Long, & Mio, 1989). On other occasions, the implied criticism is more lighthearted or teasing and works to bring speakers and listeners closer together. I evaluated each utterance as to whether it was viewed as negative, mocking, and/or humorous. Although some theorists claim that irony works to mute criticism, in some cases, especially for sarcasm, the speakers' comments may be seen as very negative. Not surprisingly, how critical or humorous an utterance is depends on whether it was jocular, sarcastic, a rhetorical question, a hyperbole, or an understatement.

The final analysis concerned addressees' responses to irony. My first interest here was to examine whether addressees gave any behavioral indication that they understood the speakers' ironic messages. My expectation was that listeners would respond to what speakers say by laughing, especially when they hear jocularity, or, most notably, they may say something ironic in return. I was specifically interested to determine to what extent students would engage in ironic banter in which each person jabs one another with an ironic or teasing remark, perhaps in the attempt to "top" one another in playful verbal battle. In this way, speaker and listener actively collaborate to create ironic scenes in which each participant plays a specific role. As the conversations described earlier clearly indicate, addressees will respond to more humorous ironic comments by speaking ironically themselves. Students may respond ironically more so when these statements are viewed as jocular or teasing than when the comments are sarcastic and more negative.

METHOD

Participants

The participants were 149 undergraduate students and their friends from the University of California, Santa Cruz community. The youngest was 19 and the oldest was 38. Most of the participants were in their early 20s. The sex of these participants is described in detail later.

Material

Sixty-two 10-min conversations were tape-recorded by 62 students in an undergraduate class on interpersonal communication at the University of California, Santa Cruz. These conversations took place in a variety of places, including student dormitories, apartments, houses, and various places nearby these locations. Several conversations occurred in more public settings, such as restaurants, coffee shops, and the university library.

Students from the class were simply asked to tape-record a single conversation that occurred between their friends or roommates. The tape recorder was clearly visible, and all participants in the conversations were aware that the recordings were intended for analysis as part of a class project. However, no mention was made of the interest in irony. Although the students doing the tape-recording participated in some of the conversations collected and analyzed, they did not speak sarcastically nor did they attempt to elicit irony, sarcasm, or both in any way. It is difficult to know to what extent the presence of the tape recorder might have influenced the participants' speech. Many sociolinguists have argued and observed that the data collected from situations where participants knew that they were being tape-recorded accurately reflect participants' ordinary social relationships and speech styles (Tannen, 1984). Conversational participants in this study appeared, according to the students in the class doing the tape recording, to soon forget about the presence of the tape recorder as they were swept up into the flow of conversation.

Transcription of the Tapes

After the 62 conversations were collected, each student from the class transcribed his or her tape according to fairly standard sociolinguistic conventions, which included attention to changes of speaker, back-channel responses, parenthetical remarks, interruptions, hesitations, false starts, and basic intonational features (Tannen, 1984). I oversaw the 62 students as they worked on their transcriptions, but it is clear that there was a good deal of variance in how accurately students completed their transcriptions. Some of this variability was due to differences in the quality of the tape record-ings. At the very least, though, the 62 transcripts reflected who said what and how addressees and overhearers may have verbally reacted in turn.

Classification of the Utterances

The practical problem of distinguishing between ironic and nonironic language, and between different forms of irony (e.g., sarcasm, jocularity, hyperbole, etc.), is very difficult to solve. As Tannen (1984) noted in her own analysis of irony in a din-ner conversation, "Clearly, there is some subjectivity involved in classifying utter-ances as ironic or not ironic" (p. 130). For this study, it was immediately clear that speakers used a variety of ironic forms in talking with their friends. Thus, people did not just speak sarcastically (as is too often assumed in psycholinguistic studies to be the ideal form of irony). In fact, people were more likely at first glance to use jocularity with humorous intent than to use sarcasm with more hostile intent.

Examination of the corpus suggested that there were, at least, five main forms of irony: (a) jocularity, where speakers teased one another in humorous ways; (b) sar-casm, where speakers spoke positively to convey a more negative intent; (c) rhetori-cal questions, where speakers literally asked a question that implied either a humorous or critical assertion; (d) hyperbole, where speakers expressed their nonliteral meaning by exaggerating the reality of the situation; and (e) understate-ment, where speakers conveyed their ironic messages by stating far less than was obviously the case. Each form of irony minimally reflected the idea of a speaker, providing some contrast between expectation and reality (Gibbs, 1994).

The first conversation mentioned earlier between Anne and Dana illustrates three of the five types of irony. Many of Anne's statements are clearly sarcastic, as when she says in reference to the visitors that "I would just love to have them here more often" and "they totally lightened up my mood." Anne's rhetorical question "Isn't it so nice to have guests here?" expresses her negative attitude toward the guests. Her comment, "They bring in the most wonderful guests in the world and they can totally relate to us," is a nice example of hyperbole, as is the following: "I was like the happiest person on earth."

The second conversation provides several examples of jocularity, such as when David in a mocking tone echoes with ironic intent Cherie's previous comment by saying, "What, wo-ah, you're dissin' my Latin." Understatement is seen in other con-versations, as when one student ironically commented, "James was just a bit late with his rent," when, in fact, James was quite tardy in paying his rent that month.

The classification of the individual utterances in the 62 conversations took place in three steps. First, each student who tape-recorded and transcribed a conversation analyzed the utterances in their transcription to find ironic utterances. They then classified each ironic utterance as reflecting one of the five types of irony men-tioned earlier. Following this, each student determined for each utterance the sex of the speaker, who the addressee was, the location in which the utterance was made, the topic of the utterance, whether the utterance was critical of someone or something, whether the utterance echoed some previously mentioned statement or belief, whether the utterance involved pretense, whether the utterance mocked someone or something, whether the utterance was viewed by someone in the conversation as humorous, whether the utterance was spoken in a special tone of voice, and how the addressee responded to the ironic utterance.

In the second part of the coding process, once the students made their classifications for their own transcript, each student traded his or her transcript with another student, and they both examined the classifications together. Cases where disagreements could not be resolved were marked. At this point in the process, 314 individual utterances across the 62 conversations were identified as jocular, sarcastic, rhetorical questions, hyperbole, or understatement.

The third step involved me going over all the transcripts and utterances and providing my own independent analysis. Because of my disagreement over the specific classification of 25 utterances, including whether or not these were at all ironic, the final corpus of ironic expressions contained 289 utterances. This corpus of 289 instances of irony probably underestimates the true level of ironic speech in these conversations given that three judges (two students and myself) had to agree on whether an individual utterance was ironic or not, as well as belonging to a particular category of irony, and classified along the various dimensions noted earlier.

There was one additional analysis that I did myself. After examining the jocular and sarcastic utterances, I determined the extent to which each one stated something positive to convey a negative ironic meaning (e.g., "You're a fine friend," *meaning* "You are a bad friend"), as opposed to the opposite (e.g., "You're a bad friend," *meaning* "You are a good friend").

RESULTS AND DISCUSSION

On average, there were 4.7 instances of irony per taped conversation, ranging from a low of 1 ironic remark in one conversation up to a high of 20 ironic comments in another. A count of the different conversational turns in the 62 conversations roughly shows that about 8% of the turns were ironic. This was about the same as found in Tannen's (1984) analysis of a conversation among adult friends (in their 20s and 30s).

Analysis of the 289 utterances revealed 145 cases of jocularity (50%), 80 cases of sarcasm (28%), 34 instances of hyperbole (12%), 24 rhetorical questions (8%), and 6 cases of understatement (2%). Table 15.1 presents the mean proportions for each question for each type of irony. I repeat many aspects of these data in my discussion later, but include the results in tabular form to make for easy cross-category comparisons. The analyses of the five types of irony along several dimensions are presented later.

TABLE 15.1

Mean Proportion for Each Type of Analysis for Each Type of Irony

	Jocularity	Sarcasm	Hyperbole	Rhetorical Question	Understatement
Frequency	.50	.28	.12	.08	.02
Speaker	—	—	—	—	—
Male	.48	.64	.41	.45	.83
Female	.52	.36	.59	.54	.17
Addressee	—	—	—	—	—
Male	.42	.45	.38	.42	.67
Female	.58	.51	.47	.36	.33
Male and female	.00	.04	.15	.25	.00
Topic	—	—	—	—	—
Situation	.32	.31	.38	.44	.33
Past event	.06	.14	.04	.06	.50
Addressee	.27	.21	.15	.29	.00
Speaker	.09	.08	.04	.08	.00
Other person	.14	.13	.21	.17	.17
Other comment	.09	.11	.15	.08	.00
Overhearer	.03	.03	.00	.00	.00
Echo	.50	.26	.29	.25	.00
Pretense	.58	.63	.62	.42	.50
Voice tone	.67	.76	.47	.67	.50
Negative	.47	.75	.59	.52	.10
Critical	.28	.54	.24	.25	.00
Mocking	.81	.90	.76	.75	.50
Self-mock	.08	.00	.00	.08	.00
Humorous	.84	.74	.74	.79	.33
Addressee response	—	—	—	—	—
Ironic	.32	.33	.21	.21	.33
Literal	.22	.23	.38	.21	.33
Laughter only	.12	.13	.21	.25	.17
Missed sarcasm	.05	.04	.00	.09	.17
Changed topic	.29	.29	.21	.33	.00

Jocularity

Speakers/Addressees. Forty-eight percent of the speakers of jocularity were men, and 52% were women. Forty-two percent of the addressees were men, whereas 58% were women. Fifty-eight of the conversations containing jocularity also included overhearers. Overall, these data revealed no specific differences in the prominence of jocularity between men and women.

Topics. Thirty-two percent of the jocularity concerned something in this physical situation of the speakers and listeners (e.g., events occurring when the participants were making dinner together). Twenty-seven percent of the jocularity concerned something specific about the addressees (i.e., something they had done, were doing, or some aspect of their personality). Fourteen percent concerned some person(s) not present in the conversation. Nine percent of these remarks related to the speaker himself or herself. Nine percent of these remarks concerned some previous utterance in the conversation. Six percent referred to some past event (e.g., something that happened to the speaker or listeners before the conversation occurred). Finally, only 3% of the jocularity concerned an overhearer (e.g., a conversational participant who was not the addressee).

These data provide strong support to the idea that irony primarily refers to human events, concerns, or both. Each of the aforementioned categories reflects different aspects of individual people (e.g., their personalities or specific characteristics) or people's involvement with particular objects or environments. Very few of the jocular comments referred to nonhuman events, and when they did, such as when a speaker sarcastically said, "This is a terrible salad," the utterances were indirectly intended as comments about other relevant people (e.g., the person who made the salad).

Echo, pretense, and tone of voice. Fifty percent of these remarks echoed a previous utterance, whereas 58% involved the speaker adopting pretense. Twenty-eight percent of the jocular remarks involved both echoic mention and pretense, whereas 21% involved neither. These data immediately reveal that all instances of irony are not characterized by echoic mention or pretense, contrary to several psychological/linguistic proposals about irony. Sixty-seven percent of the jocularity was uttered in what judges viewed were special tones of voice. Most of these instances were delivered with heavy stress on particular words, or exaggerated rhythm. About half of the jocularity with special intonation actually mimicked the addressee or some other person (real or imagined). Although it is clear that speakers can communicate their jocular statements without using any unusual intonation, a significant number of these achieved their effects in part due to these varying voice patterns.

Mockery, Criticism, and Humor. Eighty-one percent of the remarks were judged as mocking some person, object, or event. Of these instances of mockery,

8% were self-directed (e.g., said by the speaker about the speaker). At the same time, only 28% of these utterances were seen as being critical. Twenty-seven of the jocular remarks were seen as both mocking and critical. Finally, 84% of these utterances were viewed as humorous by at least one of the conversational participants (more on this later). The data show that jocularity very frequently mocks some other person, object, or event in a playful manner, even if this mockery is not necessarily viewed in a negative or critical light. This suggests one way in which the teasing associated with jocularity differs from the teasing done when one person bullies another, often with negative, critical import.

Addressee Responses.   Thirty-two percent of the time, addressees responded to jocularity by saying something ironic in return. The fact that almost one third of all responses (including nonverbal ones) to jocularity were ironic in some form illustrates the playful nature of these conversations between friends. The students often created ironic routines or scenes and eagerly engaged as actors in these temporary roles. This finding also demonstrates the collaborative nature of irony, at least to the extent that speakers and addressees tacitly coordinate to stage ironic scenes. Twenty-two percent of the responses to jocularity were literal remarks that clearly indicated some understanding of the first speaker's ironic intent. Twelve percent of the responses were simple laughter without any other linguistic utterance. This, too, reflects something of addressees' understanding of original speakers' playful, ironic intentions when using jocularity. Five percent of the responses indicated that the addressee clearly missed the speaker's ironic intent (e.g., when the addressee responded as if the speaker were serious). Although it is difficult to know what a reasonable baseline for understanding any utterance may be, a misunderstanding rate of 5% suggests that using irony, even playfully, has its risks. However, there may be occasions when speakers explicitly used irony to communicate some attitude or idea without feeling responsible for what is expressed if an addressee complains about what was stated. Finally, 29% of the time, addressees ignored the jocularity or changed the subject right away.

Asymmetry.   My own analysis of the jocular utterances showed that only 9% presented a positive statement to indirectly convey a negative message (e.g., "So you're fluent in Latin after a year"), whereas 28% presented negative statements to convey positive messages (e.g., "Dumb bitch!" said to someone who just solved a difficult problem, or "I'm not all that good in the sack, anyways, so you're not missing out on much" when the speaker was known to be a good lover). This difference was statistically significant, $z = 2.0, p < .05$. Sixty-two percent of the jocular utterances were either difficult to classify as being positive/negative or negative/positive, or simply expressed an ironic meaning not via literal opposition. This latter finding shows that theories of irony based on listeners simply assuming the opposite of what a speaker says (Grice, 1989; Searle, 1979) do not come close to capturing the richness of ironic language use, at least in terms of teasing, jocularity, or both.

Sarcasm

Speakers/Addressees.   Sixty-four percent of the sarcastic remarks were spoken by men, and 36% by women. This pattern differs from that seen with jocularity, where there was a near equal balance between men and women speakers, $\chi^2(1) =$ 6.6, $p < .05$. One might speculate that men are more likely to speak sarcastically than are women because of the hostile, aggressive content of most sarcastic remarks. In fact, one study in Norway found that men included a "sarcastic" speech style as a positive part of their social self-image, whereas women include a "funny" social style as positive (Svebak, 1975). Beyond this, 45% of the addressees of sarcasm were men, and 51% were women. Four percent of the sarcastic remarks were clearly intended for both male and female addressees. Finally, 35% of the sarcastic utterances were spoken to addressees with other overhearers present.

Topics.   Thirty-one percent of the sarcasm concerned something about the present situation, and 21% concerned something about the addressees. Thirteen percent concerned some person(s) not present in the conversation. Eight percent of these remarks related to the speaker himself or herself. Eleven percent of these remarks concerned some previous utterance in the present conversation. Fourteen percent referred to some past event. Finally, only 3% of the sarcasm concerned an overhearer. These data show that sarcasm, like jocularity, is primarily focused on human concerns.

Echo, Pretense, and Tone of Voice.   Only 26% of sarcastic remarks echoed previous utterances, whereas 63% percent involved the speaker adopting pretense, a significant difference, $z = 4.58, p < .001$. These data differ, then, from that found with jocularity, where echoic mention and pretense were nearly equal in frequency. Eighteen percent of the sarcastic remarks were judged to involve both echoic mention and pretense, whereas 24% involved neither of these two factors. The lower frequency of echoic mention for sarcasm than for jocularity may be attributed to the repetitions of what another speaker says when teasing that person. The results again show that at least some aspects of irony need not depend on echoic mention or pretense. Seventy-six percent of the sarcasm was uttered in what judges viewed as special intonation patterns. As was seen for the jocularity, most of these instances were delivered with heavy stress on particular words, or exaggerated rhythm. But far fewer of the sarcastic remarks (only 4 out of 80) were uttered with special intonation where the speaker mimicked the addressee or some other person (real or imagined).

Mockery, Criticism, and Humor.   Ninety percent of the remarks were judged as mocking some person, object, or event. Of these instances of mockery, 5% were self-directed (e.g., said by the speaker about the speaker). Fifty-four percent of these utterances were seen as being critical, which is a significant increase from the 28% seen in the jocular statements, $z = 3.85, p < .001$. Forty-six percent of the sarcastic comments were judged as both mocking and critical, a significant increase over that found for jocularity, $z = 3.0$, $p < .01$. Finally, 74% of these sarcastic utterances were viewed as humorous by at least one of the conversational participants. A very informal analysis suggested that a greater number of the sarcastic comments were viewed as being humorous to the speakers and overhearers than to the addressees, compared to what was obtained in the analysis of the jocular statements.

Addressee Responses. Thirty-three percent of the time, addressees responded to sarcasm by saying something ironic in return. The fact that almost one third of all responses (including nonverbal ones) to sarcasm were ironic in some form illustrates how the friends tacitly collaborated to create ironic routines or scenes in the conversations, even if, in some cases, the routine was less than completely playful. In addition, 23% of the responses to sarcasm were literal remarks that clearly indicated some understanding of the first speaker's ironic intent. Thirteen percent of the responses were simple laughter without any other linguistic utterance. This, too, reflects the addressee's understanding of some of the original speakers' playful, ironic intent when using sarcasm. Four percent of the responses indicated that the addressee clearly missed the speaker's sarcastic intent, a rate similar to the misunderstandings found for jocularity. Finally, 29% of the time, addressees ignored the sarcasm or changed the subject right away. Overall, this analysis of the addressees' responses to sarcasm reflects the same pattern of data seen in the jocularity data.

Asymmetry. My analysis of the sarcastic statements indicated that 69% presented positive utterances to indirectly convey a negative message (e.g., "You're just so damn smart," *meaning* "You're not very bright"), whereas 15% presented negative statements to convey positive messages (e.g., "Everyone should abandon their children," *meaning* "People need to take care of their children"), a reliable difference, $z = 6.6$, $p < .001$. Seventeen percent of the sarcastic remarks were either difficult to classify as being positive/negative or negative/positive, or simply expressed an ironic meaning not via opposition. Thus, literal opposition theories of irony fail to account for all aspects of sarcasm.

Hyperbole

Speakers/Addressees. Forty-one percent of the hyperbolic remarks were spoken by men, and 59% by women. This pattern differed from that seen with sarcasm, where more men than women spoke sarcastically, $\chi^2(1) = 7.11$, $p < .01$. Thirty-eight percent of the addressees were men, and 47% were women. Fifteen percent of the hyperbolic remarks were clearly intended for both male and female addressees. Finally, 68% of the hyperboles were spoken to addressees with other overhearers present.

Topics. Forty-four percent of the hyperboles concerned something about the present situation, 15% of the hyperboles concerned something about the addressees, 21% concerned some person(s) not present in the conversation, 8% of these remarks related to the speaker himself or herself, 15% of these remarks concerned some previous utterance in the present conversation, and 6% referred to some past event. Again, very few of the remarks addressed nonhuman concerns.

Echo, Pretense, and Tone of Voice.   Only 29% of hyperboles echoed a previous utterance, whereas 62% involved the speaker adopting pretense, a difference that is significant, $z = 2.72$, $p < .025$. Twenty-six percent of the hyperboles involved both echoic mention and pretense, and 35% involved neither of these factors. These data, once more, show that at least some aspects of irony need not depend on echoic mention or pretense. Forty-seven percent of the hyperboles were uttered in what judges viewed were special voices. This finding is significantly lower than the proportion of jocular or sarcastic utterances spoken with a special tone of voice, $z = 2.46$ and 2.93, respectively, with both $ps < .05$.

Mockery, Criticism, and Humor.   Seventy-six percent of the hyperboles were judged as mocking some person, object, or event. None of these instances of mockery were self-directed (e.g., said by the speaker about the speaker). Only 24% of the hyperboles were seen as being critical, which is also a significant decrease from the 54% found for sarcasm, $z = 5.60$, $p < .001$, but is close to the 28% of critical remarks found for jocular statements. Eighteen percent of the hyperboles were judged as both mocking and critical. Finally, 74% of the hyperboles were viewed as humorous by at least one of the conversational participants.

Addressee Responses.   Twenty-one percent of the time, addressees responded to hyperbole by saying something ironic in return, 38% of the responses to hyperbole were literal remarks that clearly indicated some understanding of the first speaker's ironic intent, and 21% of the responses were simple laughter without any other linguistic utterance. None of the responses indicated that the addressee clearly missed the speaker's ironic intent. Finally, 21% of the time, addressees ignored the hyperbole or changed the subject right away.

Rhetorical Questions

Speakers/Addressees.   Forty-six percent of the rhetorical questions were spoken by men, and 54% by women. Forty-two percent of the addressees were men, and 36% were women. Twenty-five percent of the rhetorical questions were clearly intended for both male and female addressees. Finally, 46% of the rhetorical questions were spoken to addressees with other overhearers present.

Topics.   Thirty-eight percent of the rhetorical questions concerned something about the present situation, 29% of the rhetorical questions concerned something about the addressees, 17% concerned some person(s) not present in the conversation, 4% of the rhetorical questions related to the speaker himself or herself, 8% of these remarks concerned some previous utterance in the present conversation, and 4% referred to some past event.

Echo, Pretense, and Tone of Voice. Only 25% of rhetorical questions echoed a previous utterance, whereas 42% involved the speaker adopting pretense, a nonsignificant difference. Eight percent of the rhetorical questions involved both echoic mention and pretense, whereas 41% involved neither of these factors. These data, once more, show that at least some aspects of irony need not depend on echoic mention or pretense. Sixty-seven percent of the rhetorical questions were uttered in what judges viewed were special intonational patterns.

Mockery, Criticism, and Humor. Seventy-five percent of the rhetorical questions were judged as mocking some person, object, or event. Eight percent of these instances of mockery were self-directed (e.g., said by the speaker about the speaker). Only 25% of hyperboles were seen as being critical, which is a significant decrease from the 54% found for sarcasm, $z = 6.11$, $p < .001$. Twenty-nine percent of the rhetorical questions were viewed as both mocking and critical. Finally, 79% of the rhetorical questions were viewed as humorous by at least one of the conversational participants.

Addressee Responses. Twenty-one percent of the time, addressees responded to rhetorical questions by saying something ironic in return. Twenty-one percent of the responses to rhetorical questions were literal remarks that clearly indicated some understanding of the first speaker's ironic intent. Twenty-five percent of the responses were simple laughter without any other linguistic utterance. None of the responses indicated that the addressee clearly missed the speaker's ironic intent. Finally, 33% of the time, addressees ignored the hyperbole or changed the subject right away.

Understatements

Speakers/Addressees. Eighty-three percent of the understatements were made by men, and 17% by women. Sixty-seven percent of the addressees were men, and 33% were women. Finally, 50% of the understatements were spoken to addressees with other overhearers present.

Topics. Fifty percent of the statements referred to past events. Thirty-three percent of the understatements concerned something about the present situation. Seventeen percent concerned some person(s) not present in the conversation. None of the understatements concerned something about the addressees.

Echo, Pretense, and Tone of Voice. None of the understatements echoed a previous utterance, whereas 50% involved the speaker adopting pretense. These data, once more, show that at least some aspects of irony need not depend on echoic mention or pretense. Fifty percent of the understatements were uttered in what judges viewed were special voices.

Mockery, Criticism, and Humor.   Fifty percent of the understatements were judged as mocking some person, object, or event. None of the understatements were seen as being critical, which is also a significant decrease from the percentages seen for the other types of irony. Finally, 33% of the understatements were viewed as humorous by at least one of the conversational participants.

Addressee Responses.   Thirty-three percent of the time addressees responded to understatements by saying something ironic in return. Thirty-three percent of the responses to understatements were literal remarks that clearly indicated some understanding of the first speaker's ironic intent. Seventeen percent of the responses were simple laughter without any other linguistic utterance. Seventeen percent of the responses indicated that the addressee clearly missed the speaker's ironic intent (a high proportion, but based on only one error).

Summary of Analyses Across Different Types of Irony

I have selectively reported some of the most notable differences that arise across the analyses of the five main types of irony. For the most part, the statistical tests reported earlier were those that related to specific empirical hypotheses. This section briefly summarizes these findings as they relate to the specific aims of the study outlined in the introduction. Because of the small number of understatements, I have excluded these in what follows.

First, the most frequent type of irony found in this corpus was jocularity, followed by sarcasm, hyperbole, rhetorical questions, and understatements. Second, the most notable sex difference in the use of irony was that men spoke more sarcastically than did women, as opposed to women using hyperbole more so than men, while there were no significant differences in the patterns of men and women using jocularity and rhetorical questions. Third, the topics mentioned in speakers' ironic utterances didn't change noticeably across the five types of irony. In each case, the topic of each utterance type was invariably focused on some, usually immediate, human concern, most often having to do with the conversational participants or some person or event known to the participants.

There were differences in the degree to which the speakers' ironic utterances involved echo, pretense, or were spoken in a special tone of voice. The main differences here were that people using sarcasm and hyperbole adopted pretense much more so than they echoed a previous statement, whereas speakers of jocularity employed pretense and echo mention with near equal frequency. Speakers often used various special tones of voices with each type of ironic utterance, especially with sarcasm, jocularity, and rhetorical questions.

Overall, speakers of sarcasm were significantly more critical and mocking of others than were speakers of jocularity, hyperbole, and rhetorical questions. Almost all of the ironic utterances, with the exception of understatements, were viewed as humorous. Most notably here, there appears to be a strong association between an ironic utterance mocking someone or something and it being viewed as humorous.

Another interesting finding was that addressees frequently responded to speakers' ironic statements by saying something ironic in return. This averaged from 21% to 33% across the five types of irony. There were fairly consistent numbers of addressees laughing in response to the five types of irony, ranging from 12% to 25%.

Finally, an important difference across the various types of irony concerned asymmetry. For jocular utterances, speakers more frequently presented a negative statement to convey a positive message than they spoke positively to express negative meaning. On the other hand, a far greater number of sarcastic utterances were stated positively to convey negative messages than the reverse.

GENERAL DISCUSSION

The research reported here illustrates some of the important complexities in ironic talk among friends. My study departs from traditional sociolinguistic and ethnographic analyses in that I have collected a large number of conversations and systematically analyzed these along a number of quantifiable dimensions. Although my conclusions are restricted to how college students speak to one another in the late 1990s, it seems clear that the present findings reveal the prominence of irony in interpersonal communication. Speaking ironically 8% of the time demonstrates that irony is not a specific rhetorical device only to be used in unusual circumstances. People comfortably use various forms of irony (i.e., jocularity, sarcasm, hyperbole, rhetorical questions, and understatement) to convey a wide range of both blatant and subtle interpersonal meanings.

Irony is not a single category of figurative language, but includes a variety of types, each of which is motivated by slightly different cognitive, linguistic, and social factors, and conveys somewhat different pragmatic meanings. My analysis of the college student corpus did not even distinguish irony from sarcasm, hyperboles, understatement, and so on, but sees irony as a more general category under which various subtypes of irony exist. Most notably, I've emphasized the crucial role that jocularity (or ironic banter or teasing) plays in ordinary language use. All five types of irony studied here mocked other people or objects to a high degree, especially sarcasm. Yet all five forms of irony were viewed as being quite humorous to at least some of the addressees and overhearers, with jocular utterances overall being the most often humorous. Sarcastic remarks were seen as more critical and somewhat more mocking than are jocularity, hyperbole, rhetorical questions, and understatements. The fact that judges did not see the nonsarcastic remarks as being all that critical illustrates the playful nature of many aspects of irony, where speakers tease one another without the intention to seriously harm or criticize. Even the more critical sarcastic comments were often viewed as critical only 50% of the time, with close to 75% of all sarcastic remarks being viewed as humorous. Sarcastic remarks also exhibited a distinctive asymmetry in that these are far more often stated by men than are the other forms of irony. The five types of irony considered here are clearly used to address human concerns, and thus, possibly differ from metaphor in that metaphorical utterances refer to a wide range of human and nonhuman events and issues (Katz, 1996b).

One of the debates in psycholinguistics over the best theory for irony understanding centers on the importance of echoic mention, pretense, and allusional reminders (and pretense) in conveying ironic meaning. The data presented here do not provide a clear solution to which of these perspectives best accounts for ironic language use. My results strongly indicate that not all ironic utterances rely on echoic mention or pretense, with some ironic expressions having nothing to do with either of these factors. There are differences among the five types of irony such that jocular remarks involve significantly greater degrees of echoic mention than do the other forms of irony, while pretense, overall, is seen as more important for irony than is echoic mention. Kumon-Nakamura et al.'s (1995) allusional pretense theory may provide the more comprehensive theoretical umbrella under which to fit the diverse forms of ironic language use revealed in these conversations among friends. In particular, the two main conditions for irony, according to the allusional-pretense view, that ironic language calls attention to some expectation that has been violated and critically involves pragmatic insincerity, may handle a variety of cases, ranging from lighthearted teasing to negative sarcastic remarks. I was not able to look closely in any systematic way at the different ways that the 289 ironic utterances alluded to failed expectations and were reflective of pragmatic insincerity precisely because it is almost impossible from the outside to know with any certainty what conversational participants mutually believe or know. Yet it seems clear that almost every ironic utterance in the corpus examined here alluded to speakers' and listeners' expectations and indirectly conveyed speaker's attitudes through some form of pragmatic insincerity. One tentative step toward finding more convincing evidence in favor of this idea, in addition to the laboratory data presented by Kumon-Nakamura et al., is to actually interview conversational participants about what they said, specifically looking for information as to their own understandings of the groups' expectations when each ironic utterance was stated.

Although speakers need not convey their ironic messages in a special tone of voice, the speaker's intonation is often seen as an important clue to ironic meaning. One difficulty with this conclusion is that there appears not to be a single pattern of prosodic cues when people speak ironically. Certain words are sometimes stressed, and there often is an exaggerated emphasis, occasionally accompanied by a slowing down of the speaking rate, for certain phrases, especially for sarcasm. But the wide variety of prosodic cues noted by judges in this study suggests that no single pattern accounts for all uses where people believed that an ironic utterance was spoken in a special tone of voice. Moreover, my own belief is that listeners will often perceive that a speaker's ironic message was stated with special prosodic cues, but that judgment may often be determined after the listener has understood what is said as having ironic meaning. Nonironic utterances may conceivably share similar intonational qualities with some ironic remarks, yet people tend not to see these as particularly special given that the speaker's message is not ironic. This observation suggests that future work needs to examine the exact role that intonational cues play in a listener's online processing of ironic messages. As Gibbs (1986a, 1986b), for one, showed, people can easily understand sarcastic comments without special intonational cues. This does not deny that tone of voice is one of a set of heuristics that listeners may use to infer ironic meaning (Kreuz, 1996). But exactly how this works, and how important tone of voice is for comprehending irony, as compared to literal utterances stated in the same tone of voice, are questions for future research.

Perhaps the most interesting findings from this project were the large degree to which addressees responded to a speaker's irony by saying something ironic in return. This result has not been previously noted, but suggests how irony is as much a state of mind jointly created by speakers and listeners, as it is a special kind of figurative language. The give-and-take nature of irony also illustrates the importance of collaboration and coordination in psychological models of speaking and listening (Clark, 1996). Yet people's conceptual understanding of various people, events, and objects as being ironic (Gibbs, 1994; Lucariello, 1994) underlies a great part of why speakers choose to express their beliefs and attitudes via different forms of ironic language. These ironic conceptualizations are often part of speakers' and listeners' common ground such that people will create ironic routines to exploit, and indeed celebrate, their mutual recognition of life's ironies.

ACKNOWLEDGMENTS

I thank Albert Katz and Herbert Colston for their helpful comments on an earlier draft of this article.

REFERENCES

Baxter, L. (1992). Forms and functions of intimate play in personal relationships. *Human Communication, 18*, 336–363.
Clark, H. (1996). *Using language.* New York: Cambridge University Press.
Clark, H., & Gerrig, R. (1984). On the pretense theory of irony. *Journal of Experimental Psychology: General, 113*, 121–126.
Colston, H. (1997a). "I've never seen anything like it;" Overstatement, understatement, and irony, *Metaphor and Symbol, 12*, 43–58.
Colston, H. (1997b). Salting a wound or sugaring a pill: The pragmatic functions of ironic criticisms. *Discourse Processes, 23*, 24–45.
Colston, H., & Keller, S. (1998). "You'll never believe this:" Irony and hyperbole in expressing surprise. *Journal of Psycholinguistic Research, 27*, 499–513.
Coser, R. (1959). Some social functions of laughter. *Human Relations, 12*, 171–182.
Cutler, A. (1974). On saying what you mean without meaning what you say. In *Papers from the Tenth Regional Meeting, Chicago Linguistics Society* (pp. 117–127). Chicago: University of Chicago.

Dews, S., Kaplan, J., & Winner, E. (1995). Why not say it directly? The social functions of irony. *Discourse Processes, 19,* 347–367.

Drew, P. (1987). Po-faced receipts of teases. *Linguistics, 25,* 219–253.

Ducharme, L. (1994). Sarcasm and interactional politics. *Symbolic Interaction, 17,* 51–62.

Dunn, J., & Brown, J. (1994). Affect expression in the family: Children's understanding of emotions and their interactions with others. *Merrill—Palmer Quarterly, 40,* 120–137.

Gibbs, R. (1986a). Comprehension and memory for nonliteral utterances: The problem of sarcastic indirect requests. *Acta Psychologica, 62,* 41–57.

Gibbs, R. (1986b). On the psycholinguistics of sarcasm. *Journal of Experimental Psychology: General, 115,* 3–15.

Gibbs, R. (1994). *The poetics of mind: Figurative thought, language, and understanding.* New York: Cambridge University Press.

Graesser, A., Long, D., & Mio, J. (1989). What are the cognitive and conceptual components of humorous texts? *Poetics, 18,* 143–163.

Grice, H. (1989). *Studies in the way of words.* Cambridge, MA: Harvard University Press.

Harris, M., & Knight-Bohnhoff, K. (1996). Gender and aggression: I. Perceptions of aggression. *Sex Roles, 35,* 1–26.

Jorgensen, J. (1996). The functions of sarcastic irony in speech. *Journal of Pragmatics, 26,* 613–634.

Katz, A. (1996a). Experimental psycholinguistics and figurative language: Circa 1995. *Metaphor and Symbol, 11,* 17–37.

Katz, A. (1996b). On interpreting statements as metaphor or irony: Contextual heuristics and cognitive consequences. In J. Mio & A. Katz (Eds.), *Metaphor: Implications and applications* (pp. 1–22). Mahwah, NJ: Lawrence Erlbaum Associates.

Keltner, D., Young, R., Heerey, E., Oeming, C., & Monarch, N. (1998). Teasing in hierarchical and intimate relations. *Journal of Personality and Social Psychology, 75,* 1231–1247.

Kierkegaard, S. (1965). *The concept of irony.* Bloomington: Indiana University Press.

Kreuz, R. (1996). The use of verbal irony: Cues and constraints. In J. Mio & A. Katz (Eds.), *Metaphor: Implications and applications* (pp. 23–38). Mahwah, NJ: Lawrence Erlbaum Associates.

Kreuz, R., & Glucksberg, S. (1989). How to be sarcastic: The echoic reminder theory of verbal irony. *Journal of Experimental Psychology: General, 118,* 374–386.

Kreuz, R., Long, D., & Church, M. (1991). On being ironic: Pragmatic and mnemonic implications. *Metaphor and Symbolic Activity, 6,* 149–162.

Kreuz, R., & Roberts, R. (1995). Two cues for verbal irony: Hyperbole and the ironic tone of voice. *Metaphor and Symbolic Activity, 10,* 21–30.

Kreuz, R., Roberts, R., Johnson, B., & Bertus, E. (1996). Figurative language occurrence and co-occurrence in contemporary literature. In R. Kreuz & M. MacNealy (Eds.), *Empirical approaches to literature and aesthetics* (pp. 83–97). Norwood, NJ: Ablex.

Kumon-Nakamura, S., Glucksberg, S., & Brown, M. (1995). How about another piece of pie: The allusional pretense theory of discourse irony. *Journal of Experimental Psychology: General, 124,* 3–121.

Lee, C., & Katz, A. (1998). The differential role of ridicule in sarcasm and irony. *Metaphor and Symbol, 13,* 1–15.

Leggitt, J., & Gibbs, R. (in press). Emotional reactions to verbal irony. *Discourse Processes.*

Lucariello, J. (1994). Situational irony. *Journal of Experimental Psychology: General, 123,* 129–145.

Mooney, A., Cresser, R., & Blatchford, P. (1991). Children's views on teasing and fighting in junior schools. *Educational Research, 33,* 103–112.

Pogrebin, M., & Poole, E. (1989). Humor in the briefing room. *Journal of Contemporary Ethnography, 17,* 183–209.

Reddy, V. (1991). Playing with others' expectations: Teasing and mucking about in the first year. In A. Whiten (Ed.), *Natural theories of mind* (pp. 143–158). Oxford, England: Blackwell.

Roberts, R., & Kreuz, R. (1994). Why do people use figurative language? *Psychological Science, 5,* 159–163.

Ruvelson, L. (1988). The empathetic use of sarcasm: Humor in psychotherapy from a self-psychological perspective. *Clinical Social Work Journal, 16,* 297–305.

Searle, J. (1979). Metaphor. In A. Ortony (Ed.), *Metaphor and thought* (pp. 92–123). New York: Cambridge University Press.

Seckman, M., & Couch, C. (1989). Jocularity, sarcasm, and relationships. *Journal of Contemporary Ethnography, 18,* 327–344.

Slugoski, B., & Turnbull, W. (1988). Cruel to be kind and kind to be cruel: Sarcasm, banter, and social relations. *Journal of Language and Social Psychology, 7,* 101–121.

Sperber, D., & Wilson, D. (1995). *Relevance: Communication and cognition* (2nd ed.). Cambridge, MA: Blackwell.

Svebak, S. (1975). Styles of humor and social self-images. *Scandinavian Journal of Psychology, 16,* 79–84.

Tannen, D. (1984). *Conversational style.* Hillsdale, NJ: Lawrence Erlbaum Associates.

Wilson, D., & Sperber, D. (1992). On verbal irony. *Lingua, 87,* 53–76.

CHAPTER 16

From "Blame by Praise" to "Praise by Blame:" Analysis of Vocal Patterns in Ironic Communication

Luigi Anolli
Rita Ciceri
Maria Giaele Infantino
Catholic University of Milan, Italy

From a communication psychology point of view, irony is not only a rhetorical figure or a cunning linguistic device, but also an articulated strategy for a flexible negotiation of meaning as well as for establishing and maintaining relations with others. Within the "irony family" phenomena, our attention is focused on the sarcastic irony generated in a conflict context ("praise by blame") and on the kind irony produced in a cooperation context ("blame by praise"). The effects of the variability of contextual cues on the vocal variables (Fo, energy, time) of irony were studied. Through the analysis of the vocal features of standard phrases in a conflict or cooperation context, an ironic dominant pattern has been found consisting of caricatured vocal traits, although differences referring to the two ironic expressions came out. From a subject-by-subject analysis, four ironic patterns were obtained: (1) in the cooperation context (a) a rather high and changeable pitch and strong energy ("bantering" joy) were observed, as well as (b) a low and monotone pitch and strong energy (emphatic mark of tenderness); (2) in the conflict context (a) a very high and changeable pitch, strong energy, and slow rate of articulation ("accented banter") were found, as well as (b) a low and not very changeable pitch, slow rate of articulation, and steadily soft energy (like scorn and cold anger). Following these four vocal patterns, the ironic voice could be defined as a "voice of banter." In such a way, irony appears as a method used to manipulate the weight of indirect speech, which allows the efficacy of the word and the innocence of silence. Moreover, the ironist can be described as an able director of his own image, able to play with the voice. Within social relationships,

---

This chapter was previously published as "From "blame by praise" to "praise by blame": Analysis of vocal patterns in ironic communication" (L. Anolli, E. Ciceri, & M. Infantino) in *International Journal of Psychology, 37,* 266–276. Copyright © [2002] by the International Union of Psychological Science. Reprinted with permission.

in fact, he can use his own voice for calibrating strategically his ways of (un)-masking himself to the others.

Examining irony as a rhetorical figure or as a crafty linguistic device is an important way of understanding this typical human process. But irony could also be analyzed as a way of establishing and maintaining relations on a psychological level. In fact, irony appears to be a communicative strategy that aims to safeguard one's own image, leaving several degrees of freedom for managing both meanings and relationships (Allemann, 1956; Ducrot, 1972; Mizzau, 1984). Through irony people can negotiate the sense of an utterance by the prerogative (typical of indirect speech) of tingeing the borders of meaning. Hence, it is simpler to calibrate one's own action (of attack, too) strategically according to the standards of social interaction in a certain culture.

In particular, irony can be used as an ambiguous kind of communication, in order to renegotiate the meaning because of the flexibility of indirect discourse. The speaker can resort to the idiosyncrasy of irony to play with the "effectiveness of the word and the innocence of silence" (Ducrot, 1972), so that he/she has the opportunity to change in his/her own favor the border between various semantic interpretations, from the manifest level to the hidden one (Dolitsky, 1983, 1992; Haiman, 1998; Mizzau, 1984). Because of the ambiguity of irony, the speaker does not assume the whole responsibility of what he/she says, and consequently, he/she does not compromise himself/herself (Jorgensen, 1996). In this way, he/she has the opportunity to create an "escape hatch" of sorts (Keenan & Quigley, 1999). To recognize the speaker's intention, it is necessary to interpret the sense of his/her message according to the sociocultural standards and his/her communicative pattern (Katz & Pexman, 1997).

As regards the contextual environment, it is worth highlighting the role of context in the communication of irony (Almansi, 1978; Attardo, 2000; Barbe, 1995). According to Wilson and Sperber's (1992) *echoic theory,* an ironic remark is a mention of social beliefs (contextual reference) or previously stated utterances (textual reference). In such a way, an ironist can produce some change within his/her social situation while being influenced by it. In such a perspective, irony is a method that is used to *manipulate the weight of indirect speech,* sometimes lightening it, sometimes intensifying it. Some scholars have proposed the "tinge hypothesis" in which an ironic utterance has the function of attenuating and softening the negative evaluation and the attack against the partner (Dews, Kaplan, & Winner, 1995; Dews & Winner, 1995). A criticism carried by an ironic phrase is apparently lighter and less offensive than an open insult; similarly, an ironic expression of praise is less positive than an explicit one. There is a kind of "regression to the center," in which, on one hand, the exultation is lessened, and, on the other, the aggressive charge is attenuated.

On the contrary, other scholars have underlined the "intensification hypothesis" according to which, in a *conflict context,* irony represents an effective device to achieve one's objectives in a more pointed and accurate manner (Jorgensen, 1996;

Oring, 1994). In this sense, irony is considered as a cold way to wound the victim more harshly; unlike an open insult produced in a moment of rage, a sarcastic comment is more calculated, as it arises from rational and intentional planning. Alternatively, in a *cooperation context,* an ironic expression of praise can have a more harmonious and less formal effect than a direct one. This happens because social expectations are invariably positive and so the use of an apparently "negative" speech to express an intention of praise is socially available only among "informal" relationships of relatives, friends, and peers (Clift, 1999; Gibbs, 1999, 2000; Oring, 1994).

Ironic communication emerges as an eminently vocal process, as it is the result of a contrastive synergy between the linguistic (verbal) pattern and the prosodic (vocal nonverbal) one. In fact, the ironic value arises from the synthesis between the lexical meaning of a statement and the suprasegmental profile superimposed on it with an opposite sense. The contrastive game between these patterns represents the distinctive structural aspect of irony, common to all its forms. On this basis, using irony, you can say what you mean without meaning what you say (Cutler, 1974), because of the distinction between sentence meaning and intended meaning.

Deepening this point, irony can be considered as a set of communicative phenomena and processes in which what is said and what is meant are different according to the speaker's intention referring to the contextual constraints (Anolli, Ciceri, & Infantino, in press; Anolli, Infantino, & Ciceri, 2002). In this "irony family," a basic, although not exhaustive, distinction is between the ironic vocal expression of praise (*kind irony*) in a cooperation context, vs. the ironic vocal expression of blame (*sarcastic irony*) in a conflict context (Anolli, Ciceri, & Infantino, 2000; Anolli & Infantino, 1997; Brown & Levinson, 1987; Kreuz, 2000; Kreuz & Glucksberg, 1989). As Knox (1961) pointed out, in its essence, irony is *praise by blame* and *blame by praise.* In the first case, we have an expression of *kind irony,* in which the speaker intends to commend an action of the addressee by resorting to reproof (censure) with a joking intonation; in the second, we have a form of *sarcastic irony* in which the praise is pronounced by the speaker in such a way that it means exactly the opposite.

Up till now, the ironic expression has usually been analyzed from a perceptual point of view on the ground of the judges' evaluation, and has been described as a "bantering voice," characterized by a lengthening of the rate of articulation, strengthening of the intensity accent, a special sort of nasal articulation, and a high and changeable pitch (Cutler, 1974; Haverkate, 1990; Kreuz & Roberts, 1995). Fónagy (1971) has determined three phases in the Hungarian ironic sentence: an initial "chest voice" with very low pitch ("creak") due to pharyngeal constriction, an intermediate "head voice" with a high rise in pitch, and a final "chest voice" with compressed and renewed creak.

In particular, the kind ironic voice has been described as full of empathic involvement with a fondling, soft, and tender intonation (Debyser, 1981; Kerbrat-Orecchioni, 1980). Conversely, sarcastic irony is associated with an attitude of scornful judgment, by means of which the speaker can convey colder and sharper censure than through the direct expression of blame (Clark & Gerrig, 1984; Kumon-Nakamura, Glucksberg, & Brown, 1995). As a consequence, the voice of irony is sometimes described as bantering and caricatured, sometimes as tender and fondling, and sometimes as harsh and shrill.

These few perceptual studies on prosodic characteristics of irony, although they obtained interesting and promising outcomes, should be integrated with an acoustical analysis of vocal variations of ironic comments in terms of pitch, energy, and time. Moreover, in light of the different ironic functions outlined, it is worth considering their influence on the speaker's vocal pattern off (1) the dimension of "conflict/cooperation" context, (2) the speaker's intention to mitigate or intensify the weight of indirect speech, and (3) his/her estrangement from the interlocutor, in terms of greater or smaller empathy (Giora, 1995, 1999; Giora, Fein, & Schwartz, 1998; Glucksberg, 1995).

The general aim of this research is to analyze and describe the variability of the vocal patterns of different ironic communication strategies related to different interactive contexts. In particular, we mean to verify the following: (1) if, within the ironic comment, according to the perceptual studies mentioned earlier, there are suprasegmental differences in terms of acoustic parameters (pitch, energy, and time) in comparison with normal speech, and what kind they are; (2) if the suprasegmental pattern (or profile) of an ironic utterance included in a conflict context (intention of blame, empathy in negative: *sarcastic irony*) is systematically different at the acoustic level from that of an ironic utterance included in a cooperation context (intention of praise, positive empathy: *kind irony*); and (3) if, within each kind of irony, it is possible to determine more defined types of vocal patterns in connection with the speaker's intention and communicative strategy, if he/she means to stress or attenuate his/her own praise or blame, in order to obtain interactive calibration.

Referring to these aims, the following research hypotheses can be formulated: (1) as a rule, the ironic expression is characterized by a specific suprasegmental profile that distinguishes it from normal speech when regarding the acoustic parameters of pitch, energy, and time; (2) suprasegmental patterns of irony change notably according to the conflict or cooperation context (*"indexicality" value of irony*); (3) within the two contexts (conflict vs. cooperation), different kinds of vocal profiles of irony emerge connected to the speaker's different communicative intentions (lightening vs. intensification and empathic involvement vs. estrangement).

METHOD

Participants

Fifty male reader-actors, randomly chosen from the student population of the Catholic University of Milan, were recruited. The subjects' ages ranged from 18 to 25 years, with an average of 21.44 years ($SD = 1.63$ years). They belonged to a middle socioeconomical class. Professional actors were not employed, to avoid the risk of acoustic bias due to their emphatic and overstressed vocal performance, and non-professional actors were preferred for reasons of ecological validity (Barker, 1968; Bronfenbrenner, 1979). They did not have a difficult task, since they had only to read short, plain pieces in a natural and spontaneous manner.

Moreover, a male sample was chosen to control voice variability better, as the fundamental frequency for the male voice typically ranges between 100–125 Hz, compared to 200–250 Hz for the female voice. As a consequence, it is possible to obtain very thick harmonics for the male voice in the sonographic analysis, allowing us to obtain more reliable results (Scherer, 1984).

Material

Two inducing texts were prepared, each of which clearly concerned a defined contextual situation: the former referred to an interactive *conflict context* (see Appendix, Text B); the latter described an interactive *cooperation context* (see Appendix, Text C). The readings, expressly produced for the experiment, were formulated according to the following linguistic criteria. Stylistically, the inducing texts were narratives, written in a simple, immediate, everyday language, concerning ordinary people's actions (De Beaugrande, 1980; Eco, 1985). They revolved around the figure of a boy interacting with another person; the situations described were well known and experienced by the reader-actors (the university exam situation).

To give relevance and consistency to the texts, as Lang (1984, 1986) suggested, information relevant to the situation, information relevant to the answer, and information about sense were included in them. The pieces were also structured in agreement with the phases of the ironic script (Anolli et al., 2002). In the first part (nearly two thirds of the text), there was a description of the contextual assumptions (the store of knowledge and cultural expectations shared by the interlocutors), and in the second part, the focal event was described (the "trigger" element, the object of the ironic communication). In this way, the texts could reach a high index value due to the definition and richness of contextual cues in the description of interaction between the partners (Gumperz, 1996; Hanks, 1996; Lucy, 1992). The third part of the pieces, with a conversational structure, was organized on the dialogic comment (the ironic utterance), in which the standard phrase that one speaker directs to another is included. The pieces finished with a conclusive sequence that described the ironic effect (the outcome of the ironic utterance, the manner in which it was reinterpreted by the addressee). In such a way, irony induced by this kind of stimulus is basically different from the irony of reported speech, in which sometimes—if not often—the speaker's voice can assume a "caricatured" pitch (Holt, 1996).

For acoustic analysis, in the third part of each reading two different but phonetically calibrated standard phrases were employed, in order to evaluate and compare how two opposite contexts influenced the management of the ironic communication, and consequently, the use of the suprasegmental features of the standard phrases. In the conflict context, a boy called Pete mocked the lack of success of Steve, an insolent, superficial, and presumptuous companion, who took an exam unwisely and failed it (standard phrase: *"Do you know: You're a real genius,"* in Italian, 9 consonants and 11 vowels). In the cooperation context, Matt, another boy, although he was well prepared, expressed his own fear for the forthcoming exam. The examination turned out to be a success and Jon, the friend who had heard Matt hesitate, teased him affectionately and jokingly (standard phrase: *"Do you know: You're a real donkey,"* in Italian, 9 consonants and 11 vowels).

The verb phrase "Do you know," followed by quite a strong punctuation mark (:), allowed the phrase to be divided into two segments, so that the fixed pause between them could be analyzed. Because the Italian prosody for the word "donkey" is, of course, different from the one for "genius," a statistical matching was carried out to verify the absence of any significant difference for all the parameters considered (pitch, energy, time) between these two words pronounced in a normal situation. Subsequently an analysis of variance (ANOVA) confirmed this absence of significant difference between them [e.g., Fo mean $F(1, 48) = 1.48$, *ns*]. Moreover, as we shall see further, in the subject-by-subject analysis (Ekman, O'Sullivan, Friesen, & Scherer, 1991), kind irony (*"Do you know: You're a real donkey"*) and sarcastic irony (*"Do you know: You're a real genius"*) were never directly compared. On the contrary, the matching was carried out only between each ironic phrase and the corresponding normal phrase.

To build the baseline value for the acoustic variables considered (pitch, energy, time), a preliminary "beginning text" (Appendix, Text A) was elaborated, made up of a set of different phrases of a comparable length, extracted from a quiz contest.[1] Among other utterances, characterized by a descriptive and plain style, the same standard phrases used in the inducing Texts B and C were randomly included, that is, the following: *"Do you know: You're a real donkey"* and *"Do you know: You're a real genius."* The former was called "normal speech 1," and the latter "normal speech 2." It is worth specifying that the denomination of "normal voice" attributed to the baseline arises from a conventional choice. In fact, it could also be defined as "neutral setting" or "modal voice," according to Laver's terminology (1979/1996).

The situation of a quiz contest was chosen because the utterances can be short, easy, and plain in their meaning, disconnected from each other and related to quite different topics. In this way, the speakers are induced to interpret these sentences according to their lexical meaning, since they are presented as a list of independent phrases. In this situation, it was expected that the participants would have read Text A with their usual, "normal" profile of voice. Text A was calibrated in length and it was distributed in three parts, in order to make it similar in structure to inducing Texts B and C (Appendix).

Procedure

The appointments were given singly. The recording sessions, which took place in a quiet room, lasted about 15 minutes, during which the participants were asked to read the texts one by one, first in silence and then aloud. Text A (Appendix) was read first; Texts B and C were read following a counterbalanced order. In the written instructions, the experiment was described as part of a study of the human voice. Each subject was asked to read the texts in a spontaneous manner, according to his/her style, interpreting them so that other people could understand the meaning of the pieces.

The subjects were warned that their reading would be recorded (digital recorder DAT TASCAM DA-30 MKII, 90' DAT Digital Audio Tape SONY, mixer TASCAM M-06ST, unidirectional microphone RCF MD 3500 X, headphones SENNHEISER HD 265). The measure of energy was calibrated according to the procedure described by Walbott (1982), in order to get a high-quality recording. Unidirectional microphones were used and each subject was seated on an adjustable chair, so that his mouth was 20 cm from the microphone. To make the experimental situation less artificial, some books and other items were placed on the table in addition to the microphone.

Once the recording protocols had been established, the standard phrases were extracted from Texts A, B, and C. There were four standard phrases for each subject: irony in a cooperation context, irony in a conflict context, and the two corresponding baseline phrases, conventionally defined "normal speech 1" and "normal speech 2." Afterwards, acoustic analysis was carried out using CSL (Computerized Speech Lab, model 4300 B, version software 5.X, Kay Elemetrics Corps). Results are reported both for the group of subjects as a whole and for a detailed subject-by-subject analysis.

Analysis of the Acoustic Features

In order to verify the differences between normal and ironic speech, as well as between kind and sarcastic irony, an acoustic analysis of the recording protocols was carried out on the basis of time, pitch, and energy parameters, which are the usual physical parameters employed in this field of research (Laver, 1980; Scherer, 1986).

Referring to the dimension of *time,* measured in milliseconds, the following dependent variables were considered: the length of the standard phrase (in seconds, given by the interval between the pause that preceded the acoustic signal and the end of the spoken segments without considering the final pause), the length of the pauses (in seconds), the length of the spoken segments (in seconds, derived by subtracting the duration of the pauses from the overall duration of the phrase), the number of pauses (in units), the rate of articulation (in syllables per second, given by the relationship between the number of syllables and the length of the spoken segments).[2]

With reference to the dimension of *pitch,* the fundamental frequency (Fo) was measured in hertz, extracted by means of the spectral clipping method and the zero crossing analysis (with the appropriate parameters relative to the amplitude of segments and to the length of the windows). Once extracted, the mean, the minimum Fo, the maximum Fo, the Fo range, and the standard deviation (as a measure of the Fo variability) were calculated.

Last, referring to the dimension of *amplitude,* the energy diagram was employed that traces in dB the sound wave value (with the parameters relative to the amplitude of segments and to the length of the windows). To get the values of the spoken segments only, the pauses were eliminated (initial and inner ones) from the complete acoustic signal, using the "trim" procedure provided by the CSL. Once extracted, the mean, the minimum, the maximum, the range, and the standard deviation of dB were calculated.

Subject-by-Subject Analysis

To check out the existence of different vocal profiles of irony for the communicative patterns of each speaker, a "subject-by-subject analysis" was carried out (Ekman et al., 1991). Five parameters of Fo and of energy were analyzed, i.e., the mean, the range (minimum, maximum, and range), and the standard deviation, and, among the variables of the parameter of time, only the rate of articulation, which synthetically measures both the duration and the tempo of an utterance.

The subject-by-subject analysis was divided into three phases:

1. In order to find out the differential idiosyncratic values (specific of each subject) of the 11 dependent variables, the differences were calculated between the irony values in a context of both cooperation and conflict, respectively, and the baseline values, i.e., the corresponding "normal" speech.

2. In order to determine the threshold values to build categories of vocal profiles, the criteria employed by Ekman et al. (1991) were followed, taking twice the standard error as the "threshold value," calculated for each variable among the 11 examined.

3. In order to define the categories of profiles, for each variable we determined the three categories considered by means of the method of the standard error: the subjects presenting positive differences greater than twice the standard error ("+ subject"), the subjects presenting negative differences greater than twice the standard error ("– subject"), and the subjects presenting differences included in the "intermediate" zone between the two former levels ("= subject"). In such a way, it was possible to distinguish *high-pitched* vs. *low-pitched voice* for the pitch, *changeable* vs. *monotone voice* for the pitch variability, *loud* vs. *soft voice* for the energy, and *slow* vs. *fast voice* for the rate of articulation.

ANALYSIS OF THE DATA

Analysis of the Acoustic Features

In order to verify the suprasegmental differences between irony and normal speech, as well as between kind and sarcastic irony, the data acquired in the four conditions of the experimental design (normal speech 1, normal speech 2, irony in a cooperation context, and irony in a conflict context) were submitted for the one-way repeated measures ANOVA (SAS for WINDOWS, version 6.12). The analysis was replicated for the 15 dependent variables (vocal features dealing with time, pitch, and energy).

As can be observed from the mean values (Table 16.1), pitch was the most sensitive parameter in distinguishing the vocal profile of irony compared with that of normal speech. On the one hand, there was a general increase in the mean values, the range, and the standard deviation of Fo in each form of irony in comparison with normal speech. Moreover, differences between the Fo values of irony in a conflict vs. co-operation context were observed. In fact, in sarcastic irony, Fo mean values and standard deviation were higher than in kind irony. ANOVA (Table 16.2) points out the significance of the main effect in all the Fo variables. In particular, from the post hoc analysis of contrasts, it emerges that the two ironic forms differed significantly from normal speech, as the two ironic forms do from each other, in all the Fo variables except for the minimum.

As for voice energy, there was an increase of the mean values and of the range but not of the standard deviation in comparison with normal speech, whereas there

TABLE 16-1
Mean Values of the Acoustic Parameters: Fo, Energy, and Time ($N = 50$)

	Normal Speech 1	Kind Irony	Normal Speech 2	Sarcastic Irony
Fo (Hz)				
Mean	123.31	131.27	124.68	138.45
Maximum	157.14	179.60	157.56	198.84
Minimum	99.84	98.32	99.30	95.94
Range	57.30	81.28	58.26	102.90
SD	16.98	24.82	18.12	30.76
Energy (dB)				
Mean	53.43	55.48	54.55	56.37
Maximum	65.05	68.00	65.34	69.17
Minimum	33.63	35.27	33.64	35.48
Range	31.42	32.73	31.70	33.70
SD	8.05	8.09	8.03	8.14
Time				
Duration of speech (s)	1.74	1.67	1.77	1.67
Duration spoken segments (s)	1.30	1.34	1.31	1.37
Number of pauses (n)	1.06	1.14	0.94	1.14
Pauses length (s)	0.44	0.33	0.46	0.30
Rate of articulation (syll/s)	6.92	6.72	6.87	6.57

Note. (s) = seconds, (n) = number, (syll/s) = syllables per second.

TABLE 16-2
Fo: Main Effects and Contrast (One-Way Repeated Measures, Analysis of Variance)

	Error	F	p
Mean			
Main effect	119.10	19.37	< .000
Normal 1 — normal 2	75.29	1.17	n.s.
Normal 1 — kind	288.22	10.61	< .002
Normal 2 — sarcastic	305.11	29.70	< .000
Kind — sarcastic	183.62	13.24	< .001
+ Range			
Main effect	730.42	26.81	< .000
Normal 1 — normal 2	277.42	0.03	n.s.
Normal 1 — kind	1692.91	14.79	< .000
Normal 2 — sarcastic	1894.60	43.94	< .000
Kind — sarcastic	1420.36	12.46	< .001
– Range			
Main effect	57.56	2.89	< .038
Normal 1 — normal 2	92.72	0.11	n.s.
Normal 1 — kind	150.59	0.79	n.s.
Normal 2 — sarcastic	125.03	5.24	< .026
Kind — sarcastic	59.22	5.41	< .024
Range amplitude			
Main effect	700.09	33.24	< .000
Normal 1 — normal 2	280.13	0.13	n.s.
Normal 1 — kind	1549.63	18.47	< .000
Normal 2 — sarcastic	1879.37	52.50	< .000
Kind — sarcastic	1446.61	15.75	< .000
SD			
Main effect	66.24	30.29	< .000
Normal 1 — normal 2	25.34	2.46	n.s.
Normal 1 — kind	160.18	19.16	< .000
Normal 2 — sarcastic	167.52	46.49	< .000
Kind — sarcastic	121.56	13.65	< .001

were no significant differences between the two ironic forms (Table 16.1). ANOVA showed significant values of the main effect for the mean, $F(2, 96) = 7.93, p < .000$; the maximum, $F(2, 96) = 16.59, p < .000$; the minimum, $F(2, 96) = 4.15, p < .008$;

and the range, $F(2, 96) = 3.34, p < .021$; in the standard deviation, there were no significant differences between the utterances. The analysis of contrasts pointed out that the significance concerned the differences between normal speech 1 and kind irony: mean, $F(1, 48) = 7.73, p < .008$; maximum, $F(1, 48) = 12.86, p < .001$; as well as between normal speech 2 and sarcastic irony: mean, $F(1, 48) = 6.88, p < .012$; maximum, $F(1, 48) = 27.47, p < .000$; minimum, $F(1, 48) = 8.18, p < .006$; range, $F(1, 48) = 6.41, p < .015$; but not between the two ironic forms.

Referring to the parameter of time, irony was qualified globally by a shorter length in the pauses in comparison with normal speech (Table 16.1), which was significant from ANOVA, main effect: $F(2, 96) = 5.91, p < .001$. The analysis of contrasts showed the presence of significant differences between normal speech 1 and kind irony, $F(1, 48) = 5.14, p < .028$, as well as between normal speech 2 and sarcastic irony, $F(1, 48) = 8.79, p < .005$.

Subject-by-Subject Analysis

Table 16.3 summarizes the percentages of those subjects who were classified in the vocal categories as *high* vs. *low, changeable* vs. *monotone, loud* vs. *soft,* and *slow* vs. *fast voice,* according to the aforesaid criteria. As for pitch, in both ironic contexts most subjects (66% kind irony, 78% sarcastic irony) showed a high pitch. Nevertheless, there also emerges an ironic voice, albeit to a lesser degree, which was characterized by a low pitch, especially for the expression of kind irony. This twofold trend was confirmed for energy too: The predominance of those subjects who employed a stronger energy (66% kind irony, 68% sarcastic irony) than in normal speech was contrasted by a smaller group of subjects who were characterized

TABLE 16-3

Percentages and Chi-Square Test for Fo, Energy, and Rate of Articulation ($N = 50, df = 2$)

	High Voice	Low Voice	Intermediate	χ^2	p
Fo					
Kind irony	66%	24%	10%	26.44	< .001
Sarcastic irony	78%	10%	12%	44.92	< .001
	Loud Voice	Soft Voice	Intermediate	χ^2	p
Energy					
Kind irony	66%	26%	8%	25.48	< .001
Sarcastic irony	68%	30%	2%	32.92	< .001
	Fast Voice	Slow Voice	Intermediate	χ^2	p
Rate of articulation					
Kind irony	24%	52%	24%	7.84	< .020
Sarcastic irony	28%	48%	24%	4.96	ns

by a reduction in the voice energy, in almost analogous percentages in both ironic forms. Last, for the rate of articulation there was a greater concentration of subjects in the category of the slow vocal profile (52% kind irony, 48% sarcastic irony), whereas the remaining subjects were equally distributed among those who used a normal rate of articulation (24% in both cases) and those who increased it significantly (24% kind irony; 28% sarcastic irony). A chi square test pointed out the significance of differences for each considered parameter, except for "fast" vs. "slow" vocal profile in sarcastic irony (Table 16.3).

In order to get a more analytic description of the ironic patterns, we resorted to disassembling further the categories according to the indicators of variability for pitch and energy only. Our goal was to focus on five vocal profile categories for Fo (high/changeable, high/monotone, low/changeable, low/monotone, intermediate) and five for energy (strong/variable, strong/stable, soft/variable, soft/stable, intermediate).

As regards pitch in the expression of kind irony (Table 16.4), two vocal profiles that were very different from each other were observed: one belonging to those who used a high changeable pitch, and which constituted the prevalent form (58%), and the other belonging to those who spoke in a low monotone pitch (20%). Alternatively, in expressing sarcastic irony, 70% of subjects used a high changeable pitch, whereas in the "low monotone" category, there were only 10% of speakers. For

TABLE 16.4
Percentages for the Vocal Profiles Referring to Fo and Energy ($N = 50$)

	High Voice	Low Voice
Fo		
Kind irony		
Monotone voice	8%	20%
Changeable voice	58%	4%
Sarcastic irony		
Monotone voice	8%	10%
Changeable voice	70%	0%
	Loud Voice	Soft Voice
Energy		
Kind irony		
Stable voice	32%	22%
Variable voice	34%	4%
Sarcastic irony		
Stable voice	34%	20%
Variable voice	34%	10%

both ironic forms, the Mantel-Haenszel test confirmed that the distribution of the frequencies was not random: kind irony, $\chi^2 = 73.14$, $p < .001$; sarcastic irony, $\chi^2 = 74.93$, $p < .001$. Moreover, from a one-way ANOVA with repeated measures for multiple response categorical data, applied to both distributions considering the factor of irony at its two levels, there emerged a significant difference between the two ironic forms, $F(2, 96) = 8.20$, $p < .042$.

Regarding energy, a higher similarity was observed between the expression of kind and sarcastic irony. In fact, in the context of both cooperation and conflict, the presence of three different prevailing forms was registered: there were subjects who employed a strong and stable energy (respectively, 32% for kind irony and 34% for sarcastic irony), subjects who used a loud (strong energy) but very variable voice (34% for both ironic forms), and subjects who used a uniformly soft voice (respectively, 22% for kind irony and 20% for sarcastic irony). It should be stressed that only in the expression of sarcastic irony, 10% of subjects used a moderately soft but very variable energy of the voice. Within each ironic form, the Mantel-Haenszel statistic test confirmed the significance of the distribution of the frequencies: kind irony, $\chi^2 = 55.46$, $p < .001$; sarcastic irony, $\chi^2 = 51.19$, $p < .001$. Conversely, the differences between the two ironic forms were not significant in the application of a one-way ANOVA with repeated measures for multiple response categorical data.

DISCUSSION OF THE RESULTS AND CONCLUSIONS

Before discussing the results, some caveats about the limits of the present research have to be pointed out. First, the collected data were gathered by a tightly controlled group of participants reading constructed passages of text. This standard experimental setting, however, tends to place the data obtained at some distance from everyday speech that is produced spontaneously (Holt, 1996). Second, for the reasons mentioned earlier, the experimental group included only male subjects. This fact limits the possibility of generalizing our results. Third, the participants were non-actors. Though this condition could have strengthened the ecological validity of the present research, it might have raised some problems regarding their quality of performance because of their lack of preparation in acting.

Nevertheless, in agreement with what has already been pointed out in literature, the results of the present research confirm the existence of a suprasegmental profile that implies irony as being basically different from normal speech. From both acoustic characteristics and from a subject-by-subject analysis, one can perceive a modal vocal pattern that involves the combination of a *high pitch,* a *strong energy,* and a *lengthened rate of articulation.* Therefore, the ironic voice seems to be qualified as a caricatured stress of the suprasegmental features by means of which irony is a device to "play with the voice" (Cutler, 1974; Fónagy, 1971; Haverkate, 1990; Kreuz & Roberts, 1995). It is employed not in a natural but a "studied" way, i.e., both "premeditated" and "affected." The emphatic form, in which the different suprasegmental characteristics of the voice are jointly stressed, allows one to convey, along with the message, the contradiction between the lexical meaning of the words and the speaker's communicative intention.

However, the present research also points out a multiplicity and a differentiation of ironic vocal profiles with reference to the relational context (cooperation vs. conflict). In fact, in the conflict context, a high and changeable pitch emerges, whereas in the cooperation context there is a "smoother" and more attenuated pitch. Irony is not a homogeneous communicative process, but a flexible and articulated strategy, planned according to the situation and to the relationship with the addressee. As a consequence, it is possible to foresee a family of ironic voices, among which the speaker can choose the most effective and appropriate one to express higher intention. In fact, though based on the same communicative rules (contrastivity and suprasegmental stress), the two ironic forms here examined—kind and sarcastic irony—are characterized by different goals and motivations (praise in the first case and blame in the second one), which lead to different expressive suprasegmental patterns.

In particular, our results show that each ironic form basically presents a twofold path. In the cooperation context the participants, through a rather high and changeable pitch, a strong energy, and a slow rhythm, mainly express kind irony. However, a few subjects, through a rather strong energy, a slow rate of articulation, and a low and monotone pitch, also express kind irony in a subordinate way. These last acoustic features are similar, to some extent, to those of tenderness (Anolli & Ciceri, 1997), in agreement with those studies that describe the voice of kind irony as soft and tender (Debyser, 1981; Kerbrat-Orecchioni, 1980; Koevecses, 1990). The rather high value of energy in kind irony, which is not consistent with tenderness, could be explained as a consequence of emphatic stress: It is likely that a speaker who communicates ironic praise as "tenderness" imitates the voice of tenderness in a caricatured way.

Similarly, in the conflict context, most subjects, by means of a very high and changeable pitch, a strong energy, and a slow rate of articulation, have mainly expressed sarcastic irony. These suprasegmental traits are in line with researchers' hypothesis about the ironic form being included in the general field of the emphatic banter (Frijda, 1987; Oatley & Johnson-Laird, 1987; Scherer, 1984). However, a few subjects show sarcastic irony by using a secondary vocal pattern, characterized by the combination of a low and not very changeable pitch as well as a slow rate of articulation. It includes suprasegmental aspects that are similar to those of blame and cold anger, and that confirm the perceptual description of the ironic voice as scornful (Scherer, 1984).

These four vocal patterns in the expression of kind and sarcastic irony allow a more precise definition of the perspective of the ironic voice as a "voice of banter," as it has been stressed by the perceptual analysis scholars (Fónagy, 1971; Haverkate, 1990; Kreuz & Roberts, 1995). The ironic voice is certainly a "bantering" voice, acoustically defined as a high-pitched, changeable, and loud voice with a slow rhythm, as really is the case for most subjects; but it can also assume other acoustic profiles according to the relational context and the speaker's intention, as in the case of a scornful voice for sarcastic irony and a tender voice for kind irony.

The speaker's communicative choice among these different vocal patterns is linked with both degrees of the empathic involvement and the context. He/she can adjust the level of emphasis of the ironic comment according to the intensity with which he/she means to affect his/her interlocutor (Gibbs, 2000). As summarized in Figure 16.1, it is useful to take into account two dimensions: *context and empathy.* For the first one, the two ends consist of *conflict* and *cooperation;* for the other, involvement and estrangement represent the two ends. In both conflict and cooperation contexts, according to the degree of empathic involvement with his/her partner, the speaker can measure the weight of the indirect speech, choosing whether to strengthen his/her own intention, or, instead, to weaken it. In the first case, when he/she wants to reinforce indirectly his/her intention, he/she can resort to a scornful voice to carry sharp blame or to a tender voice to express affectionate praise. In the second case, when he/she intends to minimize his/her comment, he/she can employ a bantering voice to express both criticism and commendation.

Going into this matter thoroughly, the bantering voice, both kind and sarcastic, represents an effective way to cope with the inducing event, tingeing and mitigating the situation by means of an empathic estrangement. By means of a bantering

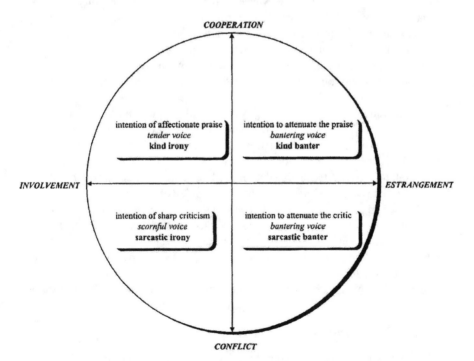

Figure 16.1.   Hypothesis on the components and the process of the ironic communication.

voice, the speaker weakens his/her communicative intention in a compliant way without exposing him/herself openly: He/she can censure a certain action of the interlocutor without attacking him/her, or, on the contrary, he/she can praise the interlocutor without exalting him/her and without putting him/her in an awkward situation (attenuation condition). However, the speaker can also strengthen his/her intention through ironic comment (intensification condition). In a conflict context, for instance, he/she can deeply offend the partner by resorting to a sarcastic comment pronounced in a scornful voice (that is, a low and monotone pitch, a slow rhythm and a stressed articulation of words) in a cold way, without showing an apparent emotional arousal (Brown & Levinson, 1987; Kumon-Nakamura, Glucksberg, & Brown, 1995). Likewise, in a cooperation context, the speaker can praise the partner through an ironic utterance pronounced with a tender voice in order not to exhibit verbally his/her own emotion for reasons of discretion.

This segmentation of acoustic patterns of irony could help to explain and reconcile some differences in the theoretical models proposed until now. On the one hand, irony has been seen as a way to lighten tension through the attenuation of praise and the mitigation of blame according to the so-called "tinge hypothesis" (Almansi, 1978; Haverkate, 1990; Kerbrat-Orecchioni, 1980; Kumon-Nakamura et al., 1995). On the other, irony has been considered as a calculated and shrewd strategy that adds weight to the relevance of indirect speech in line with the "intensification hypothesis" (Jorgensen, 1996; Oring, 1994). Actually, these perspectives are not two opposite alternatives, but two different communicative paths, which are both not only feasible, but also effective and favorable according to the context and to the speaker's intention. In fact, in order to manage interpersonal relationships, the speaker can play on both sides, appealing to the several components of the acoustic pattern of irony.

Irony assumes the shape of a complex and kaleidoscopic communicative device. From time to time, it can be employed in order to stress or to weaken implied meaning. By means of an ironic comment the speaker, director of his/her own image within social relationships, can adjust communicative patterns with which to (un)mask himself/herself to the other, trying to reduce the risk of being "twisted around the other's finger." From this point of view, irony has a high value of indexicality in the regulation of the weight of indirect speech. Because of the family of ironic forms, characterized by strong flexibility and compliance in connection with his/her aims (Gumperz, 1996), the speaker can adjust his/her communicative target in a subtle way according to the nature of the relationship with the partner, to the contingent context, and to his/her intention. In the ironic exchange, on the one hand, the speaker must be able to say and not to say his/her evaluation of the situation; on the other, the interlocutor must be able to detect and unmask the speaker's intention.

ACKNOWLEDGMENTS

This research was funded by a contribution from Fondazione Ferrero (Alba, Italy) and was carried out at the Center for Communication Psychology, Catholic University of Milan.

ENDNOTES

1. In order to achieve a normal voice, especially with strong semantically oriented utterances like ours, the only way to neutralize and "narcotize" the semantic aspects of theirs has been to include them among other phrases, in a list of "instructions for a quiz contest."
2. The calculation of the number of syllables followed phonetic, rather than grammatical, rules. The phonetic syllable is composed of an initial articulation (consonant), a vocal nucleus, and a stop articulation: CVS, or also only CV (Scherer, 1982).

REFERENCES

Allemann, B. (1956). *Ironie und dichtung* [Irony and poetry]. Pfullingen, Germany: Günther Neske.

Almansi, G. (1978). L'affaire mystérieuse de l'abominable "tongue-in-cheek" [The mysterious case of the abominable "tongue-in-cheek"]. *Poétique, 36,* 413–426.

Anolli, L., & Ciceri, R. (1997). *La voce delle emozioni* [The voice of emotions]. Milan: Angeli.

Anolli, L., Ciceri, R., & lnfantino, M. G. (2000). Irony as a game of implicitness: Acoustic profiles of the ironic communication. *Journal of Psycholinguistic Research, 29,* 275–311.

Anolli, L., Ciceri, R., & Infantino, M. G. (in press). Behind "dark glasses." Irony as a strategy for indirect communication. *Genetic, Social, and General Psychology Monographs.*

Anolli, L., & Infantino, M. G. (1997). La pelle della volpe. L'ironia come strategia di comunicazione conveniente [The skin of the fox. Irony as a strategy to communicate in a seemly way]. *Studi Italiani di Linguistica Teorica e Applicata, 26,* 57–85.

Anolli, L., Infantino, M. G., & Ciceri, R. (2002). "You're a real genius!": Irony as miscommunication strategy. In L. Anolli, R. Ciceri, & G. Riva (Eds.), *Say not to say: New perspectives on miscommunication* (pp. 142–163). Amsterdam: IOS Press.

Attardo, S. (2000). Irony as a relevant inappropriateness. *Journal of Pragmatics, 32,* 793–826.

Barbe, K. (1995). *Irony in context.* Amsterdam: Benjamins.

Barker, R. G. (1968). *Ecological psychology. Concepts and methods for studying the environment of human behaviour.* Stanford, CA: Stanford University Press.

Bronfenbrenner, U. (1979). Contexts of child rearing: Problems and prospects. *American Psychologist, 34,* 844–850.

Brown, P., & Levinson, S. C. (1987). *Politeness.* Cambridge, MA: Cambridge University Press.

Clark, H., & Gerrig, R. (1984). On the pretense theory of irony. *Journal of Experimental Psychology: General, 113,* 121–126.

Clift, R. (1999). Irony in conversation. *Language in Society, 28,* 23–553.

Cutler, A. (1974). On saying what you mean without meaning what you say. In *Papers from the tenth regional meeting of the Chicago Linguistic Society* (pp. 117–127). Chicago: Department of Linguistics, University of Chicago.

De Beaugrande, R. A. (1980). *Text, discourse and process.* Norwood, NJ: Ablex.

Debyser, F. (1981). Les mécanismes de l'ironie. *Lectures, 9,* 141–157.

Dews, S., Kaplan, J., & Winner, E. (1995). Why not say it directly? The social functions of irony. *Discourse Processes, 19,* 347–367.

Dews, S., & Winner, E. (1995). Muting the meaning: A social function of irony. *Metaphor and Symbolic Activity, 10,* 3–19.

Dolitsky, M. (1983). Humor and the unsaid. *Journal of Pragmatics, 7,* 39–48.

Dolitsky, M. (1992). Aspects of unsaid in humor. *Humor: International Journal of Humor Research, 5*, 33–43.

Ducrot, O. (1972). *Dire et ne pas dire* [To say and not to say]. Paris: Hermann.

Eco, U. (1985). *Lector in fabula* [Reader in fable]. Milan: Bompiani.

Ekman, P., O'Sullivan, M., Friesen, W. V., & Scherer, K. R. (1991). Invited article: Face, voice and body in detecting deceit. *Journal of Nonverbal Behavior, 15*, 125–135.

Fónagy, I. (1971). The functions of vocal style. In *Literary style. A symposium* (pp. 159–174). New York: Oxford University Press.

Fónagy, I. (1978). A new method of investigating the perception of prosodic features. *Language and Speech, 21*, 34–49.

Frijda, N. H. (1987). Emotion, cognitive structure, and action tendency. *Cognition and Emotion, 1*, 115–143.

Gibbs, R. W., Jr. (1999). Speakers' intuitions and pragmatic theory. *Cognition, 69*, 355–359.

Gibbs, R. W., Jr. (2000). Irony in talk among friends. *Metaphor and Symbol, 15*, 5–27.

Giora, R. (1995). On irony and negation. *Discourse Processes, 19*, 239–264.

Giora, R. (1999). On the priority of salient meanings: Studies of literal and figurative language. *Journal of Pragmatics, 31*, 919–929.

Giora, R., Fein, O., & Schwartz, T. (1998). Irony: Graded and indirect negation. *Metaphor and Symbol, 13*, 83–101.

Glucksberg, S. (1995). Commentary on nonliteral language: Processing and use. *Metaphor and Symbolic Activity, 10*, 47–57.

Gumperz, J. J. (1996). The linguistic and cultural relativity of conversational inference. In J. J. Gumperz & S. C. Levinson (Eds.), *Rethinking linguistic relativity* (pp. 374–406). Cambridge, England: Cambridge University Press.

Haiman, J. (1998). *Talk is cheap: Sarcasm, alienation, and the evolution of language.* Oxford, UK: Oxford University Press.

Hanks, W. F. (1996). Language form and communicative practices. In J. J. Gumperz & S. C. Levinson (Eds.), *Rethinking linguistic relativity* (pp. 232–270). Cambridge, UK: Cambridge University Press.

Haverkate, H. (1990). A speech act analysis of irony. *Journal of Pragmatics, 14*, 77–109.

Holt, E. (1996). Reporting on talk: The use of direct reported speech in conversation. *Research on Language and Social Interaction, 29*, 219–245.

Jorgensen, J. (1996). The functions of sarcastic irony in speech. *Journal of Pragmatics, 26*, 613–634.

Katz, A. N., & Pexman, P. M. (1997). Interpreting figurative statements: Speaker occupation can change metaphor to irony. *Metaphor and Symbol, 12*, 19–41.

Keenan, T. R., & Quigley, K. (1999). Do young children use echoic information in their comprehension of sarcastic speech? A test of echoic mention theory. *British Journal of Developmental Psychology, 17*, 83–96.

Kerbrat-Orecchioni, C. (1980). L'ironie comme trope [Irony as a trope]. *Poétique, 41*, 108–127.

Knox, N. (1961). *The word irony and its context, 1500–1755.* Durham, NC: Duke University Press.

Koevecses, Z. (1990). *Emotion concepts.* New York: Springer-Verlag.

Kreuz, R. J. (2000). The production and processing of verbal irony. *Metaphor and Symbol, 15*, 99–107.

Kreuz, R. J., & Glucksberg, S. (1989). How to be sarcastic: The echoic reminder theory of verbal irony, *Journal of Experimental Psychology: General, 118*, 374–386.

Kreuz, R. J., & Roberts, R. M. (1995). Two cues for verbal irony: Hyperbole and the ironic tone of voice. *Metaphor and Symbolic Activity, 10*, 21–31.

Kumon-Nakamura, S., Glucksberg, S., & Brown, M. (1995). How about another piece of pie: The allusional pretense theory of discourse irony. *Journal of Experimental Psychology: General, 124,* 3–21.

Lang, P. J. (1984). Cognition in emotion: Concept and action. In C. Izard, J. Kagan, & R. Zajonc (Eds.), *Emotion, cognition and behavior* (pp. 192–226). New York: Cambridge University Press.

Lang, P. J. (1986). Anxiety and memory. In B. E Shaw, Z. V. Segal, T. M. Vallis, & F. E. Cashman (Eds.), *Anxiety disorders. Psychological and biological perspectives* (pp. 51–66). New York: Plenum.

Laver, J. (1979/1996). The description of voice quality. In J. Laver (Ed.), *The gift of speech* (pp. 184–208). Edinburgh, Scotland: Edinburgh University Press.

Laver, J. (1980). *The phonetic description of voice quality.* Cambridge, England: Cambridge University Press.

Lucy, J.A. (1992). *Language diversity and thought: A reformulation of the linguistic relativity hypothesis.* Cambridge: Cambridge University Press.

Mizzau, M. (1984). *L'ironia. La contraddizione consentita* [Irony. The allowed contradiction]. Milan: Feltrinelli.

Oatley, P., & Johnson-Laird, P. (1987). Towards a cognitive theory of emotions. *Cognition and Emotion, 1,* 29–50.

Oring, E. (1994). Humor and the suppression of sentiment. *Humor: International Journal of Humor Research, 7,* 7–26.

Scherer, K. R. (1982). Methods of research on vocal communication: Paradigms and parameters. In K. R. Scherer & P. Ekman (Eds.), *Handbook of methods in nonverbal behavior research. Studies in emotions and social interaction.* Cambridge, England: Cambridge University Press.

Scherer, K. R. (1984). On the nature and function of emotion: A multicomponent process approach. In K. R. Scherer & P. Ekman (Eds.), *Approaches to emotion* (pp. 293–317). Hillsdale, NJ: Lawrence Erlbaum Associates.

Scherer, K. R. (1986). Vocal affect expression: A review and a model for future research. *Psychological Bulletin, 99,* 143–165.

Walbott, H. G. (1982). Audiovisual recording: Procedures, equipment and troubleshooting. In K. R. Scherer & P. Ekman (Eds.), *Approaches to emotion.* Hillsdale, NJ: Lawrence Erlbaum Associates.

Wilson, D., & Sperber, D. (1992). On verbal irony. *Lingua, 87,* 53–67.

APPENDIX

Text A—Preliminary Text: Instructions for a Quiz Contest

Only one among the following phrases, the computer randomly selected, can open the safe. Please, read the eight phrases in a simple way and, then, choose one among them: Good luck! / This dress is red / The weather is getting better / *Do you know: You're a real genius* / You really made me die with laughter / Do you know: You've finished soon / The result was the one you hoped / *Do you know: You're a real donkey* / The situation was going on and on/.

Text B—Irony in a Context of Conflict

Pete and Steve were university mates. Pete was hardworking and usually achieved good results, without being arrogant. Steve, however, exhibited his ability in having success without studying so much, and mocked people that were studying very hard. Pete could not stand Steve's behaviour, and hoped this "spoiled child" was going to pay for his arrogance, sooner or later. The "proof of the pudding" arrived when Steve, sitting an exam although he did not study anything, failed. In fact, the professor realized his shallowness and blamed him. Pete was happy; so, he waited for Steve outside the classroom and made fun of him with a sarcastic comment: "Bravo! Compliments. What a good exam! *Do you know: You're a real genius!*" For the first time, Steve felt the bitterness of a defeat, which his rival's derision made even more piercing.

Text C—Irony in a Context of Cooperation

Jon and Matt, both close friends and university mates, studied seriously and with enthusiasm. Jon was more determined than his friend, and tried to encourage him when he was afraid. Matt, in his turn, tried to make his ambitious friend more careful. Jon and Matt helped each other even during the exams. Once, Matt was afraid to sit a difficult exam, although he was really prepared. He repeated to Jon: "I'll fail, yeah, this time will be wrong, I feel it! I'll look a proper donkey!" As usual, Jon tried to give him strength. The exam was a success, and the professor openly expressed his praise to Matt, who was gratified, as was Jon, who ironically expressed his congratulations and affection: "Sure, you are right, what a poor figure! Do you know: You're a real donkey!" This witty remark amused Matt, who was happy to see Jon sharing his own joy.

CHAPTER 17

Responding to Irony in Different Contexts:
On Cognition in Conversation

Helga Kotthoff
Freiburg University of Education, Germany

My article deals with responses to irony in two different contexts. As an interaction analyst, I am interested in what interlocutors do with the ironic in the
co-construction of the ongoing conversational sequence. Many reactions to an
ironic act reveal that, in irony, a gap in evaluative perspective is communicated
as the most central information. The said represents a perspective which is
combined with a counter-perspective—the intended. Listeners can in principle
react to both perspectives. Reacting to the said continues the play with clashing
perspectives and confirms the gap. I combine data analytic methods from
interactional sociolinguistics with questions from cognition theory. I shall
point out how an interaction analysis of different responses to an ironic act contributes to the development of irony theory. A look at two data sets (informal
dinner conversations among friends, and pro and con TV debates) provides interesting differences in responses to irony. From the format of the responses,
we can often (though not always) access the processing of irony. If there are responses to the literal meaning, this does not necessarily indicate that the listener was not able to bridge the ironic gap (as former theories of irony have
suggested), but most often that both the implicated and the literal message are
processed. The data confirm that there are definitely different types of responses to irony: from responses to the literal level of the ironic act, to the implicated, mixed, or ambiguous reactions, to just laughter. The data further
confirm that the different types of responses to irony create different activity
types. Responses to the literally said (the dictum) develop a humorous discourse type of joint teasing; they cultivate the clash of perspectives and are frequent in dinner table conversations among friends. In the context of pro and con
debates, responses within the group differ in accordance with the line of arguing. Here, responses to the implicatum are more frequent; they recontextualize
the serious debate.

This chapter was previously published as "Responding to irony in different contexts: On cognition in
communication" (H. Kotthoff) in *Journal of Pragmatics, 35,* 1387–1411. Copyright © [2003] by
Elsevier. Reprinted with permission.

In this chapter, I intend to contribute to a neglected area of irony research, the reception of irony in contexts of face-to-face interaction. I would like to show that the reception of irony in different conversational contexts can give us insights into the way irony is processed. I cast a critical glance at cognition-oriented irony research which works with data from lab settings. The greatest differences between lab situations and natural conversations are that in the former, the irony recipients (a) are not affected by the ironic act, and (b) have no opportunity to continue the interaction and thus to shape and co-construct it. As to the latter, I have reasons to think that the way an addressee is affected by the ironic act influences her or his response. I discuss irony in two different contexts: in private conversations among close acquaintances, and in pro and con television discussions. I will show that in private conversations (where friendly irony is displayed), people react more to what is said in the ironic act, while in television discussions of controversial issues, they react more to what is meant by the (critical) ironic act. Previous irony research has underestimated the fact that people normally can react to both levels of meaning: to what is said and to what is implicated, and thereby shape the meaning of the emergent conversational sequence.

In particular, the double responses (to the dictum and the implicatum), which are present in both data sets, suggest furthermore that both levels of expression are recognized. This again indicates that irony is a special case of communicating a gap between the two levels of dictum and implicatum. This gap has to do with an evaluative contrast.

Let us first take a short glance at the long history of irony theory. In antiquity, ironists were viewed, on the one hand, as deceivers, hypocrites, and self-righteous pretenders. and, on the other hand, as sensitive, modest persons who employ understatement. In his *Institutio Oratoria,* Quintilian classifies irony as a trope, a figure of speech.

> Irony, however, is a type of allegory in which the opposite is expressed. The Romans call it "illusio" (mocking). One recognizes this either from the tone in which it is spoken, or from the person affected, or from the nature of the subject; for if something contradicts what is said, it is clear that the speech wishes to say something different. (VII, 6, 54, my translation)

In irony, Quintilian maintained, building upon Cicero's comments on irony, the speaker states the opposite of what he means and at the same time communicates that the stated message is not the one intended. In the further history of the concept, this aspect of "dissimulatio"[1] was emphasized more strongly (Lapp, 1992, p. 22). Lapp (1992, p. 24) summarized the ancient concept of irony as follows:

1. What is said is the opposite of what is meant.
2. One says something other than what one thinks.
3. Criticism through false praise, praise through apparent criticism.
4. Every type of making fun and ridicule.

Quintilian has emphasized points 1 and 3.

Later debates focused on the motive for the ironic, the specific quality of the contrast expressed in irony, its recognizability, and the question of the necessity of irony signals. Weinrich (1970) postulated the latter in *Linguistik der Lüge* (Linguistics of the Lie). In contrast to this, most researchers assume that indicators of a prosodic, mimetic, kinetic, or purely contextual nature are usually the case. They emphasize, however, that there are no signals which point exclusively to irony, but rather there are distancing procedures which, among other things, can block a direct understanding of the message and suggest perceiving it as ironic or sarcastic (Haiman, 1990). I suggest treating these distancing procedures as contextualization cues in the sense of Cook-Gumperz and Gumperz (1976) and Gumperz (1982).

The question of motives is answered in quite different ways. Many linguists regard irony as an aggressive form of communication (see on this the overview by Lapp, 1992). Brown and Levinson (1987) and Barbe (1995) have maintained, to the contrary, that ironic critique is less face threatening than direct. They thus view politeness as a reason for using irony. I regard as unfounded not only the general statement that irony is aggressive, but also the claim that it is always more polite than other speech activities. Above all, these assertions do not clarify what is uniquely specific about irony. I would like to show that what is specific about irony is the communication of a cleft between what is said and what is meant as the primary message.

ON WHAT LEVEL DO WE FIND THE IRONY-SPECIFIC OPPOSITION?

The view that in irony the said and the meant form an opposition is commonplace. But the question is on what level the opposition should be located: on that of semantics, of speech acts, or of evaluation?

Recently positions have been developed which conceptualize the relationship between the said and the meant as essentially one of the opposition between positive and negative evaluation (Elstermann, 1991; Hartung, 1998). They emphasize that the specific opposition is located not simply on the level of the proposition or illocution, but rather on the level of evaluation. I have reason to agree with this view.

Hartung's (1998) concept of evaluation can be summarized as follows:

1. An evaluation is a mental activity in which a person assigns an object a value on a continuous scale between the poles of positive and negative. The object can be any given entity: object, action, utterance, event, person, etc.
2. An evaluation is made from a perspective which takes specific attributes as relevant and assigns them a normative value. It is based on a comparison between the concrete object and a mental standard consisting of the relevant attributes, their normative value, and their weighting.
3. Between the individual components of object, evaluation aspect, and standard there are conventional relationships, which develop from the practical

activities in which the object is integrated. Without this evaluation knowledge, neither joint activity nor communication would be possible.

Evaluations can be communicated as predicates, or by certain formulations (choice of words, prosody, mimicry, repetition, syntactical (in)completion, presupposition, etc.). Hartung (1998) concluded that ironic utterances are perceived as negative evaluations, supposedly directed against the person who is associated with the object of the evaluation (which is not necessarily the addressee). However, irony is not always a form of negative evaluation: rather, it is a way of communicating an *evaluation gap*. Thus, irony can very well express positive evaluations by stating them negatively, as when (in my data from dinner conversations) the following remark is laughingly made by a guest as a comment on a sumptuous menu: "Once again something simple out of a can." As evaluation, this message is negative, but it makes everybody laugh. The hostess/cook replies as follows: "I certainly do know how to open cans." The background knowledge to which the ironic remark alludes is that this hostess often invites people to "something small." Normally, the dinner she then offers is quite elaborate and extensive; she is known to be a good cook. The implicatum accordingly consists of something like the following: "Once again, such a wonderful meal that you announced much too modestly"—a positive evaluation. The hostess reacts to the level of wording, thereby continuing the sequence as ironic. The implicatum of her ironic reply is something like the following: "I know a lot more than to open a can." Among close friends, irony very often alludes to group knowledge, just as it is the case here. According to Hartung (1998), irony allows us to re-affirm the in-group relations among friends, because both the ironist, his/her addressee, and the public rely on shared knowledge about a joint interaction history.

Irony as Echo?

One answer to the question of why people use irony is that given by Sperber and Wilson (1981), who stated that an additional comment is expressed in irony. Stempel (1976) assumed that the ironic speaker relies on his/her partner's assumptions for the opposition potential of irony. That is, if a mother says to her son, when he comes home dirty, "You are really a hero," she is attributing to her son the assumption that he may find himself heroic, whereas she holds the opposite view.

Drawing on the Freudian situation of telling a "dirty" joke, many irony analysts operate with a three-person interaction model (Groeben & Scheele, 1984; Stempel, 1976): The first person (speaker) explicitly refers in an affirming manner to a second person (addressee), whom he in reality attacks through an implicit denial of the affirmation, thereby exposing the latter vis-à-vis a third person (another hearer). Researchers often speak of exposing and ridiculing the object of irony (Stempel, 1976); however, irony does not necessarily imply ridicule.

Sperber and Wilson (1981), Sperber (1984), and Wilson and Sperber (1992) viewed irony as the prototypical speech act which does not "use" the literal meaning to transmit a message, but rather "mentions" it (transmits it as an "echo"), at the same time expressing a specific attitude toward it. Accordingly, irony is a variety of implicit echoic interpretive use, in which the communicator dissociates himself/herself from the opinion echoed by communicating a re-evaluation of the said. Though reasonable at first glance, Wilson and Sperber's limitation of irony to interpretive use is, however, not acceptable; vice versa, not all forms of echoic uses are ironic. In 1981, Sperber and Wilson assumed that the ironic utterance "what a lovely party," made at a very boring gathering, alluded to the already expressed expectation of a hearer who had expected a lovely party; while the ironist shows that this expectation was not fulfilled at all. In their (Wilson & Sperber, 1992) paper, the authors expand their concept of irony as "echo" and "mention" to apply to every attribution of a position to someone from which the speaker distances himself/herself. Here, the authors come very close to Stempel's (1976) concept of irony (although they seemingly do not know his work): they simply stipulate that the ironic utterance could be attributed to anybody (whether present or not).

In Kotthoff (1998b, 2000), I argued against conceptualizing irony as a prototypical case of mentioned speech (to be exact: of quasi-citation, that is, of unintroduced, citation-like speech). Double voicing through unintroduced quasi-citation, and the complex conversational inferencing needed to find out what was actually meant, are not limited to irony, however: they also occur in many other forms of polyphonic communication (in the Bakhtinian sense [Bakhtin, 1981]), above all, in conversational parody, which is quite often a feature of reported speech (Kotthoff, 1998b, 2000).[2] While for me, irony is just one case of "staged intertextuality," for Sperber and Wilson it seems to be the only case, or at least the prototypical one.

Researchers in interactional sociolinguistics have shown that we always contextualize our utterances in a specific way in order to control conversational inferencing (Cook-Gumperz & Gumperz, 1994). It is not enough to just distinguish "bona fide" and "non bona fide" communication (Raskin, 1985). Rather, it is necessary to go into the details of formatting talk in such a way that a specific understanding is obtained. Contextualization research starts from the assumption that we always conversationally create the frames (or contexts) in which we act. For humor research, this approach has been carried out by Davies (1986, 2002), Norrick (1993), and Kotthoff (1998a). Along very similar lines, Clift (1999) proposed to base the study of irony on Goffman's (1981) concept of "footing." [3]

Do We Only Process What Is Meant in Perceiving Irony?

In addition to asking what makes the ironic opposition specific, it is also important to ask whether the intended, the said, or both levels are processed. For Wilson and Sperber (1992, p. 75), only the level of what is meant, counts: "It is a variety of echoic interpretive use, in which the communicator dissociates herself from the opinion echoed with accompanying ridicule or scorn." "What a lovely party!" echoes a specific or imagined meaning, and simultaneously conveys that this meaning is absurd: this message is proclaimed as the most relevant one. In contrast to this,

Giora (1995), Giora and Kotthoff (1998), Kotthoff (1998a), and Giora and Fein (1999a, 1999b) assumed that irony does not erase what is said (the implicitly contrasted message), but rather that it communicates the difference between the dictum and the implicatum as being the most relevant information.

I consider the special achievement of irony to be its ability to signal a contrast in evaluation. An attitude is attributed to the addressee (or a third person) from which the ironist wishes to contrastively distance himself/herself. The gap between the said and the meant is conveyed as constituting the most relevant message.

Empirical Research on Irony

Irony has seldom been studied in live interaction. The majority of the literature reviewed in Lapp (1992) and Hartung (1998) used artificial examples and works with isolated individual activities (often taken from literary texts). Not even Barbe (1995) systematically takes into account responses to the ironic act. Empirical studies have been done by Engeler (1980), Giora and Gur (in press), Groeben and Scheele (1984), Groeben et al. (1985), Groeben (1986), Rundquist (1990), Schütte (1991), Barbe (1995), Hartung (1998), and Clift (1999). Among these, only Hartung, Giora and Gur, and Clift systematically analyzed the reactions of the addressee to the ironic act; so far, theirs are the only studies of conversational irony in context. As we will see below, how irony is processed can often be inferred from the responses to it; the latter co-construct the sequence.

Groeben and his colleagues (1985) combined a speech-act framework with psychological approaches to situational and personal conditions of irony. Analyzing questionnaires involving situational conditions and effects of irony, the authors found the following types of irony: defensive irony, protective irony, critical irony, friendly irony, and arrogant irony. The study showed that ironic acts are perceived quite differently by addressees, depending on general social interpretations (such as friendly, helpful, or critical intentions).

In a few cases, these authors were able to show, on the basis of observations, how the high creativity potential of the ironic utterances made these everyday examples much more creative (and funny!) than the invented ones used in lab studies (often limited to saying "nice weather today" on a stormy day). Here is an example from a natural context (Groeben & Scheele, 1984, p. 36, my translation):

> A teacher calls on a student who, despite a warning, has continued to talk to his neighbor and asks him what he has just said; the student, who has no idea, answers: "Well, uh ... ." The teacher retorts: "Correct so far."

We can classify this example under the rubric "critical." Such comments require a "bisociation" typical of humor (the student cannot be wrong up to this point because he has said nothing/the teacher does not expect more to come).

Schütte (1991) treated irony in general as a form of humorous communication. In a professional context of orchestra musicians, irony is found to represent a subversive means of denouncing a perspective or expectation attributed to a powerful partner. The partner's perspective is thereby implicitly rejected. By means of irony, the institutional power structure in the orchestra may be circumvented, e.g., the orchestra director could be indirectly attacked or criticized. In contrast, making sarcastic remarks turned out to be the exclusive right of the conductor, the person with highest status, who occasionally evaluates the performances of musicians in this way. Schütte viewed irony in a professional context as a social procedure for avoiding conflict and securing cooperation despite divergent interests and expectations. Schütte (1991), Hartung (1998), and Kotthoff (1998a, 1998b) have shown that irony is very often woven into complex humorous sequences.[4]

The processing of irony has usually been studied in laboratory situations, in which subjects were given dialogues to read and questions to answer (Gibbs, 1986; Gibbs & O'Brien, 1991). In various reading-time studies, these authors concluded that the "standard pragmatic model," such as the approaches due to Grice and Searle, does not satisfactorily explain the process of generating meaning. The standard pragmatic model offers a three-step procedure consisting of understanding the literal meaning, recognizing its inappropriateness in the current context, and finally generating a suitable meaning. However, processing irony in this way would take more time than processing literal utterances—something which is not borne out by the experiments. The authors draw the conclusion that irony is not understood by taking the roundabout route of processing the said, but that, in the appropriate context, it is grasped relatively directly (for a different view, see Colston & Gibbs, 2002). What interests us here is the question of whether, in fact, normal understanding only concerns the intended.

IRONY IN PRIVATE CONVERSATIONS AND TELEVISION DISCUSSIONS

First of all, we must realize that simply understanding irony and reacting to it are two different things. While cognitive psychologists (like Gibbs) and psycholinguists (like Giora) test for comprehension, as interaction analysts we are interested in *responses* to irony, in what is done with the ironic in the co-construction of the whole conversational sequence.

Responses to Irony in Dinner Table Conversations

Here, I will place particular weight on the way the reception of irony co-creates the specific quality of the ongoing conversational sequence. Before I demonstrate this in transcripts of talk, I will construct an example of a dialogue between A and B. A is handing out glasses to guests and gives B a kitschy glass with a horrible pink foot.[5] A says the following to B: "You get the most beautiful glass." Among B's possible responses are the following:

1. B: You are always so nice to me. (Response to the said)
2. B: Is that ever ugly! (Response to the meant)
3. B: Quite charming ... Isn't that ugly! (Mixed response)
4. B Thanks. (Ambiguous response)
5. B: HAHAHA (laughter)

Response 1 refers to what is positively *said* in the ironic act, and is received as such. One can easily imagine further comments continuing the irony, e.g., "We both have the same excellent taste." Obviously, reactions to what is said in irony have the potential to lead to playful discourse (teasing). The response to the said shows that this potential is activated, but it does not change the discourse frame: on the contrary, the irony is reframed.[6] Response 2 refers to what is *meant* by the ironic act. In this standard reaction, the frame switches back to ordinary discourse. Response 3 contains both types of reaction. As to response 4, it is not clear whether and how the irony was perceived, as the reaction is ambiguous. It could simply refer to the act of passing the glass, but it could also express an ironic stance to what is said. Response 5 responds only to the humor inherent in the ironic act.

Responses to the Said

In conversations with several participants, we often find mixed and complex responses by various conversational participants; the result is longer sequences. Example (1) below in addition contains various responses to what had been said in a preceding ironic act.

(1) (Conversation 14, Episode 6)
David (D), Ernst (E), Inge (I), Johannes (J), Katharina (K), Maria (M), Rudolph (R), several (s)

1 M:	Du hasch grad son opulentes [Sozialleben.
2 R:	[(? ?)
3 D:	total. total was los grad, well ich nämlich initiativ
4	geworden bin [jetzt.
5 M:	[HAHAHAHAHAHA
6 K:	[hab ich schoHn erzäHhlt. HAHA[HAHAHA
7 s:	[HAHA =
8 s:	HAHAHAHAHAHA[HAHAHAHA
9 E:	[was sagt er, er freut sich schon auf
10	Weihnachten und Silvester.
11 a:	HAHAHAHAHAHAHAHAHAHAHAHAHAHAHAHA[HAHAHAH AHA
12 E:	[munkelt
	man. munkelt man.
13 D:	ich hab angeregt entweder, oder. hab ich angeregt.

```
14 s:         HEHEHEHEHEHEHE
15 K:         wenn nichts los sei, Weihnachten und Silvester, dann
16            würde er (-) verreisen, hat er gesagt. [dann fliegt er
17 D:                                              [mhm dann flieg ich.
18 E:         in die Karibik. Karibik. HEHEHE[HEHEHE
19 s:                                         [HA[HAHAHAHAHAHA
              HAHA
20 M:                                            [HEHEHEHEHE
```

```
1 M:          You are having such a rich [social life lately.
2 R:                                     [(? ?)
3 D:          a lot. a lot is going on lately, because I
4             have taken the initiative [now.
5 M:                                     [HAHAHAHAHAHA
6 K:                                     [I told you already. HAHA[HAHAHA
7 s:                                                              [HAHA =
8 s:          HAHAHAHAHAHA [HAHAHAHA
9 E:                        [what is he saying, he is already
              looking forward to
10            Christmas and New Years.
11 a:         HAHAHAHAHAHAHAHAHAHAHAHAHAHAHA[HAHAHAH
              AHA
12 E:                                        [the rumors
              are. the rumors
13 D:         I have suggested either. or. I have suggested.
14 s:         HEHEHEHEHEHEHE
15 K:         if nothing is happening, Christmas and the New Year's,
16            then he would (-) take a trip. he said. [then he flies
17 D:                                                 [uhm then I fly.
18 E:         to the Caribbean. Caribbean. HEHEHE[HEHEHE
19 s:                                             [HA[HAHAHAHAHA
              HAHAHA
20 M:                                                [HEHEHEHEHE
```

The meal at which Maria makes this ironic remark to David happened at Katharina and David's apartment. Maria comments to David on his "rich social life." David normally prefers to enjoy his peace and quiet. Recently, however, he has participated in two social gatherings (Christmas and New Year's), which took place at his house (something he would otherwise have avoided). Maria's formulation is marked ("rich") and highly exaggerated. In her irony, Maria assigns David a "perspective" in which he himself would find his social life "rich."[7] Doing this, she implicitly distances herself from this evaluation, thus indicating a *gap*. David likewise ironically reacts to what Maria says and thus (sort of) confirms the existence of this gap (3/4).

In this connection, I want to maintain, first, that David is not reacting to the implicatum of the irony, but rather to the dictum: in reacting to what is said, one enters the playful frame which can recreate friendly irony.

Next, the question is what is ironic about David's response. First of all, the expression "have taken the initiative" is borrowed from Maria and David's girlfriend Katharina; the latter immediately provides an affirmative reaction and laughs (6). Maria laughs, too, since she knows how Katharina and David negotiate the "social life" topic. She knows that Katharina's opinion that David does not take enough "initiative" (Maria thinks so, too) is not shared by David himself. David's self-directed irony thus draws its potential from Maria's and Katharina's attitudes.

One also has to know that David did not take any "initiative" at all: he has only graciously submitted to his fate, since it was Katharina who had planned the parties, and David, living with Katharina, could hardly avoid them. The others present also know about David's and Katharina's differing levels of sociability.

In lines 7 and 8, several persons laugh. David's response is a classical example of echoic irony (Sperber & Wilson, 1981; Sperber, 1984). In lines 9 and 10, Ernst ironically alludes to "Christmas" and "New Year's," which further expands the ironic frame and the teasing. The shared knowledge is that Katharina had invited many people for Christmas and New Year's Eve, including those present, and that David had manifestly expressed his displeasure about this. So everyone laughs at the ironic joke that he was already looking forward to "Christmas" and "New Year's," for which supposedly big parties are being planned. At the time of conversation, it was already clear that it was David's expressed wish that there would be no such parties this year.

In line 13, David seriously reports on his preference. From line 15 on, Katharina ironically links David's distaste for a "rich social life" with his equally familiar dislike of travel. David intensifies the teasing with self-directed irony (17), as in fact he vehemently objects to flying. Ernst then further exaggerates this by indicating a travel goal (the Caribbean), which David himself has recently ridiculed, when Ernst took a flight to this very region. Again people laugh; David is teased and teases back. Interwoven in this complex scene are irony, self-irony, and playful attack. David, the target of the irony, also participates in the ridiculing (e.g., in line 17; here, he demonstrates the ability to laugh at himself).

People talk about David in the third person, which is typical of teasing (Günthner, 1996a; Straehle, 1993). The speakers communicate extensive knowledge of one another and teasingly confirm themselves as in-group members. Actual differences can be dealt with playfully and marked as such; they are thereby also accepted.

Combined Responses

Combined responses are common not only in my corpus of dinner table conversations, but also in the television debates to be discussed below (however, there are also differences, as we will see). Many examples from the dinner conversations can be characterized as forms of friendly-playful irony (just as was the case for those mentioned above). Thus, for example, ironic predicates are employed (e.g., "orderly" for a nearly unfurnished room or "healthy" for a dessert that is not too tasty), which also have negative connotations ("too little furniture" "does not taste good"). Example (2) shows such a combined response:

(2) (Conversation 12, episode 2)
Annette (A), Bernd (B)
Bernd shows the guests his new apartment.

| A: | seHEhr übersichtlich. doch. schöHN üHÜbersichtlich. HE |
| B: | ja:::HA SO kann mans auch sagen. also bald steht hiern größerer Tisch ... |

| A: | veHRy orderly, really. Neat and orderly. HE |
| B: | yeah:::HA THAT is one way to put it. well soon there will be a large kind of table here ... |

Annette laughingly says something to Bernd which is generally positive in its connotations, but which in this context does not necessarily have a positive meaning. Her positive evaluation (from Bernd's point of view) of the relatively empty apartment communicates a *gap:* she herself finds the apartment too empty. The laughter (integrated in the words of both speakers) contextualizes the ironic contrast between these phrases as funny. Bernd responds both to the dictum and to the implicatum; he accepts the positive wording by "yeah ... HA that is one way to put it" (reacting to the said), and then explains what must still be done in the apartment: "soon there will be a large kind of table here ..." (reacting to the implicatum). The wording "orderly" (*übersichtlich*) intertextually alludes to a sketch by the German comedian Loriot. Loriot and a girlfriend have ordered a *nouvelle cuisine* dish and receive a plate with a small piece of fish and two pea pods. They then comment as follows: "very orderly." Annette uses a quasi-quotation here (an echoic irony in the sense of Sperber and Wilson).

Ambiguous Responses

In the next episode, Sylvia expresses a very specific wish for a drink. Fritz does not have this drink and reacts ironically to her wish. This irony would have to be interpreted, according to Brown and Levinson (1987), as off-record politeness. The irony is, however, made clear gradually and thereby transferred from the off-record into the on-record domain. Example (3) below shows an ambiguous response.

(3) (Conversation 9, episode 3)
Anton (A), Beate (B), Fritz (F), Helena (H), Kilian (K), Sylvia (S)

1 S: ICH will, (-) en Orangensaft mit Mineralwasser.

2 K:	obs hier Orangensaft gibt?
3	(2.0)
4 F:	wie wärs mit Pfirs Pfirsich Maracuja?
5 K:	aber ich trink doch [einen Wein.
6 F:	[aus unserer REICHhaltigen Bar.
7 S:	SEHR gut.
8 K:	[HAHAHA
9 F:	[HAHAHA ich glaub Du spinnst.
10 H:	HAHAHA
11 S:	(? ?)
12 F:	also, O-Saft hab ich noch. aber Mineralwasser,
13 S:	DANN mit Wasser gemischt. DANN misch ich selber.

1 S:	I would like, (-) an orange juice with mineral water.
2 K:	is there any orange juice?
3	(2.0)
4 F:	how about pea- peach maracuja?
5 K:	but I could have [wine.
6 F:	[from our WELL-stocked bar.
7 S:	VERY well.
8 K:	[HAHAHA
9 F:	[HAHAHA you must be out of your mind.
10 H:	HAHAHA
11 S:	(? ?)
12 F:	well, I have o-juice. but mineral water,
13 S:	THEN mixed with water. THEN I will mix it myself.

Sylvia very directly expresses her wish for a specific mixed drink. Kilian, the other invited friend, expresses doubt as to its availability. Then the host, Fritz, asks whether an even more unusual drink ("peach maracuja") would be acceptable. Independently of this dialogue, Kilian makes his own drink request, and Fritz adds a characterization of the place where he plans to get the drink ("our well-stocked bar"). Fritz lives in a student co-op and it is consequently quite obvious that they do not have a "well-stocked bar." (At this point, it becomes clear that Fritz had already reacted ironically in line 4).

In line 7, Sylvia welcomes the suggestion. We cannot infer from her *very well* whether she welcomes the proposed drink or whether her remark is placed in a playful frame; it is ambiguous. Kilian and Fritz laugh. At least Kilian has grasped the subtle irony in Fritz's words; possibly also Sylvia is playing along (however, this is not clear). When Fritz laughingly says "you must be out of your mind," it becomes fully apparent that he has reacted ironically to her request, thus defining it as excessive. Fritz himself makes sure that his irony will be gradually recognized for what it is. Helena also laughs. Then Fritz states seriously what kinds of drinks he has, and Sylvia accepts a different beverage already before he has completed his statement.

When Fritz, in line 4, proposes an exotic drink combination in the context of a student household, he implies that Sylvia's first wish has been excessive. His ironic remark adopts her perspective and assigns it a negative evaluation (see below). His rejection in line 9 is highly implicit, but certainly no more polite than rejecting the request for a drink by suggesting another one. A more polite way of turning down this request would have involved an expression of great regret ("I am terribly sorry," etc.). The laughter introducing his reply "you must be out of your mind" contextualizes this impoliteness as not unfriendly. (Helena also laughs in response). In the given context, it is clear that Fritz's remark further indexes the unusualness of Sylvia's request.

Let us examine a last scene from the dinner conversation corpus.

Laughter As a Response

Example (4) shows laughter as response to irony and as repartee to what had been said ironically by another participant. After practice, a judo group has gathered to share beer and pretzels. Of the members, Gisela was in charge of arranging the pretzels. Normally, in South Germany, pretzels are buttered; there is, however, hardly any butter on the pretzels at hand. Helmut teasingly claims that Gisela bought butter for sixty pretzels, which would mean that they have far too much butter for the twenty pretzels they are about to eat. Obviously, the contrary is the case. In line 42, Helmut's ironic act starts out by creating a fiction as if Gisela had bought too much butter. Gisela laughs.

(4)
All (a), Gisela (G), Helmut (H), Nadine (N)

```
42 H:    und für sechzig Butter gekauft hier.
43 G:    HA[HAHAHA
44 H:        [wo wir doch sowieso alle gesagt haben,
45       wir WOLLN nich soviel Butter.
46 a:    HAHAHAHAHAHAHAHAHA
47 N:    die is dein Problem (? ?) HEHE
48 G:    HAHAHAHAHA
49 H:    ha is doch wahr. [soviel BUTTer das is doch
50       wirklich nich gesund.
```

```
42 H:    and bought butter for sixty here.
43 G:    HA[HAHAHA
44 H:        [even though we all said anyway,
45       we DON'T want so much butter.
46 a:    HAHAHAHAHAHAHAHAHA
47 N:    that is your problem (? ?) HEHE
48 G:    HAHAHAHAHA
```

49 H: ha it's really true. [so much BUTTer that is
50   really not healthy.

In line 44/45, Helmut further intensifies the irony by claiming that everyone had said that they "don't want so much butter." Helmut ironically pretends to disagree with the supposedly large amount of butter made available. In reality, he objects to the fact that there is almost no butter on the pretzels. As the person responsible for the pretzels and the butter, Gisela is the chief addressee of Helmut's irony. She laughs, and the rest of the group laughs with her in line 46. Nadine reacts on the level of Helmut's ironical reply by saying "That is your problem"—which, in this context, means the following: "You are too fat, and therefore butter is a problem for you." Gisela in particular, the victim of Helmut's irony, laughs at Nadine's response. Nadine's response is again ironic, since she reacts to what is being said, not to what is meant. In line 49, Helmut reaffirms what Gisela has just said: "so much butter is really not healthy."

Irony and Teasing

The ironic utterances examined here all occur in the context of friendly relationships. No wonder, then, that very often, in responding to the ironic act, a teasing sequence is constructed. Teasing plays an important role in informal talk among friends. As Straehle (1993) has pointed out, we normally tease people we know quite well. Since teasing is a communicative activity that combines "bonding and biting" (Boxer & Cortés-Conde, 1997), people seem to prefer to tease those with whom they feel secure enough to practice "playful biting."

All such activities are humorous, because each time the ironic act sets a playful key, which is then reaffirmed. Nevertheless, differences of opinion are definitely being communicated, but they are kept socially acceptable. Teasing reveals a lot about the communicative construction of friendship,[8] which is apparently not entirely oriented toward displaying harmony. Friends have to find strategies that can help them deal with their mutual differences. Friendly irony and teasing seem to be a very productive way of communicating such differences (e.g., standards of sociability, attitudes towards traveling, or just different situational expectations, such as the need for furniture in a room, the drinks one can expect to get, the amount of butter needed on pretzels, and so on). Irony always marks a deviation from the normal standard, which, at the same time, it implicitly creates. Hence, the evaluation gap which is always constructed in irony, integrates the gap separating the normal from the not-normal.

Thirty hours of dinner table conversation exchanges, containing 51 ironic sequences, were transcribed and examined.[9] In the following, I present a quantitative summary of the responses to irony in this dinner conversation corpus:

Responses to the said: 26
Responses to the implicated: 4
Mixed reactions by the addressee of the irony: 10

Ambiguous reactions: 5
Laughter only: 6

Half of the responses in this corpus refer to the level of the said, and, as we have seen, turn into playful teasing sequences. Reactions to the implicatum, as we will see in the next section, do not develop a playful key, but instead, continue on a serious note.

Irony in Television Debates

Quite another situation occurs in television debates. I have examined 20 hr of the Austrian TV program "Club II" and found 24 examples. Club II discussions were held every Tuesday evening, and were transmitted live and open-ended. They are topic-centered and organized around controversies on political, cultural, and social subjects. Interestingly, in public debates, there seems to be less irony than in private conversations, even though irony is traditionally attributed more to the public domain.

Responses to the Implicatum

Since the discussions are contentious, irony plays a role here within the staging of the controversy. Here, we find the critical type of irony which so often inappropriately is viewed as the prototype. Let's look at the data. One discussion turns around the joys and dangers of riding a motorcycle. Active motorbikers are present, who defend the sport in every regard. The other party features people who would prefer to restrict biking for reasons of excessive noise and danger. The moderator, Gerd, has already stated that he is more on the side of the critics and regards the sport as dangerous. The active motorcycle enthusiast, Theo, encourages him to at least try it.

(5) (TV-Discussion on motorbiking)
Dolly (D), Ell (E), Gerd (G), Fiona (F), Theo (T), Rudi (R), several (s)

1 T:	fahrn Sie doch mal im Sommer. jetzt ist ja Sommerclub.
2 G:	ja, ich hab eh nicht vor die PeHnsiHon zu eHerleHEben.
3 s:	HEHEHE[HE
4 T:	[aber ich bitte Sie. schauns eh eh ich bin doch auch kein Verrückter.

1 T:	… do take a trip in the summer. now we're having the summer club.
2 G:	yes, I do not intend to liHEve unHEtil reHEtirement.
3 s:	HEHEHE[HE
4 T:	[but I beg your pardon. look here uh uh I really am not crazy either.

In these "summer clubs," excursions are being organized. Theo suggests that Gerd participates in one of them. Gerd agrees ironically: he does not intend anyway to live long enough to make it until retirement. The implicatum here is this: instead of enjoying the ride, he fears he could suffer a fatal accident. The people who share his opinion laugh. Theo and the other bikers do not share in the laughter. Theo employs two independent starter formulas which are very popular in Austrian German (*aber ich bitte Sie. schauns*—"but I beg your pardon. look here"). Then he reacts to the implicatum that all bikers drive so crazily that they will not survive to retirement. After two further hesitation signals, he starts to defend himself against the implicatum: "I really am not crazy either."

According to the graded salience hypothesis (Giora, 1997), it should be more difficult to process irony than direct forms of speech. This hypothesis would be confirmed if we can show that responses to the implicatum are more difficult to process than those to the said. We see in example (6) that Theo takes time to react. First, the laughter sequence offers him time to formulate a response, and then he starts hesitatingly. In the TV data, in four of the cases, others laugh before the addressee of the irony reacts.

In this TV-context, when someone reacts to the implicatum, the response is either somewhat delayed, or otherwise a simple reversal occurs, as when a pro-motorcycle speaker portrays the sport as erotic. Ell, a professor, presents some shocking accident statistics, to which Fiona, a psychologist, reacts in an ironic fashion.

(6)
1   Fiona: das ist ja[10] die Erotik. HEHE
2   Rudi: das ist nicht die Erotik.

1   Fiona: that is what we know is erotic. HEHE
2   Rudi: that is not what is erotic.

With her irony, Fiona joins Ell's line of arguing. They both belong to the anti-motorcycling party. Thus, her irony has two different addressees: she allies with the contra group and she mocks the pro group. Normally, we would not think that a high accident rate makes a sport erotic. One can, however, very well portray danger psychologically as an erotic feature. The irony in Fiona's response lies in the local context, which relates the erotic to the accidents. The active motorbiker, Rudi, immediately states that this is not the eroticism they experience in motor-biking. A simple countering of the type "It is X" in response to "It is not X" apparently is easy to manage, even under the stressful conditions of a pro and con TV-debate. Alternatively, starters and other "fillers" provide the time needed to produce an adequate reaction.

In another discussion, where the topic is whether there is any liberalism in the Austrian People's Party (Freiheitliche Partei Österreichs, FPÖ, an ultra-conservative political party, which at the time was led by Jörg Haider), critics of the party portray the anti-liberal activities of Haider and other FPÖ politicians. Discussant

Reiderer (R), a political scientist, criticizes the FPÖ's drawing on anti-liberal politicians like Schober as ancestors. Mölzer (M), an FPÖ official, asks (in lines 7 and 8) whether Reiderer then would be ready to deny that Schober was a liberal. Reiderer then repeats some facts about Schober's role in the historical movement of the thirties, referred to as "Austro-fascism," which leads to the following ironic statement: "a fine liberal, I can only say to that:"

(7) (TV discussion on liberalism)
Mölzer (M), Reiterer (R), others.

1 R:	als der Herr Steger an liberalen Ahnherrn suchen wollte,
2 M:	mhm mhm
3 R:	auf wen hat er zurückgegriffen? auf den alten Schober.
4 M:	mhm
5 R:	auf den alten [Schober, der autoritärer
6 M:	[also dem sprechen Sie den Liberalismus
7	auch ab.
8 R:	der autoritärer Bundespolizei eh Direktor in Wien war,
9	der kurzfristig eh im Austro also unmittelbar in der
10	Überleitung zum Austrofaschismus Bundeskanzler war,
11	(H) der also genau die Büttelarbeit für den
12	Austrofaschismus eigentlich geleistet hat.
13	a schöner Liberaler. kann ich da nur sagn.
14 M:	also das sehn wir aus unserem Geschichtsverständnis
15	anders, da gilt Schober also schon als an sich DAS
16	Beispiel eines Nationalliberalen in [der österreichischen Geschichte.

1 R:	when Mr. Steger wanted to find liberal ancestors
2 M:	mhm mhm
3 R:	whom did he look back to? to old Schober.
4 M:	mhm
5 R:	to old [Schober, the authoritarian
6 M:	[thus you deny liberalism
7	to him too.
8 R:	who was the authoritarian Federal police uh chief in Vienna,
9	who for a short time was uh in the Austro- I mean immediately up to and in the
10	transition to the Austro-fascist period was Federal Chancellor,
11	(H) the very man who thus did the police work for
12	Austro-fascism actually.
13	a fine liberal. I must say.
14 M:	well in our understanding of history we see this
15	differently, for us Schober is thus indeed THE

16   example of a national liberal in Austrian history.

The evaluation "a fine X" ("a fine friend you are," etc.) can be seen as a standardized ironic wording. The reinforcement "I must say" signals that the preceding predicate is meant ironically. The FPÖ representative, Mölzer, responds to the implicatum by stating the following: "well in our understanding of history we see this differently." (A reaction to the dictum could have been an affirmation in the form of "Yes, Schober was a fine liberal").

In the television corpus, there are fourteen reactions to the implicatum—more than half of the responses. Such responses seem appropriate if one understands the response as a critique of speaker's position. Interestingly, we also find many examples there of inappropriate responses, implying that the rubric "ambiguous reactions" is differently realized in both corpora. (Compare that in the dinner conversation corpus, the ambiguous responses are always coherent, even though it may be hard to determine whether they are more coherent with the dictum or with the implicatum).

Ambiguous or Incoherent Responses

Ambiguous reactions are those to which we cannot assign a specific meaning, as it is unclear to what aspects of the previous comments they react. Also in this category belong a number of entirely unrelated, hence incoherent reactions. In the case of these responses, it is not evident whether we have to do with irony, and if yes, how the irony was processed.

The following example stems from a debate on the imprisoned Viennese action artist Otto Mühl. Mühl had led a commune in which very controversial social experiments were performed. The panel included an art professor (Oswald Oberhuber) and an art critic (Regina Wyrwoll), who both defended Mühl; moreover, an ethics professor (Robert Prantner) and three former commune members (Nikolaus Hel-bich, Wencke Mühleisen, and Nadja Reyne), who all criticized him. Prantner's first contribution is very ironic. He presented it immediately, after Wencke Mühleisen gave a very critical report on life in the commune.

(8) (TV-Discussion VII)
Mühleisen (M), Oberhuber (O), Prantner (P), several (s)

1 P:	Frau Wencke Mühleisen hat mich jetzt davon eh davor bewahrt,
2	doch in ihrer realistischen Erinnerung,
3	in lyrischer Nostalgie und fast Reue zu schwelgen,
4	nicht den gleichen Weg zu diesem vielleicht doch
5	großen Otto gefunden zu haben, eh ich [verstehe
6 s:	[HEHEHEHEHE
7 P:	den Herrn Kollegen, der ein berühmter
8	eine berühmte Persönlichkeit in der europäischen Kunstszene ist,

9		aber sein Tiroler Herz vielleicht doch nicht ganz verleugnen kann,
10		wenn er auch von zersetzenden Problemen oder Elementen bei Künstlern spricht.
11		das spricht für Sie.
12	M:	HEHEHE
13	P:	ich verstehe aber weder Sie Herr Kollege Oberhuber, [noch viele andere
14	O:	[des hab ich jetzt net ganz gemeint. muß i dann antworten darauf.

1	P:	Ms. Wencke Mühleisen has just prevented me in uh, from
2		actually by her realistic reminiscences,
3		from wallowing in lyric nostalgia and near-regret,
4		from not having found the same path to this perhaps after all
5		great Otto. eh I [understand
6	s:	[HEHEHEHEHE
7	P:	my colleague, who is a famous
8	a:	famous figure on the European art scene,
9		but perhaps cannot entirely deny his Tyrolean heart,
10		when he also speaks of the destructive problems or features of artists.
11		that speaks well for you.
12	M:	HEHEHE
13	P:	but I understand neither you dear colleague Oberhuber, [nor many others
14	O:	[I did not really mean that. must I then reply to this.

It is perfectly clear that even without Ms. Mühleisen's remarks, Professor Prantner would not have wallowed in regret that he had not found his way to the great Otto, since he regards the great Otto as a criminal. Interestingly, the two persons present who take the position of acknowledging Mühl, do not react to this critical irony at all; in contrast, the three panelists who also hold critical attitudes toward Mühl laugh in line 6. When the targets of his irony do not react, Prantner addresses Professor Oberhuber directly. His remark, "[he] is a famous figure … , but perhaps cannot entirely deny his Tyrolean heart," is also critically ironic. The implication is that of a contradiction: fame makes people cruel. Oberhuber reacts in a vaguely corrective manner (it is clear that he did not imply this) and asks the moderator whether he has to answer. Prantner, however, has already continued and Oberhuber cannot answer at all.

In this case, the response to the irony is very late and unclear. It is evident, however, that Prantner is insinuating that for Oberhuber, artistry and heart are a contradiction (just as it is the case for the latter's friend Mühl). It is also clear that Oberhuber himself does not subscribe to this contradiction. Oberhuber's reaction in line 14 is therefore redundant and no one reacts to it.

It seems to be more difficult to respond to critical irony, as Oberhuber's lack of reaction to Prantler's irony in line 11 shows. While the laughter of Mühl's critics may be taken as an indication that they indeed understood the irony, it is not clear from his reaction whether Oberhuber got it. Most likely, he simply did not understand the irony.

Other examples of critical irony also display responses which are not really appropriate to irony. They indicate that the target of the irony either has not understood the irony, or does not want to understand it, or is unable to react quickly. Thus, in example (9), a book by Volker Elis Pilgrim (a participant in the discussion) is the subject of the debate. The author claims that fatherless sons who are overprotected by their mother could later become dangerous, especially in positions of power (for example, as politicians). All the guests on the show disagree with this claim. A psychologist, Riess, asks what mothers should do when there is no father. Christian Enzensberger, the philologist, answers ironically that they should try to keep their sons from becoming politicians, and rather encourage them to be poets.

(9) (TV-Discussion IX)
Enzensberger (E), Pilgrim (P), Riess (R)

1 R:	das würd also bedeuten, jetzt, ich bin auch Mutter,
2	daß Sic sagen,
3 P:	ja?
4 R:	würd ich Sie fragen, was sollte ich tun,
5 P:	ja
6 R:	ja jetzt nicht dies wir und man sollte tun,
7 P:	ja
8 R:	jetzt wir, die betroffenen Mütter, =
9 P:	mhm
10 R:	= die es ja so angeht, wa was =
11 P:	mhm
12 R:	= sollten die Mütter tu:n, damit sich was verändert.
13 E:	wenn Sie ihn zu sehr eh eh unter Ihrer Fuchtel haben, dann =
14 R:	ja:
15 E:	= sollen Sie zu ihm sagen, werde Dichter und nicht
16	Politiker. [HAHAHA HEHE HEHEHEHEHEHEHEHEHE HEHE
17 P:	[NA::IN HE Politiker is sehr was Wichtiges
18	und wir brauchen [positive Politiker.
19 E:	[aber doch nicht diese Sorte HAHAHA
1 R:	that would then mean, now, I am also a mother
2	that you are saying,
3 P:	yes?
4 R:	if I asked you, what I should do,
5 P:	yes

6 R:	well now not this what we and one should do,
7 P:	yes
8 R:	now we, the mothers in question, =
9 P:	mhm
10 R:	= who really have to deal with it, you know, wh- what =
11 P:	mhm
12 R:	= should the mothers do:, for something to change.
13 E:	if you have him too much under your thumb, then =
14 R:	yes:
15 E:	= you should tell him, become a poet and not
16	a politician. [HAHAHA HEHE HEHEHEHEHEHEHEHEHE HEHE
17 P:	[NO::: HE a politician is something very important
18	and we need [positive politicians.
19 E:	[but not this kind though HAHAHA

Ms. Riess asks Pilgrim several questions to which Enzensberger provides an answer (starting in line 13). This answer ironically simplifies Pilgrim's position. It totally ignores Pilgrim's complex psychoanalytical argumentation and brings it to the level of simple advice. He laughs at his own suggestion, the others smile. Pilgrim's response in line 17 is not fully coherent, because he ignores Enzensberger's ironic simplification. The suggestion to eliminate the problem of overaggressive boys by advising them to choose harmless professions implicitly attacks Pilgrim's theory. Pilgrim's rebuttal in lines 17/18 is only locally coherent: it neither responds to the dictum nor to the implicatum; in line 19, Enzensberger corrects his statement.

It turns out that in pro and con TV debates, a different type of irony, namely critical irony, dominates, compared with what is the case in meetings among friends; the two types of irony provoke different reactions.

CONCLUSION: INTERPRETATION OF THE DIFFERENCES

Compare the following findings:

30 hours of dinner conversations, 51 ironical sequences
Responses to the said: 26
Responses to the meant: 4
Mixed responses of the addressee: 10
Ambiguous reactions: 5
Laughter only: 6
20 hours of TV debates, 24 ironical sequences
Responses to the said: 1
Responses to the meant: 14
Mixed responses of the addressee: 2
Ambiguous responses: 5

Laughter only: 2

What apparently distinguishes these two corpora is the difference in reactions to the said and to the implicated under the different circumstances (see Fig. 17.1). In informal situations among friends, the preferred strategy is to continue in the humorous key and respond to the said. Mixed reactions and laughter-only are also responses along these lines. In contrast, in the TV corpus, the level of the said plays no important role in reactions to irony. In these public discussions, which are framed as pro and con debates, irony is heard as critical, and humorous potentials are not attended to. Given that in the TV data, the salient meaning has not been addressed, we have no evidence that it has been processed at all. But neither do we have evidence to the contrary. On the whole, findings show that reactions to irony seem to be more difficult in a frame of public competition, perhaps because it involves addressing the implicated, that which is non-salient, i.e., not coded in the mental lexicon.

This study of responses to irony supports a basic claim of interaction research, namely that listening is not just listening; rather, it is "listening for speaking," as Goodwin (1995) and also Clark (1996) have pointed out. This dimension of reception in context can hardly be studied under laboratory conditions.

Another basic claim of contextualization research also has gained support, namely that conversational inferencing is an ongoing process which works with assumptions that are continually readjusted. This also means that ironic activities are always interpreted in connection with the ongoing conversation, not as isolated acts. Among close friends, they tend to be understood in a playful frame, to be ex-

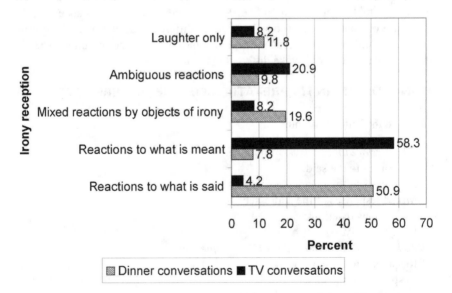

Figure 17.1.   Reception of irony in various contexts.

panded through mutual responses. Under conditions of public competition, responding to irony seems to be more difficult. Here one's own face must be defended. In a controversy, a much stronger pressure to act is involved than is the case in informal talk.

In conclusion, my data show that, in irony, in principle, both levels of the utterance are processed, not just the implicated (let alone chiefly the implicated). The dinner table conversations suggest that the salient meaning is indeed accessible; the TV data suggest that the less salient meaning is less easily accessed, but still retrievable.

The data further support another hypothesis, namely that, besides the pragmatics of irony, a meta-pragmatics[11] is of great importance in guiding the overall evaluation of the ongoing interaction on the level of relationship management. On this level, it is decided whether the irony is more supportive/friendly or competitive/aggressive. In the latter case, the reaction to irony becomes indeed more difficult. Irony thus performs quite different things in different contexts. It can communicate "bonding and biting," that is, a positive management of social differences. But it can also make it more difficult for an opponent to react.

Transcription Conventions

(-)	one hyphen indicates a short pause
(- -)	two hyphens indicate a longer pause (less than half a second)
(0.5)	pause of half a second; long pauses are measured in half seconds
(? what ?)	indicates uncertain transcription
(? ?)	indicates an unintelligible utterance
..[..	
..[..... .	indicates overlap or interruption
=	latching onto an utterance without interruption
HAHAHA	laughter
HEHEHE	slight laughter
gooHd	integrated laughter
(H)	audible exhalation
('H)	audible inhalation
?	rising intonation
.	falling intonation
,	continuing intonation
:	indicates lengthening
° blabla°	lower amplitude and pitch
COME ON	emphatic stress (pitch and volume shift)
?	high onset of pitch
((sits down))	nonverbal actions or comments

ENDNOTES

1. *Dissimulatio* means consciously pretending, or pretending to be dumb in such a way that the other will detect it on his own.
2. On double voicing in reported speech, see Günthner (1996b) and Couper-Kuhlen (1998).
3. In his chapter on "footing," Goffman (1981) analyzed the participant structure of dialogues, assigning them different degrees of responsibility for the message. His approach has some overlaps with Bakhtin's concept of dialogic polyphony.
4. However, not all irony is humorous. Especially the highly standardized and critical sorts of irony lack the surprise dimension typical of humorous discourse. Irony and humor overlap to a great extent, but are not coterminous.
5. A similar example is found in Hartung (1998).
6. I use the term *frame* in Goffman's (1974) sense, which comes close to Gumperz's (1982) notion of context.
7. On perspectivation in discourse, see Graumann (1989) and Sandig (1996). In Kotthoff (1998b), an irony theory is presented which works with the concept of perspectivation.
8. Studying irony and teasing among friends generally requires a combination of interaction analysis and ethnography. Only knowledge of the group enables us to decide whether or not the teasing has harmed the friendship. In many cultures, either po-faced or amused reactions to teasing are preferred (Drew, 1987). We must assume that the victim of a teasing may react with laughter locally, only to later on possible express a feeling of being hurt. Therefore, the conversation analytic structures of local production are too limiting when we analyze the construction of social relationships.
9. The sequences contain only clear cases of irony, that is, such as communicate an evaluation gap.
10. The modal particle "ja" cannot be directly translated into English. Modal particles have no lexical meaning, but influence the semantics of the whole phrase. The particle "ja" adds a consensual flavor to the whole utterance.
11. On differentiating between pragmatics and metapragmatics, see Verschueren (1995). Metapragmatics is concerned with how societal interpretation frameworks influence the identity construction of speakers in discourse. Without going into details here, it should be noted that, in irony, more is at stake than comprehending the ironic act. An assessment of the relationship between ironist, object, and public plays an important role. Metapragmatics goes beyond the textual level.

REFERENCES

Bakhtin, M. M. (1981). *The dialogic imagination* (C. Emerson & M. Holquist, Eds.). Austin: University of Texas Press.
Barbe, K. (1995). *Irony in context.* Amsterdam: Benjamins.
Boxer, D., Cortés-Conde, F. (1997). From bonding to biting: conversational joking and identity display. *Journal of Pragmatics, 27,* 275–294.
Brown, P., & Levinson, S. (1987). *Politeness: Some universals in language usage.* Cambridge, England: Cambridge University Press.
Clark, H. H. (1996). *Using language.* Cambridge, England: Cambridge University Press.
Colston, H. L., & Gibbs, R. W. Jr. (2002). Are irony and metaphor understood differently? *Metaphor and Symbol, 17,* 57–80.
Clift, R. (1999). Irony in conversation. *Language in Society, 28,* 523–553.
Cook-Gumperz, J., & Gumperz, J. (1976). *Context in children's speech. Papers on language and context* (Working Papers No. 46). Berkeley, CA: Language Behavior Research Laboratory.

Cook-Gumperz, J., & Gumperz, J. (1994). The politics of conversation: conversational inference in discussion. In A. D. Grimshaw (Ed.), *What's going on here? Complementary studies of professional talk* (pp. 373–395). Norwood, NJ: Ablex.

Couper-Kuhlen, E. (1998). *Coherent voicing. On prosody in conversational reported speech.* In List-Arbeitspapier Nr. 1, Fachgruppe Sprachwissenschaft der Universität Konstanz.

Davies, C. (1986). Joint Joking. Improvisational humorous episodes in conversation. *Berkeley Linguistic Society, 10,* 360–371.

Davies, C. E. (2003). How English-learners joke with native speakers: An interactional sociolinguistic perspective on humor as collaborative discourse across cultures. *Journal of Pragmatics, 35,* 1361–1385.

Dews, S., Kaplan, J., & Winner, E. (1995). Why not say it directly? The social functions of irony. *Discourse Processes, 19,* 347–367.

Drew, P. (1987). Po-faced receipts of teases. *Linguistics, 25,* 219–253.

Engeler, U. P. (1980). Sprachwissenschaftliche Untersuchung zur ironischen Rede. Dissertation Universität Zürich.

Elstermann, M. (1991). Über verschiedene Arten indirekten Kommunizierens. In H. Wolfdietrich (Ed.), *Kommunikation und Wissen. Annäherungen an ein interdisziplinäres Forschungsgebiet* (pp. 296–313). Berlin, Germany: Akademie- Verlag.

Freud, S. (1985). *Der Witz und seine Beziehung zum Unbewu8ten.* Fischer, Frankfurt.

Gibbs, R. (1986). On the psycholinguistics of sarcasm. *Journal of Experimental Psychology: General, 115,* 3–15.

Gibbs, R., & O'Brien, J. (1991). Psychological aspects of irony understanding. *Journal of Pragmatics, 16,* 523–530.

Giora, R. (1995). On irony and negation. *Discourse Processes, 19,* 239–265.

Giora, R. (1997). Understanding figurative literal language: The graded salience hypothesis. *Cognitive Linguistics, 7,* 183–206.

Giora, R. (2003). *On our mind: Salience, context and figurative language.* New York: Oxford University Press.

Giora, R., & Kotthoff, H. (1998). *Report on the research project. The graded salience hypothesis of irony.* Lion Foundation, University of Tel Aviv/University of Konstanz.

Giora, R., & Fein, O. (1999a). Irony: context and salience. *Metaphor and Symbol, 14,* 241–257.

Giora, R., & Fein, O. (1999b). Irony interpretation: the graded salience hypothesis. *HUMOR, 12,* 425–436.

Giora, R., & Inbal, G. (2003). Irony in conversation: Salience and context effects. In B. Nerlich. (Ed.), *Polysemy.* Berlin, Germany: Walter de Gruyter.

Goffman, E. (1974). *Frame analysis. An essay on the organization of experience.* New York: Harper & Row.

Goffman, E. (1981). *Forms of talk.* Philadelphia: University of Pennsylvania Press.

Goodwin, C. (1995). Sentence construction within interaction. In U. Quasthoff (Ed.), *Aspects of oral communication* (pp. 198–220). Berlin, Germany: Walter de Gruyter.

Graumann, C. F. (1989). Perspective setting and taking in verbal interaction. In R. Dietrich & C. F. Graumann (Eds.), *Language processing in social context* (pp. 95–122). Amsterdam: North-Holland.

Groeben, N. (1986). Ironie als spielerischer Kommunikationstyp? Situationsbedingungen und Wirkungen ironischer Sprechakte. In K. Werner (Ed.), *Kommunikationstypologie* (pp. 172–192). Schwann, Düsseldorf.

Groeben, N., Hanne, S., & Drinkmann, A. (1985). Produktion und rezeption von ironie. Bd. II: Empirische Untersuchungen zu Bedingungen und Wirkungen ironischer Sprechakte. Tübingen: Niemeyer.

Groeben, N., & Scheele, B. (1984). Produktion und rezeption von ironie. Bd. 1: Pragmalinguistische Beschreibung und psycholinguistische Erklärungshypothesen. Tübingen: Niemeyer.

Günthner, S. (1996a). Zwischen Scherz und Schmerz. Frotzelaktivitäten im Alltag. In H. Kotthoff (Ed.), Scherzkommunikation. Beiträge aus der Empirischen Gesprächsforschung (pp. 81–109). Westdeutscher Verlag, Opladen.

Günthner, S. (1996b). The contextualization of affect in reported dialogue. In S. Niemeyer & R. Dirven. (Eds.), The language of emotions (pp. 247–277). Amsterdam: Benjamins.

Gumperz, J. (1982). Discourse strategies. Cambridge, England: Cambridge University Press.

Haiman, J. (1990). Sarcasm as theater. Cognitive Linguistics, 1, 181–205.

Hartung, M. (1998). Ironie in der Gesprochenen Sprache. Eine Gesprächsanalytische Untersuchung. Westdeutscher Verlag, Opladen.

Kotthoff, H. (1996). Impoliteness and conversational joking: On relational politics. Folia Linguistica, 30/3–4, 299–327.

Kotthoff, H. (1997). Review of Katharina Barbe: Irony in context. Studies in Language, 21, 703–706.

Kotthoff, H. (1998a). Spass Verstehen. Zur Pragmatik von Konversationellem Humor. Niemeyer, Tübingen.

Kotthoff, H. (1998b). Irony, quotation, and other forms of staged intertextuality (LIST-Working Paper No. 7). University of Konstanz. (2002 In C. Graumann & W. Kallmeyer, Eds., Perspectivity in discourse. Amsterdam: John Benjamins), 201–233.

Kotthoff, H. (2000). Konversationelle parodie. Über komische Intertextualität in der Alltagskommunikation. Germanistische Linguistik, 153, 159–186.

Lapp, E. (1992). Linguistik der ironie. Narr, Tübingen.

Norrick, N. (1993). Conversational joking. Humor in everyday talk. Bloomington: Indiana University Press.

Quintilianus, M. F. (1975). Institutiones oratoriae, hg. und übersetzt von Helmut Rahn. Wissenschaftliche Buchgesellschaft, Darmstadt.

Raskin, V. (1985). Semantic mechanisms of humour. Dordrecht, The Netherlands: Reidel.

Rundquist, S. (1990). Indirectness in conversation: Flouting Grice's maxims at dinner. Proceedings of the Berkeley Linguistic Society, 16, 509–518.

Sandig, B. (1996). Sprachliche Perspektivierung und perspektivierende Stile. Zeitschrift für Literaturwissenschaft und Linguistik, 102, 36–63.

Schütte, W. (1991). Scherzkommunikation unter Orchestermusikern. Niemeyer, Tübingen.

Sperber, D. (1984). Verbal irony: pretense or echoic mention. Journal of Experimental Psychology: General, 113, 130–136.

Sperber, D., & Wilson, D. (1981). Irony and the use/mention distinction. In P. Cole (Ed.), Radical pragmatics (pp. 295–318). New York: Academic.

Stempel, W-D. (1976). Ironie als sprechhandlung. In W. Preisendanz & R. Warning, R. (Eds.), Das Komische (pp. 205–237). Munich, Germany: Wilhelm Fink.

Straehle, C. A. (1993). "Samuel?" "Yes, dear?": Teasing and conversational rapport. In E. Tannen (Ed.), Framing in discourse (pp. 210–229). New York: Oxford University Press.

Verschueren, J. (1995). Metapragmatics. In J. Verschueren, J.-O. Östman, & J. Blommaert. (Eds.), Handbook of pragmatics (pp. 367–371). Amsterdam: Benjamins.

Weinrich, H. (1961). Linguistik der Lüge. Schneider, Heidelberg.

Wilson, D., & Sperber, D. (1992). On verbal irony. Lingua, 87, 53–76.

PART V

DEVELOPMENT
OF IRONY UNDERSTANDING

CHAPTER 18

A Developmental Test of Theoretical Perspectives on the Understanding of Verbal Irony: Children's Recognition of Allusion and Pragmatic Insincerity

Marlena A. Creusere
University of Texas at Austin

The "allusional pretense" theory of verbal irony (Kumon-Nakamura, Glucksberg, & Brown, 1995) claims that irony can be characterized as having 2 main features: (a) *allusion* to behavioral expectations, prior thoughts utterances, social conventions, and so forth; and (b) *pragmatic insincerity*. Following a brief review of what is currently known about children's comprehension of irony, the focus of this article is on description of a developmental study testing the allusional pretense theory. One result of this study is that, just like adults, 8-year-old children were found to be able to recognize both allusion and pragmatic insincerity behind ironic speech acts. The potential effect of propositional form on irony comprehension is also discussed.

In a review of the literature pertaining to irony, Creusere (1999) claimed that both linguistic theorists and researchers should consider the evidence for adults' and children's comprehension of irony and that, for the most part, past discussion of nonliteral language has been limited to either one, but seldom both, groups. Authors have generally assumed that adults demonstrate a full understanding of irony and sarcasm. This assumption might be incorrect. For example, as data from Demorest, Meyer, Phelps, Gardner, and Winner (1984) demonstrated, adults are quite capable of misinterpreting irony and sarcasm; in that study, adults interpreted the investigators' exemplars of sarcasm as deception 46% of the time. Similarly,

---

This chapter was previously published as "A developmental test of theoretical perspectives on the understanding of verbal irony: Children's recognition of allusion and pragmatic insincerity" (M. Creusere) in *Metaphor and Symbol, 15,* 29–45. Copyright © [2000] by Lawrence Erlbaum Associates. Reprinted with permission.

adult participants in Ackerman's (1982) study failed to detect sarcasm in scenarios that included contradictory context-utterance information about 29% of the time. The intent of the subsequent section is to summarize the evidence for children's understanding of ironic speech acts.

Developmental studies of irony and sarcasm comprehension can be placed loosely into five categories. First, many of these studies have explored children's understanding of the different forms of nonliteral language (e.g., metaphor, irony, hyperbole, deception) versus literal speech acts. Sincere comments appear to be easy to interpret early on, at least by the age of 6 (Demorest et al., 1984), but more likely much earlier in development. The investigators also found that the ability to recognize deception appears slightly later. As for other forms of nonliteral language, the order of acquisition is similes, then simple metaphors, sarcasm, and finally irony (e.g., Andrews, Rosenblatt, Malkus, Gardner, & Winner, 1986; Happé, 1993). Earlier studies differed in their evidence of the approximate ages that children begin to understand irony; estimates ranged from between the ages of 6 (e.g., Winner & Leekam, 1991) and 12 (Capelli, Nakagawa, & Madden, 1990). More recent investigations have indicated that a proportion of children are quite good at recognizing at least some of the components of ironic speech acts by 5 or 6 years of age (e.g., Creusere, 1997; Creusere & Echols, 1996; Dews et al., 1996; Sullivan, Winner, & Hopfield, 1995). Winner et al. (1987) suggested that there are actually three types of irony—that is, sarcasm, hyperbole, and understatement—and that sarcasm is the easiest kind of irony to understand. In contrast, understatements appear to be the most difficult type of irony for children to grasp. An interesting finding across all of these studies is that deception is the most common form of misinterpretation of irony and sarcasm; the exception is ironic understatements, which were, in the Winner et al. study, commonly understood as literal true statements.

The second issue investigated in developmental investigations of nonliteral language understanding is the role of contextual information placement and memory on children's recognition of ironic speech acts. Ackerman (1982), for example, investigated the effects of contextual information placement and memory on children's comprehension of ironic sarcasm. The results of this study suggested that memory alone was not responsible for children's difficulty in comprehending sarcasm and that placement of contextual information affected only his youngest participants' (i.e., first-graders') performance on the task. Ackerman claimed that placement of contextual information after ironically sarcastic utterance highlights the context-utterance discrepancy, thereby aiding young children's detection of this discrepancy. Winner et al. (1987) also found that memory was not a major factor in children's inability to recognize ironic sarcasm, but that it did interact with cognitive load to affect comprehension of this speech act.

The third developmental topic involves investigating the role played by theory of mind in understanding irony and sarcasm. A number of studies (Creusere, 1997; Happé, 1993, 1995; Sullivan et al., 1995; Winner, Brownell, Happé, Blum, & Pincus, 1998; Winner & Leekam, 1991) have indicated that a second-order theory of mind ability (e.g., ability to predict what Person X knows that Person Y knows) is associated with children's and adults' understanding of irony and sarcasm. More specifically, difficulties in recognition of these speech acts by autistic children, normally developing children, and adults with right-hemisphere brain damage is found to coincide with an inability to make predictions regarding second-order mental states. For example, Sullivan et al. (1995) found that children's success or failure at distinguishing between ironic jokes and lies was associated with their performance on a theory of mind task that measured whether or not participants understood that the actions of Character X in the story were dependent on his knowledge of Character Y's knowledge of the relevant facts of the scenario.

A fourth line of research, the role of intonation and facial expression in the recognition of irony and sarcasm, has been a particularly thorny area of investigation. Ackerman (1986), Gibbs and O'Brien (1991), Winner and Leekam (1991), and Winner et al. (1987) suggested that intonation is not a necessary or useful cue to irony and sarcasm detection. However, data from other studies (Ackerman, 1983; Capelli et al., 1990; Creusere, 1997; Creusere & Echols, 1996; de Groot, Kaplan, Rosenblatt, Dews, & Winner, 1995; Demorest et al., 1984; Dews et al., 1996) have indicated that intonation does facilitate comprehension of at least certain components of ironic speech acts; the evidence suggests that the cue is important for recognizing ironic speaker meaning (de Groot et al., 1995) and the attitude that distinguishes ironic versus ironically sarcastic speakers (Creusere, 1997). Furthermore, speakers' facial expressions may also mediate perceptions of "nice" versus "mean" ironic speaker attitude (Creusere & Echols, 1999).

The fifth category of developmental research related to irony and sarcasm understanding is the social and communicative functions of the speech acts. In reality, there have been few developmental studies in which these issues were investigated. One proposed communicative function of irony is to reveal information about a speaker's attitude toward a situation or person (Andrews et al., 1986; Dews, Kaplan, & Winner, 1995; Giora, 1995; Kreuz & Glucksberg, 1989; Kumon-Nakamura, Glucksberg, & Brown, 1995; Sperber & Wilson, 1995). Results from early studies seem to provide contradictory results regarding children's recognition of ironic and sarcastic speaker attitude. For example, Andrews et al. (1986) found that children were able to recognize the speaker attitude behind irony, even if they were not also able to grasp the speaker intent behind the utterance. In contrast, Winner and Leekam (1991) claimed that children had to detect first the speaker's second-order intention before being able to recognize ironic speaker attitude. One factor to take into account when considering these results is that both sets of authors considered ironic speaker attitude to be "mean" rather than "nice," even though recent studies with adults have indicated that one function of irony is humor (e.g., Dews et al., 1995; Kreuz & Glucksberg, 1989; Kumon-Nakamura et al., 1995). However, the actual reason for why the results of Andrews et al. and Winner and Leekam's investigations differ is not clear. Two other developmental studies (Creusere, 1997; Creusere & Echols, 1996) indicated that intonation and facial expression serve as cues for distinguishing the attitude behind ironic sarcasm and nonsarcastic irony (in which the contextual information and the actual words across the paired exemplar utterances were held constant).

Two other functions of irony and sarcasm are humor (e.g., Dews et al., 1995; Littman & Mey, 1991) and muting of the speaker's intended meaning (e.g., Dews & Winner, 1995). Dews et al. (1996) tested young children's ability to grasp these functions of ironic speech acts. The experimenters found that children as young as 5, as well as adults, rated literal criticisms as "mean" more often than they did ironic criticisms. In addition, ironic criticisms characterized by flat or negative tones of voice were perceived as meaner than similar remarks spoken with positive intonation. However, Dews et al. concluded that recognition of the humor function of irony increases over age, especially between the years of 5 and 8, and that instances of irony delivered with a positive (or sincere) intonation were considered overall to be more funny than ironic exemplars characterized by deadpan or sarcastic tones of voice.

Finally, investigations of children's understanding of the perlocutionary effect (i.e., the effect of an utterance on the target of the utterance) have indicated that children recognize that an instance of ironic sarcasm will generally leave its recipient feeling worse than an instance of nonsarcastic irony (Creusere, 1997; Creusere & Echols, 1996). This and other developmental studies concerned with the functions of ironic speech acts (e.g., Andrews et al., 1986; Dews et al., 1996; Winner & Leekam, 1991) have provided intriguing evidence that children are able to recognize at least some of the communicative goals and social effects of a speaker's choice to employ irony and sarcasm. Specifically, there exists evidence that sensitivity to the potentially humorous, muting, and informative nature of the speech acts begins to develop between the ages of 5 and 6.

The aforementioned review suggests that developmental researchers have acquired an abundance of information regarding children's comprehension of irony and sarcasm. The potential theoretical value of this research cannot be taken for granted. For example, an inclusive theory (or set of theories) developed to describe how people, in general, process discourse irony should be able to account for both adults' and children's ability to recognize and interpret the speech act. Furthermore, such a theory should also be able to explain the factors that influence situations in which listeners of all ages misinterpret ironic speech acts. One trend until very recently, however, has been a failure by theorists interested in adults' processing and use of ironic speech acts to incorporate developmental data into their accounts of discourse irony (Creusere, 1999). Yet information regarding children's growing ability to comprehend irony and sarcasm is necessary for a more complete understanding of the characteristics and communicative purposes of these speech acts. In addition, developmental researchers have seldom used their opportunities to study children to test these theories, thereby leading to an even deeper divide between developmental and adult lines of literature concerning irony and sarcasm. The study to be reported was designed with the intent to explore one account of discourse irony, the "allusional pretense" theory (Kumon-Nakamura et al., 1995), and to use concepts from this account to compare aspects of children's understanding of irony and data from Kumon-Nakamura et al.'s (1995) study with adults.

   In their investigation, Kumon-Nakamura et al. (1995) challenged the traditional (e.g., Grice, 1975) definition of irony, which is that the implied meaning of an ironic utterance is the opposite of the speaker's surface-level meaning (Clark, 1996). In addition, the experimenters questioned claims that ironic utterances clearly include echoic mention or reminding of behavioral expectations, societal conventions, or prior utterances (Kreuz & Glucksberg, 1989; Sperber & Wilson, 1995). Early investigations of irony understanding most commonly employed counterfactual assertions (i.e., situations in which ironic speakers do, in fact, say something the opposite or different from their implied meaning) as exemplars of ironic statements (Creusere, 1999). For example, Demorest et al. (1984) assumed that the communicative goal of the ironic speaker is characterized by opposition. An example of the kind of questions they used to measure speaker intention was "Did Mary want Joe to think his haircut was good or bad?" (p. 1529).

   Kumon-Nakamura et al. (1995) noted that irony can be conveyed not only through counterfactual assertions, but also by (a) true assertions, such as "You sure are hungry," to a person who just ate half of a pizza meant to be shared among five people; (b) over-polite requests, such as "I hate to bother you, but would it put you out too terribly much if you refrained from walking naked in front of your living room window," from a neighbor with kids who frequently play in their front yard across the window; (c) questions, such as "Would you like another beer?" to a guest who apparently already had enough to drink and was becoming obnoxious; and (d) offerings, such as "Here, warm up with a few practice balls," to a bowling opponent who had just thrown three strikes in a row. To test their claim that irony can be expressed in more than one propositional form, Kumon-Nakamura et al. gave adults a series of literal and potentially ironic scenarios. After reading each scenario, participants were asked to rate how ironic the speakers' utterances were on a 7-point scale, ranging from X (*not at all ironic*) to 7 (*most ironic*). Data from the experiment indicated a reliable difference such that the adults rated the literal stories as significantly less ironic than the nonliteral ironic stories (2.35 vs. 5.61). In addition, nontraditional examples of irony (i.e., utterances that were not counterfactual assertions, but had the potential to be perceived as ironic) were rated as high as counterfactual assertions on their ironic Likert-type scale.

   Another aspect of Kumon-Nakamura et al.'s (1995) study was to provide a definition of irony, one that differed from traditional (e.g., Grice, 1975) and echoic reminding theories (e.g., Kreuz & Glucksberg, 1989; Sperber & Wilson, 1995). The investigators claimed that utterances such as those given earlier appear to be more allusive than echoic in nature, and that allusion differs from echoing in the sense that the latter refers to relevant information in a direct manner, whereas the former can make reference either directly or indirectly. Kumon-Nakamura et al. suggested that the notion of echoic reminding is too narrow to account for all possible forms of irony and that the former concept may be considered as one type of *allusion* to behavior, societal expectations, prior thoughts, and so forth. Furthermore, Kumon-

Nakamura et al. took the position that "oppositional" definitions of irony were also inadequately narrow to characterize the various forms that ironic utterances may take. Instead, Kumon-Nakamura et al. proposed that irony entails a notion of *pragmatic insincerity,* a concept that entails violation of the conventional communicative function of different types of speech acts. For example, speakers should use assertions to speak the truth and to add new information to the dialogue, requests at a politeness level appropriate to the situation, questions when they desire an answer, and offers only if they want them to be accepted. Kumon-Nakamura et al. were able to provide support for their claim that the characteristics of *allusion* and *pragmatic insincerity* underlie perceptions of irony; adult participants mentioned these characteristics for ironic versions of scenarios more often than for literal versions of the same scenarios.

One goal of the present study was to build a link between developmental investigations of pragmatic understanding and the adult literature by using child participants to test aspects of the "allusional pretense" theory of irony (Kumon-Nakamura et al., 1995). It is well established that children can comprehend the pragmatic insincerity underlying counterfactual assertions. As noted earlier, children as young as 5 or 6 are surprisingly proficient at detecting that the implied meaning and second-order intention of this form of irony is the opposite of speakers' surface meanings (e.g., Creusere, 1997; Dews et al., 1996; Winner & Leekam, 1991). Although developmental research has not directly tested the claim that irony involves allusion to prior thoughts, behavior, or societal conventions, indirect developmental support for this claim exists. For example, Capelli et al. (1990) measured children's understanding of ironic speaker intent by asking the question "Why did [character's name] say that?" (p. 1827). Some of the first- and third-graders' responses to the question are allusive in nature, such as one child's remark that the speaker "was making fun of the other guy because she thought that he got scammed on by his older brother, and I think he did too [laughs]" (p. 1839). Therefore, one prediction regarding the following study was that 8-year-old children, who appear to be old enough to answer open-ended questions, would be able to recognize in ironic utterances the characteristics of allusion and pragmatic insincerity.

A second goal of the study was to investigate whether or not children can detect irony in statements other than counterfactual assertions. As discussed previously, a review of developmental studies in irony understanding indicates that many children are able to understand some components of ironic and sarcastic speech acts beginning from between 5 and 6 years of age (Ackerman, 1982, 1983, 1986; Andrews et al., 1986; Creusere, 1997; Creusere & Echols, 1996; de Groot et al., 1995; Dews et al., 1996; Winner & Leekam, 1991; Winner et al., 1987). However, the only kinds of potentially ironic utterances systematically tested in these studies have been counterfactual assertions. This investigation, therefore, was the first developmental investigation to examine systematically whether or not children are able to perceive irony in true assertions, offerings, questions, and expressions of appreciation ("thankings"). The second prediction regarding the results of this study was that counterfactual assertions would be more easily comprehended than offerings, true assertions, questions, and expressions of thanks. The basis of this prediction was the experimenter's assumption that counterfactual assertions are more direct and prototypical examples of irony than are the other forms of irony, which all appear to be somewhat more indirect in the manner in which they convey irony.

The third goal of the following study was to determine whether or not the form of an ironic utterance would affect participants' interpretations of speaker "humor" and "meanness." Prior research has suggested that intonation influences how "funny" and "mean" is a given utterance (Creusere, 1997; Creusere & Echols, 1996; Dews et al., 1996). However, the influence of ironic form on ratings of speaker humor and meanness have yet to be examined, with the exception of Dews et al.'s (1996) finding that children consider subtle forms of indirect irony meaner than "obvious" forms of the speech act. In addition, the experimenters found that their child participants interpreted obvious exemplars of irony as funnier than indirect instances of irony. Consequently, the expectation was that certain types of irony (e.g., "thankings") would be perceived as more "mean" than other types of irony, such as counterfactual assertions. Similarly, counterfactual assertions, due to their characteristic of context-utterance discrepancy, would be interpreted as particularly "funny" instances of irony. The basis for this latter expectation was Attardo's (1993) claim that discrepancy and ambiguity are both important features of good jokes, and one goal of irony is humor (Dews et al., 1995; Dews et al., 1996; Kreuz & Glucksberg, 1989; Kumon-Nakamura et al., 1995; Littman & Mey, 1991).

METHOD

Participants

Participants in this study were forty 8-year-olds ($M = 8-1$, range 7–10 to 8–4, equal number of boys and girls) recruited from the database at the Children's Research Laboratory of the University of Texas at Austin. Although several studies (e.g., Creusere, 1997; Dews et al., 1996; Winner & Leekam, 1991) have indicated that children as young as 5 or 6 are able to understand irony, piloting of this study indicated that participants within this age range had difficulty answering the open-ended questions measuring Speaker Purpose and Meaning. Capelli et al.'s (1990) work suggested, however, that open-ended questions similar to those used here do not pose difficulty for 8-year-olds.

Materials and Procedure

Materials consisted of four tape-recorded stories that ended with one of five forms of a potentially ironic utterance, a questionnaire designed to measure components of irony comprehension, and a camcorder for recording responses.

Stories. Five brief audiotaped scenarios were constructed, each ending with an ironic remark by one of the two characters. An example of one of the scenarios follows:

One day Sue was sitting in the kitchen talking to a friend on the phone. Bill came into the kitchen and started taking a bunch of pots out of the cabinets. Every time he put a pot down, it made a loud clanging noise. Sue had to raise her voice so that her friend could hear her on the phone. Finally, Sue got flustered, told her friend "bye" and hung up the phone. When she turned toward Bill, he said "good morning." Sue said to Bill [either Version A, B, C, D, or E]:

A. *Counterfactual assertion:* "Oh hi. I didn't *even notice* you were here."
B. *True assertion:* "Oh hi. You know, I couldn't *help noticing* already that you were here."
C. *Question:* "Oh hi. Did you *notice* that I was trying to talk on the phone a second ago?"
D. *Offering:* "Oh hi. Here's *another* pot. You can bang it too!"
E. *Thanking:* "Thanks *a lot* for banging the pots while I was on the phone."

Four counterbalancing conditions were constructed so that participants listened to all four scenarios, each including a final remark in a different form than were the remarks of the other three scenarios.

Questionnaire.   After listening to each scenario, children answered questions related to speaker meaning, purpose, first-order belief, second-order intention, and to the "humor" and "meanness" of the utterance. The questionnaires were tailored for the scenario at hand and for the specific form of the final remark. Questions 8 and 9 were presented with a 4-point Likert-type picture of schematic faces corresponding to each possible response (see Dews et al., 1996). The questionnaire for the aforementioned scenario, Version E, is given here:

1. *Fact:* Was Bill quiet or did he make a lot of noise with the pots?
2. *Memory:* What did Sue say to Bill? _____
   _____
3. *Purpose:* Why did Sue say that to Bill? _____
   _____
4. *Meaning:* What did Sue mean when she said that to Bill? _____
   _____
5. *Sincerity:* Did Sue appreciate Bill banging the pots?   (circle)   Y   N
6. *First-Order Belief:* Did Sue think that Bill was quiet or noisy?   Y   N
7. *Second-Order Intention:* Did Sue want Bill to know what she was thinking?
   Y   N
8. How funny was Sue's comment?
   Very, Very   Very   A teeny bit   Not at all
9. How mean was Sue's comment?
   Very, Very   Very   A teeny bit   Not at all

After participants finished the irony task, the experimenter asked them four questions designed to measure whether or not they were familiar with the societal convention being referred to in the final remark of each scenario. Responses to all parts of the questionnaires were then coded individually by two people. A few differences in coding for individual items were resolved through discussion. Early in the coding process, it became apparent that the Speaker Purpose (Q3) and Speaker Meaning (Q4) measures had to be combined for one rating, to distinguish adequately between allusive (value = 3), deceptive (value = 2), sincere (value = 1), and other (value = 0) responses. For example, one child answered the Purpose question for the "banging pots" scenario with "Cuz she wanted to talk but she had to raise her voice," and the Meaning question with "I would like you to be a little quieter when I talk on the phone," thereby receiving a 3 on the allusion measure. A pragmatically insincere answer to the Speaker Sincerity (Q5) question received a value of 1; a sincere response received a value of 0.

The alternative measures of irony understanding, Speaker First-Order Belief (Q6) and Speaker Second-Order Intention (Q7), were evaluated by examining them together and categorizing them in the following manner: (a) a child who recognized both the speaker's belief and second-order intent was coded as having detected the irony behind the remark (value = 3); (b) a child who understood the speaker's belief, but not her second-order intention, received a deceptive value of 2; and (c) a child who got both measures "wrong" was coded as having interpreted the remark as sincere (value = 1). All other responses were assigned a value of 0. Ratings from the "humor" (Q8) and "meanness" (Q9) scales were coded from 0 (e.g., "not at all mean") to 3 (e.g., "very, very mean").

RESULTS

Allusion and Pragmatic Insincerity Scores

The mean total score for the two combined questions measuring the characteristic of allusion was 2.79 (with highest allusion score being 3). The mean proportion of allusive responses was .84 (134/160), and was significantly different from chance (Binomial test, $p < .0001$). The data from test items Q3 and Q4 indicated that the 8-year-old children in this study referred to allusion very frequently in their descriptions of Speaker Purpose or Meaning. Participants were also able to recognize the pragmatic insincerity behind ironic utterances. The mean total score for the Speaker Insincerity/Sincerity item (Q5) was .70 (with highest insincerity score being 1). The mean proportion of pragmatically insincere responses was .65 (104/160) and was also significantly different from chance (Binomial test, $p < .0001$). Thus, children were able to recognize the pragmatically insincere component of ironic remarks (Kumon-Nakamura et al., 1995).

Because this was the first developmental study in which irony was defined in terms of allusion and pragmatic insincerity, it was necessary to compare responses on the measures of these two characteristics with combined values from the Speaker First-Order Belief (Q6) and Speaker Second-Order Intention (Q7) items, which are commonly used for measuring irony comprehension in developmental studies (e.g., Creusere, 1997; Winner & Leekam, 1991). The mean total score from these two items was 2.67 (with a full ironic response being 3). The mean proportion of ironic responses was .72 (115/160) and was significantly different from chance (Binomial test, $p < .0001$). The values from the allusion (Q3 and Q4) and pragmatic insincerity (Q5) items were summed for each trial. The proportion of responses in which participants recognized both of these characteristics for a given trial was .62 (99/160) and was significantly different from chance (Binomial test, $p < .0001$). The correlation between ironic responses on the allusion + pragmatic insincerity items and the speaker first-order belief and second-order intention items was .28 ($z = 3.586, p = .0003$), suggesting that the two theoretical ways to measure irony comprehension appear to be associated with each other. However, it should be noted that under 10% of the common variance was accounted for, and therefore, it is still possible that the measures tap into somewhat different aspects of irony. Nevertheless, the data from both of these indicators of irony confirm the first prediction regarding the results of this study: They suggested that 8-year-olds are quite capable of recognizing various characteristics of this speech act.

Effect of Propositional Form on Children's Comprehension of Irony

A two-way analysis of variance (ANOVA) yielded that there was not a main effect of form on responses to the allusion measures (Q3 and Q4), $F(4, 155) = 1.867, ns$. Thus, the second prediction made regarding this study, that counterfactual assertions would be more easily comprehended than offerings, true assertions, questions, and expressions of thanks, was not confirmed. However, two t-test analyses revealed significant differences between responses for "offerings" and "questions," $t(62) = -2.29, p = .0253$, and "offerings" and "true assertions," $t(62) = -2.08, p = .0419$. Figure 18.1 shows the interaction bar plot for the effect of propositional form on responses to the Speaker Insincerity/Sincerity item (Q5).

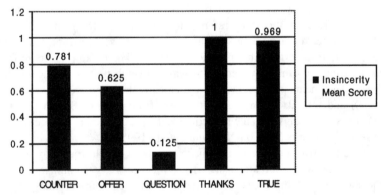

Figure 18.1.   The effect of ironic utterance form on responses to the Pragmatic Insincerity/ Sincerity item.

A two-way ANOVA indicated a main effect of form, $F(4, 155) = 35.917$, $p <$ .0001, on responses to this question. The "true" and "thanks" forms of irony were rated as most insincere. Although they did not differ in perceived similarity from one another, they were rated as more insincere than the other three forms of irony. Similarly, the "counterfactual" and "offering" forms of irony did not differ in insincerity from one another, but both were rated as more insincere than were "questions," which were rated as most sincere of the five forms. A possible explanation for the low mean (.125) for this category of irony will be offered in the discussion section of this article.

No main effect of propositional form on scores on the combined Speaker First-Order Belief and Second-Order Intention measures (Q6 and Q7) was revealed through a two-tailed ANOVA, $F(4, 155) = .784$, ns. Consideration of all of the analyses related to the second prediction of this investigation, that the propositional form of an utterance would affect children's comprehension of the irony behind these utterances, was partially confirmed and partially disconfirmed. The influence of form on recognition of the various characteristics appears to depend on which particular characteristic to which one refers (e.g., allusion vs. pragmatic insincerity).

Humor and Meanness Ratings

The mean total score for the Speaker "Funniness" item (Q8) was .375 (with the highest in humor score being 3). A single-sample t test demonstrated that participants responded at a level significantly different from chance, $t(159) = 7.280$, $p <$ .0001. A two-tailed ANOVA indicated that there was no main effect of form, $F(4, 155) = 1.183$, ns. An unpaired t-test analysis, grouped on the basis of form, revealed a trend toward differences between the means of "counterfactual assertion" and "thanking" responses on this humor measure, $t(62) = 1.899$, $p = .0623$. Similarly, there was a trend toward differences between the scores for "offering" and "thanking" responses, $t(62) = 1.729$, $p = .0889$. Figure 18.2 shows that the mean rating for humor was the lowest for "thankings" than for any of the other test forms of ironic utterances. No other t-test comparisons were significant.

The mean total score for the Speaker "Meanness" measure (Q9) was 1.075 (with the highest meanness score being 3). Another single-sample t test also demonstrated that the 8-year-old children responded at a level significantly different from chance, $t(159) = 14.234$, $p < .0001$. For this item, a two-tailed ANOVA indicated that there was a main effect of form, $F(4, 155) = 6.594$, $p < .001$. Figure 18.3 demonstrates the nature of the pattern of responses to the Speaker Meanness measure.

Whereas the "thanking" form of ironic utterances received the lowest mean score on the Speaker Humor measure, it received the highest mean score on the Speaker Meanness item. Single-sample t tests showed a trend toward a significant difference between "thanking" and "counterfactual" forms of irony, $t(62) = -1.79$, $p = .0790$, and significant differences between "thanking" and "offering," $t(62) = -4.18$, $p < .0001$; "question," $t(62) = -4.19$, $p < .0001$; and "true," $t(62) = 3.36$, $p <$

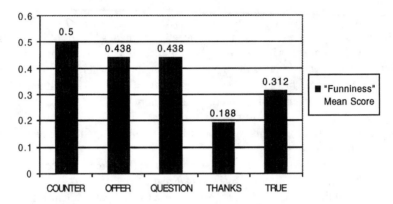

Figure 18.2.   The effect of ironic utterance form on responses to the Speaker Humor item.

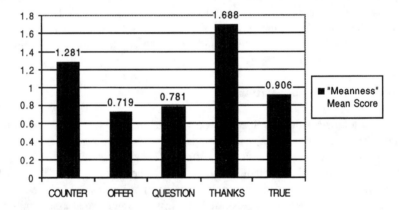

Figure 18.3.   The effect of ironic utterance form on responses to the Speaker Meanness item.

.002, forms of irony. The latter three forms did not differ in perceived meanness from one another. However, the "offering" and "question" forms were both rated as less mean than the "counterfactual" forms of irony. Thus, the "counterfactual" and "thanking" forms were perceived as most mean overall.

The data from the Speaker Humor and Speaker Meanness measures indicate that the third prediction of this study, an effect of propositional form on speaker humor and speaker meanness interpretations, was partially confirmed. Certain types of irony (e.g., "thankings") were perceived as more "mean" than other types of irony, such as offers. However, counterfactual assertions were not interpreted as particularly "funny" instances of irony. The data only suggest that "thankings" were found to be the least humorous example of irony.

Because the evidence supplied by Dews et al. (1996) indicated that older children and adults can consider some ironic utterances as both "funny" and "mean," a correlation between ratings on the Speaker Humor and Speaker Meanness scales was calculated. The correlation between these items was $-.136$ ($z = -1.591$, *ns*); thus, the scores on these scales do not appear, overall, to be related to each other. Presumably, the 8-year-old participants in this study were not yet able to recognize that irony can be simultaneously humorous and mean in nature. It should be noted, however, that the scores for both relevant items were relatively low in general; few children gave either item, in particular Speaker Humor, the maximum score of 3. The results from this measure are consistent with Dews et al.'s claim that sensitivity to the humor function increases over age. However, it is necessary to include an older group of participants to confirm this claim.

DISCUSSION

This study demonstrated that 8-year-olds can grasp the first characteristics of irony proposed by Kumon-Nakamura et al. (1995), allusion to behavioral expectations, social conventions, and so forth. Furthermore, a failure to recognize this aspect of irony was not associated with participants' awareness of the social conventions behind the four test scenarios. Impressively, 100% of the children passed all of the questions testing the relevant social conventions, whereas 84% of the participants' responses to the Speaker Purpose + Speaker Meaning questions included mention of the speaker's allusion to social conventions. In addition, children were able to recognize the pragmatic insincerity behind irony—for example, that offers should be made only if the speakers want them to be accepted. The validity of the assumption that allusion and pragmatic insincerity are associated with ironic speech acts was tested by comparing the results of these measures with more traditional items of irony comprehension, speaker first-order belief, and second-order intention. Correlational analyses suggested, in fact, that the two operational definitions of irony are associated in some manner. As was mentioned previously, however, it has yet to be demonstrated that the two indicators of irony actually measure the same aspects of irony.

That the propositional form of an utterance would affect children's comprehension of the irony behind these utterances was partially confirmed and partially disconfirmed. There was no major effect of ironic form on recognition of allusion and speaker first-order belief/second-order intention. However, a significant difference between allusion responses for "offerings" and "questions" and for "offerings" and "true assertions" was found. In contrast, there was a main effect of form on scores for the item measuring pragmatic insincerity/sincerity; all mean differences of the item were significantly different, except for between "counterfactual assertion" and "offering" scores and between "thanking" and "true assertion" scores.

As was indicated previously, children had a particularly difficult time recognizing the pragmatic insincerity behind questions (e.g., "Did you notice I was trying to talk on the phone just a moment ago?"). An example of the type of item used to measure pragmatic insincerity was "Did the woman want the man to answer her question?" During the development stage of this study, the decision to test pragmatic insincerity for ironic questions in this manner was based on Kumon-Nakamura et al.'s (1995) statement that "questions should be asked only when an answer is desired" (p. 5). Perhaps this decision failed to take into account the possibility that 8-year-olds are not yet aware that questions can be posed rhetorically or that a possible interpretation of "Did the woman want the man to answer her question?" is whether or not the speaker expected an explanation for the target's behavior. If either one of these suggestions is correct, then the significant results for pragmatic insincerity/sincerity (i.e., that the form of an utterance influences interpretations of the pragmatic insincerity behind irony) may be an artifact of methodology. Additional research will have to be conducted to sort out this issue.

The expectation that propositional form would influence children's ratings of speaker humor and speaker meanness were partially confirmed. Results indicated that there was not a main effect of form on interpretations of speaker funniness. However, there was a main effect of form on perceptions of speaker meanness. For example, ironic expressions of thanks were considered to be more mean than any other form of irony. Correlational tests indicated that there was negative association between speaker humor and funniness, but because the ratings for these items were lower than had been expected, it is difficult to make strong claims regarding the implications of this finding.

As was discussed previously, one goal of this investigation was to build a link between developmental studies of pragmatic understanding and the literature pertaining to adults' comprehension of discourse irony. More specifically, child participants were employed here to test aspects of the "allusional pretense" theory of irony (Kumon-Nakamura et al., 1995). In their study, Kumon-Nakamura and colleagues (1995) concluded that "utterances that allude to a failed expectation and that are pragmatically insincere can communicate irony" (p. 18). Not only adults are able to detect these characteristics; this study suggests that children as young as 8 are also able to understand ironic speech acts in terms of allusion and pragmatic insincerity.

The results of Kumon-Nakamura et al.'s (1995) experiments indicated that, contrary to the assumption commonly made in prior investigations of discourse irony, assertions are not the prototypical type of ironic utterances; the mean irony rating for assertions was not significantly different from the mean irony rating for all other forms of irony tested. Similarly, the children in this study did not find counterfactual and true assertions any more difficult to comprehend than offerings, expression of thanks, and questions (exempting the pragmatic insincerity issue discussed earlier). A fact that should be noted at this point is that, in both Kumon-Nakamura et al.'s and this investigation, not all participants recognized the irony behind all of the test utterances—defining a "mature" understanding or irony in terms of the assumption that adults understand all instances of verbal irony. Overall, the adult and child studies concerned with the "allusional pretense" theory complement each other nicely. Thus, this new theory appears to be a valid conceptu- alization of the features of ironic statements.

Clearly, developmental studies can be used to test specific components of the various theories of discourse irony. The results from this experiment indicate that it is beneficial to consider findings from irony studies that have adult versus child participants. Furthermore, it is possible that adults should not be used only as controls in developmental studies; it is necessary ultimately to explain why adults sometimes misinterpret irony, not just to compare their performance on irony tasks with the performance of children. A benefit for evaluating data from adults and children in both a descriptive and evaluative manner is that it provides the opportunity for theorists and researchers to reconstruct their arguments for any claim regarding the understanding and use of ironic speech acts.

ACKNOWLEDGMENTS

Preparation of this article was aided by National Institute for Child and Human Development Grant 26–1625 to Catherine Echols.

I am grateful to Albert Katz for his constructive comments on an earlier version of this article.

REFERENCES

Ackerman, B. P. (1982). Contextual integration and utterance interpretation: The ability of children and adults to interpret sarcastic utterances. *Child Development, 53,* 1075–1083.

Ackerman, B. P. (1983). Form and function in children's understanding of ironic utterances. *Journal of Experimental Child Psychology, 35,* 487–508.

Ackerman, B. P. (1986). Children's sensitivity to comprehension failure in interpreting a nonliteral use of an utterance. *Child Development, 57,* 485–497.

Andrews, J., Rosenblatt, E., Malkus, U., Gardner, H., & Winner, E. (1986). Children's abilities to distinguish metaphoric and ironic utterances from mistakes and lies. *Communication & Cognition, 19,* 281–298.

Attardo, S. (1993). Violation of conversational maxims and cooperation: The case of jokes. *Journal of Pragmatics, 19,* 537–558.

Capelli, C. A., Nakagawa, N., & Madden, C. M. (1990). How children understand sarcasm: The role of context and intonation. *Child Development, 61,* 1824–1841.

Clark, H. H. (1996). *Using language.* Cambridge, England: Cambridge University Press.

Creusere, M. A. (1997, April). *The conceptual underpinnings of children's understanding of ironic speech acts.* Poster session presented at the biennial meeting of the Society for Research in Child Development, Washington, DC.

Creusere, M. A. (1999). Theories of adults' understanding and use of irony and sarcasm: Applications to and evidence from research with children. *Developmental Review, 19,* 213–262.

Creusere, M. A., & Echols, C. H. (1996, July). *Children's understanding of attitude and effect in ironic sarcasm and non-sarcastic irony.* Poster session presented at the annual meeting of the American Psychological Society, San Francisco.

Creusere, M. A., & Echols, C. H. (1999). *The role of intonation and facial expression in detecting the different speaker attitudes behind ironic sarcasm and non-sarcastic irony.* Manuscript in preparation.

de Groot, A., Kaplan, J., Rosenblatt, E., Dews, S., & Winner, E. (1995). Understanding versus discriminating nonliteral utterances: Evidence for a disassociation. *Metaphor and Symbolic Activity, 10,* 255–273.

Demorest, A., Meyer, C., Phelps, E., Gardner, H., & Winner, E. (1984). Words speak louder than actions: Understanding deliberately false remarks. *Child Development, 55,* 1527–1534.

Dews, S., Kaplan, J., & Winner, E. (1995). Why not say it directly? The social functions of irony. *Discourse Processes, 19,* 347–367.

Dews, S., & Winner, E. (1995). Muting the meaning: A social function of irony. *Metaphor and Symbolic Activity, 10,* 3–19.

Dews, S., Winner, E., Kaplan, J., Rosenblatt, E., Hunt, M., Lim, K., et al. (1996). Children's understanding of the meaning and functions of verbal irony. *Child Development, 67,* 3071–3085.

Giora, R. (1995). On irony and negation. *Discourse Processes, 19,* 239–264.

Grice, H. P. (1975). Logic and conversation. In P. Cole & J. L. Morgan (Eds.), *Syntax and semantics: Vol. 3. Speech acts* (pp. 41–58). New York: Academic.

Happé, F. G. E. (1993). Communicative competence and theory of mind in autism: A test of relevance theory. *Cognition, 48,* 101–119.

Happé, F. G. E. (1995). Understanding minds and metaphors: Insights from the study of figurative language in autism. *Metaphor and Symbolic Activity, 10,* 275–295.

Kreuz, R. J., & Glucksberg, S. (1989). How to be sarcastic: The echoic reminder theory of verbal irony. *Journal of Experimental Psychology: General, 118,* 374–386.

Kumon-Nakamura, S., Glucksberg, S., & Brown, M. (1995). How about another piece of pie: The allusional pretense theory of discourse irony. *Journal of Experimental Psychology: General, 124,* 3–21.

Littman, D. C., & Mey, J. L. (1991). The nature of irony: Toward a computational model of irony. *Journal of Pragmatics, 15,* 131–151.

Sperber, D., & Wilson, D. (1995). *Relevance: communication and cognition.* Cambridge, MA: Harvard University Press.

Sullivan, K., Winner, E., & Hopfield, N. (1995). How children tell a lie from a joke: The role of second-order mental state attributions. *British Journal of Developmental Psychology, 13,* 191–204.

Winner, E., Brownell, H., Happé, F., Blum, A., & Pincus, D. (1998). Distinguishing lies from jokes: Theory of mind deficits and discourse interpretation in right hemisphere brain-damaged patients. *Brain and Language, 62,* 89–106.

Winner, E., & Leekam, S. (1991). Distinguishing irony from deception: Understanding the speaker's second-order intention. *British Journal of Developmental Psychology, 9,* 257–270.

Winner, E., Windmueller, G., Rosenblatt, E., Bosco, L., Best, E., & Gardner, H. (1987). Making sense of literal and nonliteral falsehood. *Metaphor and Symbolic Activity, 2,* 13–32.

CHAPTER 19

Children's Comprehension of Critical and Complimentary Forms of Verbal Irony

Jeffrey T. Hancock
Philip J. Dunham
Dalhousie University, Halifax, Canada

Kelly Purdy
McGill University, Montreal, Canada

The existing research on children's comprehension of verbal irony has focused exclusively on children's understanding of ironic criticisms. Two experiments examined 5- and 6-year-old children's ability to detect the nonliteral nature and intended meaning of both ironic criticism and ironic praise as depicted in short, videotaped stories. Considered together, the results from these experiments permit several conclusions: First, the data confirm earlier research suggesting that children's detection of nonliteral utterances and their interpretation of the speaker's pragmatic intent are separable components of early irony comprehension. Second, children's ability to detect ironic statements is asymmetrical across critical and complimentary forms of irony. Finally, although children more readily detect ironic criticisms, explicit echoic cues play an important role in facilitating uniquely their detection of ironic compliments. We discuss these results in the context of social pragmatic theories of early communicative development (e.g., Bruner, 1983; Tomasello, 1992, 1995) and with reference to a recent allusional—pretense model of irony comprehension proposed for mature speakers (Kumon-Nakamura, Glucksberg, & Brown, 1995).

Verbal irony is a commonly used form of nonliteral speech in which the speaker's intended meaning is communicated indirectly. Although verbal irony can take many forms (Kumon-Nakamura et al., 1995), perhaps the simplest and most common form occurs when the speaker's intended meaning is the opposite of the literal

This chapter was previously published as "Children's comprehension of critical and complimentary forms of verbal irony" (J. Hancock, P. Dunham, & K. Purdy) in *Journal of Cognition and Development, 12,* 227–240. Copyright © [2000] by Lawrence Erlbaum Associates. Reprinted with permission.

statement. The specific forms such counterfactual statements can take include ironic criticisms and ironic compliments. An ironic criticism is a positive statement meant to convey a negative meaning, and an ironic compliment is a negative statement meant to convey a positive meaning. To illustrate, a girl who is playing basketball exclaims to her father, "Hey Dad, watch me play basketball." The girl then shoots the ball and misses the basket. The father replies, "You sure are a good basketball player" (ironic criticism). Conversely, if the girl makes the same initial statement to her father, then shoots the ball and makes the basket, the father might reply, "You sure are a bad basketball player" (ironic compliment). Note that in both forms, the ironic statement is counterfactual.

Although, in principle, ironic compliments and ironic criticisms are equally viable pragmatic options for a mature speaker, traditional theories emphasize that the usual purpose of verbal irony is to express a negative evaluation or attitude (e.g., Sperber & Wilson, 1981). Although available theories differ as to why this asymmetry exists, the general implications are (a) that ironic criticisms are more likely to be encountered in our daily discourse than ironic praise, and (b) that, with some exceptions, ironic criticism tends to be detected and interpreted by mature conversationalists more readily than ironic praise (cf. Clark & Gerrig, 1984; Kreuz & Glucksberg, 1989; Sperber & Wilson, 1986). Kumon-Nakamura et al. (1995) suggested the following:

> People can almost always express irony by using a positive assertion, such as "This is a terrific performance" when in fact the performance in question is terrible. The reverse, using a negative statement such as "This is a terrible performance" when the performance is actually quite good, seems anomalous. (p. 11)

In this article, we focus on these issues during an early period of communicative development when children are just beginning to detect the nonliteral nature of ironic speech and to understand the pragmatic intent of the speaker. First, we note that the available developmental data concerned with the early comprehension of verbal irony are reasonably consistent. Dews and Winner (1997) reviewed a substantial amount of research concerned with how and when children's ability to comprehend verbal irony emerges during early development, and across a wide range of procedures and materials, they concluded that children are beginning to comprehend simple counterfactual forms of verbal irony between 5 and 6 years of age (e.g., Ackerman, 1981, 1983; Andrews, Rosenblatt, Malkus, Gardner, & Winner, 1986; Demorest, Meyer, Phelps, Gardner, & Winner, 1984; Happe, 1993; Sullivan, Winner, & Hopfield, 1995).

Although the data are more limited, it is interesting to note in this context that children's early experiences with verbal irony may also be biased in the direction of ironic criticism. Dews, Winner, Nicolaides, and Hunt (as cited in Dews & Winner, 1997) estimated the frequency of ironic criticism and ironic praise in two types of television shows designed for children. These television shows averaged 2.75 instances of irony per 30-min segment. The utterances were predominantly critical in intent with only 6% judged as ironic praise. Although these data do not capture all of the discourse settings in which a child might encounter irony, the results imply that children, like adults, encounter ironic criticisms more frequently than ironic praise.

Given this background, our primary question of interest was whether children, during this early period of communicative development, display a bias similar to adults in their comprehension of ironic criticism and ironic praise. To the best of our knowledge, the literature concerned with children's early comprehension of irony has not addressed this question. Instead, researchers have focused exclusively on ironic forms with negative intent (i.e., ironic criticism). As such, an answer to this question fills a fundamental gap in our knowledge about the early development of irony comprehension.

A second question of interest in this study arises from measurement issues. In his early landmark research, Ackerman (1981, 1983) established the now-popular procedure of reading children various short stories that end in a terminal evaluative comment. The stories were constructed so that the final comment could be interpreted as either literal or ironic (as noted previously, all ironic endings were in the form of criticisms). His research indicated that detecting the literal versus nonliteral property of the final comment (e.g., was the statement accurate) and inferring the intent of the speaker (e.g., was the speaker angry or happy) were separable components of irony comprehension in young children. Although this dissociation is disputed in the context of adult comprehension research (cf. Dews & Winner, 1997; Gibbs, 1994), Ackerman's developmental observations are compelling. We therefore designed a procedure that permitted us to measure separately whether the children detected the nonliteral nature of a final comment (detection question) and whether they correctly inferred the intent of the speaker (intent question). The question of interest arising in the context of this measurement issue is whether any asymmetry observed in children's comprehension of ironic criticism and ironic praise would be consistent across both components of comprehension (detection and inference).

To address these questions, we focused specifically on 5- and 6-year-old children. As noted earlier, the existing literature establishes this as the period during which children are just beginning to comprehend ironic statements. As such, we expected any differences in their sensitivity to ironic praise and ironic criticism to be most evident during this period when comprehension is well below ceiling levels of performance. Similarly, if, as has been suggested, children's detection of irony and their inferences about the pragmatic intent of the speaker are separable processes, this dissociation should also be most evident during this early transition period when performance is below ceiling levels.

EXPERIMENT I

Method

Participants.   Participants were recruited from a database of volunteer families maintained in the Dalhousie University Infant Development Laboratory. Twenty-four English-speaking, middle-class, 5- to 6-year-olds participated in the study (16 girls, 8 boys). The 12 older children (7 girls, 5 boys) ranged in age from 74 to 78 months ($M = 76.17$, $SD = 1.75$). The 12 younger children (9 girls, 3 boys) ranged in age from 59 to 69 months ($M = 66.50$, $SD = 2.94$). The mean age for these groups combined was 71.33 months ($SD = 5.47$).

Materials.   Nine short stories were videotaped using four adult actors (two men, two women). Each story included two actors, A and B, engaged in an event familiar to a child, such as reciting the alphabet or playing baseball. In the initial scene, A boasted of a particular ability (e.g., I am a good basketball player). In the next scene, A either failed or succeeded at the task identified in the boast. If A succeeded at the task, B then offered either a literal or an ironic compliment; if A failed at the task, B offered either a literal or an ironic criticism. Nine such stories were filmed four times to include each of the four possible endings. Table 19.1 provides a sample of these stories as they were modified to create each of the four treatment conditions.

When filming the stories, the ironic and literal endings were identified for the actors. Although the existing literature suggests that children at this age are not particularly sensitive to the various prosodic cues that mark irony when the context is salient (cf. Milosky & Ford, 1997; Winner & Sullivan, 1991), the actors were encouraged to employ natural changes in intonation that they would normally associate with the production of the literal and ironic statements.

Design.   Each participant watched 16 stories: Four ended with a literal criticism, 4 with an ironic criticism, 4 with a literal compliment, and 4 with an ironic compliment. Half of the children saw stories ending in criticisms first (i.e., literal or ironic), and the other half saw stories ending in compliments first (i.e., literal or ironic). The literal and ironic endings were presented in random order. As such, the completely crossed design was a 2 (criticisms vs. compliment) × 2 (literal vs. ironic endings) × 2 (treatment order) × 2 (5 vs. 6 years of age) mixed factorial with treatment order and age as the only between-subject factors. We note at this point that neither the age factor nor the order of treatment factor accounted for a significant amount of variance in this comprehensive model; consequently, these factors were excluded from our final data analysis strategy.

Procedure.   Participants were tested individually, and all sessions were videotaped. A practice story was employed prior to presenting each set of eight stories to illustrate the procedure. After the child watched each story, three questions were posed. The first question assessed the child's ability to detect the literalness of the speaker's final statement. This first-order belief question was either "Did B really think that A was a good (e.g., basketball player)?" or "Did B really think that A was a bad (e.g., basketball player)?" The order in which the *good* and *bad* queries were presented was randomized for each participant. The second question, "Was B being mean or nice?" assessed the child's comprehension of the speaker's intent. The

TABLE 19.1
Examples of Stories

The Weight Lifter Story

Critical version

   A: I'm good at lifting weights. [A fails to lift the weights]

   B: You are bad at lifting weights.   (Literal condition)

      or

      You really are good at lifting weights.   (Ironic condition)

Complimentary version

   A: I'm good at lifting weights. [A lifts the weights]

   B: You are good at lifting weights.   (Literal condition)

      or

      You really are bad at lifting weights.   (Ironic condition)

The Birthday Candles Story

Critical version

   A: I'm good at blowing out candles. [A fails to blow out candles on a cake]

   B: You are bad at blowing out candles.   (Literal condition)

      or

      You really are good at blowing out candles.   (Ironic condition)

Complimentary version

   A: I'm good at blowing out candles. [A blows out candles on a cake]

   B: You are good at blowing out candles.   (Literal condition)

      or

      You really are bad at blowing out candles.   (Ironic condition)

order in which *mean* and *nice* queries were presented was randomized. Pictorial representations were used to assess the child's comprehension of the speaker's intended meaning. When asked if the final statement in the story was mean or nice, children could respond to the question verbally and by pointing to one of two pictures: one of a happy, nice face and the other of a mean, angry face. For literal statements, the semantic content was congruent with the intended meaning. For nonliteral statements, the semantic content was incongruent with the intended meaning. For example, if an ironic criticism was detected as nonliteral, the second question determined whether the child correctly interpreted a positive statement as negative (mean). Conversely, if an ironic compliment was detected as nonliteral, the second question determined whether the child correctly interpreted a negative statement as positive (nice).

Finally, a third question was asked—either "Do you think that A was a good (e.g., basketball player)?" or "Do you think that A was a bad (e.g., basketball player)?" These questions confirmed whether participants understood the factual context of the story. Again, the order in which the good and bad queries were presented was randomized for each participant.

After children watched the first 8 stories in a randomized order, each participant played a brief game with the experimenter as a distraction while the tapes were changed. The game was a modified version of the Bear-and-Dragon game often used to assess inhibitory control in children (Kochanska, Murray, Jacques, Koenig, & Vandegeest, 1996). After this game, the second set of stories and the previously described procedures were repeated.

Results

No additional analyses were required on results obtained from the third question in the procedure. All participants correctly answered this control question, demonstrating that they were able to represent accurately the factual context of each story (e.g., that a person who scrambles the letters in the alphabet does not know the alphabet). Given the specific questions outlined in the rationale for this study, we proceeded directly to the simple effects tests required to answer these questions (Keppel & Zedick, 1989, pp. 233–234). Because the scores were limited in range (0–4 for each condition), nonparametric, Wilcoxon signed-rank tests were employed for these simple effects tests.

Children's responses to the first question indicated whether they correctly detected the speaker's beliefs about the final utterance in each story (i.e., was the speaker being literal or nonliteral when making this comment?). Table 19.2 presents these scores converted to proportions for each of the four conditions. Consider first the stories with literal endings. As the data in Table 19.2 indicate, when asked, children clearly understood that the speaker was being literal when either a literal criticism was employed appropriately to make a negative comment about a poor performance (96%) or a literal compliment was employed appropriately to make a positive comment about a good performance (99%). The near-perfect comprehension of these comments as literal statements confirms (along with results from Question 3) that the children both remembered the factual context and comprehended the sequence of events in these scenarios.

Consider next the stories ending in ironic statements. When the speaker praised a partner's failure (i.e., ironic criticism), the children correctly inferred that the speaker's praise should not be taken literally on 47% of these trials. The appropriate control against which to compare performance in the ironic criticism condition is performance in the literal compliment condition. Children are reacting to the identical statement in both of these conditions (e.g., You sure are a good basketball player). When they encountered this statement in the literal compliment condition, they correctly interpreted the statement as literal on 99% of the trials. In other words, when children encounter the identical statement as an ironic criticism, they are willing to reject their otherwise consistent literal interpretation of the same positive statement and switch to a nonliteral interpretation on approximately half of the trials. A nonparametric Wilcoxon test reveals that scores for the identical statement in the literal praise (99%) and nonliteral ironic criticism conditions (47%) were significantly different ($z = 3.62$, $p < .001$).

A similar pattern of results was observed in the ironic compliment condition. When the speaker criticized a partner's success (i.e., ironic compliment), the children correctly decided that the speaker's criticism should not be taken literally on 25% of the trials. The appropriate control against which to compare performance in the ironic compliment condition is performance in the literal criticism condition. Children are reacting to the identical statement in both of these conditions (e.g., You sure are a bad basketball player). When they encountered this statement in the literal criticism condition, they correctly interpreted the statement as literal on 96% of the trials. In other words, when children encounter the identical statement as an ironic compliment, they are willing to reject a literal interpretation of this same negative statement and switch to a nonliteral interpretation on one fourth of the trials. A nonparametric Wilcoxon test reveals that their scores for the identical statement in the literal criticism (96%) and the nonliteral ironic compliment conditions (25%) are significantly different ($z = 4.06$, $p < .001$).

In presenting these comparisons, we should perhaps note that an interesting interpretive issue arises with respect to the criterion that should be used to evaluate the children's ability to detect the nonliteral nature of the ironic statements. As Ackerman (1983) pointed out, a 50% chance hypothesis is one possible criterion (e.g., the children either detect or do not detect the nonliteral nature of the final comment). By this criterion, the children detected the nonliteral nature of ironic compliments at levels significantly below chance and detected the nonliteral nature of ironic criticisms at levels roughly equivalent to chance. However, this criterion of performance fails to acknowledge that for most children beyond 3 years of age, the literal form of the comment is perceived as appropriate, relevant, and truthful during most forms of discourse (Dunham & Dunham, 1996; Grice, 1975). Consequently, the more appropriate criterion proposed by Ackerman (1983) and adopted in this study acknowledges this bias to interpret comments literally and measures responses to the ironic statements in terms of their deviation from their literal form as a baseline.

In addition to these comparisons, there are two important points to note in the previously described results. First, there is an asymmetry in the children's performance when detecting the nonliteral nature of the ironic criticisms and compliments. A nonparametric Wilcoxon test confirms this asymmetry indicating that they were more likely to reject a literal interpretation of the ironic criticisms ($z = 2.32$, $p < .02$). This difference in the mean scores is further confirmed by the number of children who managed to detect correctly at least one ironic comment. Fifteen of the children met this criterion for ironic criticisms, whereas only 9 reached this criterion for ironic praise (McNemar test, $p < .03$). Furthermore, no participants met this criterion for detection of ironic praise without also meeting this criterion for detection of ironic criticisms. Considered together, the children's asymmetric performance across the ironic criticism and ironic praise conditions reveals that children are more likely to believe incorrectly that a speaker is being literal with an ironic compliment than with an ironic criticism. The second, more general point is that the absolute levels of detection in both the praise and criticism conditions are well below ceiling levels. Children fail to detect ironic criticisms on 53% of the trials and fail to detect ironic praise on 75% of the trials.

Children's responses to the second question assessed whether they correctly comprehended the speaker's pragmatic intent (i.e., did the speaker intend to be mean or nice when making this comment?). Again, individual scores on this question could range from 0 to 4 in each of the four possible story endings. The number of critical statements rated as mean and complimentary statements rated as nice were converted into proportions and are presented in Table 19.3. Note that only those participants who detected the nonliteral nature of one or more of both ironic criticisms and compliments were included in the analysis of pragmatic intent ($n = 9$). Note also that these proportions refer only to items in which the speaker's nonliteralness was correctly detected.

Consider first the responses to the mean versus nice question for stories with literal endings. As the data in Table 19.3 indicate, when asked, children always (100% of the time) inferred that the speaker was being nice when a successful performance ended with a literal compliment. Children inferred that the speaker was being mean when a poor performance ended with a literal criticism on 81% of the trials.

Turning next to the stories ending in ironic statements, when the speaker praised a partner's failure (i.e., ironic criticism), the children correctly decided that the speaker's praise was in fact a criticism and judged it as mean on 44% of these trials. Again, the appropriate control against which to compare performance in the ironic criticism condition is performance in the literal compliment condition. The children are reacting to identical statements in both conditions (e.g., You sure are a good basketball player). When they encounter this statement in the literal compliment condition, they interpret the speaker's intent as mean on none of the trials. In other words, when children encounter the same statement as an ironic criticism, they are willing to reject a literal interpretation of the speaker's intent as nice and switch to an interpretation of the speaker's intent as mean on approximately half of the trials. A nonparametric Wilcoxon test reveals that children's ratings of the same statement as mean in the literal praise (0%) and ironic criticism conditions (44%) were significantly different ($z = 2.68$, $p < .01$).

A similar pattern of results is observed in the ironic compliment condition. When the speaker criticized a partner's success (i.e., ironic compliment), the children correctly decided that the speaker's criticism was in fact complimentary and judged it as nice on 58% of the trials. The appropriate control against which to compare performance in the ironic compliment condition is performance in the literal criticism condition. The children are reacting to identical statements in both conditions (e.g., You sure are a bad basketball player). When they encounter the same statement in the literal criticism condition, they interpret the statement as nice on only 19% of the trials. In other words, when children encounter the same statement as an ironic compliment, they are willing to reject their literal interpretation of the speaker's intent as mean and switch to an interpretation of the speaker's intent as nice on approximately half of the trials. A nonparametric Wilcoxon test reveals that children's ratings of the same statement as nice in the literal criticism (19%) and ironic praise conditions (58%) were marginally different ($z = 1.78$, $p = .075$).

Among the 9 children who had detected that a speaker was being nonliteral in the ironic conditions, the ability to judge correctly a speaker's intent tended to be symmetrical across ironic criticisms and ironic compliments. A comparison of the relevant difference scores revealed that children were as likely to reject a nice interpretation of a positive statement in the ironic criticism condition (0%–44% = 44%) as they were to reject a mean interpretation of a negative statement in the ironic compliment condition (19%–58% = 39%). A Wilcoxon test on these difference scores indicated this difference was not significant. Considered together, these data suggest that for this age group, attributions of intent presuppose detection, and the ability to attribute intent once nonliteralness is detected is essentially equivalent for ironic criticisms and ironic compliments.

The preceding analyses of the children's responses to the mean versus nice question included only those children who managed to detect the nonliteral nature of at least one ironic criticism and one ironic compliment in response to the first question. It is also of some interest to look at the responses to the mean versus nice question provided by children who completely failed on the first question to detect the nonliteral nature of the ironic criticisms ($n = 9$) and the ironic compliments ($n = 15$). Essentially, the children who failed to detect any form of irony described 100% of the positive statements (e.g., You sure are a good basketball player) as nice whether that statement was encountered in an ironic or literal context. They described 100% of the negative statements (e.g., You sure are a bad basketball player) as mean whether that statement was encountered in an ironic or a literal context. These data confirm that these particular children, in contrast to those participants who were able to detect nonliteralness, are simply interpreting every statement made during these stories as literal, and they attribute the positive and negative intent of the speaker accordingly on every trial.

Discussion

The objective of this experiment was to determine whether children's emerging abilities to detect the nonliteral nature of ironic statements and to understand pragmatic aspects of irony are symmetrical across ironic criticisms and ironic praise. We should again acknowledge that the children's absolute performance in detecting the nonliteral nature of these ironic comments was not spectacular. They are clearly in the early stages of comprehending that adults do not always mean what they say. However, in spite of this, the data from the first experiment indicate that rejecting literal interpretations is in fact easier in the context of ironic verbal criticisms than it is in the context of ironic verbal praise. Fifteen of the 24 children detected at least one ironic criticism, whereas only 9 achieved this criterion for ironic compliments, and only those children who detected an ironic criticism were also able to detect ironic compliments. Similarly, these children rejected literal interpretations of ironic statements more frequently when they were intended as critical (44%) than when they were intended as complimentary (25%).

It is also the case that detection of the nonliteral nature of an ironic comment at this age does not guarantee that the correct inference will be made about the speaker's pragmatic intent. These data confirm Ackerman's (1983) observations indicating that detection and intent are separable components of irony comprehension and that children find the latter more difficult than the former. More important, in this study, the asymmetry evident in the detection performance was not observed in the children's comprehension of the speaker's intent to be either mean or nice. Children who correctly detected that the speaker was nonliteral in the ironic conditions were as likely to reject nice interpretations for ironic criticisms (i.e., You sure are a good basketball player) as they were to reject mean interpretations of ironic compliments (i.e., You sure are a bad basketball player). In other words, participants appropriately switched to an interpretation of the speaker's intent as opposite to the semantic content for ironic criticisms and compliments on approximately the same proportion of trials.

Why do these young children find it easier to detect the nonliteral nature of an ironic criticism? The data described earlier by Dews et al. (1997) indicating that children have more experience with ironic criticism during early development offer one possible explanation for the asymmetry observed in this experiment. This asymmetry would be predicted by theories of early communicative development that place a heavy emphasis on social–cultural learning mechanisms (Bruner, 1983; Tomasello, 1988, 1992, 1995) operating during adult–child social interactions across early development. From a social-learning perspective, the more exposure children have to the various social and linguistic structures that mark verbal irony, the more proficient they should be at detecting nonliteral speech acts and the pragmatic intent of the speaker. As such, the asymmetry can be attributed in a straightforward manner to the differential amount of experience that children have with these two ironic forms during early communicative development. Questions of course remain about the relevant social–pragmatic markers involved in such learning and the optimal social–cultural conditions under which children will acquire these skills.

Although the social learning explanation is intuitively compelling, it is important to note that another factor may also be operating in this situation. In the procedure employed in Experiment 1, there is a potentially important difference in the cues present in the ironic criticism and compliment conditions. Recall that the initial statement in each story was a boast by the first partner (e.g., I'm a *good* basketball player). Although this boast is an identical antecedent statement that sets the context for either an ironic or a literal comment at the end of the story, the speaker's final comment echoes this initial boast *uniquely* in the ironic criticism condition (e.g., You sure are a *good* basketball player). In contrast, the speaker's final statement in the ironic compliment condition (e.g., You sure are a *bad* basketball player) does not echo the initial boast.

This difference is potentially important because studies of irony comprehension in mature conversationalists have suggested that echoic markers may be particularly important in the detection and comprehension of ironic compliments (Kreuz & Glucksberg, 1989; Sperber & Wilson, 1986). Although these theories differ on the exact "nature" of the echoic marker, when Kreuz and Glucksberg presented adults with stories ending with counterfactual negative statements (e.g., the phrase "What awful weather" uttered on a sunny day), these statements were rated as more sarcastic and more sensible when a negative antecedent (e.g., It's probably going to rain tomorrow) was explicitly "echoed" by the ironist. These authors proposed that, for ironic compliments, directly echoing a negative statement facilitates irony comprehension. If, like adults, children at this age are relying on some form of echoic marker to detect ironic compliments, the absence of an explicit negative antecedent in the ironic compliment condition in Experiment 1 may account for the asymmetry we observed in children's ability to detect an ironic compliment as nonliteral.

EXPERIMENT 2

In the second experiment, to test the importance of the previously described echoic factor—the initial boast (e.g., I'm a good basketball player) employed in Experiment 1—stories was replaced with a self-critical statement (e.g., I'm a bad basketball player). This self-critical statement creates an antecedent that will be *uniquely* echoed by an ironic compliment after a successful performance (e.g., You sure are a bad basketball player). If children are using this echoic marker as an important cue for detecting the nonliteral nature of ironic comments, with all other factors equivalent across these two experiments, an interesting reversal in the results should be observed in this second experiment. The addition of the echoic factor to the ironic compliment condition should boost children's ability to detect ironic compliments, and the absence of the echoic factor in the ironic criticism condition should undermine their performance. As such, these results would be the opposite of those observed in Experiment 1.

Method

Participants. Twenty-four English-speaking, middle-class, 5- to 6-year-olds, again recruited from the database of volunteer families, participated in the study (16 girls, 8 boys). The 12 older children (6 girls, 6 boys) ranged from 76 to 80 months ($M = 77.3$, $SD = 1.2$), and the 12 younger children (10 girls, 2 boys) ranged from 65 to 68 months ($M = 67.0$, $SD = 1.0$). The mean age for all children was 72.2 months ($SD = 5.4$).

Materials. The nine short stories from Experiment 1 were modified by substituting the initial boast statement made by A with an initial self-critical statement. This was accomplished by dubbing the appropriate critical statement (e.g., I'm a bad basketball player) over the boast (e.g., I'm a good basketball player) for each story. All other aspects of the story (i.e., the action and B's final statement) remained unchanged. Note, however, that in these stories, B's final statement now explicitly echoed the initial statement only in the literal and ironic compliment conditions (e.g., You sure are a bad basketball player).

Design and Procedure.   The design was identical to that of Experiment 1. Each participant watched 16 stories: Four ended with a literal criticism, 4 with an ironic criticism, 4 with a literal compliment, and 4 with an ironic compliment. The complete design was a 2 (criticisms vs. compliment) × 2 (literal vs. ironic endings) × 2 (treatment order) × 2 (5 vs. 6 years of age) mixed factorial design with treatment order and age as the only between-subject factors.

The procedure employed in Experiment 1 was replicated as exactly as possible. The stories illustrated in Table 19.1 were employed again with the previously described change to the initial statement. After the child watched each story, the same three questions described in Experiment 1 were again posed.

Results

As in Experiment 1, initial analysis of the complete model revealed that age and order of treatment factors had no significant effects on any of the dependent measures, and they did not interact with other independent variables. Consequently these variables were dropped from all subsequent analyses. Similarly, no additional analyses were required on results obtained from the third question in the procedure, as all participants correctly answered this control question regarding the factual context of each story.

Children's responses to the first question indicated whether they correctly detected the speaker's beliefs about the final utterance in each story (see Table 19.4). Consider first the stories with literal endings. Children clearly understood that the speaker was being literal when either a literal criticism was employed appropriately to make a negative comment about a poor performance (95%) or a literal compliment was employed appropriately to make a positive comment about a good performance (100%).

TABLE 19.2
Mean Proportion of Speakers' Beliefs Correctly Detected for Each Story Ending

Criticism				Compliments			
Literal		Ironic		Literal		Ironic	
M	SD	M	SD	M	SD	M	SD
.96	.12	.47	.44	.99	.05	.25	.39

Note. n = 24.

TABLE 19.3

**Mean Proportion of Correct Comprehension of Speaker's Intended Meaning
for Each Story Ending**

	Criticisms Rated Mean				Compliments Rated Nice		
Literal		Ironic		Literal		Ironic	
M	SD	M	SD	M	SD	M	SD
.81	.24	.44	.37	1.0	0.0	.58	.46

Note. These proportions only refer to items in which the speaker's belief was correctly detected;. $n = 9$.

TABLE 19.4

Mean Proportion of Speakers' Beliefs Correctly Detected for Each Story Ending

	Criticisms				Compliments		
Literal		Ironic		Literal		Ironic	
M	SD	M	SD	M	SD	M	SD
.95	.21	.44	.42	1.0	0.0	.35	.38

Note. $n = 24$.

Consider next the stories ending in ironic statements. When the speaker praised a partner's failure (i.e., ironic criticism), the children correctly inferred that the speaker's praise should not be taken literally on 44% of these trials. A nonparametric Wilcoxon test again revealed that their scores for the identical statement (e.g., You sure are a good basketball player) in the literal praise (100%) and nonliteral ironic criticism conditions (44%) were significantly different ($z = 3.83$, $p < .001$). In the ironic compliment condition, when the speaker criticized a partner's success (i.e., ironic compliment), the children correctly decided that the speaker's negative comment should not be taken literally on 35% of the trials. A nonparametric Wilcoxon test revealed that their scores for the identical statement (e.g., You sure are a bad basketball player) in the literal criticism (95%) and the nonliteral ironic compliment conditions (35%) were significantly different ($z = 3.47$, $p < .001$).

The important point to note in these results is that the children's performance when detecting the nonliteral nature of the ironic criticisms and compliments in the second experiment is now essentially symmetrical. A nonparametric Wilcoxon test reveals that the difference in detection rates between the ironic conditions is not significant ($z = 1.03$, ns). The symmetry is confirmed further by the number of children who managed to detect correctly at least one ironic comment. An equal number of children met this criterion for both ironic criticisms ($n = 15$) and ironic praise ($n = 15$). Furthermore, participants were as likely to detect an ironic compliment and no ironic criticisms as they were to detect an ironic criticism and no ironic compliments. Considered together, the children's symmetrical performance across the ironic conditions suggests that children are equally likely to detect either an ironic criticism or an ironic compliment as nonliteral *if* a self-critical antecedent is echoed in the ironic compliment condition.

Children's responses to the second question assessed whether they correctly comprehended the speaker's pragmatic intent. The number of critical statements rated as mean and complimentary statements rated as nice were converted into proportions and are presented in Table 19.5. Only those participants who detected the nonliteral nature of one or more of both ironic criticisms and compliments were included in the analysis of pragmatic intent ($n = 11$), and the proportions presented refer only to items in which the speaker's nonliteralness was correctly detected.

Consider first the responses to the mean versus nice question for stories with literal endings. As the data in Table 19.5 indicate, children always (100% of the time) inferred that the speaker was being nice when a successful performance ended with a literal compliment. Children inferred that the speaker was being mean when a poor performance ended with a literal criticism on 84% of the trials. Turning next to the stories ending in ironic statements, when the speaker praised a partner's failure (i.e., ironic criticism), the children correctly decided that the speaker's praise was in fact a criticism and judged it as mean on 43% of these trials. When they encountered this statement (e.g., You sure are a good basketball player) in the literal compliment condition, they interpreted the speaker's intent as mean on none of the trials. A nonparametric Wilcoxon test reveals that their ratings of the same statement as mean in the literal praise (0%) and ironic criticism conditions (43%) were significantly different ($z = 2.21, p < .05$).

A similar pattern of results is observed in the ironic compliment condition. When the speaker criticized a partner's success (i.e., ironic compliment), the children correctly decided that the speaker's criticism was in fact complimentary and judged it as nice on 46% of the trials. When they encounter this statement (e.g., You sure are a bad basketball player) in the literal criticism condition, they interpret the statement as nice on only 16% of the trials. A nonparametric Wilcoxon test reveals that their ratings of the same statement as nice in the literal criticism (16%) and ironic praise conditions (46%) were significantly different ($z = 2.03, p < .05$).

TABLE 19.5

Mean Proportion of Correct Comprehension of Speaker's Intended Meaning for Each Statement Type

Criticisms Rated Mean				Compliments Rated Nice			
Literal		Ironic		Literal		Ironic	
M	SD	M	SD	M	SD	M	SD
.84	.32	.43	.48	1.0	0.0	.46	.47

Note. These proportions only refer to items in which the speaker's belief was correctly detected; $n = 11$.

For the 11 children who had detected that a speaker was being nonliteral in both ironic conditions, the ability to judge correctly the speaker's intent tended to be symmetrical across ironic criticisms and ironic compliments. A comparison of the relevant scores revealed that children were as likely to reject a nice interpretation of a positive statement in the ironic criticism condition (0%–43% = 43%) as they were to reject a mean interpretation of a negative statement in the ironic compliment condition (16%–46% = 30%). Although this numerical difference continues to favor the ironic criticism condition, a Wilcoxon test on these difference scores indicated this difference was not significant. Considered together, these data suggest again that, for this age group, the ability to attribute intent, once they have detected correctly the nonliteralness of an ironic statement, is essentially equivalent for ironic criticisms and ironic compliments.

The preceding analyses of the children's responses to the mean versus nice question include only those children who managed to detect the nonliteral nature of at least one ironic criticism and one ironic compliment in response to the first question. Responses to the mean versus nice question provided by children who completely failed to detect the nonliteral nature of the ironic criticisms ($n = 9$) and the ironic compliments ($n = 9$) were again of interest. Essentially, the children who failed to detect any form of irony described 100% of the positive statements (e.g., You sure are a good basketball player) as nice whether that statement was encountered in an ironic or literal context. They described 100% of the negative statements (e.g., You sure are a bad basketball player) as mean whether that statement was encountered in an ironic or a literal context. These data confirm that these particular children, in contrast to the participants who were able to detect nonliteralness, are simply interpreting every statement made during these stories as literal, and they attribute positive and negative intent to the speaker accordingly on every trial.

Discussion

As predicted, modifying the stories so that the ironic compliments uniquely echoed a previous negative statement increased the number of children able to detect at least one ironic compliment from 9 children in the first experiment to 15 in the second, whereas the number of children detecting ironic criticisms did not change (Pearson $\chi^2 = 3.00$, one-tailed; $p < .04$). In addition, the echoic cue increased the proportion of ironic compliments detected from 25% in the first experiment to 35% in the second (Mann–Whitney $U = 227$, $p = .09$). Note, however, that removing the echoic factor from the ironic criticism condition in this second experiment did not undermine detection performance. An equal number of children were able to detect at least one ironic criticism in both experiments ($n = 15$), and the proportion of ironic criticisms detected was essentially equivalent across experiments (47% vs. 44%).

Considered together, these data suggest that the echoic factor plays an important, specific role in helping children detect the nonliteral nature of ironic compliments. Indeed, the positive effect of the echoic factor in this second experiment was sufficient to reduce significantly the asymmetry between detection of ironic criticisms and compliments we observed in Experiment 1. The data compared across experiments also indicate, however, that the echoic factor is not particularly important when processing ironic criticisms. Performance did not decline in this second experiment when the explicit echoic factor was removed from the story. Indeed, putting the echoic factor aside, if we simply average detection rates across the two experiments, ironic criticisms generally continue to be detected more frequently (45% vs. 30%) than ironic compliments ($z = 2.33$, $p < .02$).

The results concerned with the comprehension of the speaker's intent to be either mean or nice confirmed the data from Experiment 1. Again, the intent question was more difficult for children than the detection question, and performance across the ironic conditions was again symmetrical when children did correctly infer intent. Children who detected that the speaker was nonliteral in the ironic conditions were as likely to reject nice interpretations for ironic criticisms (e.g., You sure are a good basketball player) as they were to reject mean interpretations of ironic compliments (e.g., You sure are a bad basketball player).

GENERAL DISCUSSION

The primary question addressed in this study was whether children, during this early transition period of irony comprehension, display a bias in their ability to detect nonliteral forms of criticisms and compliments. When the data concerned with the detection question are considered across both experiments, two conclusions are suggested. First, the superior performance in the ironic criticism condition in Experiment 1 cannot be attributed to the advantage offered by an echoic marker in that condition. Experiment 2 revealed that children performed equally well in detecting ironic criticisms whether the echoic marker was present (Experiment 1) or absent (Experiment 2). Second, the data from Experiment 2 also suggest that the presence of an echoic marker did uniquely and significantly enhance the children's ability to detect the nonliteral nature of ironic compliments.

How does one explain this interaction and the relative advantage enjoyed by the critical ironist in these data? As discussed earlier, one suggestion is that the asymmetry in children's performance reflects their differential experience with this particular form of irony (Dews & Winner, 1997). As such, the results are in general consistent with social–pragmatic theories of early communicative development (e.g., Bruner, 1983; Tomasello, 1988, 1992, 1995) that would attribute these asymmetrical competencies to differential exposure.

Although early social–pragmatic experiences may contribute directly to the differences we have observed, the unique influence of the echoic factor on ironic compliments observed in the second experiment suggests that a simple social-learning mechanism may be an oversimplification. Recent attempts to explain a similar asymmetry in mature conversationalists' comprehension of various forms of verbal irony (Kreuz & Glucksberg, 1989; Kumon-Nakamura et al., 1995) potentially provide a more elaborate explanation for the results of these two experiments. Specifically, Kumon-

Nakamura et al. (1995) outlined an allusional pretense theory of irony that is also grounded in our social–cultural experiences but explains the asymmetry in terms of the differential extent to which ironic criticisms and ironic praise echo or allude to some antecedent event, social norm, or shared expectation. Starting from the assumption that our social norms, preferences, and desires tend to be positive (e.g., people desire good weather, expect polite behavior, etc.), allusional pretense theory suggests that ironic criticisms do not require explicit antecedent statements. Instead ironic criticisms *implicitly* echo or allude to our presumed positive expectations (e.g., "Another gorgeous day" uttered in a downpour). In contrast, ironic compliments (e.g., "You sure are a terrible friend" after receiving a gift) are assumed to require explicit antecedents (e.g., "You won't get a gift from a terrible friend like me") because these negative utterances are less effective reminders of our implicit positive expectations or norms.

The data presented in this article suggest that 5- and 6-year-old children are operating in exactly the manner predicted by allusional pretense theory. The explicit echoic statement was influential in the context of the ironic compliments but had no effect in the context of ironic criticisms. More specifically, when a negative antecedent remark was directly echoed in the ironic compliment condition (Experiment 2), the children's detection performance was enhanced and the asymmetry between the two forms of ironic statements was diminished. Equally important, a reciprocal decrease in detection performance was not observed in the ironic criticism condition when the explicit, positive antecedent remark was removed. Apparently, as the allusional pretense model would predict, the positive antecedent condition can be implicitly *assumed* by the critical ironist.

It is also important to emphasize that our extension of allusional pretense theory to these data implies that the wide variety of positive social norms, preferences, and expectations presumed by this model are also in place at this young age. Indeed, it is possible that children's early, differential social–pragmatic experiences with these two forms of verbal irony (Dews & Winner, 1997) are contributing directly to the emergence of the shared expectations that are central to the allusional pretense model. We suspect, however, that some caution is in order with respect to this assumption. Our own view, and something to investigate in further research, is that children may have acquired some positive norms and expectations at this young age, but we would expect this bias to be more domain specific than the general norms assumed for adults.

Finally, we suggest that the allusional pretense model also offers a viable explanation for earlier findings, suggesting that echoic cues do not play an important role in young children's comprehension of irony (e.g., Dews et al., 1996). Recall that all prior research has considered only children's comprehension of ironic criticisms. From the perspective of the allusional pretense model (and consistent with our data), ironic criticisms are assumed to be less dependent on *explicit* antecedents. Consequently, it is perhaps not surprising that echoic cues have failed to play a role in prior developmental studies.

The second question of interest in this article is the degree to which detection and understanding pragmatic intent are separable components of irony comprehension during this early period of communicative development. Ackerman (1983) first suggested that the detection of the nonliteral form could be dissociated from the process of inferring the intent or attitude of the speaker. His conclusion was based, in part, on the observation that 6-year-olds were able to detect the nonliteral nature of an ironic criticism more frequently than they were able to infer the negative intent of the ironist. Our results are similar. When responses are averaged across the ironic conditions and experiments, our children were able to detect that a speaker was being nonliteral more frequently (38%) than they were able to correctly infer the speaker's intent (28%), and this difference was significant ($z = 3.02$, $p < .01$).

One would not expect this difference if these two processes were dependent on the same underlying process, and one would not expect the asymmetry in children's performance to occur only in response to the detection question. One admittedly speculative explanation for these results is that our two questions are tapping separable components of irony comprehension that are systematically associated with a fundamental change in social cognition that is also in transition during this period of development. Specifically, a considerable amount of converging evidence suggests that a child's ability to understand the mental states of others is a minimally necessary condition for the comprehension of ironic statements. As Dews and Winner (1997) noted, to understand a nonliteral utterance as ironic, the hearer must make two determinations about the speaker's mental state. First, the hearer must correctly determine the speaker's belief about the situation under discussion. Consider, for example, an ironic criticism ("You sure are a good weight lifter") delivered after a failure to lift the weights. To detect the nonliteral nature of this statement, the listener must correctly infer the speaker's actual belief about the listener's weight-lifting skills. If the listener infers that the speaker does not really believe the positive statement, the listener has inferred the "true" belief of the speaker. This process is indexed by our detection question and is typically described as first-order reasoning about other's belief states. In addition, once this first-order inference is made, to determine the speaker's pragmatic intent or attitude (e.g., is the speaker being mean or nice or possibly lying to the listener), the listener must also infer the *speaker's belief* about the listener's actual knowledge of the situation. Again, in the context of an ironic criticism delivered after a failure to lift the weights, the listener must infer what the speaker believes about the listener's actual knowledge state. In this example, correctly inferring that the speaker believes that the listener knows he or she has failed the weight-lifting task permits correct inferences about the intent of the nonliteral statement (i.e., is the speaker being mean or nice). This process is typically described as second-order reasoning about belief states, and it is indexed by our inference question (Winner & Leekam, 1991).

Several types of evidence also suggest that a child's understanding of irony appears to be constrained by the ability to make these first- and second-order belief attributions. For example, in addition to descriptive data indicating that the ability to infer second-order belief attributions and inferences about the pragmatic intent of an ironist tend to emerge at about the same age (see Dews & Winner, 1997), more direct research on individual differences has demonstrated that children who fail or pass independent second-order false belief tasks also differ in their ability to comprehend the intent of an ironist (Happe, 1993; Leekam, 1991; Sullivan, Winner, & Hopfield, 1995; Winner & Leekam, 1991).

Given that first-order reasoning skills emerge prior to second-order reasoning skills during early development (e.g., Frye, Zelazo, & Palfai, 1995), we would suggest, consistent with Ackerman's (1983) earlier claims, that the detection of non-literalness may be a first-order stage of the underlying reasoning process that is separable from and necessary for second-order inferences about the speaker's pragmatic intent. Although this model runs contrary to some current theories of adult irony comprehension (e.g., Gibbs & O'Brien, 1991), it is consistent with the data we have obtained from these young children (see also deGroot, Kaplan, Rosenblatt, Dews, & Winner, 1995). Some of the children in our procedure are clearly able to detect both the nonliteral nature of the ironic comment (first-order attribution) and infer the speaker's intent (second-order attribution). Others, however, detect only the nonliteral nature of the speech and are not consistently able to engage in the second-order reasoning required to infer intent. There are also a substantial number of children at this age who are unable to detect nonliteral speech. These children appear content to take everyone at their word in every context.

Finally, we can conclude this somewhat speculative analysis by returning for a moment to allusional pretense theory and describing its implications in the context of the two-stage process of early irony comprehension previously outlined. Although further research employing a wider age range will be required to address the issue, our data suggest that the mechanisms outlined by allusional pretense theory must be operating specifically on the detection stage of the comprehension process. It is at this stage that we observe the asymmetry in children's comprehension. Once children have detected the nonliteral nature of an ironic compliment or an ironic criticism, if they also possess the second-order belief attribution skills required to infer pragmatic intent, the advantage ascribed to the critical ironist and the role of implicit and explicit echoic antecedents apparently disappears, and children who can manage second-order belief attributions find it equally easy to infer the intent of both forms.

ACKNOWLEDGMENTS

This research was supported by a grant from the Social Sciences and Humanities Research Council of Canada. We thank Fran Dunham for her valuable comments and technical support, and we are grateful to Aimee Hancock, Susan Boehnke, and Jack Loney for their assistance in constructing the stories. Thanks also to all of those families who so generously volunteered to participate in our research program.

REFERENCES

Ackerman, B. P. (1981). Young children's understanding of a speaker's intentional use of a false utterance. *Developmental Psychology, 17*, 472–480.

Ackerman, B. P. (1983). Form and function in children's understanding of ironic utterances. Journal of Experimental *Child Psychology, 35*, 487–508.

Andrews, J., Rosenblatt, E., Malkus, U., Gardner, H., & Winner, E. (1986). Children's abilities to distinguish metaphoric and ironic utterances from mistakes and lies. *Communication and Cognition, 19*, 281–298.

Bruner, J. (1983). *Child's talk*. New York: Norton.

Clark, H. H., & Gerrig, R. J. (1984). On the pretense theory of irony. *Journal of Experimental Psychology: General, 113*, 121–126.

DeGroot, A., Kaplan, J., Rosenblatt, E., Dews, S., & Winner, E. (1995). Understanding vs. discriminating non-literal utterances: Evidence for a dissociation. *Metaphor and Symbolic Activity, 10*, 255–273.

Demorest, A., Meyer, C., Phelps, E., Gardner, H., & Winner, E. (1984). Words speak louder than actions: Understanding deliberately false remarks. *Child Development, 55*, 1527–1534.

Dews, S., & Winner, E. (1997). Attributing meaning to deliberately false utterances: The case or irony. In C. Mandell & A. McCabe (Eds.), *The problem of meaning: Behavioral and cognitive perspectives* (pp. 377–414). Amsterdam: North-Holland/Elsevier Science.

Dews, S., Winner, E., Kaplan, J., Rosenblatt, E., Hunt, M., Lim, K., et al. (1996). Children's understanding of the meaning and functions of verbal irony. *Child Development, 67*, 3071–3085.

Dunham, P., & Dunham, F. (1996). The semantically reciprocating robot: Adult influences on children's early conversational skills. Social Development, 5, 261–274.

Frye, D., Zelazo, P. D., & Palfai, T. (1995). Theory of mind and rule-based reasoning. *Cognitive Development, 10*, 483–527.

Gibbs, R. W. (1994). Figurative thought and figurative language. In M. Gernsbacher (Ed.), *Handbook of psycholinguistics* (pp. 411–446). San Diego, CA: Academic.

Gibbs, R. W., & O'Brien, J. (1991). Psychological aspects of irony understanding. *Journal of Pragmatics, 16*, 523–530.

Grice, H. P. (1975). Logic and conversation. In P. Cole & J. Morgan (Eds.), *Syntax and semantics 3: Speech acts* (pp. 41–58). New York: Academic.

Happe, F. (1993). Communicative competence and theory of mind in autism: A test of relevance theory. *Cognition, 48*, 101–119.

Keppel, G., & Zedick, S. (1989). *Data analysis for research designs*. New York: Freeman.

Kochanska, G., Murray, K., Jacques, T., Koenig, A., & Vandegeest, K. (1996). Inhibitory control in young children and its role in emerging internalization. *Child Development, 67*, 490–507.

Kreuz, R. J., & Glucksberg, S. (1989). How to be sarcastic: The echoic reminder theory of verbal irony. *Journal of Experimental Psychology: General, 18*, 374–386.

Kumon-Nakamura, S., Glucksberg, S., & Brown, M. (1995). How about another piece of pie: The allusional pretense theory of discourse irony. *Journal of Experimental Psychology: General, 124*, 3–21.

Leekam, S. (1991). Jokes and lies: Children's understanding of intentional falsehood. In A. Whiten (Ed.), *Natural theories of mind: Evolution, development, and simulation of everyday mindreading* (pp. 159–174). Cambridge, MA: Blackwell.

Milosky, L. M., & Ford, J. A. (1997). The role of prosody in children's inferences of ironic intent. *Discourse Processes, 23*, 47–61.

Sperber, D., & Wilson, D. (1981). Irony and the use–mention distinction. In P. Cole (Ed.), *Radical pragmatics* (pp. 295–318). New York: Academic.

Sperber, D., & Wilson, D. (1986). *Relevance: Communication and cognition.* Cambridge, MA: Harvard University Press.

Sullivan, K., Winner, E., & Hopfield, N. (1995). How children tell a lie from a joke: The role of second-order mental state attributions. *British Journal of Developmental Psychology, 13*, 191–204.

Tomasello, M. (1988). The role of joint attentional processes in early language development. *Language Sciences, 10*, 69–98.

Tomasello, M. (1992). The social bases of language acquisition. *Social Development, 1*, 68–87.

Tomasello, M. (1995). Joint attention as social cognition. In C. Moore & P. Dunham (Eds.), *Joint attention: Its origins and role in development* (pp. 103–130). Hillsdale, NJ: Lawrence Erlbaum Associates.

Winner, E., & Leekam, S. (1991). Distinguishing irony from deception: Understanding the speaker's second-order intention. *British Journal of Developmental Psychology, 9*, 257–270.

CHAPTER 20

Children's Perceptions of the Social Functions of Verbal Irony

Melanie Harris Glenwright
Penny M. Pexman
University of Calgary, Canada

Verbal irony can serve many social functions: speakers can mute the aggression conveyed by criticism or temper the praise conveyed by a compliment (the Tinge Hypothesis; Dews, Kaplan, & Winner, 1995), and speakers can also bring humor to a situation. A full understanding of ironic language requires one to make complex inferences about speaker intent, a task that can be challenging for children. The present study was devised as a developmental test of the Tinge Hypothesis. Two experiments assessed 5- to 6- and 7- to 8-year-old children's abilities to detect and interpret the aggressive and humorous intent of speakers who made ironic criticisms, literal criticisms, ironic compliments, and literal compliments depicted in puppet shows. When children detected the use of irony, their aggression ratings provided support for the Tinge Hypothesis but their humor ratings indicated that the humor function was not recognized.

Consider the following situation: Martha, a 7-year-old girl, and her father spent an entire Saturday cleaning the house and cutting the lawn. Upon returning home and observing the completed work, Martha's mother commented to Martha's father, "You sure have been lazy today." Can children like Martha recognize this remark as an ironic compliment? Can children recognize and interpret the humor intended in this sort of remark? These are some of the issues explored in the present research.

SOCIAL FUNCTIONS SERVED BY VERBAL IRONY

Why would a speaker use verbal irony instead of literal language to convey a message? Here we use the term *verbal irony* to refer to counterfactual language that is

This chapter was previously published as "Children's perceptions of the social functions of irony" (M. Harris, & P. Pexman) in *Discourse Processes, 36,* 147–165. Copyright © [2003] by Lawrence Erlbaum Associates. Reprinted with permission. *Note:* The first Author's name has changed to: Melanie Glenwright (nee Harris).

447

often labeled as sarcasm. Psycholinguists suggest that verbal irony is used to achieve complex social and communicative goals (Kreuz & Roberts, 1995; Leggit & Gibbs, 2000). For instance, one may choose ironic language over literal language in order to bring humor to a situation (Kreuz & Glucksberg, 1989; Kreuz, Long, & Church, 1991, Kumon-Nakamura, Glucksberg, & Brown, 1995; Long & Graesser, 1988; Roberts & Kreuz, 1994). Examinations of adults' perceptions indicate that ironic remarks are often viewed as funnier and more playful than literal remarks (Gibbs, 2000; Kreuz et al., 1991) and that ironic speakers tend to be viewed as humorous (Pexman & Olineck, 2002a).

Ironic utterances might also be made when speakers wish to indirectly convey their attitudes towards a particular individual or event (Giora, 1995; Sperber & Wilson, 1986). In the case of ironic criticisms (saying something positive to mean something negative) that attitude is generally critical, but irony allows the criticism to be expressed indirectly, thereby allowing the speaker to mute the force of one's meaning. This effect has been termed the *muting function* (Dews & Winner, 1995). Dews, Kaplan, and Winner (1995) examined the muting function and the humor function of ironic criticisms, reporting that adults rated ironic criticisms as less mean and more funny than literal criticisms. Dews et al. concluded that "the two overarching functions of irony … [are] to save face and to be funny" (p. 366).

There are now several theories that have been devised to explain verbal irony comprehension and processing. These include the Echoic theories (Kreuz & Glucksberg, 1989; Sperber & Wilson, 1981, 1986), Pretense (e.g., Clark & Gerrig, 1984), and Allusional Pretense theories (Kumon-Nakamura et al., 1995), the Graded Salience Hypothesis (e.g., Giora, 1997), Implicit Display Theory (Utsumi, 2000), and Colston's (2002) theory of Contrast and Assimilation. These theories have not tended to focus on the social functions of irony. In contrast, the Tinge Hypothesis (e.g., Dews et al., 1995) was devised to explain these functions. This hypothesis asserts that for ironic criticisms, the positive literal meaning of the utterance tinges the interpretation of the speaker's intended (negative) meaning and results in a less negative tone. The Tinge Hypothesis is also relevant to interpretation of ironic compliments. Whereas an ironic criticism is a positive statement made with a negative meaning intended (e.g., saying "You're so graceful" in response to someone tripping and falling), an ironic compliment is a negative statement with a positive meaning intended (e.g., saying "You're so clumsy" in response to someone executing a perfect dive off the diving board). Dews et al. reported that ironic compliments were rated as more insulting than literal compliments. According to the Tinge Hypothesis, this is because the negative literal meaning of ironic compliments results in a less positive interpretation. Thus, the Tinge Hypothesis holds that irony mutes the negativity of criticism and tinges the positivity of praise. Dews et al. also reported that ironic statements were perceived to be funnier than literal statements and argued that the humor function of irony results from "surprise yielded by the disparity between what is said and what is meant" (p. 348).

Challenging the Tinge Hypothesis, recent data indicates that irony does not always soften criticism. For instance, it has been reported that adults perceive ironic criticisms as more condemning than literal criticisms (Colston, 1997), and that the interpretation adults give to irony depends on the consequences of the situation for the listener (Colston, 2002). Pexman and Olineck (2002b) found that when adults rated speaker intent, they perceived ironic criticisms as more mocking than literal criticisms. In contrast, when they made other ratings that tapped the social impression created by the statements, the same ironic criticisms were rated as more polite and more positive than literal criticisms. Furthermore, adults perceived ironic compliments as less mocking, less polite, and less positive than literal compliments. Pexman and Olineck argued that these results supported the Tinge Hypothesis for ironic compliments but suggested that the muting function is relevant only to the social impression created by ironic insults, and not to adults' ratings of underlying speaker intent.

In summary, it seems that perceptions of the social functions of ironic criticisms and ironic compliments require complex social inferences. Now consider young Martha's situation. How will she perceive the ironic compliment that her mother directed at her father? Will she have an understanding of the tinge function and thus perceive that irony renders praise less positive? In the present study we examined whether the Tinge Hypothesis is an accurate description of children's understanding of verbal irony.

CHILDREN'S UNDERSTANDING OF VERBAL IRONY

To date, the majority of developmental research regarding verbal irony has focused on variables that contribute to children's comprehension (for a review, see Creusere, 1999). Although younger children may be able to detect the use of verbal irony, it is generally agreed that the ability to recognize the intent behind ironic statements develops between the ages of 5 and 6 years (Creusere, 2000; de Groot, Kaplan, Rosenblatt, Dews, & Winner, 1995; Winner et al., 1987). Developmental data indicate that a child must understand what the speaker's ironic statement means (speaker belief) before she/he can determine why the speaker chose to use irony (speaker intent; Demorest, Meyer, Phelps, Gardner, & Winner, 1984; Winner & Leekam, 1991).

Although several developmental experiments have assessed children's understanding of speaker intent, few have assessed children's understanding of the social functions of verbal irony. Notably, Dews and colleagues (1996) found that 5- to 6-year-old and 8- to 9-year-old children rated ironic criticisms as less "mean" or less aggressive than literal criticisms, and therefore, showed recognition of the muting function of ironic criticisms. In fact, Dews et al. argued that recognition of the muting function, but not the humor function, is evident as soon as children can understand irony. These researchers also observed that 5- to 6-year-olds showed a "halo effect" by rating literal compliments as funny whereas 8- to 9-year-olds found ironic criticisms funnier than literal criticisms. These data suggest that children detect the humor function of verbal irony around 8 years of age.

Creusere (2000) recently compared the extent to which 8-year-old children found different kinds of ironic speech forms aggressive ("mean") and humorous. In addition to simple counterfactual statements (but not criticisms or compliments), children heard more sophisticated utterances such as over-polite requests, expressions of thanks, ironic questions, and ironic offerings. When 8-year-olds gave "meanness" and humor ratings to each of these speech forms, they rated the expressions of thanks as the meanest and the least humorous speech form. Questions and offerings were rated as less mean than the counterfactual statements, but the children's humor ratings did not differ significantly among the speech forms. Creusere concluded that further research was required regarding the development of the notion that some ironic remarks can be interpreted as simultaneously aggressive and humorous.

Most research on children's understanding of verbal irony has included only critical forms of irony. To our knowledge, there has been just one examination of children's understanding of ironic compliments. Hancock, Dunham, and Purdy (2000) found that 5- and 6-year-olds more accurately detected ironic criticisms than ironic compliments. Furthermore, only children who detected the use of irony could identify that speakers who made ironic criticisms intended to be "mean" and speakers who made ironic compliments intended to be nice. This supported previous findings that detection of verbal irony precedes attribution of speaker intent.

The Present Research

The primary goal of the present research was to investigate the development of children's understanding of the social functions of verbal irony, including both ironic criticisms and ironic compliments. As such, we sought to explore whether children's perceptions of irony show understanding of the tinge function by examining their understanding of the aggressive function of ironic criticisms and ironic compliments. We examined *both* the aggression and humor functions of irony because, as noted by Creusere (2000), the development of an understanding that irony is intended to be both mean and funny requires more thorough research.

Given that Hancock et al. (2000) reported that 5- and 6-year-old children are just beginning to understand ironic compliments, we chose 5- to 6-year-old children and 7- to 8-year-old children as participants to investigate whether comprehension improves immediately beyond this critical age period.

In Experiment 1, each child watched eight puppet shows in which one character made an ironic or literal *criticism* in response to the failure of the other character. In Experiment 2, each child watched eight puppet shows depicting similar events as those in Experiment 1 except one character made an ironic or literal *compliment* in response to the success of the other character. In both experiments, children were questioned regarding their interpretations of the character's intent behind the remark (literal/ironic) and were then asked to rate the remarks on scales that ranged from (a) mean to nice and (b) funny to serious.

EXPERIMENT I

Purpose

The purpose of Experiment 1 was to examine children's understanding of the muting and humor functions of ironic criticisms (compared to literal criticisms).

Based on findings from Dews et al. (1996), we anticipated that children's ratings in Experiment 1 would indicate that they perceived irony to mute the aggression of criticism and that they would rate ironic criticisms as less mean than literal criticisms. Given the Dews et al. findings, we also predicted that recognition of the muting function would coincide with correct recognition of speaker belief for ironic criticisms. If these effects were not observed, there would be at least two possible interpretations: either children don't recognize the tinge function, or they are attending to some situational cues or perspectives that neutralize the tinge.

Dews et al. (1996) argued that young children believe that anything nice is also funny (a type of halo effect), and consequently they will have difficulty seeing critical statements as funny. Thus, we predicted that younger children would perceive ironic criticisms to be quite serious and that only older children would rate ironic criticisms as funnier than literal criticisms.

Method

Participants.   Sixteen 5- to 6-year-old children ($M = 6.1$, range 5.1–6.11, 8 males, 8 females) and sixteen 7- to 8-year-old children ($M = 7.11$, range 7.1–8.8, 8 males, 8 females) participated. All participants were from English speaking and primarily middle-class families.

Materials.   Eight puppet show scenarios, which each ended in either an ironic criticism or a literal criticism, were depicted. Eight male and eight female characters comprised the cast for the puppet shows and small props were used for each scenario (e.g., a garden). We tried to choose scenarios that would be familiar to 5- to 8-year-old children (see Table 20.1 for examples). Both characters were introduced to the children before the show began. The first character did not perform any significant actions but always made a criticism in response to the failure of the other character. Dialogues for the puppet shows were pre-recorded by a narrator such that ironic criticisms were made with a mocking and insincere intonation and literal criticisms were made with a blunt and factual tone of voice.

In order to assess children's judgments of the aggression and humor conveyed in the critical remark, two rating scales from Dews et al. (1996) were modified to include extended ranges. The Mean/Nice Scale was used to assess the aggressive intent of the speaker and the Funny/Serious Scale was used to assess the humorous intent of the speaker (see Fig. 20.1).

TABLE 20.1

Sample Puppet Show Scenarios

The Garden Scenario

Bob has a flower garden in his backyard. Sam is the gardener for Bob's garden.

Sam was weeding the garden one day.

Experiment 1: Sam finished quickly, pulling out all of the flowers instead of the weeds.

    Bob said: You are an awful gardener.   (Literal criticism)

    or

    You are a great gardener.   (Ironic criticism)

Experiment 2: Sam finished quickly, pulling out all of the weeds.

    Bob said: You are a great gardener.   (Literal compliment)

    or

    You are an awful gardener.   (Ironic compliment)

The Painting Scenario

Anne wanted a painting. Jane is an artist. Anne told Jane that she wanted a painting of a beautiful rose.

Experiment 1: Jane painted a messy painting that did not look like a rose.

    Anne said: You are a horrible painter.   (Literal criticism)

    or

    You are an awesome painter.   (Ironic criticism)

Experiment 2: Jane painted the perfect painting of a beautiful rose.

    Anne said: You are an awesome painter.   (Literal compliment)

    or

    You are a horrible painter.   (Ironic compliment)

NICE   MEAN

FUNNY   SERIOUS

Figure 20.1.   Mean/Nice Scale and Funny/Serious Scale.

452

Procedure. Children were individually trained on both of the rating scales to ensure their understanding of what each face represented and that the entire range of the scale was to be used.

After every puppet show, each child was asked three questions. The speaker belief question assessed whether the children interpreted the speaker's statement as a positive or negative evaluation (e.g., "When Bob said *You are a great gardener* did Bob think that Sam was a good gardener or a bad gardener?"). The second question referred to the Mean/Nice Scale and children were requested to rate the aggression intended by the ironic speaker's final remark (e.g., "Now point to one of the faces to show how mean or nice Bob was trying to be when he said *You are a great gardener*"). The third question referred to the Funny/Serious Scale and children were requested to point to one of the faces to show how funny or serious the character who made the final remark was trying to be (e.g., "Now point to one of the faces to show how funny or serious Bob was trying to be when he said *You are a great gardener*"). When the second and third questions were posed, the experimenter repeated the criticism with the intonation in the accompanying dialogue.

Design. Each child watched one of two possible endings for each scenario for a total of eight puppet shows containing four literal criticisms and four ironic criticisms. All of the stories and characters were crossed so that, across participants, every character appeared in every story. For the speaker belief question, the order of positive and negative descriptions (e.g., good gardener/bad gardener) was randomized between puppet shows for each child. For the speaker intent questions, the order of mean/nice and humorous/serious labels were alternated between puppet shows, as was the order of the second and third questions requiring the Mean/Nice Scale and the Funny/Serious Scale. Thus, the design was a 2 (Age Group: 5–6, 7–8) × 2 (Criticism type: Ironic, Literal) mixed model with age as a between-subjects factor.

Coding System. When participants indicated that a criticism was a negative evaluation, his/her response was coded as a correctly interpreted speaker belief. Proportions were calculated for correct responses to the speaker belief questions for ironic and literal criticisms. Each child's Mean/Nice Scale ratings and Funny/Serious Scale ratings were coded on a 1 to 5 range. Scores on the Mean/Nice Scale were coded so that 1 = *very nice;* 2 = *nice;* 3 = *a little bit nice, a little bit mean;* 4 = *mean;* and 5 = *very mean.* Similarly, scores on the Funny/Serious Scale were coded so that 1 = *very funny;* 2 = *funny;* 3 = *a little bit funny, a little bit serious;* 4 = *serious;* and 5 = *very serious.* For puppet shows in which the speaker belief was correctly attributed, the coded scale ratings were used to calculate a mean Mean/Nice rating and a mean Funny/Serious rating.

Results

Responses from females and males were combined for all analyses reported here because no main effects of gender or interactions with gender were found.

Speaker Belief.   As predicted, children accurately understood ironic criticisms as negative evaluations (see Table 20.2). The mean proportions of correct speaker belief responses for the 5- to 6- year-olds and 7- to 8-year-olds were compared with a 2 (Age Group: 5–6, 7–8) × 2 (Criticism type: Ironic, Literal) mixed model analysis of variance (ANOVA) with age as a between subjects factor. This analysis yielded a significant age by criticism type interaction, $F(1, 30) = 6.28, p <$ .05, $MSE = .27$. Planned comparisons with a Bonferroni correction (alpha = .025) indicated the interaction was due to the fact that older children correctly interpreted significantly more ironic criticisms ($M = .92, SD = .20$) than did younger children ($M = .64, SD = .42$); $t(30) = 2.33, p < .025$. In contrast, both older children ($M = .95$, $SD = .11$) and younger children ($M = .94, SD = .14$) were near ceiling for interpretation of literal criticisms, $t(30) = .36, p > .025$. The main effects of criticism type and age were also significant, $F(1, 30) = 9.70, p < .05, MSE = .41$; and $F(1, 30) = $ 572.38, $p < .001, MSE = .33$, respectively.

The mean proportions of correct responses to the first, second, third, and fourth speaker belief questions for ironic criticisms were compared with a repeated measures ANOVA with order as a within subjects factor. This analysis indicated that children did not become increasingly accurate at interpreting speaker belief as more ironic criticisms were presented ($F < 1$) and that order was therefore not a confounding factor. In addition, we checked for item effects by comparing speaker belief responses for ironic statements made across the eight puppet show scenarios to explore whether the proportion of correct interpretations varied. In Experiment 1, correct speaker belief responses ranged from .73 for the garden puppet show scenario to .88 for the clothing store puppet show scenario and the proportion of correct responses did not significantly differ across puppet shows.

Mean/Nice Scale Ratings.   Mean ratings for each criticism type for all children and by age group are shown in Table 20.3. A 2 (Age Group: 5–6, 7–8) × 2 (Criticism type: Ironic, Literal) mixed model ANOVA with age as a between subjects

TABLE 20-2

Average Proportion of Correctly Attributed Speaker Belief for Ironic and Literal Criticisms and Compliments Overall and As a function of Age Group

	Experiment 1 Criticisms				Experiment 2 Compliments			
	Ironic		Literal		Ironic		Literal	
Age Group	M	SD	M	SD	M	SD	M	SD
Overall	.79	(.36)	.95	(.12)	.38	(.37)	.96	(.11)
5- to 6-year-olds	.65	(.42)	.94	(.14)	.38	(.33)	.97	(.09)
7- to 8-year-olds	.92	(.20)	.95	(.11)	.38	(.42)	.96	(.13)

Note. Values enclosed in parentheses are standard deviations.

TABLE 20.3

Average Scale Ratings for Ironic and Literal Criticisms and Compliments Overall and As a Function of Age Group

| | Experiment 1 Criticisms | | | | Experiment 2 Compliments | | | |
| | Ironic | | Literal | | Ironic | | Literal | |
Age Group	M	SD	M	SD	M	SD	M	SD
Mean/Nice ratings:								
Overall	3.35	(1.30)	4.19	(0.58)	2.67	(1.29)	1.78	(.43)
5- to 6-year-olds	3.11	(1.61)	4.22	(0.62)	2.67	(1.53)	1.27	(0.58)
7- to 8-year-olds	3.58	(0.89)	4.15	(0.59)	2.68	(1.06)	1.08	(0.19)
Funny/Serious ratings:								
Overall	3.96	(0.97)	4.35	(0.61)	3.40	(1.28)	3.80	(0.96)
5- to 6-year-olds	3.78	(1.19)	4.40	(0.58)	3.98	(1.15)	3.62	(1.06)
7- to 8-year-olds	4.13	(0.67)	4.31	(0.66)	2.75	(1.14)	3.99	(0.85)

Note. Mean ratings were calculated only when speaker belief was correctly attributed. Values enclosed in parentheses are standard deviations.

factor yielded a significant main effect of criticism type, $F(1, 30) = 12.17$, $p < .005$, $MSE = 11.32$. Children rated literal criticisms as significantly more mean ($M = 4.19$, $SD = .58$) than ironic criticisms ($M = 3.45$, $SD = 1.30$), thus demonstrating their understanding of the tinge function, wherein the aggression of ironic criticisms is muted compared to the aggression of literal criticisms. Neither the main effect of age, $F(1, 30) = 1.29$, $p > .05$, $MSE = 1.20$, nor the interaction was significant ($F < 1$).

To explore the nature of children's misperceptions of ironic criticisms, we also examined mean ratings for ironic statements to which children offered incorrect speaker belief responses. Whereas children who detected the nonliteral nature of ironic criticisms viewed these remarks as slightly mean, children who derived a literal interpretation of these remarks indicated that they perceived ironic criticisms as nice ($M = 1.93$, $SD = 1.03$).

Funny/Serious Scale Ratings. Mean ratings for the Funny/Serious Scale were also compared with a 2 (Age Group: 5–6, 7–8) × 2 (Criticism type: Ironic, Literal) mixed model ANOVA with age as a between subjects factor. The significant main effect of criticism type, $F(1, 30) = 6.00$, $p < .05$, $MSE = 2.57$, showed that literal criticisms ($M = 4.35$, $SD = .61$) were rated as significantly more serious than ironic criticisms ($M = 3.96$, $SD = .97$). Although children perceived ironic criticisms as less serious than literal criticisms, they clearly did not recognize the humorous intent behind ironic criticisms because their mean rating corresponded to the "serious" face on the scale. It was predicted that older children would rate ironic criticisms as funnier than literal criticisms, but the age by criticism type interaction was not significant, $F(1, 30) = 1.92$, $p > .05$, $MSE = .80$. The effect of age was also not significant because both age groups had similar perceptions of the seriousness of speakers who made literal and ironic criticisms ($F < 1$).

When children offered incorrect speaker belief responses for ironic criticisms, their ratings indicated that these misinterpreted criticisms were perceived as close to the "a little bit serious, a little bit funny" point on the scale ($M = 3.39$, $SD = 1.09$).

Discussion

Results from this experiment are in agreement with the growing body of evidence which indicates that children's comprehension of verbal irony continues to develop between 5 and 8 years of age (Creusere, 2000; Demorest et al., 1984; Dews et al., 1996). In Experiment 1, many children produced ratings indicating that ironic criticisms were perceived as less aggressive than literal criticisms. This finding supports the Tinge Hypothesis, which suggests that the positive literal meaning of an ironic criticism tinges the perceived meaning to be less negative.

In Experiment 1, we also addressed whether children recognize a speaker's humorous intent when an ironic criticism is uttered. Dews and colleagues (1996) found that only older children (8- to 9-year-olds) rated ironic criticisms as funny; however, older children in the present study (7- to 8-year-olds) rated ironic criticisms as somewhat serious. This discrepancy between Dews and colleagues' findings and the results of Experiment 1 could be attributed to differences in participant age groups, stimuli, or procedures. Perhaps an appreciation of the humor implied by ironic criticism continues to develop beyond 8 years of age. It is also possible that the scenarios and remarks used in the present research did not illustrate the kinds of humorous situations appreciated by 5- to 8-year-old children. Whereas Dews et al. showed children cartoon clips (e.g., The Little Mermaid), we showed children puppet shows depicting scenarios in which an employee performed a task for an employer or customer. These "professional" scenarios may have influenced the perceived seriousness of the situations. Also, Dews et al. used a 4-point rating scale that included the following labels: "not at all funny," "a teeny bit funny," "very funny," and "very, very funny." Thus, 3 of the 4 labels involved a perception of humor, and were scored as such. In contrast, our 5-point humor scale included the following labels: "very funny"; "funny"; "a little bit funny, a little bit serious"; "serious"; and "very serious." It seems possible that, in relation to our scale, Dews et al.'s scale may have been somewhat skewed toward a perception of humor, or was particularly sensitive to that perception.

EXPERIMENT 2

Purpose

The purpose of Experiment 2 was to examine children's understanding of the muting and humor functions of ironic compliments (compared to literal compliments).

To our knowledge, this was the first investigation of children's perceptions of ironic compliments. As such, it represents a new test of the Tinge Hypothesis. Although Dews et al. (1996) found that recognition of the muting function of ironic criticisms coincided with recognition of verbal irony, they did not test whether the same was true for ironic compliments.

Previous research has demonstrated that adults tend to rate ironic compliments as less positive than literal compliments and therefore show an understanding of the muting function of ironic compliments (Dews et al., 1995; Pexman & Olineck, 2002b). We anticipated that, if children similarly showed an understanding of the muting function of ironic compliments, they would rate ironic compliments as less nice than literal compliments in Experiment 2. If recognition of the muting function of ironic compliments coincides with detection of irony, then children should rate ironic compliments as less nice than literal compliments as soon as they can correctly attribute speaker belief for those utterances.

Using somewhat similar age groups as the present experiments, Dews et al. (1996) reported that younger children found literal compliments funny (halo effect). Accordingly, it was predicted that younger children in the present research would also rate literal compliments as funny.

Method

Participants.   Thirty-two children who did not participate in Experiment 1 comprised the participant groups for Experiment 2. Sixteen 5- to 6-year-old children (M = 5.11, range 5.0–6.9, 10 males, 6 females) and sixteen 7- to 8-year-old children (M = 7.9, range 7.1–8.8, 6 males, 10 females) were recruited from English speaking, primarily middle-class families.

Procedure and Design.   The same puppets, props, and scenarios from Experiment 1 were used. Each child was trained on the two scales and then watched eight puppet shows in which four ended with an ironic compliment and four ended with a literal compliment (see Table 20.1). As in Experiment 1, the statements in this experiment were prerecorded. Ironic compliments were made with a positive and joking intonation whereas literal compliments were made with a positive and praising tone of voice.

Results

No main effects of gender or interactions with gender were found; thus, responses from females and males were combined for all of the reported analyses.

Speaker Belief for Ironic Compliments.   Children's mean proportions of correct responses to the speaker belief question for the ironic compliments and literal compliments are shown in Table 20.2. The proportions of correct responses for the 5- to 6- and 7- to 8-year-old children were compared with a 2 (Age Group:

5–6, 7–8) × 2 (Compliment: Ironic, Literal) mixed model ANOVA with age as a between subjects factor. There was a significant main effect of compliment type, $F(1, 30) = 75.15$, $p < .001$, $MSE = 5.57$, such that speaker belief responses for ironic compliments ($M = .38$, $SD = .37$) were significantly less accurate than speaker belief responses for literal compliments ($M = .96$, $SD = .11$). Neither the main effect of age nor the age by compliment type interaction reached significance ($Fs < 1$). The ability to correctly interpret speaker belief for ironic compliments did not significantly differ between the groups of 5- to 6- and 7- to 8-year-old children. Younger and older children produced exactly the same mean proportion of correct speaker belief responses, and, as such, a power analysis could not be performed to determine whether null age differences resulted from the small sample sizes.

The mean proportions of correct responses to the first, second, third, and fourth speaker belief questions were compared with a repeated measures ANOVA with order as a within subjects factor. This analysis indicated that children did not become increasingly accurate across trials in interpreting speaker belief, $F(1, 30) = 2.07$, $p > .05$, $MSE = .27$. We also compared children's proportions of correct responses to the speaker belief for each puppet show scenario and found that children least often correctly interpreted the ironic compliments made in the painting puppet show scenario (.31), whereas they most often correctly interpreted ironic compliments made in the haircut puppet show scenario (.50). The proportion of correct responses did not significantly differ across scenarios.

Mean/Nice Scale Ratings.   Mean ratings on the Mean/Nice Scale are shown in Table 20.3. A 2 (Age Group: 5–6, 7–8) × 2 (Compliment type: Ironic, Literal) mixed model ANOVA with age as a between subjects factor yielded a significant main effect of compliment type, $F(1, 19) = 25.29$, $p < .001$, $MSE = 22.62$. Mean ratings for both compliment types fell towards the nice pole of the scale but, importantly, and in agreement with the Tinge Hypothesis, children tended to rate ironic compliments ($M = 2.67$, $SD = .29$) as less nice than literal compliments ($M = 1.21$, $SD = .11$). Neither the main effect of age nor the age by compliment type interaction were significant ($Fs < 1$).

When children incorrectly interpreted ironic compliments as negative evaluations, their Mean/Nice ratings indicated that they perceived these remarks as mean ($M = 4.09$, $SD = 1.08$). This suggests that when children misinterpreted ironic compliments, they based their impressions of speaker intent on their literal interpretations rather than randomly choosing faces on the scale.

Funny/Serious Scale Ratings.   Mean ratings on the Funny/Serious Scale were analyzed with a 2 (Age Group: 5–6, 7–8) × 2 (Compliment type: Ironic, Literal) mixed model ANOVA with age as a between subjects factor and resulted in a significant age group by compliment type interaction, $F(1, 19) = 31.48$, $MSE = 9.98$, $p < .001$. Planned comparisons with a Bonferroni correction (alpha = .025) indicated that the interaction occurred because 5- to 6-year-olds and 7- to 8-year-olds gave significantly different humor ratings for ironic compliments, but not for literal compliments. Older children rated ironic compliments as slightly funny ($M = 2.75$, $SD = 1.14$) whereas younger children rated ironic compliments as serious ($M = 3.98$, $SD = 1.15$); $t(19) = 2.48$, $p < .025$, $SE = .50$. It was predicted that younger children would rate literal compliments as funny (halo effect), but both younger children ($M = 3.62$, $SD = 1.06$) and older children ($M = 3.98$, $SD = .84$) tended to rate literal compliments as serious, $t(30) = 1.08$, $p > .05$, $SE = .34$. The main effect of compliment type was significant $F(1, 19) = 10.06$, $MSE = 3.19$, $p < .01$, but the main effect of age was not ($F < 1$). These results show that only older children found ironic compliments to be slightly humorous, whereas younger children perceived ironic compliments to be just as serious as literal compliments.

When children misinterpreted ironic compliments as negative evaluations, their Funny/Serious Scale ratings indicated that they perceived these remarks as serious ($M = 3.93$, $SD = 1.20$) as their mean rating fell close to the point of the scale that represented "serious."

Discussion

Experiment 2 represents a new contribution to the verbal irony literature because it is, to our knowledge, the first investigation of children's perceptions of the social functions of ironic compliments. As predicted, children perceived ironic compliments as less nice than literal compliments. This result concurs with adult ratings of ironic compliments (e.g., Dews et al., 1995; Pexman & Olineck, 2002b) and lends support to the Tinge Hypothesis (Dews et al., 1995). Accuracy of recognition of the intended negative tinge of ironic compliments did not differ between 5- to 6-year-olds and 7- to 8-year-olds. We acknowledge that the age range used in the present study was not large. It is possible that our participant groups were simply too close in age to find a developmental difference in the comprehension of ironic compliments. It is also possible, however, that appreciation of ironic compliments is a skill that emerges over quite a long developmental period.

It was also predicted that children would perceive ironic compliments as funnier than literal compliments. However, only older children perceived ironic compliments as slightly funny, with the average humor rating falling close to the "a little bit funny, a little bit serious" point on the scale. Similarly, we did not find support for the halo effect described by Dews et al. (1996), because younger children rated ironic compliments and literal compliments as equally serious. Although these findings suggest only a modest appreciation for the humor function, they provide some evidence that recognition of the humor function of ironic compliments is beginning to emerge between 7 and 8 years of age. This claim is speculative and should be tested with an older group of children.

Results from Experiment 2 suggest that correct comprehension of speaker belief is accompanied by an understanding of the negative tinge of ironic compliments. Furthermore, these results suggest that children can recognize the negative tinge of ironic compliments before they can perceive ironic compliments as funny.

GENERAL DISCUSSION

The goal of the present study was to investigate whether children's understanding of the muting function of ironic criticisms and compliments lend support for the Tinge Hypothesis. Dews et al. (1996) argued that children are sensitive to this function as soon as they are able to detect verbal irony possibly because they tend to rely more heavily on speakers' literal meanings in interpreting irony than do adults. Whereas Dews et al. provided evidence for this claim with regards to ironic criticisms, we replicated this finding and then extended this research to include children's detection and perceptions of ironic compliments.

The results of our experiments demonstrated that 7- to 8-year-olds more readily grasped the meaning of ironic criticisms than 5- to 6-year-olds, yet children of both age groups experienced the same degree of difficulty in understanding the meaning of ironic compliments. There are several possible explanations for this observation, but our data do not allow us to distinguish among them. This finding might point to the importance of previous experience with ironic speech forms because ironic compliments are used less typically in daily discourse than are ironic criticisms (Gibbs, 2000; Hancock et al., 2000). Interpretation of ironic compliments might also be more difficult because, although ironic insults tend to implicitly allude to conventions about politeness and saying nice things about other people, ironic compliments do not (Gibbs, 1986; Kreuz & Glucksberg, 1989). Therefore, we suspect that the absence of a self-critical statement in the scenarios used in the present study disadvantaged the children's comprehension rates in Experiment 2, as self-critical statements often precede ironic compliments in daily conversations (Kreuz & Glucksberg, 1989). For instance, consider the following modification of Experiment 2: Sam says, "I'm an awful gardener," then he succeeds at gardening by pulling out all of the weeds. In response to Sam's success, Bob says, "You sure are an awful gardener." When Hancock et al. (2000) added this type of self-critical statement to ironic compliment scenarios in their second experiment, children's comprehension of speaker belief increased from 25% to 35%. Presumably, the addition of self-critical statements in the present Experiment 2 would have yielded a similar enhancement of ironic compliment comprehension.

Another possible explanation for children's difficulty in understanding ironic compliments could be that these statements involve double negation. According to Giora (1995), understanding irony of any type involves negation of the literal (salient) meaning. This negation is prompted by discrepancy between the preceding context and the surface meaning of the statement. With ironic compliments, the surface meaning of the statements is also negative, and it may be more difficult to negate negative statements and comprehend the irony involved (Giora, 1995).

The present results also support the Tinge Hypothesis. For both ironic criticisms and ironic compliments, comprehension of speaker belief was accompanied by recognition of the tinge. When children derived a non-literal meaning, which occurred more often for ironic criticisms than for ironic compliments, they modulated their impressions of the aggression intended by the ironic speaker. An important question, however, concerns the manner in which the tinge is conveyed. Dews and colleagues (1995) argued that the tinge results from the listener processing the surface (literal) meaning of an utterance, and from that surface meaning coloring interpretation of the speaker's underlying intent for an utterance. Presumably, speaker intent for such utterances is cued by the preceding events and by the speaker's intonation.

The extent to which providing participants with intonations for ironic criticisms and ironic compliments influences their perceptions of these remarks is currently an unresolved issue. Adult ratings for ironic criticisms and literal criticisms made with characteristic prosodies have provided support for the Tinge Hypothesis (Dews & Winner, 1995), whereas ratings for these statement types made without prosodic cues have produced both consistent (Pexman & Olineck, 2002b) and inconsistent findings (Colston, 1997). Nonetheless, we wanted to address the possibility that the narrator's intonation could have influenced children's ratings of the aggression conveyed by ironic remarks. Recall that in the present study, ironic criticisms were made in a mocking and insincere tone and ironic compliments were made in a positive and joking tone. In a post hoc test, we asked ten graduate students to make ratings on the Mean/Nice Scale for four statement types sampled from the audiotapes used in Experiments 1 and 2. These ratings indicated that adults perceived the intonation used for ironic criticisms to be slightly less mean than the intonation used for literal criticisms and that the intonation used for ironic compliments was perceived to be somewhat less nice than intonation used for literal compliments. Based upon these findings, it appears that the intonation alone could predispose children to produce ratings in support of the Tinge Hypothesis. However, when we compared the ratings for children who correctly and incorrectly answered the speaker belief item, only children who correctly interpreted ironic remarks produced ratings demonstrating recognition of the tinge function. Children who offered literal interpretations for the ironic statements did not rate intent in a way that was consistent with intonation cues. Thus, we speculate that intonation is an important cue to irony, and that it may facilitate recognition of the tinge, but it is not the only basis for ratings of speaker intent. Developmental research has shown how children also rely on, for instance, the inconsistency between context and what is said (Ackerman, 1986) and explicit echoic markers of previous statements (Keenan & Quigley, 1999).

These results also support research indicating that the ability to infer the ironic speaker's belief is a prerequisite to understanding the speaker's intent, although here children who understood the ironic speaker's intention to be more or less aggressive still failed to infer the speaker's intention to be more funny. With the exception of the older children's perceptions of ironic compliments (found to be slightly funny), literal and ironic statement types were perceived as equally serious. This research generally indicates that recognition of the humor function of ironic criticisms and ironic compliments does not emerge before 8 years of age.

As mentioned, we suspect that children in the current studies may have perceived the professional scenarios depicted in the puppet shows as very grown up and serious. We would also surmise that children might be more familiar with making mean/nice distinctions than with making funny/serious distinctions. For instance, parents and teachers often call upon behavioral examples of what is nice and what is mean, whereas adults make attributions of what is funny and what is serious less frequently.

Additionally, the perspective children adopted in the task may have influenced their perceptions of the lack of humor conveyed by our scenarios. Toplak and Katz (2000) found that adults tended to view ironic criticisms differently depending on whether they were asked to take the perspective of the ironic speaker or the perspective of the addressee. Developmental research has not yet explored whether children also adjust their perceptions of verbal irony according to such perspectives. There is evidence that children can recognize that addressees of sarcastic irony feel worse than addressees of nonsarcastic irony (Creusere, 1997; Creusere & Echols, 1996, as cited in Creusere, 2000), and that children do not tend to enjoy teasing or use teasing in a playful way until 11 to 12 years of age (Keltner et al., 2001). If children in the present studies were interpreting the ironic remarks from the perspective of the addressee in each scenario and were reflecting back upon instances in which they were teased, they certainly would not have found the ironic remarks to be funny. Future research regarding children's impressions of the social functions of ironic compliments and ironic criticisms should control for this possibility by explicitly informing children what perspective to take when making their evaluations (e.g., observer, speaker, addressee), and by examining how the perspective taken influences their impressions of the aggression and humor implied in verbal irony. This manipulation would also allow investigation of whether children's recognition of the tinge function is dependent on taking a certain perspective.

In light of results from the present research, reconsider how a child like Martha might interpret an ironic compliment. It seems unlikely that a 7-year-old would recognize the speaker's intention to be ironic. Instead, she would probably interpret the statement literally—as an insult. If she did understand the remark as ironic, it is likely that she would perceive the utterance to be less nice than a literal compliment. Finally, it is very unlikely that she would find her mother's compliment to be funny.

CONCLUSION

The results of this research suggest that children have a fairly sophisticated understanding of the tinge function of verbal irony and that this understanding coincides with their ability to detect the use of irony. Their understanding of the humor function is, however, one that continues to develop through middle childhood. The implication of this finding is that it is not typical for a 5- to 8-year-old to "get" an ironic joke in the same manner as an adult. We hope that future research will better explicate the development of children's sense of humor.

ACKNOWLEDGMENTS

This research was supported by a grant from the Social Sciences and Humanities Research Council of Canada (SSHRC) awarded to Penny M. Pexman. This research was presented on April 24, 2003, at the biennial meeting of the Society for Research in Child Development, in Tampa, FL.

REFERENCES

Ackerman, B. P. (1982). Contextual integration and utterance interpretation: The ability of children and adults to interpret sarcastic utterances. *Child Development, 53,* 1075–1083.

Clark, H. H., & Gerrig, R. J. (1984). On the pretense of irony. *Journal of Experimental Psychology: General, 113,* 121–126.

Colston, H. L. (1997). Salting a wound or sugaring a pill: The pragmatic functions of ironic criticisms. *Discourse Processes, 23,* 24–45.

Colston, H. L. (2002). Contrast and assimilation in verbal irony. *Journal of Pragmatics, 34,* 111–142.

Creusere, M. A. (1999). Theories of adults' understanding and use of irony and sarcasm: Applications to and evidence from research with children. *Developmental Review, 19,* 213–262.

Creusere, M. A. (2000). A developmental tests of theoretical perspectives on the understanding of verbal irony: Children's recognition of allusion and pragmatic insincerity. *Metaphor and Symbolic Activity, 15,* 29–45.

de Groot, A., Kaplan, J., Rosenblatt, E., Dews, S., & Winner, E. (1995). Understanding versus discrimination nonliteral utterances: Evidence for a dissociation. *Metaphor and Symbolic Activity, 10,* 255–273.

Demorest, A., Meyer, C., Phelps, E., Gardner, H., & Winner, E. (1984). Words speak louder than actions: Understanding deliberately false remarks. *Child Development, 55,* 1527–1534.

Dews, S., Kaplan, J., & Winner, E. (1995). Why not say it directly? The social functions of irony. *Discourse Processes, 19,* 347–367.

Dews, S., & Winner, E. (1995). Muting the meaning: A social function of irony. *Metaphor and Symbolic Activity, 10,* 3–19.

Dews, S., Winner, E., Kaplan, J., Rosenblatt, E., Hunt, M., Lim, K., et al. (1996). Children's understanding of the meaning and functions of verbal irony. *Child Development, 67,* 3071–3085.

Gibbs, R. W. (1986). On the psycholinguistics of sarcasm. *Journal of Experimental Psychology: General, 115,* 3–15.

Gibbs, R. W. (2000). Irony in talk among friends. *Metaphor and Symbolic Activity, 15,* 5–27.

Giora, R. (1995). On irony and negation. *Discourse Processes, 19,* 239–264.

Giora, R. (1997). Discourse coherence and theory of relevance: Stumbling blocks in search of a unified theory. *Journal of Pragmatics, 27,* 17–34.

Hancock, J. T., Dunham, P. J., & Purdy, K. (2000). Children's comprehension of critical and complimentary forms of verbal irony. *Journal of Cognition and Development, 1,* 227–248.

Keenan, T. R., & Quigley, K. (1999). Do young children use echoic information in their comprehension of sarcastic speech? A test of echoic mention theory. *British Journal of Developmental Psychology, 17,* 83–96.

Keltner, D., Capps, L., Kring, A. M., Young, R. C., & Heerey, E. A. (2001). Just teasing: A conceptual analysis and empirical review. *Psychological Bulletin, 127,* 229–248.

Kreuz, R. J., & Glucksberg, S. (1989). How to be sarcastic: The echoic reminder theory of verbal irony. *Journal of Experimental Psychology: General, 118,* 374–386.

Kreuz, R. J., Long, D. L., & Church, M. B. (1991). On being ironic: Pragmatic and mnemonic implications. *Metaphor and Symbolic Activity, 6,* 149–162.

Kreuz, R. J., & Roberts, R. M. (1995). Two cues for verbal irony: Hyperbole and the ironic tone of voice. *Journal of Experimental Psychology: General, 118,* 372–386.

Kumon-Nakamura, S., Glucksberg, S., & Brown, M. (1995). How about another piece of pie: The allusional pretense theory of discourse irony. *Journal of Experimental Psychology: General, 124,* 3–21.

Leggit, J. S., & Gibbs, R. W. (2000). Emotional reactions to verbal irony. *Discourse Processes, 29,* 1–24.

Long, D. L., & Graesser, A. C. (1988). Wit and humor in discourse processing. *Discourse Processes, 11,* 35–60.

Pexman, P. M., & Olineck, K. (2002a). Understanding irony: How do stereotypes cue speaker intent. *Journal of Language and Social Psychology, 21,* 245–274.

Pexman, P. M., & Olineck, K. (2002b). Does sarcasm always sting? Investigating the impact of ironic insults and ironic compliments. *Discourse Processes, 33,* 199–217.

Roberts, R. M., & Kreuz, R. J. (1994). Why do people use figurative language? *Psychological Science, 5,* 159–163.

Sperber, D., & Wilson, D. (1981). Irony and the use-mention distinction. In P. Cole (Ed.), *Radical pragmatics* (pp. 296–318). New York: Academic.

Sperber, D., & Wilson, D. (1986). *Relevance: Communication and cognition.* Cambridge, MA: Harvard University Press.

Toplak, M., & Katz, A. N. (2000). On the uses of sarcastic irony. *Journal of Pragmatics, 32,* 1467–1488.

Utsumi, A. (2000). Verbal irony as implicit display of ironic environment: Distinguishing ironic utterances from nonirony. *Journal of Pragmatics, 32,* 1777–1806.

Winner, E., & Leekam, S. (1991). How children tell a lie from a joke: The role of second order mental state attributions. *British Journal of Developmental Psychology, 13,* 191–204.

Winner, E., Windmueller, G., Rosenblatt, E., Bosco, L., Best, E., & Gardner, H. (1987). Making sense of literal and nonliteral falsehood. *Metaphor and Symbolic Activity, 2,* 13–32.

PART VI

SITUATIONAL IRONY

CHAPTER 21

Situational Irony:
A Concept of Events Gone Awry

Joan Lucariello
Boston College

An event can be classified as *situationally ironic* when it deviates from routine in certain ways. In Study 1, a taxonomy of situational ironic event kinds was developed and features of these events were identified. Features included unexpectedness, human frailty, opposition, and outcome (the experience of loss or win). Study 2, category production, and Study 3, goodness-of-exemplar ratings, showed that individuals have a situational irony concept, consisting of representations of event kinds. The events exhibit typifying features, giving the concept graded structure. On this basis, knowledge of ironic events is claimed to be a form of event knowledge, along with *but distinct from* the event schema or script. The processing of ironic events, their relation to humorous and tragic events, and the relation between situational and verbal irony are discussed.

Think of the soldier who returns home safely from a long stint in combat only to be killed days later in a car accident. Observe the pickpocket whose own pocket is picked. Notice the barefoot shoemaker.

In Western society at least, most individuals would dub such events *ironic.* A rudimentary definition of *situational irony* has been provided by Muecke (1969), who cited the *Oxford English Dictionary.* Therein, situational irony is stated to be a condition of events opposite to what was, or might naturally be expected, or a contradictory outcome of events as if in mockery of the promise and fitness of things. Although the present research shows that this definition is only a partial one, the definition does capture a couple of key features of narrative events. One is unexpectedness. The second is human fragility, carried in the idea that ironic events "mock" the normal order of things. Situational irony, then, flags those situations that should not be. It is a theory of the irregularities in human activity. Said differ-

---

This chapter was previously published as "Situational irony: A concept of events gone awry" (J. Lucariello) in the *Journal of Experimental Psychology: General, 123,* 129–145. Copyright © [1994] by the American Psychological Association. Reprinted with permission.

ently, it may be thought a theory of the world's undependability, capturing our understanding that we cannot rely on ourselves, on others, or on events to run a standard course. Although ironic events are many and diverse, in one way or another they signal the vulnerability of the human condition—intentionality, actions, states, outcomes.

Such irony is related to, but is not the same as, the more familiar *verbal irony*. The classical account of verbal irony is that of saying one thing and meaning the opposite. On this definition of verbal irony, situational and verbal irony could be said to be alike in exhibiting a duality, characterized by an opposition of terms. Both entail a juxtaposition of incompatibles—what is said (literal meaning) versus what is intended (nonliteral meaning) in the verbal case and what occurred versus what was expected to occur in the situational case. An added similarity between the two forms of irony is that verbal irony, like situational, entails unexpectedness. Verbal irony has been thought to be based on the violation of a norm. On Grice's (1975, 1978) analysis, a speaker implicates the opposite of what he or she said by deliberately flouting a conversational maxim—quality. More specifically, a hearer expects a speaker to be truthful, and when that expectation is violated, the hearer constructs an alternative (nonliteral) interpretation for the utterance.

Despite these likenesses, however, the two forms of irony are not equivalent. Verbal irony implies an ironist, a speaker who deliberately uses a technique, hence Muecke (1969) termed it *intentional irony*. An ironist is entailed even on Sperber's (Jorgensen, Miller, & Sperber, 1984; Sperber & Wilson, 1986) recent "echoic" account of verbal irony, an account challenging the classical view. Situational irony does not imply an ironist but an observer of a condition of affairs that is seen as ironic. Muecke noted that we make the distinction between verbal and situational irony when we say, on the one hand, "He or she is being ironical" and on the other hand, "It is ironic that ... ."

Situational irony is well-established in contemporary culture. In daily talk, people often note ironic happenings, as do newscasters when reeling off newsworthy events. That ironic events are of interest is also evidenced by their linguistically marked status. Reference to such events is typically prefaced "Ironically ... ." Moreover, such activity is commonly the stuff of stories. Indeed, "story" seems reserved for twists and turns in human activity (Bruner, 1990; Burke, 1969; Lucariello, 1990; Mandler, 1983). These bends are often thought of as ironic. As a theory of irregularities, situational irony not only makes story events recognizable, even predictable, it also occasions storytelling itself.

We rely on situational irony, then, in our interpretation of events, actual and fictional, and indeed rely on it in the construction of events when creating fiction. How does one learn about irony and recognize events as ironic? In psychological terms, situational irony may be thought of as a concept. There are two components of conceptual coherence (Medin & Wattenmaker, 1987; Murphy & Medin, 1985). The first component involves the internal structure of a concept. The second concerns the concept's external structure, that is the position of the concept in the complete knowledge base. In considering situational irony, one could ask first, does this concept exhibit internal structure, and second, how is knowledge of ironic events related to knowledge of other event kinds? The answer to the first question will affect the answer to the second.

Both questions must be considered in relation to the larger domain of event knowledge involving human activity. *Expectedness* is one significant dimension on which a vast array of events, entailing sequenced situated action by intentional agents, is differentiable. Some events unfold prescriptively, and others take a striking turn. Regarding the former, for example, one form of event knowledge is the script (Schank & Abelson, 1977). The script is a general knowledge structure or schema for events that realize a high reliability of expectation. "Scripts may contain an implicit theory of the entailment relations between mundane events" (Murphy & Medin, 1985, p. 290). Scripts underlie frequently enacted activities, such as going to a restaurant, or conventional ones, such as getting married. They entail goal-driven, sequenced actions, appropriate to given spatiotemporal contexts, that are performed by central characters. "A script is a mental representation of 'what is supposed to happen' in a particular circumstance" (Ashcraft, 1989, p. 338). Accordingly, scripts have to do with our sense of regularity or control in the world.

There are other events wherein expectation is violated. These events are not supposed to happen. When such violations are culturally recognized rather than idiosyncratic, the events are ones for which we presumably establish a general knowledge structure or schema. This is proposed to be the case for ironic events. For example, self-inflicted loss, particularly where an individual's own plan for success has backfired to cause the loss, is apparently considered ironic. A schema for such an event would specify the intention or goal of the person, the goal-driven actions, and the outcome that is at odds with both. This schema would be applicable across all events of this type whether they concerned a housewife preparing a meal or a corporation undergoing streamlining. Ironic events entail, among other things, discordance among goals and actions and outcomes (as in self-inflicted loss), inconsistency in actions and states across spatiotemporal contexts, and action sequences unfounded in conventional and causal relations. These event characteristics diverge with those represented by script structure.

On the basis of what evidence can knowledge of ironic events be claimed as a distinct form of knowledge within the domain of event knowledge involving human activity? This is arguable if situational irony exhibited typical features and internal structure, making it identifiable as a culturally recognized class of anomalous happenings. Situational irony would then expand the domain of event knowledge, from a near-exclusive focus on prescriptive events in the direction of general knowledge structures for unexpected events. This may be likened to the challenge presented by verbal irony to semantic theories of meaning based on literal meaning and truth conditions, and to the pursuant focus on pragmatic meaning (Grice, 1975, 1978; Searle, 1975, 1979).

Alternatively, if situational irony failed with regard to the first component of conceptual coherence, that is, if it did not exhibit typifying features and internal structure, it would not be classifiable as a distinct form of event knowledge. Such is the case with other script-anomalous happenings. For example, some script-deviant and hence unexpected occurrences within an event (generally rendered in prose passages) are assimilated and regularized within script organization. In recall, the missing actions and goals of an event are inferred, and scrambled action sequences are restored to canonical order (see Mandler, 1983, for review). Other script-deviant occurrences, such as atypical actions unrelated to or inconsistent with the generic script (e.g., putting a pen in one's pocket or wiping one's eyeglasses in the restaurant script) become "tagged" (Graesser, Gordon, & Sawyer, 1979; Graesser, Woll, Kowalski, & Smith, 1980; Nakamura, Graesser, Zimmerman, & Riha, 1985; Schank & Abelson, 1977). These tagged activities are not interrelated through the generic script with various typical actions. Rather, they represent functionally separate organizational units. The tagged behavior, although it is distinct from the generic script, is defined only relationally in terms of the script, as a deviation. It has no particular conceptual organization or internal structure that would make it identifiable as a concept in its own right.

The research goal in the present article is to examine whether situational irony is a commonly shared concept that exhibits typifying features and internal structure. If situational irony is so definable, its place in the knowledge base within the domain of event knowledge involving human activity becomes clearer. It can be seen as a theory of events, in addition to and distinct from the script and possibly other event kinds. In Study 1, a taxonomy of situational irony is developed, and its salient features are identified. Study 2, category production, and Study 3, goodness-of-exemplar judgments, were conducted to explore whether adults share a concept of situational irony, and, if so, to determine whether this concept has internal structure. Moreover, in Study 3, the place of ironic events in the domain of events was examined. Ironic events are pitted against other event kinds, such as scripted ones, to ascertain whether ironic events are distinctively recognized as such. These studies represent the first systematic psychological study of situational irony and are part of a larger programmatic effort aimed at defining the concept of situational irony, and ultimately of exploring its development in children.

STUDY I: A TAXONOMY OF SITUATIONAL IRONY TYPES

The first step in the articulation of the irony concept was the collection of examples of irony. The experimenter recorded situations mentioned as ironic by individuals. These included examples provided by newscasters, ordinary conversationalists, and literary critics. In addition, a number of examples Muecke (1969) had provided in his text on irony also were recorded. These instances were categorized in terms of the ways in which the described events violated the structure of scripted events. The preliminary taxonomy of ironic event types based on this analysis is presented in Table 21.1. Although a wide variety of situations is typically classified as ironic, seven major types were identified according to their typifying characteristics: Imbalances, Losses, Wins, Double Outcomes, Dramatic, Catch-22, Coincidence.

TABLE 21-1

Taxonomy of Situational Ironic Event Kinds

Type	Definition and Example
Imbalances	Tags cases of inconsistency or opposition in human behavior or borne by situational elements.
Temporal	Intraindividual opposition over time (past vs. present). *Example:* The wimp who grows up to be a lion tamer.
Contextual	Intraindividual opposition across context, hence simultaneous. *Example:* The poor banker.
Role reversal	Interpersonal opposition wherein traits, behaviors, and so forth of one person ought to be another's, and vice versa. *Example:* The laboring children can see the men at play.
Situational	Event-based opposition wherein constituent elements of an event reflect a state of affairs opposite to convention or reason. *Example:* A kiss that signifies betrayal.
Losses	Individual faces only a loss. The key feature of such losses is their cause, either self- or fate-inflicted.
Planned	Self-inflicted losses resulting from the backfiring of the individual's goal-driven, planned action. *Example:* A man died the day before a hurricane hit, when it was sunny and calm. He was electrocuted while removing the TV antenna from his roof, as a precaution against the storm.
Spontaneous	Self-inflicted losses resulting from the individual's natural, nonintentional behavior. *Example:* While driving students to a practice site, a driving teacher made a wrong turn down a one-way street. The car bore signs all over with the auto school's name.
Change of mind	Self-inflicted losses resulting from a change of mind. *Example:* Jim long wanted new skis, but then decided he'd rather have a bike. That night, his wife presents him with skis.
Self-betrayal	Self-inflicted losses occurring when a person unwittingly reveals his or her own weakness through own words or deeds. *Example:* The Pharisee prays "God, I thank Thee that I am not a sinner as other men are."
Fluke	Fate-inflicted losses resulting from so improbable a factor that it seems the loss must be "in the cards." *Example:* May's apartment has been robbed twice. So May invests in alarms, locks, bars. She is robbed soon after; the robbers blew a hole in the wall to get in.
Foreshadowed	Fate-inflicted losses wherein fate provides a "peek" at a loss to come. Hence it seems that the loss is "in the cards." *Example:* A man had dreams about dying for a week, and he expressed his concerns to his wife. The next week he was out doing his usual gardening, when a car ran over the curb, hitting and killing him.
Deserved	Self- and fate-inflicted losses. Non-noble behavior invites an appropriate, punitive "zap" from fate. *Example:* Bob ridicules a coworker for clumsiness, then trips over the wastebasket.

(continued)

471

TABLE 21-1 *(continued)*

Type	Definition and Example
Wins	Events wherein an individual ends up with a win outcome.
Instrumental	The means to losing become the means to winning. *Example:* A man is in a car accident with a woman, who as a consequence intends to sue him. They have a meeting and she decides not to sue. A year later they marry.
Fluke	Person wins inadvertently, that is, as the result of unintended, nonplanful, fluke actions. *Example:* A karate student pauses during a test trying to remember a move. The student gets the best score because it happens that a pause should occur at just that point.
Double outcomes	The individual experiences two outcomes that are related, either loss—loss or win—loss.
Loss → Loss Recurrence	A highly unusual loss improbably recurs; these losses share no causal or conventional relation. *Example:* When Bud and Jill married in April, a rare, late blizzard occurred, dampening events. On their 25th anniversary party, another blizzard dampens festivities.

Win and Loss
 (simultaneous)
     Prize not what
     it's cracked
     up to be
	A win firmly in hand is uncharacteristically wanting.
	 Example: After playing for years, Ben finally wins the lottery. Incredibly, there are 100 other winners, thereby drastically reducing his take.

Wins
     belittling
     winner
	Individual wins but effort or concern to that end is rendered needless, leaving winner feeling foolish.
	 Example: Bill shops all over for the sweater his mom wants, but cannot find it. Tiredly, he pops into a store right across from his apartment, and finds the exact sweater.

Contrastive	A context of winning ways foregrounds a loss. *Example:* Susan is very gregarious and popular. Despite this, she has always basically felt so lonely.
Win → Loss *(sequential)* Instrumental	The means to winning become the means to losing. *Example:* A marathon runner, famous for popularizing jogging, dies of a heart attack while jogging.

Think the
     win is "in
     hand"
	Individual has reason to believe a win is had, but it turns out not to be.
	 Example: Rita gives a friend advice on love, saying the advice worked like a charm for her. The friend takes the advice. Later Rita's boyfriend calls and breaks up with her.

Loss → Win *(sequential)* Fruitless win	Person seeking a win gets a loss instead. Then the win arrives but too late to count. *Example:* Paul's wife refuses his advice over and over for years until her decisions bring the family to financial and emotional ruin. Then she turns to Paul for counsel.
Win and Loss *(interpersonal)* Distribution	Win and loss outcomes distributed across persons, in a manner opposite to justice, convention, or reason. *Example*: John spends years trying to get a green card legally. His friend Peter lives in the United States underground as an illegal alien. Peter gets the card by an amnesty program. John is deported.

Type	Definition and Example
Dramatic	Events wherein an observer (audience, reader, overhearer, etc.) knows what a victim has yet to find out.
Doomed agent	Person unaware or misinformed, relative to observer, where this state leads or can lead to loss. *Example:* Romeo killing himself over the "dead" Juliet.
Devious agent	Person intentionally tries to keep others "in the dark," but turns out also to be "blinded," amounting to a loss. *Example:* A junior law partner seeks a new job secretly so not to appear disloyal to his firm. While looking, the senior partners tell him something they had known a while. The firm is closing, and he must get a job elsewhere.
Pathetic agent	Person unaware, relative to observer, of loss outcome already happened. *Example:* Examiner has already failed the student, whom he overhears expressing a confident hope of passing.
Catch—22	Loss outcome as an unavoidable result of all available avenues of necessary and appropriate action. *Example:* The harder one tries to think of answers on a test, the more impossible it becomes to think of any.
Coincidence	Assorted events, such as co-occurrences or sequences of actions having no conventional or causal basis.
Anticipated	A current happening prefigures an improbable event occurring later. *Example:* Molly had thought about a friend from grammar school just days before she unexpectedly saw her for the first time in 9 years.
It's a small world	Inadvertent discovery of unknown interpersonal links. *Example:* Mitch chats on the ski lift with a stranger, a pretty young woman. She is from a town where a nephew lives that Mitch has not seen in years. Mitch asks if she knows his nephew, and it turns out she just started dating him.
Other	

Subtypes were identified within these types, for a total of 28 different ironic forms. These types and subtypes are discussed in turn.

There appear to be four characteristic features of ironic events. Unexpectedness is a feature shared by all ironic situations, in that ironic events are surprising ones. Although unexpectedness may be a necessary feature, it is not a sufficient one, because irony is not equivalent to surprise. An additional feature common to all ironic events is the component of human frailty. Ironic events signal fragility in the human condition—in intentionality, action, states, outcomes. Two other features characterize some but not all ironic events. These are outcome (e.g., loss, win) and opposition. The breakdown by features of types and subtypes is displayed in Table 21.2.

Imbalances are an ironic event type in which opposition is a critical feature. Contextual and Temporal Imbalance events (see Table 21.1) capture oppositions or inconsistencies, or contradictions in the behavior of persons, objects, institutions,

TABLE 21.2

Ironic Event Types, Subtypes, and Associated Category Features

Type	Feature
Imbalances	**Unexpectedness** **Human frailty** *Temporal, Contextual:* flimsy or fickle quality of human action, intentions, or states. *Role Reversal, Situational:* disorder in human events. **Opposition** *Temporal, Contextual:* intrapersonal "strong" opposition. *Role Reversal:* interpersonal "weak" opposition. *Situational:* event-based "strong" opposition.
Losses	**Unexpectedness** **Human frailty** Self-inflicted subtypes: being victim to oneself, inadvertently responsible for own loss. Fate-inflicted subtypes: being victim to extrahuman forces seemingly responsible for one's loss. **Outcome:** single loss (qualified as to cause: self, fate)
Wins	**Unexpectedness** **Human frailty** *Fluke:* inadvertently responsible for own win. *Instrumental:* individual arrives at win scathed, that is, through loss. **Outcome** *Fluke:* single win **Opposition in relation to outcome: two contrasting outcomes (loss and win)** a. discrete Win—Loss experiences = "strong" opposition 1. *Instrumental:* sequential (loss → win)

Double outcomes	**Unexpectedness**
	 Human frailty
	 Recurrences: being victim to extrahuman forces seemingly responsible for one's losses.
	 Opposition Win—Loss forms: win as a fragile state
	 Outcome: two related outcomes
	 Recurrence: two like outcomes (losses)
	 Opposition in relation to outcome: two contrasting outcomes (win and loss)
	 a. simultaneous Win—Loss experience = "weak" opposition
	    Prize Not What it's Cracked Up to Be; Wins Belittling Winner; Contrastive
	 b. discrete Win—Loss experiences = "strong" opposition
	    1. *Instrumental: Think Win Is "In Hand":* sequential (win → loss)
	    2. *Fruitless wins:* sequential (loss → win)
	    3. *Distribution:* interpersonal (win to X, loss to Y)

Dramatic	**Unexpectedness** **Human frailty** All subtypes: the disempowerment engendered by the individual's impoverished knowledge state. **Outcome: loss**
Catch—22	**Unexpectedness** **Human frailty:** trapped state of the individual. **Outcome**: loss
Coincidence	**Unexpectedness** **Human frailty** All subtypes: being subject to extrahuman forces that are seemingly arranging things.

and so on. Such oppositions may be embodied in the relation between states, as in the Contextual Imbalance example, or between goals and actions, as when an administrator has an aim that all recently released psychiatric patients be well-integrated into the community, while simultaneously authorizing that the vehicles transporting them be boldly lettered PSYCHIATRIC TRANSPORT, or between actions, as when a person who nurtures stray animals sports a fur coat, or between identity and actions, as when a gay supervisor abuses only minority employees. A sharp *canceling out* dynamic operates in such ironies, wherein one action or state negates or opposes another, or an action opposes a goal, and so on. Hence these ironies exhibit strong opposition. Such ironic events show human frailty in that they depict the unwitting forcelessness of human behavior. These ironic events diverge from scripted ones both in depicting behavior as it occurs across distinct spatiotemporal contexts and depicting behavior wherein actions conflict with each other or with goals.

Imbalance events of the Role Reversal kind, like Contextual and Temporal Imbalances, embody person-based contradictions. In Role Reversals, however, this contradiction is inter- rather than intrapersonal. This appears to mitigate the canceling out dynamic, and causes such events to carry only weak opposition. Imbalances of the Situational kind flag event-based (non-person-based) opposition. Different components of an event may carry the opposition. Actions can bear meanings opposite to convention (see example in Table 21.1), means—ends relations can be reversed (e.g., advertisements as a turn-off to products), and juxtapositions of incongruous elements, such as action and setting, can occur (e.g., a brutal crime in an idyllic setting).

Loss events, the second of the seven major ironic types, exhibit another key category feature—outcome. In these ironic situations, people face loss. That this outcome does not follow from goals and actions distinguishes these events from scripted ones. These losses may be differentiated with respect to cause. They may result from a person's own behavior and hence have the qualifying feature of self-infliction. Planned, Spontaneous, Change Of Mind, and Self-Betrayal (this last defined by Muecke, 1969) are losses of the self-inflicted variety. In such events, human frailty lies in people being victim to themselves. The most striking illustration of the impotency of human intentionality and action in attaining desired outcomes—or rather, its potency in securing undesired ones—is Planned Loss events. In these situations, an individual operates on the basis of an explicitly formulated goal, planning and taking all sensible action to meet the goal and to secure victory, only to have these very measures bring on defeat.

A second kind of Loss event entails losses that appear to be brought about by forces outside of and indifferent to the individual's own behavior, hence seeming fate- inflicted. These extrahuman forces, to which humans are victim, are conceivable as fate, or destiny, the gods, life, or chance. Fluke and Foreshadowed Loss are example cases.

In a third kind of Loss event, termed Deserved Loss, loss appears to result from both causes, being both self- and fate-inflicted. In these events, individuals are subject to the forces of fate and hence are frail, but are so by virtue of their own behavior, which has invited a relevant and punitive response from fate. "Poetic justice" strikes.

Wins, the third of the seven major event types, are clearly distinguishable as the only ironic events wherein the individual ends up winning. These ironic events are characterized by the outcome feature. This may be a single win, as in Fluke Win events, wherein persons experience wins that come as the result of unintended, unplanned, or fluke actions. In this detachment between outcome and action or between outcome and intention, these events are distinguishable from scripted events. Indeed, these events may be seen as counterpart to single outcome loss events in general, and to Planned Loss events in particular. As in Planned Loss, the human frailty evident in Fluke Win is in the poor control persons have over outcomes.

Another kind of ironic Win event, Instrumental Wins, exhibits the outcome feature. Also characteristic of Instrumental Wins, however, is the opposition feature, which functions in relation to outcome. In these events, a loss yields a win, hence there are two discrete and contrasting outcomes. If such events had ended on the first outcome, the expected loss, they would resemble scripted events.

Double Outcomes, the fourth of the seven major ironic event types, also exhibit the outcome feature and actually display two outcomes. In one type, Recurrence, these outcomes are of the same kind, that is, both losses ($L \rightarrow L$). Recurrence events share with fate-inflicted losses the depiction of people as victims to extrinsic forces, such as fate, because there is no causal or conventional relation between the losses.

The remaining types of Double Outcome events, though they exhibit the two-outcomes feature, also exhibit opposition. In these events, the two outcomes are contrastive, win and loss. The opposition feature in such Double Outcome events can be more or less salient, however, depending on (sub)type. *Weak* opposition events are ones that embody a simultaneous or intertwined win–loss ($W–L$) experience. The individual experiences neither a true win nor a true loss but a diluted outcome, one seasoned with both win and loss. Here an outcome is mutually constituted of win and loss. Three subtype events display a diluted outcome: Prize Not What It's Cracked Up To Be, Wins Belittling Winner, and Contrastive. The mixed outcome distinguishes these events from scripted ones.

Other win–loss Double Outcome events can be classified as *strong* opposition events. In situations such as these, win and loss outcomes are discrete and hence are sharply contrastive; there is an experience of win separate from an experience of loss. This happens when these outcomes occur in temporal succession, as in the Instrumental subtype ($W \rightarrow L$), Think The Win Is In Hand subtype (believed $W \rightarrow$ actual L), and the Fruitless Win subtype ($L \rightarrow W$ [not really]), or when they occur interpersonally, as in Distribution events. Here again, as with Instrumental Wins ($L \rightarrow W$), it is the second outcome that makes these events unexpected and hence distinct from scripted events.

Double Outcome events exhibit human frailty in rendering win as fragile. In simultaneous W–L events (Prize Not What It's Cracked Up To Be, Wins Belittling Winner, Contrastive), win is inextricably linked to loss. In discrete W–L forms, win is opposed by loss (Instrumental) or is elusive, never really had (Think The Win Is In Hand, Fruitless Win).

The three remaining ironic event types, in contrast with those already discussed, have been described and named prior to this research (see Muecke, 1969, among others). The *Dramatic* type exhibits the category feature of outcome, in terms of loss. Such ironies are generally associated with the theater. Plays present life's parade in which the audience does not interfere but over which it exercises the control of knowledge (e.g., the audience, not Romeo, knows Juliet is alive). This is a case of the Doomed Agent subtype. The protagonist's blinded state leads to his doom. Dramatic ironies are not bound to the theater. Life's spectacle might be actual, and the in-the-know observer could be anyone. Human frailty rests in the impoverished knowledge state of individuals, a state handicapping blinded persons as they engage life.

Catch-22 ironic events (termed *irony of dilemma* by Muecke [1969]) also exhibit the outcome feature, entailing loss that is inevitable. Loss is the natural, unavoidable result of all available alternatives for action, when action must be taken. Catch-22 events are double-bind situations. The trapped state signals human frailty. These situations are usually distinctly labeled with the Catch-22 name.

Coincidence event types, though ironic, lack the typical category features of outcome and opposition. A hodgepodge of peculiar situations form this category. Many are sequences or co-occurrences of action that have no causal or conventional basis, making them quite distinct from scripted events (Anticipated subtype, see Table 21.1) or Simultaneities (Other category, see Table 21.1; e.g., Jane looks out a bus window at the exact moment her cousin is walking by). Like Catch-22 events, these events are often distinctly labeled, as coincidences.

Situational irony, then, encompasses a strikingly broad range of event types or instances. On the probabilistic model of conceptual structure, not all of these would be equally good concept exemplars. To illustrate, opposition and outcome seem like highly typical category features. Hence Imbalances, Losses, Wins, and Double Outcome events might be expected to be highly typical instances. On the other hand. Coincidence and Catch-22 events would be expected to be peripheral instances. They carry two category names, Irony and Coincidence or Catch-22. The fact that these events bear two names may be taken to indicate that they are members of two categories. Highly prototypical category members are those with the least resemblance to other categories (Rosch, 1978). Moreover, Coincidence events lack the category features of opposition and outcome.

Study 1 articulated the constituent features and resulting types of the ironic instances that had been informally collected. The goal of Studies 2 and 3 was to examine whether the ironic forms identified informally are recognized as ironic by subjects, which would suggest a conventional concept of situational irony. If so, also to be determined was whether this concept has internal structure. Methods from category structure paradigms are used. The category production task of Study 2 required adults to generate concept instances. In Study 3, in a category recognition and judgment task, adults rated concept instances (ironic events) and non instances (scripted events and unexpected nonironic events) for their goodness as exemplars.

STUDY 2: SUBJECT PRODUCTION OF IRONY

To determine whether individuals share a concept of situational irony, a category production task that required subjects to list concept instances was used. No information about the concept was provided to the subjects, assuring that they would respond on the basis of independent knowledge. Several questions were addressed: Is there a concept of situational irony, to be evidenced by naive subjects ably responding to the request for category instances? To what extent will the kinds of irony specified by the investigator appear in these responses? If a concept of situational irony is found, will it exhibit internal structure? Category structure will be ascertained by item dominance data, a reliable measure of such (Glass, Holyoak, & O'Dell, 1974; Mervis, Catlin, & Rosch, 1976; Rosch, 1973, 1975; Smith, Shoben, & Rips, 1974).

Method

Subjects.　　The subjects were 39 adults (12 men and 27 women). Twenty-three were psychology graduate students in an introductory cognitive development class and 16 were undergraduates in a psychology seminar.

Procedure.　　Subjects were given 20 min of in-class time to participate in a category production task. They were presented with a sheet of paper bearing the following instructions:

> Describe (in a few sentences for each situation) 5 separate situations that you think of as IRONIC. These can be situations that you have actually experienced or situations that you know about through secondary sources. For example, you could know about the situation by hearing it from a friend or on the news, by reading about it in a newspaper or a novel, or by seeing it in a film, a play, or a TV show. Provide enough detail so that another person, who doesn't know anything about these situations, could follow what happened. Of course, you needn't provide actual names or other personal details. Be sure to list only situations that you think of as ironic. If you cannot think of 5 situations, that's okay. Do not add what you consider to be non-ironic situations in order to get to the total of 5. Describing less than 5 is fine. If you are uncertain about whether a given situation is ironic, and cannot provide one in its place of which you are certain, then describe this situation any way and note below it that you have some uncertainty about its ironic status. Please *exclude* from consideration those situations that consist in an individual's uttering (or writing) ironic remarks, as, for example, when a husband says to his wife, "This is what I call a peaceful way to spend the evening," in the midst of unsuccessful attempts to keep their cranky four-year-old from throwing food in a restaurant. What is of interest are those events, or episodes, or stones that upon becoming aware of them, you might say "Now, that's ironic."

Results

Coding. There was a total of 150 responses. These were analyzed for ironic status. First, they were coded as ironic or nonironic. If ironic, they were coded as one of the seven event types, and within these seven event types by subtype. Two responses (from different subjects) were omitted from the irony analyses, one because of illegibility, the other for beating too little information to determine its ironic status. This left 148 responses. A single response could be coded by more than one ironic type or subtype if it incorporated two distinct situations that each reflected a distinct form of irony, or if a single situation reflected more than one ironic form. This happened in 9 responses, leading to 157 codes (148 plus 9).

As ironic type (subtype) categories are new to the literature, interrater reliability was calculated three times; that is, the experimenter's coding was compared with that of three individuals, who worked independently of one another. These persons were provided with the same 25% of responses (37 of 148), chosen randomly but with the constraint that all seven ironic event types and nonironic responses be represented. Interrater reliabilities were based on subtypes, a more stringent criterion than type. There were 20 distinct codes or categories represented in the list of 37 responses. The coders received a written version of the coding scheme, which defined and provided examples of all ironic forms. Interrater reliabilities were 92%, 86%, and 84%. These percentages may be thought particularly high, considering the many coding categories (20) represented among the responses to be coded.

Concept Accessibility. This was defined as how readily responses were given to the request for concept instances. Accessibility was measured by tallying the mean number of responses provided per subject. The closer the mean value was to 5 (the maximum number of responses requested), presumably the greater the accessibility of a concept of irony. The mean here was 3.85. The graduate student subjects' mean equaled 3.65 and the undergraduate student subjects' mean was 4.13, not significantly different, nor was there a significant sex difference. These subgroups are not further distinguished except in the case of significant differences. More than half of the sample (51.3%) provided four or more responses. All subjects gave a minimum of two responses, and 3 subjects gave more than five.

Concept Availability. This was defined as the extent to which responses were coded as ironic, thus as concept instances. As shown in Table 21.3, only 10.9% of responses were coded as nonironic, indicating that the vast majority (nearly 90%) were coded as ironic.

Concept Structure. This was ascertained through item dominance data. The mean percentage of responses coded as ironic by event type is also shown in Table 21.3. Imbalances were the most frequently produced ironic event type, followed by Losses, Double Outcomes, Dramatic, Coincidence, Catch-22s, and finally Wins. Item dominance can be considered a prototypicality index, suggesting that Imbal-

TABLE 21.3

Mean Percentage and Total Number of Responses by Ironic Type

	Total	
Type	Percentage	Number of Responses
Imbalances	37.3	63
Losses	18.8	29
Double outcomes	13.2	21
Dramatic	8.1	13
Coincidence	5.0	8
Catch-22	4.5	5
Wins	2.2	3
Nonironic	10.9	15
Total	100	157

ances are the most prototypical type. They account for over one third of the responses. Coincidences, Catch-22s, and Wins are peripheral concept instances, by this measure, accounting for 5% or less of responses. Graduate students produced more Double Outcome events than did undergraduates, $t(37) = 2.37$, $p < .025$.

Because the major ironic event types are composed of subtypes, the response data were further analyzed by subtype, as shown in Table 21.4. All subtypes were produced. The two most frequently generated—Contextual and Temporal Imbalances—may be thought the most prototypical. The next most frequently produced forms were Situational Imbalances, Planned and Deserved Losses, and the Doomed Agent Dramatic form. Each was produced by 18% of the sample. Ten subtypes were produced by only 1 or 2 subjects, suggesting that these are less prototypical than others.

Concept Breadth.   The mean number of ironic event types (of the seven) produced by each subject was 2.08. Almost one third of the sample (30.8%) produced three or more types. Only 1 subject produced no types (all responses nonironic).

Discussion

This experiment provided evidence for a common concept of situational irony. Without benefit of any concept definition or example, naive subjects generated all types and subtypes identified in Study 1 (see Table 21.1). Moreover, the concept was accessible, with nearly four responses provided by each subject. There was some breadth to concept knowledge, with two distinct event types produced per person.

TABLE 21.4

Number of Subjects Producing Responses by Ironic Subtype

Type and Subtype	N	Type and Subtype	N
Imbalances		Wins belittling winner	3
Contextual	20	Recurrence	3
Temporal	13	Think win is "in hand"	2
Situational	7	Prize not what it's cracked up to be	1
Role reversal	5	Contrastive	1
Losses		Dramatic	
Planned	7	Doomed agent	7
Deserved	7	Devious agent	2
Change of mind	4	Pathetic agent	2
Spontaneous	3	Coincidence	
Fluke	3	Anticipated	3
Foreshadowed	2	Other	3
Self-betrayal	1	It's a small world	1
Double outcomes		Catch-22	3
Instrumental	4	Wins	
Distribution	4	Instrumental	2
Fruitless wins	3	Fluke	1

The category of situational irony was also found to exhibit internal structure. Those event types exhibiting the important category features of opposition (Imbalances), outcome (Losses), and opposition in relation to outcome (Double Outcomes) were more frequently produced than those event types that lack key category features (Coincidence) and those that straddle the border of two categories (Coincidence and Catch-22). Participation in two categories is an index of peripheral category membership. The only exception to this pattern is the Wins event type, which bears the important category feature of outcome, yet was only minimally produced.

A glance at the subtype data also revealed some interesting patterns. Among Imbalances, the three forms Temporal, Contextual, and Situational were the most frequently produced. As already discussed, these event kinds, particularly Temporal and Contextual Imbalances, were considered to exhibit strong opposition, based on the opposition being intrapersonal and hence more sharply contrastive. In contrast, Role Reversal Imbalances, where opposition was considered attenuated because of occurrence interpersonally, were much less frequently generated. Among Losses, self-inflicted loss forms (with the exception of Self-Betrayal) were more frequently generated than were fate-inflicted forms, such as Fluke and Foreshadowed Loss.

Hence it seems that self-inflicted loss amounted to a better case of irony than fate-inflicted loss. Self-Betrayal events may have been an exception to this pattern because of their greater complexity as an ironic form. These events, unlike other ironic events, often entail linguistic, specifically pragmatic understanding. To appreciate the irony in the event of the Pharisee who says "I thank thee God that I am not a sinner as other men are," a listener must understand a couple of things. The first is that utterance meaning can go beyond literal meaning (e.g., that the Pharisee is sinless and thankful for that state), as in metaphor and irony. Moreover, and unlike the case of metaphor and irony, the listener must appreciate that the nonliteral meaning (e.g., that the Pharisee is indeed a sinner by virtue of the pride, vanity, and harshness toward others revealed in his declaration of himself as sinless and superior) is unintended by the speaker. Deserved Loss, another highly produced form, partakes of both forms of causation. Apparently, events wherein self and fate conspire to produce a loss were also thought highly ironic.

The Doomed Agent Dramatic form, also frequent, may owe its salience, relative to other Dramatic forms, to its greater familiarity. It is a form of situational irony already well-recognized as such, and one long associated with the theater and literature.

This experiment, which used a production task, was informative in that it showed adults to have a concept of situational irony, and the concept to have internal structure. In production tasks, subjects must recall concept instances. The typicality of ironic kinds might vary, however, if subjects were not required to generate them. Study 3's judgment task was designed to complement the findings from Study 2. Moreover, Study 3 served as a means to establish the reliability of Study 2's data. A significant percentage of the present generated ironies served as instances to be rated for ironic status in Study 3. Finally, in Study 3, the place of ironic events within the domain of events involving human activity is explored.

STUDY 3: SUBJECT JUDGMENT OF IRONY

Subjects were asked to rate concept instances for their goodness-as-examples. This method complemented that of Study 2. "Item dominance" and "goodness ratings" measures are correlated (Glass et al., 1974; Mervis et al., 1976; Rips, Shoben, & Smith, 1973; Smith et al., 1974). This allows data from the present task on the typicality of ironic instances to be compared with those from Study 2. Additionally, this method provided a more sensitive measure of the internal structure of the concept of situational irony. "Goodness-of-example" ratings yield more articulated data on category structure in that typicality ratings for each ironic (sub)type were produced. Moreover, with regard to concept breadth, it is likely that subjects can recognize more ironic types than they can produce. Hence breadth may be underestimated in production tasks but is less likely to be so here.

Also, the placement of situational irony in the larger domain of events involving human activity was explored. Within this domain, event kinds may be differentiable on the dimension of expectedness. The script is a schema for events that realize a high reliability of expectation. In contrast, ironic events may be classified as *unex-*

pected events. They are unexpected, however, in a culturally recognized way, making them purportedly events for which a general knowledge structure is formed. Ironic events, then, are distinct from events wherein expectation is violated in an idiosyncratic manner. The differentiability of these three kinds of events (expected-scripted, unexpected-ironic, unexpected-nonironic) was tested by asking subjects to rate exemplars of each kind for how ironic they were.

Method

Subjects.   Fifty-one adults (14 men and 37 women) participated. Forty-three were psychology graduate students and 8 were advanced undergraduates. The two samples were combined to increase sample size, as almost no differences by educational level were found in Study 1.

Procedure.   Subjects were given a packet of 10 to 11 pages, with a face sheet bearing the following instructions, modeled after Rosch (1973, 1975):

> This study has to do with what we have in mind when we use words which refer to categories. Let's take the word *red* as an example. Close your eyes and imagine a true red. Now imagine an orangish red … imagine a purple red. Although you might still name the orange red or the purple red with the term *red,* they are not as good examples of red (as clear cases of what *red* refers to) as the clear "true" red. In short, some reds are redder than others. The same is true for other kinds of categories. Think of dogs. You all have some notion of what a "real dog," a "doggy dog" is. To me a retriever or a German shepherd is a very doggy dog while a Pekinese is a less doggy dog. Notice that this kind of judgment has nothing to do with how well you like the thing: you can like a purple red better than a true red but still recognize that the color you like is not a true red. You may prefer to own a Pekinese without thinking that it is the breed that best represents what people mean by dogginess.
>
> On this form you are asked to judge how good an example of a category various instances of the category are. The category is *irony (ironical situations).* Situations (instances) are listed. After each is a blank. You are to rate how good an example of the category each situation is on a 7-point scale. A *1* means that you feel the situation is a very good example of your idea of what the category is. A *7* means you feel the situation fits very poorly with your idea or image of the category (or is not a member at all). The numbers in between *1* and *7* represent the range in between a very good and very poor fit—for example, the number *4* represents a moderate fit. (See scale below.) For example, one of the members of the category *fruit* is *apple.* If *apple* fit well your idea or image of *fruit,* you would put a 1 after it; if *apple* fit your idea of *fruit* very poorly you would put a 7 after it; a 4 would indicate moderate fit. Use the other numbers of the 7-point scale to indicate intermediate judgments.
>
> Don't worry about why you feel that something is or isn't a good example of the category. And don't worry about whether it's just you or people in general who feel that way. Just mark it the way you see it. Assign only one number for each instance.

Time to complete task was not viewed as a meaningful variable, hence some subjects (30 of the 51) were allowed to do the task at home, within 1 week's time.

The remaining subjects did the task in class time and were given approximately 20 to 25 min to do so. The effect of task condition on rating behavior was tested but showed no significant effect, as reported below.

Materials.   Subjects rated 96 events, which were rendered as vignettes. Vignette length ranged from 20 to 53 words and one to three sentences. Half (48) of the vignettes depicted ironic events and half (48), the foils, depicted nonironic events.

Ironic vignettes tested 27 ironic forms, including one event type (Catch-22) and 26 event subtypes. Twenty subtypes of these 26, and the Catch-22 form, were tested by having two tokens/vignettes depict the irony, yielding 42 (21 × 2) ironic vignettes. The two tokens per ironic subtype varied in thematic content to test generalizability of ironic ratings. Additionally, there were two foil (nonironic) vignettes for each of these 21 ironic forms, leading to 42 foil vignettes. One foil, termed the *nonironic-expected,* was similar in thematic content and identical in length to one of the ironic tokens but the event depicted was normative, occurring in accord with expectation. There were 21 such foils. The second foil, termed the *nonironic-unexpected,* was similar in thematic content and identical in length to the remaining ironic token for the given form but depicted an unexpected event consigned to be nonironic by failing to conform to the concept as previously analyzed. There were 21 such foils. Hence the vignette pattern for each of these 21 tested forms included two ironic tokens, one nonironic-expected foil, and one nonironic-unexpected foil. This pattern is shown for Planned Losses in Table 21.5.

The 6 remaining subtypes of the 26 were tested by the use of only one token/vignette to represent the irony. These 6 additional ironic vignettes yielded the total of 48. This collapsed testing was adopted to reduce task unwieldiness. It was applied to the subtypes of three event types (Wins, Dramatic, Coincidence) because all subtypes of these events (except Doomed Agent Dramatic) were weakly produced (by 3 or fewer subjects) in Study 2 (see Table 21.4). For each of these three event types, there was a single four-vignette test pattern. One of the two ironic tokens represented one subtype and the second represented another subtype. A third vignette represented the nonironic-expected foil, which matched one ironic subtype token in thematic content and length, and the fourth, the nonironic-unexpected foil, matched the other subtype token in thematic content and length. This yielded 24 foils of each kind (21 + the 3 in collapsed format testing), and the total of 48 foil vignettes. For Wins, ironic tokens depicted the Fluke and Instrumental subtypes. For Dramatic, they represented the Doomed Agent and Devious Agent forms. The Pathetic Agent subtype was omitted. For Coincidence, ironic tokens depicted the Anticipated and It's A Small World subtypes.

The 27 ironic forms tested included all those in Table 21.1, with some exceptions. Self-Betrayal Loss was omitted because it is distinct from other ironic events in that it often entails linguistic knowledge. Moreover, because Temporal and Contextual Imbalance forms so predominated in Study 2, these subtypes were refined, adding to tested forms. For Temporal Imbalances, events showing inconsistency in past and present actions and states were included, as these were the most frequently

TABLE 21.5

Illustration of Four-Vignette Test Format for Planned Loss Ironic Subtype

Vignette Type	Vignette
Ironic token 1	A corporation hires consultants to suggest ways of streamlining and saving money. The consultants recommend disbanding a long-established department and assigning its function to an outside firm. This is done, and it happens that the outside firm charges twice as much as the company originally spent in the department.
Nonironic—expected	A corporation hires consultants to suggest ways of streamlining and saving money. The consultants recommend disbanding a long-established department and assigning its function to an outside firm. This is done, and it happens that the corporation saves a significant amount of money with the outside firm.
Ironic token 2	A man died the day before a hurricane hit, when it was sunny and calm. He was electrocuted while removing the TV antenna from his roof, as a precaution against the storm.
Nonironic—unexpected	A man died the day a hurricane hit, when it was windy and rainy. He was electrocuted while mowing the lawn, apparently due to an electrical short in the power mower.

produced. For Contextual Imbalances, events showing inconsistency in action across context and in goals and action were tested for the same reason.

Of the 48 ironic vignettes, just over half (28, or 58.3%) were taken from among the 133 ironic responses (148 total responses minus 15 coded as nonironic) generated in Study 2. Hence 21% of those responses were subjected to a reliability check for ironic status. Those responses included for testing were chosen randomly with the requirement that they meet vignette length parameters. When the supply of responses that met these requirements was exhausted, responses continued to be selected randomly, but these were subject to adaptation. They were shortened or lengthened, as appropriate, by modifying syntax while maintaining the semantics or meaning of the utterances. All 48 ironic token/vignettes were not drawn from Study 2 for two reasons. First, that would not be desirable as it allows the argument that ironic judgments pertain only to those specific situations described in these responses and therefore are not generalizable. Second, in the case of some ironic subtypes, only one response was generated in Study 2, necessitating the construction of a second token/vignette for testing purposes in Study 3.

The 28 responses drawn from Study 2 included both tokens for seven subtypes (14), 1 token for eight additional subtypes (8), the 1 token for five of the six subtypes tested by only one token/vignette (5); the exception being It's A Small World among Coincidence, and 1 token of the two for the Catch-22 type. The experimenter constructed the remaining 20 ironic tokens.

Two orders of the 96 vignettes, the revere of each other, were used with the stipulation that vignettes of the same ironic subtype not be contiguous.

Results

Mean Ratings for the Ironic (2) and Foil (2) Vignette Types.   The mean ratings for each of the four vignette types—ironic token 1 (I-1). nonironic-expected (NIE) foil, ironic token 2 (I-2), nonironic-unexpected (NIU) foil—are presented in Table 21.6.

The mean ratings for the I-1 and I-2 vignette types were those closest to 1.0, the ironic end of the scale, and were nearly identical. The mean rating for the NIE vignette type was that closest to 7.0, the nonironic end of the scale. The mean rating for the NIU vignette type fell between the values of the ironic vignette type (I-1 and I-2) means and the NIE mean. Correlated (paired) t tests revealed no significant difference between the mean ratings for the two sets of ironic tokens. As the two tokens for each ironic form were randomly assigned to either the I-1 or I-2 vignette types, no reliable difference between the mean ratings of these items would be expected. Significant differences were found between the mean ratings for each set of ironic tokens and the NIE foils: I-1 versus NIE, $t(50) = 30.19$, $p < .001$; I-2 versus NIE, $t(50) = 26.43$, $p < .001$. Differences were also found between the mean ratings for each set of ironic tokens and the NIU foils: I-1 versus NIU, $t(50) = 27.93$, $p < .001$; I-2 versus NIU, $t(50) = 23.35$, $p < .001$. Finally, there was a significant difference in mean ratings across the nonironic foil vignettes: NIE versus NIU, $t(50) = 11.78$, $p < .001$. Independent t tests showed no effects of test order, sex, education, and task completion condition (in or out of class) on mean ratings.

The range of the mean ratings for the four vignette types was obtained. The range for I-1 ironic tokens was 1.61 (Instrumental Double Outcomes) to 5.18 (Role Reversal Imbalance), and for I-2 tokens it was 2.06 (Planned Loss) to 4.55 (Foreshadowed Loss). The score for the ironic vignette that secured the least ironic rating, 5.18, which indicates a poor (score of 5.0) concept instance, was well-removed from the ideal nonironic score of 7.0. That all ironic vignettes received ironic ratings confirmed the ironic coding of 21% of the ironic responses from Study 2. Indeed, the ironic tokens/vignettes for Role Reversal Imbalances and Foreshadowed Losses, the tokens receiving the least ironic ratings, were not among those responses taken from Study 2.

Table 21.6

Mean Ratings for Ironic and Nonironic (Foil) Tokens

Token	Rating	
	M	*SD*
Ironic 1	3.01	0.82
Nonironic-expected	6.50	0.53
Ironic 2	3.03	0.95
Nonironic-unexpected	5.54	0.72

The coefficient alpha for I-1 items was .84, for I-2 items it was .88, and for all 48 ironic items it was .93. These data indicate a high level of interitem consistency.

The range in mean ratings for NIE foils was tight, 5.71 to 6.92. None of the expected items was mistaken as even poorly (score of 5.0) ironic by subjects. Moreover, there was no overlap in mean ratings for ironic and expected vignettes. The coefficient alpha for these 24 items was .86, indicating high interitem consistency. The range in mean ratings for NIU foils was 4.12 to 6.82. No unexpected item was deemed a very good (1.0), pretty good (2.0), or good (3.0) instance of irony. There was some overlap between those ironic items with the least ironic mean rating and those unexpected foil items with the most ironic ratings. The coefficient alpha for the NIU items was .81, indicating high interitem consistency.

Analyses of Ironic Subtypes.   There were two indexes of typicality judgments for ironic forms. First, a mean rating for each of the 27 ironic forms was derived. To get a single mean rating for the 21 forms tested by the use of two tokens/vignettes, the means of the I-1 and I-2 tokens (as calculated in the range analysis) were added and the total was divided by 2. These data are shown in Table 21.7.

There were few differences in mean ratings per ironic (sub)type by educational level (1), sex (2), and order (4). These data are available from Joan Lucariello. None of these differences reflected differences in ironic versus nonironic judgments, with all subtype means rating as ironic (4.54 was the least ironic score). The greatest disparity in mean ratings was 1.16. The effect of vignette length on ratings was tested by comparing the 12 longest ($M = 47.2$ words) and 12 shortest ($M = 25.5$ words) of the 48 ironic vignettes. Means were 3.37 (short) versus 3.01 (long) and did not differ.

A second index of typicality judgments was the percentage of subjects coding a subtype as ironic, which was defined as assigning a rating between and including 1 (*very good fit to the concept*) and 4 (*moderate fit to the concept*) to both of its tokens (I-1 and I-2). This was calculated for 21 ironic forms. The six additional subtypes (two for each of the Wins, Dramatic, and Coincidence event types) tested by the use of only one token were considered, for the purposes of this analysis, in relation to the second token of the type, though it was different in subtype. In these cases, the percentage of subjects coding the type as ironic was assessed. These data also are shown in Table 21.7.

Ironic Status of Tested Forms.   All 27 ironic forms were judged by subjects to be ironic. Only 2 forms had mean ratings above 4.0: Foreshadowed Loss = 4.24, and Role Reversal Imbalance = 4.44. These scores represented a fit to the concept just beyond moderate, heading to poor. Such scores do not seem high enough to merit reclassifying these event kinds as noninstances of the concept, a status ideally represented by a 7.0 score. Rather, these events appeared to be peripheral concept instances. Their status as ironic, if peripheral, is secured by the second measure, percentage of subjects coding subtypes as ironic. Foreshadowed Loss was judged

TABLE 21.7

Ironic Subtypes by Mean Rating and Percentage of Subjects Rating Them As Ironic

Subtype	M rating	Percentage of Subjects
Wins		
Instrumental (2)[a]	2.16	
Fluke (3)[a]	2.25	
Type	2.21	84
Imbalances		
Temporal: states (4.5)	2.37	76
Temporal: actions (6)	2.47	80
Contextual: actions (10)	2.53	75
Situational (14)	2.81	71
Contextual: goal-action (17)	3.12	63
Role reversal (27)	4.44	26
Losses		
Planned (4.5)	2.37	76
Deserved (8)	2.49	84
Spontaneous (12)	2.75	72
Change of mind (19)	3.27	61
Fluke (24)	3.84	41
Foreshadowed (26)	4.24	43
Double outcomes		
Instrumental (7)	2.48	70
Fruitless wins (9)	2.50	80
Distribution (11)	2.65	67
Think win is "in hand" (15)	2.87	69
Wins belittling winner (16)	3.04	55
Prize not what it's cracked up to be (18)	3.19	69
Recurrence (22)	3.70	43
Contrastive (25)	3.87	33
Dramatic		
Doomed agent (1)[a]	1.88	
Devious agent (21)[a]	3.47	
Type	2.68	69
Coincidence		
It's a small world (13)[a]	2.76	
Anticipated (23)[a]	3.78	
Type	3.27	63
Catch-22 (20)	3.35	45

Note. Subtype's rank orderings, from most ironic (1) to least ironic (27) are in parentheses.
[a]Ironic rating based on single token due to collapsed testing format.

488

ironic by more than 40% of the subjects, and Role Reversal Imbalance was judged ironic by just over a quarter of the subjects.

Concept Structure.   Ironic forms are differentiable on these measures, revealing the concept to have internal structure. On the mean ratings measure, the mean for the nine most ironic forms (top one third) was 2.33, and the mean for the nine least ironic forms (bottom one third) was 3.77. The second index, the percentage of subjects rating ironic forms as ironic, ranged from 84% to 26%.

Concept Structure Data Across Studies.   In general, the present internal structure data verified those of Study 2. The six event subtypes most frequently produced by subjects in Study 2 were rated highly ironic in this study. These forms, along with their rank order from 1 (most ironic) to 27 (least ironic), based on mean ratings, were as follows: Doomed Agent Dramatic (1), Planned Loss (4.5), Temporal Imbalance (States and Actions; 4.5 and 6, respectively), Deserved Loss (8), Contextual Imbalance (Actions) (10), and Situational Imbalance (14). All of these placed in the most ironic half (top 13 or 14) of forms, with Situational Imbalance straddling the border. Their mean ratings ranged from 1.88 to 2.81.

The status of less ironic forms also was consistent across studies. In Study 2, 10 event subtypes were generated very infrequently, that is, produced by just 1 or 2 subjects, making them atypical category members. Eight of these were tested in Study 3 (Self-Betrayal Loss and Pathetic Agent Dramatic were not), and 6 placed in the least ironic half of forms, with It's A Small World Coincidence (13) straddling the dividing line. The mean ratings spanned 2.76 to 4.24.

Two of the eight forms infrequently generated in Study 2 were, however, rated as highly ironic in Study 3, ranking in the top third. These were the two subtypes within the Wins event type, Fluke and Instrumental.

Cohesion.   This refers to how closely matched were the means for the I-1 and I-2 tokens. The I-1 and I-2 vignette types represented the ironic forms to be tested. The two tokens for each of 21 forms tested (the Catch-22 type and 20 subtypes) were distributed such that one appeared among I-1 vignette types and the other appeared among I-2 vignette types. Hence the scores attained on these two vignette types should be highly correlated. Pearson *r*s were calculated among the means for I-1, I-2, NIU, and NIE vignette types. The results are presented in Table 21.8.

The strongest correlation (.88) was between I-1 and I-2 scores. The strength of this correlation is even more impressive in light of the fact that in the case of three event types tested (Wins, Dramatic, Coincidence), distinct subtypes appeared across I-1 and I-2 vignette types. Hence 3 of the 24 ironic tokens/vignettes among I-1 tokens did not have a counterpart form among I-2 vignettes and vice versa. This value may be compared with those obtained between other vignette types. The next-strongest correlation between scores should be observed between I-1 and I-2 vignette types and the NIU vignette types, as unexpectedness is a feature of irony. These correlations were .66 and .60, respectively. Scores for the foil vignette types

TABLE 21.8
Intercorrelations Among Ironic and Nonironic (Foil) Tokens

Measure	1	2	3	4
1. Ironic 1	—	.31*	.88**	.66**
2. Nonironic-expected		—	.30*	.60**
3. Ironic 2			—	.60**
4. Nonironic-unexpected				—

* $p < .05$. ** $p < .001$.

(NIE and NIU) also should show a strong correlation, as these vignette types are alike in representing nonironic items, and such was the case (.60). Finally, as NIE vignette types represent those events most discrepant from ironic events, the correlations between the I-1 and NIE and the I-2 and NIE scores should be the weakest, and they were (.31 and .30, respectively).

Concept Breadth. The number of ironic types (of 7) manifested per subject was calculated by noting for each subject which of the 24 (sub)types were coded as ironic (assigned a rating between and including 1 to 4 for tokens I-1 and I-2) and determining the number of types evidenced across these subtypes. The mean per person was then tallied; it equaled 5.53, indicating a very extensive range of concept knowledge.

Concept Depth. The depth of conceptual knowledge can be measured most reliably for those ironic types for which individual subtypes were subjected to a full (noncollapsed) test. These included Imbalances, Losses, and the Double Outcomes types, and excluded Wins, Dramatic, and Coincidence. (The Catch-22 type entails no subtypes.) The mean numbers of subtypes were derived from the calculations that were conducted for the breadth analysis. They were as follows: Imbalances, $M = 3.90$ of 6; Losses, $M = 3.75$ of 6; and Double Outcomes, $M = 4.84$ of 8. Hence, more than half of the subtypes for each of these types were shown per subject, indicating substantial depth.

Discussion

The present data verified and extended those yielded by Study 2. Subjects who were not given any information on situational irony nonetheless rated all of the event kinds identified by the investigator (see Study 1 taxonomy) as ironic, providing strong evidence for a shared concept of situational irony. A little more than half (58%) of the tokens representing these ironic event kinds in Study 3 were drawn from the responses to the request for ironic instances in Study 2. The result was that 21% of those responses were rated for ironic status in Study 3. Their status as ironic was confirmed when they were rated as ironic by naive subjects, lending further support to Study 2's findings. Concept knowledge, as measured in Study 3, was broad. Subjects recognized more than five of the seven ironic event types. Such knowledge was also deep, with types understood in terms of many subtypes.

As in Study 2, the concept of situational irony manifested internal structure. Highly typical ironic event kinds were defined as those forms ranking in the top one third of ironic forms, based on mean ratings. The mean ratings for the nine most ironic forms ranged from 1.88 to 2.50. These event kinds exhibit salient category features.

Strong opposition is borne by Temporal Imbalances of the States and Actions variety, wherein one action or state cancels out or opposes another. Similarly, strong opposition in relation to outcome typifies Double Outcome events of the Fruitless Wins and Instrumental kinds, and Wins events of the Instrumental variety. In these events, the contrasting win—loss outcomes are discrete and hence are more sharply contrastive.

The category feature of outcome is shared by several forms. Fluke Wins and Planned Loss are counterpart forms in that they share the human fragility feature. Outcome is incidental to intentionality and planful action, highlighting the impotency of the latter. Planned and Deserved Loss, as in Study 2, have highly ironic status, again showing self-inflicted and the mix of self- and fate-inflicted loss respectively to be very ironic. The Doomed Agent Dramatic event also bears a loss outcome and had highly typical status in this study, as in Study 2. As noted, this form of irony is among the most familiar. It has long been recognized as ironic and as a striking dimension of literature and theater.

Of these 9 highly typical forms, only Fluke Wins and Instrumental Wins ranked among the least frequently generated forms (those 10 forms produced by just 1 or 2 subjects) in Study 2. Their highly ironic status in this study, however, is predictable on the basis of a featural analysis. Judgment tasks wherein instances need only be recognized provide a more complete inventory of concept instances than production tasks and are likely to yield at least some cases of a highly recognizable instance that had been only weakly produced.

Least typical ironic event kinds may be defined as those ranking in the bottom one third of ironic forms rated, based on mean ratings. The mean ratings for the nine least ironic forms ranged from 3.27 to 4.44. None were among the six most frequently generated or typical forms in Study 2. Indeed, they were weakly generted, with seven produced by 3 or fewer subjects. These event kinds are either lacking significant category features or bear them in weak or attenuated form.

Anticipated Coincidence and Catch-22 event kinds were expected to be less typical category members, as they participate in membership in more than one category. They are categorized as ironies, and as Coincidences and Catch-22s, respectively. Moreover, Coincidence events lack the critical category features of opposition and outcome.

Other event kinds, among the least ironic, bear no or only weak opposition. They include Recurrences and Contrastive Double Outcomes and Role Reversal Imbalances (see Table 21.2).

The remaining forms of the least ironic nine exhibit the category feature of a loss outcome. The fate-inflicted loss forms Fluke and Foreshadowed are among these, repeating the Study 2 findings showing fate-inflicted loss to be less ironic than both self-inflicted loss and the mix of fate- and self-inflicted loss. Moreover, fate-inflicted loss forms share with the also-atypical Recurrence Double Outcomes the human fragility feature in persons appearing victim to extrahuman forces. Change Of Mind Loss, the only self-inflicted form to rank among the least ironic, is the most ironic of these nine forms, hence it ranks as more ironic than the fate-inflicted forms (see Table 21.7). Finally, Devious Agent Dramatic, though bearing the feature of a loss outcome, is less familiar than the Doomed Agent form.

The data on mean ratings for the four vignette types (I-1, NIE, I-2, NIU) supported the proposal that, within the domain of events involving human activity, event kinds are distinguishable on the criterion of expectedness. Expected events, which are presumed to be represented by the script structure, were rated least ironic. Unexpected ironic events, which are said to violate expectation in well-defined, culturally recognized ways, were rated most ironic. Unexpected nonironic events, wherein expectation is violated in idiosyncratic ways, were rated as more ironic than expected events but as less ironic than ironic ones. This pattern demonstrates the specified nature of ironic deviation from expectation.

GENERAL DISCUSSION

Situational irony is a phenomenon of considerable cultural significance. Daily, ironic events are a topic of conversation and news. They often are the basis for stories that are told by ordinary folk and authors. Muecke (1969) stated that the emotional and dramatic power of ironic situations has long been recognized and noted that classical drama bears witness to a highly developed sense of irony.

In Study 1, a taxonomy was developed that explicated the structure of the concept of situational irony. Nearly 30 distinct ironic event kinds from seven major event types were identified and their category features delineated. The data from Studies 2 and 3 show that adults share a concept of situational irony, in the form described, and that the concept has internal structure. Event types exhibiting the key features of opposition and outcome, such as Imbalances, Losses, Double Outcomes, and Wins, were typical category instances, and those lacking these features, or that belong in other categories as well, such as Catch-22 and Coincidence, were peripheral category members. Typicality effects for subtypes were also predictable on the basis of a featural analysis.

In being a concept with internal structure, situational irony meets one component of conceptual coherence (Medin & Wattenmaker, 1987; Murphy & Medin, 1985). This leads necessarily to asking about its external structure, the second component of conceptual coherence (Medin & Wattenmaker, 1987; Murphy & Medin,

1985). This refers to the place of the concept of situational irony in the complete knowledge base. On the basis of situational irony's internal structure, one could claim that a general knowledge structure or schema is established for ironic events. These are unexpected events, within the domain of events involving human activity. Such knowledge would exist along with other event knowledge structures, such as the script, which is a representation for events that realize a high reliability of expectation. Indeed, the data from Study 3 show that subjects can reliably differentiate among three event kinds: expected events, for which presumably there is a script; unexpected ironic events, which are a culturally recognized pattern of unexpected events and for which a general knowledge structure is established; and unexpected nonironic events, which are idiosyncratic events presumably not associated with a general knowledge structure.

Indeed, as to the latter set of event kinds, surely not all script-anomalous occurrences require positing an event knowledge structure beyond that of the script. When these violations or variations from script structure fail to exhibit internal structure, a claim for a new form of event knowledge has not been made. For example, deviations (rendered in prose passages) such as missing actions, goals, or scrambled action sequences tend to be regularized and assimilated within script structure during recall (see Mandler, 1983, for review). Similarly, other script-atypical information, such as unrelated actions, becomes tagged. This tagged material represents functionally separate organizational units, distinct from the generic script structure (Graesser et al., 1979; Graesser et al., 1980; Nakamura et al., 1985; Schank & Abelson, 1977). Although script distinct, this information is defined only relationally in terms of the script, as a deviation, and does not represent a concept (of occurrences) in its own right.

As a distinct event-based concept, situational irony may challenge our normative theory of events as verbal irony challenges semantic theories of meaning (Grice, 1975, 1978; Searle, 1975, 1979). Before the study of situational irony, the script was one of the few event knowledge structures that received significant attention. One possible result was that the domain of event knowledge be erroneously conceived as largely comprised of knowledge for prescriptive events. Accordingly, just as verbal irony is a case for meaning beyond literal, semantic meaning, so situational irony is event knowledge beyond that for normative events.

The domain of event knowledge, then, can be presumed to incorporate knowledge of a vast array of events, differentiable on the dimension of expectedness. The script is a representation for events that unfold prescriptively, and situational irony is a general knowledge structure for at least some events that take a striking turn. Knowledge of other culturally recognized nonprescriptive events, such as tragic and humorous ones, must also have a place in the knowledge base, within the domain of events. Although humorous and tragic events are not coextensive with ironic ones, many ironic events are themselves classifiable as humorous or tragic.

What accounts for an ironic situation being construed as humorous? Humor is said to require that two disparate planes of thought coexist in relation to some experience (Apter, 1982; Koestler, 1964). Additionally, this incongruity must be resolved through reinterpretation of the situation, wherein the reality implied by the new situation stands in a diminished relation, in some way, to that implied by the original or purported one (Apter, 1982; Wyer & Collins, 1992; see the latter for discussion of how the diminishment assumption both subsumes and constrains disparagement theories of humor). For example, in slapstick humor, wherein protagonists are bludgeoning one another with two-by-fours, diminishment arises from the realization that the protagonists are not really hurt. Humor is elicited because the actual situation turns out to be more mundane than the purported one. Verbal irony has already been described as "humorous," holding a place in a taxonomy of "wit" (Long & Graesser, 1988). In attempting to explain its humorous quality, Wyer and Collins (1992) noted that intended meaning is often diminished relative to literal meaning. Hence in their example, "The Swiss Alps certainly can't compare to central Illinois," the literal meaning is that central Illinois is a scenic landscape, and the intended meaning is that it is flat and dreary.

A similar analysis may apply to some cases of situational irony, if the event that actually happened is considered the new situation and the event that was expected to happen is considered the original or purported one. In many ironic events, the reality implied by what actually happened is diminished in some way with regard to expected reality. This may account for the humor in these events. In such situations, persons become undone and look a bit ridiculous when compared with their basically capable status in the expected event. Think of the toothless dentist.

Some cases of situational irony that lack humor are among those events that we consider tragic. In the case of tragedy, it may be proposed that the reality implied by what actually happened is *augmented* in some way with regard to expected reality. People are lent import in these ironic events. They become tragic, heart-rending victims. This signals a departure from their status as average figures in the expected event. Consider parents who have lost one child in a plane crash caused by terrorists, who years later lose their remaining child, killed by uncovering a live grenade while playing (news story).

A final issue to be raised, but again only speculatively, is the processing of ironic events. Apparently, two processing routes are possible. First if processing were serial, script knowledge, that is, knowledge of what was expected to happen, would be activated when events are first experienced. If script-based expectations were violated, then knowledge of nonprescriptive events, such as ironic ones, would be activated to interpret the experience. This processing path might be likened to the one proposed by some theorists for interpreting nonliteral language, such as metaphor and verbal irony (Grice, 1975, 1978; Searle, 1975, 1979). In language, the confrontation of literal meaning is proposed to be a necessary step in the path to comprehending speakers' utterances. Only when literal meaning is inconsistent with the context is the hearer led to seek an alternative, or nonliteral (ironic) meaning. It may also be likened to what is proposed to occur in processing humor, on the *serial processing* model (see Long & Graesser, 1988). Serial processing presumes that literal meaning is processed first, and that alternative, figurative meaning is constructed only when there is a discrepancy between the punch line and the preceding context.

For example, Raskin (1984) proposed that a joke begins with the presentation of a text consistent with one script. Second, a script-switch trigger (e.g., the punch line) is presented that is inconsistent with the currently evoked script. This provokes the listener to search for an alternative script with which the text is compatible. Humor results from the overlap of scripts. See Suls (1972) for a similar two-stage processing model for humor.

On an alternative processing route, both script knowledge (knowledge of what was expected to happen) and ironic event knowledge (knowledge of what actually happened) are accessed when a person experiences events. An ironic judgment is made—that is, the ironic schema is activated—if the script structure does not account for the experience at hand and the ironic event schema does. This processing route may be the more likely one for several reasons. First, it seems that irony comprehension requires the simultaneous juxtaposition of representations of what actually happened and what was expected to happen and hence requires access to both forms of event knowledge. Moreover, assessing the humorous quality of an event presumes dual access, as the relation between these two representations (e.g., diminishment) must be considered. Third, if processing is affected by preceding context, as some researchers claim (see, e.g., Gildea & Glucksberg, 1983), the context generally preceding the experience of ironic events would foster dual access. Ironic events are often experienced in linguistically marked discourse contexts. These include, for example, discourse episodes wherein a speaker appeals to a story (e.g., "Oh, listen to this story") or begins an utterance with "Ironically ... ," or uses an exaggerated intonation. Marked contexts also include episodes of reading a story, seeing a film, or hearing a news clip. On these occasions, one expects to experience a troubled or nonroutine event. This expectation should lead to the more likely access of the ironic event schema, as opposed to the script.

A similar processing path, termed *parallel-race,* has been proposed for humor (Long & Graesser, 1988). In this model, both literal and alternate literal or figurative text meanings are accessed. A humor judgment is made if Meaning 2 of a word or phrase makes sense given the preceding text and Meaning 1 does not. Humor comprehension can also occur if both Meaning 1 and Meaning 2 are compatible with the preceding text, as in double entendre. The parallel-race processing path is also applicable to the processing of nonliteral language, namely metaphor. Glucksberg, Gildea, and Bookin (1982) showed that figurative meanings may be accessed and processed at the same time as literal meanings. Moreover, the *literal meaning* hypothesis (or the *serial processing* view) has been challenged by evidence suggesting that listeners do not automatically construct a level of representation solely in terms of the literal meaning of an utterance or sentence (Gibbs, 1979, 1983, 1984).

Additional research is necessary to gain information on the processing of ironic events. Other fruitful areas for future inquiry include the definition and description of other nonprescriptive events in the domain of events and the relations among these event kinds.

ACKNOWLEDGMENTS

I would like to thank Lois Bloom, Michael Schober, Katherine Nelson, and Bill Hirst for very insightful comments on drafts of this article. I would also like to thank Brad Richards and Cynthia Couphos for help in data analysis.

REFERENCES

Apter, M. J. (1982). *The experience of motivation: The theory of psychological reversals.* San Diego. CA: Academic.

Ashcraft, M. H. (1989). *Human memory and cognition.* Glenview, IL: Scott, Foresman.

Brunet, J. (1990). *Acts of meaning.* Cambridge, MA: Harvard University Press.

Burke, K. (1969). *A grammar of motives.* Berkeley: University of California Press.

Gibbs, R. (1979). Contextual effects in understanding indirect requests. *Discourse Processes, 2,* 1–10.

Gibbs, R. (1983). Do people always process the literal meanings of indirect requests? *Journal of Experimental Psychology: Learning, Memory, and Cognition, 9,* 524–533.

Gibbs, R. (1984). Literal meaning and psychological theory. *Cognitive Science, 8,* 275–304.

Gildea, P., & Glucksberg, S. (1983). On understanding metaphor: The role of context. *Journal of Verbal Learning and Verbal Behavior, 22,* 577–590.

Glass, A., Holyoak, K., & O'Dell, C. (1974). Production frequency and the verification of quantified sentences. *Journal of Verbal Learning and Verbal Behavior, 13,* 237–254.

Glucksberg, S., Gildea, P., & Bookin, H. (1982). On understanding nonliteral speech: Can people ignore metaphors? *Journal of Verbal Learning and Verbal Behavior, 21,* 85–98.

Graesser, A. C., Gordon, S. E., & Sawyer, J. D. (1979). Recognition memory for typical and atypical actions in scripted activities: Tests of a script pointer + tag hypothesis. *Journal of Verbal Learning and Verbal Behavior, 18,* 319–332.

Graesser, A. C., Woll, S. B., Kowalski, D. J., & Smith, D. A. (1980). Memory for typical and atypical actions in scripted activities. *Journal of Experimental Psychology: Human Learning and Memory, 6,* 503–515.

Grice, H. P. (1975). Logic and conversation. In P. Cole & J. Morgan (Eds.), *Syntax and semantics: Vol. 3. Speech acts* (pp. 41–58). New York: Academic.

Grice, H. P. (1978). Some further notes on logic and conversation. In P. Cole (Ed.), *Syntax and semantics: Vol. 9. Pragmatics* (pp. 113–128). New York: Academic.

Jorgensen, J., Miller, G., & Sperber, D. (1984). Test of the mention theory of irony. *Journal of Experimental Psychology: General, 113,* 112–120.

Koestler, A. (1964). *The act of creation.* New York: Macmillan.

Long, D. L., & Graesser, A. C. (1988). Wit and humor in discourse processing. *Discourse Processes, 11,* 35–60.

Lucariello, J. (1990). Canonicality and consciousness in child narrative. In B. Britton & A. Pellegrini (Eds.), *Narrative thought and narrative language* (pp. 131–149). Hillsdale, NJ: Lawrence Erlbaum Associates.

Mandler, J. M. (1983). Representation. In P. H. Mussen (Series Ed.) & J. H. Flavell & E. M. Markman (Vol. Eds.), *Handbook of child psychology: Vol. 3. Cognitive development* (pp. 420–494). New York: Wiley.

Medin, D. L., & Wattenmaker, W. D. (1987). Category cohesiveness, theories, and cognitive archeology. In U. Neisser (Ed.), *Concepts and conceptual development: Ecological and intellectual factors in categorization* (pp. 25–62). Cambridge, England: Cambridge University Press.

Mervis, C., Catlin, J., & Rosch, E. (1976). Relationships among goodness-of-example, category norms, and word frequency. *Bulletin of the Psychonomic Society, 7,* 283–284.

Muecke, D. (1969). *The compass of irony.* London: Methuen.

Murphy, G. L., & Medin, D. L. (1985). The role of theories in conceptual coherence. *Psychological Review, 92,* 289–316.

Nakamura, G. V., Graesser, A. C., Zimmerman, J. A., & Riha, J. (1985). Script processing in a natural situation. *Memory & Cognition, 13,* 140–144.

Raskin, V. (1984). *Semantic mechanisms of humor.* Boston: Reidel.

Rips, L., Shoben, E., & Smith, E. (1973). Semantic distance and the verification of semantic relations. *Journal of Verbal Learning and Verbal Behavior, 12,* 1–20.

Rosch, E. (1973). On the internal structure of perceptual and semantic categories. In T. E. Moore (Ed.), *Cognitive development and the acquisition of language* (pp. 111–144). New York: Academic.

Rosch, E. (1975). Cognitive representations of semantic categories. *Journal of Experimental Psychology: General, 104,* 192–233.

Rosch, E. (1978). Principles of categorization. In E. Rosch & B. B. Lloyd (Eds.), *Cognition and categorization* (pp. 27–48). Hillsdale, NJ: Lawrence Erlbaum Associates.

Schank, R. C., & Abelson, R. (1977). *Scripts, plans, goals and understanding.* Hillsdale, NJ: Lawrence Erlbaum Associates.

Searle, J. (1975). Indirect speech acts. In P. Cole & J. Morgan (Eds.), *Syntax and semantics: Vol. 3. Speech acts* (pp. 59–82). New York: Academic.

Searle, J. (1979). Metaphor. In A. Ortony (Ed.), *Metaphor and thought* (pp. 92–123). Cambridge, England: Cambridge University Press.

Smith, E., Shoben, E., & Rips, L. (1974). Structure and process in semantic memory: A featural model for semantic decisions. *Psychological Review, 81,* 214–241.

Sperber, D., & Wilson, D. (1986). *Relevance.* Cambridge, MA: Harvard University Press.

Suls, J. M. (1972). A two-stage model for the appreciation of jokes and cartoons: An information-processing analysis. In J. H. Goldstein & P. E. McGhee (Eds.). *The psychology of humor* (pp. 81–100). New York: Academic.

Wyer, R. S., & Collins, J. E. (1992). A theory of humor elicitation. *Psychological Review, 99,* 663–688.

CHAPTER 22

Verbal Irony As Implicit Display of Ironic Environment: Distinguishing Ironic Utterances From Nonirony

Akira Utsumi
Tokyo Institute of Technology, Japan

This chapter proposes an implicit display theory of verbal irony in order to provide a plausible explanation of how irony is distinguished from nonirony. The implicit display theory claims that verbal irony is an utterance or a statement that implicitly displays ironic environment, a proper situational setting in the discourse context, and that verbal irony is a prototype-based category. The notion of implicit display provides typicality conditions characterizing the prototype of verbal irony; the similarity between the prototype and an utterance is formulated as the degree of ironicalness. In order for an utterance to be interpreted ironically, the utterance must be recognized as achieving implicit display through the process of assessing the degree of ironicalness, and the discourse situation must be identified as ironic environment through the process of checking or inferring its constituent events/states. If these two criteria are satisfied, the utterance is judged to be ironic, otherwise it is judged to be non-ironic. This paper also argues that the implicit display theory overcomes several difficulties of the existing irony studies and that it is consistent with the empirical findings from psycholinguistics. These arguments indicate that the implicit display theory is a more adequate and comprehensive theory of verbal irony than the traditional pragmatic theory, the echoic interpretation theory, the pretense theory, and other theories.

Verbal irony is an intelligent, witty figure of speech found in many language activities. It has attracted the interest of linguists, philosophers, psychologists, rhetoricians, and other scholars. Researchers in linguistics (e.g., Grice, 1975; Haverkate, 1990; Giora, 1995) have paid much attention to the relation (e.g., opposition, insincerity, negation) between the surface meanings of ironic utterances and their in-

---

This chapter was previously published as "Verbal irony as implicit display of ironic environment: Distinguishing ironic utterances from nonirony" (A. Utsumi) in the *Journal of Pragmatics, 32,* 1777–1806. Copyright © [2000] by Elsevier. Reprinted with permission.

tended meanings, while psychological or cognitive studies (e.g., Sperber & Wilson, 1981; Clark & Gerrig, 1984; Kreuz & Glucksberg, 1989; Wilson & Sperber, 1992; Gibbs, 1994; Kumon-Nakamura, Glucksberg, & Brown, 1995) have been devoted to the properties of irony (e.g., echoic mention/interpretation, pretense, ironic tone of voice) which facilitate ironic interpretation.

However, it appears to me that none of the previous irony theories can distinguish ironic utterances from nonironic ones completely, i.e., they do not provide a sufficient explanation of how people judge whether an utterance is ironic or not. The reason for this incompetence lies in the implicit nature of verbal irony. Verbal irony is fundamentally implicit, not explicitly expressed. As Haverkate (1990, p. 79) pointed out, verbal irony cannot be expressed by referential expressions like "I ironically inform you that ..." or "It is ironic that ... ," and it may be empirically inferred from the fact that there does not exist a verb like "ironize."[1] The implicit nature of irony causes serious difficulty in drawing a clear boundary between irony and nonirony, in spite of a number of previous attempts to define irony by common properties shared by all ironic utterances: "irony possesses no easily identifiable independent criteria. As much as we would like to find them, there are no signals that can be considered purely signals of irony" (Barbe, 1995, p. 71).

This chapter proposes an *implicit display theory* of verbal irony which provides a more plausible explanation of how irony is distinguished from nonirony. The main claim underlying the theory is threefold. First, ironic language presupposes an *ironic environment,* a certain situational setting in the discourse context. Verbal irony is a language-related phenomenon, but it cannot be discussed outside of a situation. Although the importance of situation in verbal irony has been pointed out by some notable studies (Littman & Mey, 1991; Gibbs & O'Brien, 1991; Gibbs, O'Brien, & Doolittle, 1995), these studies make a fatal mistake in that they confuse situations which cause verbal irony (i.e., situations which make statements ironic) with ironic situations or situational irony (Lucariello, 1994; i.e., situations which are ironic). I argue that though closely related, these two kinds of situations represent different concepts and should be addressed separately. Because this chapter focuses on verbal irony, I define ironic environment as a situational setting which motivates verbal irony.

Second, verbal irony is viewed as an utterance/statement that *implicitly displays* ironic environment. It means that ironic communication presumes an implicit display of ironic environment, and because of this presumption, people understand an ironic intention that is not explicitly expressed. Implicit display provides neither a necessary nor a sufficient condition for distinguishing verbal irony from nonirony. Rather, it is a presumption according to which people judge whether an utterance is ironic, and infer an ironic intention so that the current situation meets the requirements of an ironic environment.

Third, verbal irony is a prototype-based category characterized by the notion of implicit display. Implicit displays are achieved by certain linguistic properties, but to different degrees, and irony does not always have all the properties for implicit display. Thus, the notion of implicit display provides typicality conditions characterizing the prototype "verbal irony," and as prototype theory (e.g., Rosch & Mervis, 1975; Lakoff, 1987) predicts, utterances with more properties of implicit display are perceived as being more ironic. It follows that people judge whether an utterance is ironic by assessing the similarity between the prototype and the utterance.

The rest of this chapter is organized as follows: Section 2 discusses the existing irony theories that have so far been proposed, and shows that they are too specific to cover all ironic utterances, and, at the same time, too general to exclude all nonironic utterances. Section 3 then elaborates on the implicit display theory of verbal irony and explains how it distinguishes irony from nonirony. Sections 4 through 6 lend support to the implicit display theory by showing that it can cope with several problems posed by the previous irony theories and account for the empirical findings from psycholinguistics.

CRITICISM OF PREVIOUS APPROACHES TO IRONY

2.1 Violation-Based Approach

According to the traditional pragmatic view of irony (Grice, 1975; Searle, 1979b; Haverkate, 1990), people detect ironic meanings by becoming aware of an apparent violation of the maxim of quality (Grice, 1975) or felicity conditions for surface speech acts (Searle, 1979b; Haverkate, 1990); as a result, they substitute the surface-literal meaning with its opposite meaning. This view explains some typical ironies like the following utterance (1a):

[Situation 1] A mother asked her son to clean up his messy room, but he was lost in a comic book. After a while, she discovered that his room was still messy, and said to her son:

(1) a.   This room is totally clean!

The mother's utterance (1a) violates the maxim of quality in that it obviously contradicts the situation and she does not believe what is literally said.

However, the violation-based view fails to cover many ironic utterances: hearers understand ironic intention even when an utterance does not include such a violation or when they are not aware of such a violation. For example, irony can be communicated by various expressions that do not include the violation, such as a literally true assertion (1b) and an understatement (1c) uttered in the same situation as Situation 1.

(1) b.   I love children who keep their rooms clean.
     c.   This room seems to be messy.

Likewise, in the following example, Peter is unaware of the events of Brenda's morning and thus he cannot decide whether her utterance (2) includes a violation or not. Nevertheless, he can appreciate that her utterance is ironic, especially when it is accompanied by prosodic cues (Barbe, 1995; Milosky & Ford, 1997).

[Situation 2] Peter sees his friend Brenda at work for the first time that day, and she says the following:

(2)   I've had a great morning!

These examples indicate that violation is not a necessary property of irony.

Moreover, violation is not a sufficient property, either. The violation-based view cannot discriminate irony from other nonliteral utterances (e.g., metaphors, indirect speech acts) which include the violation. In addition, the claim that irony conveys the opposite of the literal meaning is problematic: irony is far more than mere opposition. For example, the ironic utterance (1b) cannot be seen as communicating the opposite of what is literally said, such as "I hate children who keep their rooms clean" or "I love children who do not keep their rooms clean."

Mention-Based Approach

The mention theory proposed by Sperber and Wilson (1981) denied the traditional approach and focused on the allusive nature of irony. The recent version of the mention theory, the echoic interpretation theory (Sperber & Wilson, 1986, 1998; Wilson & Sperber, 1992), has argued that verbal irony is a variety of echoic interpretations of someone's thought, utterance, expectation, or cultural norm, in which the speaker dissociates herself from the echoed materials with accompanying ridicule or scorn. For example, Peter's reply (3a) of the following exchange is a typical example of echoic irony.

[Situation 3] Jesse said "I'd be promoted before you" to his colleague Peter. This elicited the following reply:

(3) a.   Oh! You'd be promoted before me.

However, the echoic interpretation theory is still incomplete as a comprehensive framework for irony. One problem is that Sperber and Wilson's notions of echoic interpretation and of dissociation from an echoed material are too narrow, and therefore unable to explain all cases of irony. In other words, the echoic interpretation theory cannot explain that irony need not necessarily be interpretively echoic, as shown by, e.g., Giora (1995) and Kumon-Nakamura et al. (1995). For example, the utterance (1b) "I love children who keep their rooms clean" is ironic, but we cannot easily find the echoed material from which the mother dissociates herself.[2] A more convincing example is the following where, given the situation that makes the echo (3a) of Jesse's preceding utterance ironic, the following nonechoic utterance (3b) also communicates irony.

(3) b.   Thank you for informing me of your priceless opinion.

According to Wilson and Sperber (1992), an utterance is an echoic interpretation of, or interpretively resembles, another thought or utterance to the extent that these two propositions share logical and contextual implications. Hence, the reply (3b) cannot be analyzed as an interpretive echo, because it hardly shares any implications with Jesse's preceding utterance, nor does it share them with general norms/ universal desire.

Another problem that makes the echoic interpretation theory incomplete is that it provides no plausible explanation of how irony is distinguished from interpretive echoes used for nonironic purposes. For instance, the utterance (4b) in the following exchange is echoic (i.e., it mentions the Prime Minister's utterance and simultaneously expresses Mira's negative attitude), but it is not ironic (Giora, 1995, p. 248).

(4) a.   Dina: I missed the last news broadcast. What did the Prime Minister say
         about the Palestinians?
    b.   Mira (with ridiculing aversion): That we should deport them.

Other mention-based approaches have recently been proposed which extend the mention theory to cover a wider range of verbal irony. Kreuz and Glucksberg's (1989) echoic reminder theory emphasized the reminder function of ironic utterances: verbal irony reminds addressees of what has been expected by alluding to that expectation. Their theory implies that not all ironic utterances are echoic, and because of this it may be a more adequate theory than the mention theory. However, it suffers from the same difficulties because the authors' notion of reminder reveals no more features of verbal irony than does the mention theory. Kumon-Nakamura et al.'s (1995) allusional pretense theory integrated both the mention-based and the violation-based approaches, and claimed that all ironic utterances allude to a failed expectation and violate one of the felicity conditions for well-formed speech acts. The allusional pretense theory has a powerful ability to explain more ironic utterances than both other approaches, resolving some of their difficulties. However, it still suffers from similar problems. First, the allusional pretense theory, just like the violation-based approach, cannot explain the fact that hearers interpret ironic utterances without recognizing their violations. Second, their notion of allusion is not clear enough to distinguish between irony and nonirony. Third, it does not address the role of ironic cues in interpreting irony (Glucksberg, 1995).

Pretense-Based Approach

In an attempt to criticize the mention theory, Clark and Gerrig (1984) proposed a seemingly different approach, the pretense theory of irony. The pretense theory views an ironist as "pretending to be an injudicious person speaking to an uniniti- ated audience" (Clark & Gerrig, 1984, p. 121). For example, the ironist of Situation

1, the mother, pretends to be an imaginary person, perhaps an indulgent mother who never reprimands her children, by exaggerating how ridiculous is her behavior. When addressees recognize this pretense, they understand that the speaker is expressing the intended derogatory attitude ironically.

However, pretense is not a necessary property of irony. If one says "What lovely weather" when the weather is miserable, the pretense theory explains, the speaker is pretending to be an unseeing person, like a TV forecaster, exclaiming to some uncomprehending audience how beautiful is the weather. However, do hearers really identify such persons in interpreting irony? What is worse, the authors' argument about the victim of irony makes the pretense theory less convincing. The pretense theory posits two kinds of victims—the person the speaker pretends to be and the ignorant audience accepting what is said—but it is more likely to say that the utterance above has no victims (Sperber, 1984). Furthermore, in the case of Situation 1, the victim is obviously the mother's son, but it seems unreasonable to suppose that she pretends to be her son or that he is an ignorant acceptor of what is said. These facts reveal that the claim that the ironist is pretending to be an imaginary person is very doubtful, and thus, irony need not necessarily include pretense.

Pretense is not a sufficient property of irony, either. One typical example of non-irony with pretense is parody: "What they offer as a theory of irony is a straightforward theory of parody" (Sperber, 1984, p. 135). Moreover, as Kreuz and Glucksberg (1989) pointed out, the notion of pretense is too powerful for an adequate theory of irony in that it applies to all indirect speech acts.

The recent version of the pretense theory by Clark (1996) argued that irony is viewed as joint pretense. The joint pretense view assumes an imaginary situation, rather than an imaginary person, in which the speaker of irony is performing a serious communicative act directed at the addressee. Irony is caused by their joint pretense in the actual situation that the event in the imaginary situation is taking place. Hence, on this view, the mother and her son in Situation 1 jointly pretend that she praises him for his clean room.

However, the joint pretense view still fails to distinguish irony from nonirony. First, the joint pretense view poses a different serious problem: it assumes that the addressee of irony must share the ironic intention with the speaker beforehand in order to pretend jointly; however, in many cases (such as Situation 1), this is an inappropriate assumption. Hence, joint pretense is not a necessary property of irony. Second, the theory cannot distinguish irony from parody and other nonironic utterances for the same reason as in the case of the original pretense theory, and thus joint pretense is not a sufficient property. Finally, Clark (1996) stated nothing about how joint pretense treats the victims of irony (although the joint pretense view seems to explain victimless irony, such as the "weather" irony, since it does not assume that an ironist pretends to be an imaginary person).

IMPLICIT DISPLAY THEORY

This section presents an implicit display theory of irony which overcomes the problems of the previous approaches. To begin with, section 3.1 introduces the ironic environment as a prerequisite for the speaker to be ironic, while section 3.2 describes how ironic utterances achieve an implicit display of the ironic environment by linguistic and paralinguistic means. Section 3.3 then explains why the prototype-based view of irony is required, by showing that implicit display need not be recognized completely in interpreting ironic utterances; it illustrates how the prototype-based view is incorporated into the implicit display theory by giving a formula for calculating the degree of ironicalness as a similarity measure. Finally, section 3.4 describes how the implicit display theory distinguishes irony from nonirony.

Ironic Environment

Given two temporal locations t_0 and t_1 that temporally precede the time when an utterance (or a statement) is given, ironic environment consists of the following three events/states.

1. The speaker has a certain expectation E at time t_0.
2. The speaker's expectation E fails (i.e., E is incongruous with reality) at time t_1.
3. The speaker has a negative emotional attitude (e.g., disappointment, anger, reproach, envy) toward the incongruity between what is expected and what actually is the case.[3]

When the discourse context includes these three events/states, I say that the situation is surrounded by an ironic environment. In order for an utterance/statement to be ironic, the speaker must deliver it in the situation surrounded by the ironic environment.[4] For example, Situation 1 is surrounded by an ironic environment since the ironist, the mother, has an expectation that her son's room is clean (this is implied by her action of asking him to clean the room), but her expectation has not been fulfilled and it can be reasonably assumed that she is disappointed or angry at the result that the room is still messy.

Hence, when a discourse context is not surrounded by ironic environment, such that a speaker is not given the reason for being ironic, none of the utterances given in that context have an ironic intention.[5] For example, in the following situation, the mother's utterances (5a)—(5c) are not ironic though they are the same expressions as (1a)—(1c).

[Situation 4] A mother asked her son to clean up his messy room, which he then did completely. After a while, she discovered that his room was clean, and said the following to her son:

(5) a. This room is totally clean!
   b. I love children who keep their rooms clean.
   c. This room seems to be messy.

The utterances (5a) and (5b) are literal complimentary statements and (5c) is a literal complaint with no ironic/sarcastic intention. Situations like Situation 4 can be readily recognized not to be surrounded by ironic environment, because it is quite obvious to hearers that the speaker's expectation is fulfilled, and that the speaker believes that. On the other hand, in many situations which are surrounded by ironic environment such as Situation 1, all three components of the ironic environment are easily recognized by hearers.

The speaker's expectation deserves special mention. The important point to note is that, on my view, the speaker of an ironic statement must have a failed expectation for his/her utterance to be ironic. In other words, all expectations which motivate irony must be attributed to or possessed by the speaker. For example, in the case of Situation 3, unless the speaker Peter expects addressee Jesse to know that his opinion expressed in the preceding utterance is false, utterance (3a) should not communicate irony, even though it echoes Jesse's preceding utterance with a negative attitude. This point essentially differentiates the implicit display theory from the mention-based approach, as will be discussed further in section 4.2.

Implicit Display

The main claim of the implicit display theory is that verbal irony implicitly displays the fact that the situation is surrounded by ironic environment. Implicit display of the three components of the ironic environment is typically accomplished in such a way that an utterance U

1. Alludes to the speaker's expectation E.
2. Includes pragmatic insincerity by intentionally violating one of the pragmatic principles.
3. Expresses indirectly the speaker's negative attitude toward the failure of E.

The term *display* was first used in the context of irony research by Williams (1984, p. 128): "What the ironist does, then, is to *display* the situation to the listener." However, the notion of display in the present paper essentially differs from hers and is better for at least two reasons. First, Williams's notion of situation includes only two components—i.e., incongruity of two or more elements and a person who does not see the incongruity—which is not enough to explain verbal irony, and at the same time she confuses the ironic situation with the situation which triggers verbal irony. Second, she does not explain how irony displays the situation.

According to the notion of implicit display, utterances are clearly nonironic when they *directly* express at least one of the three components of ironic environment. Thus, the following utterances are not perceived as ironic even if they are spoken in Situation 1, which is surrounded by ironic environment.

(1) d.   I've expected a clean room.
     e.   I'm disappointed with the messy room.

Neither utterance implicitly displays an ironic environment: (1d) directly expresses the speaker's expectation, while (1e) directly expresses the speaker's true attitude.

In sections 3.2.1–3.2.3, I describe in detail the notions of allusion, pragmatic insincerity, and indirect expression of negative attitudes.

3.2.1 Allusion

The notion of allusion in this chapter can be captured in terms of coherence relations—e.g., *volitional-cause, non-volitional-cause, enable, prevent*—similar to the relations of rhetorical structure theory (Mann & Thompson, 1987). Given the propositional content P of an utterance U, P's constituents P_i (I assume $P—P_0$) and the speaker's expected event/state Q, the utterance U *alludes* to the speaker's expectation E if and only if

1. There is a path that coherently relates P_i to Q (i.e., a sequence of coherence relations leading from P_i to Q).
2. U does not directly express the speaker's expectation E using such expressions as "I've expected … ."

Note that the notion of allusion subsumes mention as a special case: U mentions E when Q and P_i are identical, as in the case of (1a).

For example, the ironic utterance (1b) in Situation 1 alludes to the speaker's expectation, as the action of keeping rooms clean *volitionally causes* the expected state that the room is clean. Similarly, (1c) alludes to the expectation by referring to the state (i.e., the room is messy), which *motivates* the action (of cleaning up the room) *volitionally causing* the expected state. The following ironic utterances also show various ways of allusion.

[Situation 5] Candy had baked a pizza to satisfy her hunger. When she was dishing it up, her husband entered the kitchen and gobbled up the whole pizza. Candy said the following to her husband:

(6) a. I'm not hungry at all.
  b. I'm really happy to eat the pizza.
  c. Have you seen my pizza on the table?
  d. I don't want to eat any more.
  e. How about another small slice of pizza?

The allusion to the speaker Candy's expectation of satisfying her hunger is accomplished as follows:

Q = [Candy is not hungry] (speaker's expectation).
A = [Candy eats a pizza] (action that volitionally causes Q, i.e., *volitional-cause* (A, Q)).

B = [Candy's husband eats the whole pizza] (action that prevents A, i.e., *prevent* (B, A)).

Y = [Candy does not want to eat any more] (state non-volitionally caused by Q, i.e., *non-volitional-cause* (Q, Y)).

X = [Candy's pizza is on the table] (state that enables A, i.e., *enable* (X, A)).

In (6a) P and Q are identical.

In (6b) *volitional-cause*(P_i, Q) where P_i ("to eat the pizza") and A are identical.

In (6c) *enable*(P_i, A) ^ *volitional-cause* (A, Q) where P_i and X are identical.[6]

In (6d) *non-volitional-cause*(Q, P) where P and Y are identical.

In (6e) *prevent*(P_i, A) ^ *volitional-cause*(A, Q) where P_i and B are identical.

Pragmatic Insincerity

Pragmatic insincerity is an extension of the concept of surface incongruity as caused by a violation of norms. An ironic utterance is pragmatically insincere when it violates at least one of the pragmatic principles. Many ironic utterances like (1a) intentionally violate one of the preconditions (such as the sincerity, preparatory, and propositional content conditions) that need to hold before their illocutionary speech acts are accomplished but even ironic utterances that do not violate these preconditions often violate other pragmatic principles.

For example, understatements like (1c) are pragmatically insincere since they do not provide as much information as required and thus violate the maxim of quantity.[7] Requests often become insincere when they are over-polite such as the following ironic statement (1f) uttered in Situation 1 (Kumon-Nakamura et al., 1995).

(1) f.   Would you mind if I asked you to clean up your room, please?

This utterance violates the politeness principle, or, more precisely, the convention in linguistic politeness that any utterance should be made at an appropriate level of politeness. According to Brown and Levinson's (1987) model, the mother of Situation 1 does not have to make an indirect request (in accordance with the politeness strategy, "do the act on-record with negative politeness redress") because the mother and her son are intimate and he has no power over her. Nevertheless, she makes the indirect request by saying (1f); consequently, (1f) includes pragmatic insincerity. Some kinds of true assertion like (1b) might also be seen as pragmatically insincere (Haverkate, 1990), although to a much lesser degree than do other insincere utterances. Such assertions are generalized statements that attribute properties to certain sets of objects, but when the properties cannot be attributed to any objects in the discourse situation, their explicit contents are not relevant as they stand (e.g., the son in Situation 1 does not belong to the class of children expressed by the generalized statement 1b).

Indirect Expression of Negative Attitudes

Speakers of irony use a variety of cues, many of which are called "ironic cues," for indirectly expressing their negative attitudes (see Table 22.1). These cues include hyperbolic words/phrases and intensives (Kreuz & Roberts, 1995; e.g., "totally" in 1a and "really" in 6b), interjections (e.g., "Oh" in 3a), prosodic features (e.g., intonation, tone of voice, exaggerated stress, and nasalization), and nonverbal cues (e.g., facial expressions and behavioral cues). Implicit display can also be accomplished by certain speech acts like "thank" as in the case of (3b) (i.e., the verbal cue 4 of Table 22.1). Such utterances can be seen as implying a negative attitude by explicitly expressing the counterfactual, pleased emotion that speakers would experience if their failed expectation was satisfied.

Prototype-Based View and the Degree of Ironicalness

Typical ironies can be recognized as satisfying all the three conditions for implicit display. For example, both (1a) and (1c) satisfy the three conditions (although 1c should be accompanied by prosodic and/or nonverbal cues).

However, many ironic utterances in genuine communicative interactions are not so straightforward. It is difficult or impossible to recognize all the conditions. For example, the ironic utterance (1b) is not so pragmatically insincere as is (1a) (or people do not recognize it as easily to be insincere). More important is the fact that hearers, because they are not sure whether the situation is surrounded by an ironic environment before interpreting an utterance, cannot recognize some of the properties of implicit display. In Situation 2, for example, the addressee Peter is incapable of identifying the incongruity between Brenda's expectation and the events of her morning before interpreting the utterance (2). Nevertheless, Peter can appreciate her ironic remark in some cases. The following example serves to further elucidate the point.

[Situation 6] (To someone acting inappropriately for his or her age)

(7)   How old did you say you were? (Kumon-Nakamura et al., 1995).

In this case, it is unlikely that the addressee of (7) knows the speaker's expectation beforehand. Rather, after recognizing the ironic intention involved in (7), the ad-

TABLE 22.1

Examples of Cues for Implicitly Displaying Negative Attitudes

Verbal cues	1. hyperbole, exaggeration—adjectives (e.g., amazing, splendid), adverbs (e.g., certainly, really, absolutely), metaphors
	2. interjection—'Oh!,' 'ah!,' 'O!,' 'Dear me!,' 'Oh dear!,' 'huh'
	3. prosody (paralinguistic cues)—accent, intonation contour, exaggerated stress, slow speaking rate, tone of voice, nasalization
	4. speech acts for expressing counterfactual pleased emotions—thank, compliment
Nonverbal cues	1. facial expression—quizzical, sneering, deadpan
	2. behavioral cues—gesture, pointing, laughing

dressee becomes aware of the speaker's expectation—e.g., the speaker expects the addressee to conform to some social norm saying "Be your age"—together with her/his inappropriate behavior. These examples clearly show that people do not have to see all the three conditions for implicit display in order to interpret irony, nor do they have to notice ironic environment beforehand, as long as there is a possibility that the situation is surrounded by ironic environment.

A close parallel can be drawn between the difficulty in distinguishing irony from nonirony and the difficulty in distinguishing members of a category from non-members. In the classical theory of categorization, it is assumed that a category is defined by common properties that all members of that category share. However, in accordance with current lines of thought in psychology and cognitive linguistics (e.g., Lakoff, 1987; Taylor, 1989), this view cannot explain our categorization ability. Similarly, the ironic examples (2) and (7) indicate that people do not decide whether an utterance is ironic by identifying all the conditions for implicit display.

I conclude that developing a method for assessing the similarity between an ironic utterance and a prototype of irony is a much more appropriate strategy for distinguishing irony from nonirony than defining irony by common properties shared by all ironic utterances which the previous irony studies have attempted to find. Along the lines suggested by Wittgenstein (1953), Rosch (1973), and Rosch and Mervis (1975), the notion of implicit display provides typicality conditions— e.g., allusion, pragmatic insincerity, indirect expression of negative attitude—characterizing the prototype of irony, and consequently, utterances with more typicality conditions are recognized to be more ironic, which is intuitively plausible.

To formulate, a measure of similarity between each utterance and the prototype, I consider the following three values, which correspond to the three conditions of implicit display.

d_a: the degree of allusion of an utterance U—to what degree U is coherently related to the speaker's expectation E.

d_i: the degree of pragmatic insincerity of U—to what degree U violates pragmatic principles.

d_e: the degree of indirect expression of negative attitude of U—how many cues (e.g., such as listed in Table 22.1) accompany U.

In this chapter, I assume that each of these values can be measured on a scale of 0 to 1, because these three properties of implicit display are achieved to different degrees.[8] Concerning the degree of allusion d_a, it can be assumed that d_a takes a greater value for an utterance whose P_i is related to Q by the smaller number of coherence relations. Thus, an utterance has the maximum value (i.e., $d_a = 1$) when it mentions the speaker's expectation (i.e., $P_i = Q$), and $d_a = 0$ when it does not allude to the expectation. For example, d_a of the utterance (1a) is greater than that of (1c) because (1a) mentions the expectation, whereas (1c) is connected to the expectation by two coherence relations. The degree of insincerity d_i can be determined according to the seriousness of violation or ease of recognition of the violation: $d_i = 0$

when an utterance does not include any violation, and otherwise $d_i > 0$. Also, d_e takes a greater value when an utterance includes more cues listed in Table 22.1, but $d_e = 0$ when it includes none of these. It must be noted that I am interested in the values of these factors that a hearer (i.e., a person who interprets an utterance) assesses before judging whether the utterance is ironic. The hearer's evaluation of these values often differs from that of the speaker who intends irony. Hence, for example, $d_a = 0$ and $d_i = 0$ are here intended to mean that the hearer can find no allusion to the expectation and no pragmatic insincerity, respectively.[9]

Using these factors, the similarity between an utterance U and the prototype is roughly calculated as the degree of ironicalness $d(U)$ by the following formula:

(8) $\quad d(u) = d_a + d_i + d_e$

The formula reflects the prototype-based view that an utterance satisfying more conditions for implicit display is recognized as being more ironic.

Although the formula (8) seems to work well, I must in fact consider other factors and a more complex composition of these factors so that the degree of ironicalness is consistent with an important feature of irony: its asymmetry. As many studies (e.g., Kreuz & Glucksberg, 1989; Kumon-Nakamura et al., 1995) have pointed out, positive utterances (e.g., "this room is clean") are, in general, recognized to be more ironic than negative utterances (e.g., "this room is messy"). This suggests that the polarity of an utterance plays an important role in assessing the degree of ironicalness. Furthermore, Kreuz and Glucksberg (1989) showed that negative utterances were also perceived appropriately as ironic when the speaker's negative expectation, which was incongruous with a positive event, was obvious to the hearer. For example, people generally expect that New York subways are dirty, so if one encounters a clean train, the negative remark "New York subways are dirty" communicates irony. This finding implies that the obviousness or the manifestness of the expectation also affects the way in which ironic utterances are interpreted: when an expectation is obvious to the hearer, an utterance which alludes to that expectation can be recognized to be ironic regardless of the polarity.

Hence, in order to incorporate the above findings on the asymmetry of irony into the formula for the degree of ironicalness, I will consider the following two factors:

d_d: the degree of context-independent desirability (i.e., polarity) of an utterance U—how positive is the content of U.
d_m: the degree of manifestness of the speaker's expectation E—to what degree the speaker's expectation, which can constitute ironic environment, is manifest to the hearer before interpreting U.

These degrees are also assumed to be measured on a scale of 0 to 1, for the same reason as mentioned above. The degree of desirability d_d takes a positive value (i.e., $1 \geq d_d > 0$) when the content of an utterance is positive, and $d_d = 0$ when it is not positive. The degree of manifestness takes a positive value (i.e., $1 \geq d_m > 0$) when the speaker's expectation is already manifest to the addressee (i.e., he/she knows the expectation), and $d_m = 0$ when it is not manifest at all to the addressee before interpreting an utterance (i.e., he/she does not know the expectation).[10] Presence or absence of allusion is closely related to manifestness of the expectation. If an allusion is recognized by the addressee (i.e., $d_a > 0$), it follows that the alluded expectation, which can motivate irony, is more or less manifest to the addressee, and thus $d_m > 0$.[11] On the other hand, the fact that no allusion can be recognized (i.e., $d_a = 0$) entails that there is no manifest expectation which can constitute ironic environment, and thus $d_m = 0$.[12]

Using the five factors listed in Table 22.2, the degree of ironicalness $d(U)$ can be redefined, as expressed by the following formula:

(9) $d(U) = d_m \bullet d_a + (1 - d_m) \bullet d_d + d_i + d_e$

This formula reflects the asymmetry of irony.[13] Other things (i.e., d_m, d_a, d_i, d_e) being equal, positive utterances are more ironic than negative utterances. At the same time, when the expectation is fully obvious to the hearer (i.e., $d_m = 1$), formula (9) is identical to formula (8); this is consistent with Kreuz and Glucksberg's (1989) finding that utterances alluding to an explicit expectation can be recognized ironically regardless of their polarity. On the other hand, when $d_m = 0$, formula (9) becomes the following:

(10) $d(U) = d_d + d_i + d_e$

Formula (10) means that when the speaker's expectation is not manifest at all before an utterance, the polarity of the utterance greatly affects the degree of ironicalness. Note that it does not mean that irony can be communicated even when there is no speaker's expectation. It merely says that people do not have to know the expectation beforehand in order to understand irony; in such cases, the utterance must include an allusion so that the expectation must be inferred from the utterance, and consequently, positive utterances can facilitate this inference process, as I will explain in the next section.

TABLE 22.2

The Five Factors Determining the Degree of Ironicalness

d_a	the *Degree* of *Allusion* of an utterance to the speaker's expectation
d_i	the *Degree* of pragmatic *Insincerity* involved in an utterance
d_e	the *Degree* of indirect *Expression* of the negative attitude of an utterance
d_d	the *Degree* of context-independent *Desirability* (or polarity) of an utterance
d_m	the *Degree* of *Manifestness* of the speaker's expectation which motivates irony ($d_a = 0$ is equivalent to $d_m = 0$, but $d_a > d_m$ when $d_a, d_m > 0$.)

Distinguishing Irony From Nonirony

According to the implicit display theory, irony is distinguished from nonirony in accordance with the two conditions mentioned earlier:

1. The implicit display condition—irony implicitly displays an ironic environment.
2. The ironic environment condition—irony is given in the situation surrounded by the ironic environment.

When a hearer cannot recognize that an utterance meets both conditions, he/she judges that it is nonironic.

The implicit display condition is checked on the basis of the prototype-based view of irony: implicit display of an utterance U is achieved to the extent that its degree of ironicalness $d(U)$ is high. Given a certain threshold value C (for example, a middle value $C = 1.5$), it is reasonably assumed that an utterance does not implicitly display ironic environment (and thus is not ironic) when its ironicalness value is less than C. For example, the utterance (1a) satisfies the implicit display condition: it mentions the speaker's expectation, which is manifest to the addressee (i.e., $d_a = 1$, $d_m = 1$), it is an obviously insincere statement (i.e., $d_i > 0$; > means "much greater than"), it includes a hyperbolic word (i.e., $d_e > 0$), and thereby, $d(U)$ is estimated at a higher value than C by (9). At the same time, when an utterance directly expresses ironic environment, as in the cases of (1d) and (1e) in section 3.2, it is judged not to achieve implicit display, and thus, to be nonironic.

When the implicit display condition is satisfied, the ironic environment condition is then checked, using the information about how the utterance achieves implicit display. The reason for checking the implicit display condition in advance of the ironic environment condition is that hearers cannot decide whether the known expectation motivates irony (i.e., whether it is a constituent of the ironic environment) unless they know whether the utterance alludes to that expectation. When hearers readily recognize an allusion to the speaker's expectation, they only examine whether the known expectation constitutes an ironic environment. Then, if the hearers can recognize or presuppose both the incongruity of the known expectation and the negative attitude, they simultaneously judge the utterance as ironic. On the other hand, if the hearers perceive that the expectation cannot constitute an ironic environment (e.g., the expectation is fulfilled in the situation, as in the case of Situation 4 in section 3.1), they judge the utterance as being nonironic.

In case the hearers do not know the speaker's expectation beforehand or they cannot find any allusion to the known expectation (i.e., d_m is 0 or very small), the ironic environment must be inferred from the information about how the utterance achieves implicit display by a process of hypothesis formation and evaluation.[14] In the inference process, an assumption about the speaker's expectation is derived from the content of the utterance and checked for whether it is attributable to the speaker and relevant to the situation (the expectation condition), whether it is incompatible to the situation (the incongruity condition), and whether a negative attitude can be elicited (the negative attitude condition). If the hearers recognize through the inference process that there is a reason to suppose that the discourse situation is surrounded by ironic environment, they judge the utterance as ironic and end up sharing the ironic environment with the speaker. On the other hand, when the hearers fail to infer the speaker's expectation (which constitutes an ironic environment), they judge the utterance as being nonironic even though they recognize that the implicit display is achieved.

For example, the addressee Peter perceives Brenda's utterance (2) in Situation 2 (where $d_m = 0$) as ironic if he can recognize that the two conditions are met. Indeed, utterance (2) satisfies the implicit display condition: it has high values of d_d (a positive statement) and d_e (especially when it is accompanied by prosodic cues), and thus $d(U)$ is estimated at a higher value than C by (9). Therefore, when Peter (and other hearers) can infer without contradiction that Brenda expected a good morning, but the morning was terrible and she felt unhappy, he interprets (2) ironically, and as a result, he ends up knowing that Situation 2 is surrounded by an ironic environment. On the other hand, the following utterance (1g) cannot be perceived as ironic when it is uttered by the mother in Situation 1.

(1) g.   Hawaii is really beautiful!

This utterance meets the implicit display condition since it does not allude to the known expectation that the room is clean (i.e., $d_m = 0$) and thus it obtains high values for d_d, d_i, d_e. Nevertheless, the utterance is nonironic in accordance with the ironic environment condition: hearers cannot assume the speaker's expectation to be relevant to Situation 1 from the content of (1g) and thus cannot presuppose the ironic environment that makes (1g) ironic.

From the above discussion, I conclude that to interpret irony is to know that the discourse situation is surrounded by an ironic environment: irony communicates the information about .the ironic environment to the addressees. In the case of typical irony, since the addressee already knows that the three conditions for ironic environment hold in the situation, interpretation of irony results in confirmation of the most uncertain information, that is, the speaker's negative attitude. That is why the previous irony theories argue that irony communicates the speaker's negative attitude. On the other hand, when the addressee does not recognize the ironic environment beforehand, he/she also obtains any new information that the unrecognized components hold in the current situation.

SUPERIORITY OVER THE PREVIOUS APPROACHES TO IRONY

Superiority Over the Violation-Based Approach

In section 2.1, I showed that violation of pragmatic principles is neither a necessary nor a sufficient property of irony, which is why the violation-based approach fails to distinguish irony from nonirony. Although pragmatic insincerity in this paper does not significantly differ from the violation of the maxim of quality or felicity conditions in the case of speech acts, the implicit display theory, in particular the prototype-based view, can solve the problems described in section 2.1.

First, the implicit display theory correctly accounts for ironic utterances which include no pragmatic insincerity or which hearers cannot recognize as including pragmatic insincerity such as (1b) and (2). Although the degree of insincerity d_i is 0 for these utterances, then ironicalness values can be high enough to meet the implicit display condition when other factors (e.g., d_a, d_d, d_e) have high values (of course, at the same time, the ironic environment must be satisfied). Second, the implicit display theory distinguishes ironic utterances from nonironic ones, including those based on violation/insincerity: situations in which such nonironic utterances are given are not surrounded by any ironic environment, or the degrees of ironicalness of those utterances are assessed at relatively small values. Third, the implicit display theory does not assume that irony conveys the opposite of the literal meaning. Verbal irony implicitly conveys the information about the three events/states in the current situation surrounded by the ironic environment.

Allusion and Echoic Interpretation

In section 2.2, I showed, using the examples of nonechoic irony and nonironic echo, that Sperber and Wilson's (1986; Wilson & Sperber 1992) echoic interpretation is neither a necessary nor a sufficient property of irony. In this section, I will show that my notion of allusion essentially differs from echoic interpretation, and consequently that the implicit display theory is successful in explaining nonechoic irony and nonironic echo.

The most important difference between allusion and echoic interpretation lies in what sources are allowed to be echoed/alluded to by irony, in particular, whether only the speakers' expectation is assumed to trigger irony. The echoic interpretation theory argues that irony echoes not only the speaker's expectation but also other sources such as other person's utterances, opinions, or even general norms. However, because of this argument, the theory cannot provide a consistent explanation for a variety of ironic utterances such as (3a) and (3b), as described in section 2.2.

[Situation 3] Jesse said "I'd be promoted before you" to his colleague Peter. This elicited the following reply:

(3) a. Oh! You'd be promoted before me.
    b. Thank you for informing me of your priceless opinion.

Furthermore, in the following exchange between Peter and his other colleague, James, who does not know what Jesse had said

(3) c. James: What did Jesse said to you?

    d. Peter (with ridiculing aversion): He'd be promoted before me.

Peter's utterance (3d) echoes Jesse's preceding utterance and Peter simultaneously dissociates himself from Jesse's opinion, echoed in the same way as (3a), but no irony results. Hence, the sources which the echoic interpretation theory assumes irony to echo are too general to exclude nonironic echoic utterances. According to the implicit display theory, every ironic utterance alludes to the speaker's, not other person's, expectations. Therefore, in the cases of (3a) and (3b), the ironic intention is provoked by the speaker's expectation concerning Jesse's utterance or opinion, not by Jesse's utterance itself. The speaker's expectation in Situation 3 is something like that Jesse should know that his preceding utterance (and the opinion expressed) is false.[15] The reason that (3d) is not ironic is that the addressee James does not (or cannot) assume any irony-motivating expectation of the speaker relevant to the current exchange and thus it does not meet the ironic environment condition (and it may not meet the implicit display condition since he knows no manifest expectations, it is not a positive statement for James, and it does not include insincerity).[16] For the same reason, the echo (4b) in section 2.2 is not ironic.

    Another point that differentiates allusion in the framework of the implicit display theory from Sperber and Wilson's echoic interpretation is what relations are allowed between an ironic utterance and an echoed/alluded source. As I mentioned in section 2.2, the relation between an echoic interpretation and its echoed source is characterized by a sharing of implications; however, some ironies such as (3b) cannot be analyzed as a sharing of implications. On the other hand, the implicit display theory argues that the relation between an ironic utterance and an alluded expectation is best analyzed by coherence relations. For example, the utterance (3b) is coherently related to the speaker's expectation, because it refers to Jesse's action of informing that Jesse would be promoted before Peter and that action precludes the speaker's expected state of affairs. Hence (3b) alludes to the speaker's expectation and as a result it is ironic.

Pretense and Victims

In section 2.3, I explained that the pretense theory (including the joint pretense view) cannot distinguish irony from nonirony and thus fails to account for how people become victims of irony. Since I already have shown the superiority of the implicit display theory with respect to the irony–nonirony distinction, I will show in this section that the implicit display theory provides a plausible explanation for how irony creates its victims.

    My explanation of the victims' predicament is quite simple: victims of irony are persons (or agents, in terms of artificial intelligence) who performed intentional actions because of which the ironist's expectation was not realized. Thus, victimless ironies such as "What lovely weather" in the rain have no victims because, the ironist's expected states of affairs (i.e., fine weather) accidentally failed without someone's intentional actions. Moreover, although pretense theory cannot explain that the mother's son is the victim of ironies in Situation 1, the implicit display theory assumes him to be the victim because his action of reading a comic book prevented him from cleaning up the room and as a result the mother's expectation of the room being clean was not fulfilled.

This view of irony victims has its merit in that it does not need to posit different explanations for different victims. All victims are explained in the same way: anybody who precludes the realization of the speaker's expectation becomes a potential victim. Imagine, for instance, the following situation:

[Situation 7] Against Judy's advice, Bill bought what a crooked art dealer told him was a true Picasso. Roger, claiming to be competent, vouched for the painting's authenticity. Other friends of Bill's were much impressed by the painting until a genuine expert at last showed it to be a fake. Judy then says the following to them:

(11)   That was a truly beautiful Picasso! (Sperber, 1984, p. 134)

In this case, Bill, Roger, and Bill's friends are the victims of the irony (11). Although Sperber (1984) stated that they are victims in different ways, in my view they are victims for one and the same reason: they all precluded the realization of Judy's expectation. For example, Bill's action of buying the fake painting precluded Judy's expectation that Bill should not buy it, and thus he is a victim. Furthermore, on account of the speaker's expectation about the addressee's thought or utterance (as in the case of Situation 3), the addressee becomes a victim in that his/her action of expressing or informing his/her own thought or opinion can be seen as precluding the expectation. Therefore, Roger and Bill's friends are also victims. Roger vouched for the authenticity, which simultaneously precluded Judy's expectation that Roger should know his incompetence. In the same way, Bill's friends canceled Judy's expectation that they should know that their opinion is false.

Understanding Irony With and Without Ironic Cues

Some studies (e.g., Cutler, 1974; Clark & Gerrig, 1984) assume that irony can be recognized by ironic cues, in particular, ironic tone of voice or ironic intonation. There is little doubt that these cues often accompany ironic utterances, but these cues are neither sufficient nor necessary properties of irony. Empirical studies have demonstrated the following:

- People can interpret ironic statements without any special intonational cues, since irony is perceived in written discourse (Gibbs & O'Brien, 1991).
- These cues can also be used for nonironic purposes (Barbe, 1995): both ironic and nonironic interpretations are derived from the use of the same intonational contour in different contexts (Ward & Hirschberg, 1985).

The implicit display theory is consistent with these findings. An utterance without ironic cues (i.e., $d_e = 0$) is ironic when values of other factors (e.g., d_a, d_d, d_i) are high enough for its ironicalness value to meet the implicit display condition (and when the discourse context meets the ironic environment condition). On the other hand, an utterance accompanied by these cues (i.e., with a high d_e value) is nonironic when the values of the other factors are so low that the utterance does not satisfy the implicit display condition, or when the discourse context does not meet the ironic environment condition.

PSYCHOLOGICAL VALIDITY OF THE IMPLICIT DISPLAY THEORY

The implicit display theory makes the following predictions about irony rating and about the comprehension time of irony:

1. More prototypical ironies (i.e., ironies with greater degrees of ironicalness) are perceived as more ironic and are processed faster.
2. Ironies given in a situation that is more easily identified as ironic environment are processed faster (e.g., ironies in the context where the speaker's expectation is manifest to the addressees are processed faster than ironies in the contexts where the expectation is not known beforehand or less manifest).

The first prediction indicates that ironic utterances vary greatly as to their rating and comprehension time. Concerning irony rating, each property of implicit display has been examined separately in a number of psychological experiments, although there are no experimental studies which directly examine the interaction of the five factors with respect to the degree of ironicalness. For instance, Kumon-Nakamura et al. (1995) demonstrated that allusion and pragmatic insincerity differentiate ironic utterances from literal ones, and Kreuz and Roberts (1995) revealed that hyperbole facilitates the perception of irony. These results can be seen as empirical support for my first prediction about irony rating. On the other hand, there are no on-line studies which examine the first prediction about comprehension time. The second prediction suggests that context can greatly affect the processing time of ironies. Some experimental studies (e.g., Jorgensen et al., 1984; Gibbs, 1986) which attempted to show the effect of echoic mention can be seen as examining this prediction.

The rest of this section and section 6 show how the predictions of the implicit display theory are consistent with the existing psychological findings on irony.

Allusion and Expectation

Gibbs (1986) conducted an experiment, which assessed comprehension times (and reaction times for making the paraphrase judgments) for ironic utterances in explicit and implicit contexts. Each explicit context contained the statements motivating an explicit echoic mention of some belief or expectation whereas the implicit contexts contained no such statements. Examples of the story contexts and the target sentences presented in Gibbs are as follows:

[Explicit context (Situation 8)] Gus just graduated from high school and he didn't know what to do. One day he saw an ad about the Navy. It said that the Navy was not just a job, but an adventure. So, Gus joined up. Soon he was aboard a ship doing all sorts of boring things. One day as he was peeling potatoes he said the following to his buddy:

(12)   "This sure is an exciting life."

[Implicit context (Situation 9)] Gus just graduated from high school and he didn't know what to do. So, Gus went out and joined the Navy. Soon he was aboard a ship doing all sorts of boring things. One day as he was peeling potatoes he said the following to his buddy:

(13)   "This sure is an exciting life."

The result was that subjects significantly took less time understand ironic remarks (and to make paraphrase judgments) in the explicit contexts than they did to process the same remarks in the implicit contexts.

This finding can be explained by the implicit display theory (i.e., the second prediction mentioned above). In the explicit contexts, the speaker's expectations (e.g., in the above story, the speaker Gus expected an adventurous and exciting life in the Navy) are quite manifest to hearers (and the subjects of the experiment), but in the implicit contexts the speaker's expectations are much less manifest. In other words, it can be reasonably assumed that the degrees of manifestness d_m for the explicit contexts are much greater than those for the implicit contexts (possibly $d_m = 0$). Therefore, in the implicit contexts, the subjects (and hearers) must identify the speaker's expectation through an additional inference process, while in the explicit contexts, they recognize an allusion to the manifest expectation without difficulty, as I explained in section 3.4. As a result, the ironic remarks in the explicit contexts take less time to process than in the implicit contexts.

Asymmetry of Irony and Expectation

As I mentioned in section 3.3, the degree of ironicalness is designed to accord with the asymmetry of irony. In the present section, I will explain how the formulation of the degree of ironicalness and the implicit display theory are consistent with further psychological findings about the asymmetry of irony.

Kreuz and Glucksberg (1989) showed that the availability of a victim is more important for negative sarcastic remarks than for positive ones: when an explicit victim was available, appropriateness ratings of positive and negative sarcastic statements did not differ, while when there were no available victims, sentence polarity had a considerable effect (i.e., positive statements were rated as more appropriate than negative ones). Since (as they assumed) the availability of victims provides one measure of explicitness/manifestness of an expectation, such interaction between victim availability and sentence polarity can be seen as the interaction between d_m and d_a, such that in fact the degree of ironicalness predicts the interaction: the term $(1-d_m)$ d_a of the formula (9) indicates that, other things being equal, d_a has little effect on $d(U)$ when $d_m \gg 1$ (i.e., $1-d_m \approx 0$), but has a considerable effect when $d_m = 0$ (i.e., $1-d_m = 1$).

More importantly, Kumon-Nakamura et al. (1995) showed that counterfactual positive utterances were still recognized to be ironic even when the speaker's negative expectation was obvious to the addressees. This finding indicates that when a positive ironic utterance does not allude to the known negative expectation, an alternative (positive) expectation of the speaker is inferred so that the utterance includes an allusion. Furthermore, Gibbs (1986) showed that when there were no explicit expectations, counterfactual positive utterances were rated as more ironic and processed faster than counterfactual negative ones. Taken together, these results support the implicit display theory and the formula for the degree of ironicalness. When a hearer does not recognize that an utterance alludes to the speaker's expectation (i.e., $d_a = d_m = 0$), the degree of ironicalness is considerably affected by sentence polarity (as formula 9 indicates), where a positive utterance facilitates the inference process of the speaker's expectation.

PROCESSING TIMES FOR IRONIC AND LITERAL UTTERANCES

A number of studies have proposed comprehension models of figurative language which make different predictions about processing times for literal versus figurative utterances. For irony comprehension, Gibbs (1986) demonstrated that people did not take any longer to interpret ironic sentences than they did to interpret nonironic literal equivalent sentences. This result seems to imply that the traditional pragmatic view (or the so-called standard pragmatic model, e.g., Grice, 1975; Searle, 1979a) is incorrect, inasmuch as it predicts that ironic expressions would always take more time to process than literal language. On the other hand, Giora (1995) contended that a reanalysis of Gibbs's (1986) findings evinces that ironic utterances take longer to process than nonironic ones. The point of her reanalysis is that it is the processing times of the same sentence embedded in different (literally/ironically motivating) contexts which should be measured, while Gibbs (1986) arrives at his conclusion by comparing different (ironic/literal) sentences with the same implicated meaning in the same context. Moreover, Giora (1997) maintained that such reinterpreted findings are consistent with the so-called graded salience hypothesis, according to which salient meanings are processed first before less salient meanings are activated.

Although I agree with Giora's critique of the comparison method for measuring comprehension time differences and even though I accept her graded salience hypothesis, I do not agree with one point: viz., that irony always takes longer to process than nonironic literal language.[17] I believe that while sometimes ironic interpretation proceeds slower than literal interpretation, at other times an ironic interpretation does not take longer to process than its literal counterpart. I will therefore try to show that Gibbs's (1986) experimental results can be interpreted differently by means of Giora's (1995) comparison method, so that irony does not always take longer to process. In addition, I will explain that the predictions of the implicit display theory, as shown in section 5, suggest such a result.

In Gibbs's (1986) experiment (Experiment 1), four types of texts—sarcastic and nonsarcastic sentences in negative contexts and literal and compliment sentences in positive contexts—were used to measure comprehension times for ironic versus literal sentences. Here is a sample of the texts presented in Gibbs (1986):

[Negative context (Situation 10)] Harry was building an addition to his house. He was working real hard putting in the foundation. His younger brother was supposed to help. But he never showed up. At the end of a long day, Harry's brother finally appeared. Harry was a bit upset with him. Harry said the following to his brother:

(14) a. [Sarcastic target] You're a big help.
     b. [Nonsarcastic target] You're not helping me.

[Positive context (Situation 11)] Greg was having trouble with calculus. He had a big exam coming up and he was in trouble. Fortunately, his roommate tutored him on some of the basics. When they were done, Greg felt he'd learned a lot. "Well," he said to his roommate

(15) a. [Literal target] You're a big help.
     b. [Compliment target] Thanks for your help.

If Giora's argument for the time-course of irony comprehension is right, the sarcastic (ironic) utterances (e.g., 14a) should take longer than the nonironic literal uses of the same sentences (e.g., 15a). However, the result does not support this prediction: the differences in comprehension times were not significant (Gibbs, 1986, p. 6). Giora (1995) explained the result of the equal comprehension times in terms of discourse well-formedness. For instance, the sarcastic utterance (14a) is highly informative in Situation 10; in contrast, the literal utterance (15a) in Situation 11 states the obvious. Hence, the longer reading times for the sarcastic utterances predicted by the graded salience hypothesis are offset by the relative well-formedness of the sarcastic utterances as compared to the literal uses of the same sentences. Giora (1995) therefore claimed that the sarcastic utterances (e.g., 14a) should be compared with the literal compliment utterances (e.g., 15b) because, for example, both (14a) and (15b) are equally informative (i.e., they are thanking ironically/literally); also, Gibbs's result indeed shows that the sarcastic utterances took significantly longer to comprehend than the compliment ones. However, such a comparison does not justify Giora's claim as to the time-course of ironic and literal comprehension: there is a possibility that ironic uses of the compliment sentences (e.g., saying "Thanks for your help" ironically) would not take longer to process than literal uses of the same sentences (e.g., 15b).

The observed equal reading times for the sarcastic sentences and the literal use of the same sentences can be explained by the implicit display theory. Sarcastic sentences like (14a) are highly prototypical ironies (i.e., they can be readily recognized as satisfying all the conditions for implicit display) and the negative contexts like Situation 10 are easily identified as ironic environments (i.e., all the components of the ironic environment are manifest to the subjects). Therefore, comprehension of these ironies does not need an additional inference process, and for this reason, there would be little time difference between the sarcastic utterances and the literal appropriate utterances like (15a).

On the other hand, another of Gibbs's (1986) experiments (Experiment 3), in which the following texts were used, demonstrated that the sarcastic utterance of both sentence types took longer to process than the nonsarcastic use of the same sentences.

[Normative (negative) context (Situation 12)] Billy and Joe were long-time pals. But one time when Billy was away on a business trip, Joe slept with Billy's wife, Lynn. When Billy found out about it afterwards, he was upset. He confronted Joe and said the following to him:

(16) a. [Sarcastic target] You're a fine friend.
    b. [Nonsarcastic target] You're a terrible friend.

[Non-normative (positive) context (Situation 13)] Billy and Joe were long-time pals. One time Billy was in desperate need of money. His car had broken down and he needed $300 to fix it. So, he asked Joe for a loan. Joe said he could lend Billy the money. This made Billy happy and he said the following to Joe:

(17) a. [Sarcastic target] You're a terrible friend.
    b. [Nonsarcastic target] You're a fine friend.

This result, too, can be explained by the implicit display theory. The stories used in the experiment are constructed so that there are no explicit expectations (Gibbs, 1986), and thus, ironic interpretation in both types of context needs the additional process of inferring the speaker's expectation. Taken together with the observation referred to above that there is no significant time difference between ironic and literal utterances, when the speaker's expectation is manifest, the second prediction in section 5 implies that ironic utterances without manifest expectations take longer to process than literal utterances.

Giora's (1997, 1999) graded salience hypothesis is a general principle that governs literal and figurative language comprehension. According to the graded salience hypothesis, the most salient meaning is processed first, and if it is rejected as the intended meaning, a less salient meaning is then processed. Thus, this view assumes no priority with respect to literality, and I agree with the graded salience hypothesis in this respect. Concerning irony comprehension, Giora (1997) stated that the ironic meaning of unconventional irony is less salient than its literal meaning: "Even if irony were a widespread practice, ironic meanings have not for the most part been conventionalized, i.e., made salient (though context may contribute to their salience)" (pp. 192–193). The graded salience hypothesis, she argued, then predicts that (unconventional) ironic utterances always take more time to process than the same utterances used literally. Giora et al. (1998) showed findings in favor of this prediction: ironic utterances (e.g., "You are just in time" when a student is late for the lecture) took longer to read than the same utterances used literally (Experiment 1), while the literal meanings of the ironic utterances were activated first and were not suppressed even when the ironic meanings were activated (Experiments 2 and 3).

However, I do not agree with Giora's argument about the time difference between ironic and literal utterances being explained by the graded salience hypothesis, because Giora underestimates the important role of context in language comprehension. It is doubtful that the fact that the literal meaning of irony is activated first entails that the whole literal interpretation of a literal sentence is processed faster than the whole ironic interpretation of the same sentence. The implicit display theory provides an alternative explanation of the time difference, one that is consistent with Giora et al.'s (1998) findings. According to the implicit display theory, the ironic interpretation of an ironic utterance requires the presence of the literal sentence meaning, because people must assess the degree of ironicalness and/or infer the speaker's expectation in order to interpret the irony (the view that irony requires computation of the literal meaning is also consistent with Giora's [1995] indirect negation view of irony). Hence, after the literal meaning of irony is computed first, the ironic interpretation is derived from the information provided by the literal meaning and the contextual information.

As to literal interpretation, this is carried out along the same lines: literal interpretation is also inferentially derived from the immediately computed literal meaning and the contextual information (for a similar view of literal and nonliteral interpretation, see Récanati, 1995). Therefore, the processing time difference between the ironic and the literal interpretation can be attributed to the time difference in the process of discourse interpretation in which the speaker's meaning is derived from the sentence meaning and context. This view of literal and ironic comprehension is consistent with the second prediction of the implicit display theory presented in section 5. The longer comprehension times of irony shown by Giora et al. (1998) may then be explained as the result of the discourse contexts for irony being less easily identified as ironic environment; as the above discussion of Gibbs's findings shows, irony would be easily processed if it were given in a situation where the ironic environment is manifest to the hearers.

From these discussions, one important point becomes clear: there seem to be no principles common to all ironies that would decide on a priority of ironic over literal language with respect to ease of processing (this point must be justified by further empirical research). More prototypical ironies in the contexts in which the speaker's expectation is manifest would be processed faster than, or as fast as, literal language, and the less prototypical ironies in contexts in which the speaker's expectation is not manifest would be processed slower than literal language.

CONCLUSION

In order to provide a reliable explanation of how people distinguish ironic utterances from nonironic ones, this chapter has proposed the implicit display theory of verbal irony. The essential points of the theory are as follows:

1. Verbal irony presupposes a proper situational setting, which has been described in terms of ironic environment. An ironic environment consists of the speaker's expectation, an incongruity between expectation and reality, and the speaker's negative attitude toward this incongruity.
2. Verbal irony is a verbal expression (utterance or statement) that implicitly displays an ironic environment. This implicit display of the ironic environment is, in the most prototypical cases, achieved by an utterance which alludes to the speaker's expectation, violates one of the pragmatic principles, and is accompanied by indirect cues.
3. Verbal irony is distinguished from nonirony in accordance with both the ironic environment condition and the implicit display condition: in order for an utterance to be interpreted ironically, the utterance must be recognized as achieving implicit display through the process of assessing the degree of ironicalness, and the situation must be identified as an ironic environment through the process of checking or inferring the three components. The degree of ironicalness is quantitatively defined as a measure of similarity between the prototype of irony and an utterance; it embodies the prototype-based view of irony that the ironical character of an utterance is a matter of degree.

These points permit the implicit display theory to overcome the difficulties involved in previous irony theories, and to be much more comprehensive. The main problem with the previous studies is that they have attempted to provide necessary and/or sufficient properties for distinguishing irony from nonirony; however, there appear to be no such properties shared by all ironic utterances. On the other hand, the prototype-based view taken by the implicit display theory does not need such common properties. Rather, it takes the comparative view in which the property of irony implicit display is achieved to the extent that the degree of ironicalness is high. Furthermore, the implicit display theory argues that only the expectations possessed by speakers can motivate them to use language ironically. When the speaker has no expectation which is identifiable and relevant to the situation, his/her utterance is not perceived as ironic even if it echoes other persons' utterances, opinions, or general norms. Echoic irony should similarly be analyzed by an allusion to the speaker's expectation concerning someone's opinion or utterance. This view of echoed sources gives the implicit display theory an advantage over Sperber and Wilson's (1986; Wilson & Sperber, 1992) echoic interpretation theory, which has been the dominant view of irony.

The implicit display theory is consistent with several empirical findings. The ironic environment condition indicates the important role of context in interpreting irony. It predicts that ironies in a context where the speaker's expectation is known by hearers beforehand are interpreted faster than ironies in contexts where such expectation is not available; the psychological findings about echoic mention support this prediction. On the other hand, the degree of ironicalness $d(U)$ explains the observed interaction between sentence polarity and expectation availability. Furthermore, the degree of ironicalness poses interesting questions for further empirical research. For example, formula (9) would predict that exceedingly positive statements in the context where no speaker's expectation is available (i.e., $d_m = 0$; $d_d = 1$) are judged to be more ironic than statements related to the fully manifest expectation by a number of coherence relations (i.e., $d_m = 1$; $d_a < 1$). The question is, if this really is the case. This question notwithstanding, the implicit display theory would also hold promise as the basis for a psychologically testable theory of verbal irony.

Of course, I do not suppose that this chapter gives a complete theory of verbal irony: the implicit display theory has its limitations. One crucial limitation is that the theory does not address the functions of irony, which is a recent topic to emerge in the empirical studies of irony (Roberts & Kreuz, 1994; Dews & Winner, 1995; Dews et al., 1995; Jorgensen, 1996; Ito & Takizawa, 1996). Irony offers an effective way of accomplishing various communication goals that are difficult to achieve literally: positive goals (e.g., to be humorous, to emphasize a point) and negative goals (e.g., to be sarcastic, to give pain, to criticize). One interesting question that arises here is how a speaker's intended goals affect the decision on how to accomplish implicit display, i.e., which of the coherence relations should be used for allusion, which of the pragmatic principles should be violated, and what cues should be used to convey the attitude. To take a simple example, ironic utterances employed to achieve the goal of giving pain to an addressee or of being sarcastic seem to have some common properties—they refer to a victim's action (or one of its premises/effects), which precludes the speaker's expectation, they have a surface speech act of expressives like thanking, and they express the counterfactual pleased emotion toward the victim's action—although this hypothesis has, as yet, no empirical support. It would be interesting to try and extend the implicit display theory so as to account for the functions of irony. In a related development, I am trying to develop a computational model of irony interpretation based on the implicit display theory in order to obtain further evidence in favor of the theory (Utsumi, 1996, 1999).

ACKNOWLEDGMENT

I would like to thank two anonymous reviewers for their helpful comments and suggestions.

ENDNOTES

1. Of course, we can give explicit expressions like the following utterance to convey ironic intention to hearers with little common ground or to avoid the risk of misinterpretation: "I am going to be ironic now: I just love people who have all the money for warfare but none for welfare" (Barbe, 1995, p. 140). However, such irony loses its effectiveness and it is pragmatically un-well-formed.
2. Sperber and Wilson (1998) argued that (1b) ironically echoes the higher order explicature that the utterance is relevant in the circumstances, e.g., that the room is clean and the mother praises her child sincerely. However, such an explanation would lead the echoic interpretation theory astray. If the explanation by the higher order explicature is right, many other cases of irony like (1a) for which they provide different explanations (e.g., echo of someone's utterance, expectation, or general norms) can also be explained along the same line (e.g., 1a can also be seen as an echo of the same higher order explicature). Hence, they must explain why they do not apply the echo of the higher order explicature to such cases of irony.
3. All examples of ironic environment include the speaker's negative attitude (or some kind of criticism in terms of Barbe, 1995), but there are negative attitudes of different degrees and types. Some are strong, and others are weak; some are serious, but others are joking.
4. As I mentioned in the introduction, ironic environment differs from both ironic situation and situational irony. The example of Situation 1 serves to recognize the difference: outside Situation 1, the utterances (1a)—(1c) cannot have ironic meanings, but Situation 1 is not at all ironic. It is very unlikely for someone to say "It's ironic that a mother discovered that her son did not clean up his room in spite of her advice."
5. It must be noted here that by this phrase, I mean that the possibility that a discourse context is surrounded by ironic environment is denied. Therefore, it does not rule out the cases (e.g., Situation 2) in which hearers are not sure whether the situation is surrounded by ironic environment.
6. When the propositional content includes variables (e.g., the contents of WH-questions), "being identical" can be replaced by "being unifiable." That P and X are unifiable means that they become identical when we simultaneously replace each occurrence of the variable in P and X by the same constant.
7. Some understatements such as (1c) can also be analyzed as violations of the maxim of quality or truthfulness. However, which of Grice's maxims is violated is not important here.
8. The numerical values ranging from 0 to 1 are here intended only as a model of relative measures of proportions of these factors. Therefore, I do not intend to claim that these values should be measured on a scale of 0 to 1, nor do I intend to claim that such scale is psychologically plausible. The point I want to clarify here is that the three properties of implicit display are of different degrees of achievement and thus should be quantitatively measured. A similar view is taken by Sperber and Wilson (1981, p. 309) about the echoic nature of irony: "there are echoic mentions of many different degrees and types."

9. How these values should be determined for real examples is a complicated problem. One possible solution would be that they are empirically determined through a statistical method for training on naturally occurring examples or for human ratings used in the field of natural language processing.

10. Manifestness of the expectation is also a matter of degree, although it is much more difficult to determine such values. For example, expectations the speaker previously has mentioned to the addressee—i.e., when mutual knowledge about the expectations is established by linguistic co-presence, in Clark and Marshall's (1981) terms—would be more manifest than expectations the speaker did not mention (but the addressee knows).

11. It does not follow that $d = d$, since allusion is a property of an utterance (i.e., relevance of an utterance to the expectation), while manifestness is a property of an expectation (i.e., addressee's ease of access to the expectation). Therefore, though closely related, these two factors should be separately considered.

12. There are two cases in which no allusion can be found. One case is when the addressee does not know any speaker's expectations beforehand; the other case is when the addressee knows some speaker's expectations, but judges that none of the known expectations are alluded to by an utterance. In both cases, the speaker's expectation which can trigger irony is not known beforehand, and thus $d = 0$.

13. How formula (9) is consistent with the asymmetry of irony will be elaborated on in section 5.2.

14. Some inferences are also required when the hearers recognize an allusion to the known expectation, but are not sure of the incongruity and/or the negative attitude. However, such an inference process differs from the process of inferring the expectation here. The former process only tests whether the known expectation constitutes an ironic environment, but the latter process needs a generate-and-test procedure to infer the expectation.

15. Kaufer (1981) mentioned a similar view in his discussion of what assumptions about the context may ironize clearly false utterances like "Columbus discovered America in 1900." He argued that, in order to be perceived as irony, such utterance must be given in the contextual setting in which "the ironist knows the utterance is false (and thus rejects it), knows that the addressee does not know this, and (most importantly) also *believes that the latter should know it*" (p. 503, italics added). This argument also applies to utterances the speaker believes to be false, such as the echo (3a) of Jesse's preceding utterance. Especially the last assumption in Kaufer's argument, viz., that the ironist believes that the addressee should know that the utterance is false, obviously corresponds to the speaker's expectation of echoic irony as explained here.

16. The echoic utterance (3d) is also an appropriate answer to James's question, which can be another reason that (3d) is not interpreted as ironic. This explanation of such nonironic echoes is given by Giora (1995) in terms of discourse well-formedness.

17. The graded salience hypothesis also predicts that conventional/familiar ironies do not take longer to process than equivalent literal sentences, because their ironic and literal meanings are equally salient (Giora, 1999). In the rest of this section, I argue against the claim that unconventional ironic utterances, whose ironic meanings are less salient, always take longer to process than nonironic literal expressions

REFERENCES

Barbe, K. (1995). *Irony in context.* Amsterdam: Benjamins.

Brown, P., & Levinson, S. C. (1987). *Politeness: Some universals in language usage.* Cambridge, England: Cambridge University Press.

Clark, H. H. (1996). *Using language.* Cambridge, England: Cambridge University Press.

Clark, H. H., & Gerrig, R. (1984). On the pretense theory of irony. *Journal of Experimental Psychology: General, 113,* 121–126.

Clark, H. H., &. Marshall, C. R. (1981). Definite reference and mutual knowledge. In A. Joshi, B. Webber, & I. Sag (Eds.), *Elements of discourse understanding* (pp. 10–63). Cambridge, England: Cambridge University Press.

Cutler, A. (1974). On saying what you mean without meaning what you say. In M. Lagaly, R. Fox, & A. Bruck (Eds.), *Papers from the tenth regional meeting of the Chicago Linguistics Society* (pp. 117–127). Chicago: University of Chicago Press.

Dews, S., Kaplan, J., & Winner, E. (1995). Why not say it directly?: The social functions of irony. *Discourse Processes, 19,* 347–367.

Dews, S., & Winner, E. (1995). Muting the meaning: A social function of irony. *Metaphor and Symbolic Activity, 10,* 3–19.

Gibbs, R. W. (1986). On the psycholinguistics of sarcasm. *Journal of Experimental Psychology General: 115,* 3–15.

Gibbs, R. W. (1994). *The poetics of mind.* Cambridge, England: Cambridge University Press. Gibbs, R. W., & O'Brien, J. (1991). Psychological aspects of irony understanding. *Journal of Pragmatics, 16,* 523–530.

Gibbs, R. W., O'Brien, J., & Doolittle, S. (1995). Inferring meanings that are not intended: Speakers' intentions and irony comprehension. *Discourse Processes, 20,* 187–203.

Giora, R. (1995). On irony and negation. *Discourse Processes, 19,* 239–264.

Giora, R. (1997). Understanding figurative and literal language: The graded salience hypothesis. *Cognitive Linguistics, 8,* 183–206.

Giora, R. (1999). On the priority of salient meanings: Studies of literal and figurative language. *Journal of Pragmatics, 31,* 919–929.

Giora, R., Fein, O., & Schwartz, T. (1998). Irony: Graded salience and indirect negation. *Metaphor and Symbol, 13,* 83–101.

Glucksberg, S. (1995). Commentary on nonliteral language: Processing and use. *Metaphor and Symbolic Activity, 10,* 47–57.

Grice, P. H. (1975). Logic and conversation. In P. Cole & J. Morgan (Eds.), *Syntax and semantics Vol. 3: Speech acts* (pp. 41–58). New York: Academic.

Haverkate, H. (1990). A speech act analysis of irony. *Journal of Pragmatics, 14,* 77–109.

Ito, A., & Takizawa, O. (1996). Why do people use irony?: The pragmatics of irony usage. *Proceedings of the International Workshop on Computational Humor (IWCH'96),* 21–28.

Jorgensen, J. C. (1996). The functions of sarcastic irony in speech. *Journal of Pragmatics, 26,* 613–634.

Jorgensen, J. C., Miller, G. A., & Sperber, D. (1984). Test of the mention theory of irony. *Journal of Experimental Psychology: General, 113,* 112–120.

Kaufer, D. (1981). Understanding ironic communication. *Journal of Pragmatics, 5,* 495–510.

Kreuz, R. J., & Glucksberg, S. (1989). How to be sarcastic: The echoic reminder theory of verbal irony. *Journal of Experimental Psychology: General, 118,* 374–386.

Kreuz, R. J., & Roberts, R. M. (1995). Two cues for verbal irony: Hyperbole and the ironic tone of voice. *Metaphor and Symbolic Activity, 10,* 21–31.

Kumon-Nakamura, S., Glucksberg, S., & Brown, M. (1995). How about another piece of pie. The allusional pretense theory of discourse irony. *Journal of Experimental Psychology: General, 124,* 3–21.

Lakoff, G. (1987). *Women, fire, and dangerous things: What categories reveal about the mind.* Chicago: University of Chicago Press.

Littman, D. C., & Mey, J. L. (1991). The nature of irony: Toward a computational model of irony. *Journal of Pragmatics, 15,* 131–151.

Lucariello, J. (1994). Situational irony: A concept of events gone awry. *Journal of Experimental Psychology: General, 123,* 129–145.

Mann, W. C., & Thompson, S. A. (1987). Rhetorical structure theory: Toward a functional theory of text organization. *Text, 8,* 167–182.

Milosky, L. M., & Ford, J. A. (1997). The role of prosody in children's inferences of ironic intent. *Discourse Processes, 23,* 47–61.

Récanati, F. (1995). The alleged priority of literal interpretation. *Cognitive Science, 19,* 207–232.

Roberts, R. M., & Kreuz, R. J. (1994). Why do people use figurative language? *Psychological Science, 5,* 159–163.

Rosch, E. (1973). Natural categories. *Cognitive Psychology, 4,* 328–350.

Rosch, E., & Mervis, C. (1975). Family resemblances: Studies in the internal structure of categories. *Cognitive Psychology, 7,* 573–605.

Searle, J. (1979a). *Expression and meaning.* Cambridge, England: Cambridge University Press.

Searle, J. (1979b). Metaphor. In A. Ortony (Ed.), *Metaphor and thought* (pp. 92–123). Cambridge, England: Cambridge University Press.

Sperber, D. (1984). Verbal irony: Pretense or echoic mention? *Journal of Experimental Psychology: General, 113,* 130–136.

Sperber, D., & Wilson, D. (1981). Irony and the use-mention distinction. In P. Cole (Ed.), *Radical pragmatics* (pp. 295–318). New York: Academic.

Sperber, D., & Wilson, D. (1986). *Relevance: Communication and cognition.* Oxford, England: Blackwell.

Sperber, D., & Wilson, D. (1998). Irony and relevance: A reply to Seto, Hamamoto and Yamanashi. In R. Carston & S. Uchida (Eds.), *Relevance theory: Applications and implications* (pp. 283–293). Amsterdam: Benjamins.

Taylor, J. R. (1989). *Linguistic categorization: Prototypes in linguistic theory.* Oxford, England: Clarendon.

Utsumi, A. (1996). A unified theory of irony and its computational formalization. *Proceedings of the 16th International Conference on Computational Linguistics (COLING'96),* 962–967.

Utsumi, A. (1999). A computational model of irony interpretation *Proceedings of the Fourth Conference of the Pacific Association for Computational Linguistics (PACLING'99),* 312–323.

Ward, G., & Hirschberg, J. (1985). Implicating uncertainty: The pragmatics of fall-rise intonation. *Language, 61,* 747–776.

Williams, J. (1984). Does mention (or pretense) exhaust the concept of irony? *Journal of Experimental Psychology: General, 113,* 127–129.

Wilson, D., & Sperber, D. (1992). On verbal irony. *Lingua, 87,* 53–76.

Wittgenstein, L. (1953). *Philosophical investigations.* New York: Macmillan.

CHAPTER 23

The Bicoherence Theory
of Situational Irony

Cameron Shelley
University of Michigan

Situational irony concerns what it is about a situation that causes people to describe it as ironic. Although situational irony is as complex and commonplace as verbal and literary irony, it has received nowhere near the same attention from cognitive scientists and other scholars. This chapter presents the *bicoherence* theory of situational irony, based on the theory of conceptual coherence (Kunda & Thagard, 1996; Thagard & Verbeurgt, 1998). On this theory, a situation counts as ironic when it is conceived as having a bicoherent conceptual structure, adequate cognitive salience, and evokes an appropriate configuration of emotions. The theory is applied to a corpus of 250 examples of situational ironies gathered automatically from electronic news sources. A useful taxonomy of situational ironies is produced, new predictions and insights into situational irony are discussed, and extensions of the theory to other forms of irony are examined.

When people say that they find a situation *ironic,* they mean that their conception of it defies the normal way in which situations fit with their repertoire of concepts, that this misfit is noteworthy in some way, that it evokes a particular kind of emotional response, and, perhaps, that it has a special, moral significance. Consider the situation of the firefighters of Station 20 in Las Vegas, Nevada, who had a fire in their kitchen due to some chicken fingers left cooking while they went out to answer a fire alarm.[1] The spokesman for the Clark County Fire Department put it as follows:

'It just shows that if it can happen to us, it can happen to anyone,' La-Sky said of the November 10th fire. 'The irony's not lost in it.'

We usually think of firefighters as people who put out fires, not as people who start them. The fact that these firefighters did start a fire made the national Associated

This chapter was previously published as "The bicoherence theory of situational irony" (C. Shelley) in *Cognitive Science, 25,* 775–818. Copyright © [2001] by the Cognitive Science Society. Reprinted with permission.

Press news feed, as have many similar incidents of firefighters causing fires, failing to keep their buildings up to the local fire code, etc. This situation evokes a particular emotional response, namely mirth, and conveys a cautionary moral message which La-Sky summarized in the quotation given above.

Regrettably, no current theory of irony takes all these factors into account. Of course, most current theories treat situational irony only in passing if at all, focusing instead on literary irony or verbal irony.[2] Theories of literary irony typically adopt a rhetorical or Aristotelian approach—that is, they define irony as some configuration of dramatic roles and plot structures and thus ignore its cognitive content. Muecke (1969, 1982), for example, took irony to be a kind of distance between appearance and reality brought about by an ironist and perpetrated on a victim. Booth (1974) treated irony as the recognition or reconstruction of a literary device analogous to the recognition of figures of speech such as metaphors, allegories, and puns. Hutcheon (1995) defined irony as a strategy of "discursive politics" in the rhetoric of texts. In all of these accounts, it is assumed that literary irony is the paradigm case and that situational irony is a special case of life imitating art.

Theories of verbal irony take a more cognitively plausible approach but concentrate solely on irony as a conversational strategy. Grice (1975, 1977) characterized irony as a particular kind of conversational implicature in which intended meaning is inferred from literal meaning by reference to maxims of conversation (see also Giora, 1995). Sperber (1984) and Wilson and Sperber (1981, 1992) treated irony as an expression having an "interpretive resemblance" to an unexpressed opinion, in accord with the principle of relevance (see section 6.4.). These views enjoy some experimental support (see Clark & Gerrig, 1984; Jorgensen, Miller, & Sperber, 1984; Gibbs & O'Brien, 1991; Winner, 1988; Winner & Leekam, 1991) but apply solely to discourse and therefore omit situational irony altogether.

Only two attempts have been made to give cognitively plausible accounts of situational irony, namely those by Littman and Mey (1991) and Lucariello (1994). Littman and Mey adopted a view of human cognition as a plan-recognition system of the sort well known in artificial intelligence. Their theory combines elements from theories of literary and verbal irony: They proposed that humans construe situations as twists in story plots (literary irony) from which thwarted intentions are inferred (verbal irony). Certain combinations of plot twists and thwarted intentions constitute irony. This account has at least three important drawbacks. First, it distinguishes only three types of situational irony based on the number of plot twists counted: zero, one, or two. No independent justification is given as to why the number of plot twists should be regarded as significant. Second, this account gives logical priority to literary and verbal irony by borrowing plot twists and communicative intentions from them. Littman and Mey simply did not consider any cognitive model *not* based on these forms of representation. Third, Littman and Mey offered no evidence that their three categories of irony exhaust all the possibilities or are typical of situational ironies as a whole.

Lucariello (1994) adopted a view of human cognition as a schema-recognition system in which people comprehend events by fitting them to given schemata such as scripts (Schank & Abelson, 1977). Some schemata represent people's expectations about how events should unfold *normally,* whereas other schemata represent an alternative theory about how events may unfold ironically. Ironic schemata are activated when some combination of the following four features are detected in a situation: *unexpectedness, human frailty, outcome,* and *opposition.* A taxonomy of 28 ironic schemata is proposed, organized into eight basic groups. Lucariello presented experimental evidence that people do hold a concept of irony that might be realized as a collection of schemata, and that her taxonomy reliably covers that concept—that is, that her taxonomy includes ironic situations and excludes nonironic situations. This theory is richer and more plausible than Littman and Mey's (1991) and does a much better job of unpacking the concept of situational irony. However, by aiming solely at producing a taxonomy, Lucariello missed the opportunity to find any principled relationship between situational irony and other cognitive phenomena. Consider the following two problems with her theory. First, the relationship between the taxonomy and typical features of ironic situations is not clarified. The eight basic groups of ironies cannot be predicted from the four features given, neither can the features be explained by examination of the groups. Second, the theory fails to elucidate the difference between ironic and nonironic situations, other than to say that they happen to fit with different schemata. Overall, the theory fails to explain the distinctions among ironies and between irony and non-irony. What we want, ultimately, from any cognitive theory of situational irony, is not simply a taxonomy that fits the data but a theory that also explains the data.

This aim is the goal of the bicoherence theory proposed below. On this theory, human cognition is viewed as a system of concepts organized by maximal conceptual *coherence* (see Thagard, 1989; Thagard & Verbeurgt, 1998; Thagard, 2000). A situation is recognized as ironic when it activates concepts in a particular, submaximal, or *bicoherent* pattern. Conceptual coherence involves maximizing constraint satisfaction on a set of elements in view of positive and negative constraints between pairs of those elements. In the bicoherence theory of situational irony, the elements are the concepts activated by a situation and the positive and negative constraints are relations of coherence and incoherence as specified below. In addition, the bicoherence theory takes account of the effects of the salience of and emotional reactions to situations. The bicoherence theory has several advantages. First, it does not characterize situational ironies in terms of literary or verbal ironies. Second, it explains the relation between irony and non-irony through use of the general theory of conceptual coherence in cognitive science and association with the theory of causal attribution in social psychology. Third, it enjoys empirical support from a corpus study of real-world examples of situational irony.

Section 2 presents the bicoherence theory. The general concept of bicoherence is defined in section 2.1, while the specific kinds of coherence and incoherence involved in it are described in sections 2.2 and 2.3. Salience and the role of ironic schemata in situational irony are outlined in section 2.4. The importance of emotions to situational irony is discussed in section 2.5, where *manner* is defined and used to describe how emotions are evoked in certain ironic situations. The corpus study, in which the theory is used to explain a body of situational ironies gathered from news articles, is presented in section 3. Results of the corpus study are given in section 4. A discussion of further issues and predictions arising from the theory is provided in section 5, along with speculations concerning the extension of the theory to other forms of irony.

THE BICOHERENCE THEORY

Situational irony is recognized when the accepted interpretation of a situation displays a bicoherent conceptual structure, affords adequate cognitive salience, and evokes an appropriate configuration of emotions. These criteria are explained, in order, in this section.

Bicoherence

Bicoherence is most easily understood as the reverse of coherence, so this section begins with an explanation of coherence. In general, coherence constitutes the way in which a set of elements can be partitioned such that the positive and negative relations existing between pairs of the elements are maximally satisfied. Coherence may be informally defined as follows:

1. Elements are representations specific to the cognitive domain in question. Conceptual coherence, for example, concerns *concepts*.
2. Pairwise, elements can cohere (fit together) or incohere (resist fitting together). Conceptual coherence relations include *positive association* between concepts, that is, when there are several objects to which two concepts both apply. Conceptual incoherence relations between concepts include *negative association,* that is, when there are few or no objects to which two concepts both apply.
3. If two elements cohere, then a positive constraint holds between them. Conversely, if two elements incohere, then a negative constraint holds between them.
4. Elements are to be divided into two classes, namely *accepted* and *rejected.*
5. A positive constraint between two elements is best satisfied either by accepting both elements together or by rejecting both elements together. Conversely, a negative constraint between two elements is best satisfied only by accepting one element and rejecting the other one. In other words, positively constrained elements are best treated the same, whereas negatively constrained elements are best treated differently.
6. A coherence problem consists of dividing a class of elements into accepted and rejected sets in a way that best satisfies these constraints.

A formal, mathematical characterization of coherence is given in Thagard and Verbeurgt (1998), along with computational algorithms for solving coherence problems in the general case. Specific coherence theories in the explanatory, analogical, deductive, visual, and conceptual domains are discussed in Thagard (2000).

Bicoherence is the same as coherence but with the rule given in step 5 above exchanged for its reverse. Consider the two parts of this rule again:

i. If two elements a and b cohere, then a and b belong to the same class (e.g., *accepted* or *rejected*).

ii. If two elements a and b incohere, then a and b belong to different classes.

These rules stipulate (i) that any pair of elements in the same class should cohere with each other, and (ii) that any pair of classes that share the same element should cohere with each other. Now consider the reverse of these stipulations, in order, obtained by exchanging the roles of coherence and incoherence:

i'. If the same class contains two elements, then those elements incohere with each other.

ii'. If different classes contain the same element, then those classes incohere with each other.

Plug this rule into the informal description of coherence given above and you will get bicoherence.

Consider examples of elements and classes arranged according to this new rule. First, consider the class of books by one author, call her Anne O'Nymous. Anne's opus includes the following titles: *The travail of life in an imperfect world, Why would God allow evil?* and *Curious George goes ape!* The class of Anne's books is bicoherent in the sense that it groups a light-hearted children's book together with all her weighty works on existential alienation. Thus, the class of Anne's books may be called a *bicoherent class* because it is a class that contains two elements that are incoherent with each other, in accord with rule i' above. A visual representation of this situation is given in Figure 23.1.

Second, consider Anne's latest work, *Curious George seeks the way.* This book is bicoherent in the sense that bookstores stock it in both the children's section (because of its funny pictures and Curious George's hilarious antics) and the philosophy section (because of the accessible manner in which it addresses important life

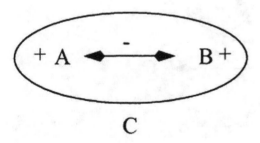

Figure 23.1. The works of Anne O'Nymous as a bicoherent class. A = "Why would God allow evil?" B = "Curious George goes ape!" C = the works of Anne O'Nymous. The "+" signs indicate that A and B both cohere with C (to which they belong), and the "—" indicates that A and B incohere with each other.

issues). These two classes do not otherwise intersect, and therefore count as incoherent. Thus, Anne's new book may be called a *bicoherent element* because it belongs to two classes that incohere with each other, in accord with rule ii' above. A visual representation of this situation is given in Figure 23.2.

In summary, bicoherence is simply coherence with the reverse rule for constraint satisfaction. Situational irony requires that concepts in the *accepted* set of a coherence solution (see rule 4 above) are activated in a bicoherent pattern. Having specified what is meant by bicoherence, it is necessary to specify what is meant by *conceptual* bicoherence. In other words, the coherence and incoherence relations that apply to conceptual bicoherence must be specified. These are outlined below.

Conceptual Coherence Relations

A list of conceptual coherence relations is given in Table 23.1. The basic kind of conceptual coherence relation is positive *association* (Kunda & Thagard, 1996; Thagard, 2000). Two concepts are positively associated if there are objects to which both apply. For example, the concepts of politician and lawyer are positively associated because many politicians are also lawyers.

Similarity is a broad kind of positive association between concepts. Two concepts are similar if there are attributes in which both participate, that is, if they share some attributes. Beavers and muskrats are similar, for example, because, they are small, round, brown, aquatic rodents. There are a variety of more specialized or derivative forms of similarity that it is useful to distinguish. *Analogy* holds between two concepts when they participate in the same abstract relational structures (Gentner, 1983; Holyoak & Thagard, 1995). Despite their superficial dissimilarities, penguins and camels are analogous in the sense that they are both highly specialized for extreme climates. *Coincidence* holds between two concepts when there is a time during which both occur. A picnic and a thundershower may occur at the same time, which is therefore a coincidence (although it may not seem so to the picnickers). *Collocation* holds between concepts when there is a place in which they are both located, either physically or metaphorically. Lions and zebras are positively associated because they are both found in the African savannahs.

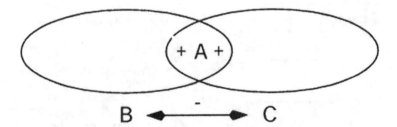

Figure 23.2.   "Curious George seeks the way" as a bicoherent element. A = "Curious George seeks the way," B = children's books, C = philosophy books. The "+" signs indicate that A coheres with both B and C (to which it belongs), and the "—" indicates that B and C incohere with each other.

TABLE 23.1

The Coherence Relations in Bicoherent Ironies Arranged According to Types and Subtypes

Type	Subtypes	Causal Attribution
Similarity		—
	Analogy	
	Coincidence	
	Collocation	
Policy		Consistency
	Intention	
Constitution		Distinctiveness
Type		Consensus
	Role	
	Status	
	Title	
	Model	

Note. All coherence relations are different forms of positive association between concepts. The kind of causal attribution corresponding to each type of coherence relation is given in the rightmost column (see section 6.1).

Policy is a positive association between a person or an institution and a code of conduct adopted by them. A person and a policy are positively associated if there are actions done by the former in accord with the latter. Appeasement is the policy associated with Neville Chamberlain, especially because pursuing it caused him to sign the famous Munich accord with Hitler. *Intention* is a specialized form of policy in which a plan with specific steps is laid out in pursuit of a policy or goal.

Constitution is a positive association between a concept and the temperaments, traits, and dispositions that it possesses. A machine and a trait, say, are positively associated if there are events brought about by the machine that are caused by the fact that the machine has a particular trait. A subway locomotive may often stall in winter because it has a cooling fan that sucks snow into the engine, for instance (Ferguson, 1977).

Type is a positive association between two concepts due to the conceptual structure in which they exist. Whereas constitution associates a concept and its *intrinsic* qualities, type associates a concept and its *extrinsic* qualities. A concept often inherits a quality transitively because it is subsumed by another concept that possesses the quality.[3] Thus, for example, philosophy professors are thought of as absent-minded—that is, as being absent-minded people—because philosophy professors are university professors and university professors are thought of as absent-minded people. *Role* holds between two concepts when one is a quality of the other in virtue of a position held by the other. For example, a person may be thought to be protective if he is seen to occupy the role of a father figure. *Status* holds between two concepts when one is a quality of the other by designation. A status is often, although not invariably, a kind of role for inanimate objects. For example, a mat may be considered welcoming simply because it is one of those objects with the expression "welcome" printed on it. *Title* is a specialized kind of status granted by a fixed, conventional designation. A person is associated with the title "President" simply because she is one of those people who have been elected president of a country, say. *Model* holds between two concepts if one possesses a quality because it is based on something else that possesses that quality. For example, the movie *Apocalypse Now* (Coppola, 1979) is positively associated with Joseph Conrad because it is modeled on the book *Heart of Darkness,* which was written by Conrad (1902).

Conceptual Incoherence Relations

A list of conceptual incoherence relations is given in Table 23.2. The basic kind of conceptual incoherence relation is *negative association* (Kunda & Thagard, 1996; Thagard, 2000). Two concepts are negatively associated if objects that fall under one concept usually do not fall under the other concept. So, for example, the concepts of book and stone are negatively associated because there are few books that are also stones.

Antisymmetry is a kind of negative association between two concepts. Two concepts are antisymmetric if there is a relation such that the first concept stands in that relation to the second concept, but the second concept stands in the opposite relation to the first one. In mathematics, a relation R is antisymmetric with a relation R' when $aRb \equiv bR'a$ and R' is the inverse or opposite relation from R. For example, the greater-than "$\geq$" relation is antisymmetric with the lesser-than "$\leq$" relation of arithmetic, as may be seen in expressions such as $5 > 4 \equiv 4 \leq 5$ where $\leq$ is the inverse of $>$. Outside mathematics, consider the relations *is-taller-than* and *is-shorter-than* and two people, Greg and Phil, chosen at random from a large population such that Greg

TABLE 23.2
The Incoherence Relations in Bicoherent Ironies Arranged According to Types and Subtypes

Type	Subtypes
Antisymmetry	
	Symmetry + mutual exclusion
	Antireciprocity
Antonymy	
Disproportion	
Dissimilarity	

Note. All incoherence relations are different forms of negative association between concepts.

is taller than Phil. Clearly, Greg and Phil are related antisymmetrically in terms of height since Greg is taller than Phil and Phil is shorter than Greg. This relation is a negative association since few people who, like Greg, fall under the concept of *taller-than-Phil* are likely to also fall under the concept of *shorter-than-Greg*. *Symmetry plus mutual exclusion* is a weak form of antisymmetry in which two concepts are symmetrically related, but only under different circumstances. In mathematics, a relation R is symmetric when $aRb \equiv bRa$, as may be seen in arithmetical relations such as multiplication where, for example, $4 \times 5 = 5 \times 4$. Outside mathematics, consider the relation *is-meaner-than* as in *Darth Vader is meaner than a junkyard dog*. This relation holds true during the first two *Star Wars* movies (Lucas, 1977, 1980), but is not true by the end of the third movie (Lucas, 1983). In fact, by the end of the third movie, it is true that a junkyard dog is meaner than Darth Vader. So, Darth Vader and a junkyard dog occupy a symmetric relationship, each is meaner than the other, but only under mutually exclusive circumstances, that is, at different times. A relation of symmetry plus mutual exclusion can always be recast as a formal antisymmetry. For example, the above example can be recast as an antisymmetry by using the relations *is-first-meaner-than* and *is-then-meaner-than,* as in *Darth Vader is first meaner than a junkyard dog* and *A junkyard dog is then meaner than Darth Vader*. *Antireciprocity* is a specialized form of antisymmetry in which the antisymmetric relations are forms of *give* and *take*. Giving and taking are important forms of social interaction and failures to reciprocate, as when one person gives something to another but the other does not give anything back, are especially liable to attract notice and disapproval (see Ekeh, 1974).

Antonymy is a kind of negative association that holds between concepts that are opposite in meaning. The concepts of *good* and *evil* are antonymous and negatively associated since those things that are good are also not evil.

Disproportion is a kind of negative association between two concepts in which each concept has the magnitude usually associated with the other. Consider the situation in Robert Bolt's play *A Man for all Seasons* (Bolt, 1962, p. 71) in which the Duke of Norfolk attempts to persuade his friend Thomas More to swear allegiance to Henry VIII as the head of the Church of England, thereby giving up his allegiance to the Pope. More explains that he cannot give in because it would not be like him to do so; Norfolk then responds as follows:

> And who are you? Goddammit, man, it's disproportionate! *We're* supposed to be the arrogant ones, the proud, splenetic ones—and we've all given in! Why must you stand out?

In other words, it is disproportionate for a man of *low* birth like More to demonstrate such *great* probity when a man of *high* birth like Norfolk demonstrates such *little* probity. Disproportion may be viewed as a way in which one antisymmetry in magnitudes leads us to expect another. Consider one antisymmetry involving More: *Norfolk's birth is higher than More's birth* and *More's birth is lower than Norfolk's birth*. As Norfolk implies, we expect *Norfolk* and *More* to occupy the same places if *probity* is substituted for *birth* (because probity and nobility are positively associated). But the opposite is the case: *More's probity is greater than Norfolk's probity* and *Norfolk's probity is less than More's probity.* The double antisymmetry of *disproportion* and its reference to the metaphorical magnitudes of concepts make it a very interesting form of incoherence.

Dissimilarity is a kind of negative association between two concepts simply because those objects that fall under dissimilar concepts tend themselves to be dissimilar to one another.

Salience and Schemata

Cognitive salience is a measure of how important or noticeable something is in contrast to other things. The salience of a situation varies according to the *contents* of the situation itself and how those contents *relate* to the individual conceiving them. As far as the contents of a situation are concerned, salience is generally a result of our biological and cultural dispositions (Lyons, 1977, pp. 247–249). Biological salience is exemplified in the color concepts employed across cultures, which systematically divide up the color spectrum according to a progressive set of universal distinctions among hues (see D'Andrade, 1995, pp. 106–115). Cultural salience is exemplified in human kinship terms, which emphasize whatever distinctions are regarded as important in the culture at hand (see D'Andrade, 1995, pp. 19–30).[4]

The salience of a situation is enhanced where a schema is readily applicable to it, and diminished otherwise (Higgins, 1996, p. 136). For instance, the story of a biker-gang member who stops by the side of a road to help push an old lady's Buick out of the ditch is salient partially because the man is behaving like the Good Samaritan described in the Gospel of Luke 10.30–7, in that he goes against a negative stereotype and helps someone in need. Indeed, he may be called a "Good Samaritan" for this very reason. Lucariello (1994) showed that the salience of situational ironies is enhanced where ironic schemata are readily applied.[5] The effects of schemata on irony recognition are discussed in section 3.

Emotions and Manner

Emotional configuration is as central to situational irony as conceptual structure. This position may seem controversial because emotions are regarded as peripheral in the best-known theories of irony. Grice's (1975) account of irony omits emotions entirely, since conversational implicature is intended strictly as a theory of rational action in conversation. Similarly, emotions occupy a strictly peripheral role in Sperber and Wilson's account of irony. On this account, emotions are held to act through *weak implicature* (Sperber & Wilson, 1986, pp. 199–200) and poetic effects (Sperber & Wilson, 1986, pp. 222; see also Pilkington, 1992), which is to say that emotions are of secondary importance in normal language and characteristic of unusual language (see also Hutcheon, 1995, pp. 37–43). Leggitt and Gibbs Jr. (2000) showed that this position does not accurately represent the role of emotions in everyday sorts of verbal irony.

Recent work in cognitive science (e.g., Oatley, 1992; Damasio, 1994) indicates that, unless there is specific evidence to the contrary, we should assume that emotions are an integral feature of any cognitive phenomenon. As of yet, work on integrating emotions into coherence theory is not far enough advanced (but see Thagard, 2000) to elucidate exactly how emotions and conceptual bicoherence interact in situational irony. Therefore, a simple framework for describing emotions and their eliciting conditions is adopted in this paper, based on the *communicative theory* of emotions proposed by Oatley (1992). Observations made here within this framework can be revised appropriately as work proceeds on emotions in conceptual coherence.

Emotions relate to situational irony in at least two ways. First, some kinds of situational irony may be associated with particular emotions only. Some kinds of irony may evoke only mirth and not sadness, for example. This issue is discussed further in sections 3 and 5.

Second, heightened emotional response tends to increase the salience of a situation and thus may increase the sense that the situation is ironic (section 2.4). Emotional response, in turn, depends upon how the situation measures up to the cognizer's goals (Oatley, 1992), concerns (Frijda, 1986, pp. 335–340), or preferences (Damasio, 1994, pp. 198–200). Muecke (1982, p. 55) expressed this point nicely in an economic metaphor:

> Other things being equal, ironies will be more or less forceful in proportion to the amount of emotional capital the reader or observer has invested in the victim or topic of the irony.

Consider the following example from a recurring sketch on the American television show *Mad TV*, broadcast February 28, 1998. In the sketch called *Talkin' American*, the pop singer Alanis Morissette is taken to task precisely for violating the emotional salience criterion for using "rain on your wedding day" as an example of irony in her song *Irony*. Mr. Dakai, a host of *Talkin' American*, castigates Morissette for this failing, as follows:

> And you do not even know what the word "irony" means. Let me tell you something: When it rained on *my* wedding day, and a mudslide washed away my hut, my two goats and my fourth spouse … Oh! now *that* is irony!

Humor is derived from the fact that Dakai is a non-native English speaker (he pronounces "irony" as eye-RON-ee) who is scolding a native speaker for her incompetence in the English language (and from the fact that Dakai's spouse figures *after* his hut and goats). The substance of Dakai's complaint is simply that rain falling during a wedding is not a sufficient departure from his goals, concerns, or preferences for a marriage to evoke his sense of irony. A much greater catastrophe is required.

For present purposes, *manner* is adopted as the main measure of the distance between a situation and the goals, concerns, and preferences that a cognizer applies to it. Manner consists of two, discretely valued scales, namely *physical* and *moral*. On the physical scale, an agent that achieves its goal dead on could be said to have acted *capably*. Take, for example, a salesman who meets his quota for the month. A goal may remain unachieved because the task aimed to achieve it is done (1) *improficiently*—left incomplete, (2) *incapably*—left utterly incomplete, or (3) *excessively*—taken too far. Similarly, on the moral scale, an agent that achieves its goal in a permissible way could be said to have acted *rightly*.[6] Take, for example, a politician who gets elected without lying about his financial holdings. A goal may remain unachieved because someone pursues it (1) *licentiously*—outside the bounds of custom or authority, (2) *maliciously*—by voluntarily choosing to do wrong, or (3) *overzealously*—by applying a moral principle beyond its proper place.[7]

The connection between manner and the emotions that it elicits has not been systematically investigated by psychologists. However, some studies show, for example, that "people provoking anger [in others] were most often seen as doing something voluntarily that they had no right to do, or as doing something they could have avoided had they been more careful" (Oatley, 1992, p. 209). In other words, anger may be elicited when people see others acting licentiously or incapably. The emotional valuation of manners applied in this chapter is made in accord with such evidence as currently exists in the literature on the psychology of emotions. Revisions may be necessary in the future as circumstances warrant.

Emotions are important to situational irony because (1) some ironies are conditioned by particular emotions, and (2) emotional arousal increases cognitive salience. Manner describes in what ways situations tend to elicit emotions as those emotions are relevant to irony.

THE CORPUS STUDY

A corpus of ironic situations was gathered electronically from newspaper articles that contain the term *irony* and its relatives. The object was to collect instances of situations described simply and briefly and labeled as ironic without the solicitation of the experimenter (i.e., the author). Situations were classified into a taxonomy based on the coherence and incoherence relations active in the representation of each situation. This taxonomy does not *embody* the bicoherence theory but rather serves as a convenient tool for analyzing ironic situations *according to* the theory. Illustrations from each category are discussed in order to show how the theory accounts for the variety of ironic situations commonly found in the real world.

Method

The corpus discussed here consists of newspaper articles containing the term *irony, ironic, ironical,* or *ironically.*[8] These articles were collected each weekday morning by a program that searched the Internet sites of various press associations such as the Associated Press and Reuters for relevant articles posted within the previous 24 hr. The program, called ksearch, then retrieved the appropriate articles, labeled them, and emailed them to the experimenter for analysis. This search was carried out roughly from May 1997 through May 1998.

Articles that were duplicates or did not concern situational irony were discarded. So, for example, articles in which the term *ironic* was applied to remarks, commentary, speeches, music (not lyrics), demeanors, outlooks, persons, generation-X, corporations, nations, literary works, and so forth were classified as non-situational and excluded from the corpus. Also discarded were articles whose sole use of *irony* was to offer a definition of it, as were articles that labeled something as *ironic* without providing clarification, discussion, or context.

The remaining articles were arranged by a dynamic *pile sort*. Each instance of irony was added to a pile containing only similar instances. Ironies were moved from pile to pile, and piles were created or destroyed as necessary to keep similar ones together and dissimilar ones apart. The process was completed when no more shuffling had occurred for two months. The *ad hoc* nature of this procedure implies that the distribution of examples in the resulting corpus does not have precise statistical significance (see section 4). However, this procedure has the advantage that the distinctions afforded by the examples themselves could be represented without difficulty by creating or amalgamating separate piles. Since the resulting taxonomy is intended only as an analytical convenience, this method is wholly appropriate.

The result is a collection of articles arranged into two groups according to the kind of bicoherence represented, namely bicoherent classes and bicoherent elements. Subgroups are given where specific coherence or (in the case of disproportion) incoherence relations are emphasized. Sixteen categories are given in all. This scheme is represented graphically in Figure 23.3. An illustration of each kind of situational irony is discussed below in sections 3.2. and 3.3.

Bicoherent Class Ironies

Basic

A basic bicoherent class irony concerns things that are simply positively associated under one concept but are negatively associated in some way when considered pairwise. Consider the situation created by a court ruling in British Columbia, Canada, to the effect that immigrant representatives must be lawyers, unlike government representatives.[9] The resulting inequity caused a private immigration advocate of 27 years experience, Mr. Mangat, to complain about an irony in the situation:

> Mr. Mangat pointed out the irony in the court requiring an immigrant's representative to be a lawyer, although many of the adjudicators are not lawyers and often have minimal formal education.

Mr. Mangat, and others like him, are legally barred from their former occupation from the time of the ruling onward.

Mr. Mangat and the government adjudicators are positively associated in that both fall under the concept of advocates recognized in the British Columbia immigration court. However, Mr. Mangat and the government adjudicators are related

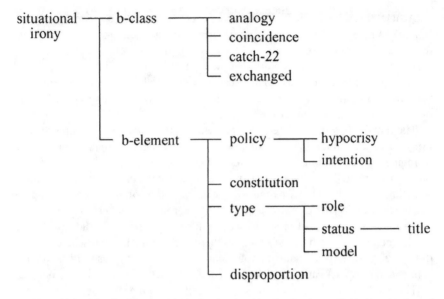

Figure 23.3.   The classification scheme for situational ironies. Ironies are divided into two ba-sic types: bicoherent class (*b-class*) and bicoherent element (*b-element*). These types are then di-vided into subtypes according to tree structure displayed here.

antisymmetrically to each other in that although the adjudicators should be at least as qualified as Mr. Mangat (to do the same job), Mr. Mangat is actually much more qualified than the they are (in terms of experience).

The salience of this example is raised in two ways: first by the unfairness and undeservedness of the blow to Mr. Mangat, and second by activation of the common schema of a large impersonal entity, the government, running roughshod over the little guy.

Beyond the surprise and perhaps shock of an unfavorable ruling, the dominant emotions of this irony are bitterness and anger. Bitterness is a complex form of disgust experienced when a joint plan or activity (joint in the sense of shared with other people) is discontinued by others (Oatley, 1992, pp. 212–213). In creating this antisymmetric situation, the British Columbia court discontinued its standing relationship with Mr. Mangat, causing him to feel bitter. The anger apparent in Mr. Mangat's attribution of irony proceeds from the salience of being deprived of his livelihood. Anger typically arises from the "unattainability of a life goal" (Frijda, 1986, p. 338), and, where irony is concerned, results in a form of moral outrage. But bicoherent class ironies need not all involve bitterness and anger.

Analogy

An irony of analogy concerns elements that fall under one concept analogically but are nevertheless dissimilar. Consider the situation of Paul Valleli, a private citizen of Burlington, Massachusetts, who, with no special training, located the leak in a water main that several professional bodies had failed to locate over the span of the previous week.[10] An official of the Boston Sewer Commission put it as follows:

> The irony is that despite all our crews and help from the MWRA [Massachusetts Water Resource Authority] with all sorts of detection crews, it was a Town Meeting member who discovered the break and reported it to officials.

The article emphasizes that Valleli had no training as a plumber, but located the leak using his skills as a Boy Scout leader (as indicated by the pun in the article's title) and within 20 min after leaving the Town Meeting where he resolved to try his luck on the problem. Mr. Valleli and the members of the MWRA, the Boston Sewer Commission, and other local authorities all fall under the concept of plumbers by virtue of analogy of their activities. However, Mr. Valleli is very dissimilar to the other plumbers in their tools, training, and success. There is also a disproportion in the fact that Valleli took only 20 min to find the leak whereas the professional plumbers could not do so in a full seven days.

The salience of this example is raised by the *egg-on-the-face* schema that applies to the various Massachusetts authorities. Who does not enjoy seeing people in authority embarrassed in such an abject manner? All the examples of ironic analogy collected in this corpus are humorous, although those that involve the frustration of life goals present the relevant authorities in a very scornful light.

Irony of analogy is the complement of irony of model (see section 3.3.).

Coincidence

An irony of coincidence concerns elements that fall under one concept and are also positively associated in a second but surprising way. Consider the situation in which Joe Carter, a longtime designated hitter for the Toronto Blue Jays American League baseball team, made his 2,000th career hit at Veterans Stadium, home of the Philadelphia Phillies National League team. Carter described the situation thus:[11]

> It's ironic to get it here. I don't know when I'll be back.

The preamble emphasizes that Carter also got his 1st and 1,000th professional hits in the same ballpark.

All three of these hits fall under the concept of signal career events. However, they are all collocated as well, that is, they occurred in the same ballpark, against all likelihood, since Carter played in the American League and Veterans Stadium is a National League ballpark. So, the positive conceptual relation of collocation simulates a negative relation because of the negative valence of surprise attached to it.

The salience of this situation derives from the importance conventionally assigned to events attached to millennial numbers like 2000. In domains such as sports and finance, statistics are an important form of knowledge whether they are of practical or merely numerological significance.

Beyond surprise, ironies of coincidence appear to take on the emotional quality of their subject matter. Thus, the deaths of Gianni Versace and Princess Diana, two celebrity friends whom it also happens were killed within a few weeks of each other, is perceived as a sad or tragic irony of coincidence because that is the emotional quality attached to each occasion.[12] If an irony is extremely salient, then it may be perceived as completely *non*-coincidental. For example, a television producer described Tiger Woods's victory at the Masters golf tournament as "fate or irony."[13] Fate is the opposite of coincidence—the first describes the outcome of a grand design whereas the second describes the outcome of a mere accident—which underlines the importance of salience to the recognition of coincidences as ironies. Jung (1973) discussed this concept of ironic fate in terms of *synchronicity* or *meaningful coincidence.*

People sometimes express irritation with ironies of coincidence brought to their attention by others. For example, the *Pedantry Hotline* received the following question:[14]

> Why do people say "ironically" when they mean "coincidentally" or even "surprisingly"? A friend is forever saying things like, "I saw her last month at the Bar Marmont and ironically I ran into her a week ago at the Hot Tin Roof." Should I try to correct her?

The reporter recommended correction but wisely avoided offering a definition of irony for the purpose. There are a number of reasons one might object to ironies of coincidence: (1) a positive association with a negative valence of surprise is not a proper negative association, or (2) the unlikelihood is not high enough to be salient. The first objection, exemplified by the *Pedantry Hotline* example, is true but indeed pedantic in view of the commonness of ironies of coincidence in the corpus. The second objection reflects *egocentricity bias* (Falk 1989), a tendency for people to rate coincidences that involve themselves as being more salient than coincidences that do not. This bias would cause people to find coincidences involving others to be nonsalient and therefore nonironic, as is apparent from both examples given above.

Catch-22

A Catch-22 irony concerns elements that fall under one concept, namely the fact that each is an ironic element irony (section 3.3.), and are negatively associated by antisymmetry. This kind of irony is really a meta-irony that has gained currency from the Joseph Heller novel of the same title. Consider the situation of prisoners under the supervision of the Massachusetts Department of Correction (DOC). In order to save money and alleviate overcrowding, the DOC has a contract with the Dallas (Texas) County Jail that allows DOC prisoners to be held in Dallas.[15] Anthony Doniger, a Boston lawyer representing several Massachusetts prisoners in the Dallas County Jail who are challenging the constitutionality of sending them out of state, characterizes the policy in this way: Doniger said the fact that the contract with Dallas says that only "model prisoners" will be accepted is "beyond ironic—it is punitive." "It's a strange message for them to be sending," said Doniger. "It's like they are saying, 'If you're good you get exiled from your family; if you're bad, you stay.'"

The article noted that prisoners who have access to education and family members while incarcerated have the lowest recidivism rate.

The "good" and "bad" prisoners fall under and exhaust the concept of DOC prisoners. The two groups of prisoners are related antisymmetrically in that the good prisoners deserve to receive better treatment than the bad ones but the bad ones actually receive better treatment than the good ones. In addition, each element is caught in a policy irony (section 3.3.) in the sense that being good results in punishment and being bad results in a (comparative) reward.

There are three sources of salience in this example. First, there is now a ready schema for such situations, derived from Heller's novel (Muecke, 1982, p. 12). Second is the compounded nature of this irony. Not only is the whole situation ironic, but each of its components constitutes an irony in its own right. Third, the infrequency of Catch-22 ironies in the corpus also suggests that this kind of irony is highly unexpected and therefore grabs attention for this reason also.

The emotions attached to this situation are sadness and anger. These prisoners are losing important forms of encouragement, namely their familial support and their prospects for rehabilitation. Losses of this kind typically generate sadness (Oatley, 1992, pp. 294–296). Anger is generated by the unfairness of the ruling and the recognition of the schema of a large, uncaring entity running roughshod over individuals. Some anger also results in the reward received by bad prisoners who are undeserving (see section 2.5.).

Exchanged Places

An irony of exchanged places concerns two elements that fall under the same concept by collocation but are also related antisymmetrically. Consider the situation of members of "Generation X" as they turn 30 years old and begin to emulate their parents in finding jobs, spouses, and responsibility. Meanwhile, their parents have begun to pull up stakes, cohabitate, and drive fast cars.[16] Saul Wisnia of Brookline, for example, drives a Honda Accord, is engaged to be married, lives in the suburbs, and edits business books for a living, whereas his 60-year-old mother drives sports cars and speedboats, lives with her boyfriend, and works out at the gym:

> To understand this irony it's crucial to know how most people who are turning 30 in the 1990s perceive the passage: as a time to buckle down and—yipes—become an adult.

As the article's title suggests, members of Generation X and their parents have exchanged places.

The Generation Xers and their parents both occupy a traditional, American family household or "nest." However, exemplars of these two groups stand in an antisymmetric relation to each other: Saul Wisnia is acting more responsibly than his mother and his mother is acting less responsibly than he is.

The salience of this situation is raised by at least two factors. First, each element occupies the traditional household in successive and exclusive periods of time only. This succession through time is conceived as a "twist" in the course of events. A twist is a schema that readily evokes the sense of irony (see Lucariello, 1994). Second, the exchange of places between parents and children is a stock comic schema and is found, for example, in the movies *Freaky Friday* (Nelson, 1977), *18 Again!* (Flaherty, 1988), and *Vice Versa* (Gilbert, 1988).

Surprise is always conveyed in ironies of exchanged places, which seems to derive from the perceived unlikelihood of the turn of events. Ironies of exchanged places also typically evoke mirth, probably from the salience of the comic schema so frequently applied to them, one which emphasizes incongruous elements jockeying for each other's positions in life.

Bicoherent Element Ironies

Basic

A basic bicoherent element irony concerns an element to which two concepts apply but which are negatively associated with each other. Consider the following example concerning Sanford Wallace, the Internet "Spam King" notorious for inundating millions of Internet users with a flood of unsolicited electronic junk email (spam).[17] In late October 1997, Wallace was disconnected by his Internet provider AGIS. Wallace's reaction was to sue for damages. In reaction to AGIS's actions, Wallace said he will "aggressively pursue litigation against AGIS" for damages. Among the allegations he cited was, ironically enough, a "loss of reputation and good will."

Shabbir Safdar, of the Voters' Telecommunications Watch, is quoted describing Mr. Wallace as "the despised figurehead" of Internet spammers.

Sanford Wallace falls under two concepts, namely reputable people and despised people, which are related antonymously.

The salience of this situation is heightened by the patent absurdity of Wallace's presumption that he enjoyed any reputation and good will that could suffer damage.

There are two emotional qualities attached to this example, namely mirth and a feeling of moral superiority. Mirth derives from an enjoyment of the minor misfortune of others. The feeling of moral superiority to Mr. Wallace probably derives from what Bazerman (1998, pp. 94–99) called the *positive illusions,* our tendency to see confirmation of our positive self-images when we observe the moral failings of others.

Basic bicoherent element ironies are essentially bicoherent element ironies that could not be fitted into any particular subcategory because the ironic situation could not have been anticipated simply from knowledge about the element. In this case, no one could have anticipated that Mr. Wallace would consider himself a reputable person. His predicament could have qualified as an irony of status had he declared this opinion himself in advance.

Policy

An irony of policy concerns an element, usually a person or institution, that falls under one concept due to a policy on its part and another concept due to its actions. Consider the situation of Paul Newman who obtains salsa for his brand of *Newman's Own* foods from a wholly-owned subsidiary named *Cantisano Foods*.[18] Newman has a strict policy of not purchasing products made with child labor. But, it turns out that the company which supplies Cantisano with chili peppers routinely employs child labor in growing them.

Newman said the situation is ironic, considering that his company gave $9 million to charities this year, much of it to help children.

Cantisano Foods falls under the two, antonymous concepts of those whose policy is to promote child welfare and those whose actions serve to exploit child labor.

The salience of this example is raised by its objectionable subject matter, namely child labor. Also, salience is increased by the commitment to the promotion of child welfare otherwise displayed by Cantisano Foods, to the tune of $9 million.

The emotion most clearly associated with this example is disappointment with the failure of Cantisano to apply its policy of nonexploitation. Also, as is typical for policy ironies, this policy is shown to have completely failed to be applied exactly where the conditions for its application are met. Thus, the policy is applied incapably. Other ironies of policy display improficient or even excessive applications of the policies in question. A policy applied in an excessive manner arises in examples such as the *Sharp* corporation's drop in profits due, ironically, to an *increase* in production that inadvertently caused an oversupply of LCD screens.[19] Such examples are usually humorous.

Hypocrisy

An irony of hypocrisy is a special case of ironic policy in which a policy is exercised maliciously and in which the two concepts in question are related antisymmetrically. Consider the situation of Emilio Valdez and Alfredo Hodoyan, two hitmen for a notorious Mexican drug cartel, who were arrested by American authorities in California on charges of drug trafficking.[20] The Mexican Attorney General's Office (PGR) successfully launched an extradition request, which was subsequently appealed by Valdez and Hodoyan on the grounds that they had confessed only after torture and violations of their human rights. The California judges rejected the appeal. The PGR stated the following:

> (One judge) added that it would be ironic to think that the appellants invoked
> claims to human rights when, in addition to linking them to an organization dedi-

cated to drug trafficking, they are accused of being the executioners of the organization and don't respect the human rights of their victims.

Valdez and Hodoyan (V&H) collectively fall under the concepts of those whose
policy is to respect human rights and also those who egregiously violate human
rights. As such, V&H place themselves in an antisymmetric relation with other
people insofar as V&H believe that others need to respect the human rights of V&H
but also believe that V&H need not respect the human rights of others.

The salience of this situation is increased by two factors. First is the high contrast
between the characterization of V&H as perpetrators of extreme violence and their
own characterization of themselves as the victims of violence. Second is the
schema activated by V&H's appeal, which fits the well-known stereotype of a lawyer baldly advancing any outrageous claim on behalf of even (or especially) the
most despicable client.

This irony evokes disgust, a revulsion to V&H because they are murderers. Anger is also evident in the judge's description of their appeal, which amounts to nothing but an attempt to obstruct the legal process whereby they would get their just
desserts. In other words, V&H's professed policy was practiced maliciously, deliberately aimed at avoiding a good outcome.

Intention

An irony of intention is a special case of an irony of policy in which the policy is
deliberately put into effect (i.e., it constitutes a plan) and fails due to physical and
not moral defects in manner of practice. Consider the situation of the Nile Perch, a
hefty, carnivorous fish that was introduced into Lake Victoria by British officials in
the 1950s in order to improve the local fishery.[21] But the voracious perch has hunted
half the native cichlid fishes to extinction. In the absence of these cichlids, the in-
sects and algae they used to eat have boomed in population, creating a plague of
bugs around the lake and choking out other water plants, thus killing off more fish.
Furthermore, the Perch must be cooked rather than sun-dried, meaning that local
forests have been denuded for firewood. The increased erosion from the absence of
trees has filled the lake with sediment, creating still more problems.

> Perhaps most ironic, as the Nile Perch destroyed species after species of cichlids,
> the perches no longer had the abundant food supply that they did initially. With-
> out sufficient food, they stopped growing to the enormous and profitable sizes
> they had once attained.

As a result, the ecology of Lake Victoria and the fishery that depends on it are near a
state of collapse.

The introduction of the Nile Perch into Lake Victoria falls here under two antonymous concepts, namely, promotion of the fishery on Lake Victoria and destruction
of the fishery on Lake Victoria.

The salience of such situations is heightened by the law-like schema of futility
into which they fit. The Nile Perch story is described by the reporter as an exemplar

of the "Law of Unexpected Consequences." Another reporter uses the term *Laurel-and-Hardiness*.[22] Terms like *backfired* and *counterproductive* often occur in the description of intention ironies. Littman and Mey (1991, p. 137) pointed out that the salience of this kind of irony (which they call *intentional* irony) also depends upon the initial reasonableness of the intention before it is disastrously played out. So, for example, the introduction of the Nile Perch into Lake Victoria is all the more ironic because it appeared to be such a reasonable move at the time. Although there are no examples in the corpus, it is possible that plans which are initially unreasonable and work out very well could also be seen as ironies of intention. Perhaps all that is required is sufficient contrast between the reasonableness of the plan and the desirability of its actual outcome.

Ironies of intention evoke mirth at the folly of people fumbling to control situations that they do not comprehend. This emotion could be regarded as a kind of Schadenfreude or shameful joy in the misfortune of another. Not surprisingly, ironies of intention are always viewed as the result of actions carried out incapably, which is associated with a sense of superiority on the part of the person reviewing the intention. Mention of metaphysical principles like the "Law of Unexpected Consequences" suggest a belief, if only jokingly, in the idea that the cosmos rewards the deserving, and, more importantly, punishes the over-confident. In this respect, irony of intention resembles some of the examples of irony of coincidence (section 3.2.).

Constitution

An irony of constitution concerns an element that falls under one concept because of its intrinsic qualities and another concept because of actions. Consider the situation of Timothy McVeigh, who was put on trial for first degree murder in the bombing of the Murrah Federal Building in Oklahoma City on April 19, 1995.[23] As his trial drew to a close, the main uncertainty of the outcome was whether or not McVeigh would be sentenced to death. Scott Robinson, a Denver trial attorney who had been analyzing the trial, made the following comment:

> This case is so fraught with irony. Unlike most first degree murder cases where the defendant is someone utterly without redeeming social values … . Here we have someone who was a helpful student, not a bully, had a sense of humor. They have enormous mitigation, but the aggravation is so overwhelming that it doesn't matter.

McVeigh also had an excellent service record in the U.S. Army.

Timothy McVeigh falls under the antonymous concepts of people of good social character (the mitigation) and people guilty of first degree murder (the aggravation).

This situation is salient for at least two reasons. First is the spectacular nature of the crime, resulting in a huge loss of life and damage to property. Second, as Robinson mentions, is the high contrast between McVeigh's character as portrayed by his record and his character as reflected in his crime. In addition, the article raises the issue of the death penalty, which is contentious and apt to raise salience as well.

The emotion portrayed in this example is a combination of puzzlement and disgust that might be called chagrin. How could someone of apparently good character turn around and decide on such a villainous course of action? From his track record, we can only assume that McVeigh realized the vicious nature of his attack and chose to go through with it anyway. Unquestionably, McVeigh acted maliciously. Anger is generated in considering this fact, and is evident in the death sentence that McVeigh ultimately received.

Constitution ironies appear to be highly generalized in nature, having no configuration of affect or subject matter peculiar to themselves. Anything possessing intrinsic characteristics, people, institutions, and also animals, may be the subject of these ironies, as the following example about horse evolution shows (Prothero & Schoch, 1989):

> In terms of numbers of individuals, number of species, or ability to spread geographically, *Equus* is undoubtedly the most successful perissodactyl[24] that ever lived. Ironically, it became extinct in its homeland, North America, during the megafaunal extinctions at the beginning of the Holocene.

In this case, the modern horse *Equus* went extinct in the very location for which its evolutionary history suited it. In this case, the modern horse would seem to have incapably exercised the adaptations it had acquired for living in North America.

Type

An irony of type concerns an element that falls under one concept due to its being of a particular kind and falls under a second concept due to circumstances. Consider the aftermath of the death of Johnathan Melvoin, keyboardist of the rock band *Smashing Pumpkins,* who was found dead of a heroin overdose in a New York City hotel room in July 1996.[25] News of the death had at least one odd consequence: Ironically, New York City police reported that Melvoin's death had spurred a rise in demand for the brand of heroin that killed him.

Melvoin's death falls under two concepts, namely warnings against the use of heroin and inducements for the use of heroin. These two concepts are related antisymmetrically in the sense that Melvoin's death shows that heroin kills people, while it also shows that people like heroin.

The salience of this situation is enhanced by two schemata that it activates. First there is the schema of *sex, drugs, and rock 'n roll,* as the article's title suggests. Second, the situation reveals a rule-like perversity in people's behavior as triggered by their attitudes towards celebrities: What celebrities do is desirable to do, no matter how stupid it is.

This situation evokes sadness at the folly of New Yorkers. In a literal sense, Melvoin's death has acted incapably as a type of warning against the use of heroin. But in a metaphorical, personified sense, his death has acted maliciously in advertising heroin rather than cautioning against it. There is also a kind of amusement at the automatic nature of the reaction of those New Yorkers who flock to heroin like the proverbial lemmings to the ocean just because a celebrity did so. Bergson (1900/1913) noted that inappropriately inflexible behavior in others is often the cause of mirth.

Beyond a general tendency to be funny for this reason, ironies of type take on the affect suggested by their subject matter. For example, Marc Philippoussis acted improficiently as an Australian at the 1997 Wimbledon Tennis Championship by being the only one of five Australians defeated in the first elimination round; a slight irony of little salience. If four other Australians could do it, then why couldn't he?[26] Watergate, although it should have served as an affirmation that "the system worked," was instead the event that fixed distrust of government in the public mind; a very unhappy irony for government observers.[27]

Role

Ironies of role are essentially the same as ironies of type except for the fact that the type in question is specialized to an office, position, or rank (e.g., professor, author, president). Consider the Mexican artist Diego Rivera, famous for his murals relating to the Mexican Revolution:[28]

> Ironically, Rivera spent most of the 1910–19 Mexican Revolution in Paris, but he is the artist most commonly associated with the agrarian uprising. In the years after his return to Mexico, his murals celebrated socialist ideas, workers and indigenous peoples.

Diego Rivera is regarded as an icon of the Mexican Revolution, although he worked as a Parisian painter during the Revolution and took no part in it. There are a number of incoherence relations that could be applied to this situation depending upon which aspect of it is emphasized. The most obvious incoherence relation is a simple negative association: people who are symbols of a movement would usually also be participants in it. This reading emphasizes the defeated expectation generated by Rivera's role as a symbol of the Revolution. The situation could also be read as antireciprocal: Whereas Rivera's work did not a advance the Revolution, the Revolution did advance Rivera. This reading emphasizes the costs and benefits arising from the situation. Finally, the situation could also be read as a disproportion: although Rivera was of *little* help to the Revolution, the Revolution was of *much* help to Rivera.

The salience of this situation depends on which reading is represented cognitively. None of these readings alone produce a particularly high salience, except perhaps for art history buffs. However, multiple readings could act collectively to heighten its salience enough so that the situation is recognized as ironic. But, by the same token, multiple readings tend to confuse the conceptual structure assigned to this situation and would thus prevent it from easily matching any particular ironic schema. This inhibitory effect should then lower the salience of the situation. The bicoherence theory, then, predicts that although this situation may be acceptable as an irony, few people would describe it as a good or strong example.

This situation evokes some mirth. On the simple incoherence reading, Rivera would be said to have improficiently fulfilled the role of symbol of the Revolution, in view of his inactivity in that regard. On the antireciprocal reading, Rivera would be said to have licentiously profited from the Revolution, since he did not contribute directly to it. Ironies of role are generally amusing and may be exploited for comic effect, as in the following example from *Saturday Night Live:*[29]

> Famed anthropologist Mary Leakey died last Monday at the age of 83. Leakey was buried near her home, where she will rest in peace, until some nosy anthropologist digs her up.

This situation is clearly antisymmetric and also portrays Leakey as acting licentiously as an anthropologist, just like her "nosy" tormentor.

Status

An irony of status concerns an element that falls under one concept because of some declaration or commitment to that effect and falls under another concept because of its actual performance. It functions similarly to an irony of role but for inanimate objects. Consider the crash of an Aerosweet Yakovlev-42 passenger jet on a regular run from Kiev to Odessa to Salonika in the mountains of northern Greece on December 17, 1997.[30] Aerosweet First Deputy Director Mykola Nykytenko commented that the route is normally serviced by their Western-built aircraft, but that the Boeing 737 in use on that day had to be grounded at Odessa due to technical problems:

> We decided not to continue the flight with the Boeing because of safety considerations, so we called up a Yakovlev 42 from (the western Ukrainian city of Lviv) to continue the flight. Who could have foreseen such a terrible irony?

The Yak-42 aircraft falls under the antonymous concepts of aircraft judged able to provide a safe flight and of aircraft that crash.

The salience of this situation is high for at least three reasons. First, the loss of life was high, thus making this flight stand out. Second, the issue of flight safety is thrown into high relief by the fact that the Yak-42 was chosen over a Boeing 737 for precisely this reason. Third, the situation follows a version of Murphy's Law: Anything that can go wrong will go wrong, and under the worst possible circumstances. The plane crashed in a mountainous area that made rescue efforts especially difficult.

The emotion most obvious in this situation is sadness. Much of this emotion results from the loss of life involved, but some also seems to result from being frustrated in the goal of providing a safe flight. The Yak-42 incapably lived up to its end of the bargain, as it were, which it entered into when it was given its flight-ready status. If we take this personification more seriously, the Yak-42 might be considered to have acted maliciously, deceiving officials into declaring it flight-ready and then betraying them on that count. This reading would be confirmed if Nykytenko and other Aerosweet officials felt bitter or angry after the crash.

Ironies of status are typically tragic, evoking emotions of sadness and bitterness. The sadness may be a result of the fact that ironies of status often expose the defeat of deliberate declarations, presumptions, and announcements. This situation gives rise to a depressing sense of futility or what Frijda (1986, pp. 211–212) referred to as loss of *controllability*. Ironies of status often appear to encourage inanimate objects to be personified, which makes their situations more concrete and easier to understand (Lakoff & Johnson, 1980, pp. 33–34), in this case by construing a physical misfortune as a social letdown. However, where the salience remains sufficiently low, status ironies may be humorous, as in the case of Robbie Fowler, the Liverpool soccer player who was condemned by UEFA (the European soccer association) and praised by FIFA (the world soccer association) at one and the same time, albeit for different reasons.[31]

Title

An irony of title is an irony of status in which the status of an element is fixed simply by a name other than institutionalized description. Consider the situation of Susan John, a representative in the New York State Assembly, and, until May 1997, chair of the Assembly's Alcohol and Drug Abuse Committee:[32]

> In Albany, N.Y., Susan John has been asked to resign as chairwoman of the State Assembly's *Alcohol and Drug Abuse Committee* following her arrest on drunk-driving charges. On the bright side for John, she has been asked to chair the Assembly's Committee on Irony.

The Committee on Irony is, of course, fictitious.

Susan John falls under two antonymous concepts, namely a prominent official who opposes alcohol abuse and a prominent person who indulges in alcohol abuse.

The salience of this situation is increased by the egg-on-the-face effect above (section 3.3.). John also readily fits the stereotype of the duplicitous government official saying one thing and doing its opposite. Also, Littman and Mey (1991, p. 138) noted that the salience of title ironies (which they called *competence* ironies) is increased where the element is not impelled or pushed into an incoherent situation but rather goes of its own accord.

The emotion of mirth is associated with this situation. This quality may be explained by our reaction to the automatism displayed by the element which puts itself into an ironic situation, as with the example of a type irony discussed above. Because title ironies involve an incoherence between an element and its institutional description, the element is conceived as acting licentiously. Title ironies are always humorous and often rely on puns. Title ironies may be imposed upon sad or tragic situations, but have a forced or made-up feel as a result. Ironies of title resemble ironies of policy and role in some respects, except that a title is a much more tenuous way than a policy or role for an element to fall under a concept. If we were to examine Susan John's situation more closely, we might find that she expressed an explicit policy of eliminating drunk driving, or that her role as Chair formally compels her to condemn her own actions. These things may be true and ironic, but they are not raised in the story above. It is sufficient that she has a particular title associated with her name.

Model

A model irony is a special form of type irony in which an element derives its type from being modeled on something else. Consider the *Native American Graves Protection and Repatriation Act* (NAGPRA), a federal American law which requires museums and other institutions to return artifacts and skeletal remains to the appropriate Native American bands.[33] This act was modeled on a Massachusetts state law brought into existence through the efforts of John Peters, the supreme medicine man of the Mashpee Wampanoag tribe. Shortly after John's death, his brother made the following observation about the NAGPRA: "Ironically, it excluded [the Mashpee Wampanoags] because we're not federally recognized," said Russell Peters.

The NAGPRA falls under the antonymous concepts of legislation modeled on the Massachusetts law and legislation significantly dissimilar to the Massachusetts law. But, as suggested by the content of Russell Peters's quotation, the situation can also be understood metaphorically as follows: The Mashpee Wampanoags helped bring the NAGPRA into existence but the NAGPRA failed to help bring the Mashpee Wampanoags into existence—as a federally recognized entity.

The salience of this irony is increased by the fact that it concerns the legacy of a recently deceased person whose life project, authorizing the claim of Native Americans to their artifacts, failed in a personally important respect due to an arbitrary difference in state and federal laws.

The dominant emotion attendant on this situation is sadness. The modeling process which produced the NAGPRA from the Massachusetts legislation appears therefore to have been flawed, which is to say that it was carried out improficiently. On the metaphorical reading, the relation between the Mashpee Wampanoags and the NAGPRA is antireciprocal, and the modeling process was carried out licentiously. There might also be some *dark humor* in this reading in the sense that this licentious behavior on the part of the NAGPRA was the result of a mechanical kind of legal problem, and mechanical failures in behavior tend to be funny (see the discussion of type irony above).

Model irony is the complement of analogy irony (section 3.2.). In other words, ironies of one kind may be re-represented as ironies of the other kind through a process of *irony shift* (see section 6.3.). In this case, the model irony could have been represented as a class of laws regarding Native Americans, two elements of which are ironically dissimilar. However, the emphasis in this example, to judge from the phrasing chosen by Russell Peters, is primarily on the NAGPRA itself.

Disproportion

An irony of disproportion concerns an element that has the magnitude usually associated with some other element. This category is very different from the others discussed above as it features an incoherence relation, namely *disproportion,* rather than a coherence relation such as *type.* Ironies of disproportion seem to stand out in the corpus, however, so the creation of a special category seems warranted. Consider, for example, the fact that heart disease is the number one killer of women in the United States, a fact that most American women do not appreciate.[34] The National Council on the Aging and the Center for Risk Communication, which uncovered this fact in a study, made the following remark about it: "When asked which disease they fear most, more than half the women in the survey (61%) cited cancer," the Council said in a statement. "Ironically, only 9% said they feared heart attack, the No. 1 killer of women."

Heart disease here falls under two concepts, namely the top cause of death among American women and the also-ran causes of concern among American women. Obviously, the two concepts are related by disproportion. Since heart disease is the top killer of women, it should be the most feared, but cancer, which is not the top killer, generates that level of fear instead.

The salience of this irony comes from at least two sources. First, it concerns life-threatening diseases, so fundamental health issues are at stake. Second, women's ignorance about heart disease increases their vulnerability to it.

The emotions conveyed by this example are sadness and frustration. Sadness stems ultimately from the lack of controllability (see the discussion of status irony above) inherent in the fact that although we expect things to be proportioned in one way, they come proportioned in a contrary way. Frustration results from difficulties in correcting the situation. The National Council on Aging shows this frustration by blaming doctors and the media for not effectively communicating the facts about heart disease to women.

But, beyond an initial tendency to sad affect, disproportions take on the emotional tone imposed by their subject matter. Some ironies of disproportion may be humorous, as in well-known T-shirt slogans such as "My brother went to Disneyland, and all I got was this lousy T-shirt."

This example could have been classified as a type irony on the basis that, being a No. 1 killer, heart disease is exactly the type of thing that American women should fear most. While this assignment would be valid, it would only capture half of the irony. It is not only important that women's fear of heart disease is out of proportion to its threat, but that heart disease and cancer seem to have *each other's* proportion of that fear. This fact points to the conclusion that irony of disproportion is the complement of irony of exchanged places (section 3.3.). So, the irony could be described as applying to a class, fatal diseases, of which heart disease exceeds cancer in real fatalities, but of which cancer exceeds heart disease in imagined fatalities.

RESULTS

The Taxonomy

A total of 217 articles, containing a total of 250 separate instances of irony, were collected over the course of the study. A taxonomy of 16 categories of situational irony was generated from pile-sorting every instance in the corpus. Each category is defined by a unique combination of coherence relations, incoherence relations, and manner consistent with the bicoherence theory. Five categories of bicoherence class ironies (including the basic class) and eleven categories of bicoherent element irony (including the basic class) were generated.

The Distribution of Ironies

The distribution of ironies into each category is given in Table 23.3. The distribution highlights the class/element distinction that is fundamental to the conceptual structure of ironies according to the bicoherence theory. There are roughly twice as many bicoherent element ironies (165) as there are bicoherent class ironies (85). This roughly 2-to-1 ratio is probably explained by the similar ratio of *categories* of element ironies (11) to class ironies (5). Roughly speaking, there are twice as many element ironies than class ironies in the corpus because there are twice as many ways to find an element irony in a situation than there are ways to find a class irony in it.

But it is not clear why there are twice as many categories of bicoherent element ironies as bicoherent class ironies. In fact, the reason for this disparity may rest outside the purview of the bicoherence theory. The cognitive resources at work in finding a situation ironic are also recruited for other purposes, such as causal attribution (see section 6.1). All the cognitive functions, including situational irony, that share or compete for these resources do therefore affect each other indirectly. Thus, there are undoubtedly facts about situational irony that are not explicable within any theory of situational irony, properly speaking, but only within a more general cognitive theory. The 2-to-1 ratio in categories of irony may well be one such fact.

Typicality and Representativeness

Certain kinds of irony stand out as typical in relation to the corpus as a whole. Ironies of coincidence comprise approximately 38% of the total number of bicoherent class ironies. Ironies of policy, type, and title comprise 13%, 16%, and 14% of bicoherent element ironies, respectively. These forms of irony appear to typify the subgrouping of irony in which they each occur. The distribution of ironies into these subgroupings is given in Table 23.4. This table indicates that ironies depending on

TABLE 23.3

The Distribution of Ironies in the Study Corpus is Given According to Category

Type and Subtype	N
B-class/basic	23
Analogy	6
Coincidence	32
Catch-22	2
Exchanged	22
Subtotal	85
B-element/basic	11
Policy	21
Hypocrisy	16
Intention	14
Constitution	20
Type	26
Role	7
Status	9
Title	23
Model	3
Disproportion	15
Subtotal	165
Total	250

Note. A total of 250 ironies were counted in 217 news articles. Ambiguous ironies and complement ironies were counted only once.

TABLE 23.4

The Distribution of Ironies According to Subcategory, in Order of Descending Frequency

Subgrouping	N
Type	70
Similarity	62
Policy	51
Constitution	20
Disproportion	15

various forms of similarity, policy, and type are fairly evenly represented in the corpus as a whole, whereas ironies featuring the constitution coherence relation and the disproportion incoherence relation are much less frequent.

This notable division in frequency may be explicable by the particular demands made by ironies of constitution and disproportion. First, disproportion is a fairly complex coherence relation (see section 2.3.) that might not be applied to a situation when it is sufficient for a simpler relation to be applied. In other words, where different representations compete to be applied to a situation, complex representations including disproportion are at a disadvantage and may lose out. Second, constitution usually implies knowledge of how someone or something has behaved in the past (see section 2.2.). A reporter describing an ironic situation may decide, for the sake of brevity, to omit any description of someone's past history in favor of, say, a remark on what type of person that person is. So, it is often quicker to describe someone as "lazy" than to state that she leaves work early most days, drives rather than walks to the end of her block to get to the convenience store, and likes porridge because she doesn't have to chew it. Space is often at a premium in news articles, so there may well be a tendency among reporters to avoid describing constitutions where shorter descriptions based on types, for example, are available.

This potential source of bias raises the issue of the representativeness of the corpus as a whole. That is, how well does the distribution of ironies, as given in Tables 23.3 and 23.4, represent the true distribution of situational ironies in the minds of people at large? The question is impossible to answer since the true distribution of ironies is not known. Comparison with future corpus studies would seem to be the most promising way to address this issue.

Of course, the representativeness of the current study could be questioned by taking sources of reporter bias into account. Reporters and editors do not select stories at random for distribution. Harriss, Leiter, and Johnson (1992, pp. 27–33) stated that newsworthy situations are those that display at least some of the following "values:" conflict, progress, disaster, consequence, prominence, novelty, human interest, timeliness, proximity, sex, and animals. It may be that sensitivity to these values introduces a bias in the sample that reporters take of the overall population of ironic situations. It is also possible that people in general are sensitive to the same values in their view of situations so that the reporters' sampling is really unbiased after all.

Exhaustiveness

In addition to representativeness, there is the issue of the exhaustiveness of the taxonomy discussed in section 3. It is possible that there are categories of situational irony that simply did not turn up in the collection of the present corpus. Without denying this possibility, there are good reasons to believe that the corpus is comprehensive.

At 250 ironies, the corpus is extensive and was collected over an entire year from a broad variety of sources and covers many, varying situations. The expectations of the experimenter exerted no influence over the generation or collection of the ironies. Most appear to have been generated spontaneously either by the reporter or a person quoted by the reporter.

Finally, as noted in section 3.1., collection of new examples had continued for two months prior to the end of the experiment without requiring the addition or deletion of any taxonomic categories.

All this evidence suggests that the taxonomy is exhaustive. It should also be remembered, as pointed out at the outset of section 3, that the taxonomy is *not* identical with the bicoherence theory, but is an analytical convenience defined in accordance with the theory. Revisions to the taxonomy need not be injurious to the theory, provided they can be made within the framework laid out in section 2. Thus, although the exhaustiveness of the taxonomy is an important issue, it is not paramount for current purposes.

Reliability

A modest study of interrater reliability was undertaken to assess the clarity of the taxonomic categories. A pilot study indicated that training subjects in the entire theory is too onerous a task for this purpose. So the study was broken into five independent substudies in which the subject was trained to make a single distinction between two types of situational irony and asked to apply this distinction to five examples drawn from the corpus described above. The nine most populous, nonbasic categories were chosen for this purpose. Coincidence was used twice in hopes of contrasting its repeated appearances. Categories were paired to represent a full range of taxonomic distances, with distance calculated as the number of branchings separating two categories in the hierarchy given in Figure 23.3. Other things being equal, greater distance should imply greater ease of making the distinction in question.

The study was constructed as a set of Web pages so that volunteers could be solicited over the Internet. (The experimenter does not have access to a pool of subjects.) Efforts were made to maximize the likelihood of casual participation: subjects were asked to undertake only as many of the substudies as they wished; in each substudy, one example of two kinds of situational irony (drawn from the examples covered in section 3.) were described in nontheoretical terms; the subjects were asked to categorize five further examples into one or the other training category; these five examples were selected randomly from the corpus, provided only that they occupied no more than one, brief paragraph. Respondents were solicited by "word-of-mouth" through email and postings to Internet newsgroups. None of the respondents had any prior knowledge of the bicoherence theory. Responses consisted of a list of categorizations of the examples in each substudy and were emailed by the respondent directly to the experimenter. The study was conducted during November 2000. The results are summarized in Table 23.5.

The table shows strong agreement between the experimenter and the respondents. Agreement of the respondents with the experimenter in each substudy was

TABLE 23.5

Rater Agreement As a Function of Taxonomic Distance

Distance	Distinction	Respondents	Agreements/Response	
			Ratio	Percentage
1	Policy vs. hypocrisy	10	38/47	81%
2	Coincidence vs. exchanged	16	75/78	96%
3	Constitution vs. intention	10	42/46	91%
4	Disproportion vs. title	12	45/57	79%
4x	Coincidence vs. type	10	43/47	91%

Note. The distance 4x denotes a distance of 4 that stretches across the element/class branches of the taxonomy. Each study (row of the table) contained five examples for categorization.

typically on the order of 90%. (The 79% agreement of the disproportion vs. title substudy is attributable to a single example for which only 4 of 11 responses agreed with the categorization of the experimenter.) This result indicates that the contrasts between categories of situational irony offered by the bicoherence theory are robust and reliable. The expected correlation between agreement and categorical distance, however, is not evident. It may be that the number of respondents was simply too low for this effect to appear, or it may be that the restriction of problem examples to short excerpts confounded it. The shortest examples are often the most stereotyped, leaving little opportunity for the details of their conceptual structure to affect how they are processed.

Respondents' comments revealed other interesting aspects of this study that should be taken into consideration in further studies of this kind. First, some respondents have strong ideas about irony that they brought into the study. Some effort should be made to assess and adjust for this fact in the future. Second, as predicted in section 2.4., respondents are reluctant to categorize as ironic situations that they do not perceive to be salient. It might be more informative to compare ironic situations that are perceived as equally salient, or to adjust for assessments of salience. Third, respondents sometimes have strong notions of hypocrisy or coincidence, so that it would be best to avoid using these terms in labeling categories of irony for study purposes.

Manner and Rhetoric

The distribution of manners into the specific kinds of element ironies (excluding basic and disproportion) is given in Table 23.6. The table gives an indication of how the various forms of irony relate to the manners considered. Some ironies, such as hypocrisy and title, seem directed mostly toward moral failings, whereas policy and intention relate mostly to physical failings and the rest show a fairly even distribution. The manners are fairly evenly distributed overall, but with *licentiously* as a clear favorite and *excessively* by far the least represented.

Manner is key to understanding the emotional responses of people to the perceived physical and moral qualities of situational ironies (see section 2.5.). As such, manner is key to understanding the rhetoric of irony—that is, the study of how ironies affect or bring about persuasion. Accusing someone of hypocrisy, for example, can be an effective rhetorical device to persuade others that that person deserves punishment. A study of the rhetoric of irony would go a long way in answering the need for research on how bias affects the reporting of ironies noted in section 4.3.

DISCUSSION

The corpus study provides empirical support for the bicoherence theory of situational irony. The theory explains why the situation described in each article is labeled as *ironic*. The term *irony* and its lexical relatives, when used spontaneously by reporters to describe a situation, signal the activation of a bicoherent conceptual structure, a certain level of cognitive salience accompanied by a particular configuration of emotions, and often a physical or moral evaluation.

A comprehensive classificatory scheme for situational ironies was derived from the bicoherence theory by grouping ironies according to the coherence or incoherence relations prominent in each case. This scheme shows not only that the theory applies well to the data collected in the corpus, but that it provides a tool useful for analyzing the kinds of ironies that crop up under a variety of circumstances. In or-

TABLE 23.6
The Joint Distribution of Manners in Specific Bicoherent Element Ironies

Irony	Manner				
	Improficiently	Incapably	Excessively	Licentiously	Maliciously
Policy	7	5	6	2	0
Hypocrisy	0	0	0	0	16
Intention	5	8	2	0	0
Constitution	5	2	0	6	3
Type	7	13	1	9	8
Role	1	0	1	5	0
Status	3	5	1	1	5
Title	1	0	0	20	0
Model	1	0	0	1	1
Total	30	33	11	44	33

Note. Ironies with metaphorical readings have been counted for both literal and personified senses.

der to analyze a situational irony, the following questions need to be addressed: Is the emphasis on one thing (bicoherent element) or two things and the contrast between them (bicoherent class)? Which incoherence relation is involved? What makes this irony salient? Which emotions are attached to it? Which moral or physical evaluation is placed on the irony? Finding answers to these questions is guided by the theory and provides a thorough understanding of the irony in question.

The study revealed a number of issues not anticipated in the initial statement of the bicoherence theory. Ironies of coincidence, for example, do not include an incoherence relation from the list given in section 2.2. In addition to a coherence relation, however, they do include a second coherence relation accompanied by the emotion of surprise. In order to apply the bicoherence theory to these examples, it must be assumed that a coherence relation accompanied by surprise can simulate or act in place of a real incoherence relation. It is supposed that the negative valence attached to surprise allows a surprising coherence relation to activate the concept of irony. This additional hypothesis saves the bicoherence theory but enjoys, as yet, no independent empirical support. If this solution seems *ad hoc,* it might by the same token explain the common view that ironies of coincidence are not proper ironies.

As far as emotional configurations are concerned, situational ironies may be divided up into two types. First are the *opaque* types that are usually associated with one or two particular emotions. Hypocrisy, for example, is generally accompanied by emotions of disgust and anger, and a manner of being maliciously brought about. Second are the *opace* or transparent types of irony that usually take on the emotional qualities suggested by the situation itself. Ironies of constitution are of this type: Such ironies about funny situations evoke mirth whereas such ironies about tragic situations evoke sadness. The emotional opaqueness or opacity of situational ironies has not been considered by previous researchers. Some researchers have simply used emotions to distinguish taxonomic categories, effectively assuming that all ironies must be opaque in the sense that a particular emotion is invariably attached to each category. The bicoherence theory indicates that this assumption is unfounded.

The study also offers a solution to a the problem of defining hypocrisy, a concept that has resisted such attempts since Aristotle (Szabados & Soifer, 1998). Traditionally, hypocrisy has been defined as a kind of moral defect of character and has not been connected with situational irony. This study suggests a connection and the following definition: Hypocrisy, as a character trait, is that disposition which causes a person to put himself in a particular kind of ironic situation by maliciously applying a policy. Although this definition does not clarify the whole issue, it does offer a way of connecting the concept of hypocrisy as a character trait with current theories of human cognition via the bicoherence theory.

Muecke (1982, p. 1) stated that the kind of irony described in news articles, which he called *folk irony,* "generally offers no great challenge." The corpus study shows that this view could not be further from the truth. The explanation of folk irony requires, at least, the use of cognitive theories like the coherence theory, psychological theories like the communicative theory of emotions, along with accounts of cognitive salience and new theoretical apparatus such as manners. Clearly, folk irony offers challenges great enough to merit serious consideration.

FURTHER ISSUES

Irony and Causal Attribution

The bicoherence theory of situational irony enjoys a number of connections with theories of social psychology. It is based on the theory of conceptual coherence used by Kunda and Thagard (1996) to give a model of social impression formation. Their model shows how stereotypes and other sources of information constrain each other during the process through which people evaluate each other's traits and characters.

The bicoherence theory enjoys another connection with social psychology in the form of the *principle of causal attribution* (see Nisbett & Ross, 1980, pp. 113–115). This principle states that people use three kinds of information in order to explain the behavior of others, namely *consistency, distinctiveness,* and *consensus*. These sources map exactly onto the three main subgroups of bicoherent element ironies, namely policy, constitution, and type.

People apply the consistency criterion when they judge someone in one situation by comparison with how that person has behaved in the *same* situation in the past. This criterion corresponds to the policy coherence relation in the bicoherence theory. A policy is, after all, a way people have of making their behavior consistent over time. If someone has a policy of helping little old ladies across the street, then she will do so on each appropriate occasion. Departures from one's policy are counted as inconsistencies in one's behavior.

People apply the distinctiveness criterion when they judge someone in one situation by comparison with how that person has behaved in *similar* situations in the past. This criterion corresponds to the constitution relation in the bicoherence theory. Having a particular constitution or temperament means that a person will behave in a similar manner in a broad class of similar situations. If we observe that someone becomes nauseous in courtyards and in parking lots, for example, we may conclude that he has agoraphobia, which would also cause him to become queasy in a baseball stadium.

People apply the consensus criterion when they judge someone in one situation by comparison with how *other* people have behaved in the same situation in the past. This criterion corresponds to the type relation of the bicoherence theory. Knowing what type of person someone is means knowing how everyone of the same type is apt to behave. If we know that someone is a thrill-seeker and we have seen that other thrill seekers enjoy bungee-jumping, then we may conclude that she will also enjoy bungee-jumping.

Both the principle of causal attribution and the bicoherence theory describe ways in which people explain behavior in a given situation. Their congruence, then, suggests that the bicoherence theory is consistent with the account of causal reason-

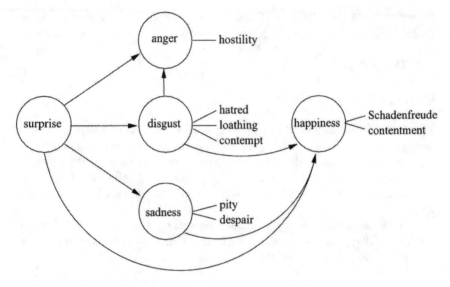

Figure 23.4.   A transition diagram displaying the possible developments in emotions from surprise over the course of considering a situational irony.

ing given by the principle of causal attribution. Indeed, the bicoherence theory may suggest refinements for the principle, since it makes finer distinctions among sources of information and covers not only people, but objects, institutions, and events.

This congruence also produces a prediction about cultural variation in situational irony. The principle of causal attribution has been shown to be applied differently in different cultures (see Ross & Nisbett, 1991, pp. 184–186). Similarly, people in different cultures should have different concepts of situational irony. This matter is clearly one for further investigation.

There is one incongruity between the principle of causal attribution and the bicoherence theory. The bicoherence theory includes a group of similarity relations comprising the bicoherent class ironies. There is no corresponding criterion of causal attribution. Social psychologists do, however, recognize a corresponding *departure* from causal attribution called the *fundamental attribution error* (see Ross & Nisbett, 1991, pp. 125–139), the tendency of people to explain the misfortunes of others as the results of some personal defect rather than simple coincidence. So, for example, if someone stumbles, then we are apt to attribute it to clumsiness rather than to an innocuous lump in the rug. There is a curious analogy here: Just as people devalue coincidence as a kind of situational irony, they devalue coincidence as an explanation of the behavior of others. Coincidence, at least, appears to hold a similar position in both theories.

Irony and the Course of Emotions Over Time

Situational ironies are accompanied by some configuration of emotion or affect. This fact is not the end of the story, however. The emotions evoked by an irony tend to develop in particular ways over the time the irony is considered, a fact that shows up occasionally in the news articles in the corpus. The course of emotions over this time is shown in Figure 23.4 and is outlined in this section.

Ironies tend to begin with surprise. Lucariello (1994) showed that unexpectedness is the feature most reliably associated with situational ironies. This fact is explicable in the bicoherence theory by noting that bicoherence represents a pattern of concept activation diametrically opposed to coherence, the pattern that arises when our concepts fit well with the world. A pattern of concepts that show the worst fit with the world is naturally unexpected.

Although surprise is ubiquitous in situational ironies, this fact does not mean that surprise and irony can be equated. For a surprising situation to be ironic, the surprise must be due to conceptual incoherence and not some other factor, and the situation must be sufficiently salient. You might be surprised to notice a square manhole cover on a manhole but this situation is not ironic unless it was important to you that the cover be round as usual.

Ironies frequently proceed from surprise to sadness, a state of affairs often pointed out in news articles by the adjectives *sad, tragic,* and *grim.* Complex emotions such as pity and despair typically result: pity for those persons caught in a sad situation, and despair that situations such as the one in question may often turn out contrary to expectation.

Other ironies are disagreeable and proceed from surprise to disgust. These ironies are often described as *bitter.* The complex emotions related to disgust, such as hatred, loathing, and contempt may be felt by a person towards an offending object or situation from which he desires to distance himself. Expressions of disgust in the corpus indicate the wish of the person affected for the ironic situation to simply go away or cease to exist.

Some ironies go from surprise to anger in the form of accusations of negligence, wrong-doing, and immorality. The complex form of anger aimed at a particular target could be called hostility. Hostility is especially evident in ironies of hypocrisy, in which a person or institution is reviled. Some cases of hostility seem to arise not directly from surprise but as a development of disgust when a disagreeable situation persists and thereby frustrates the desire that it should go away. In this case, the disagreeable entity becomes not something to be avoided but something to be removed.

A few ironies result in a feeling of happiness or satisfaction. There are three different routes that lead to this result. First, happiness may result from a kind of *Schadenfreude* or shameful joy in the misfortunes of another, especially an enemy. Second, contentment may follow from the appearance of *poetic justice,* when a disagreeable situation reaches a satisfactory outcome. Third, happiness occasionally appears to follow directly from surprise in the form of a *happy coincidence.* Some happy coincidence ironies are described as delicious, which suggests that they are happy partly because the anticipated feeling of disgust has been thoroughly reversed.

Fear is the basic emotion conspicuous by its absence from situational irony. No clear indications of fear or related emotions occur in the corpus. There are two possible explanations for the absence of fear. First, it may be that fear is incompatible with irony. Frijda (1986, p. 350) argued that unusual or unfamiliar situations tend to elicit fear if we feel that we have no ways of coping with them. (Otherwise, unusual situations tend to produce interest or curiosity.) Finding an unusual situation to be ironic may count as a way of coping with it, in which case fear is inhibited. Reacting fearfully to a situation likewise results in irony being inhibited.

Second, Ortony, Clore, and Collins (1988, p. 109) pointed out that fear is primarily a prospect-based emotion—that is, a reaction to a future situation that we expect to be unpleasant and unavoidable. Situational irony is primarily retrospective—that is, a reaction to a past situation. Because fear is prospective whereas irony is retrospective, it may simply be the case that irony and fear develop from incompatible circumstances. The second explanation seems more forceful than the first, but further research is needed to clarify the relation between fear and situational irony.

6.3. Changes in Conceptual Structure

The relationship in conceptual structure between class and element ironies suggests a novel prediction about situational ironies, namely that class and element ironies are interconvertible. Consider again the following descriptions of bicoherent elements and classes:

- *Bicoherent element:* An element that belongs to two incoherent classes.
- *Bicoherent class:* A class that includes two incoherent elements.

Note that each description is the *dual* of the other—that is, each description may be obtained from the other by transposing the terms *element* and *class,* and *belong to* and *include,* respectively. This duality implies that element and class ironies may be interconverted by a similar transposition. Of course, the duality of conceptual structure is no guarantee that salience or emotional quality will be preserved in the process.

This section lays out manipulations of the conceptual structure of ironies consistent with the bicoherence theory. The workability of these manipulations, which may be called *irony shift* and *irony elimination,* helps to confirm that the theory correctly describes the conceptual structure of situational ironies.

6.3.1. Irony Shift

The process of shifting from one form of irony to another, *irony shift,* is easily understood graphically as shown in Figure 23.5. The procedure for class-to-element shift may be described as follows:

1. Select one of the two class elements on which to concentrate.
2. Remove the unselected element and its attendant incoherence relation from the description of the given situation.
3. Add the description of a class to which the unselected element does not belong but to which the selected element does belong, such that the two classes incohere.

The procedure for element-to-class shift is simply the reverse of the above procedure.

For example, consider the case of Mr. Mangat described as a basic, bicoherent class irony (section 3.2.). The irony concerned the fact that immigrant representatives like Mr. Mangat were required to be lawyers, although the government adjudicators—who belonged to the same class of immigration court advocates—were not so required. This irony may be shifted to an element irony as follows:

1. Concentrate on Mr. Mangat.
2. Forget about the government adjudicators.
3. Note that Mr. Mangat remains a court advocate and must *also* be a lawyer.

Read in this way, Mr. Mangat is caught in a type irony (section 3.3.) since, as an immigration court advocate, he can only function improficiently as a lawyer. Put another way, it would be ironic for Mr. Mangat to go to law school and become a lawyer only to perform a job for which his special skills make him grossly overqualified. When represented as an element irony, the situation is less salient as it does not enjoy the sharp contrast between Mr. Mangat and the government adjudicators nor a particularly sad affect. Undoubtedly, the maximization of salience is a major reason why the situation is described as a class irony by Mr. Mangat himself.

It is evident that irony shift, which depends primarily on the conceptual structure of irony, does not necessarily preserve salience or affect. The fact that irony shift is possible as the bicoherence theory predicts offers further support for the conceptual structure of irony proposed in the theory. The fact

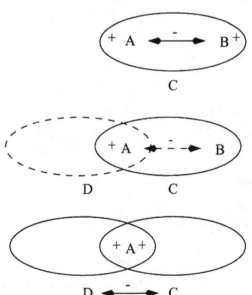

Figure 23.5. The procedure for irony shift. The shift class-to-element is shown top-down, and the element-to-class shift is shown bottom-up.

that salience and affect are not preserved underlines the importance of their place in the theory as well.

Irony Elimination

A different implication of the conceptual structure of situational irony is that irony may be eliminated by changing the conceptual representation of a situation so that no incoherence is apparent. A bicoherent element irony, for example, may be eliminated by replacing the two incoherent concepts which the element falls under with a single concept which it falls under. This procedure of *irony elimination* is displayed graphically in Figure 23.6. The procedure of *irony introduction* is simply the reverse of elimination.

Consider the case of Jimmy Bulger, a mobster who was used by the FBI as an informant on organized crime in Boston.[35] As a mob informant, Bulger obtained more information from his handlers about local FBI activity than he ever gave out about mob activity. He sometimes even wore a wire to his FBI meetings and recorded the proceedings on tape. Needless to say, the fact that Bulger was able to exchange places with his FBI handlers was an embarrassing irony for the FBI. But, more basic even than this irony is the fact that Bulger was a known criminal in the employ of the FBI, a federal law-enforcement agency. It is ironic, in general, for someone who earns a living from organized crime to draw a paycheck from the police in virtue of this same fact. However, this irony plays no immediate role in the situation as presented above precisely because Bulger is described as a *mob infor-*

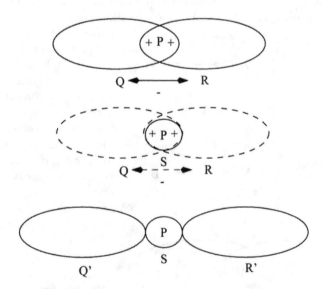

Figure 23.6.   The procedure for irony elimination. The classes Q and R are eliminated in favor of Q' and R', and the class S is introduced such that it contains P but excludes classes Q' and R'. The procedure for irony introduction would be the reverse procedure.

mant. The fact that he is represented under this concept makes Bulger appear to fall under the concept of mob informants, rather than a person at the intersection of the concepts mobster and law-enforcement personnel. In effect, the overlap and the attendant irony have been eliminated by replacement with a new concept, as shown graphically in Figure 23.6.

Situational ironies appear to depend upon details of conceptual representations as the bicoherence theory predicts. Ironies may be created or destroyed through manipulations of the concepts applied to represent a situation. The details of irony shift and irony elimination need to be further investigated by experiment.

Irony and Modality

The bicoherence theory gives a solid account of situational irony. Naturally, it is interesting to consider how the bicoherence theory might be applied to other kinds of irony, such as verbal or dramatic irony. This section presents a cursory examination of irony in nonsituational modalities to assess the prospects for applying or extending the bicoherence theory to account for them. Extending the theory and thus unifying the different kinds of irony is left as a project for another time.

In addition to situations, irony also occurs in the visual modality in terms of ironies conveyed by pictures. Consider the irony conveyed in a picture taken by photographer James Nachtwey:[36]

> Irony abounds in his work. The foreground of one photo shows a young couple strolling casually, engrossed in quiet conversation, the woman pushing a stroller in which a baby sleeps. The child's mouth is plugged by a pacifier, a gadget whose very name means "peace." In the background the skeleton of a fire-bombed truck still burns. This is Northern Ireland.

This photograph is ironic in the sense that it depicts a basic element irony: a single scene (element) combining components coherent with peaceful and violent activities (concepts), parceled out into foreground and background. The elaboration on pacifier hints at a congruent title irony. The irony of the photograph falls nicely under the bicoherence theory when its contents are given as the description of a situation.

There are also ironic gestures and expressions. Consider the facial expression that Ekman (1984, pp. 323–324) called a miserable smile. Such a smile is one that a person fakes in order to indicate that he or she feels miserable rather than happy (Ekman, 1984, p. 323):

> Suppose the dentist tells a patient that a root canal is needed, which is going to hurt a lot and cost a lot of money. A good patient will greet such news with a miserable smile. It is a "grin and bear it" smile. It lets the other person know one is not going to show the distress or fear that one feels. It acknowledges one's misery.

The miserable smile may be considered as the element in a model irony—that is, it is an expression modeled on a genuine smile, but also including elements of a distress grimace sufficient to show that it is not a genuine expression of pleasure. Normally, a smile and a grimace express antonymic emotions. As Ekman (1984) noted, the smile bears a resemblance to the verbal irony of stating something contrary to what one means, in this case a verbal assurance like "A root canal? Oh great!"

Irony is also present in music. Monson (1994), for example, discussed several instances of musical irony which are characterized, interestingly, in terms of "doubleness" or "repetition with a difference." For example, Monson cited John Coltraine's rearrangement of Rodgers and Hammerstein's *My Favorite Things,* otherwise canonically associated with Julie Andrews's performance of it in the movie *The Sound of Music* (Wise, 1965). Coltraine's swinging jazz version seems to mock the "vapid" rendition given by Andrews (Monson, 1994, p. 292*n*26). In fact, the mere *selection* of a song whose lyrics concern so many white things, for example, girls in white dresses, snowflakes on eyelashes, silver white winters, and cream-colored ponies, by a Black musician seems ironic in itself (Monson, 1994, p. 298). The description of this irony as "repetition with a difference" suggests that this irony is a model irony in which Coltraine's arrangement is the target element that takes *The Sound of Music's* arrangement for its source.

The notion of repetition with a difference recalls the interpretive resemblance theory of Wilson and Sperber (1992), on which an utterance counts as ironic if the speaker uses it to (a) implicitly attribute an opinion to someone while (b) expressing an attitude of dissociation or disapproval towards that opinion. The implicit attribution of (a) is evidenced by the resemblance of the content of the utterance to the content of the opinion in question. So, for example, if Bill is described to Mary as "an officer and a gentleman" and Bill subsequently behaves like a jerk towards her, then Mary might be apt to remark "An officer and a gentleman, indeed" (Wilson & Sperber, 1992, p. 60). The remark counts as ironic because Mary uses it to refer to an opinion previously stated to her which, we may infer, she has found to be misleading.

In terms of the bicoherence theory, this characterization of verbal irony could be recast as follows: condition (a) identifies the source of a concept that applied bicoherently to the situation in question, while (b) registers a negative emotional reaction from the speaker. On this view, a verbal irony counts as ironic because it draws attention to an irony in some situation. Consider the Bill-and-Mary example. Mary's remark refers to a type irony: She expected Bill to be the polite and gallant type but discovered him to be a jerk instead. Mary's remark, then, is ironic because it draws attention to the fact that Mary finds the situation to which it refers to be an ironic one. Perhaps, as Littman and Mey (1991, p. 134) speculated, all verbal ironies presuppose an ironic situation in this sort of way.

There are a couple of things to note about this characterization of verbal irony. First, the remark is not ironic if it explicitly identifies its subject as ironic. For example, if Mary had said, "Ironically, the 'officer and a gentleman' turned out to be a big jerk," then this remark itself would not count as an ironic one, in spite of the fact that it describes that same situation as the alternative, "an officer and a gentleman, indeed." Apparently, the remark itself is ironic only if it does *not* directly indicate that the relevant situation is ironic in the speaker's view. Perhaps this condition is what Sperber (1994) referred to when he described irony as metarepresentational—that is, inferred from an utterance and its context. Second, not all ironic remarks express dissociation or disapproval. After all, some ironies are happy ones. Consider an understatement such as "Tiger Woods had a pretty good day" by an approving TV producer to describe Woods's win in the 1997 Masters golf tournament (see the discussion of coincidence in section 3.2.). Obviously, this remark would not be wholly consonant with the producer's reaction to Woods's victory, but there is no dissociation or disapproval. Instead, the use of understatement apprises the hearer of the high salience that the speaker perceives so acutely in this satisfying situation. Here, the speaker of an ironic remark simply expresses an appropriate emotional reaction to the situation remarked upon. Since most situational ironies involve negative emotional reactions, most ironic remarks do so as well.

Probably, however, the relationship between emotions and types of verbal ironies is more complex than this statement suggests, resembling the relationship between emotions and types of situational ironies. In other words, types of verbal ironies are probably opaque to particular emotions, a situation that appears to be consistent with the results of Leggitt and Gibbs Jr. (2000).

Discussing verbal ironies in terms of the bicoherence theory would appear to provide a detailed and cognitively plausible way of understanding ironic remarks. The example above suggests that verbal ironies are constituted by qualitative reattachment—that is, the ironic quality of a situation is remarked upon in such a way that this quality is detached from the situation and attached instead to the remark itself. Thus, this account explains the ironic quality of verbal irony by linking it systematically to situational irony.

CONCLUSIONS

The bicoherence theory of situational irony provides a reasonably clear explanation of what it is about some everyday situations that leads people to call them ironic. Ironic situations activate concepts in a bicoherent pattern in a way that is adequately salient and produces a fitting emotional response.

Empirical support for the theory comes from the corpus study described above, in which the theory was applied to 250 unsolicited instances of situational irony. By sorting these instances into piles sharing similar coherence and incoherence relations, a comprehensive taxonomy has been generated. The taxonomy demonstrates the application of the theory and provides a useful tool for further analysis of situational ironies.

The bicoherence theory also introduces novel concepts into irony theory in general, such as manner, the emotional opacity or opaqueness of irony, and the possibilities for irony shift and elimination. These aspects of irony suggest the fecundity of the bicoherence theory and also directions for experimental investigation of situational irony.

The bicoherence theory relates situational irony to other theories of human psychology and cognition, such as the communicative theory of emotions, conceptual coherence theory, and causal attribution theory. These connections show that situational irony is simply part of the way in which humans evaluate and deal with situations, particularly those that do not fit with their normal expectations.

This fact also addresses perhaps the most basic question about irony: Why irony at all? Why is there irony instead of nothing? This question has dogged research in irony. Verbal irony, for example, is puzzling because it seems simply perverse to use an ironic expression where a literal one might always be used instead (Morgan, 1990, pp. 192–193). The bicoherence theory suggests that, in the case of situations, a sense of irony informs us when our concepts and the world to which they apply are saliently out of sync. Our emotions are engaged to prepare us to respond to the problem. Coherence tells us when our concepts mesh with the world, bicoherence tells us when they do not. This kind of problem is one that any cognitive agent might need drawn to its attention, in order to expend special efforts in dealing with the situation, or by revising its conceptual repertoire. Irony, then, is as useful a part of cognition as a smoke alarm is of a fire station.

ENDNOTES

1. From untitled article, November19, 1998, Associated Press.
2. Muecke (1969, pp. 99–115) discussed situational irony from a literary standpoint. For criticism of Muecke's approach, see Knox (1972, pp. 56–7). On the history of irony in general, see Muecke (1982, pp. 14–32), and O'Connor and Behler (1993).
3. Think of the inheritance of features in the network memory model of Quillian (1968).
4. Higgins (1996, pp. 135–6) argued that *salience* should be restricted to comparative distinctiveness among percepts, e.g., the tendency of a black sheep to grab attention when seen in a field of white sheep, independently of which concepts a perceiver happens to apply to those percepts. The term *salience,* or *cognitive salience,* is used here to designate an analogous quality concerning the readiness with which certain concepts tend to stand out when active.
5. Lucariello (1994) then *identified* irony with ironic schemata, which this study shows to be an error (section 1).
6. Experimental evidence suggests that children learn to make moral or "deontic" evaluations of situations by analogy with physical evaluations of them. It is therefore reasonable to treat both kinds of manner in the same way. See Sweetser (1990, pp. 49–68) for discussion of this topic.
7. The manner *overzealously* does not happen to figure in the corpus described in section 3, although there is no reason why it should not.
8. Cf. the corpus studies of Knox (1961) and Lucariello (1994).
9. From *B.C. court ruling halts hearings on immigration: Decision bars non-lawyers who charge a fee from representing foreigners,* Robert Matas, August 20, 1997, Globe and Mail.
10. From *Resident scouted out water break: He found what agencies couldn't,* Jennifer Mcmenamin, June 25, 1997, Boston Globe.
11. From *Quote of the day for Monday, June 16th,* June 16, 1997, Reuters.
12. From *Donatella and Naomi weep for Versace,* Kathryn Hone, October 9, 1997, Reuters.

13. From *Woods' showing sends television ratings' soaring,* Howard Manly, April 15, 1997, Boston Globe.
14. From *Pedantry hotline,* Diane White, July 28, 1997, Boston Globe.
15. From *25 more convicts are going to Texas,* Alisa Valdes, April 29, 1997, Boston Globe.
16. From *Who's the grown-up now? Trading places with their parents, 30-somethings settle down just as Mom and Dad are fleeing the nest,* Nathan Cobb, November 19, 1997, Boston Globe.
17. From *Spam king unplugged from Internet,* Jennifer Eno, October 20, 1997, Reuters.
18. From *America's secret world of child labor,* David Foster and Farrell Kramer, December 15, 1997, Associated Press.
19. From *Sharp seen posting its first profit drop in 5 years,* Miki Shimogori, September 24, 1997, Reuters.
20. From *California to extradite alleged drug hit men to Mexico,* January 18, 1998, Reuters.
21. From *The cautionary tale of the Nile Perch,* Mitzi Perdue, May 13, 1997, Scripps Howard News Service.
22. From *Chuck the 'reforms,'* Martin F. Nolan, March 3, 1997, Boston Globe.
23. From *Oklahoma bombing trial goes to summations,* Judith Crosson, June 12, 1997, Reuters.
24. A perissodactyl is a hoofed mammal with an odd number of toes.
25. From *Sex, drugs and rock 'n roll,* July 18, 1996, Reuters.
26. From *Sampras, Hingis win; Chang ousted at Wimbledon,* June 25, 1997, Robert Kitson, Reuters.
27. From *Watergate's hangover,* June 13, 1997, David Shribman, Associated Press.
28. From *Getty not the only art show in L.A.,* Steve James, December 9, 1997, Reuters.
29. From *Weekend Update,* Norm MacDonald, December 14, 1996, Saturday Night Live.
30. From *Foul weather hampers search for plane,* George Georgiopoulos, December 18, 1997, Reuters.
31. From *UEFA fines Fowler $1,400,* March 27, 1997, Reuters.
32. From Weekend Update, Norm MacDonald, May 10, 1997, Saturday Night Live.
33. From *John Peters,* October 29, 1997, Associated Press.
34. From *Too few women aware of their heart risk, study finds,* November 19, 1997, Reuters.
35. From *Jimmy Bulger: Fox in FBI coop,* Mike Barnicle, June 24, 1997, Boston Globe.
36. From *Eloquent witness,* Christine Temin, Boston Globe, September 19, 1997.

ACKNOWLEDGMENTS

Thanks to Ray Gibbs, Paul Thagard, and the anonymous reviewers for comments on earlier versions of this paper, and to Colleen Seifert for her encouragement and advice with this project. This research is supported by the Social Sciences and Humanities Research Council of Canada.

REFERENCES

Bazerman, M. H. (1998). *Judgment in managerial decision making* (4th ed.). New York: Wiley.

Bergson, H. L. (1900). *Le rire: Essai sur la signification du comique* [Laughter, an essay on the meaning of the comic]. Paris: F. Alcan.

Bergson, H. L. (1913). *Laughter, an essay on the meaning of the comic* (C. Brereton & F. Rothwell, Trans.). London: Macmillan. (Original work published 1900)

Bolt, R. (1962). *A man for all seasons.* New York: Random House.

Booth, W. C. (1974). *A rhetoric of irony.* Chicago: University of Chicago Press.

Clark, H. H., & Gerrig, R. J. (1984). On the pretense of irony. *Journal of Experimental Psychology: General, 113,* 121–126.

Conrad, J. (1902). *Youth, a narrative, and two other stories.* London: W. Blackwood and Sons.

Coppola, F. F. (1979). *Apocalypse now* [Film]. (Available from Zoetrope Studios).

Damasio, A. R. (1994). *Descartes' error: Emotion, reason, and the human brain.* New York: Putnam.

D'Andrade, R. (1995). *The development of cognitive anthropology.* Cambridge, England: Cambridge University Press.

Ekeh, P. P. (1974). *Social exchange theory: The two traditions.* London: Heinemann Educational.

Ekman, P. (1984). Expression and the nature of emotion. In K. R. Scherer & P. Ekman (Eds.) *Approaches to emotion* (pp. 319–343). Hillsdale, NJ: Lawrence Erlbaum Associates.

Falk, R. (1989). Judgment of coincidences: Mine versus yours. *American Journal of Psychology, 102,* 477–493.

Ferguson, E. (1977). The minds eye: Nonverbal thought in technology. *Science, 197,* 827–836.

Flaherty, P. .(1988). *18 again!* [Film]. (Available from New World Entertainment.

Frijda, N. (1986). *The emotions. Studies in emotion and social interaction.* Cambridge, England: Cambridge University Press.

Gentner, D. (1983). Structure-mapping: A theoretical framework. *Cognitive Science, 7,* 155–170.

Gibbs, J. R. W., & O'Brien, J. (1991). Psychological aspects of irony understanding. *Journal of Pragmatics, 16,* 523–530.

Gilbert, B. (1988). *Vice versa* [Film]. (Available from Columbia Pictures)

Giora, R. (1995). On irony and negation. *Discourse Processes, 19,* 239–264.

Grice, H. P. (1975). Logic and conversation. In P. Cole & J. L. Morgan (Eds.), *Syntax and semantics: Speech acts number 3 in syntax and semantics series* (pp. 41–58). New York: Academic.

Grice, H. P. (1977). Further notes on logic in conversation. In J. L. Morgan (Ed.), *Syntax and semantics: Pragmatics number 9 in syntax and semantics series* (pp. 113–127). New York: Academic.

Harriss, J., Leiter, K., & Johnson, S. (1992). *The complete reporter: Fundamentals of news gathering, writing, and editing* (6th ed.). New York: Macmillan.

Higgins, E. T. (1996). Knowledge activation: Accessibility, applicability, and salience. In E. T. Higgins & A. W. Kruglanski (Eds.), *Social psychology: Handbook of basic principles* (pp. 133–168). New York: Guilford.

Holyoak, K. J., & Thagard, P. (1995). *Mental leaps: Analogy in creative thought.* Cambridge, MA: MIT Press.

Hutcheon, L. (1995). *Irony's edge: The theory and politics of irony.* New York: Routledge.

Jorgensen, J., Miller, G. A., & Sperber, D. (1984). Test of the mention theory of irony. *Journal of Experimental Psychology: General, 113,* 112–120.

Jung, C. G. (1973). *Synchronicity: An acausal connecting principle.* Princeton, NJ: Princeton University Press.

Knox, N. (1961). *The word "irony" and its context, 1500–1755.* Durham, NC: Duke University Press.

Knox, N. (1972). On the classification of ironies. *Modern Philology, 70,* 53–62.

Kunda, Z., & Thagard, P. (1996). Forming impressions from stereotypes, traits, and behaviors: A parallel-constraint-satisfaction theory. *Psychological Review, 103,* 284–308.

Lakoff, G., & Johnson, M. (1980). *Metaphors we live by.* Chicago: University of Chicago Press.

Leggitt, J. S., & Gibbs, R. W., Jr. (2000). Emotional reactions to verbal irony. *Discourse Processes, 29,* 1–24.

Littman, D. C., & Mey, J. L. (1991). The nature of irony: Toward a computational model of irony. *Journal of Pragmatics, 15,* 131–151.

Lucariello, J. (1994). Situational irony: A concept of events gone awry. *Journal of Experimental Psychology: General, 123,* 129–145.

Lucas, G. (1977). *Star wars* [Film]. (Available from Lucasfilm Ltd.)

Lucas, G. (1980). *The empire strikes back* [Film]. (Available from Lucasfilm Ltd.)

Lucas, G. (1983). *Return of the Jedi* [Film]. (Available from Lucasfilm Ltd.)

Lyons, J. (1977). *Semantics.* Cambridge, England: Cambridge University Press.

Monson, I. (1994). Doubleness and jazz improvisation: Irony, parody, and ethnomusicology. *Critical Inquiry, 20,* 283–313.

Morgan, J. L. (1990). Comments on Jones and Perrault. In P. R. Cohen, J. L. Morgan, & M. E. Pollack (Eds.), *Intentions in communication* (pp. 187–194). Cambridge, MA: MIT Press.

Muecke, D. C. (1969). *The compass of irony.* London: Methuen.

Muecke, D. C. (1982). *Irony and the ironic. The critical idiom* (2nd ed.). London: Methuen.

Nelson, G. (1977). *Freaky Friday* [Film]. (Available from Walt Disney Productions).

Nisbett, R. E., & Ross, L. (1980). *Human inference: Strategies and shortcomings of social judgment. Century Psychology series.* Englewood Cliffs, NJ: Prentice Hall.

Oatley, K. (1992). *Best laid schemes: The psychology of emotions.* Cambridge, England: Cambridge University Press.

O'Connor, W. V., & Behler, E. H. (1993). Irony. In A. Preminger & T. V. F. Brogan (Eds.), *The new Princeton encyclopedia of poetry and poetics* (pp. 633–635). Princeton, NJ: Princeton University Press.

Ortony, A., Clore, G. L., & Collins, A. (1988). *The cognitive structure of emotions.* Cambridge, England: Cambridge University Press.

Pilkington, A. (1992). Poetic effects. *Lingua, 87,* 29–51.

Prothero, D. R., & Schoch, R. M. (1989). *The evolution of perissodactyls. Volume 15 of Oxford monographs on geology and geophysics.* New York: Oxford University Press.

Quillian, M. R. (1968). Semantic memory. In M. Minsky (Ed.), *Semantic information processing* (pp. 216–260). Cambridge, MA: MIT Press.

Ross, L., & Nisbett, R. E. (1991). *The person and the situation: Perspectives of social psychology.* Philadelphia: Temple University Press.

Schank, R. C., & Abelson, R. (1977). *Scripts, plans, goals and understanding.* Hillsdale, NJ: Lawrence Erlbaum Associates.

Sperber, D. (1984). Verbal irony: Pretense or echoic mention? *Journal of Experimental Psychology: General, 113,* 130–136.

Sperber, D. (1994). Understanding verbal understanding. In J. Khalfa (Ed.), *What is intelligence?* (pp. 179–198). Cambridge, England: Cambridge University Press.

Sperber, D., & Wilson, D. (1986). *Relevance: Communication and cognition. The Language and Thought series.* Cambridge, MA: Harvard University Press.

Sweetser, E. E. (1990). *From etymology to pragmatics: Metaphorical and cultural aspects of semantic structure. Volume 54 of Cambridge Studies in Linguistics.* Cambridge, England: Cambridge University Press.

Szabados, B., & Soifer, E. (1998). Hypocrisy after Aristotle. *Dialogue, 37,* 545–570.

Thagard, P. (1989). Explanatory coherence. *Behavioral and Brain Sciences, 12,* 435–467.

Thagard, P. (2000). *Coherence in thought and action.* Cambridge, MA: MIT Press.

Thagard, P., & Verbeurgt, K. (1998). Coherence as constraint satisfaction. *Cognitive Science, 22,* 1–24.

Wilson, D., & Sperber, D. (1981). Irony and the use-mention distinction. In P. Cole (Ed.), *Radical pragmatics* (pp. 295–318). New York: Academic.

Wilson, D., & Sperber, D. (1992). On verbal irony. *Lingua, 87,* 53–76.

Winner, E. (1988). *The points of words: Children's understanding of metaphor and irony.* Cambridge, MA: Harvard University Press.

Winner, E., & Leekam, S. (1991). Distinguishing irony from deceptional understanding of the speaker's second-order intention. *The British Journal of Developmental Psychology, 9,* 257–270.

Wise, R. (1965). *The sound of music* [Film]. (Available from 20th Century Fox)

PART VII

CONCLUSION

CHAPTER 24

The Future of Irony Studies

Raymond W. Gibbs, Jr.
University of California, Santa Cruz

Herbert L. Colston
University of Wisconsin–Parkside

The articles presented in this reader represent some of the finest work on irony within the cognitive sciences over the last 20 years. As is evident in the organization of this volume, there have been several topics/themes that have attracted the attention of most irony scholars with particular attention paid to issues of immediate irony comprehension and the social/pragmatic functions of irony in discourse. Our aim in this final chapter is to comment on several of these themes and to suggest additional topics and ideas that will be important to empirically study in future irony studies. Some of our suggestions refer to questions and topics that are typically far removed from the interests of most cognitive scientists, especially psycholinguists and linguists. Nonetheless, we believe that examining irony in the myriad ways that it is found in language, thought, and culture is an important step toward formulating more detailed theories of irony as linguistic, cognitive, and social phenomena.

IRONY AND THE PROBLEM OF LITERAL MEANING

Most experimental studies on irony comprehension contrast irony interpretation against understanding of roughly equivalent literal speech. This strategy makes some sense given that traditional theories of figurative language understanding, most generally, and irony understanding, more specifically, make explicit assumptions about the relative difficulty in processing nonliteral as opposed to literal language. For the most part, scholars also assume that literal processing reflects the standard, default mode of linguistic processing, while irony, and other forms of indirect and nonliteral language, require either special mechanisms to properly interpret, or at the very least requires the activation of sufficient contextual and/or conceptual information in order to be easily understood.

But there are several problems with this approach to studying irony comprehension that we, and others, have struggled to deal with. First, irony scholars have not had much at all to say about what actually constitutes literal processing. For example, in studies showing that literal and ironic utterances can be understood equally fast, or that indicate that ironic meanings arise as quickly during online processing as do ironic ones, scholars sometimes conclude that these null results (e.g., no difference in processing literal and figurative sentences) necessarily provide evidence in favor of a parallel processing model. Moreover, studies showing that some aspects of ironic meanings emerge more slowly than do standard literal meanings are assumed to reflect the outputs of two entirely different linguistic processes (e.g., literal vs. ironic). The possibility remains, however, that activation of different kinds of meaning (i.e., literal vs. ironic) may arise from a single unified linguistic process. The fact that scholars label one kind of meaning as "literal" and another "ironic" doesn't necessarily indicate that different processes operate (i.e., a literal processing mode and ironic processing mode) to access these meanings (either in a serial or parallel manner). More generally, scholars looking at processing of other kinds of nonliteral meaning, such as metaphoric, idiomatic, metonymic, and so on, often assume that each meaning type is the output of special processes devoted to understanding these specific types of tropes. Across the hundreds of experimental studies on figurative language processing, then, there have been numerous types of processing modes postulated to account for the different results in each set of experiments.

We should resist interpreting the findings of different on-line studies of sentence processing, including those looking at so-called literal meaning in figurative language understanding, as necessarily demonstrating different linguistic processes. An important consequence of this idea is that differences in the activation of literal and figurative meanings should not be viewed as evidence for the primacy of literal processing in utterance interpretation. One need not postulate different literal and figurative processing modes to account for any of the data obtained in these studies.

Another reason to question whether different linguistic meanings reflect different linguistic processes is the fact that there are numerous types of figurative meaning, including metaphoric, idiomatic, metonymic, ironic, satirical, proverbial, hyperbolic, oxymoronic, and so on (Gibbs, 1994). Scholars often assume within the context of a single set of studies that there are two processes at work during figurative language understanding, such as literal vs. idiomatic, literal vs. metaphoric, or literal vs. metonymic, and so on. Yet if there are numerous types of meaning, must there be dozens of types of linguistic processes all at work, or potentially at work, when language is understood? Psycholinguists have not addressed this question primarily because they focus too narrowly in their individual studies on only one kind of figurative meaning against a simple view of literal meaning.

In fact, it is not clear what the operational definition of "literal" meaning is in most psycholinguistic experiments. These studies individually compare metaphor vs. literal meaning, irony vs. literal meaning, idiomatic vs. literal meaning, metonymy vs. literal meaning, and so on. But across the vast number of empirical studies that compared "literal" and "nonliteral" meaning, the variety of forms for literal utterances is as great as are the differences between metaphors, metonymies, ironies, and so on. Yet scholars continue to assume that the literal meaning they examine empirically somehow is the same variable that other researchers investigate in their respective experiments. We urge scholars not to refer to any linguistic expression as "literal" unless theoretical reasons can be clearly stated as to what makes this type of meaning different from all other kinds of meaning (e.g., ironic, metaphoric, metonymic, poetic, and so on).

A related problem in contrasting ironic and literal language is that these two forms of expression are simply not equivalent. After all, people use irony for different rhetorical purposes that reflect a tacit choice over using literal speech. For example, to say to someone sarcastically that "You're a fine friend" indirectly conveys various beliefs, expectations, attitudes that are not simply captured by the typical literal paraphrase "You're a bad friend." Although it is reasonable to contrast understanding of a specific expression, such as "You're a fine friend" when used "ironically" or "literally," it is always problematic to assume that the meaning of any ironic utterance can somehow be adequately paraphrased by an equivalent expression of the same length (a requirement for reading time experiments). We are not sure how to remedy this problem, which is found throughout the experimental literature on figurative language understanding. But we are hopeful that irony scholars will take on the challenge of thinking more about this issue than has been the case in the past.

Finally, one of the greatest puzzles in theories of irony is that it is not clear what role literal meaning actually plays in nonliteral language understanding. For the most part, literal meanings are only rejected along the way to understanding what speakers actually ironically imply. Psycholinguistic studies usually say little about how literal meaning functions to derive speaking meaning, regardless of whether literal meaning is processed first or in parallel to understanding indirect or figurative meaning. In this way, figurative language scholars of all types have ignored a critical aspect of the very theory they espouse, namely that nonliteral processing has something to do with the literal analysis of words and expressions. But little attention has been given to elaborating in the exact relation of literal meaning to nonliteral understanding. Perhaps the lack of attention to this question reveals a deeper problem with the very notions of "literal" and "nonliteral" in the first place.

DOES IRONY HAVE A SPECIAL TONE OF VOICE?

Traditional theories of irony have often suggested that a person's tone of voice is a special clue toward recognizing that he/she is speaking ironically. For example, Grice (1975) claimed that after a listener sees that a person's utterance is literally inappropriate in some context, the person's tone of voice was the important sign that a speaker meant the opposite of what his/her utterance meant. Various scholars have speculated since then that irony must have a specific intonational pattern that distinguishes it from other kinds of literal and nonliteral meaning, such as slower speaking rate, heavy emphasis and nasalization on certain words. But as pointed out in several chapters in this volume (see Gibbs), people can readily understand ironic utterances without any intonational cues.

Where does the impression that irony is often conveyed with a special tone of voice come from? One recent set of experimental studies examined this question by having participants judge whether utterances that had been acoustically altered to remove high or low frequency information were ironic or not (Bryant & Fox Tree, 2005). Listeners could not identify any individual words when hearing these filtered statements, but could recognize various prosodic contours still present in the utterances. Not surprisingly, participants could generally recognize that filtered utterances which were originally ironic were indeed ironic more so than were the originally non-ironic filtered expressions. However, when people listened to the same stimuli and made a variety of different judgments (e.g., say whether the speaker of this utterance was angry, expressing doubt, being authoritative, and so on), people also tended to choose the filtered utterances that were originally recognized as ironic. Thus, the tone of voice associated with at least some ironies is not specific to ironic communication, but is associated with a wide range of interpersonal affective styles.

We think that this is a topic that demands a great deal more research. One problem with past studies on this topic is that judgments about tone of voice are given after an utterance has been completely heard, and often explicitly recognized as communicating ironic meaning. But the understanding of irony may lead people to falsely assume that these utterances must have a special tone of voice, just as people associated a speaker's angry attitudes from his or her tone of voice. What is needed is online studies that explicitly investigate how prosodic information is used moment-by-moment in inferring that a speaker is being ironic. Moreover, there is also still a great need for naturalistic speech analyses to uncover the range of prosodic contours that are used when people speak ironically in the multiple ways they do.

Moving Downward: Specifying the Subtypes of Irony

One problem that surfaces in the irony literature concerns the definition of irony. To some extent, many authors embrace a global view of irony expressing the opposite of what speakers literally say, although several contributions in this collection expressed more nuanced definitions, including recognition that many ironies allude to expectations and do not always simply contradict the truth of what is said (see chapters by Gibbs; Kumon-Nakamura, Glucksberg, & Brown; Wilson & Sperber; Curco). But there is still a tendency in the literature to conceive of irony solely in terms of classic sarcasm by which a speaker intends to criticize or wound an addressee. Yet sarcasm is only one form of irony. People also use jocularity, rhetorical questions, hyperbole, and understatement, among others, to express different sorts of ironic meanings. Although these fit under the larger umbrella of irony, these forms are not entirely equivalent as they express different sorts of interpersonal meaning and elicit different kinds of affective reactions from listeners.

One form of irony that is little studied within cognitive science is self-mockery. Self-mockery usually involves a speaker making an utterance and then immediately denying or invalidating its consequence, often by saying something like "No, I was just kidding" (in English). This form of irony differs from sarcasm, jocularity, hyperbole, and so because it does not involve contempt for others, does not echo anyone else's speech or thoughts, and because the speaker may actually believe the utterance he/she invalidates (Suziki, 2001). One analysis of self-mocking in Japanese demonstrates that several factors contribute to the complex meanings of self-mockery, such as the double-voice associated with utterances invoking pretense, the presence of certain lexical items that highlight speakers' lack of commitment to what they are saying, and the use of pause or other framing devices to signal that a speaker wishes to dissociate himself or herself from the content of the utterance. No experimental studies have examined listeners' understandings of self-mockery, even though this form of irony may be rather prevalent in some people and some social circles.

We remain open to the possibility that there may not be a single theory of irony that is capable of explaining the comprehension of, and pragmatic functions of, these different forms of ironic speech. This possibility, we hasten to add, does not imply that there must be entirely different mechanisms underlying, for example, understanding of hyperbole and understanding of jocularity. But the time is right for continued exploration into the cognitive processes involved in interpreting various ironic forms, how these different forms reflect different conceptualizations of events, and the emotional and pragmatic effects these different ironic forms have in discourse.

Moving Upward: Irony, Satire, and Parody

Irony is often compared to the related tropes of satire and parody. Satire is generally defined as a specific formal genre in which a person speaking in the first person attacks one or more individuals, institutions, or social customs. In many cases, satire is aimed at revealing the folly in someone holding particular beliefs. Parody, on the other hand, is closely related to satire, but more specifically engages in exaggerated mimicry of the person(s) being attacked.

There are thousands of wonderful examples of both satire and parody in literature and film, ranging from selected work of Shakespeare to movies such as "Dr. Strangelove or How I Learned to Love the Bomb." Like irony, both satire and parody run the risk of being misunderstood for either being taken too seriously, or being offensive toward the person or ideas being mocked. Perhaps the most famous American satirist at the moment is the lovable, and incorrigible, television character Homer Simpson. "The Simpsons" has enjoyed amazing success as an animated series on television, partly because of Homer Simpson's hilarious satire of "Everyman." The program is filled with ironic social commentary that cuts to the core of many American values, and the ironic manner in which many Americans manifest these in their ordinary behaviors. For instance, the strictness and limitations of religion are often targets for ironic commentary on "The Simpsons." In one episode,

Homer creates his own religion and refuses to attend church. But he then has a dream in which God speaks to him and seemingly supports Homer's actions (Groening, 1997, p. 94):

Homer: "I'm not a bad guy. I work hard and I love my kids. So why should I spend half my Sunday hearing about how I'm going to hell?"
God: "Hmmm, you've got a good point there. You know, sometimes even I'd rather be watching football. Does St. Louis still have a team?"
Homer: "No. They moved to Phoenix."

By showing that God may be more caring and understanding of the "ordinary guy," "The Simpsons" satirizes the strictness of religion in regimenting people's lives. God's question about whether St. Louis still has a football team even deflates God from a position of someone who is all-knowing to, once more, a person who really is just another "average guy."

There have, unfortunately been no empirical studies examining the extent to which people recognize the satire in widely watched television programs such as "The Simpsons," nor have there been any studies comparing understanding of irony with satire and parody, although there have been a select few studies on interpretation of satirical texts (Pfaff & Gibbs, 1997; also see Simpson, 2003).

Parody is also a neglected topic. A quick glance at any comedy or variety show on television, such as "The Simpsons," will show that people love to engage in parody which others find enormously funny. To take a simple example, there is a contest each year where people submit their best parodies of the writings of William Faulkner and Ernest Hemingway. These two writers have extremely different, and unique, styles that make them excellent targets for comic imitation. Consider the opening paragraph from the winning Hemingway entry for the 2005 contest, titled "Da Moveable Code" ("The Pun Also Rises," 2005):

> Paris could be very fine in the winter when it was clear and cold and they were very young and in love but that winter of 1924 they quarreled badly and she left for good. Paris, the city of light, turned dark and sodden with sadness. But it was still a damn fine place and he hated to leave it so he sat in the cafes all day and drank wine and thought about writing clean short words on bright white paper. (p. 51)

Nobody familiar with Ernest Hemingway could deny the dual aim here to both celebrate Hemingway as a great writer and to mock him for his tendency to glorify art and life in the 1920s in Paris (e.g., "A moveable feast"), as well as his insistence on writing rather stark, simple prose in a rather masculine style. As with all parodies, the victim is exposed for his/her faults, even when these partly contribute to the positive reasons for why we admire the person being parodied. The ironic nature of the teasing here, and its reliance on a type of "echoing," is similar to irony and satire, although these clearly differ to some degree.

We believe that such comparisons between closely related tropes is much needed to not only reveal comprehension differences between irony, satire, and parody, but also to uncover the different modes of thought that each of these mocking attitudes reveal. Not surprisingly, work on these topics will require moving to a level of analysis beyond the single sentence as most instances of satire and parody are extended through some discourse.

Moving Beyond the Single Utterance

Consider the following letter to the editor published in "The Chronicle of Higher Education" (August 15, 2003):

> Fire the Professors, Give the Coaches Bonuses
> To the Editor:
>
> Times are tough at the University of Nebraska, "The Chronicle" reported that the university is seeking to eliminate the jobs of 15 tenured professors due to budget cuts ("U. of Nebraska Seeks to Lay Off 15 Tenured Faculty Members" July 4). If the measure goes through, some of these faculty members will be fired outright
> …
> Given the bleakness of that news, it's cheering to learn that the budget situation in Nebraska isn't so desperate that Cornhusker athletic coaches will be affected. The Associated Press reported on July 9 that despite Nebraska's worst football season in 41 years, the university will be paying its football coaches $153,163 in incentive bonuses. Other coaches did very well, too … .
> Those who have observed the takeover of American higher education by commercialized athletics sometimes say that places like Nebraska are not universities but semiprofessional franchises that maintain a few classrooms for show … .
> Given the terrible budgetary situation, wouldn't it make sense simply to abolish the university and strengthen the football franchise? Just closing the library, firing all faculty members and administrators, and putting padlocks on the dormitories and dining halls would free up enough money to triple the bonuses paid to coaches and athletic-staff members.
>
> Sincerely,
> (author)
> Professor of English
> (university affiliation)

This letter is written in the spirit of Jonathan Swift, who was famous for his essay "A Modest Proposal," in which he chastised the complacency of wealthy citizens of Ireland by making the outrageous suggestion that the country can be restored to economic health if people bought and ate the babies of the destitute unemployed Catholics. Irony is a wonderful way to express outrage and is frequently seen in the letters to the editors of newspapers all over the United States and other countries.

Our point in mentioning this example is simply to encourage researchers to study irony as it exists in longer texts and conversations, and not restrict the examination of irony comprehension to single utterances/sentences. There are several good reasons for expanding irony studies in this way. First, irony probably does not come forth only in single expressions in the absence of any other ironic speech. As noted in Kotthoff (this volume) and Gibbs (this volume), speakers often engage in ironic repartee, in which individual ironic utterances are chained together, both within and across individual speakers. These "ironic chains" reflect important ironic conceptualizations of events, in addition to speakers' pragmatic aims to mock or disparage the people and situations being referred to. In this way, extended ironic discourse is a major indication of irony in thought. At the same time, there has been little work looking at immediate comprehension of "ironic chains" in both conversation and writing. We can easily speculate that recognizing that a person is speaking ironically may set up expectations where additional ironic utterances would be seen as quite relevant and appropriate.

In fact, there are many situations in which speakers, both individually and collectively, step on and off the ironic stage, so to speak, by intermixing ironic language around other forms of discourse (Gibbs, 2001). Examining comprehension effort for ironies that follow, or do not follow, other ironic statements, is something well-worth pursuing in future irony research. Finally, there may be special linguistic features of texts that give clues to some utterances as being ironical. For example, at what point in reading the above letter to the editor do you see the irony in the writer's overall argument? How does context, previous knowledge of the author, the topic, the forum of publication, all effect the easy interpretation of irony? These are clearly questions that require much further attention in future empirical work.

Nonlinguistic Expressions of Irony

As this volume makes clear, irony is a form of thought as much as it is a kind of linguistic expression. For this reason, irony is evident in many nonlinguistic expressions, including dress, pictorial advertisements, artworks, political messages, and even music. For example, musicologists have begun to explore how composers create ironic moments in their works, such as the "double-voicing" technique employed by Dmitri Shostakovich to ironically comment on the lack of artistic freedom under the Soviet regime (Gerstel, 1999). Many artists, including painters, sculptors, and performance artists, most famously Marcel Duchamp and Salvador Dali, frequently express ironic themes in their work. One collection of paintings and sculptors by American military veterans from the Vietnam War has many poignant, yet disturbing, elements of irony, such as displays of dead Vietnamese bodies heroically draped by the American flag, or skeletal remains of American soldiers covered with decorations for their military valor (Sinaiko, 1998). Each of these ironies is deeply critical of war in general, in addition to American governmental policies during, and after, the Vietnam War.

One of our favorite cases of nonlinguistic irony comes from the work of the artist J. S. G. Boggs (Weschler, 1999). Boggs is obsessed with money and has the wonderful talent of being able to accurately draw money on actual paper notes in the denominations of standard currencies around the world. Rather than selling these artworks to museums and collectors, Boggs tries to get merchants to accept his drawings in lieu of cash for wares and services. In doing so, Boggs creates this elaborate set of transactions that raise fundamental questions about the value of art, the value of real money, and why we place such trust in something like paper money. Not surprisingly, Boggs encounters many difficulties with treasury police around the world who sometimes prosecute Boggs for counterfeiting crimes, when all Boggs has really done is traded art drawings for wares and goods.

Boggs's artworks, and what he does with them, act to destabilize contemporary values in the art and financial world by posing contrasts between what is expected and what is given, and thus dissolves the rigid distinction between what is real and what is imagined. In this manner, Bogg's artworks cultivate our awareness of the absurdity in many aspects of ordinary life, especially in terms of our obsession with material possessions and money.

Images used in political ads make both adept and not so subtle use of irony in their attempt to propagate messages and disdain enemies. One image from the 2004 U.S. election juxtaposed a photograph of President George Bush on the deck of an aircraft carrier under a banner declaring "mission accomplished," with a listing of the number of American soldiers and civilians killed after the date of the photograph. This image contrasts the conceited and indeed often described as arrogant, attitude of the Bush Administration with the reality of the progress of the American war in Iraq.

A cover of *The New Yorker* magazine (Cover image, 2000), well-known for its powerful and compact cover images, depicts a drawing of Martin Luther King, Jr., attempting to hail a taxi cab, as seen from the perspective of the driver. In the corner of the image, the driver's face can be seen reflected in the rear view mirror, with a frightened expression of trepidation at an "African American" seeking a cab. This image poignantly displays the irony in continued difficulties in race relations in the United States, as reflected in the well-documented struggle people of color have in hailing taxis in some American cities, nearly forty years after King's now-celebrated campaign to eliminate racism ended in his assassination.

Advertisements frequently make use of irony in both their images and texts (as well as among both), whether intentional or not. Consider a billboard advertisement seen in Wisconsin with a very well-intentioned public health message concerning depression treatment. The ad showed a woman in a clearly despondent mood with her head in her hands with the text under the picture reading, "Depression, you don't have to live with it." Following this text an undeniably insensitive yet nonetheless clever observer had spray-painted the words, "yeah, try suicide," with a drawing of a rope noose.

Once again, there is a simply lack of basic information on the degree to which people comprehend, and consciously recognize, the irony in nonlinguistic objects, images, and events. Although it may seem more difficult to experimentally control pictorial stimuli, say, compared to what is done with verbal materials in psychological experiments, we think the time is ripe for empirical studies of nonverbal irony both in constructed and natural contexts. Attention to nonlinguistic irony also forces us to acknowledge life's ironies that we often cause ourselves through our interactions with and valuing of various objects and events.

Ironic People

Have you ever known someone that was especially ironic or sarcastic? We all have encountered such people and some of us readily admit to being especially prone to irony in our speech. Some empirical research suggests that ordinary college students assume that people in some types of occupations tend to be more ironic in their speech compared to other occupations (Pexman & Katz, 2001).

It is not clear as to what personality characteristics make someone more prone to speaking ironically, or even what kinds of situations, most generally, elicit ironic speech. These are clearly interesting topics for future research. But there are certain individuals who have been noted for their irony, not only in terms of their speech, but in terms of their beliefs and actions. Charlie Chaplin, Woody Allen, Plato, Andy Kaufman are representative of this category, to mention just a few (see Gibbs, 1994). We believe that case study analyses of such individuals would illuminate special qualities of "the ironic mind." Consider just two instances, both personal favorites of ours.

Fernando Pessoa (1888–1935) was a Portuguese poet who wrote under numerous "heteronyms" or literary alter egos. Unlike many other early twentieth-century writers (Pound, Rilke, Valery) who used alter egos in their writing, Pessoa devoted his life to conferring substance to each alter ego, giving each a personal biography, psychology, politics, aesthetics, religion, and physique. Albert Caeiro was an

> ingenious, unlettered man who lived in the country and had no profession. Richard Reis was a doctor and classicist who wrote odes in the style of Horace, Alvardo de Campos, a naval engineer, started out as an exuberant futurist with a Walt Whitmanesque voice, but over time he came to sound like a mopey existentialist. (Zenith, 1997, pp. 2–3)

Pessoa also developed several other "semiheteronyms," most notably Bernardo Soares, whose well-known fictional diary was entitled "The Book of Disquietude." As many as seventy-two names besides Fernando Pessoa were "responsible" for the thousands of pages of texts and poems discovered in Pessoa's possession when he died. These authors did not act or write alone, but collaborated, critiqued, and translated one another.

Pessoa and his "heteronyms" and their constant striving toward fragmentation of the self, were constructed as part of Pessoa's ironic skepticism in the belief in "essences," especially in regard to Romanticist notion of the heroic individual with a unified mind as the sole source of artistic creation. Consider one passage from Bernando Soares's "The Book of Disquietude:"

> I am, in large measure, the selfsame prose I write. I unroll myself in periods and paragraphs, I make myself punctuation marks; in my unbridled allocation of im-

ages I'm like a child using newspaper to dress up as a king ... I've made myself into the character of a book, a life one reads. Whatever I feel is felt (against my will) so that I can write that I felt it. Whatever I think instantly takes shape in words, mixed with images that undo it, opening it into rhythms that are something else altogether. From so much self-modeling, I've destroyed myself. From so much self-thinking, I've now my thoughts and not I ... And so, describing myself in image after image—not without truth, but also with lies—I end up more in the images than in me, stating myself until I no longer exist, writing with my soul for ink, useful for nothing except writing. (Zenith, 1997, pp. 13–14)

The levels of irony in this writing are quite complex. Some of these are obvious to readers as when Soares, who is again just a figment of Pessoa's imagination, expresses ironic statement after statement, mostly referring to the idea that the more he creates words and images, the more invisible, even non-existent, he becomes. But there is another implicit irony in all of Pessoa's heteronyms and their artistic writings, namely that we readers usually interpret so-called creative acts as if these originate from the minds of special, creative individuals who are speaking to us directly. Yet this simple belief about the nature of language and communication is completely destabilized by our struggle to understand the intentions of someone who is only fictional and solely the product of some other person's imagination. In these ways, Pessoa casts a wide ironic net to lure readers into his nest of instability where nothing is certain, and all meanings and images stand in ironic contrast to one another.

Pessoa is clearly special, compared to most speakers/writers, but his ironic mind is rooted in the same basic cognitive and linguistic processes that each of us possess. Although Pessoa wrote, and existed, in an intentional ironic manner, there are others, like Homer Simpson mentioned above, who consistently, and perhaps unintentionally, exhibit features of the ironic mind by highlighting the discrepancy between expectations and behaviors through their speech and actions. When Homer proclaims "To alcohol! The cause of ... and solution to ... all of life's problems," (Groening, 1997, p. 231), he displays both his stupidity about alcohol as a realistic solution to life's difficulties, but also sharply undercuts the more general theme in American life of excessive consumption (e.g., the desire for money, food, power), which paradoxically often leads people to feel empty, and ironically pushes people to remedy this emptiness with more false remedies, such as alcohol. Homer Simpson may not always be aware of his satirical ways, yet the writers of "The Simpsons" clearly present Homer as a master ironist in the sense of embodying "some of the classic conflicts from which all great theater and literature derives" (MacGregor, 1999, p. 27).

Contemporary music is another arena in which ironic personalities are quite prominent, especially in the way that some artists express ironic commentary on many of the widely accepted cultural and aesthetic values, such as seen in rock and roll. For example, one analysis of the work by the British rocker Bryan Ferry suggests a full-blown attempt to disparage rock and roll icons like Bob Dylan and Mick Jagger (Bailey, 2003). Irony is fundamental to Ferry's musical strategy as his cover of classic songs like "A Hard Rain's A-Gonna Fall" and "Sympathy for the Devil" feature cool, dispassionate renditions of songs that are classically viewed as passionate and romantic. Rather than representing the rock star as "working class hero" in the way suggested by Dylan, Lennon, Springsteen, and others, Ferry aims to be viewed as the "Gatsby of Rock," one whose primary mode of being is critical, distance, and indeed ironic. Ferry's appearance back in the 1970s and 1980s, where he wore a tuxedo and had short, styled hair, reinforce his ironic opposition to the ideals and practices of rockers in that time period.

Just as psychologists learn a great deal about ordinary perception from the study of visual illusions, cognitive scientists would appreciate more about the complexities of ironic thought and language from studying special ironists like Pessoa, Homer Simpson, and Bryan Ferry. More generally, irony plays an important role in how people define and negotiate their identities and this too is an open area of research for the future.

SUMMARY

Many of the topics discussed here, and the suggestions for specific areas of research, are not typically associated with the kinds of empirical research done in the main disciplines within cognitive science. But the fact that irony is so frequently found in art, literature, and culture more generally, demands a broadening of the scope of irony research. This seems especially important if we are to better understand the complexities of ironic thought as manifested in great works of art. Within more traditional research programs within cognitive science, there is still a great need for further explicit experimental studies on online irony understanding, tone of voice, and how ironic personalities influence verbal irony understanding. Yet each of these suggestions require further theoretical work as we try to better define what constitutes irony in language, thought, and situation, as well as how irony really differs from literal language (whatever that is), and other closely related forms of figurative speech.

REFERENCES

Bailey, S. (2003). Faithful or foolish: The emergence of the ironic cover album and rock culture. *Popular Music and Society, 26,* 141–161.
Bryant, G., & Fox Tree, J. (2005). Is there an ironic tone of voice? *Language & Speech, 48,* 257–277.
Cover image. (2000, January 17). *The New Yorker.*
Gerstel, J. (1999). Irony, deception, and political culture in the world of Dmitri Shostakovich. *Mosaic—A Journal for the Interdisciplinary Study of Literature, 32,* 35–51.
Gibbs, R. (2001). Metarepresentations in staged communicative acts. In D. Sperber (Ed.), *Metarepresentation: A multidisciplinary perspective* (pp. 388–410). New York: Oxford University Press.
Groening, M. (1997). *The Simpsons: A complete guide to our favorite family.* New York: HarperCollins.

MacGregor, J. (1999, June 20). More than sight gags and subversive satire. *The New York Times,* p. 27.

Pexman, P., & Katz, A. (2001). Speaker occupation and preference for irony. In J. Mio (Ed.), *Metaphor: Research and implications* (pp. 131–152). Mahwah, NJ: Lawrence Erlbaum Associates.

Pfaff, K., & Gibbs, R. (1997). Authorial intentions in understanding satirical texts. *Poetics, 34,* 145–162.

Simpson, P. (2003). *On the discourse of satire.* Amsterdam: Benjamins.

Sinaiko, E. (Ed.). (1998). *Vietnam: Reflexes and reflections.* New York: Abrams.

Suzuki, S. (2001). Self-mockery in Japanese. *Linguistics, 40,* 163–189.

The pun also rises. (2005, July). *Hemispheres Magazine,* United Airlines, 49–52.

Weschler, L. (1999). *Boggs: A comedy of values.* Chicago: University of Chicago Press.

Zenith, R. (1997). Introduction: The drama and dreams of Fernando Pessoa. In R. Zenith (Ed.), *Fernando Pessoa & Co.: Selected poems* (pp. 1–36). New York: Grove.

Author Index

Subject Index

→ Jorgensen = empirical support

Wilson & Sperber = use and mention
                          Echoing

Clark & Gerry = } Pretense

Grice

Colston = Testing empirically

Kumon
NAKAMURA
echoing =
   allusing
pretense =
   pragmatic
   insincerity

evolves into
echoic interpretation

PURE FOCUS TONICO

LANCÔME - GENIFIQUE SERUM -

GENIFIQUE CREMA